How To Use This Book

This book starts where most C tutorials leave off—just before you get into the really cool stuff! Fear not. If you are looking to take your programming knowledge to the next level, you've made the right purchase. This book provides useful tips and hands-on examples for developing your own applications with the C programming language. You get a deeper understanding of several important C concepts, such as memory allocation and complex data types; then you learn application development through the design of a personal database.

Who Should Read This Book

Anyone who knows some C—through a primer book or an introductory class—but wants to learn more will benefit by reading this book. You spend several days covering advanced topics, yet a majority of this book is dedicated to helping you apply the C language to real applications. It is this hands-on knowledge of the C language that sets this book apart from others. In addition to helping you develop an appplication, you learn the concepts involved in development. As an added bonus during the development process, you will create a library of functions that you are sure to find useful.

How This Book Is Structured

This book is intended to be read and absorbed over the course of three weeks. During each week, you'll read seven chapters that present concepts related to ActiveX.

Conventions

NOTE A Note box presents interesting pieces of information related to the surrounding discussion.

TIP: A Tip box offers advice or teaches an easier way to do something.

WARNING: A Warning box advises you about potential problems and helps you steer clear of disaster.

Do	Don't

Do/Don't boxes give you specific guidance on what to do and what to avoid doing when working with ActiveX.

- ➥Sometimes you need to type a very long, single line of code. When you see this character, a code continuation character, it means the line is continued from the preceding line, and you should type both lines as one.
- Actual code is typeset in a special `monospace` font. You'll see this font used in code examples. Explanations of code features, commands, statements, methods, and any text you see on the screen also are typeset in this font.
- Placeholders in code appear in `italic monospace` font. Replace the placeholder with the actual filename, parameter, or whatever element it represents.
- *Italics* highlight technical terms when they first appear in the text and are sometimes used to emphasize important points.

Teach Yourself ACTIVEX™ PROGRAMMING
in 21 days

Teach Yourself
ACTIVEX™ PROGRAMMING
in 21 days

Sanders Kaufman, Jr.
Jeff Perkins
Dina Fleet

201 West 103rd Street
Indianapolis, Indiana 46290

Copyright © 1996 by Sams.net Publishing

FIRST EDITION

All rights reserved. No part of this book shall be reproduced, stored in a retrieval system, or transmitted by any means, electronic, mechanical, photocopying, recording, or otherwise, without written permission from the publisher. No patent liability is assumed with respect to the use of the information contained herein. Although every precaution has been taken in the preparation of this book, the publisher and author assume no responsibility for errors or omissions. Neither is any liability assumed for damages resulting from the use of the information contained herein. For information, address Sams.net Publishing, 201 W. 103rd St., Indianapolis, IN 46290.

International Standard Book Number: 1-57521-163-7

Library of Congress Catalog Card Number: 96-69067

99 98 97 96   4 3 2 1

Interpretation of the printing code: the rightmost double-digit number is the year of the book's printing; the rightmost single-digit, the number of the book's printing. For example, a printing code of 96-1 shows that the first printing of the book occurred in 1996.

Composed in AGaramond and MCPdigital by Macmillan Computer Publishing

Printed in the United States of America

Trademarks

All terms mentioned in this book that are known to be trademarks or service marks have been appropriately capitalized. Sams.net Publishing cannot attest to the accuracy of this information. Use of a term in this book should not be regarded as affecting the validity of any trademark or service mark. ActiveX, Microsoft, and Microsoft Internet Explorer are trademarks of Microsoft Corporation.

President, Sams Publishing Richard K. Swadley
Publishing Team Leader Rosemarie Graham
Managing Editor Cindy Morrow
Director of Marketing John Pierce
Assistant Marketing Managers Kristina Perry, Rachel Wolfe

Acquisitions Editor
Sharon Cox

Development Editor
Todd Bumbalough

Software Development Specialist
John Warriner

Production Editor
Kate Shoup

Copy Editors
Kim Hannel, Carolyn Linn

Indexer
Benjamin Slen

Technical Reviewers
Dina Fleet, Brett Bonenberger, Brad Jones

Editorial Coordinator
Katie Wise

Technical Edit Coordinator
Lorraine E. Schaffer

Resource Coordinator
Deborah Frisby

Editorial Assistants
Carol Ackerman, Andi Richter, Rhonda Tinch-Mize

Cover Designer
Tim Amrhein

Book Designer
Gary Adair

Copy Writer
Peter Fuller

Production Team Supervisor
Brad Chinn

Production
Georgiana Briggs, Elizabeth Deeter, Dana Rhodes, Shawn Ring, Ian Smith, Andrew Stone

Dedications

In loving memory of Kimberly Ann Kaufman (1969–1996). An artist and a child of the universe. No less than the trees and the stars—she had every right to be here.

Sanders Kaufman, Jr.

I would like to dedicate this book to all the programmers and Webmasters on the leading edge of this technology—it's not going to be easy, but it will be fun.

Jeff Perkins

To Mom.

Dina Fleet

Overview

	Introduction		xx
Week 1 at a Glance			**1**
Day 1	Programming for the Internet		3
2	HTML & Scripting		15
3	ActiveX Scripting		41
4	The Tools of the Trade		57
5	Programming for Internet Explorer		87
6	Writing VBScripts		107
7	Writing JavaScripts		167
Week 2 at a Glance			**211**
Day 8	A VBScript Application		213
9	A JavaScript Application		259
10	Setting Up an ActiveX Web Site		291
11	Server-Side Scripting with CGI and ISAPI		311
12	WinSock—Windows Network Programming		331
13	Learning to Use the Win32 Internet API Library		349
14	Programming with Microsoft ActiveX Conferencing APIs		377
Week 3 at a Glance			**405**
Day 15	What Is an ActiveX Control?		407
16	Installing ActiveX Controls		427
17	ActiveX Control Downloading		447
18	Customizing ActiveX Control Properties		473
19	User Interaction with ActiveX Controls		491
20	Using the Internet Control Pack		511
21	Creating an ActiveX Control		537
Appendix	Answers		555
	Index		565

Contents

		Introduction	xx
Week 1 at a Glance			**1**
Day 1		**Programming for the Internet**	**3**
		Windows—The Most Widely Used Desktop Operating System	4
		Dial-Up Networking	4
		Integration of Network Technologies	7
		The Release of ActiveX	7
		Document Objects	8
		Hypertext	11
		Summary	12
		Q&A	13
		Workshop	14
		Quiz	14
	2	**HTML & Scripting**	**15**
		Overview of HTML	16
		The Basic Form	16
		Elements of HTML	17
		Overall Page Structure	18
		Working Inside the Body of the Web Page	21
		Lists	27
		Tables	29
		Forms and Inputs	31
		Summary	39
		Q&A	39
		Workshop	40
		Quiz	40
	3	**ActiveX Scripting**	**41**
		Client-Side Scripting	42
		Scripts, Hosts, and the Engines	43
		HTML Scripting	45
		The Script Element	46
		JScript and VBScript	47
		JScript	49
		VBScript	50
		The ActiveX Script Engine	50
		Host and Engine Interaction	51
		The Engine as an OLE/COM Object	52
		Summary	54
		Q&A	54

| | Workshop .... 55 |
| | Quiz .... 56 |

4 The Tools of the Trade 57

Overview of the Internet Assistant for Microsoft Word for Windows 58
Tour of the Microsoft Internet Assistant for Word 59
    Making a New Web Page 59
    Other Enhancements to Word 63
    Last Word on Word 64
Overview of HoTMetaL 64
Tour of HoTMetaL 65
    Building a Simple Web Page 65
    Toolbar by Toolbar 67
    HoTMetaL Summary 71
Overview of the IIS Add-In for Microsoft Access 71
Tour of the IIS Add-In for Microsoft Access 71
    Query and Display Page Wizard and Shameless Promotion 73
    Hacking the Script File 76
    The IIS Add-In for Access Wrap-Up 78
Overview of the ActiveX Control Pad 79
Tour of the ActiveX Control Pad 79
    Building a Page 80
    Scripting with the ActiveX Control Pad 84
Summary 85
Q&A 86
Workshop 86
Quiz 86

5 Programming for Internet Explorer 87

Why Internet Explorer? 88
    Internet Explorer Object Model 88
Summary 104
Q&A 104
Workshop 105
Quiz 105

6 Writing VBScripts 107

A Brief Background of VBScript 107
    Overview of Scripting Architecture 108
    Supported Software Platforms 108
    The Visual Basic Programming Model 108
Language Structure 109
    Comments 111
    Variables 112
    Procedures 125
    User-Built Functions 127

		Operators	128
		Built-In Functions	142
		Variants	158
		Program Flow	159
		Error Handling	163
		User Interface	164
		Resources	165
	Summary	....	165
	Q&A	....	165
	Workshop	....	166
	Quiz	....	166
7	**Writing JavaScripts**		**167**
	A Brief Background of JavaScript	....	168
		Overview of Scripting Architecture	168
		Supported Software Platforms	168
		The JavaScript Programming Model	169
	Language Structure	....	169
		General	170
		Comments	172
		Variables	173
		Procedures	179
		Operators	182
		Objects	189
		Built-In Objects	196
		Program Flow	202
		User Interface Elements	206
	Resources	....	207
	Summary	....	207
	Q&A	....	208
	Workshop	....	209
	Quiz	....	209

Week 2 at a Glance   211

Day 8	**A VBScript Application**		**213**
	Gathering Requirements for Your Application	....	213
		Can You Do It?	214
	Use Word to Create Rough Drafts of the Three Main Pages	....	215
	Design the Database in Access	....	219
		Add a Driver for the Bike Shop Database to Your System's ODBC Manager	221
	Using the Internet Information Server Add-In	....	222
	What Do You Have So Far?	....	229
		The Catalog Page	230
		The Sales Page	236

	The Order-Tracking Page 252
	Odds and Ends 256
	Summary 257
	Q&A 257
	Workshop 257
	Quiz 258
9	**A JavaScript Application** **259**
	Project Requirements 259
	Can You Do It? 260
	Use Word to Rough Out the Three Main Pages 261
	Summary 289
	Q&A 289
	Workshop 290
	Quiz 290
10	**Setting Up an ActiveX Web Site** **291**
	System Requirements 292
	Hardware 292
	Server Software 296
	Web Server 299
	Database Server 300
	Web-Site Administrator Requirements 300
	Technical Skills 300
	Internet Service Providers 304
	Selecting an ISP 306
	Summary 307
	Q&A 308
	Workshop 309
	Quiz 309
11	**Server-Side Scripting with CGI and ISAPI** **311**
	CGI 312
	CGI Creation 313
	CGI Operation 315
	Using CGIs with HTML Forms 319
	ISAPI Programming 320
	Executables Versus Dynamic Link Libraries 320
	In-Process Versus New Process 321
	HTTP and ISAPI Interaction 322
	Considerations for Building an ISAPI .DLL 325
	Converting CGI to ISAPI 327
	Summary 328
	Q&A 328
	Workshop 330
	Quiz 330

12	**WinSock—Windows Network Programming**	**331**
	What Is WinSock?	332
	Background	332
	`WinSck.OCX`	335
	Purpose of the WinSock Control	335
	Installation	335
	Creating a WinSock TCP Server	336
	Creating a WinSock Client	340
	WinSock UDP	342
	Summary	345
	Q&A	346
	Workshop	346
	Quiz	347
13	**Learning to Use the Win32 Internet API Library**	**349**
	Overview	350
	What Is the File Transfer Protocol (FTP)?	350
	The Gopher Protocol	351
	HTTP and HTML	353
	FTP and Gopher in the Future	353
	How Does the WinInet API Fit In?	354
	The API Functions	354
	The MFC Classes and WinInet	358
	Programming with MFC	360
	The First Sample Program	360
	`CInternetSession`	368
	`CInternetConnection` and the Connection Classes	368
	The `CFtpConnection` Class	369
	The FTP Sample Application	369
	Summary	375
	Q&A	375
	Workshop	376
	Quiz	376
14	**Programming with Microsoft ActiveX Conferencing APIs**	**377**
	The Goal	377
	The Standard	378
	The Technology	378
	Microsoft NetMeeting	378
	Let's Get Started	381
	System Requirements	381
	The Functions in the API	382
	Before You Get Started	383
	Let's Get to Coding	384

	The NetConferencing ActiveX Control 390
	NetConference API Structures 395
	NetConference ActiveX Objects, Properties, Methods, and Events 398
	Summary 403
	Q&A 403
	Workshop 403
	Quiz 404

Week 3 at a Glance 405

Day 15 What Is an ActiveX Control? 407

Evolution of ActiveX Controls 408
    OLE 408
    VBX—16-bit Custom Control 412
    OCX—16/32-bit Object Controls 413
    ActiveX Controls 413
How ActiveX Controls Are Used 413
    Programmatic 413
    ActiveX Scripting 414
Where to Find ActiveX Controls 418
    World Wide Web 418
    Software Distributors 419
ActiveX System Requirements 422
    Operating Systems 423
    Required Files 423
Summary 424
Q&A 425
Workshop 425
Quiz 426

16 Installing ActiveX Controls 427

HTML—Hypertext Markup Language 428
    The `<OBJECT>` Tag 430
Programmatic Installation of ActiveX Controls 437
    Visual Basic 437
    Other Languages 440
Using ActiveX Controls within ActiveX Documents 440
    Business Case 440
Summary 443
Q&A 444
Workshop 444
Quiz 445

17 ActiveX Control Downloading 447

OLE Objects 448
    Acquisition 448
    Verification 448

Contents

    Installation 448
    Component Downloading 448
  Internet Security 457
    Certificates 460
    Safety API 461
    Internet Ratings 466
  Summary 468
  Q&A 469
  Workshop 470
  Quiz 470

18 Customizing ActiveX Control Properties   473

  Built-In Controls 474
    Window Object 475
  Document Object 480
    The Color Object 481
    The Anchor Object 481
    The Link Object 481
    The Form Object 482
    The Location Object 482
    The `LastModified` Property 483
    The `Title` Property 483
    The `Referrer` Property 483
    Talking to the Document 484
  Control Attributes and Parameters 485
    Attributes—`ID`, `ClassID`, `Data` 486
    Parameters 486
  Summary 488
  Q&A 489
  Workshop 489
  Quiz 490

19 User Interaction with ActiveX Controls   491

  Interactive HTML 492
    The `<FORM>` Container Tag 492
    The `<INPUT>` Tag 494
    Image Maps 500
    User Input Via HTML Scripting 504
  User Input Via Visual Basic 505
  Summary 507
  Q&A 508
  Workshop 508
  Quiz 509

20 Using the Internet Control Pack   511

  `HTML.OCX`—Hypertext Markup Language Control 512
  `HTTPct.OCX`—Hypertext Transfer Protocol Client Control 514

SMTPct.OCX—Simple Mail Transfer Protocol Client Control 517
POP3ct.OCX—Post Office Protocol Client Control 519
NNTPct.OCX—Network News Transfer Protocol Client Control 522
FTPct.OCX—File Transfer Protocol Client Control 526
State Logic 531
   The Control State 531
   The Protocol State 531
   The DocObject State 532
Summary 532
Q&A 533
Workshop 534
Quiz 535

21 Creating an ActiveX Control   537

Editing the System Registry 538
   Windows 3.0 538
   Windows 3.1 539
   Windows 95 539
Registry Components 540
   System.DAT 540
   Reg.DAT 540
   User.DAT 540
   Editing the Registry Database 540
ActiveX and the System Registry 544
   Self-Registering and Versioning 544
ActiveX Control Features 546
   Visual J++ (Jakarta) 547
   Visual Basic 548
   Visual C++ 549
   IUnknown—The Center of ActiveX OLE 550
Summary 552
Q&A 552
Workshop 554
Quiz 554

Appendix   Answers   555

Index   565

Acknowledgments

First and foremost, I'd like to thank my mother, Judith Kaufman, and my friend, Larry Kern—each of whom subsidized a significant part of the research for this book.

I'd like to thank Holly and Mark Rice for their help in creating some of the cooler animations and static graphics found in this book and on the enclosed CD-ROM. Holly's a real artist!

I'd also like to thank my baby brother, David, for his work catching my really stupid errors (like "Computer Object Model" instead of "Component Object Model").

I'd like to thank the editors and staff at Sams.net for their courteous comments and suggestions. It took me a couple of weeks to get the hang of the fact that they really don't use a hard-line formula in producing these books. Then again, you can attribute any errors herein directly to me!

Finally, I'd like to thank the developers at Microsoft for updating and publishing the ActiveX specifications three times during the three months I worked on this tome. By keeping us developers informed of the progress of ActiveX's development, the technology was released with the advice and consent of literally thousands of software and documentation authors.

  Sanders Kaufman, Jr.

I would like to thank my family, especially my wife Leslie. They suffer more than I do during the writing process. I would also like to thank Sharon Cox, for the opportunity to write this book, and her excellent editing staff, especially Kate Shoup, for making my writing readable.

  Jeff Perkins

I would like to thank Sams.net for making this a possibility. I would like to thank Lorraine Schaffer, Sharon Cox, Kate Shoup, and Todd Bumbalough of Sams.net for their help.

I would also like to thank Wayne Berry for his support and guidance with this book.

  Dina Fleet

About the Authors

Sanders Kaufman

Sanders "Bucky" Kaufman, Jr. is an Internet Consultant in Dallas, Texas. He got his start in computers when he was 11 years old. Sanders, his little brother David, and a group of their friends used to hike down to the local Radio Shack and program TRS-80 BASIC games and animation on the demo machines—the children themselves being an important part of the demonstration.

In 1988, Sanders focused on providing new and small businesses with management information and accounting systems tailored to their already installed PC systems.

In 1994, he teamed up with some of the Executive Officers of the Richardson, Texas Telecom Corridor companies to develop an Internet-Fax system. With a strong foundation in Bulletin Board Systems and experience as a BBS System Operator, Sanders dove headlong into the broad and expanding Internet/intranet technologies.

He now lives and works out of his two-bedroom apartment in Addison, Texas. It keeps him in close contact with his brother, Ron, and mother, Judith—to whom he owes more than just his life.

Jeff Perkins

Jeff Perkins is a Senior Software Engineer with TYBRIN Corporation, and a co-author of *Teach Yourself SQL in 14 Days*. A graduate of the United States Air Force Academy, he is a veteran with over 2,500 hours of flying time as navigator and bombardier in the B-52. He has also been a programmer, team leader, and program manager.

Dina Fleet

Dina Fleet holds a bachelor's degree in Computer Science from Principia College, Elsah, Illinois. Her background includes hardware and network consulting, software development, network and database engineering, Web development, and quality control. She is originally from Midland, Texas, and now works for Microsoft in Redmond, Washington for the OLE DB team.

Dina can be contacted at dinaf@microsoft.com.

Tell Us What You Think!

As a reader, you are the most important critic and commentator of our books. We value your opinion and want to know what we're doing right, what we could do better, what areas you'd like to see us publish in, and any other words of wisdom you're willing to pass our way. You can help us make strong books that meet your needs and give you the computer guidance you require.

Do you have access to CompuServe or the World Wide Web? Then check out our CompuServe forum by typing GO SAMS at any prompt. If you prefer the World Wide Web, check out our site at http://www.mcp.com.

NOTE If you have a technical question about this book, call the technical support line at (800) 571-5840, ext. 3668.

As the team leader of the group that created this book, I welcome your comments. You can fax, e-mail, or write me directly to let me know what you did or didn't like about this book—as well as what we can do to make our books stronger. Here's the information:

FAX: 317/581-4669

E-mail: enterprise_mgr@sams.mcp.com

Mail: Comments Department
Sams Publishing
201 W. 103rd Street
Indianapolis, IN 46290

Introduction

When we were first asked to do this book, a lot of folks on the team thought ActiveX was some kind of programming language like C++, HTML, or JavaStuff. In fact, it's all of them and none of them. ActiveX is a technology—a way of using a computer's environment to communicate over the Web efficiently and reliably. HTML, C++ Visual Basic, DirectX, and many other tools can be used to take advantage of ActiveX technologies.

"Why would I want to use ActiveX?" is the question we hear the most. We've got all kinds of answers—a different one for each individual.

"To have a professional Web presence."

"So people won't have to be techies to use your site."

"So everyone's machine can work with your pages."

The $40 answer is that it allows you to use OLE over the Web. This means that you can use your Web browser as a front end for your word processor, spreadsheet, database, chat, news, mail, and other applications. With ActiveX, you don't need to have 10 zillion applications installed on your machine. Moreover, you don't need to know how to use 10 zillion applications. When the Web browser tries to load an ActiveX document and you don't have the software required to load it, your Web browser will contact the software distributor over the Net, grab the stuff you need, and install it onto your local machine. If you never use that software again, it will be automatically deleted, freeing up valuable system resources for other uses.

After browsing some of the book titles available for computer programming, we found very few like this one. That is because ActiveX is a unique concept in programming. It addresses the issues of networking by relying on standards that have been cussed and discussed by the many standards organizations out there. Microsoft has said that it will release the ActiveX technologies to an independent standards body for continued maintenance, but in fact, most of it is already in public hands.

At A Glance

During Week 1, you will gain the fundamentals of scripting in relation to the Internet. By the end of the first week, you will be ready to start writing your own ActiveX scripts.

Day 1: Programming for the Internet

Day 1 introduces programming for the Internet. In this chapter, you will learn to recognize the basic features of a hypertext document, as well as how to receive background information about ActiveX and Internet programming.

Day 2: HTML & Scripting

Day 2 illustrates basic Web-page construction. You will be introduced to the format of an HTML page and the specific tags that make each page work. After you become familiar with the basic form of an HTML page, you will be shown how to incorporate scripting languages into your Web page.

Day 3: ActiveX Scripting

Day 3 introduces the international standard for client-side scripting, and discusses how Microsoft has implemented HTML scripting into ActiveX with JScript (based on another company's script processes) and VBScript (based on Microsoft's own Visual Basic programming language). Finally, the chapter briefly discusses some of the considerations for building your own ActiveX scripting engine. This skill, however, requires an in-depth knowledge of a programming language, such as C++, and a knowledge of OLE programming in general. You are not limited to using a script language that already exists, however; if nobody makes the one you want, make it yourself!

Day 4: The Tools of the Trade

Day 4 is a hands-on tour of four tools: Internet Assistant for Microsoft Word, HoTMetaL from SoftQuad, the Internet Information Server Add-In for Microsoft Access, and the ActiveX Control Pad from Microsoft. These tools can help you cut hours from your Web-site development time.

Day 5: Programming for Internet Explorer

On Day 5, you will learn the programming environment inside Microsoft's Internet Explorer. During Day 5, you will learn how the parts of Internet Explorer are structured, and how to use them with a scripting language.

Day 6: Writing VBScripts

Day 6 is an introduction and a reference to VBScript. During Week 2, you will learn how VBScript functions by working your way through dozens of examples that demonstrate syntax and function. By the end of Day 6, however, you will know how to use VBScript inside your HTML pages.

Day 7: Writing JavaScripts

Day 7 is an introduction and a reference to JavaScript. During Week 2, you will learn how JavaScript functions by working your way through dozens of examples that demonstrate syntax and function. By the end of Day 7, however, you will know how to use JavaScript inside your HTML pages.

Week 1

Day 1

Programming for the Internet

ActiveX is not the first method designed for programming over a network, but it is the first culmination of many diverse, prior-existing technologies for programming over intranet and Internet networks.

In this chapter you will learn to recognize the basic features of a hypertext document, as well as how to receive background information about ActiveX and Internet programming, including

- ☐ Microsoft's drive to focus research on Internet technologies.
- ☐ The shift from computer-oriented programming to document-oriented programming.

Internet programming, or ActiveX, has advanced significantly due to the Microsoft-led initiative to implement the most effective processes for cross-network development.

Windows—The Most Widely Used Desktop Operating System

In its quest to provide a computer environment that would draw new users (as well as users of other operating systems), Microsoft introduced Windows 95 in late 1995. The latest version integrated technologies and interfaces exposed by competing operating systems. Microsoft hoped to draw in users of those systems by incorporating the speed, graphics and other interfaces from more successful operating systems such as Macintosh, Atari, Amiga and Commodore. By making the look and feel of Windows simple and intuitive, Microsoft hoped to also draw in folks who had never used a PC before.

When Windows 95 was in its developmental test phases (alpha and beta releases), the Internet was taking off like a rocket. The Net had been around for dozens of years, but it was not until about the time of Windows 95's release that it had become a household word. For some households (and businesses), it came as America Online, CompuServe, Prodigy, or a few local BBS systems. Others, sometimes without knowing it, used the Internet by way of a leased line, usually a frame-relay or ISDN over their office or school LAN (Local Area Network).

As Microsoft developed Windows, it could not ignore the burgeoning use of their operating system on networked computers. In acknowledgment of this, Windows 95 includes support for a wide variety of networks. By default, Windows installs itself as a client for both a Windows (such as NT) and a Netware network. This is occurring as Netware networks are being phased out in many office LANs.

Dial-Up Networking

Many Internet users are connected through independent Internet service providers, or *ISPs* (such as CompuTek Network and FishNet). Many more users are connected through dial-up accounts with information tollways. Either way, the connection is probably made through a dial-up connection over regular phone lines.

The main difference between ISPs and tollways is pricing. ISPs tend to charge a flat monthly rate (around $10 to $30 per month, depending on your calling area), and tollways usually want $2 to $10 or more for every hour online. Another difference is that ISPs don't generally provide much content or tech support, whereas tollways focus on these services. For most developers, an account with an ISP is the way to go.

Microsoft provides a hybrid of ISPs and tollways called *MSN* (The Microsoft Network). MSN acts, for the most part, as a content provider. If you can't access MSN from the Net (via another dial-up provider), Microsoft offers several levels of metered hourly usage and charges a couple of bucks per hour for it—but it gives you an Internet connection when no others are available.

Installing MSN

Windows 95 ships with the everything you need to connect to the Internet. If you don't already have the MSN connection on your desktop, take this opportunity to install it.

MSN is both an ISP and a content provider. If you have an Internet account with another provider, skip this section. MSN costs about $5 per month if you don't use it for dial-up access. If you don't have a dial-up connection to the Internet, MSN does the trick, but the fee goes up to a couple of dollars every hour you're online. Figure 1.1 presents you with the setup screen for installing MSN; to install MSN, follow these steps:

1. From the Control Panel, click the Add/Remove Programs icon.
2. From the Windows Setup tab, select Communications and press the Details command button. This displays a list of communications accessories that you can install.
3. Make sure that Dial-Up Networking and Hyperterminal are selected, then press the OK command button to return to the Windows Setup tab. The Dial-Up Networking component allows you to make any of several different types of network connections, including and especially a PPP (Point-to-Point Protocol) connection to the Internet. Hyperterminal allows you to make telnet-like dial-up connections to local BBS and UNIX shell providers.
4. Scroll down the list and select Microsoft Exchange, then press the Details command button to display a list of Microsoft Exchange programs that can be installed from the Windows95 Setup disk(s).
5. Make sure that Microsoft Exchange is selected. Do not select Microsoft Mail Services unless you already know that you are using Microsoft Mail. Microsoft Mail is not Internet Mail. Press the OK command button to return to the Windows Setup tab.
6. Scroll down the list and select The Microsoft Network, then press the OK command button to return to the Windows Setup tab for the last time.
7. Finally, press the OK command button on the Add/Remove Programs window. Windows will prompt you for disks (unless your Win95 CD-ROM or diskettes have remained in the same place as when you installed Windows). When the installation process is complete, you will be prompted to reboot your machine.
8. Launch the white MSN icon that is now on your desktop (see Figure 1.1) and follow the prompts for logging on to the Internet.

Figure 1.1.
Windows setup allows you to install MSN, or another service, as your default Internet provider.

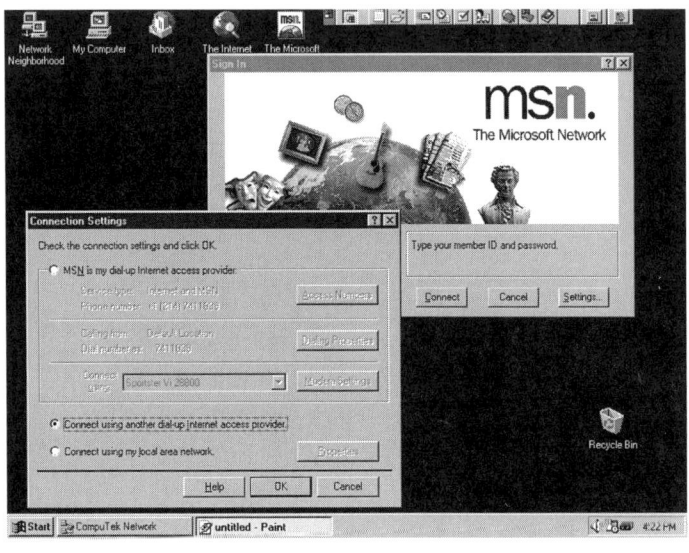

WARNING

Most online services require that you provide a valid checking- or credit-card-account number. This is like giving your account number to a cashier at an unfamiliar shop, so monitor the activity on any accounts used—be they over the Internet or elsewhere. This protects you from overcharges (these systems aren't perfect!) as well as from outright theft.

One option in Windows 95's setup process allows you to place a connection to MSN on your desktop—putting it and the Internet just a click away. Placing the MSN icon on the Windows 95 desktop consummated the marriage of the ordinary user's computer with the Internet. This marriage has placed an immediate demand on programmers to develop applications that used the distributed nature of the Internet—the capability to transmit information back and forth over wide distances and in real-time. Business owners want to use the Internet to give their business a worldwide presence on the Internet.

On previous networks, users could share documents and directories of documents, but this was limited primarily to use on LANs. This was because most technologies, such as file sharing, were only mature on LANs, not WANs. The technology was there—it just had not yet been implemented.

Integration of Network Technologies

That's when Microsoft took the ball and ran with it. To maintain dominance in the computer industry, they needed to develop applications that would allow the greatest percentage of the market to use the Internet with Windows. The task became complicated because there were many diverse entities working on the standards under which the Internet would operate.

Organizations such as IETF (Internet Engineering Task Force), the World Wide Web Consortium (W3C), Xerox PARC, France's CERN, NCSA (National Center for Supercomputing Applications), EFF (Electronic Frontier Foundation), and many others each took one or a few intranet computing concepts and developed methods and protocols to support those ideas on different systems (see Figure 1.2). These converted methods and protocols allow for file transfers, e-mail, conferencing, and news broadcasts to occur on the Net without interfering with each other, and ensure the delivery of the proper message packets to the intended recipients.

Figure 1.2.
Many different organizations are involved in defining the standards for the Internet.

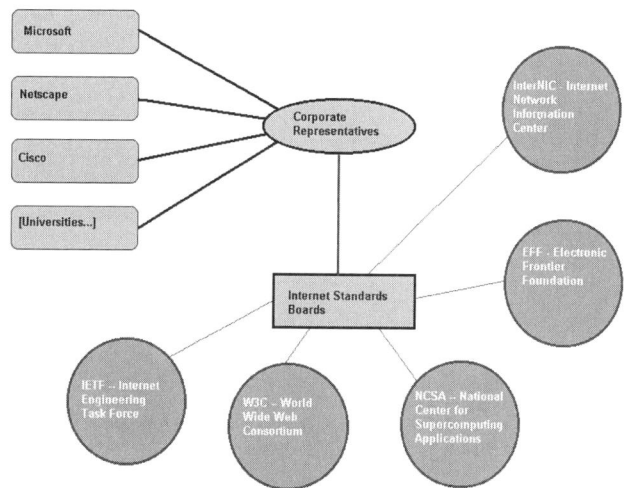

Microsoft has placed its own people on the boards of many of these bodies to ensure the representation of Windows technologies in the ongoing task of allowing cross-platform use of the Internet, and to ensure that Microsoft's products conform to any adopted standards.

The Release of ActiveX

Now that the marriage of Windows and the Internet is complete, Microsoft is turning its network-programming technologies over to the public domain. This will allow people to write applications for use on the Internet, and will bring more non-users into the fold of Windows computing.

These technologies are collectively referred to as ActiveX, reflecting Bill Gates' directive to his developmental staff to "Activate the Internet."

> **Installing the ActiveX Software Developers Kit**
>
>
>
> Before you go any further, install the ActiveX SDK on your local hard drive. You can find this tool kit, which is central to this book, on the enclosed CD-ROM. Installation is simple:
>
> 1. Locate the `ActiveX.exe` file on the enclosed CD-ROM.
> 2. Double-click this file and accept its installation defaults when prompted.
> 3. Reboot the system when prompted.
> 4. Review the directory in which the file was installed (usually `\INetSDK\`). Notice which files `ActiveX.exe` placed in that directory. You will be using these files throughout this book.

ActiveX gives the programmer the ability to enable a program to access files and messages (and even access actual *people*) over the Internet—and to be able to market that program to a *very* wide audience. This means that a user can acquire an inexpensive custom program for a specific purpose from darn near anywhere because even the most inexperienced programmers will have the tools to write applications that can manipulate data over a network right at their fingertips.

TIP

The demand for simple Web browsers and e-mail programs has peaked—everybody needs them. You probably won't be creating these basic utilities because anybody can get them free from Microsoft!

ActiveX gives you the tools to provide what the market really wants: customized, specialized products created for specific purposes. You will need to identify special demands that cannot be met by standard Internet utilities.

Document Objects

One of the paradigm shifts effected by Microsoft's input in network standards involves the idea of documents as *enhanced objects*.

In earlier operating systems, the whole focus of programming was limited by the capabilities of the user's computer. For instance, a programmer who writes a really great paint program first has to determine whether the end-user's machine will have the graphics resources (hardware, firmware, software, and so on) to run the application.

Instead of asking "What is the user's computer capable of doing?" ActiveX programmers ask "What does the user want to do?" (A very happy question!) This compelled Microsoft to adopt the slogan "Where do you want to go today?"

Certain *classes* define the different types of *objects* supported by a given computer system. The classes define what properties, methods and events are supported for an object. They also define how an object is to be implemented on the local machine. These defined objects are *instantiated* (created), then *uninstantiated* (thrown away) as needed by a program.

The Frankenstein Model

Let's take this idea to its wildest extreme: You are a mad scientist, and you want to create an object called objFrankenstein. To make it, you must have a specification (or class) for creating it. This specification defines objFrankenstein's properties, methods, and events.

objFrankenstein will have properties, such as a brain called objFrankenstein.Brain and a torso called objFrankenstein.Torso. Some of these properties will be property *arrays*, such as objFrankenstein.Eyes(Left) and objFrankenstein.Eyes(Right).

objFrankenstein will also have events that occur based on changes in a property. He might have an event called objFrankenstein_WakeUp that fires whenever he wakes up, or an event called objFrankenstein.Eyes(Left)_Wink that fires whenever he winks his left eye.

objFrankenstein's methods define how he does things. An example would be his method for sitting down. When he sits, he might use a method like the following, which is coded in VBScript (with some imaginary objects, properties, methods, and events):

```
objFrankenstein_Sit(Chair as Furniture, Distance as Height)
Select Case Chair
    Case "Bean Bag"
        objFrankenstein.move "Down" "Distance"
    Case "Couch"
        objFrankenstein.move "Down" "Distance"
    Case "Unknown"
        objFrankenstein.Look "Behind" "You"
End Select
```

All of this is defined in the class specification for the object (see Figure 1.3). In ActiveX, the methods for defining these classes on a computer are expanded to consider the distributed nature of the Internet. This gives your Frankenstein object certain advanced features, such as privacy and the capability to re-create modified versions of itself from information available at a remote location. Pretty wild, eh?

Figure 1.3.
By treating a document as a customizable bag of properties, OLE programmers can create almost anything within that document.

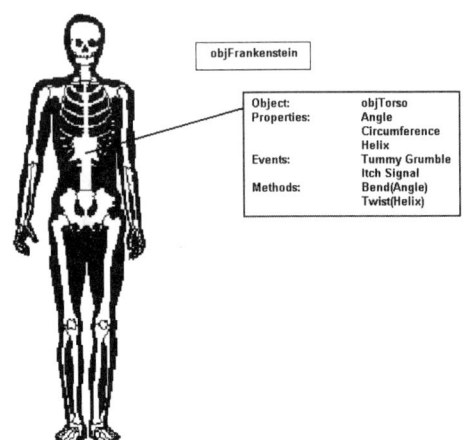

The Document Object

ActiveX technologies reference each document on the Internet as an object. By *document*, I mean an item that exists somewhere on the Net and can be transferred to another machine. This document object could be a whole program that runs on a user's machine, or a spreadsheet table, or even a word-processing document, such as a resume or a business plan.

In turn, these document objects have their own properties, methods and events. Some of the properties of the document can include Document.Page(), Document.Title, and Document.Author. Some of the events of the document can include Document_OnLoad and Document_OnUnload. Some of the methods can include Document.Save and Document.Delete.

This redefinition of the document has compelled the development of several related technologies. The OLE controls used by programmers of standalone systems were enhanced or redesigned (see Figure 1.4), which necessitated the implementation of cryptographic and other security features. Data download services were implemented to enable users who wanted to view a document that their system was incapable of downloading controls as needed. Scripting services have also been redesigned to take advantage of document-automation processes.

Figure 1.4.
Documents may just be a string of text, but if the text is formatted correctly, properties of that content can be retrieved.

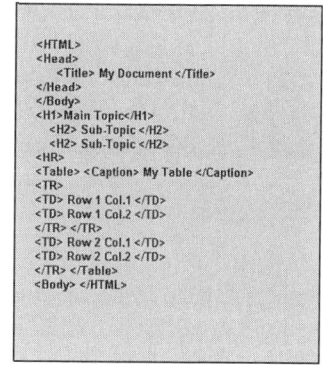
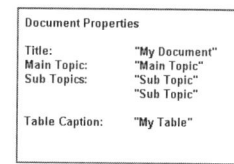

Hypertext

In and of itself, the sharing of documents over the Net is only mildly interesting. However, in the last five years, hypertext documents have become very popular—and rightly so (see Figure 1.5). *Hypertext* is a way of formatting various forms of content through the Net so that users can interact with the content regardless of the type of computer they are using. Therefore, Mac, UNIX, and Windows users can each access, interact with, and update the same information. The most common type of content that can be shared in this way is called *multimedia*.

Figure 1.5.
A hypertext document viewed in Netscape.

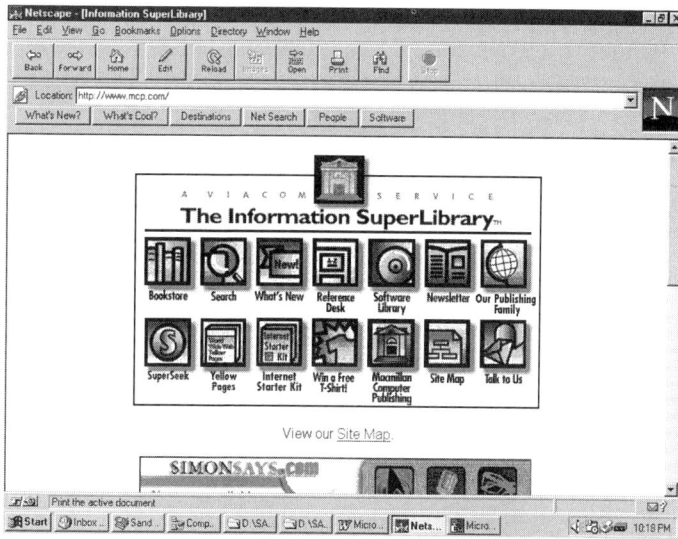

The standard format for transferring this multimedia data over the Net is referred to as *MIME* (Multimedia Internet Mail Extensions). The entire MIME specification is contained in RFC (Request For Comment) 1521 (http://ds.internic.net/rfc/rfc1521.txt) and RFC 1522 (http://ds.internic.net/rfc/rfc1522.txt). Basically, this specification defines how computers on the Internet share nontext information, such as video and sound clips. These RFC pages are the first and second halves of the MIME standard for identification and dissemination of multimedia content over the Internet.

When someone says "I'm surfing the Net" or "I'm cruising the Web," he is usually referring to viewing hypertext documents. Hypertext documents exist on a remote server system, such as NASA's, the Louvre's or the Library of Congress's. The documents then can be viewed with a Web browser, such as MSIE (Microsoft Internet Explorer) or Netscape Navigator.

These powerful document viewers allow for content like you will never see in a traditional newspaper. Instead of simple inline graphics for a news story or advertisement, content providers place inline audio and video on their pages. Also, features such as command buttons and scrolling lists allow the user to enter data (such as a name, address, and credit-card information) into the page. This user input might either be some sort of request for, or submission of, information.

The hypertext specification is the definition of how these documents are put together. Remembering that a document is nothing more than text strung together, the specification does not define what *content* is found in a document. Rather, it specifies how that content is formatted. For a full description of the hypertext specification, visit Microsoft's Internet Development site (http://www.microsoft.com/intdev), the IETF (http://www.ietf.org), or the Internet Network Information Center (http://www.internic.net).

Summary

In this chapter, you have become familiar with Microsoft's drive to integrate the diverse Internet technologies into a cohesive family of commercial-grade processes for information sharing. You also have been exposed to MSN, one of the information tollways. These new products and services add value to dial-up computing as well as leased-line services, such as corporations and research institutions.

You are now also aware of the paradigm shift involved in the ActiveX integration, which involves a change from computer-oriented to document-oriented programming. Document-oriented programming allows each document to have properties, methods, and events, within which programmers may code their programs. You have also been exposed briefly to the basics of hypertext documents.

Q&A

Q What is the best system for accessing the Internet?

A There is no best system for accessing the Internet. ActiveX is mature only on Windows 95 machines, but it is being written for Mac and UNIX as well. Each system has its own strengths and weaknesses. As a rule of thumb:

- If your task is graphics-intensive, use a Mac. You could use a more pricey solution, such as a those put out by Silicon Graphics, but for the money, Mac is the best graphics editor around.
- If your system is for desktop business, use a Windows 95 PC. You could use NT Workstation as well, but such a powerhorse would be more suited to the network administrator than the accounting department.
- If your system is a server for a LAN, use Windows NT. It supports all of the common networking features, such as e-mail and chat, and allows very stable security- and information-sharing features.
- If your system is an Internet server, use Windows NT or UNIX. NT supports the more important ActiveX server features, but unless you are relying on those features, many ISPs find a simple UNIX box gives them the most bang for their buck, and with fewer day-to-day maintenance requirements.

Q How is Windows 95 used as a dial-up network workstation?

A Most, if not all, dial-up services are usable through Windows 95 and its applets. For the old BBS-type dial-up, which uses a login screen and ANSI or ASCII text, there is the HyperTerminal program. The Windows 95 setup process adds connections for several other dial-up services, including AT&T and MCI. AOL and CompuServe require additional software, and MSN is an installation option on the desktop.

MSN has built-in support for connections to most types of other networks—LAN, WAN, TelCo (telephone company), and so on. Internet connections are usually handled through the built-in dial-up networking feature. Technically, this is a dial-up TCP/IP (Transmission Control Protocol/Internet Protocol) connection using PPP (Point to Point Protocol) over a Modem (Modulator/Demodulator) through an analog connection. MSN's e-mail program, Microsoft Exchange, has an additional networking feature called Microsoft Fax. This is a server and client for the fax network. It works over the telephone network to send and receive messages over the POTS (Plain Old Telephone System) network.

Q How is the simultaneous playing of one multimedia file by multiple systems possible?

A Although the file begins in one place (the server), it is transferred to all the machines requesting it. Each requesting machine uses programs installed on its local machine to play the file. This allows a UNIX user to use a different method for playing files than an NT user while each listens to the same sound.

Workshop

Referring to the documentation provided with the ActiveX SDK and available at their Web site, notice the standards that have been developed outside of Microsoft (such as PICS, MIME and HTML 3.2). Review and bookmark these sites. You can add a shortcut to your desktop, instead of bookmarking it, by selecting File|Create Shortcut from the Internet Explorer menu bar.

Quiz

1. What is an information tollway?
2. What two different components of Windows 95 can be used to access network services over a modem?
3. Why did Microsoft create ActiveX?
4. What conceptual shift is reflected in the ActiveX document objects features?
5. What defines an object's properties, methods and events?
6. Of what are objects composed?
7. Why is HTML such a popular presentation format?
8. What format allows multimedia content, such as audio and video, to be transmitted via the Internet?

Refer to the appendix, "Answers," for the answers to these questions.

Week 1

Day 2

HTML & Scripting

Today you start applying the theory of scripting. Web pages are written in Hypertext Markup Language (HTML). This chapter starts a crash course on HTML. You will learn how to design a basic Web page with nothing but your brain, this chapter, and a text editor. In addition to learning basic HTML functions, you will learn the mechanics of inserting scripting language and ActiveX objects on your Web pages. You are going to have fun today, so let's get started.

Overview of HTML

HTML is related to (or rather, descended from) another formatting standard for text documents called Standard Generalized Markup Language (SGML). SGML is used as a standard to share data across diverse systems. HTML is a document-type definition (DTD) of SGML. *DTD* is a fancy way of saying subset. So, HTML is a subset of SGML.

Remarkably, HTML files are written in plain ASCII text. It is probably an accident that something so useful didn't wind up in an obscure format. Or it could be that HTML's usefulness derives from its format, which is common enough for any text editor to generate. So fire up your text editor and launch your browser. Let's make Web pages!

The Basic Form

Type Listing 2.1 into your text editor.

Listing 2.1. The traditional Hello World introduction.

```
<HTML>
<HEAD>
<TITLE>Hello World</TITLE>
</HEAD>
<BODY>
Hello World
</BODY>
</HTML>
```

Save your file as `hello.html`, then launch your Web browser.

NOTE: The standard filename extension for HTML files is `*.html`. In operating systems that support three-letter file extensions, the standard is `.htm`. Other extensions won't cause the system to crash, but can cause confusion. I recommend that you stay with the standard extension.

Your creation should look something like Figure 2.1.

Figure 2.1.
Your first Web page.

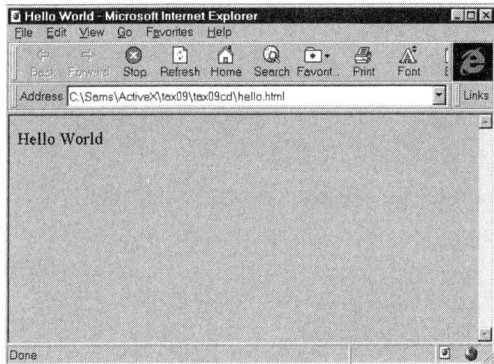

Not bad for your first try. Let's learn how to improve on this simple start.

Elements of HTML

HTML uses tags to convey ideas to the Web browser. Listing 2.1 is full of tags, such as <HTML> and <BODY>. Tags are enclosed in brackets (<>). You will look at tags during the next several pages. You will start with the most common tags and end with the tags <SCRIPT> and <OBJECT>. <SCRIPT> and <OBJECT> are the keys to using scripting language and ActiveX components. While this chapter does not cover every element of HTML, it should cover enough to build a foundation for your knowledge of how a Web page is constructed. Each HTML element that we examine will appear in the following format:

The <TAG> Tag

Description: Contains a brief description of the tag. Some tags take the form <TAG>...</TAG> to indicate the elements affected by the tags. Other tags appear as <TAG>, which normally sets an attribute of the element on the page that follows it.

Appears As: <TAG> </TAG> or <TAG>

Attributes: Properties that can be set for the tag, such as color and position. Not all tags have attributes.

Can Contain: Other tags that can be used within this tag. (Not all tags will have entries in this section.)

Can Be In: Other tags in which this tag can be used.

Example: Contains an example that illustrates the capabilities of a given HTML tag.

Overall Page Structure

There are three tags used in almost every Web page, <HTML>, <HEAD>, and <BODY>. All the action in your Web pages will take place inside these tags. Take a look at how to use them.

The <HTML> Tag

Description: The beginning and ending of an HTML document.

Appears As: <HTML> </HTML>

Attributes: None

Can Contain: <BODY>, <HEAD>

Can Be In: N/A

Example: Reduce your Hello World page to three lines using the <HTML> tag (see Listing 2.2).

Listing 2.2. The simplified Hello World page.

```
<HTML>
Hello World
</HTML>
```

Notice that the output shown in Figure 2.2 is the same as that shown in Figure 2.1.

Figure 2.2.
The simple Hello World.

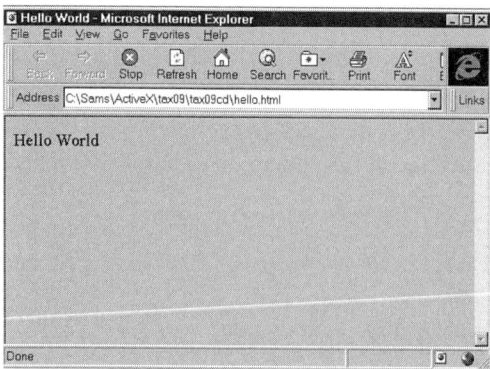

All your HTML documents will be enclosed with the <HTML> tag.

The `<HEAD>` Tag

Description: This is where you can save information about the Web page. The information stored here is not displayed. This section is loaded before other sections of the document, which makes it a great place to put `<SCRIPT>` and `<OBJECT>` tags (I'll discuss these tags later in this chapter).

Appears As: `<HEAD>  </HEAD>`

Attributes: None

Can Contain: `<BASE>`, `<ISINDEX>`, `<LINK>`, `<META>`, `<NEXTID>`, `<TITLE>`, `<SCRIPT>`, `<OBJECT>`

Can Be In: `<HTML>`

Example: Give the Web page a title inside the `<HEAD>` tags, as shown in Listing 2.3.

Listing 2.3. Giving a title to a Web page.

```
<HTML>
<HEAD>
<TITLE>MY WEB PAGE</TITLE>
</HEAD>
<BODY>
This is My Very Own Web Page
</BODY>
</HTML>
```

Notice in Figure 2.3 that the title doesn't show up on the form.

Figure 2.3.
The phantom title.

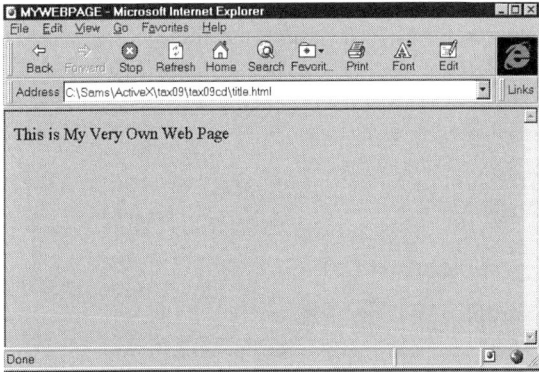

You might be saying, "If is doesn't show up, what good is it?" Well, for one thing, if someone wants to remember where your page is and adds it to his browser's "favorites" list, the browser will use the text inside the <TITLE> tags. In this case, MY WEB PAGE would be added to the list. Examine the Start bar pictured in Figure 2.4. It shows that the browser has extracted the title from this Web page and is using it as a Start bar button.

Figure 2.4.
The title on the Start bar button.

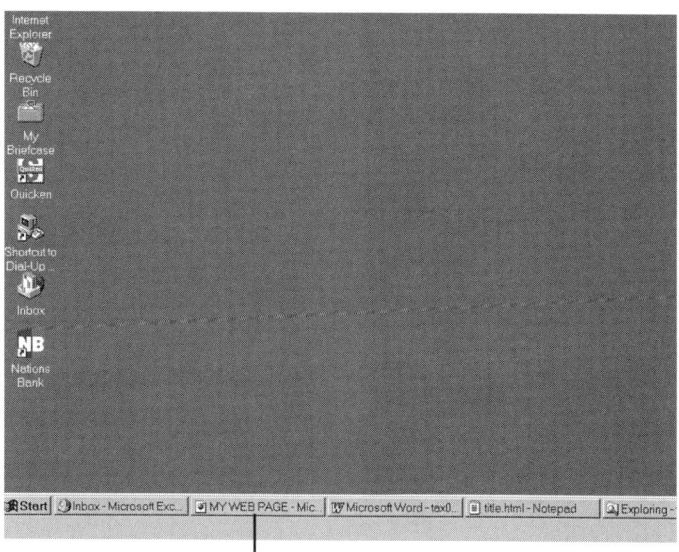

MYWEBPAGE - Mic

The <BODY> Tag

Description: Contains all the content of your Web page.

Appears As: <BODY> </BODY>

Attributes: BACKGROUND

Can Contain: <H1> through <H6>, <P>, <OL>, <UL>, <DIR>, <MENU>, <DL>, <PRE>, <BLOCKQUOTE>, <FORM>, <ISINDEX>, <HR>, <ADDRESS>

Can Be In: <HTML>

Example: Aside from containing all the content of your page, the BACKGROUND attribute is set within the <BODY> tags (see Listing 2.4).

Listing 2.4. Setting the background inside the <BODY> tags.

```
<HTML>
<HEAD>
<TITLE>STARS!</TITLE>
</HEAD>
<BODY BACKGROUND = "GoldStar.gif">
I see Stars!
</BODY>
</HTML>
```

The result of Listing 2.4 is shown in Figure 2.5.

Figure 2.5.
Setting the BACKGROUND *attribute.*

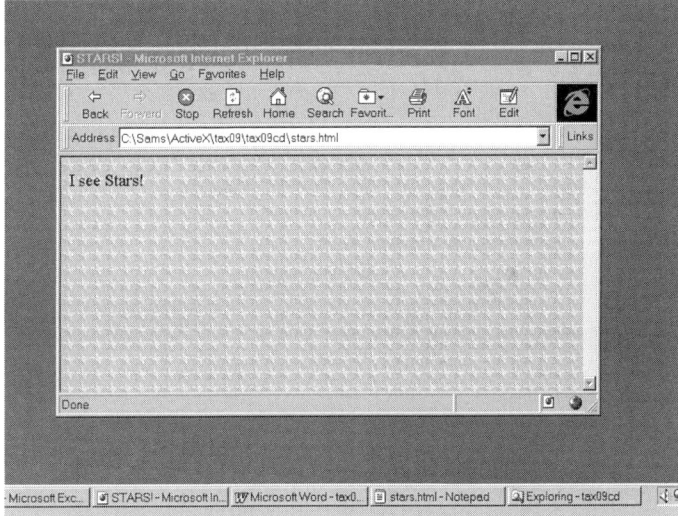

Notice the Start bar at the bottom of the picture. It contains the STARS! attribute that you saw in the <TITLE> tag. Also notice that the single star contained in the GIF file ("GoldStar.gif") was tiled to fill the entire screen.

The <HTML>, <HEAD>, and <BODY> tags are the backbone of the HTML page.

Working Inside the Body of the Web Page

Now that you have mastered the skeleton of the HTML page, take a look at some of its vital organs.

Comment Tags

Description: Those of you with a programming background were probably hoping that HTML wouldn't have any comments. The merits of comments have been debated in break rooms across the world. One school of thought is that the lack of comments has probably made more work for programmers (in general, a good thing if one wants to make a living by programming). Admittedly, I have never seen anyone lose a job due to lack of comments, but if you want to make your Web-page-building life a little easier, comments are important. When asked what a particular poem meant, the great poet Robert Frost is supposed to have said, "When I wrote this poem, only God and I knew what it meant. Now only God knows." That is because his poems didn't have comments.

Appear As: <!...>

Example: Add a comment to the previous STARS! example, as shown in Listing 2.5.

Listing 2.5. Using comment tags inside the <BODY> tags.

```
<HTML>
<HEAD>
<TITLE>STARS!</TITLE>
</HEAD>
<BODY BACKGROUND = "GoldStar.gif">
<!
Goldstar.gif came from the QuickStart Collection of Gifs
>
I see Stars!
</BODY>
</HTML>
```

The result is the same as Figure 2.5, but when you have to maintain this page you will know where the picture came from. Comments can speak to future programmers tasked to maintain or learn from your pages. The comment tags can also be used in conjunction with the <SCRIPT> tags. To keep older browsers that don't recognize the <SCRIPT> tag from seeing the code inside the <SCRIPT> tags, the <SCRIPT> tags themselves are placed inside comment tags.

Heading Tags

Description: Heading tags allow you to outline your Web page. Visually, the lower the number, the bigger the print. Avoid using large headings just to achieve the visual effect. A program building an index from your page might use the text in your index as the entry in the index.

Appear As: <H1> </H1>, <H2> </H2>, <H3> </H3>, <H4> </H4>, <H5> </H5>, <H6> </H6>

Attributes: ALIGN

Can Contain: <A>, <IMG>, <BR>, <EM>, <STRONG>, <CODE>, <SAMP>, <KBD>, <VAR>, <CITE>, <B>, <I>

Can Be In: <BLOCKQUOTE>, <BODY>, <PRE>, <ADDRESS>, <FORM>, <TH>, <TD>

Example: Create headings in your text (see Listing 2.6).

Listing 2.6. Using headings.

```
<HTML>
<HEAD>
<TITLE>SPEECH</TITLE>
</HEAD>
<BODY>
<H1>SPEECH OUTLINE </H1>

<H1>INTRODUCTION </H1>
    <H2>TELL THEM WHAT YOU ARE GOING TO TELL THEM</H2>

<H1>MAIN POINT</H1>
    <H2>DETAIL</H2>
        <H3>SUB DETAIL</H3>
            <H4>REALLY DETAILED</H4>
                <H5>SO DETAILED NO ONE UNDERSTANDS IT</H5>
                    <H6>SO DETAILED NO ONE CARES</H6>

<H1>CONCLUSION</H1>
    <H2>TELL THEM WHAT YOU TOLD THEM</H2>

</BODY>
</HTML>
```

This example shows another common use for heading tags. The title to a form is often echoed in an <H1> tag, as shown in seventh line of Listing 2.6. Listing 2.6 produces the page shown in Figure 2.6.

Paragraph Tags

Description: Paragraph tags provide a way to separate the content of your page. A paragraph tag ends any previous section, then puts some space after that section. Finally, the text inside the tag is printed as a new section.

Appear As: <P> </P>

Attributes: ALIGN

Can Contain: <A>, <IMG>, <BR>, <EM>, <STRONG>, <CODE>, <SAMP>, <KBD>, <VAR>, <CITE>, <B>, <I>, <TT>

Can Be In: <BLOCKQUOTE>, <BODY>, <PRE>, <ADDRESS>, <FORM>, <TH>, <TD>

Example: Let's throw a couple of paragraphs together and see what happens (see Listing 2.7).

Figure 2.6.
Using headings.

> **SPEECH OUTLINE**
> **INTRODUCTION**
> TELL THEM WHAT YOU ARE GOING TO TELL THEM
> **MAIN POINT**
> DETAIL
> SUB DETAIL
> REALLY DETAILED
> SO DETAILED NO ONE UNDERSTANDS IT
> SO DETAILED NO ONE CARES
> **CONCLUSION**
> TELL THEM WHAT YOU TOLD THEM

Listing 2.7. Fun with paragraphs.

```
<HTML>
<HEAD>
<TITLE>PARAGRAPHS</TITLE>
</HEAD>
<BODY>
<H1>PARAGRAPHS </H1>

<H1>FIRST PARAGRAPH </H1>
<P>Paragraph tags provide a way of separating the content of your page.
A paragraph tag first ends any previous section.  Then it puts some
space after the last section.  Finally the text inside the tag is
printed as a new section.</P>
<P>Notice the separation between this section and the last section. Also
notice how this section interacts with the plain text that follows</P>
Plain text that follows

</BODY>
</HTML>
```

Listing 2.7 produces the page shown in Figure 2.7.

Links (The <A> Tag)

Description: The <A> tag is the bread and butter of current Internet pages. It allows you to specify a new page to jump to when the user selects a certain area of the Web page.

Appears As: <A> </A>

Attributes: HREF, NAME

Can Contain: <IMG>, <BR>, <EM>, <STRONG>, <CODE>, <SAMP>, <KBD>, <VAR>, <CITE>, <B>, <I>, <TT>

Can Be In: <ADDRESS>, <B>, <CITE>, <CODE>, <DD>, <DT>, <EM>, <H1> through <H6>, <I>, <KBD>, <LI>, <P>, <PRE>, <SAMP>, <STRONG>, <TT>, <VAR>, <TH>, <TD>

Example: Make two pages. The main page source code is shown in Listing 2.8. The source code for the page you will jump to is in Listing 2.9.

Figure 2.7.
Paragraphs in action.

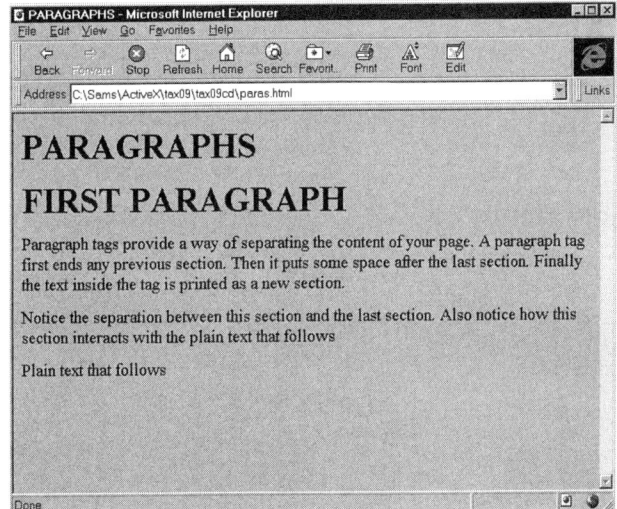

Listing 2.8. Links: the main page.

```
<HTML>
<HEAD>
<TITLE>LINKS MAIN PAGE</TITLE>
</HEAD>
<BODY>
<H1>LINKS MAIN PAGE </H1>

<H1>An Example of links </H1>
<P>Links are what make the internet interesting.  How often have
you started looking for one piece of information and wound up looking
at something like a Llama Ranch Home Page?
<A HREF="linkref.html">Click Here to Go to another page.</A></P>

</BODY>
</HTML>
```

Listing 2.9. Links: the page referenced.

```
<HTML>
<HEAD>
<TITLE>LINKS REF PAGE</TITLE>
</HEAD>
<BODY>
<H1>LINKS REF PAGE </H1>

<H1>An Example of links </H1>
<P>We made it to another page!  Congratulations on your first link.
<A HREF="linkmain.html">Now lets go back.</A></P>

</BODY>
</HTML>
```

Notice the syntax for the <A> tag. The filename of the link is placed with the beginning tag, like this: <A HREF="linkmain.html">. The text you want to associate with the tag is placed between the <A> tag and the </A> tag. The main form is shown in Figure 2.8.

Figure 2.8.
The original document.

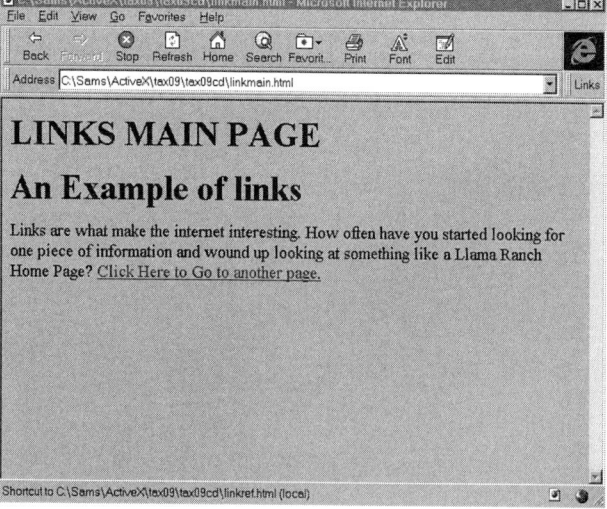

Clicking the line Click Here to Go to another page displays the page shown in Figure 2.9.

Clicking the phrase Now lets go back returns you to the main document.

Figure 2.9.
The referenced document.

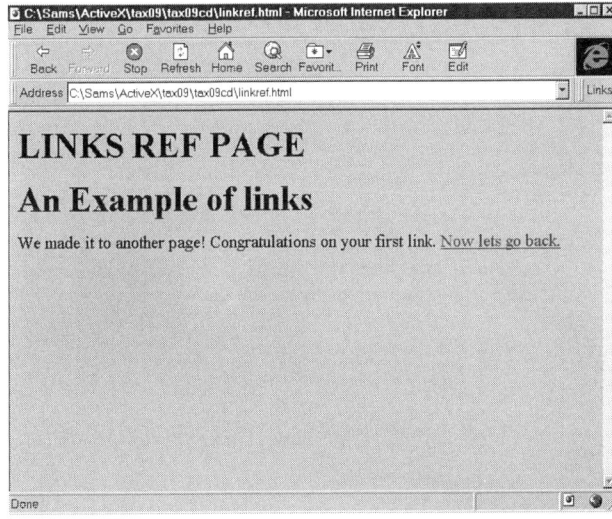

Lists

A list is a very common way of presenting data. HTML provides two mainstream ways to show them: the <OL> tag and the <UL> tag.

The <OL> Tag

Description: An ordered list. Items in this list are numbered by the Web browser.

Appears As: <OL> </OL>

Attributes: TYPE, START

Can Contain: <LI>

Can Be In: <BLOCKQUOTE>, <BODY>, <PRE>, <ADDRESS>, <FORM>, <TH>, <TD>

The <UL> Tag

Description: An unordered list. This doesn't mean the data in the list is chaotic. It means that the Web browser designates the item with a symbol.

Appears As: <UL> </UL>

Attributes: TYPE

Can Contain: <LI>

Can Be In: <BLOCKQUOTE>, <BODY>, <PRE>, <ADDRESS>, <FORM>, <TH>, <TD>

Example: Listing 2.10 shows how these two tags are used.

Listing 2.10. An ordered list and an unordered list.

```
<HTML>
<HEAD>
<TITLE>LISTS</TITLE>
</HEAD>
<BODY>
<H1>LISTS</H1>

<H1>An Example of Lists </H1>
<P>Lists are another way of organizing the content of
your page.  An ordered list of three items looks like this:</P>
<OL>
<LI> Thing One
<LI> Thing Two
<LI> Thing Three
</OL>
<P>An unordered list of same three items looks like this:</P>
<UL>
<LI> Thing One
<LI> Thing Two
<LI> Thing Three
</UL>
</BODY>
</HTML>
```

The <LI> tag denotes the items placed on the list. The output is shown in Figure 2.10.

Figure 2.10.
Displaying lists.

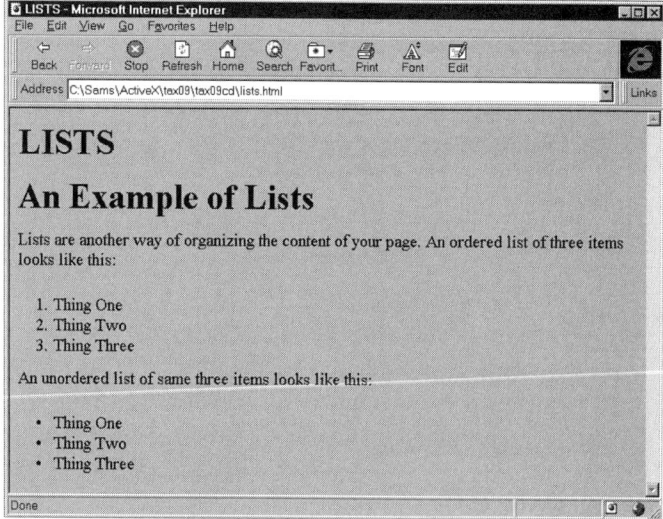

The TYPE attribute is browser dependent. TYPE allows you to change the numbering system or symbol depending on the kind of list you are building. The START attribute allows you to start the list at a particular number.

Tables

Tables are a useful way of showing any data that can be put into rows and columns. Using the <TABLE> tag allows you to do this.

The <TABLE> Tag

Description: Allows you to present the contents of your pages in column and row format.

Appears As: <TABLE> </TABLE>

Attributes: BORDER

Can Contain: <CAPTION>

Can Be In: <BLOCKQUOTE>, <BODY>, <DD>, <LI>, <FORM>

Example: Create your own table. Listing 2.11 shows the source code for a simple table in a Web page.

Listing 2.11. Web page with table.

```
<HTML>
<HEAD><Title>TABLES</Title></HEAD>
<BODY BGCOLOR="#FFFFFF">
<H1>Tables</H1>

<H3>A table of Phone Numbers</H3>
<TABLE BORDER>
<TR>
 <TH>NAME</TH>
 <TH>STATE</TH>
 <TH>PHONE</TH>
</TR>
<TR>
 <TD>Valerie</TD>
 <TD>CA</TD>
 <TD>555 555-5551</TD>
</TR>
<TR>
 <TD>Jeff</TD>
 <TD>FL</TD>
 <TD>555 555-5552</TD>
</TR>
<TR>
```

continues

Listing 2.11. continued

```
 <TD>Alton</TD>
 <TD>CA</TD>
 <TD>555 555-5553</TD>
</TR>
<TR>
 <TD>Ruth</TD>
 <TD>CA</TD>
 <TD>555 555-5554</TD>
</TR>
</TABLE>
</BODY></HTML>
```

Three tags, <TR>, <TH>, and <TD>, work inside a table. Rows in the table are defined between <TR> and </TR>. Within these rows, headings are denoted using <TH> and </TH>, and data is enclosed by <TD> and </TD>. The primary difference between a data element and a heading element is the heading element is bolded by the browser. See Figure 2.11 for the resulting page.

Figure 2.11.
A table of phone numbers.

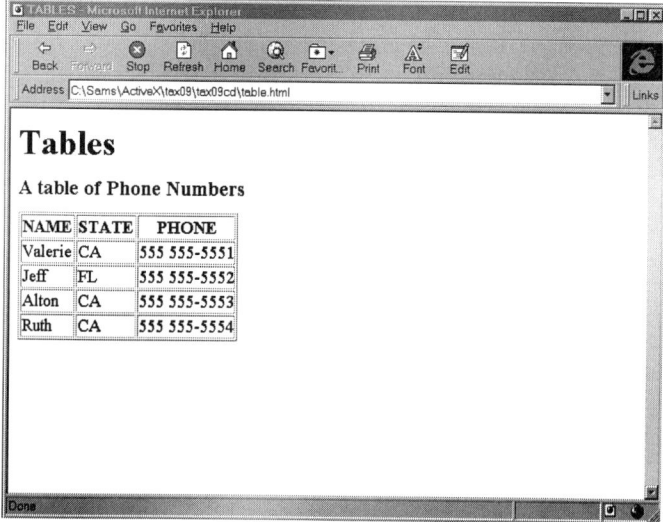

Notice the use of the BORDER attribute. If the BORDER attribute was left out, the border shown in Figure 2.11 would disappear.

Forms and Inputs

The `<FORM>` and `<INPUT>` tags work hand-in-hand to provide a way to get information from the user and pass it to your server. The `<FORM>` tag provides the framework and the `<INPUT>` tag provides the user-interface elements.

The `<FORM>` Tag

Description: `<FORM>` provides a section of page where the user can input data; that data can be collected and sent back to your server.

Appears As: `<FORM>` `</FORM>`

Attributes: ACTION, METHOD, ENCTYPE

Can Contain: `<H1>` through `<H6>`, `<P>`, `<OL>`, `<UL>`, `<DIR>`, `<MENU>`, `<DL>`, `<PRE>`, `<BLOCKQUOTE>`, `<ISINDEX>`, `<TABLE>`, `<HR>`, `<ADDRESS>`, `<INPUT>`, `<SELECT>`, `<TEXTAREA>`

Can Be In: `<BLOCKQUOTE>`, `<BODY>`, `<DD>`, `<LI>`, `<TH>`, `<TD>`

The `<INPUT>` Tag

Description: These are the user interface objects allowed by HTML. There are seven user interface objects: CHECKBOX, HIDDEN, RADIO, RESET, SUBMIT, TEXT, and IMAGE.

Appears As: `<INPUT>`

Attributes: TYPE, NAME, VALUE, SRC, CHECKED, SIZE, MAXLENGTH, ALIGN

Can Contain: N/A

Can Be In: `<FORM>`

Example: You will do two examples for these tags. The first will show all the user interface elements available from the `<INPUT>` tag, and the second will show how `<FORM>` and `<INPUT>` work together to collect data and pass data back to the server. (See Listing 2.12.)

Listing 2.12. Sample source code for `<INPUT>`.

```
<HTML>
<HEAD><Title>INPUTS</Title></HEAD>
<BODY BGCOLOR="#FFFFFF">
<H1>INPUTS</H1>

<H3>These are the Grapic Elements available through the INPUTS Tag</H3>
<! The INPUT tag only works inside a form>
<FORM>
<P>TEXT
```

continues

Listing 2.12. continued

```
<INPUT TYPE ="TEXT" NAME ="TextBox1" SIZE = "20" MAXLENGTH ="15">
</P>
<P>RADIO Buttons
<UL>
<LI><INPUT TYPE ="RADIO" NAME ="RadioButton1" VALUE = "Thing1" > Thing1
<LI><INPUT TYPE ="RADIO" NAME ="RadioButton1" VALUE = "Thing2" > Thing2
</UL>
<INPUT TYPE ="RADIO" NAME ="RadioButton2" VALUE = "Item1" > Item1
<INPUT TYPE ="RADIO" NAME ="RadioButton2" VALUE = "Item2" > Item2
</P>
<P>CheckBoxes (Choose all that apply)
<UL>
<LI><INPUT TYPE ="CHECKBOX" NAME ="Tinker" VALUE = "Thing1" > Tinker
<LI><INPUT TYPE ="CHECKBOX" NAME ="Taylor" VALUE = "Thing2" > Taylor
</UL>
</P>
<P>Image:
<INPUT TYPE ="IMAGE" NAME ="BitMapBtn" SRC = "GoldStar.gif" >
</P>
<P>RESET AND SUBMIT
<INPUT TYPE ="RESET" VALUE = "RESET VALUES" >
<INPUT TYPE ="SUBMIT" VALUE = "SEND STUFF TO SERVER" >
</P>
<P>Hidden:
<INPUT TYPE ="HIDDEN" NAME ="HiddenValue" >
</P>
</FORM>
</BODY></HTML>
```

There are a couple of things you should look at here. Notice the use of the attributes SIZE and MAXLENGTH in the line `<INPUT TYPE ="TEXT" NAME ="TextBox1" SIZE = "20" MAXLENGTH ="15">`. This sizes the text box at 20 characters and limits the user to 15 characters. If MAXLENGTH is left out, the user can type an unlimited amount of text. In general, the attribute VALUE is what is submitted along with the attribute NAME when <FORM> is sent back for processing. Also note how the two sets of radio buttons are grouped by their respective names. The page looks like Figure 2.12.

Let's see how a script is submitted using the <FORM> tag. Listing 2.13 shows how <FORM> does this.

Listing 2.13. Sending data back to the server.

```
<HTML>
<HEAD><Title>HTML document for the World Wide Web</Title>
➥</HEAD>
<BODY BGCOLOR="#FFFFFF">
<CENTER><IMG SRC="Goldstar.gif" ALT=" "></CENTER>
```

```
<H1 Align = "Center"><FONT FACE="Arial" FONT COLOR="#000000">
➥My Test Page</H1></Font><BR>
<FONT FACE="Arial" FONT COLOR="#000000">This is additonal text
➥</Font><BR>
<FORM ACTION="/scripts/testdata.idc" METHOD = "POST" >
<TABLE BORDER BGCOLOR="#FFFFFF">
<TR>
<TD ALIGN="RIGHT">ContactName</TD>
<TD><INPUT NAME="ContactName"</TD></TR><P>
<TD ALIGN="RIGHT">CompanyName</TD>
<TD><INPUT NAME="CompanyName"</TD></TR><P>
</TABLE>
<P><INPUT TYPE="SUBMIT" VALUE="Search" ALIGN="MIDDLE">
➥<INPUT TYPE="RESET" NAME="reset" VALUE="Clear all fields"
ALIGN="MIDDLE"></P></FORM>
</BODY></HTML>
```

Figure 2.12.
An <INPUT> sampler.

Pages like this can also be generated by several software tools. The IIS Add-In for Access 95, which I will talk about in some detail tomorrow, is one such tool. Remember, this is a crash course in HTML, not CGI. Between this example and tomorrow's description of the tool that created it, you will cover some CGI basics. For now, note that this form is passed to a script called `testdata.idc`, shown in Listing 2.14, and returned via a template called `testtata.htx`, shown in Listing 2.15.

Listing 2.14. `testdata.idc`.

```
Datasource: TestCust
Template: testdata.htx
DefaultParameters: ContactName=%%, CompanyName=%%
SQLStatement:
```

continues

Listing 2.14. continued

```
+Select "CompanyName", "ContactName", "Address", "City", "Region", "PostalCode",
➥"Phone"
+From "Customers"
+Where "ContactName" LIKE '%ContactName%'
+AND    "CompanyName" LIKE '%CompanyName%'
#IDC-Search FrontHTM-testdata.htm ReportHTX-testdata.htx
```

Listing 2.15. testdata.htx.

```
<HTML>
<META NAME="GENERATOR" CONTENT="IIS Add In For Access 95">
<HEAD><Title>HTML document for the World Wide Web</Title></HEAD>
<BODY BGCOLOR="#FFFFFF">
<%begindetail%>
<%if CurrentRecord EQ 0 %>
<TABLE BORDER BGCOLOR="#FFFFFF">
<TR>
<TH><B>CompanyName</B></TH>
<TH><B>ContactName</B></TH>
<TH><B>Address</B></TH>
<TH><B>City</B></TH>
<TH><B>Region</B></TH>
<TH><B>PostalCode</B></TH>
<TH><B>Phone</B></TH>
</TR>
<%endif%>
<TR>
<TD Align=Left><%CompanyName%></TD>
<TD Align=Left><%ContactName%></TD>
<TD Align=Left><%Address%></TD>
<TD Align=Left><%City%></TD>
<TD Align=Left><%Region%></TD>
<TD Align=Left><%PostalCode%></TD>
<TD Align=Left><%Phone%></TD>
</TR>
<%enddetail%>
<%if CurrentRecord EQ 0 %>
<HR=2><P>
<CENTER><B>No records were selected!<B></CENTER><P>
<%endif%>
</TABLE>
<HR=2>
<CENTER>This page was produced by using the
➥ <B>IIS Add-In for Access 95</B>.<BR>
➥<I> Copyright 1996 Microsoft Corporation</I>.</CENTER>
</BODY></HTML>
```

You have seen enough HTML to understand the basics of the template file (testdata.htx). Notice how testdata.htx sets up a <TABLE> tag, into which it puts the data the server finds.

Those of you with database backgrounds will understand the database query set up in the `testdata.idc` file pointed to in the `<FORM>` tag (`FORM ACTION="/scripts/testdata.idc" METHOD = "POST"`). Hands are waved, some pixie dust is thrown, and the page comes up looking like Figure 2.13.

Figure 2.13.
Searching for records.

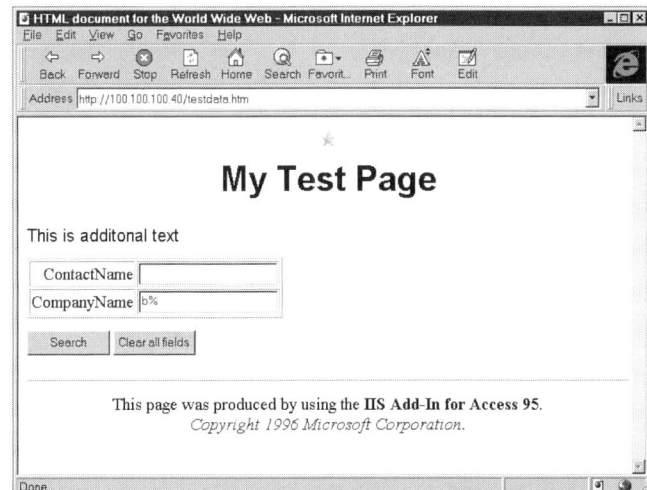

The user indicates a need to see all companies that start with the letter B by entering `b%` in the company name `<INPUT>` field. Notice in Listing 2.13 how the `<INPUT>` tags are placed in a table. The server returns the list shown in Figure 2.14.

Figure 2.14.
All the companies that start with the letter B.

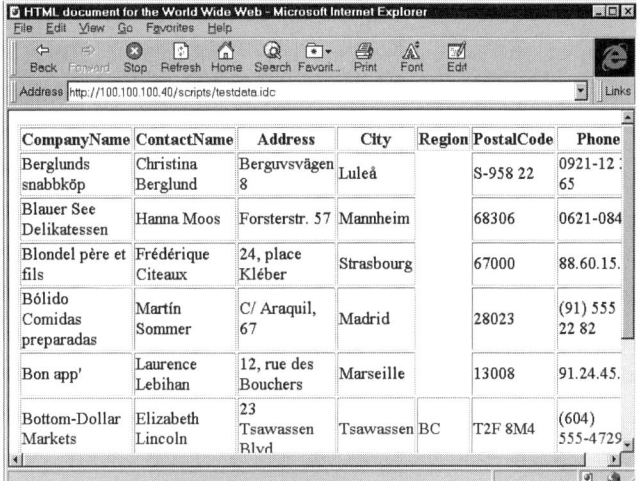

The `<SCRIPT>` Tag

Description: There are some pretty neat things you can do with `<FORM>` and `<INPUT>`, but the processing and error checking is still being conducted by the server. `<SCRIPT>` was created make your Web pages smarter.

Appears As: `<SCRIPT> </SCRIPT>`

Attributes: LANGUAGE, SRC

Can Contain: JavaScript, VBScript

Can Be In: `<HEAD>`

Example: Let's do a form that uses `<SCRIPT>` to compute and display a value. (See Listing 2.16.)

Listing 2.16. A sample script.

```
<HTML>
<HEAD>
<Title>First Scipt</Title>
<SCRIPT LANGUAGE ="JavaScript">
<!--
function calc(form)
{
  form.answer.value = form.number1.value * form.number2.value;
}
-->
</SCRIPT>
</HEAD>
<BODY BGCOLOR="#FFFFFF">
<H1>First Script</H1>

<H3>Enter two Numbers and Press the Calculate Button</H3>
<! The INPUT tag only works inside a form>
<FORM>
<P>First Number:
<INPUT TYPE ="TEXT" NAME ="Number1" SIZE = "5" MAXLENGTH ="5">
</P>
<P>Second Number:
<INPUT TYPE ="TEXT" NAME ="Number2" SIZE = "5" MAXLENGTH ="5">
</P>
<P>Answer:
<INPUT TYPE ="TEXT" NAME ="Answer" SIZE = "5" MAXLENGTH ="5">
</P>
<P>
<INPUT TYPE ="BUTTON" NAME ="Calculate" VALUE = "Multiply"
 onClick = "calc(this.form)">
</P>

</FORM>
</BODY>
</HTML>
```

Don't worry about the scripting-language syntax yet. Remember, you will have four days to study scripting in detail (one each on VBScript and JavaScript, and two projects). The important thing here is how to fit scripts into HTML. Notice that the <SCRIPT> was placed inside the <HEAD> tag. This ensures the code is loaded before the page has a chance to do anything else. Also notice that the code is enclosed in a comment tag. This prevents older browsers from trying to figure out what to do with the code. If you want to use comments inside the code, use the notation native to the language. Call this script up in your browser, enter a couple of numbers, and push the Multiply button. This form isn't long on format, but it computes well.

The <OBJECT> Tag

Description: The relatively few user interface objects supported by HTML are augmented by the <OBJECT> tag. <OBJECT> can also be used to bring in self-contained, non-visual programs that have functions and values you can access via scripting.

Appears As: <OBJECT> </OBJECT>

Attributes: ID, CLASSID, DATA, PARAM, NAME

Can Contain: N/A

Can Be In: <BODY>

Example: Listing 2.17 is a simple ActiveX text box control. It illustrates the difference between using the HTML components and the ActiveX components.

Listing 2.17. Using <OBJECT>.

```
<HTML>
<HEAD>
<TITLE>Inserting Objects</TITLE>
</HEAD>
<BODY BGCOLOR="#FFFFFF">
<H1>First ActiveX Object</H1>

<H3>This used to be an OCX but now it's ActiveX!</H3>

<P>ActiveX Text Box:
<OBJECT ID="ActiveXTextBox" WIDTH=120 HEIGHT=30
 CLASSID="CLSID:8BD21D10-EC42-11CE-9E0D-00AA006002F3">
    <PARAM NAME="VariousPropertyBits" VALUE="746604571">
    <PARAM NAME="Size" VALUE="2540;635">
    <PARAM NAME="FontCharSet" VALUE="0">
    <PARAM NAME="FontPitchAndFamily" VALUE="2">
</OBJECT>
</P>
</BODY>
</HTML>
```

Figure 2.15.
CLASSIDs *found on my system.*

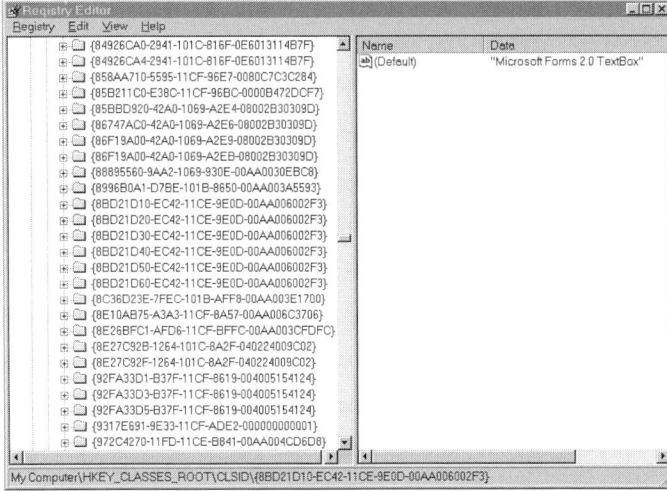

Notice the overhead has increased. And there is one very puzzling attribute, CLASSID, that looks like a cross between a VISA number and the national debt! CLASSID is an identifier for an ActiveX control. These numbers can be found by finding a control in the Windows Registry under the CLSID subdirectory. Figure 2.15 shows some of the CLASSIDs on my system, including the one used in Listing 2.17.

Run the page in your Web browser; your screen should look like Figure 2.16.

Figure 2.16.
Your first ActiveX object.

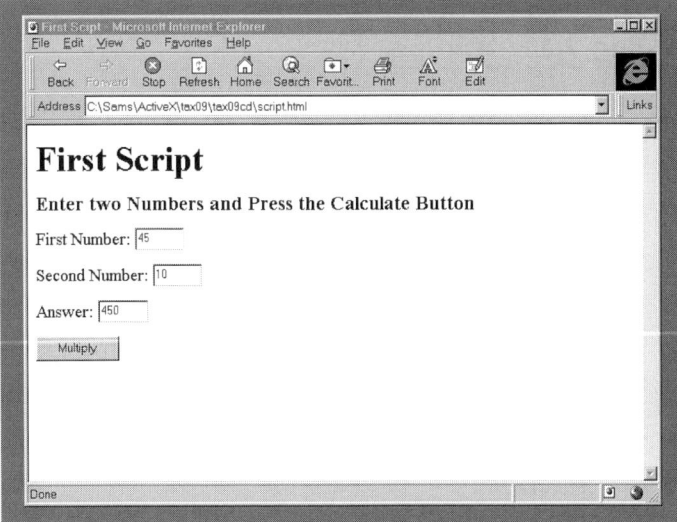

Not very impressive visually, but it does along with scripting, start a whole new era for Web pages.

Summary

Now you have some practical knowledge of basic HTML. You have also solved the mysteries of how <SCRIPT> and <OBJECT> tags are used. If you stopped reading this book today, you would have a good foundation for understanding and using current HTML technology. But do not stop, because tomorrow you will focus on several tools that go well beyond the text editor, including the most important tool available today for ActiveX programming, the ActiveX Control Pad. Before the end of the week, you'll have written two projects using scripting and ActiveX controls.

Q&A

Q Why, in Figure 2.6, in the section on headings, are all the headings left justified? Listing 2.6 shows the tags as being indented, and that is how I expected to see them.

A Listing 2.6 indented the tags for readability. The browser ignored the whitespace from the start of the line to the heading tag.

Q There are a lot of tags mentioned in the tag definitions that you didn't specifically cover. Where can I find out how they work?

A There are several books, including *Teach Yourself Web Publishing with HTML 3.0 in a Week* by Laura LeMay (published by Sams.net), and literally hundreds of Internet sites that provide HTML information. I have also started looking at the source code of the interesting Web sites I come across using the View Source function of my Web browser. I encourage you to experiment.

Q During the sections on scripting and objects, I noticed that the resulting HTML pages were getting more and more complicated. What do I gain by making my HTML universe more complex?

A The answer is diversity. The Internet and local intranets are evolving from showing static text to report retrieval to heavy user interaction. Scripting and objects support user interaction. Tools are already at hand to handle some of the details for you, and more are on the way.

Workshop

Rewrite the ordered part of Listing 2.10 to start numbering the list at 5 (hint: use the START attribute).

Quiz

1. What attribute of which tag do you use to load a background picture into your Web page?
2. Which attribute of the <TABLE> tag causes lines to be drawn around the cells in the table?
3. Where can I find the CLASSID for an ActiveX control?

NOTE Refer to the appendix, "Answers," for the answers to these questions.

Week 1

Day 3

ActiveX Scripting

You have learned that ActiveX programming involves the manipulation of documents and other objects over the Internet. You also know that the Internet consists of a diverse population of client and server machines.

With all these different types of control objects available to the programmer, a language must be used to manipulate those objects. This language should have the added functionality of being able to work well over a distributed environment like the Internet. In this section, you will learn about:

- ☐ HTML scripting
- ☐ JScript
- ☐ VBScript
- ☐ The ActiveX script engine

NOTE This section discusses ActiveX scripting technology but does not contain an in-depth discussion of ActiveX syntax and programming-specific syntax. Instead, the discussion focuses on what happens behind the scenes with ActiveX scripting. Later, you will learn more details about two forms of ActiveX scripting—VBScript and JavaScript.

Client-Side Scripting

Lights, camera, ACTION! No, that's not what scripting is about, but there are some similarities. Client-side scripting is a way to define procedures that manipulate the properties, methods, and events of an object. The script itself is executed on the user's local machine rather than on some remote server.

Running a server-side script once for each connection that requests it can be very taxing on the system resources of a busy server (such as WWW.Netscape.Com or WWW.Microsoft.Com). Memory and storage can become gobbled up, and processing speed deteriorates as more and more redundant code is loaded, run, and unloaded (see Figure 3.1).

Figure 3.1.
Too many simultaneous connections from multiple clients to the same server can result in access refusal for the latecomers.

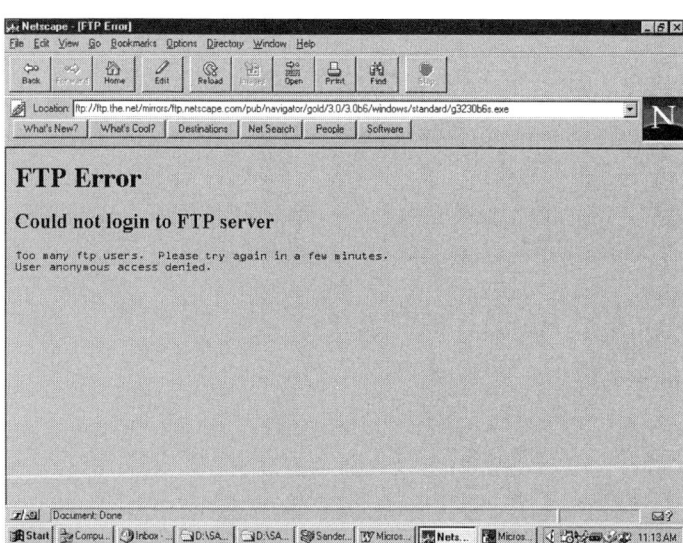

This resource drain can be relieved somewhat by the use of HTML client-side scripting. Client-side scripting shifts the code processing burden from the server (which would have to run zillions of instances at once and transmit the queries and responses back and forth over the Net) to the client (which would only have to run one instance at a time—locally). If the scripts are run on a local machine rather than the main server, client-server traffic is reduced and the server will be able to process more requests in the same time. For a graphical representation of this kind of bottleneck, see Figures 3.1 and 3.2.

Figure 3.2.
Most scripting functions are best performed by the client, rather than the server, to avoid bottlenecks.

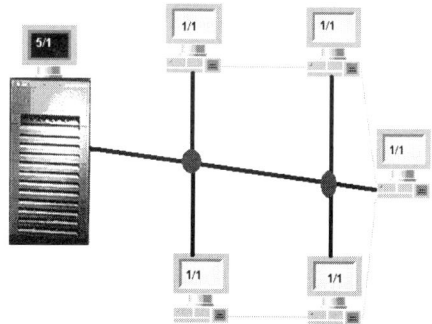

In the preceding figure, the server must run a script five times in one minute, unless the five hosts can simultaneously run one script each in one minute.

When you are browsing the Web, you are using one host to access information on any number of other hosts. Scripting can occur on either side of that connection. For example, the server to which you are connecting could run an ISAPI, CGI, Perl, or other script, and your browser could run a bit of VBScript, JScript, or other ActiveX script.

As powerful as most programming languages are at full strength, they can provide strangers on the Net more access to your system than you want them to have.

A scripting language is usually a subset of another language. For example, VBScript is a subset of Visual Basic. JScript is a subset of Visual J++ (code-named *Jakarta*). By restricting some processes that are normally available, such as features of file I/O, programmers can use a hobbled version of a programming language.

This gives you some degree of protection against malicious or undesirable programs. Features such as shelling to the operating system and formatting the hard drive are simply not available through a good script engine.

Scripts, Hosts, and the Engines

Another difference between scripting and programming is the way the finished program code is compiled and executed. A normal program is usually compiled into an executable to be run by itself, or it can be compiled into a library of features, such as a DLL (dynamic link library). A script, on the other hand, requires two things besides itself to run—a *host* and an *engine*.

> **Connection Confusion**
>
> The concepts *host*, *client*, *server*, and so on, as they apply to the Internet, can get awfully confusing.
>
> In the most basic connections, a client requests something and a server processes this request.
>
> Often confused with a server, a host is one of several systems connected to the Internet. The host might or might not be a server to other machines that then might or might not have their own connections to the Internet. Regardless of how it's connected, every system attached to the Internet is a host.
>
> On most other networks, such as LANs, a host is a dedicated server. On the Internet, however, a host can be any machine connected to the Internet with a dedicated or dynamic IP (Internet Protocol) address. That's just about everybody.

Script Hosts

In reference to scripting, a host is a program (such as Microsoft Internet Explorer or Netscape Navigator) that uses a script engine to run a script on the local machine. The host application is the intermediary program between the user and the server, and resides on the user's machine. Any OLE program can act as a script host when it implements either the IActiveScriptSite interface or the optional IActiveScriptSiteWindow interface.

Engine

In order for a host to run a bit of script, it must reference a script *engine*. This engine is usually a library or set of libraries (such as VBScript.DLL or JScript.DLL) that tells the host how to interpret the script. ActiveX scripting is Microsoft's implementation of the HTML script element. Every ActiveX script engine must implement either IActiveScript or the optional IActiveScriptParse interface.

The script engine (that is, a runtime file or files installed on the local machine) has a two-pronged approach to facilitating Internet programming.

First, script engines use all the objects in the standard Internet Explorer Object Model for Scripting. This includes the Document object, the Anchor object, the History object, and so on.

Second, script engines also support a few objects that are built into the engine itself. This extends the power of basic HTML scripts. If these JScript, VBScript, and MSIE objects are not enough, you can add other objects to your document, as you will learn in the final chapters of this book.

Script

The script itself is the code, in whatever syntax is supported by the script engine. The script can make reference to the various objects supported within the context of the document. These include the document object and other embedded objects (the final chapters of this book, which cover ActiveX controls, present these objects and object models in greater detail). For a graphical representation of how client scripting works across a net, see Figure 3.3.

Figure 3.3.
The relationships between the parts and pieces of ActiveX scripting.

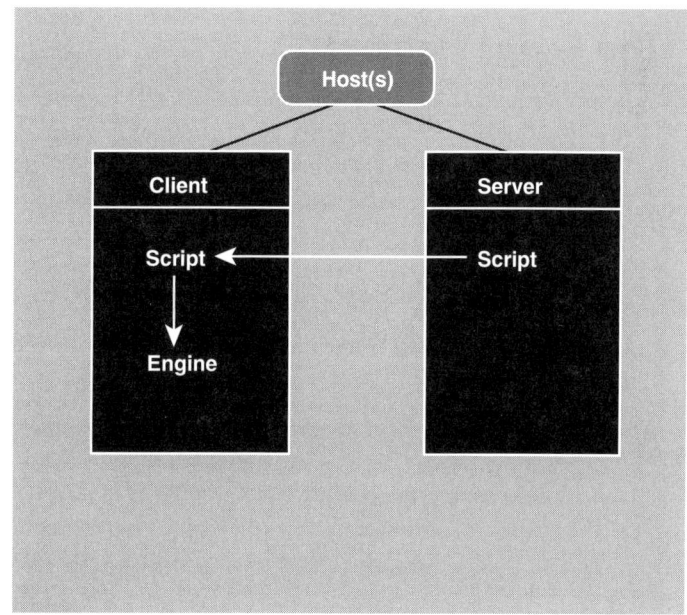

A script can be loaded into the system by one of two interfaces. The whole script can be loaded using IPersist*, or a portion of the script can be attached to an object using IActiveScriptParse.

HTML Scripting

Although it's not necessary to be a fully qualified OLE programmer to use most forms of script, it certainly helps. Programming and scripting are very similar. In fact, early versions of Basic (such as those found on the Radio Shack TRS-80 and the Commodore 64/128) were not as powerful as most of today's elemental scripting languages!

Programmers do their thing within one or several programming languages. These languages define the way you control processes on your computer, and are usually very powerful. On newer machines that have APM (advanced power management), a programmer can write a program that actually turns off the computer for the night.

Script writers, on the other hand, are dealing with a somewhat less powerful environment. This limited environment disallows most hardware control features without actually disabling them. For example, a script writer can make the user's computer play sound files in MIDI and Wave format, but the script writer cannot install the drivers that play those files. The drivers would have to already be installed on the client machine.

The Script Element

The insertion of client-side script into an HTML document requires the <SCRIPT> container tags to define pieces of text within that document that are code segments. The script element has three attributes (two of which are optional). These include the SRC, Type, and Language attributes. A <SCRIPT> tag looks something like this:

```
<SCRIPT Type="text/vbscript" Language="VBScript" src="VBScript.vbs">
</SCRIPT>
```

Because some browsers do not support the <SCRIPT> tag, it is sometimes ignored. This becomes problematic when content is displayed because the content and the script become mixed together.

Older browsers (such as Mosaic and Lynx) usually *do* support the <COMMENT> tag, so make your pages friendly to non-ActiveX browsers by adding <COMMENT></COMMENT> tags around your code. These tags are ignored by the script if the browser can run them, and filters out the text of the script if the browser cannot run them. This format for coding script looks like this:

```
<SCRIPT Language="VBScript">
<!--
    'My Code
-->
</SCRIPT>
```

The Language Attribute

The primary attribute of the script element is the Language attribute. The Language attribute is the only attribute that must always be specified. Normally this will be VBScript or JavaScript because these are the two primary script engines used by the two primary Web browsers.

The SRC Attribute

The optional SRC attribute tells the browser that the code for this entry can be found in an external file. In the preceding example, the code is in a file called VBScript.vbs in the current directory.

The Type Attribute

If you refer to an external source file in a script tag, you might need to use the Type attribute to define the MIME type for the script file. For instance, in the preceding example, the code is in a text file with a .VBS extension. The user's browser will retrieve the script the same way it retrieves text/vbscript MIME type files.

JScript and VBScript

When using script within an HTML file, the best place to put your code might be at the top of the file (within the head element). Code *can* be placed in a later portion of the document, but it must be before the </HTML> tag. One reason to place code at the top of a file is if the code actually *writes* to the file.

Often, people speak of ActiveX scripting. There is no "ActiveX script" language *per se*. ActiveX script is the name given to the use of OLE interfaces in script engines. JScript and VBScript are the usual two that are referenced, because Microsoft includes their engines with MSIE (see Figure 3.4). ActiveX script engines for Perl, LISP, and others are also being developed.

If, for instance, you were to use VBScript's Document.Write method, the text that is written would need to be figured in before the rest of the page is displayed. This ensures that the browser knows what to put where on the page when the page is viewed.

Figure 3.4.
ActiveX script shares objects, properties, methods, and events with VBScript and JScript.

Another reason to place code at the beginning of a file is for procedures that, logically, would only be launched after the page is viewed. This could include a procedure that would be launched when the user clicks a button or an image map. Since the code is vital to the operation of the page, it needs to be loaded before the rest of the page.

One school of thought says to put every bit of code in the head element to ensure that the script is available before the user needs it. Another school of thought says to put some code at the end of the page so the text will display more quickly.

Additionally, you can place code in the middle of a document, preferably near an object with which the code interacts. If you code your script this way, most browsers will load and display the content of the document as it is downloaded. When it gets to the object and the script, it will pause (or *hiccup*) as it displays the content. During this pause, the object and code are grabbed from the Net and are appropriately displayed.

Placing the code at the beginning of the document produces a pause at the beginning of the document. Depending on the size of the code, the pause could last as long as a minute before the user is able to view the first line on the page. In cyberspace, this seems like a lifetime and causes the user to choose another page.

> **Licensing the Engines**
>
> Some programs are so customizable that you need to make a whole programming language available within the application. Good examples of programs that use scripting are Telix, Qmodem, and ProComm.
>
> These dial-up terminal programs are very similar to Windows 95's HyperTerminal. To allow program users to customize the features of interactions with dial-up servers, the developers of these packages included scripting languages specifically for their package.
>
> Telix uses a scripting language called SALT (Script Application Language for Telix). SALT allows users to create custom logon/logoff processes for their dial-up connections, then takes them several steps further. Users can customize the way the program responds to different prompts from the dial-up connection. They can then automate long and complex data entry and retrieval tasks that would otherwise require a human to sit at the keyboard and make intelligent decisions.
>
> If you create an application that is very complex and powerful but requires simple decision making, you can include a script engine in your application. VBScript and JScript are licensed to everybody, provided they acknowledge Microsoft in the About box of the application. No money is required.

JScript

JScript is Microsoft's implementation of JavaScript. System support for JScript is installed by default with Microsoft Internet Explorer. Additionally, Microsoft maintains an excellent resource for up-to-date information related to JScript development at `http://www.microsoft.com/jscript`.

NOTE Microsoft's Web sites for the most up-to-date documentation and information on their two script engines are located at

`http://www.microsoft.com/jscript`

`http://www.microsoft.com/vbscript`

The ActiveX Control Pad is a handy utility for writing JScript code. Even more powerful than JScript is Visual J++ (also known as *Jakarta*), which allows users to compile Java applets, OLE-level code, and other high-power Internet tools.

Installing the ActiveX Control Pad and the ActiveX Layout Control

This would be a good time to install the ActiveX Control Pad and its co-control, the ActiveX Layout control. The installation routine for these can be found on the enclosed CD-ROM. Installing them is very simple (as is using it!). To install these utilities, follow these steps:

Step 1—Locate and double-click `SetupPad.exe`.

Step 2—Allow the setup program to install the program into its default path.

Then, for the ActiveX Layout control, follow these same steps using `SetupALX.exe`.

The URLs `ftp://ftp.microsoft.com/developr/MSDN/CPAD` and `ftp://ftp.microsoft.com/msdownload/ieinstall` take you to the FTP sites for the ActiveX Control Pad and its associated ActiveX Layout control. As ActiveX travels through its inevitable evolutions, you will want to check these sites frequently for the most up-to-date versions. You will learn more about this handy little editor in the next chapter.

As with Java, JScript is (or soon will be) available for a variety of platforms, including Mac, PC, and UNIX, and extending to Sun, HP, and even IBM platforms.

VBScript

VBScript is another big Microsoft implementation of HTML script. In many respects, VBScript is similar to JScript, with an additional twist.

VBScript is a subset of VBA (Visual Basic for Applications), which is a subset of VB (Visual Basic), and can easily port applications back and forth among the three. Going the other way, VB is a superset of VBA, and VBA is a superset of VBScript. For a less confusing, graphical representation of this relationship, see Figure 3.5.

Figure 3.5.
Visual Basic has become a hierarchical family of programming tools.

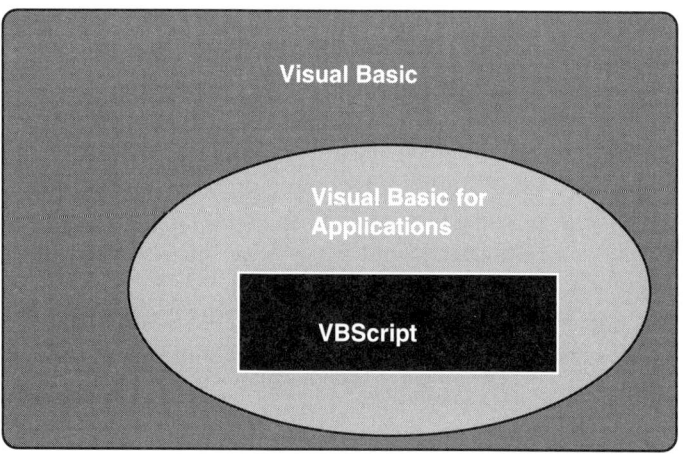

Some of the features within VBA that are not found in VBScript include DDE (Dynamic Data Exchange) link features and declarations for calls to external DLLs. VBScript also has significantly fewer debug and error handling routines. For the person creating the script, these are handy. By eliminating these features, however, the user does not need to install large runtime files on his local machines—just small runtime files.

You will learn more about VBScript later in this book.

The ActiveX Script Engine

ActiveX supports the use of customized script engines (that is, engines other than VBScript and JScript). ActiveX script engines can be created for LISP, Scheme, SALT, Perl, or even your own custom or proprietary language.

Developing your own programming language is a very complex process (don't even try it unless you know what you are doing!). Creating a script engine for a pre-existing language is only slightly less difficult.

This chapter does not go into all the details of creating your own engine. To do so requires a much larger volume. But for those of you who need your own script engine, or are developing one for the open market, there are a few features of ActiveX scripting with which you should be familiar.

If you just plan on using engines created by others, such as VBScript and JScript, you will want to be familiar with how the engine works. You will also want to know how it crashes.

Host and Engine Interaction

There are several steps involved in making a connection between a host (such as Microsoft Internet Explorer) and an engine (such as VBScript).

1. Project Creation—In this step, the document is loaded onto the local machine. The document is usually an HTML document, but can be just about anything that has your script in it.
2. Engine Creation—In this step, the host calls the CoCreateInstance() function and specifies the CLSID of the script engine. This creates an instance of the script engine, and is required before you can get the script to run.
3. Script Loading—In this step, the script itself is retrieved. If it is being retrieved from persistent data, the script is sent directly to the script engine. If the script must be retrieved from a remote site, a null script object is created. At this point, the remote script is retrieved and fed into the new script object. Only then can it be fed to the script engine itself.

TIP

Although you can place your script in a file separate from the hypertext document, you might want to place as much as possible within the document itself to speed things up.

One reason for this increase in speed is fairly obvious. When the scripts are kept in separate files, HTTP (the networking protocol) must go through the whole process of connecting with, sending requests to, and receiving responses from the server. This happens for each document and image that is in the HTML document.

A less obvious reason is connected to the local (client-side) operation of the script engine. When creating the script object, fewer IPersist* interfaces need to be coded. Also a simplified process of creating the script object is used within the HTML document itself.

4. Script Item Loading—In this step, the pieces of the script, such as forms and the engine's namespace, are loaded into the script object. This is sometimes referred to as *populating* the script properties.

5. Running the Script—During the initialization of a scripting process, the host and the script are first connected. A few changes occur, including static bindings and hooking up to events.

    ☐ Static Bindings—After the script is initialized, it uses the `GetItemInfo()` method to retrieve information from any necessary objects.

    ☐ Hooking up to Events—After static bindings are made, Connection Points are made to any relevant objects.

6. Script Invocation—Finally, the events, properties, and methods of the script itself are invoked through a standard OLE binding mechanism.

The Engine as an OLE/COM Object

If you are an OLE or COM programmer, you can create your own script engine using a program such as C++.

Required Interfaces

To qualify as an ActiveX script engine, your project must support the `IActiveScript` interface. This gives the OLE programmer access to the basic scripting features of the engine.

The control must also support at least one of the following `IPersist*` interfaces:

☐ `IPersistStorage`—If this interface is supported, the information required to run the control can be placed in a file at a remote URL and can be retrieved through the data attribute of the object element.

☐ `IPersistStreamInit`—If this interface is supported, the data attribute can use the Internet MIME encoding features for transferring various types of multimedia and other data over the Internet. This feature of the data attribute follows a format somewhat similar to `Data=base64-encoded byte stream` and is followed by the ASCII Base64 encoded stream of data for the script.

☐ `IPersistPropertyBag`—If this interface is supported, it enables an HTML author to use the `param` attribute of the object element to any several of the control's properties.

Engines and the Registry

ActiveX engines are added to the system registry in two component categories: `CATID_ActiveScript` and `CATID_ActiveScriptParse`.

If the engine's `CLSID` is entered in `CATID ActiveScript`, it must support `IActiveScript` and one of the `IPersist*` interfaces mentioned earlier. However, if the engine's `CLSID` is entered in `CATID ActiveScriptParse`, it must support `IActiveScript` and `IActiveScriptParse` interfaces.

Engine States

An ActiveX script engine can exist in any of several states. The programmer who creates the engine might find it necessary to monitor these states and to enable or disable functions of the engine as these states change. This case logic can ensure that users are not able to attempt impossible tasks, such as trying to disconnect from a server that was never successfully initialized.

Uninitialized

In this state, the engine is little more than an idea. No program has called it and no program is using it.

Initialized

In this state, the script has been initialized (that is, called) but has not yet started connecting to the referenced objects and event handlers that it will need to run.

Started

In this state, the connections have still not been made, but code that was loaded during initialization can be run automatically.

Connected

In this state, the engine is going full-tilt boogie. All the connections to objects and events have been made, code is ready to execute, states are being monitored, and events are firing.

Disconnected

In this state, the script is still loaded into the engine, but it has been disconnected from all objects and events with which it might have been communicating. The script is not automatically reset, however, because that would send everything back into the initialized state. This would cause your script to run endlessly.

Closed

In this state, the script is over with, whether it completed normally or not. If it was communicating with other objects in the system, it should tell them when it closes. If external objects try to reference it after it closes, it will just return a bunch of errors.

Figure 3.6.
The features of an ActiveX script engine.

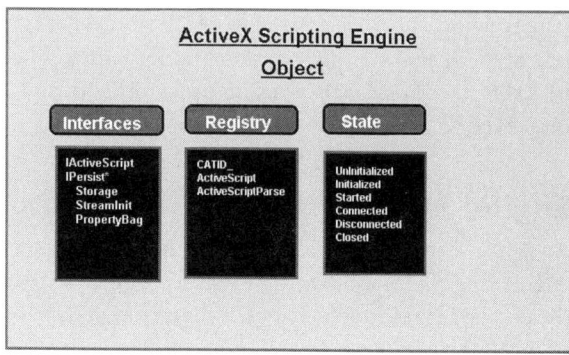

Summary

You should now have a strong familiarity with the features of ActiveX scripting. It allows the use of a variety of general and specialized scripting languages. Client-side scripting relieves an Internet server of much of the burden of processing multiple simultaneous requests.

You also know about the two major script engines supported by ActiveX, JScript and VBScript. JScript is Microsoft's implementation of Sun Microsystem's JavaScript, which was the first wide implementation of HTML scripting. VBScript, which is part of the Visual Basic family of programming languages, is very similar to JScript, but is aimed more toward today's front-end developers who use Visual Basic and Visual Basic for Applications.

You are also aware of the basic interaction between a script host, engine, and code. (A full definition of the script engine interface would include several of the OLE features represented in Figure 3.6.) A host is a program that manages scripting functions by coordinating the retrieval of a script and the processing of that script by an engine. A script is a bit of code written in a scripting language, which can be run by a script host, such as Telix, Internet Explorer, or Netscape. An engine is the files and routines required to interpret, compile, and run a script.

Prospective OLE programmers have been introduced to some of the features of a script engine, such as the processes it uses and the OLE interfaces it implements.

Q&A

Q Why does ActiveX script use two script engines instead of choosing one standard and sticking with it?

A There is no "ActiveX script" per se. ActiveX scripting is a technology, not a program. The two engines supplied with the SDK and Microsoft Internet Explorer are simply two types of script engines that can be used on the Net.

The value of implementing VBScript and JScript right off the bat is that each, to some degree, is already widely used in the programming world. JScript is based on JavaScript, which was the first wide implementation of HTML scripting. VBScript is based on the very popular Visual Basic, and is a gateway product for bringing current programmers into the Internet programming fold.

Q What IDEs can be used to program VBScript?

A The ActiveX Control Pad is probably the best utility for quick editing of VBScript within an HTML Document. Visual Basic for Applications v5.0 will support VBScript and provide online help, which the Control Pad currently does not.

Q What IDEs can be used to program JScript?

A Again, the ActiveX Control Pad is probably the best utility for quick editing of JScript within an HTML Document. Visual J++ will support JScript and provide online help, which the ActiveX Control Pad currently does not. It will also allow you to compile applets and integrate with other Visual programming applications.

Q What is the deal with `IPersist*` interfaces?

A When an object, such as a script, is created on a local machine, it has properties that need to be populated, or defined. This information is retrieved by way of an interface with a name that begins with `IPersist` (such as `IPersistStorage` or `IPersistStreamInit`). It can be retrieved from a remote host or from the local machine; either way, the `IPersist*` interface is the pipeline to that data.

Q What is the difference between an `IActiveScript` interface and an `IActiveScriptParse` interface?

A An `IActiveScript` interface defines a method for retrieving the script. An `IActiveScriptParse` interface defines a method for retrieving any portion of a script, which is useful when bits of script are placed throughout various parts of an HTML document instead of all within the head element.

Q What programming languages and IDEs can be used to create an ActiveX scripting language?

A Any programming language that can create an ActiveX control should be able to create a script engine. This includes Visual Basic 5, Visual C++, and even Delphi.

Workshop

List some of the programming features you use in Visual Basic that you would not want available in a script engine (for security's sake), then list some of the programming features you use in Visual Basic that you would consider indispensable in a script engine (for security's sake).

Quiz

1. What is the purpose of client-side scripting?
2. What ActiveX script engines are included with the SDK and Microsoft Internet Explorer?
3. Why are scripting languages usually scaled down versions of another language or hobbled in some way?
4. What two different things are described by the word *host*?
5. What three components are required in a scripting situation?
6. What groups of objects are available to VBScript?
7. What attribute of the script element must always be defined?
8. How do you keep a browser that does not support script from inadvertently viewing coded script as content?
9. Where should script that modifies the content of a document be placed?
10. What is the fee for licensing VBScript or JScript in your own applications?

NOTE Refer to the appendix, "Answers," for the answers to these questions.

Week 1

Day 4

The Tools of the Trade

On Day 2, "HTML & Scripting," you learned how to build basic HTML pages the manual way. You also manually inserted scripts and objects into HTML pages. Now it's time to leave the trusty text editor and study some new tools. First, today's lesson provides a look at the Internet Assistant for Microsoft Word—a free add-in that enables you to build HTML pages in the familiar environment of a word processor. Then you will work with SoftQuad's HoTMetaL, a tool dedicated to building Web pages. Next you will learn about the Internet Information Server (IIS) Add-In for Microsoft Access. This free add-in builds database front ends and reports for your Web pages. Finally, the tour ends with a look at the ActiveX Control Pad. The ActiveX Control Pad is specifically designed to integrate ActiveX objects and scripting into your Web pages.

These tools are representative of the two dozen or so tools available to the HTML developer today—and dozens more are on the horizon. After today you will have a working knowledge of each of these tools. You will also have a good foundation for future decisions about which tools to use for all the works that are going to be generated by ActiveX on the Internet.

Overview of the Internet Assistant for Microsoft Word for Windows

The Internet Assistant for Microsoft Word is a free add-in that gives Word the capability to read and write Web pages. Its biggest advantage is that it enables you to create Web pages in a familiar environment. To download it, set your browser to `http://www.microsoft.com/msword/Internet/IA/default.htm` and follow the download instructions. After you have it downloaded, bring up Word. If you have the toolbars selected, you will see some eyeglasses on the far left of the toolbar, next to the style drop-down list box, as shown in Figure 4.1.

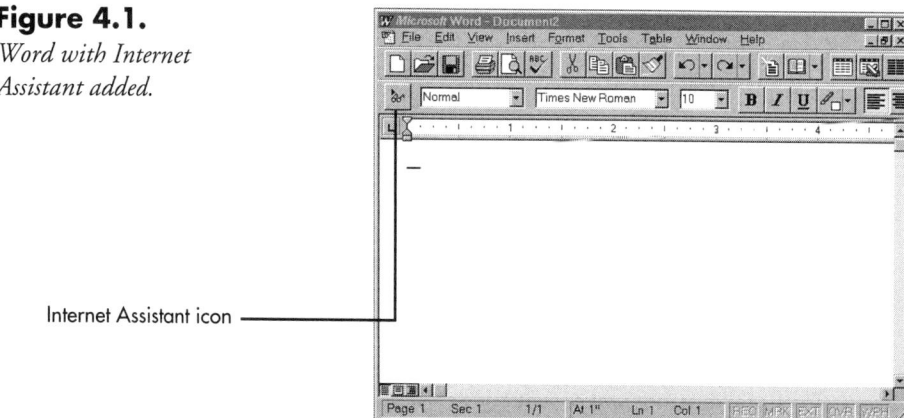

Figure 4.1.
Word with Internet Assistant added.

Internet Assistant icon

Press this button to go into Web Browse view. If you don't have the toolbars turned on, select Web Browse from the View menu. Your screen will look like Figure 4.2.

Figure 4.2.
Web Browse view.

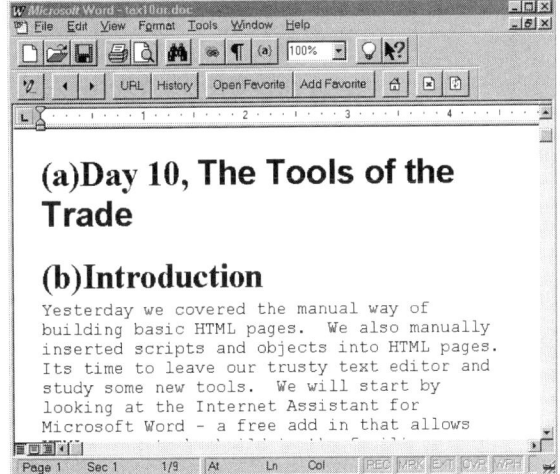

This is the screen where your tour begins.

Tour of the Microsoft Internet Assistant for Word

This tour highlights the features added by Internet Assistant to Microsoft Word. Let's start by making a new Web page.

Making a New Web Page

Choose New from the File menu to bring up the New Document dialog shown in Figure 4.3.

Figure 4.3.
New Document dialog.

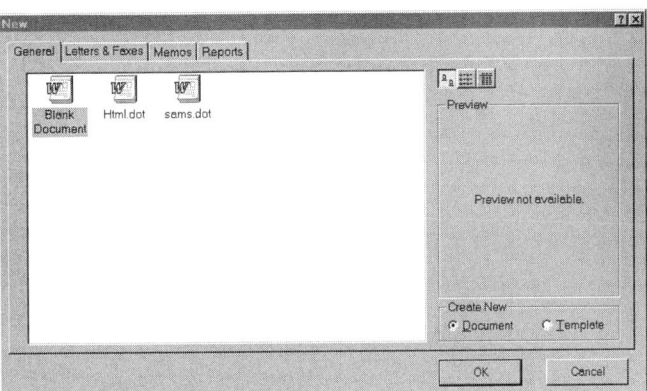

Click Html.dot. This loads the HTML style sheet. Space down toward the middle of the page and type in the text This is My First Word Web Page. Save it as FirstPage.htm. Don't fight the default extension Word wants to add. Then call it up in your Web browser.

Choose View | Source on your browser to see the Word-generated source code in Listing 4.1.

Listing 4.1. FirstPage.htm.

```
<HTML>
<HEAD>

<META NAME="GENERATOR" CONTENT="Internet Assistant for Microsoft Word 2.0z">
<TITLE>Untitled</TITLE>
</HEAD>
<BODY>
<P>
This is My First Word Web Page<BR>
</BODY>
</HTML>
```

Not bad. This code generates all the sections discussed yesterday: <HTML>, <HEAD>, <TITLE>, <BODY>, and <P> (although it did use the old-style <P>; you might remember that the one studied yesterday had the end tag </P>). If you want to see the tags in the document, go back to Word and choose HTML Source from the View menu. Your screen will change to look like the one in Figure 4.4.

Figure 4.4.
HTML view.

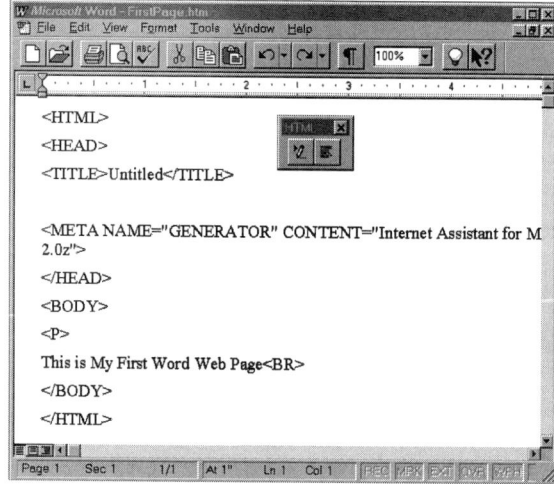

Looks like you are back in the text editor business from yesterday. Just to check this area out, add the line:

```
<INPUT TYPE ="TEXT" NAME ="TextBox1" SIZE = "20" MAXLENGTH ="15">
```

Then return to Edit mode by clicking the Return to Edit Mode button on the floating toolbar. You should see a screen like the one in Figure 4.5.

Figure 4.5.
Added field viewed in Word.

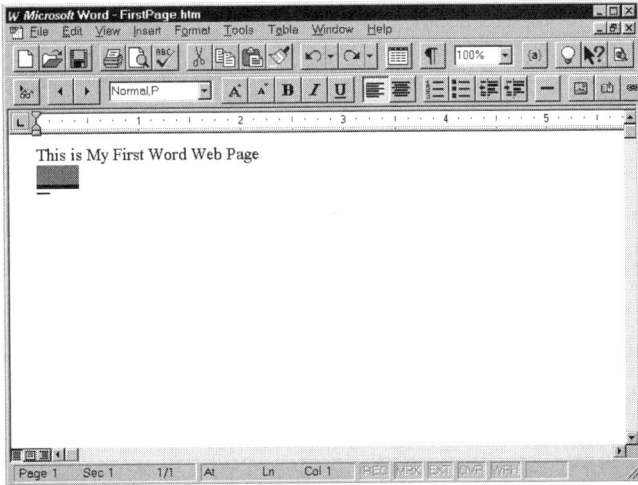

The added field is easier to see if you view it in the Web browser. You can launch the Web browser from Word. There is a button on the top toolbar, two to the right of the big light bulb, that will start your Web browser. The Web page with the <INPUT> tag on it should look like Figure 4.6.

Figure 4.6.
Added field viewed in a browser.

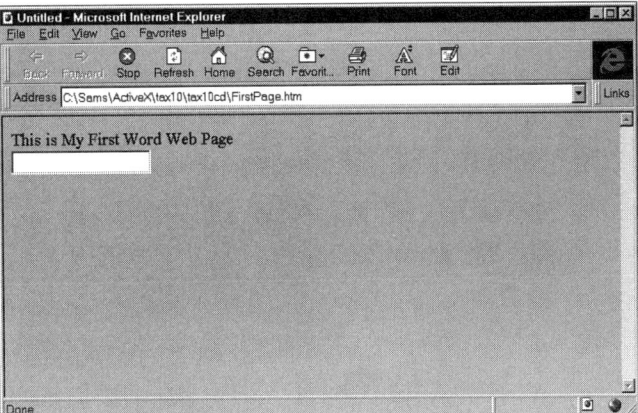

I tend to use tools that let me drop back to the source instead of their more automated cousins. Let's take a general look at what you can add to this page. Use the Bulleted and Numbered List buttons Add Image (use the `GoldStar.Gif` in the Chapter 2 subdirectory of the CD-ROM and the Alignment button to center it and the title), Add Link (link to the `FirstPage.htm` you just did), and Add Title to make your page look something like Figure 4.7. Save it as `TestPage.htm`.

Figure 4.7.
Adding other elements.

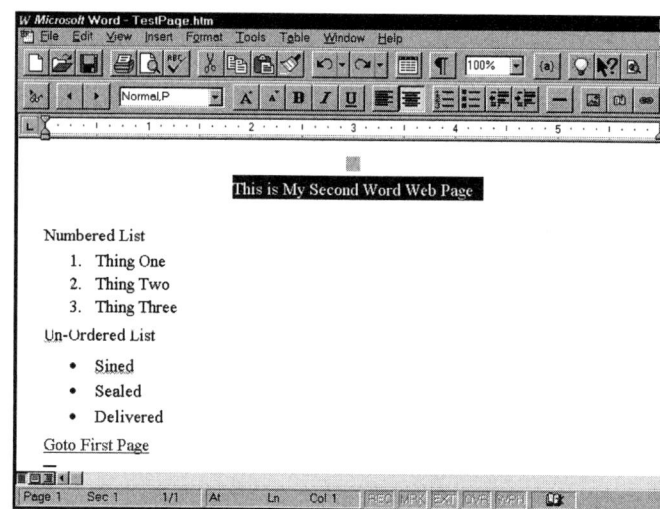

All of this adding produced the document in Listing 4.2.

Listing 4.2. The source for `TestPage.htm`.

```
<HTML>
<HEAD>
<TITLE>My First Web Page</TITLE>

<META NAME="GENERATOR" CONTENT="Internet Assistant for Microsoft Word 2.0z">
</HEAD>
<BODY>
<P>
<CENTER><IMG SRC="GOLDSTAR.GIF" ALT="Could Have Had a Picture Here"></CENTER>
<P>
<CENTER>This is My Second Word Web Page<BR>
</CENTER>
<P>
Numbered List
<OL>
<LI>Thing One
<LI>Thing Two
<LI>Thing Three
</OL>
<P>
```

```
Un-Ordered List
<UL>
<LI>Sined
<LI>Sealed
<LI>Delivered
</UL>
<P>
<A HREF="FirstPage.htm" >Goto First Page</A>
</BODY>
</HTML>
```

This source code produces a Web page that looks like Figure 4.8.

Figure 4.8.
TestPage.htm *in the browser.*

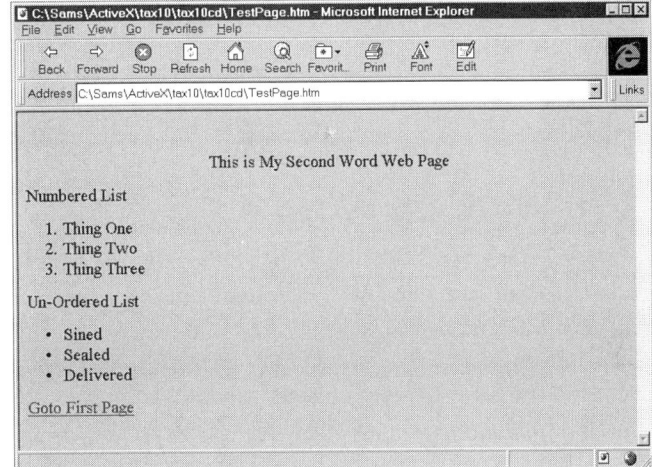

Keep experimenting to find what you can build. On the whole, the editing capabilities of Word are good, but it doesn't include support for scripts and objects.

Other Enhancements to Word

With Internet Assistant installed, you can load URLs as easily as you load a file. Pick Open URL from the File menu. Use http://www.mcp.com/sams/. This will bring the Sams home page into Word and demonstrate how Word can be used as a Web browser, as shown in Figure 4.9.

If you bring up the same page in your Web browser, you may notice (if your browser supports animation) that the book on the Sams home page is animated. Word shows it as a static picture. The Web browser capability of Word can be used to preview your pages with a less-capable Web browser to make sure your message gets across to those still using older Web browsers.

Figure 4.9.
Word as a Web browser.

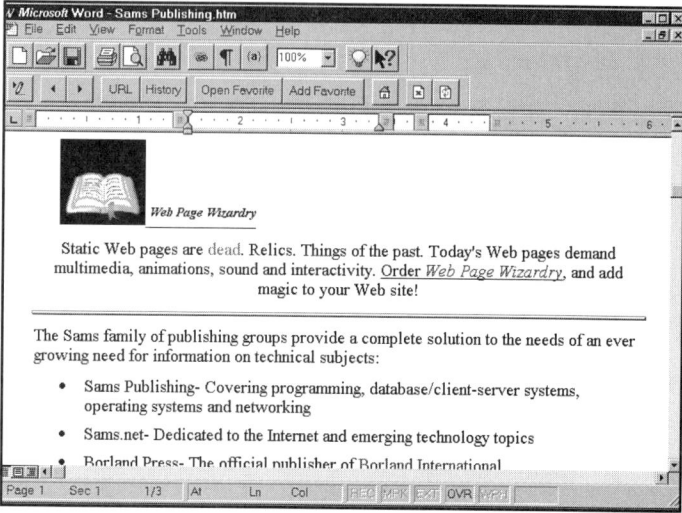

Last Word on Word

As you have seen, Word is good at creating simple HTML pages, but it doesn't include support for scripts and objects. You can put them in manually, but as you have seen, that can get really complicated really quickly. It does have a spell checker and that puts it miles ahead of most text editors. I would look for word processors and publishing programs to keep integrating HTML technologies and to compete with the specialized programs, like HoTMetL, for a share of the dollars you will spend on Web publishing.

Overview of HoTMetaL

HoTMetaL, from SoftQuad, is a dedicated HTML editing tool (see Figure 4.10). Information on the three versions—Professional, Lite, and Free—is available on the Web at http://www.softquad.com.

Figure 4.10.
SoftQuad home page.

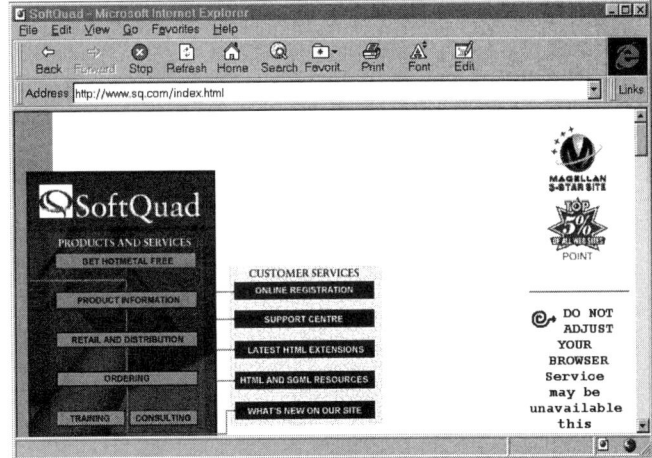

Tour of HoTMetaL

This tour covers the highlights of HoTMetaL. It is not an attempt to cover every aspect of the program, but to give you a feel for how it can help. Let's start by making a new Web page.

Building a Simple Web Page

Choose the New entry under the File menu. You will get a New dialog just like you did in Word, where you can pick from various types of templates. Choose Intranet/Intranet Home Page. You should wind up with a screen that looks like Figure 4.11.

Figure 4.11.
Choosing the intranet template in HoTMetaL.

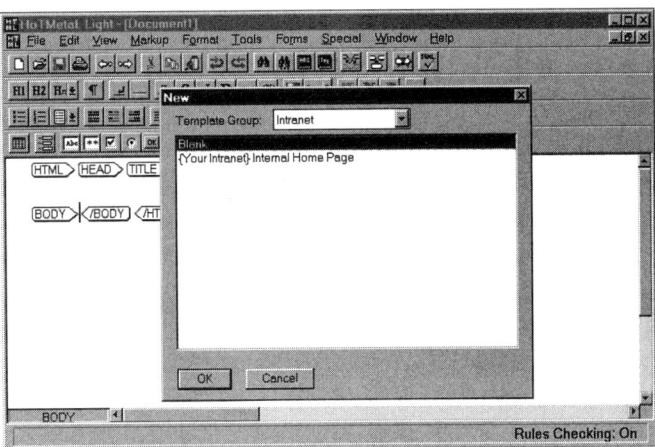

Listing 4.3 contains the source for this page.

Listing 4.3. The source for `TestPage`.

```
<!DOCTYPE HTML PUBLIC "-//SQ//DTD HTML 2.0 + all extensions//EN">
<HTML>
<HEAD>
<TITLE>{Your Intranet} Internal Home Page</TITLE></HEAD>
<BODY
BGCOLOR="#A4AE93" TEXT="#1F0291" LINK="#332E04" VLINK="#740AB4" ALINK="#332E04">
<H1 ALIGN="CENTER"><FONT COLOR="#A40052">{YOUR INTRANET}</FONT></H1><IMG
SRC="IMAGE/crumpled.gif" ALIGN="BOTTOM">
<P><FONT SIZE="+3">W</FONT><FONT SIZE="+1">elcome to {YOUR INTRANET}, the
internal
<A HREF="http://www.w3.org/hypertext/WWW/TheProject.html">World Wide Web</A>
site for {YOUR COMPANY}. Like any Web, this one will continue to grow.  Revisit
this  page from time to time and see what's new.</FONT></P>
<UL>
<LI><FONT SIZE="+2" COLOR="#A40052">The Essentials </FONT>
<UL>
<LI><A HREF="{YOUR NEWS PAGE}">{YOUR INTRANET} Electronic News
</A> -- Access to company newsgroups.  Read often!</LI>
<LI><A HREF="{YOUR DIRECTORY}">The people of {YOUR INTRANET}</A>  Who's who,
and where?</LI>
<LI><A HREF="{YOUR FACILITIES}">{YOUR INTRANET}Facilities</A> (describes
computers, networks &amp; The Internet, building systems, telephones, etc.)
</LI>
<LI>A <A HREF="{YOUR OFFICE}">map of {YOUR COMPANY}'s office space</A></LI></UL>
<P></P></LI>
<LI><FONT SIZE="+2" COLOR="#A40052">Making your job easier</FONT>
<UL>
<LI>A <A HREF="{YOUR TRAVEL PLANNER}">Travel Planner</A></LI>
<LI>An <A HREF="{YOUR EXPENSE REPORT}">Online Expense Report</A> (for when you
get back)</LI>
<LI><A HREF="{YOUR SEARCH PAGE}">Web Searching</A>: There must be fifty ways
to find your info...</LI>
<LI><A HREF="{YOUR NEWS PAGE}">Technology Watch</A> - What's new in {YOUR
INDUSTRY}</LI></UL>
<P></P></LI>
<LI><FONT SIZE="+2" COLOR="#A40052">{YOUR COMPANY}'s<A
HREF="{YOUR EXTERNAL PAGE}">External Pages</A></FONT></LI></UL><IMG
WIDTH="100%" HEIGHT="6" SRC="IMAGE/crumpled.gif" ALIGN="BOTTOM">
<P>Suggestions for changes, updates and  other resources to include are
welcome.   </P> <ADDRESS><A HREF="mailto:webmaster@your.intranet.com">
➥webmaster@your.intranet.com
</A></ADDRESS></BODY></HTML>
```

This code is more complex that the code generated by Word. You will also notice that what you see in the HoTMetaL editing screen is closer to what you get on the Web browser.

Toolbar by Toolbar

The first thing you notice about HoTMetaL are all the toolbars. There are four: Standard, Common HTML, Other HTML, and Forms. The Standard toolbar contains the normal stuff (hard to resist saying standard stuff) with the most interesting button being the last one on the right, SGML Check (see Figure 4.12).

Figure 4.12.
HoTMetaL's toolbars.

As explained yesterday, SGML is what HTML descended from. When you click the SGML button, a dialog comes up that shows you what elements have been used and if they are supported, as shown in Figure 4.13.

Figure 4.13.
SGML check.

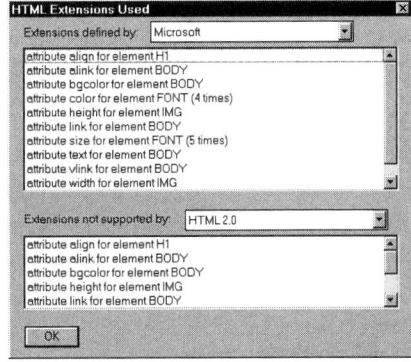

The next toolbar (see Figure 4.14) contains the common HTML commands such as headings <H1>, paragraphs <P>, alignment, and special characters. (Our HTML crash course did not address alignment.) In this menu the three alignment choices (Right, Left, and Center) are represented by three buttons. To align text or other elements, select the element you want to align and press the appropriate button. The last key, Special Characters, is new. Let's see how this works.

Figure 4.14.
Common HTML toolbar.

Open up a new, blank intranet form. Type the line Special Math Characters Include:, then click the Special Characters button. It will give you a floating dialog full of special characters. Choose what look to be special math characters. Save the form as Math.html. Your form should look like Figure 4.15 and show up in the browser looking like Figure 4.16.

Figure 4.15.
Math.html *in HoTMetaL.*

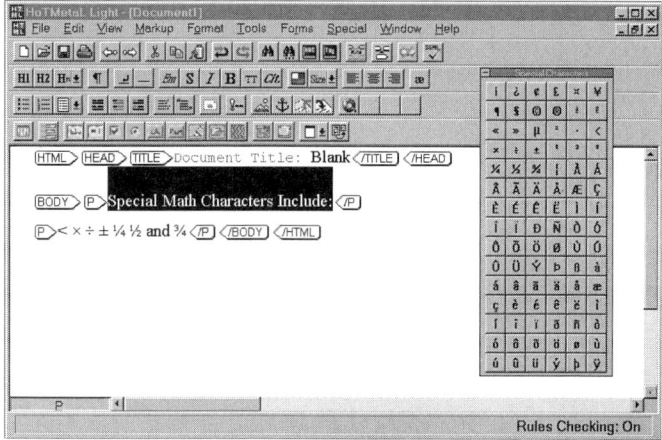

Figure 4.16.
Math.html *in the browser.*

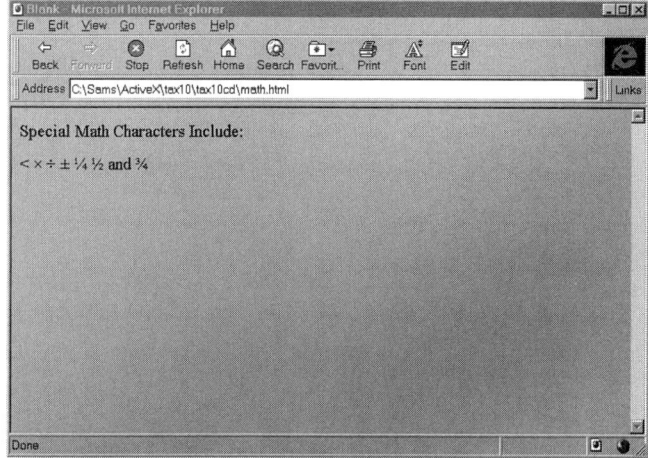

The Other HTML toolbar (see Figure 4.17) starts with lots of different ways to do lists, and then moves on to Address, Comments, Images, and Links buttons. The last group of blank buttons enables you to launch your Web browser from inside HoTMetaL. Just to see how this works, start a new form. Then add an ordered and an unordered list. For good measure, add an address at the bottom. Save it as Lists.html. The source code should look roughly like Listing 4.4.

Figure 4.17.

Other HTML toolbar.

Listing 4.4. The source for `Lists.html`.

```
<!DOCTYPE HTML PUBLIC "-//SQ//DTD HTML 2.0 + all extensions//EN">
<HTML>
<HEAD>
<TITLE>Common Html</TITLE></HEAD>
<BODY>
<P>Here are some Lists</P>
<P>First List</P>
<UL>
<LI>Thing One</LI>
<LI>Thing Two</LI>
<LI>Thing Three</LI></UL>
<P>Second List</P>
<OL>
<LI>Red Fish</LI>
<LI>Blue Fish</LI>
<LI>Old Fish</LI></OL>
<ADDRESS>myaddress@what.me.worry.com</ADDRESS></BODY></HTML>
```

This source produces a Web page that looks like Figure 4.18.

Figure 4.18.

`Lists.html` *in the browser.*

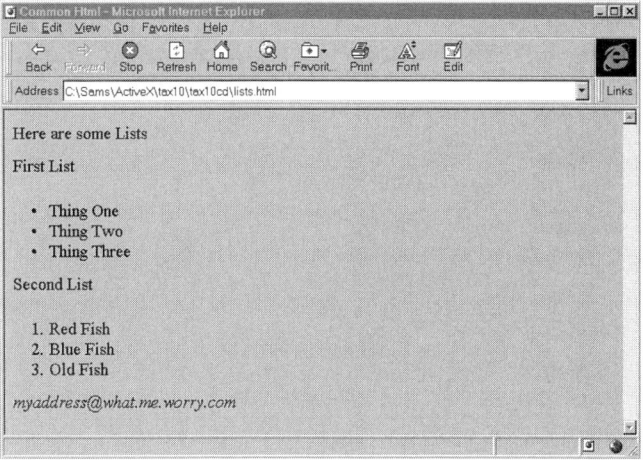

The last toolbar, Forms (see Figure 4.19), is where we move from static to interactive. You will find a button to insert a Form section as well as the familiar <INPUT> elements: Text, Check Box, Radio Button, Reset, Submit, and Hidden. There are a few elements we haven't seen, like Select List, which works like a drop-down list box, and Multiline Edit, which is just what the name implies. Make a new form called Form. Add a <FORM> tag, then add a text box, a check box, and a select list. You may remember from yesterday that there are many attributes associated with <INPUT>. How do you set them? Right-click the Check Box element, choose Element Attributes from the pop-up menu, and you will get the INPUT Attributes dialog shown in Figure 4.20. The name gives it away. This is where you set the attributes.

Figure 4.19.
Forms toolbar.

Figure 4.20.
INPUT *Attributes dialog.*

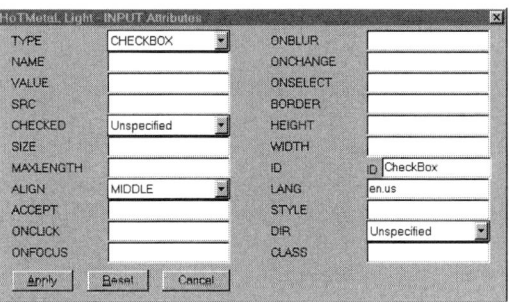

When adding the select list, double-click the button to bring up a dialog that enables you to add items to it. Your source should look like Listing 4.5.

Listing 4.5. The source for the amended `Lists.html`.

```
<!DOCTYPE HTML PUBLIC "-//SQ//DTD HTML 2.0 + all extensions//EN">
<HTML>
<HEAD>
<TITLE>Blank</TITLE></HEAD>
<BODY>
<FORM>
<P ALIGN="LEFT" ID="TextBox1">Text Box: <INPUT TYPE="TEXT" NAME=""></P>
<P ALIGN="LEFT">Check Box:
<INPUT TYPE="CHECKBOX" NAME="CheckMe" ID="CheckBox1"></P>
<P ALIGN="LEFT">
<SELECT NAME="SelectList" MULTIPLE="MULTIPLE" ID="SelectList">
<OPTION VALUE="First">First Thing</OPTION>
<OPTION VALUE="Second">Second Thing</OPTION></SELECT></P></FORM></BODY></HTML>
```

This listing might vary from what you get due to the details of how you set your form up. HoTMetaL also enables you to connect to a CGI script with the <SUBMIT> button, just like what you did yesterday in the database demo.

HoTMetaL Summary

HoTMetaL is for the professional Webmaster, someone who thinks in HTML rather that word-processing terms. I have some friends who edit newspapers for a living and they are very at home with publishing tools like Adobe PageMaker, but not as comfortable with a word processor. If they were Web editors (and their business could go that way), they would be at home in HoTMetaL.

Overview of the IIS Add-In for Microsoft Access

The IIS Add-In for Microsoft Access is a free download that enables Microsoft Access, in concert with Microsoft Internet Information Server (IIS, which comes with NT 4.0), to

- ☐ Create Web pages with information contained in an Access database
- ☐ Create database front end Web pages that enable the user to insert, update, and delete information in the database
- ☐ Create templates for database reports based on SQL statements

You can download the IIS Add-In from `http://www.microsoft.com/accessdev/itk/default.htm`

NOTE Make sure you download the IIS Add-In and not the Internet Assistant. They are two different products.

Tour of the IIS Add-In for Microsoft Access

The IIS Add-In adds itself under the Tools / Add-In menu. Before you use it, you will need to design your database and add an entry into the System DSN section of the ODBC Database Administrator. An entry using the sample NorthWind database that ships with Access is shown in Figure 4.21.

NOTE Make sure you make this entry into the System DSN. The System DSN is reached by a button on the main screen of the ODBC Database Administrator.

After you have built and installed your database, go back to Access and select the IIS Add-In from the Add-In menu. The IIS will appear in the form of a wizard, as shown in Figure 4.22.

Figure 4.21.
ODBC Database Administrator.

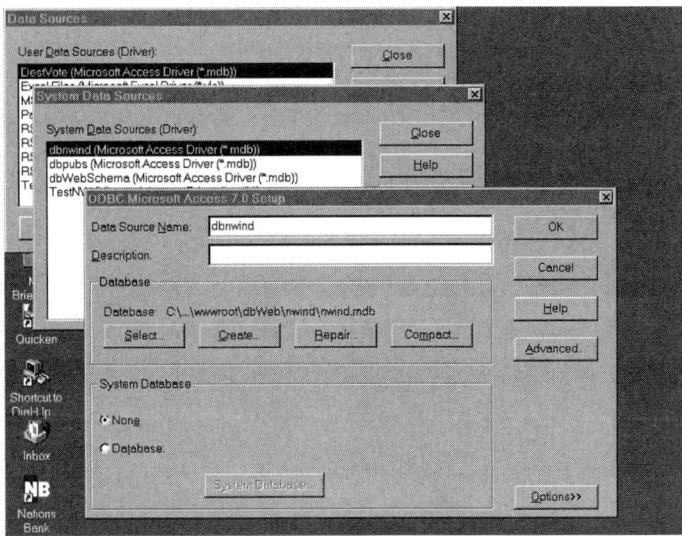

Figure 4.22.
Access Internet Wizard.

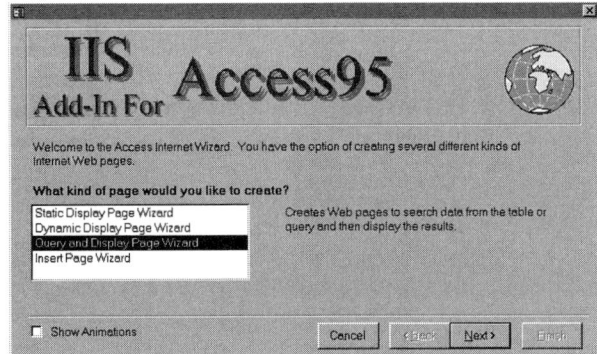

Notice there are four choices. The first choice, Static Display Page Wizard, creates a Web page with data from a database. The user will see the same data every time the Web page is opened, even if the data in the database has changed. The second option, Dynamic Display Page Wizard, creates a page that is linked to the data so that when the page is opened, it reflects the most current data in the database. These two options are interesting but not very interactive. The third option, Insert Page Wizard, allows you to insert records into databases. Let's walk through the fourth option, Query and Display Page Wizard.

Query and Display Page Wizard and Shameless Promotion

Choose Query and Display Page Wizard to bring up the screen shown in Figure 4.23.

Figure 4.23.
Query and Display Page Wizard.

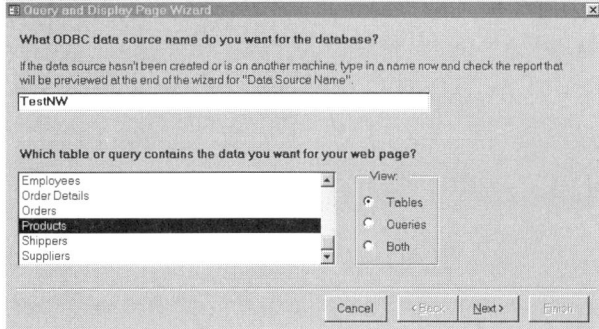

In this dialog, you type in the name of the System DSN you set up in the ODBC Administrator and choose a table to work with. Also, notice you can work with queries. If you are familiar with SQL, you know you can create a view of several different tables to relate and extract the data you want. For those of you not familiar with SQL, there are several good books on the subject, including *Teach Yourself SQL in 14 Days* (a book I co-authored by Sams Publishing). You are not limited to the data in a single table. Select the Products table and move on.

On the next page choose `ProductName` and `UnitsinStock` to search by and click the Add All Fields button to display all the fields on the form returned by the search. When you are done, the page should look like Figure 4.24. Verify your inputs, then move on to the next screen.

Figure 4.24.
Second stage.

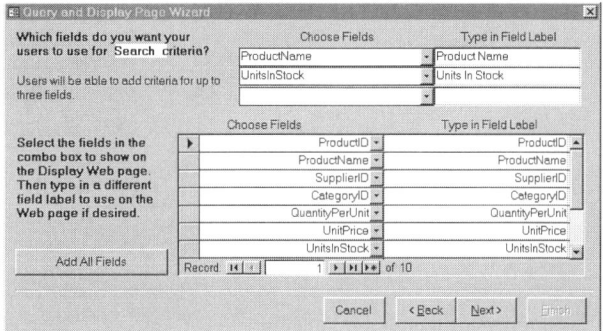

The next page gives you some control over the format of the form. You can add a title and text, and even change the appearance of the data table. I added the text This Form Allows you to Search the Product Database by Product Name and/or Units in Stock, and a title, Search of Product Database. Do what you need to do, as shown in Figure 4.25, and move on.

Figure 4.25.
Adding format.

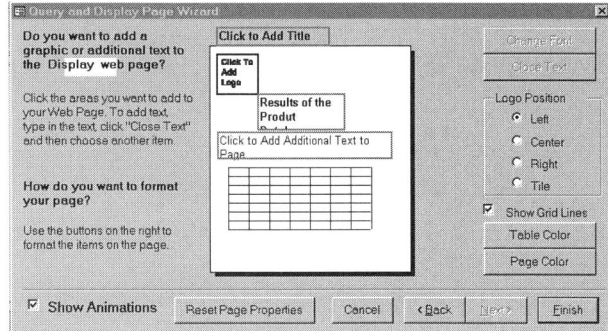

On the next and final page of the input sequence of the wizard, you can format the page returns with the results of the query. Add some kind of title—I added The Results of the Product Database Query. Then press the Finish button.

After you press Finish, IIS Add-In builds you a letter, shown in Figure 4.26, telling you what you built and where to put it.

Figure 4.26.
Summary of wizardry.

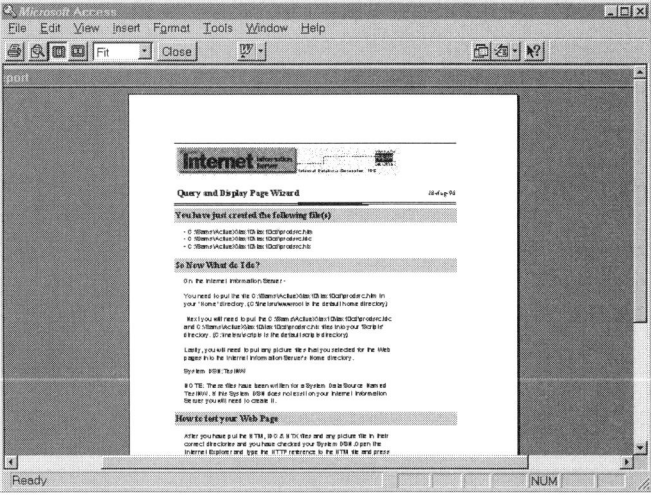

The Tools of the Trade

What you produced, according to the letter, are three files: prodsrc.htm, prodsrc.idc, and prodsrc.hdx. The first file, prodsrc.htm, is your search page and needs to be moved to your Web pages. The next two files, prodsrc.idc and prodsrc.hdx, are your script and return file templates. They go into the scripting directory. After everything is in place, call up prodsrc.htm with your Web browser through your Web server.

NOTE When you use scripts, you need to run the page through the Web server. This means using the http:\\myserver\prodsrc.htm format (assuming you put prodsrc.htm in your server's root directory) in your Web browser. Simply calling the form by double-clicking it in the Explorer or by using the File menu in your Web browser will not bring the Web server into play. You need the Web server to run the script and return the answer.

The Search form and its report are shown in Figures 4.27 and 4.28.

Figure 4.27.
Setting up the search.

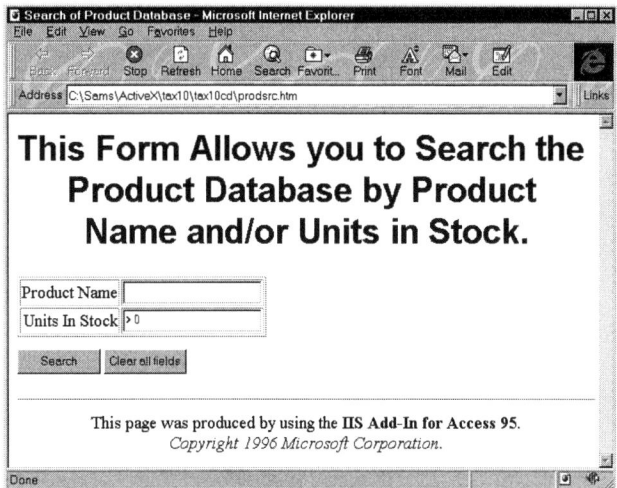

Figure 4.28.
Results of the search.

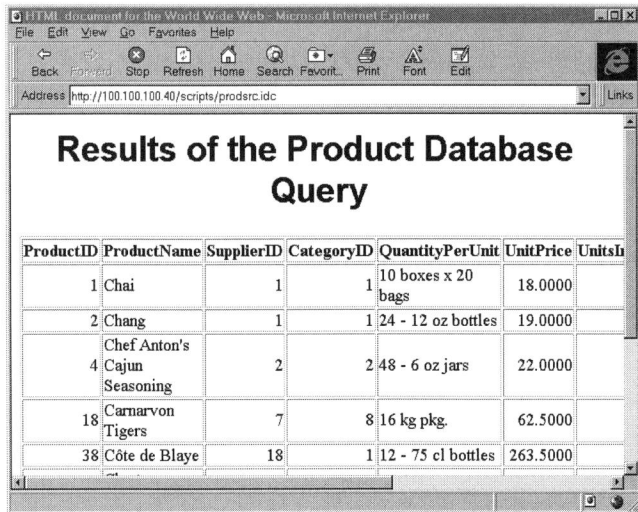

Hacking the Script File

There is a problem in paradise. Try to search using the UnitsInStock field. You only get exact matches. This is not very useful. Look at the source code for the script file prodsrc.idc, shown in Listing 4.6.

Listing 4.6. The source for prodsrc.idc.

```
Datasource: TestNW
Template: prodsrc.htx
DefaultParameters: ProductName=%%, UnitsInStock="UnitsInStock"
SQLStatement:
+Select "ProductID", "ProductName", "SupplierID", "CategoryID",
➥ "QuantityPerUnit", "UnitPrice", "UnitsInStock", "UnitsOnOrder",
➥ "ReorderLevel", "Discontinued"
+From "Products"
+Where "ProductName" LIKE '%ProductName%'
+AND    "UnitsInStock" = %UnitsInStock%
#IDC-Search FrontHTM-prodsrc.htm ReportHTX-prodsrc.htx
```

Do you see the problem? In the second to last line, after the +AND, the field "UnitsInStock" is compared with the variable UnitsInStock. Assuming these variables are passed as strings (they are) using a text editor, let's adjust the line to read:

```
+AND    "UnitsInStock"    %UnitsInStock%
```

Save the file. Make sure you edited the one in the Internet Information Server script directory. Think about it a minute. What is going to happen when you search by ProductName without using UnitsInStock? You will get an ODBC driver error because the last part of the SQL statement won't make sense to the driver. Use your text editor and put a value in the <INPUT> tag that sets up the Units in Stock Query. (I suggest VALUE = "> 0".) Your source should look like Listing 4.7.

Listing 4.7. The revised source for `prodsrc.htm`.

```
<HTML>
<META NAME="GENERATOR" CONTENT="IIS Add-In For Access 95">
<HEAD><Title>Search of Product Database</Title></HEAD>
<BODY BGCOLOR="#FFFFFF">

<H1 Align = "Center"><FONT FACE="Arial" FONT COLOR="#000000">
➥This Form Allows you to Search the Product Database
➥by Product Name and/or Units in Stock.</H1></Font><BR>
<FORM ACTION="/scripts/prodsrc.idc" METHOD = "POST" >
<TABLE BORDER BGCOLOR="#FFFFFF">
<TR>
<TD ALIGN="RIGHT">Product Name</TD>
<TD><INPUT NAME="ProductName"</TD></TR><P>
<TD ALIGN="RIGHT">Units In Stock</TD>
<TD><INPUT NAME="UnitsInStock" VALUE = "> 0"</TD></TR><P>
</TABLE>
<P><INPUT TYPE="SUBMIT" VALUE="Search" ALIGN="MIDDLE">
<INPUT TYPE="RESET" NAME="reset" VALUE="Clear all fields" ALIGN="MIDDLE">
</P></FORM>
<HR=2>
<CENTER>This page was produced by using the <B>IIS Add-In for Access 95</B>.
<BR><I> Copyright 1996 Microsoft Corporation</I>.</CENTER>
</BODY></HTML>
```

The revised line now reads:

```
<TD><INPUT NAME="UnitsInStock" VALUE = "> 0"</TD></TR><P>
```

Save your changes, making sure to save them to your `scripts` directory. Call up the Search form again. Notice that "> 0" appears in the Units In Stock field. Run the original search by entering c% in the Product Name field to make sure that part works. It should. Now blank out the Product Name field (Reset works well for that) and enter "<= 39" in the Units in Stock field, as shown in Figure 4.29. The results are shown in Figure 4.30.

While you were running the last example, you might have accidentally left the Units In Stock field blank. If you did, you got the ODBC error we spoke of earlier. You can't rely on users to be perfect, so how can you fix this problem? Scripting! As I mentioned earlier, you could use scripting to check the values before they are sent to the server. Hold this thought for a day or so and bring it up again after you learn about specific scripting languages.

Figure 4.29.
Finding products with 39 or fewer items in stock.

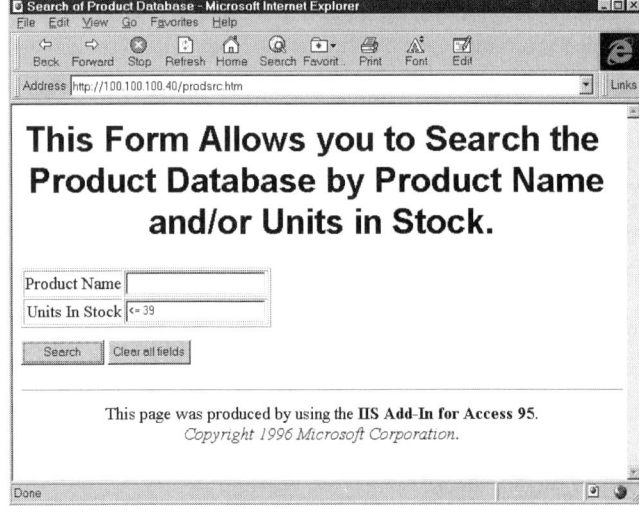

Figure 4.30.
The search result.

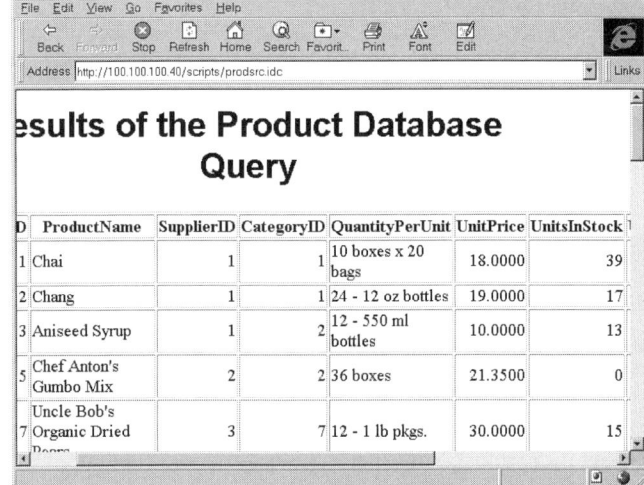

The IIS Add-In for Access Wrap-Up

The IIS Add-In for Microsoft Access is representative of several products on the market, such as

- dbWeb (http://www.microsoft.com/intdev/dbweb/)
- IntraBuilder (http://www.borland.com/intrabuilder/)
- Oracle (http://www.oracle.com)

These tools cost anywhere from nothing to a couple hundred dollars to thousands of dollars. They provide solutions ranging from your local intranet page to an Internet serving thousands of users per second. They all work by binding the Web browser and the Web server together with a database, a process that is now part of your basic knowledge—a basic knowledge that includes HTML and the common themes of the tools that manipulate HTML. You are now ready for scripting and objects.

Overview of the ActiveX Control Pad

It is good that you are ready for scripting and objects now because six months ago you would have been working with a text editor. The ActiveX Control Pad is in the front of a pack of tools that will be competing for your Web development dollars. Before you go off and spend, or recommend your company spend (my favorite thing to do), a great deal of money on new technology to support scripting and objects on the Net, let's see what you can get for free. Point your browser to `http://www.microsoft.com/workshop/author/cpad/default.htm`. Download and install the ActiveX Control Pad.

Tour of the ActiveX Control Pad

After you have it installed, open the ActiveX Control Pad. You will see a screen that looks like Figure 4.31.

Figure 4.31.
The ActiveX Control Pad.

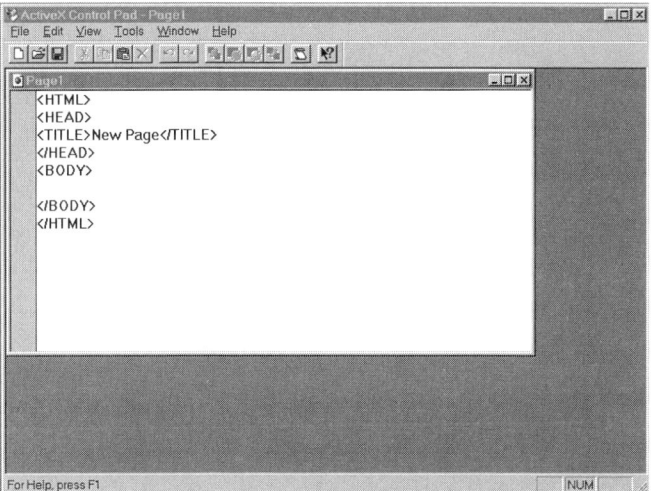

I can hear some of you saying, "Wait a second! After all of this build up, I'm looking at another text editor! We've been tricked!" Just relax for a second. Appearances, in this case, are deceiving. Within a few paragraphs, I will introduce you to more solutions than you have problems for. (I am only speaking about programming problems, personal problems are another book. Probably a big market for a book about personal problems brought on by programming…hmmm.)

Building a Page

You have already seen the text editor in the ActiveX Control Pad, and you could use it to make HTML pages using methods you have already seen. But the ActiveX Control Pad brings many new things to the table. Open the File menu and choose New HTML Layout. Your screen will look like Figure 4.32.

Figure 4.32.
New HTML Layout.

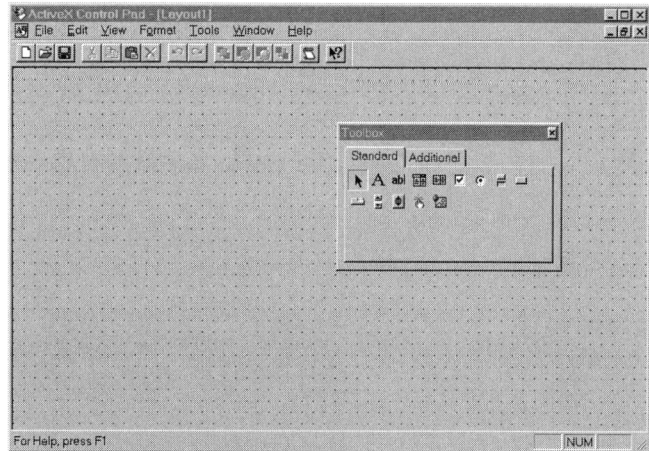

For those of you familiar with Visual Basic or Delphi, this will look familiar. One of the most important things ActiveX Control Pad brings to the table is the capability to design a true What-You-See-Is-What-You-Get (WYSIWYG) Web page. Remember how hard it was in Word to get your working screen to look like the final output on your Web browser? HoTMetal was better, but try to put two lists side-by-side. The ActiveX Control Pad enables you to build a form by selecting an object and dragging it into position. Let's build a form.

Add a label, two radio buttons, and a button. Make your page look like Figure 4.33.

Figure 4.33.
First ActiveX form.

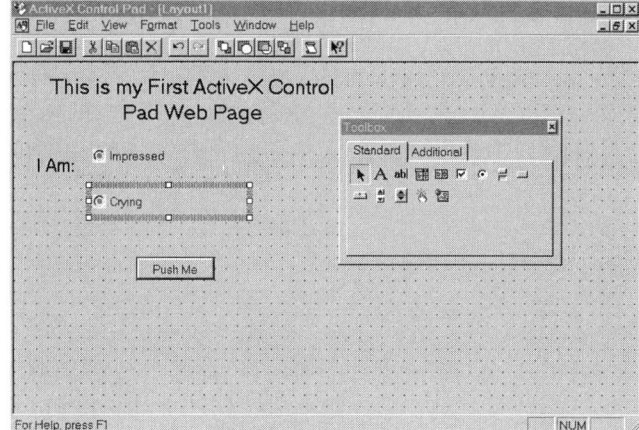

Now save it as activex1.alx. Is this some kind of proprietary format? No, we will look at its structure in a moment. When you create an HTML layout in ActiveX Control Pad, the results are saved in an ALX file and then inserted into an HTML page. Close this screen and go back to the screen that looks like a text editor (refer to Figure 4.31). Your cursor should be between the <BODY> tags. Pull down the Edit menu and click Insert HTML Layout. Your screen should look like Figure 4.34.

Figure 4.34.
The inserted HTML layout.

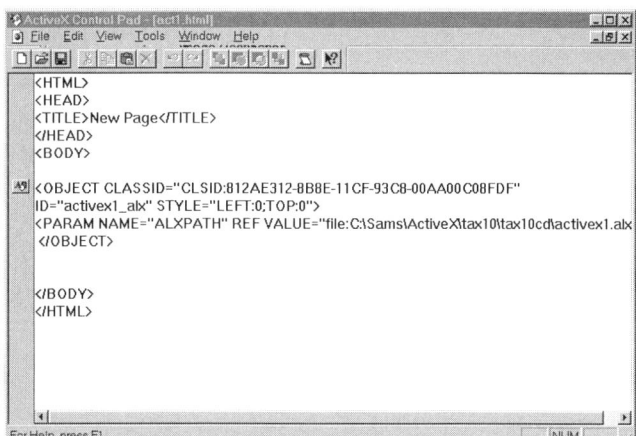

Let's see what this looks like before we take start to dissect it. Save the HTML file as act1.html. Load the file into your browser. It should look like Figure 4.35.

Figure 4.35.
The ActiveX Form in a browser.

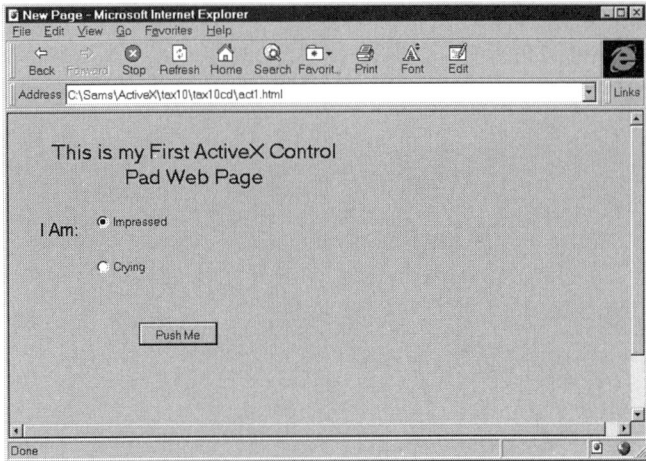

Congratulations! I'll bet you are the first one on your block to use ActiveX controls. Well, maybe the first one in your cubicle. What have you done here? Let's go back and look.

First, put `activex1.alx` into a text browser. It looks like Listing 4.8.

Listing 4.8. The source for `activex1.alx`.

```
<DIV ID="Layout1" STYLE="LAYOUT:FIXED;WIDTH:440pt;HEIGHT:239pt;">
    <OBJECT ID="Label1"
     CLASSID="CLSID:978C9E23-D4B0-11CE-BF2D-00AA003F40D0"
 ➥   STYLE="TOP:8pt;LEFT:16pt;WIDTH:218pt;HEIGHT:55pt;ZINDEX:0;">
        <PARAM NAME="Caption" VALUE=
 ➥   "This is my First ActiveX Control Pad Web Page">
        <PARAM NAME="Size" VALUE="7705;1926">
        <PARAM NAME="FontHeight" VALUE="280">
        <PARAM NAME="FontCharSet" VALUE="0">
        <PARAM NAME="FontPitchAndFamily" VALUE="2">
        <PARAM NAME="ParagraphAlign" VALUE="3">
    </OBJECT>
    <OBJECT ID="Label2"
     CLASSID="CLSID:978C9E23-D4B0-11CE-BF2D-00AA003F40D0"
 ➥   STYLE="TOP:62pt;LEFT:16pt;WIDTH:39pt;HEIGHT:16pt;ZINDEX:1;">
        <PARAM NAME="Caption" VALUE="I Am:">
        <PARAM NAME="Size" VALUE="1376;551">
        <PARAM NAME="FontHeight" VALUE="240">
        <PARAM NAME="FontCharSet" VALUE="0">
        <PARAM NAME="FontPitchAndFamily" VALUE="2">
    </OBJECT>
    <OBJECT ID="OptionButton1"
     CLASSID="CLSID:8BD21D50-EC42-11CE-9E0D-00AA006002F3"
 ➥   STYLE="TOP:55pt;LEFT:55pt;WIDTH:108pt;HEIGHT:18pt;TABINDEX:2;ZINDEX:2;">
        <PARAM NAME="BackColor" VALUE="2147483663">
        <PARAM NAME="ForeColor" VALUE="2147483666">
        <PARAM NAME="DisplayStyle" VALUE="5">
        <PARAM NAME="Size" VALUE="3810;635">
```

```
            <PARAM NAME="Caption" VALUE="Impressed">
            <PARAM NAME="FontCharSet" VALUE="0">
            <PARAM NAME="FontPitchAndFamily" VALUE="2">
    </OBJECT>
    <OBJECT ID="OptionButton2"
     CLASSID="CLSID:8BD21D50-EC42-11CE-9E0D-00AA006002F3"
➥ STYLE="TOP:86pt;LEFT:55pt;WIDTH:108pt;HEIGHT:18pt;TABINDEX:3;ZINDEX:3;">
            <PARAM NAME="BackColor" VALUE="2147483663">
            <PARAM NAME="ForeColor" VALUE="2147483666">
            <PARAM NAME="DisplayStyle" VALUE="5">
            <PARAM NAME="Size" VALUE="3810;635">
            <PARAM NAME="Caption" VALUE="Crying">
            <PARAM NAME="FontCharSet" VALUE="0">
            <PARAM NAME="FontPitchAndFamily" VALUE="2">
    </OBJECT>
    <OBJECT ID="CommandButton1"
     CLASSID="CLSID:D7053240-CE69-11CD-A777-00DD01143C57"
➥ STYLE="TOP:133pt;LEFT:86pt;WIDTH:55pt;HEIGHT:16pt;TABINDEX:4;ZINDEX:4;">
            <PARAM NAME="Caption" VALUE="Push Me">
            <PARAM NAME="Size" VALUE="1926;550">
            <PARAM NAME="FontCharSet" VALUE="0">
            <PARAM NAME="FontPitchAndFamily" VALUE="2">
            <PARAM NAME="ParagraphAlign" VALUE="3">
    </OBJECT>
</DIV>
```

Nothing very mysterious here. Looks like what we saw when we looked at the object tags. Look at Listing 4.9 for our HTML page, act1.

Listing 4.9. The source for `act1.html`.

```
HTML>
<HEAD>
<TITLE>New Page</TITLE>
</HEAD>
<BODY>

<OBJECT CLASSID="CLSID:812AE312-8B8E-11CF-93C8-00AA00C08FDF"
ID="activex1_alx" STYLE="LEFT:0;TOP:0">
<PARAM NAME="ALXPATH" REF VALUE=
➥"file: \source\chap04\activex1.alx">
 </OBJECT>


</BODY>
</HTML>
```

Here we see that `activex1.alx` is not pasted directly into our screen but is instead fed into the HTML Layout Control. (That file path is something you might want to watch as you go from development to deployment.) The HTML Layout Control then takes the form you designed and displays it exactly where you designed it.

OK, let's do some scripting.

Scripting with the ActiveX Control Pad

Aside from the first WYSIWYG method for designing Web pages, the ActiveX Control Pad supports both JavaScript and VBScript. Design a layout called `activex2.alx`. Put two radio buttons, an image, and a button on it. It should look something like Figure 4.36.

Figure 4.36.
Scripting example.

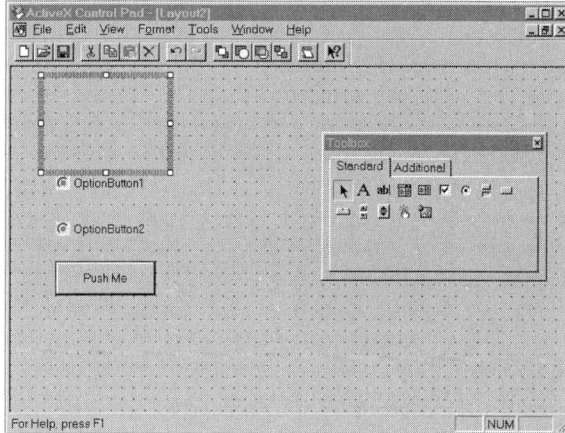

I want this program to change the picture according to which radio button is enabled when the user clicks the Push Me button. When you have the form looking like Figure 4.36, select the Script Wizard from the Tools menu. As you can see, the Script Wizard already knows what objects are on your form and what events come with them. Almost takes some of the fun out of this. The Script Wizard is shown in Figure 4.37.

Figure 4.37.
Script Wizard.

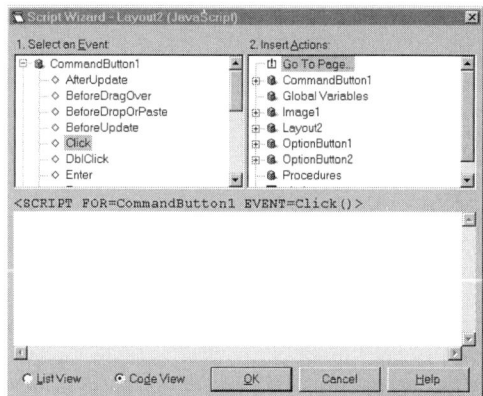

Add the following code to the `click` event of `commandbutton1`:

```
if (OptionButton1.Value)
{
  image1.picturepath = "cash.gif"
}
else
{
  image1.picturepath = "pow.gif"
}
```

Also, change the `GroupName` on both the radio buttons `Choice`. This relates the radio buttons. Notice that when you do this, the first radio button becomes active.

Save this layout to `activex2.alx`. Then insert it in a new HTML document, just like you did in the first example. Save the HTML document as `act2.html`. Run `act2.html` through the browser. You should have a screen that initially has no picture, but when you press the button, a picture appears according to what is selected in the radio button (see Figure 4.38).

Figure 4.38.
ActiveX and scripting.

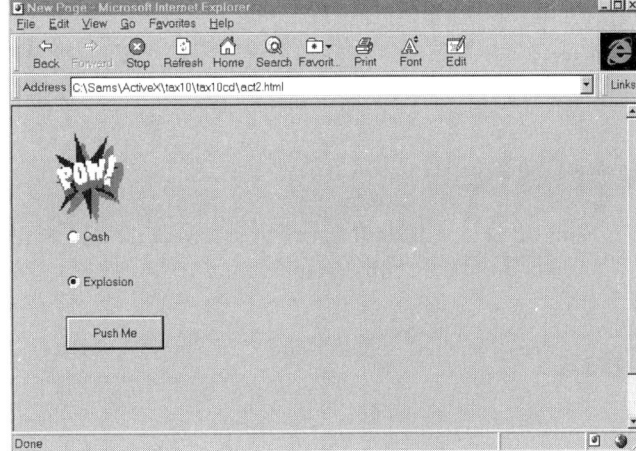

You now know how to operate the ActiveX Control Pad!

Summary

Today you learned about four tools that make creating HTML pages easier: Internet Assistant for Word, HoTMetaL, IIS Add-In for Access, and the ActiveX Control Pad. These tools are the vanguard of an army of tools that will be arriving shortly. You now have a working knowledge of how they operate and a good start toward making an intelligent decision about which tool is right for your job. During the next four days you will use them often, especially the ActiveX Control Pad tomorrow when you learn VBScript.

Q&A

Q There are so many tools. Which one do I use?

A I recommend using a tool that you are comfortable with. For example, if you are an assembly language programmer, the text pad is a familiar place. For Visual Basic and Delphi Programmers, the ActiveX Control Pad looks familiar.

Q I tried to run the ActiveX examples in my Netscape Browser and they don't work. What's wrong?

A Netscape doesn't support the ActiveX model. It probably will in the near future. Keep your eyes on Netscape's home page. Anything you learn about scripting and objects in general will help you understand any object and scripting technologies that come down the road.

Q Where is all this going?

A My guess is that before a year has passed Visual Basic, Jakarta, Delphi, Latte, and a couple of other programming environments will support Web page building. You will be placing the same controls on an area called a Web page instead of on an area called a form.

Workshop

Using Internet Assistant for Microsoft Word, build a table of name, state, and telephone number for at least three people.

Quiz

1. Does Word support `<SCRIPT>` and `<OBJECT>` tags?
2. What is a good point and click method to align text in both Word and HoTMetaL? What are the three alignment settings?
3. Can I put normal HTML `<INPUT>` controls in forms I use on the ActiveX Control Pad?

NOTE Refer to the appendix, "Answers," for the answers to these questions.

Week 1

Day 5

Programming for Internet Explorer

Today you will learn to exploit the programming power that lives inside Microsoft Internet Explorer. Internet Explorer presents a rich set of internal objects, properties, and methods, along with scripting and ActiveX components, that you can use to build smarter, more interactive Web sites. By the end of the day you will know how to use:

- [ ] The main object in Internet Explorer, Window.
- [ ] The Window object's eleven properties.
- [ ] The Window object's eight methods.
- [ ] The Window object's two events.

Why Internet Explorer?

There are several Web browsers available for the Internet today. The two primary browsers are Netscape Navigator (http://www.netscape.com/) and Microsoft Internet Explorer (http://www.microsoft.com/). Currently, Internet Explorer is the only browser that supports VBScript and ActiveX controls, so you will be running your scripts and ActiveX controls on it.

The internal object model for Netscape Navigator is similar to the one for Internet Explorer, so what you learn today will at least give you a good start if you ever wind up putting ActiveX components in Netscape Navigator Web pages.

Internet Explorer Object Model

This section has two objectives: first, to detail the objects available to the programmer; second, to show how these objects are manipulated through scripting. I will use both VBScript and JavaScript in the examples. Don't worry about the syntax, that's what Days 6 and 7 are for.

For those of you who are new to programming, an *object* is a collection of properties and methods. A window on your computer screen is an object. The window has properties, such as background color, size, and border type. The window also has methods. *Methods* are ways of doing things. A window usually has a method for expanding itself to fill the whole screen, and another method to reduce itself to an icon. *Events* are the object's methods that are triggered by the operating system. A good example of an event is clicking your mouse button when the cursor is over a button. By clicking the mouse, you cause the operating system to call the OnClick method of the button. The programmer can place code in this method. You placed code in this event in yesterday's ActiveX Control Pad example, and will be putting code inside events in almost every example you do today.

The Window: Mother of all Objects

The object at the top of the chart is the Window object. This object contains eleven properties, eight methods, and two events. Lets start with Window's properties.

Window Properties

The eleven Window object properties are

- name—This property is the name of the current window. To have a name, a window must be created by:

- Using the `window.open` method (not currently implemented):
  ```
  <SCRIPT Language="VBScript">
   window.open ( "sample.htm", "mywindow");
  ```
- Creating the window with a name using the FRAMESET element:
  ```
  <FRAMESET ROWS="50%, *">
  <FRAME NAME="firstframe" SRC="minibrws.htm">
  <FRAME NAME="secondframe" SRC ="name.htm" >
  </FRAMESET>
  ```
- Creating the window with a URL using the TARGET attribute:
  ```
  <A HREF="Name.htm" TARGET="secondframe">Launch Name Frame </A>
  ```

- parent—This property is the Window object that is the parent of the current window. Because it is a Window object, the parent property possesses all the objects, methods, and events that come with being a window.
- self—This property is the Window object of the current window. This object is redundant. For example, the current window could reference its name by either `window.name` or by `self.name`; both refer to the name of the current window.
- top—This property is the Window object of the top-most window in a collection of windows. This is the object that owns all the frames in a given browser window. For example, to get the name of the top-most window, use:

  `string1 = top.name`

- defaultstatus—This property is the default text displayed in the lower-left corner of the status bar. This doesn't currently set the default status, but it does set the text that appears in the left part of the status bar. You will shortly do an example that shows `defaultstatus` in action.
- status—This property changes the text in the lower-left corner of the status bar (not currently implemented).
- script—This property contains all the functions defined within the <SCRIPT> tags in a window. The browser uses this object to track the functions that are loaded by your scripts.
- location—This property is the location object for the window. It contains the properties `href`, `protocol`, `host`, `hostname`, `port`, `pathname`, `search`, and `hash`. The most commonly used of these properties is `href`. For example, to put the current URL in a variable called `string1` you would write:

  `string1 = window.location.href`

- frame—This property is a zero-based array of frames for the current window. The Frame object can be used like a Window object. For example, the name of the first frame is

  `window.frame(0).name`

- `history`—This property is an object that contains data from the browser's history list. This object contains three methods (`Forward`, `Back`, and `Go`) and one property (`length`). `Forward` and `Back` work just like pushing the Forward and Back buttons on the Explorer to get to other Web pages on the history list. `Go` moves you a given number of pages from the beginning of the list. `length` tells us how long the list is (currently not implemented).
- `navigator`—This property is an object that contains information about the browser. This information is contained in four properties: `appCodeName`, `appName`, `appVersion`, and `userAgent`. In the 3.0 version of Internet Explorer, these properties have the following values (notice how Internet Explorer 3.0 makes itself look like Netscape with the `appCodeName` and the `userAgent`):
  - `appCodeName`—Mozilla
  - `appName`—Microsoft Internet Explorer
  - `appVersion`—2.0 (compatible; MSIE 3.0A; Windows 95)
  - `userAgent`—Mozilla/2.0 (compatible; MSIE 3.0A; Windows 95)
- `document`—This property is an object that contains references to all of the major elements of a Web page. The properties associated with document are
  - `linkColor`, `aLinkColor`, `vLinkColor`—The color of the links, highlighted links, and visited links, respectively.
  - `bgColor`, `fgColor`—The foreground and background colors.
  - Anchors—An array of anchors (`<A>` tags) in the document.
  - Links—An array of links in the document.
  - Forms—An array of forms in the document.
  - `lastModified`—The date the page was last modified.
  - Title—The title of the document, from the `<TITLE>` Tag.
  - Cookie—A text file the document can create, store information to, and retrieve information from, like a Windows `INI` file. An in-depth discussion of cookies is beyond the scope of this book, but if you have been using Internet Explorer for a while, you will have a collection of cookies in a subdirectory named `cookies` off your Windows directory.
  - Referrer—The URL of the program that launched this Web page.

`document` methods are
- `write`—Writes data to the current document.
- `Writeln`—Writes data to the current document with a new-line character at the end. HTML ignores the new-line character unless the section is enclosed in a `<PRE>` tag.

- `Open`—Opens the document for writing. Clears the page of any current text.
- `Close`—Closes the document.
- `Clear`—Closes the document output stream and writes data to the screen. Similar to `Flush` in the C language. (Not implemented in this build.)

The following code segment would cause the `navigator` properties to be printed on the page.

```
window.document.open
window.document.writeln("<PRE>")
window.document.writeln(window.navigator.appCodeName )
window.document.writeln(window.navigator.appName )
window.document.writeln(window.navigator.appVersion )
window.document.writeln(window.navigator.useragent )
window.document.writeln("</PRE>")
window.document.close
```

Let's go through some examples to see how these properties work.

Examples

Launch the ActiveX Control Pad. Before you do anything, go to the Tools menu, choose Options, and then choose Scripting. Change the Scripting option to VBScript. The following example is built using VBScript. This is the only place you can change this option. Your screen should look like Figure 5.1.

Figure 5.1.
Changing the scripting option.

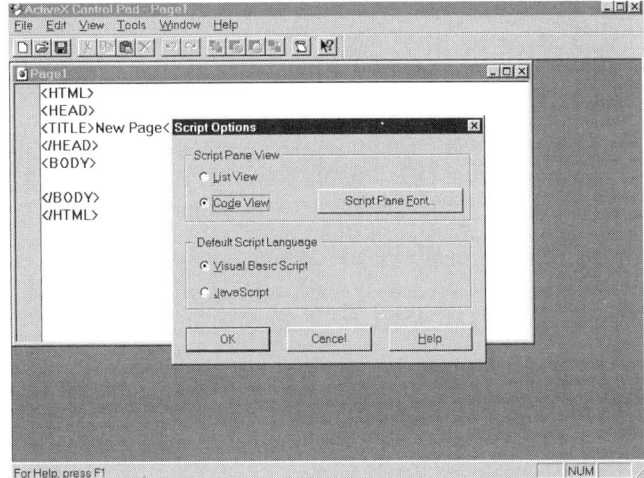

Next, build two HTML inserts. Both have a label, a text box, and a button. Make the inserts look like Figure 5.2.

Figure 5.2.
Sample window *object.*

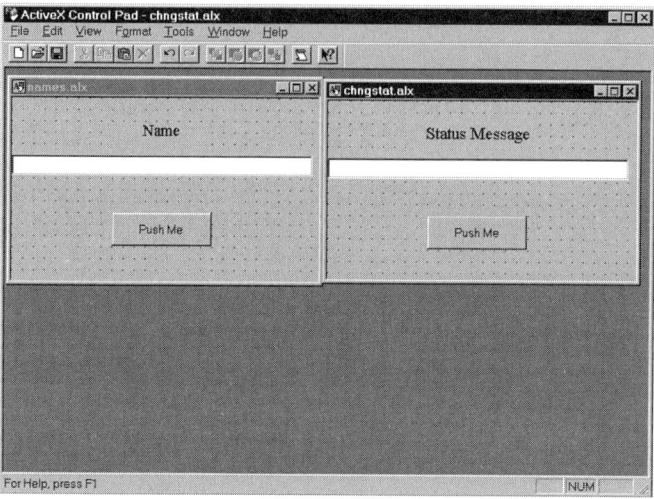

Save the insert with the Name label as names.alx, and save the other insert as chngstat.alx. In names.alx, add the following code to the click method of CommandButton1 (use the Script Wizard to find it). CommandButton1 is the default name the ActiveX Control Pad gives to the first button you put on your form.

TextBox1.Text = window.name

Then, in the click method of the CommandButton1 in names.alx, add this line of code:

Window.DefaultStatus = Textbox1.Text

Also, put some text in the Text property of TextBox1. You will get an error if you push the button without putting any text in the text box. However, it's not a fatal error, so you might want to try it when you run these forms.

Create two new HTML documents. Insert names.alx into one, and save it as names.htm. Insert chngstat.alx into the other, and save it as chngstat.htm. These documents should look like Listings 5.1 and 5.2.

Listing 5.1. Source for names.htm.

```
<HTML>
<HEAD>
<TITLE>Names</TITLE>
</HEAD>
<BODY>

<OBJECT CLASSID="CLSID:812AE312-8B8E-11CF-93C8-00AA00C08FDF"
ID="names_alx" STYLE="LEFT:0;TOP:0">
```

```
<PARAM NAME="ALXPATH" REF VALUE="file: \source\chap05\name.alx">
 </OBJECT>
</BODY>
</HTML>
```

Listing 5.2. Source for `chngstat.htm`.

```
<HTML>
<HEAD>
<TITLE>New Page</TITLE>
</HEAD>
<BODY>

<OBJECT CLASSID="CLSID:812AE312-8B8E-11CF-93C8-00AA00C08FDF"
ID="chngstat_alx" STYLE="LEFT:0;TOP:0">
<PARAM NAME="ALXPATH" REF VALUE="file: \source\chap05\chngstat.alx">
 </OBJECT>


</BODY>
</HTML>
```

The `alx` files should look like Listings 5.3 and 5.4.

Listing 5.3. Source for `name.alx`.

```
<SCRIPT LANGUAGE="VBScript">
<!--
Sub CommandButton1_Click()
TextBox1.Text = window.name


end sub
-->
</SCRIPT>
<DIV ID="Layout1" STYLE="LAYOUT:FIXED;WIDTH:215pt;HEIGHT:124pt;">
    <OBJECT ID="CommandButton1"
     CLASSID="CLSID:D7053240-CE69-11CD-A777-00DD01143C57"
    ➥STYLE="TOP:78pt;LEFT:70pt;WIDTH:70pt;HEIGHT:23pt;TABINDEX:0;ZINDEX:0;">
        <PARAM NAME="Caption" VALUE="Push Me">
        <PARAM NAME="Size" VALUE="2469;811">
        <PARAM NAME="FontCharSet" VALUE="0">
        <PARAM NAME="FontPitchAndFamily" VALUE="2">
        <PARAM NAME="ParagraphAlign" VALUE="3">
    </OBJECT>
    <OBJECT ID="TextBox1"
```

continues

Listing 5.3. continued

```
            CLASSID="CLSID:8BD21D10-EC42-11CE-9E0D-00AA006002F3"
         ➥STYLE="TOP:39pt;LEFT:0pt;WIDTH:211pt;HEIGHT:14pt;TABINDEX:1;ZINDEX:1;">
            <PARAM NAME="VariousPropertyBits" VALUE="746604571">
            <PARAM NAME="Size" VALUE="7444;494">
            <PARAM NAME="FontCharSet" VALUE="0">
            <PARAM NAME="FontPitchAndFamily" VALUE="2">
        </OBJECT>
        <OBJECT ID="Label1"
         CLASSID="CLSID:978C9E23-D4B0-11CE-BF2D-00AA003F40D0"
         ➥ STYLE="TOP:16pt;LEFT:70pt;WIDTH:70pt;HEIGHT:16pt;ZINDEX:2;">
            <PARAM NAME="Caption" VALUE="Name">
            <PARAM NAME="Size" VALUE="2469;564">
            <PARAM NAME="FontName" VALUE="Times New Roman">
            <PARAM NAME="FontHeight" VALUE="240">
            <PARAM NAME="FontCharSet" VALUE="0">
            <PARAM NAME="FontPitchAndFamily" VALUE="2">
            <PARAM NAME="ParagraphAlign" VALUE="3">
        </OBJECT>
    </DIV>
```

Listing 5.4. Source for chngstat.alx.

```
    <SCRIPT LANGUAGE="VBScript">
    <!--
    Sub CommandButton1_Click()
    Window.DefaultStatus = Textbox1.Text
    end sub
    -->
    </SCRIPT>
    <DIV ID="Layout1" STYLE="LAYOUT:FIXED;WIDTH:217pt;HEIGHT:121pt;">
        <OBJECT ID="CommandButton1"
         CLASSID="CLSID:D7053240-CE69-11CD-A777-00DD01143C57"
         ➥ STYLE="TOP:78pt;LEFT:70pt;WIDTH:70pt;HEIGHT:23pt;TABINDEX:0;ZINDEX:0;">
            <PARAM NAME="Caption" VALUE="Push Me">
            <PARAM NAME="Size" VALUE="2469;811">
            <PARAM NAME="FontCharSet" VALUE="0">
            <PARAM NAME="FontPitchAndFamily" VALUE="2">
            <PARAM NAME="ParagraphAlign" VALUE="3">
        </OBJECT>
        <OBJECT ID="TextBox1"
         CLASSID="CLSID:8BD21D10-EC42-11CE-9E0D-00AA006002F3"
         ➥ STYLE="TOP:39pt;LEFT:0pt;WIDTH:211pt;HEIGHT:14pt;TABINDEX:1;ZINDEX:1;">
            <PARAM NAME="VariousPropertyBits" VALUE="746604571">
            <PARAM NAME="Size" VALUE="7444;494">
            <PARAM NAME="Value" VALUE="Some Default Text">
            <PARAM NAME="FontCharSet" VALUE="0">
            <PARAM NAME="FontPitchAndFamily" VALUE="2">
```

```
      </OBJECT>
      <OBJECT ID="Label1"
        CLASSID="CLSID:978C9E23-D4B0-11CE-BF2D-00AA003F40D0"
        STYLE="TOP:16pt;LEFT:62pt;WIDTH:86pt;HEIGHT:16pt;ZINDEX:2;">
          <PARAM NAME="Caption" VALUE="Status Message">
          <PARAM NAME="Size" VALUE="3034;564">
          <PARAM NAME="FontName" VALUE="Times New Roman">
          <PARAM NAME="FontHeight" VALUE="240">
          <PARAM NAME="FontCharSet" VALUE="0">
          <PARAM NAME="FontPitchAndFamily" VALUE="2">
          <PARAM NAME="ParagraphAlign" VALUE="3">
      </OBJECT>
</DIV>
```

At this point, if you run names.htm and push the button, the text box remains blank. Remember that there were only three ways to name a window (window.open, <FRAMESET>, and TARGET). Let's try one of them. To get a better look at what the name property does, create a new form using <FRAMESET> and add two lines of code to your existing forms. Use a text editor and create the following as frame.htm:

Listing 5.5. Source for frame.htm.

```
<HTML>

<FRAMESET ROWS="50%, *">
<FRAME NAME="firstframe" SRC="name.htm">
<FRAME NAME="secondframe" SRC ="name.htm" >
</FRAMESET>

</HTML>
```

This splits the screen into two frames, "firstframe" and "secondframe", and loads name.htm into both frames. Now add the line

```
<A HREF="chngstat.htm" TARGET="secondframe">Change Status </A>
```

to the name.htm file on the line following the </OBJECT> tag. This line will load chngstat.htm into "secondframe". Save the file. Now add the line

```
<A HREF="Name.htm" TARGET="secondframe">Launch Name Frame </A>
```

to the chngstat.htm file on the line following the </OBJECT> tag. This calls names.htm back into "secondframe". Save the file and bring up frame.htm in your browser. After clicking both Push Me buttons, your screen should look like Figure 5.3.

Figure 5.3.
Seeing double.

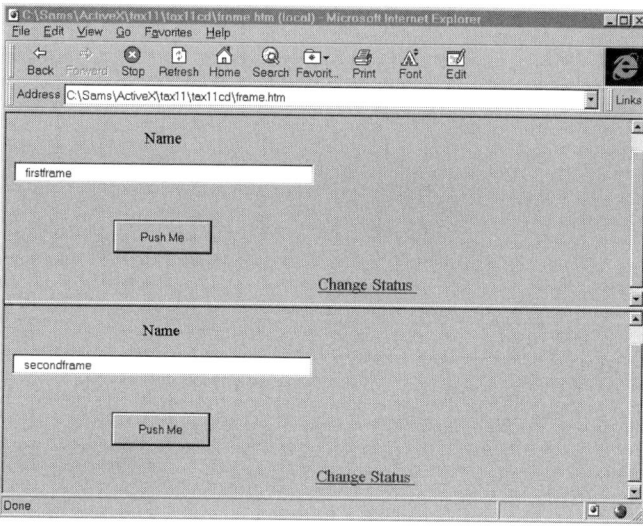

The truth comes out! windows.name is the name of the <FRAME> where the window is loaded. Clicking the Change Status link, adding some text to the text box, and pushing the button results in Figure 5.4.

Figure 5.4.
Status change.

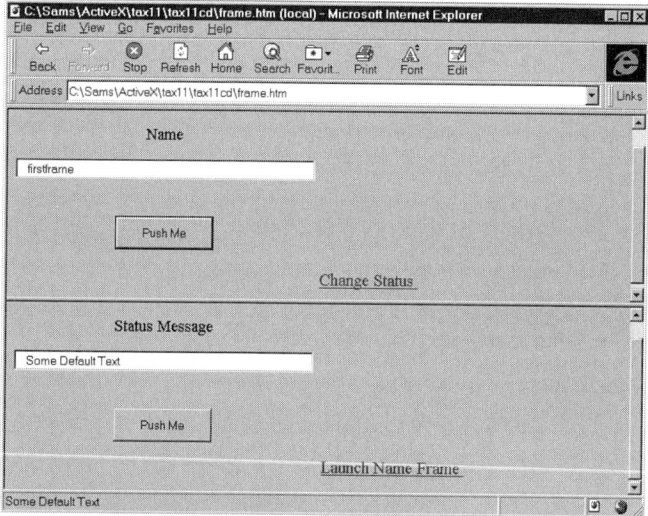

Notice the status change. Notice how the window object and the text box are manipulated the same way by VBScript. When you set the text box text, you used TextBox1.Text. You used the same syntax for window.name.

WARNING

The preceding example works just as well if you use name instead of window.name. However, this is a bad habit to get into. For example, if you misspell name as nane, VBScript uses the new variable nane. Mistakes like this can take some time to find. However, if you use window.nane, you get an error telling you window doesn't support a nane when you run the form in the browser.

Lets look at some of the other interesting properties. The following example looks simple, but it does some cool stuff.

Put three labels, a button, and a text box on a form using ActiveX. The physical layout should look like Figure 5.5.

Figure 5.5.
The physical layout.

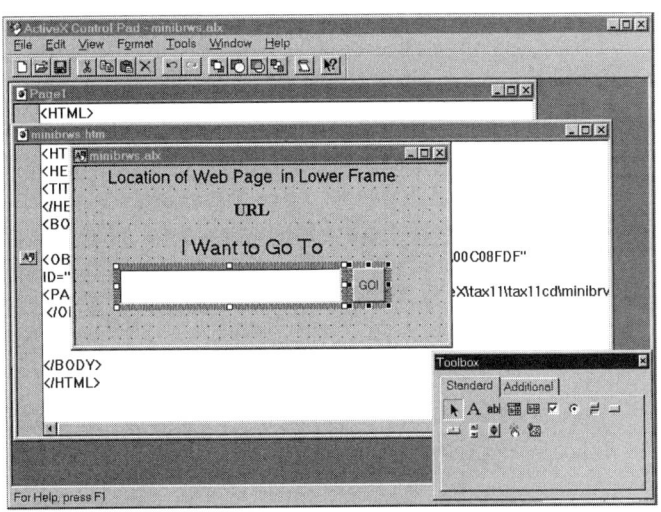

Using the Script Wizard, add the following code to the Onload event for the Layout control:

```
Label1.Caption = window.location.href
```

Then, quick like a bunny, add the following code to your friend CommandButton1's click event:

```
parent.frames(1).location.href = TextBox2.Text
label1.caption = parent.frames(1).location.href
```

Then save the insert as minibrs.alx. Your source code should look like Listing 5.6.

Listing 5.6. Source for `minibrs.alx`.

```
<SCRIPT LANGUAGE="VBScript">
<!--
Sub Layout2_OnLoad()
Label1.Caption = window.location.href


end sub
-->
</SCRIPT>
<SCRIPT LANGUAGE="VBScript">
<!--
Sub CommandButton1_Click()
parent.frames(1).location.href = TextBox2.Text
label1.caption = parent.frames(1).location.href
end sub
-->
</SCRIPT>
<DIV ID="Layout2" STYLE="LAYOUT:FIXED;WIDTH:262pt;HEIGHT:122pt;">
    <OBJECT ID="Label2"
     CLASSID="CLSID:978C9E23-D4B0-11CE-BF2D-00AA003F40D0"
    ➥STYLE="TOP:0pt;LEFT:23pt;WIDTH:203pt;HEIGHT:15pt;ZINDEX:0;">
        <PARAM NAME="VariousPropertyBits" VALUE="276824091">
        <PARAM NAME="Caption" VALUE="Location of Web Page  in Lower Frame">
        <PARAM NAME="Size" VALUE="7161;529">
        <PARAM NAME="FontHeight" VALUE="240">
        <PARAM NAME="FontCharSet" VALUE="0">
        <PARAM NAME="FontPitchAndFamily" VALUE="2">
        <PARAM NAME="ParagraphAlign" VALUE="3">
    </OBJECT>
    <OBJECT ID="Label3"
     CLASSID="CLSID:978C9E23-D4B0-11CE-BF2D-00AA003F40D0"
    ➥STYLE="TOP:47pt;LEFT:70pt;WIDTH:109pt;HEIGHT:16pt;ZINDEX:1;">
        <PARAM NAME="Caption" VALUE="I Want to Go To">
        <PARAM NAME="Size" VALUE="3845;564">
        <PARAM NAME="FontHeight" VALUE="280">
        <PARAM NAME="FontCharSet" VALUE="0">
        <PARAM NAME="FontPitchAndFamily" VALUE="2">
        <PARAM NAME="ParagraphAlign" VALUE="3">
    </OBJECT>
    <OBJECT ID="CommandButton1"
     CLASSID="CLSID:D7053240-CE69-11CD-A777-00DD01143C57"
    ➥STYLE="TOP:70pt;LEFT:195pt;WIDTH:23pt;HEIGHT:24pt;TABINDEX:2;ZINDEX:2;">
        <PARAM NAME="Caption" VALUE="GO!">
        <PARAM NAME="Size" VALUE="811;847">
        <PARAM NAME="FontCharSet" VALUE="0">
        <PARAM NAME="FontPitchAndFamily" VALUE="2">
        <PARAM NAME="ParagraphAlign" VALUE="3">
    </OBJECT>
    <OBJECT ID="TextBox2"
     CLASSID="CLSID:8BD21D10-EC42-11CE-9E0D-00AA006002F3"
    ➥ STYLE="TOP:70pt;LEFT:31pt;WIDTH:156pt;HEIGHT:24pt;TABINDEX:3;ZINDEX:3;">
        <PARAM NAME="VariousPropertyBits" VALUE="746604571">
        <PARAM NAME="Size" VALUE="5503;847">
        <PARAM NAME="FontCharSet" VALUE="0">
```

```
            <PARAM NAME="FontPitchAndFamily" VALUE="2">
        </OBJECT>
        <OBJECT ID="Label1"
         CLASSID="CLSID:978C9E23-D4B0-11CE-BF2D-00AA003F40D0"
         STYLE="TOP:23pt;LEFT:23pt;WIDTH:203pt;HEIGHT:14pt;ZINDEX:4;">
            <PARAM NAME="VariousPropertyBits" VALUE="276824091">
            <PARAM NAME="Caption" VALUE="URL">
            <PARAM NAME="Size" VALUE="7161;494">
            <PARAM NAME="FontName" VALUE="Times New Roman">
            <PARAM NAME="FontEffects" VALUE="1073741825">
            <PARAM NAME="FontHeight" VALUE="240">
            <PARAM NAME="FontCharSet" VALUE="0">
            <PARAM NAME="FontPitchAndFamily" VALUE="2">
            <PARAM NAME="ParagraphAlign" VALUE="3">
            <PARAM NAME="FontWeight" VALUE="700">
        </OBJECT>
</DIV>
```

Place `minibrs.alx` inside a new HTML page, and save it as `minibrs.htm`. Create a frame page to hold `minibrs.htm`. Use the source code in Listing 5.7, and save it as `brsfram.htm`.

Listing 5.7. Source for `brsfram.htm`.

```
<HTML>

<FRAMESET ROWS="50%, *">
<FRAME NAME="firstframe" SRC="minibrws.htm">
<FRAME NAME="secondframe" SRC ="name.htm" >
</FRAMESET>


</HTML>
```

This is just a simple modification of the frame page you used a few pages ago. Load `brsfram.htm` into the browser, then type `http://www.mcp.com` into the text box and press the Go button. You now have a browser within a browser, as shown in Figure 5.6.

The secret to this program is in the object's `parent`, `frames`, and `location`. The `parent` in this case is the window created by `brsfram.htm`. The Parent contains a zero-based (`frame(0)` is the first frame, `frame(1)` is the second, and so on) array of frames that can be addressed like the Window object in the first example. The third object you use is `location`, which has the property `href`, which you read (`label1.caption = parent.frames(1).location.href`) and wrote to (`parent.frames(1).location.href = TextBox2.Text`) in the example. Another object, `history`, gives you access to a listing of all the pages you have browsed; you can traverse this URL list by using the Forward, Back, and Go buttons. At the time of this writing, the `history` object was not yet supported by the browser.

Figure 5.6.
A browser in a browser.

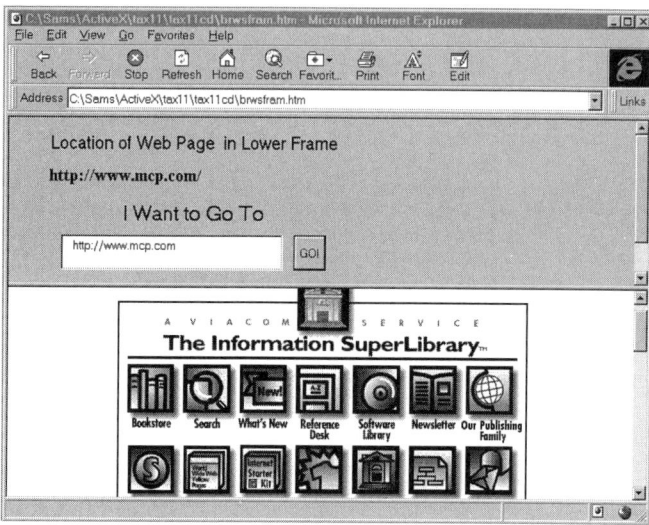

You have seen what objects are available to the developer through the browser and how to access them using VBScript. Most of the objects not covered in the last two examples will be covered during the rest of the discussion of VBScipt.

Window Methods

The Window object offers nine methods.

- Alert—This creates a dialog box with an optional string message. The command Alert brings up an empty dialog with an OK button. Coding Alert, This Space for rent puts the text on a dialog and shows the dialog on the screen (see Figure 5.7).

Figure 5.7.
Alert in action.

- Confirm—This creates a dialog box with an optional string message, OK and Cancel buttons, and a boolean return value that depends on which button the user presses.

Figure 5.8.
To confirm or not to confirm.

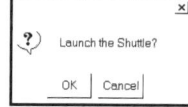

☐ Prompt—This creates a dialog with a text field that shows a default string (if defined by the programmer) and returns the string entered by the user.

Figure 5.9.
The Prompt dialog.

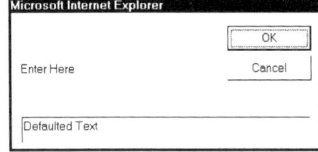

☐ Open, Close—These are used to open and close another instance of the Internet Explorer (not implemented in Internet Explorer 3.0).

☐ SetTimeout, ClearTimeout—These are used to set and clear a timer.

☐ Navigate—This is used to load a URL into a window.

Window Events

There are two Window object events:

Onload—This is fired when the window is loaded and is a good place for initialization code.

Unload—This is fired when the window is closed and is a good place for clean-up or thank-you messages.

Get out your text editor and create the following:

Listing 5.8. A collection of dialogs, boxes.htm.

```
<HTML>
<HEAD>
<TITLE>Boxes</TITLE>
<SCRIPT LANGUAGE="VBScript" >
<!--
Sub LoadMe()
 Alert "This Space for Rent"
 Answer = Confirm("Launch the Shuttle?")
 String1 = Prompt("Enter Here","Defaulted Text")
 Alert string1
end sub

Sub OutofHere()
 Alert "Thats All Folks"
end sub
-->
</SCRIPT>
</HEAD>
<BODY Language="VBS" onLoad="LoadMe" onUnload = "OutofHere">

</BODY>
</HTML>
```

Save this source code as boxes.htm and run it in the browser. Notice how the onLoad and onUnload events are assigned to the subroutines LoadMe and OutofHere in the line

```
<BODY Language="VBS" onLoad="LoadMe" onUnload = "OutofHere">
```

Also, notice how the default text for the text box (where the user can enter a value) in the prompt is entered

```
String1 = Prompt("Enter Here","Defaulted Text")
```

Let's do another example. Launch the ActiveX Control Pad and change the scripting language to JavaScript (Tools | Options | Script). Create one HTML insert, and attach an image control called Image1. Save the HTML insert as chngpix.alx. Open a new HTML file. Using the Script Wizard, add the variables MyTimer and PicState. Then add the procedure ChangePic(). In the window.onload, window.onunload, and ChangePic events, put the code shown in Listing 5.9.

Listing 5.9. Source for chngpix.htm.

```
<HTML>
<HEAD>
    <SCRIPT LANGUAGE="JavaScript">
<!--
var MyTimer

var PicState

function ChangePic()
{
if (PicState=1)
{
  chngpix_alx.Image1.PicturePath = "pow.gif";
  Picstate = 2;
}
else
{
  chngpix_alx.Image1.PicturePate = "caution.gif";
  Picstate = 1;
}
MyTimer = window.setTimeout('ChangePic()', 50000)}
-->
    </SCRIPT>
    <SCRIPT LANGUAGE="JavaScript" FOR="window" EVENT="onLoad()">
<!--
MyTimer = window.setTimeout('ChangePic()', 500);
PicState = 1;

-->
    </SCRIPT>
    <SCRIPT LANGUAGE="JavaScript" FOR="window" EVENT="onUnload()">
```

```
<!--
window.clearTimeout(MyTimer)

-->
    </SCRIPT>
<TITLE>New Page</TITLE>
</HEAD>
<BODY>

<OBJECT CLASSID="CLSID:812AE312-8B8E-11CF-93C8-00AA00C08FDF"
ID="chngpix_alx" STYLE="LEFT:0;TOP:0">
<PARAM NAME="ALXPATH" REF VALUE=
➥"file: \source\chap05\chngpix.alx">
 </OBJECT>


</BODY>
</HTML>
```

Save this as chngpix.htm. Listing 5.10 shows chngpix.alx.

Listing 5.10. Source for chngpix.alx.

```
<DIV ID="Layout4" STYLE="LAYOUT:FIXED;WIDTH:453pt;HEIGHT:275pt;">
    <OBJECT ID="Image1"
     CLASSID="CLSID:D4A97620-8E8F-11CF-93CD-00AA00C08FDF"
     ➥STYLE="TOP:16pt;LEFT:8pt;WIDTH:110pt;HEIGHT:94pt;ZINDEX:0;">
        <PARAM NAME="BorderStyle" VALUE="0">
        <PARAM NAME="SizeMode" VALUE="3">
        <PARAM NAME="Size" VALUE="3900;3302">
        <PARAM NAME="PictureAlignment" VALUE="0">
        <PARAM NAME="VariousPropertyBits" VALUE="19">
    </OBJECT>
</DIV>
```

When you run this in your browser, the picture Pow.gif will flash about one time per second and will look like Figure 5.10. (Only yours will be flashing, the one here on the page will not. You can get the same effect by opening and closing the book quickly.)

One thing to note about this code is the reference to the Image control from outside the Layout control. The Image control is referenced as chngpix_alx.Image1. It is not accessible as Image1 from outside the Layout control. This allows you to reference any piece inside the Layout control. You can create clusters of controls, such as a toolbar, and access the same alx component from many different forms.

You have seen what objects are available to the developer through the browser and how to access them using VBScript and JavaScript. During the course of the rest of the week, you will use Window and its properties, methods, and events over and over again.

Figure 5.10.
It's flashing!

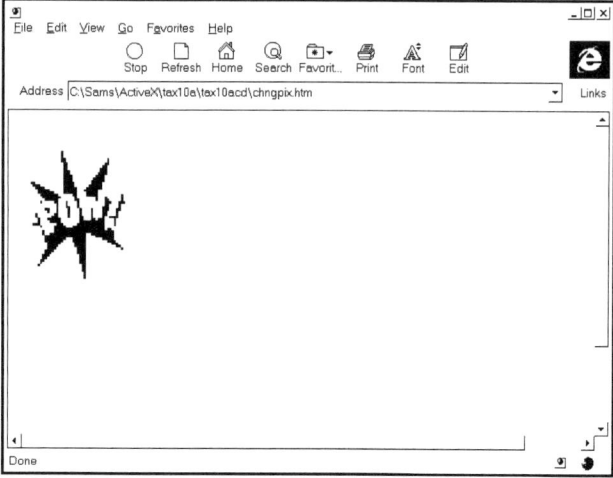

Summary

Today you looked inside the Internet Explorer and found the mother of all objects, window. You can use window's built-in functions to make your Web pages more expressive. Tomorrow you will add VBScript to your tool chest.

Q&A

Q I read in the ActiveX Help that a certain function was not implemented, but it worked when I used it. What gives?

A Browser software and the tools to support it are still in their infancy. I think you are about to see them go through a very fast adolescence. Someday they might move out of the house and leave us alone. No, wait, that last line applies to my kids. Forget that line, but remember that Internet publishing and programming are in a state of flux. Keep trying the functions that didn't work on your last beta!

Q Who is driving the Web-browser-standard boat? Everything is changing so quickly!

A The HTML standard that is the key to this technology is public. However, JavaScript, VBScript, Netscape Navigator, and Internet Explorer all represent proprietary standards. This is good and bad. The good thing is that a proprietary standard evolves more quickly than a public standard. The bad thing is that competition takes some proprietary standards out of the marketplace.

Q Will Netscape Navigator support VBScript and ActiveX?

A There is a plug-in for Netscape Navigator that supports VBScript and ActiveX.

Workshop

Rewrite the example in Listings 5.6 and 5.7 (`brsfram.htm`, `minibrs.alx`, and `minbrs.htm`) to use the Window object's `Onload` event instead of `Layout.onload`. Also, use the `window.navigate` method instead of `frame(1).location.href` to load the user-selected window. Use the `window.unload` event to display a farewell message.

Quiz

1. What would happen if you typed `window.mane` instead of `window.name`, then tried to assign it to a text box? What if you typed `mane` instead of `name`?
2. What object or function can you use to write directly to the Web page from within the Web page?
3. What HTML tag do I use to break my screen into smaller windows? What attribute inside that component sets the name of the new region?

NOTE

Refer to the appendix, "Answers," for the answers to these questions.

Week 1

Day 6

Writing VBScripts

Today you will learn VBScript. You have already used quite a bit of VBScript. You implemented VBScript both by hand coding directly on the HTML page (covered on Day 2, "HTML & Scripting") and with the three editing tools you looked at on Day 4 ("The Tools of the Trade"): Word, HoTMetaL, and the ActiveX Control Pad. Yesterday you used VBScript in some of the examples of programming inside the Internet Explorer. Today, after looking briefly at the background of VBScript, you will learn many aspects of the language from variables to error handling. By the end of the day, you will have examined dozens of examples, and you will be ready to use VBScript in a project.

A Brief Background of VBScript

VBScript grew out of Visual Basic, a programming language that has been around for several years. Visual Basic is the basis for scripting languages in Microsoft Office, Word, Access, Excel, and PowerPoint. Visual Basic is component based. You build a Visual Basic program by placing components onto a form and then using the Visual Basic language to lace them together. Visual

Basic also gave rise to the grandfather of the ActiveX control, the Visual Basic control (VBX). Visual Basic controls shared a common interface that allowed them to be placed on a Visual Basic form. This was one of the first widespread uses of component-based software. VBXs gave way to OLE Controls (OCXs), which were renamed ActiveX. So when Microsoft took an interest in Internet affairs, they moved OCX to ActiveX and modeled VBScript after Visual Basic.

Overview of Scripting Architecture

To learn VBScript you will cover the following topics. There will be several examples and a test at the end—so pay attention!

- Software platforms that support VBScript
- The VBScript programming model
- Variable types
- Operators
- Variable scope
- Functions
- Program flow structures
- User-interface elements of VBScript

Supported Software Platforms

As of this writing, only one Web browser supports VBScript: Internet Explorer from Microsoft. It can be downloaded at http://www.microsoft.com/ie/ie.htm.

Internet Explorer is freeware in its third version. The other major Web browser, Netscape, has no built-in capability to run VBScript or use ActiveX objects. However, it is very probable that by the time you read this, there will be a plug-in module for Netscape that will support both VBScript and ActiveX objects. Netscape is available at http://home.netscape.com.

Microsoft currently controls both the ActiveX and VBScript standards. However, Microsoft recently published its intention to transfer the ActiveX standard to a industry-standards body.

The bottom line is that if you need to use VBScript and ActiveX right now, you have to use the Internet Explorer as your target software platform.

The Visual Basic Programming Model

VBScript is a *procedural language*. For those of you who are new to programming, a procedural language uses subroutines as the basic unit. During previous days, you have seen many subroutines used to do work on a Web page. For example, during Day 5, "Programming for Internet Explorer," you wrote the following subroutine inside an HTML page called `boxes.htm`:

```
Sub LoadMe()
 Alert "This Space for Rent"
 Answer = Confirm("Launch the Shuttle?")
 String1 = Prompt("Enter Here","Defaulted Text")
 Alert string1
end sub
```

Everything between `Sub` and `end sub` is a procedure. VBScript and procedural languages in general are strong in the areas of ease of use, and speed of implementation. The downside of procedural languages is that large projects tend to become unmanageable. Because Web pages must be passed across the Net in a reasonable period of time, they favor small code, making VBScript is a good fit.

What about all those objects you used on Day 5? Good question! You have used objects such as `window.document.write()` and the ActiveX objects Text Box, Label, and Layout, so it is possible to use objects inside VBScript. What is not possible is creating objects with VBScript.

Language Structure

Today you will start with a discussion of the general elements of the language, and before you are through, you will cover every keyword in VBScript. Most of the examples you use to learn VBScript will be run from within the framework of template.htm, shown in Listing 6.1.

Listing 6.1. HTML code for `template.htm`.

```
<HTML>
<HEAD>
<TITLE>Example Template</TITLE>
<SCRIPT LANGUAGE="VBScript" >
<!--
Sub LoadMe()
 ' Your Code Here
end sub

Sub OutofHere()
 ' Your Code Here
end sub
-->
</SCRIPT>
</HEAD>
<BODY Language="VBS" onLoad="LoadMe" onUnload = "OutofHere">

</BODY>
</HTML>
```

Notice how the Language attribute of the <SCRIPT> tag is set to VBScript. We have covered all the elements of this Web page during the previous days of the week. As you can see, it assigns two functions to two window object events. One function, Loadme(), is assigned to the onLoad event. This causes Loadme to be run whenever the page is loaded. OutofHere() is assigned to the onUnload event and is fired every time you leave the page.

VBScript is not case sensitive. In VBScript, a Rose is a ROSE is a rose. This will be a little unsettling for those of you coming from a C or C++ programming background, but old hat for those of you familiar with Pascal or Visual Basic. You are free to capitalize at will. There will be a few situations discussed later today when I will recommend the use of capitalization, but its use is entirely up to you.

So how do you tell one line from another? In VBScript, all you have to do is start a new line. Observe the following code:

```
</SCRIPT>
<SCRIPT LANGUAGE="VBScript">
<!--
Sub CommandButton1_Click()
parent.frames(1).navigate TextBox2.Text
label1.caption = parent.frames(1).location.href
end sub
-->
</SCRIPT>
```

Notice the lines have no visible terminator. Some languages, such as C, use a semicolon (;) as the terminator for a line. Lines of code in VBScript use the line feed at the end of the line as a terminator.

If you feel the need to pack several lines of code on one line, use a colon (:) to separate them, as shown in Listing 6.2.

Listing 6.2. HTML code for `separate.htm`, packing several lines of code into one line.

```
<HTML>
<HEAD>
<TITLE>Example Template</TITLE>
<SCRIPT LANGUAGE="VBScript" >
<!--
Sub LoadMe()
 ' Your Code Here
 A = A + 1 : A = A + 1: A = A + 1
 document.open:document.write(A):document.close
end sub

Sub OutofHere()
 ' Your Code Here
end sub
```

```
-->
</SCRIPT>
</HEAD>
<BODY Language="VBS" onLoad="LoadMe" onUnload = "OutofHere">

</BODY>
</HTML>
```

Notice how this is embedded into template.htm. Running this program produces the number 3. Multiple program lines on the same physical line will annoy any programming purists you work with. I recommend that you keep to one statement per line. Keep your code well organized and easy to read.

Listing 6.2 is the only example using the entire template that I will show you. You will focus on the code inside the template.

Indentation is not required to make the language work. Compare the following code segments.

```
Sub LoadMe()
 ' Your Code Here
    A = A + 1
      A = A + 1
      A = A + 1
         document.open
         document.write(A)
         document.close
end sub
```

runs the same way as

```
Sub LoadMe()
 ' Your Code Here
A = A + 1
A = A + 1
A = A + 1
document.open
document.write(A)
document.close
end sub
```

However, the second example won't win you many points for style. I recommend that you use indentation to organize your code so that if you or others have to go back and maintain it, your code will be easier to understand. You will see examples of indentation used for clarity throughout this chapter.

Comments

Comments can make your life (or the life of someone who looks at your work later) much easier. Comments are not required in VBScript. However, if you want to leave comments

in your code you have two choices: Rem and '. Any characters from the start of the remark to the end of the line are ignored when the script is run. The next segment is an example of Rem:

```
<SCRIPT LANGUAGE="VBScript">
<!--
rem Here is rem used on a separate line
Sub CommandButton1_Click():Rem This is rem after a comment, notice the :
parent.frames(1).location.href = TextBox2.Text
label1.caption = parent.frames(1).location.href
end sub
-->
</SCRIPT>
```

If you use the Rem at the end of a line, you must use a colon (:) or you will get an error. Here is the same example using a single quote ('):

```
<SCRIPT LANGUAGE="VBScript">
<!--
'remark used on a separate line
Sub CommandButton1_Click()'This is rem after a comment, notice the there is no :
parent.frames(1).location.href = TextBox2.Text
label1.caption = parent.frames(1).location.href
end sub
-->
</SCRIPT>
```

Variables

Variables are those things you learned in high school algebra. You remember, the class you knew would never apply to your "real" life. Well, you were wrong. Without variables, computer languages could do little more than power player pianos or music boxes; they would be limited to doing preset tasks over and over. Variables are what allowed us to send people to the moon, build addictive games like DOOM, and make interactive Web pages.

Types of Variables

VBScript has only one variable type, the Variant. Variant can be any type of data. For example, the line

```
string1 = "hello world"
```

sets the value of string1 to "hello world". In the very next line you could type:

```
string1 = 2 + 2
```

Try it yourself. Add the code in Listing 6.3 to template.htm.

Listing 6.3. The `variant.htm` subroutine.

```
Sub LoadMe()
 ' Your Code Here
 string1 = "hello world"
 window.document.open
 window.document.writeln("<PRE>")
 window.document.writeln(string1)
 string1 = 2 + 2
 window.document.writeln(string1)
 window.document.writeln("</PRE>")
 window.document.close
end sub
```

Save it as `variant.htm`, then run it in the browser. You should see

```
hello world
4
```

on your Web page. Remember the `<PRE>` (Preformatted Text) tag allows the browser to execute the new line character that the `writln` function generates.

Variable Typing

This example also suggests that VBScript is *loosely typed*. This means that in VBScript you can add an `int` to a `real` without using a conversion function. A *strongly typed* language would not allow you to add an `int` to a `float`, or a `string` to an `int`. Modify the code you just typed so it looks like Listing 6.4.

Listing 6.4. Using loosely typed variables.

```
Sub LoadMe()
 ' Your Code Here
 string1 = "42"
 window.document.open
 window.document.writeln("<PRE>")
 window.document.writeln(string1)
 string2 = 2 + string1
 window.document.writeln(string2)
 window.document.writeln("</PRE>")
 window.document.close
end sub
```

Save it as `loosetyp.htm` and run it in the browser. You should see

```
42
44
```

proving that VBScript is loosely typed. The advantage to a loosely typed language is that you don't have to remember lots of conversion functions. The disadvantage is that you are at the mercy of the language interpreter. The interpreter determines what conversions need to be done and how. You need to keep an eye on these automatic conversions. In the section later today that covers the built-in functions of VBScript, you will cover conversion functions in VBScript that give you the ability to precisely change one type to another.

Variable Naming

What can you name the `Variant` variables? There are four rules for naming a VBScript variable:

- Begin with an alphabetic character.
- Do not include an embedded period.
- Do not exceed 255 characters.
- Make it unique in the scope in which it is declared.

This means a variable such as `22street` would return an error like the one shown in Figure 6.1.

Figure 6.1.

Results of an improper variable name.

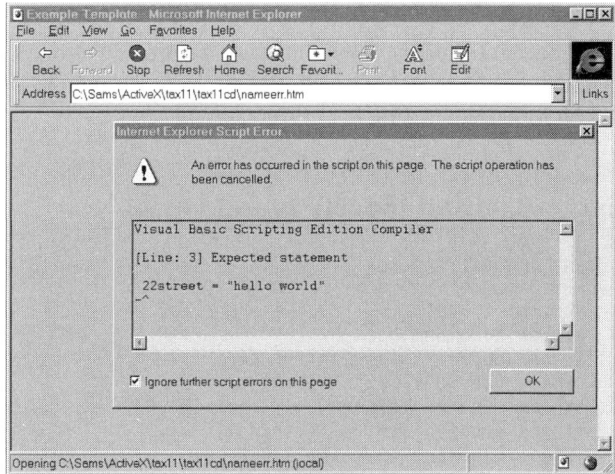

This error was generated by changing `string1` in `variant.htm` to `22street`, as shown in this pseudo code:

```
Sub LoadMe()
  ' Your Code Here
  22street = "hello world"
  window.document.open
```

```
window.document.writeln("<PRE>")
window.document.writeln(string1)
22street = 2 + 2
window.document.writeln(string1)
window.document.writeln("</PRE>")
window.document.close
end sub
```

Number of Variables Allowed

Now that you know how to name a variable, the next question is, how many variables can you use? The answer is that a particular form can have no more that 127 variables. This shouldn't be a limitation unless you do some kind of heavy-duty number crunching on the forms. But it is a small enough number that you need to remember it just in case one of your contemporaries (you would never make this mistake) puts 128 variables on a form.

Dim

`Dim` declares variables. Declaring variables is easy, and optional, in VBScript. Consider Listing 6.5.

Listing 6.5. Using the `Dim` statement.

```
Sub LoadMe()
 ' Your Code Here
 Dim string1
 string1 = "I was declared"
 window.document.open
 window.document.writeln("<PRE>")
 window.document.writeln(string1)
 string2 = "I wasn't declared"
 window.document.writeln(string2)
 window.document.writeln("</PRE>")
 window.document.close
end sub
```

Notice how `string1` is declared and `string2` is not. The form will produce the lines:

```
I was declared
I wasn't declared
```

Not declaring your variables will work, but will not sit well with programming purists. Or you may be working in a corporation that has programming standards requiring all variables to be declared. There is a way in VBScript to require all variables to be declared: `Option Explicit`.

Option Explicit

Placing Option Explicit at the beginning of a <SCRIPT> section generates an exception whenever your code tries to use a variable that is not declared. Modify the Listing 6.5 to use Option Explicit, as shown in Listing 6.6.

Listing 6.6. Using Option Explicit **to force variable declaration.**

```
<SCRIPT LANGUAGE="VBScript" >
<!--
Option Explicit
Sub LoadMe()
 ' Your Code Here
 Dim string1
 string1 = "I was declared"
 window.document.open
 window.document.writeln("<PRE>")
 window.document.writeln(string1)
 string2 = "I wasn't declared"
 window.document.writeln(string1)
 window.document.writeln("</PRE>")
 window.document.close
end sub

Sub OutofHere()
 ' Your Code Here
end sub
-->
</SCRIPT>
```

Showing this page results in the error box shown in Figure 6.2.

Figure 6.2.
Option Explicit *at work.*

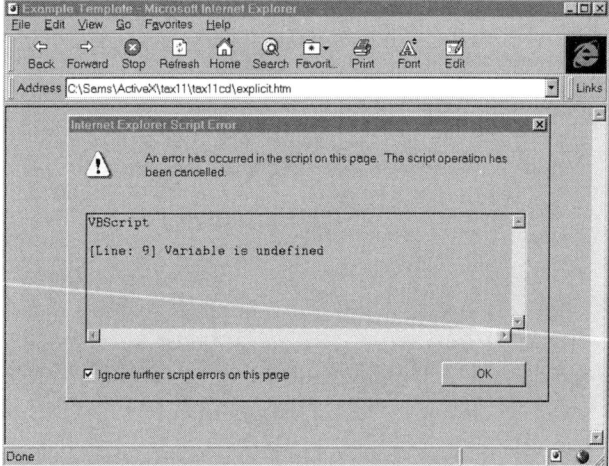

Option Explicit applies only to the <SCRIPT> section in which it is declared. Look at Listing 6.7.

Listing 6.7 Where `Option Explicit` applies.

```
<SCRIPT LANGUAGE="VBScript" >
<!--
Sub LoadMe()
 ' Your Code Here
 Dim string1, string2
 string1 = "I was declared"
 window.document.open
 window.document.writeln("<PRE>")
 window.document.writeln(string1)
 string2 = "So Was I!"
 window.document.writeln(string2)
 window.document.writeln("</PRE>")
 window.document.close
end sub
-->
</SCRIPT>
<SCRIPT LANGUAGE="VBScript" >
<!--
Sub OutofHere()
 ' Your Code Here
 exitmessage = "Thats all folks"
 window.alert(exitmessage)
end sub
-->
</SCRIPT>
```

Notice how there are two <SCRIPT> sections and only one has `Option Explicit`. Run Listing 6.7 (optexp02.htm). You will get:

```
I was declared
So Was I!
```

Notice that you leave the Web page by loading a new one; you will fire the `unload` event and get the alert box as shown in Figure 6.3.

Figure 6.3.
The Alert box fired in the unload *event.*

Uninitialized Variables

If you use Dim to declare a variable and then print that variable, what will be in it? I have spent days in other languages tracking down bugs caused by uninitialized variables where the variable was assigned to some random number. VBScript does not support this kind of frustration. Variables in VBScript are given a value of a zero-length string (" ") when they are declared in the Dim statement. Let's prove it. Enter the code in Listing 6.8.

Listing 6.8. Testing variable initialization.

```
Sub LoadMe()
 ' Your Code Here
 Dim string1, string2
 window.document.open
 window.document.writeln("<PRE>")
 window.document.write("string1 = ")
 window.document.writeln(string1)
 window.document.write("string2 = ")
 window.document.writeln(string2)
 window.document.writeln("</PRE>")
 window.document.close
end sub
```

Save it as initial.htm and run it. You will get the output:

```
string1 =
string2 =
```

which shows the initial value to be empty. Modify the code as shown in Listing 6.9 (initial2.htm).

Listing 6.9. More on initialization.

```
Sub LoadMe()
 ' Your Code Here
 Dim string1, string2
 window.document.open
 window.document.writeln("<PRE>")
 window.document.write("string1 = ")
 window.document.writeln(string1)
 window.document.write("string2 = ")
 window.document.writeln(4 + string2)
 window.document.writeln("</PRE>")
 window.document.close
end sub
```

This treats the second variable, string2, as a number and produces the following output:

```
string1 =
string2 = 4
```

The output shows that string2's initial value, when expressed as a number, is 0.

Constant Variables

In general, VBScript does not support the idea of constant variables. A *constant variable* is one of those programming oxymorons: it is a variable that cannot be changed once it is declared. A constant variable is used to hold things such as the value of pi, which should not be open to the interpretation of the programmer. This prevents the programmer from improving on pi or accidentally changing pi. Unfortunately, you don't have constant variables in VBScript, but there are ways to work around this limitation.

To implement constants in your Web pages, give them a unique identifier like PI or MAXROWS (I recommend all uppercase letters—it is the C programmer in me) and invent a stiff penalty for programmers that change them during the course of a program (I recommend reassignment as the tech writer for a group of assembly language programmers—they hate that).

After telling you that you cannot declare a constant variable, I have to tell you now that VBScript contains five built-in constant variables: Empty, Null, Nothing, True, and False. Again, I recommend that you capitalize these in your code.

Empty

The Empty keyword is used to indicate an uninitialized variable value. Let's see if it works. Type Listing 6.10 as const01.htm.

Listing 6.10. Using the Empty keyword for variables.

```
Sub LoadMe()
 ' Your Code Here
 Dim string1
 window.document.open
 window.document.write("string1 is empty ")
 if (string1 = empty) then
   window.document.writeln("<PRE>")
 else
   window.document.write("string1 is not empty ")
 end if
 window.document.writeln("</PRE>")
 window.document.close
end sub
```

Now run it. You will get this result:

```
string1 is empty
```

The same result is achieved by using the isEmpty function inside the if statement. Empty is different from the next constant Null.

Null

Null means that a variable contains no valid data. This is different than the uninitialized data that empty refers to. Assign a value of Null and then test for it using the function IsNull, as shown in const02.htm (Listing 6.11).

Listing 6.11. Using the Null constant.

```
Sub LoadMe()
 ' Your Code Here
 Dim string1
 string1 = Null
 window.document.open
 window.document.writeln("<PRE>")
 if (string1 = empty) then
   window.document.write("string1 is empty ")
 end if
 if (isNull(string1)) then
   window.document.write("string1 Null ")
 end if
 window.document.writeln("</PRE>")
 window.document.close
end sub
```

When you run Listing 6.11, it bypasses the first if statement and produces the output:

```
string1 is Null
```

A variable can be set to Null and then tested later in the program to see if any data has been put in it. A Null variant contains no data where an empty variant contains uninitialized data.

Nothing

Nothing differs from both Null and Empty in that it is applied to objects and has no associated testing function. When you set an object to Nothing, you sever any ties the variable had to the object. To set an object to Nothing, use the Set statement like so

```
Set MyObject = Nothing
```

Doing this reallocates any system memory or resources allocated to the object. You can use the following code:

```
if isObject(MyObject) then
  MyObject.document.open
  MyObject.document.write("Written by MyObject")
  MyObject.document.close
 end if

Set MyObject = Nothing
```

However, if you try to use `MyObject` after setting it to `Nothing`, you get one or two messages saying that the object is not initialized, and then you get a GP fault, which takes down your Internet Explorer. I would not use this method to de-allocate memory and resources. If you use it, I recommend that you test your objects (`if MyObject = nothing then...`) before using them. As you shall see later in the day, VBScript cleans up after itself pretty well.

True and False

The last two constants are `True` and `False`. These two are the classic boolean constant variables. In VBScript, they have the internal values of -1 for `True` and 0 for `False`. This means you can not use the old C trick of assuming true is any value that is not zero. Try the code in Listing 6.12 (const03.htm) and see.

Listing 6.12. Using True and False.

```
Sub LoadMe()
 ' Your Code Here
 Vartwo = -1
 Varthree = 10
 if Vartwo = True then
  window.document.open
  window.document.writeln("<PRE>")
  window.document.writeln("Vartwo is True")
  window.document.writeln("</PRE>")
  window.document.close
 end if
 if VarThree = true then
  window.document.open
  window.document.writeln("<PRE>")
  window.document.writeln("VarThree is True")
  window.document.writeln("</PRE>")
  window.document.close
 end if
end sub
```

As predicted, this produces the result:

```
Vartwo is True
```

Variable Scope and Global Variables

The *scope* of a variable has to do with where it is visible within the structure of a program or an HTML page. Look at Listing 6.13 (scope01.htm).

Listing 6.13. `scope01.htm` **illustrates the scopes of variables.**

```
<SCRIPT LANGUAGE="VBScript" >
<!--
Dim MyVariable
MyVariable = "Global edition of My Variable"
Sub LoadMe()
 ' Your Code Here
  window.document.open
  window.document.writeln("<PRE>")
  window.document.write("In LoadMe MyVariable is ")
  window.document.writeln(MyVariable)

  ThingOne
  ThingTwo

  window.document.writeln("</PRE>")
  window.document.close
end sub
Sub ThingOne()
  dim Myvariable
  MyVariable = "ThingOne edition of MyVariable"
  window.document.write("In ThingOne MyVariable is ")
  window.document.writeln(MyVariable)
end sub
Sub ThingTwo()
  window.document.write("In ThingTwo MyVariable is ")
  window.document.writeln(MyVariable)
end sub
-->
</SCRIPT>
```

This produces the output:

```
In LoadMe MyVariable is Global edition of My Variable
In ThingOne MyVariable is ThingOne edition of MyVariable
In ThingTwo MyVariable is Global edition of My Variable
```

The first thing you should notice is that the MyVariable declared outside of the functions is visible to all functions in the <SCRIPT>, making it *global*. Then, when a variable is declared inside ThingOne with the same name, that *local* variable is used inside procedure ThingOne. Just to prove you didn't overwrite the global MyVariable, ThingTwo writes the value of MyVariable, and you see that the global MyVariable hasn't changed. Also worth noting here is how the Window object is global. The Window object is visible from anywhere in your

HTML page. Change the code so ThingOne and ThingTwo are in a different <SCRIPT> tag (see Listing 6.14, scope02.htm).

Listing 6.14. `scope02.htm` **places** `ThingOne` **and** `ThingTwo` **in different** `<SCRIPT>` **tags.**

```
<SCRIPT LANGUAGE="VBScript" >
<!--
Dim MyVariable
MyVariable = "Global edition of My Variable"
Sub LoadMe()
  ' Your Code Here
  window.document.open
  window.document.writeln("<PRE>")
  window.document.write("In LoadMe MyVariable is ")
  window.document.writeln(MyVariable)

  ThingOne
  ThingTwo

  window.document.writeln("</PRE>")
  window.document.close
end sub
-->
</SCRIPT>

<SCRIPT LANGUAGE="VBScript" >
<!--
Sub ThingOne()
  dim Myvariable
  MyVariable = "ThingOne edition of MyVariable"
  window.document.write("In ThingOne MyVariable is ")
  window.document.writeln(MyVariable)
end sub
Sub ThingTwo()
    window.document.write("In ThingTwo MyVariable is ")
    window.document.writeln(MyVariable)
end sub
-->
</SCRIPT>
```

Run the page. The results are identical. So scope applies across <SCRIPT> sections.

Arrays and Declarations

You can also create arrays of variables. An *array* is a collection of variables of the same type. If you have an array of MyThings, you would get the first element of MyThings by writing MyThings(0). If you want the second element, type MyThings(1), and so on where 0 and 1 reflect the index of the array. VBScript uses parentheses, (), to enclose the index. Arrays can have more than one dimension. For example, Dim MYArray(10,10) creates an array with 100 possible values. Arrays where the first element is stored in the element zero are called *zero-based* arrays. Arrays in VBScript are zero based. To declare an array, use the same Dim function you used to declare a single variable.

Dim and ReDim

There are two ways to declare an array. The first is to declare the size of the array in the Dim statement, as shown in Listing 6.15 (array01.htm).

Listing 6.15. array01.htm **shows how to declare the size of an array in the DIM statement.**

```
<SCRIPT LANGUAGE="VBScript" >
<!--
Sub LoadMe()
 Dim string1(2)
 string1(0) = "This is "
 string1(1) = "the end "
 alert string1(0) & string1(1)
end sub
-->
```

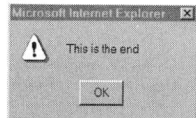

Figure 6.4.
Results of array01.htm.

This code produces an Alert dialog, as shown in Figure 6.4.

If you want to vary the memory requirements of your array at runtime, you would Dim the array without a value and then use ReDim to set and reset the size. This is shown in Listing 6.16 (array02.htm).

Listing 6.16. array02.htm **uses DIM and ReDIM to set and reset the size of and array.**

```
<SCRIPT LANGUAGE="VBScript" >
<!--
Sub LoadMe()
 Dim string1()
 ReDim string1(2)
 string1(0) = "This is "
```

```
string1(1) = "the end "
alert string1(0) & string1(1)
ReDim string1(3)
string1(0) = "This is "
string1(1) = "the end "
string1(0) = "Really "
alert string1(0) & string1(1) & string1(2)
end sub
-->
</SCRIPT>
```

Notice how the array is declared using `Dim string()`, and then redimensioned twice using the `ReDim` function. This allows you to dimension the array according to runtime requirements.

Now that you know everything about variables, or at least enough to start using variables, you can become formally introduced to the structure where you will be doing most of your work: the procedure.

Procedures

In general, a procedure contains programming instructions and can be assigned to events or called from other functions. You have seen procedures in every example today. To be more precise, you have seen one kind of procedure in every example today: the subroutine. The other kind of procedure is the function. Let's look at subroutines first.

Sub

The keyword `Sub` starts a subroutine. A *subroutine* is a collection of program statements that fall between the keyword `Sub` and the `end sub` statement, which marks the end of the subroutine. The general structure, which you have used many times already, appears in the following syntax:

```
Sub LoadMe()
 ' Declare Variables
 Dim string1()
 ReDim string1(2)
 ' Do some Work
 string1(0) = "This is "
 string1(1) = "the end "
 alert string1(0) & string1(1)
 ReDim string1(3)
 string1(0) = "This is "
 string1(1) = "the end "
 string1(0) = "Really "
 alert string1(0) & string1(1) & string1(2)
 ' Leave when we are done
end sub
```

A subroutine can also have arguments. *Arguments* are variables that are passed to the subroutine. Type in and run Listing 6.17 (`sub01.htm`).

Listing 6.17. sub01.htm contains arguments.

```
Sub LoadMe()
  ' Your Code Here
  firstnum = window.Prompt("Enter a number",10)
  secondnum = window.Prompt("Enter another number",20)
  SumONumbers firstnum, secondnum
end sub

Sub SumONumbers(a, b)
  answer = a + b
  window.document.open
  window.document.writeln("<PRE>")
  window.document.write("The Answer is -> ")
  window.document.writeln(answer)
  window.document.writeln("</PRE>")
  window.document.close
end sub
```

The idea here is pretty straightforward: Have the user enter two numbers and then call a function to add them together (use the defaults 10 and 20) and display them.

Run the page; you will get

```
The Answer is -> 1020
```

Wait a minute! Adding 10 and 20 should equal 30, not 1020! Remember before, in this discussion of variables, that you saw how the language does conversions for you. In this case the computer is treating the inputs as strings and adding them together. Later today, in the section on built-in VBScript functions, you will revisit this example and use some of VBScript's built-in procedures to make the numbers add up.

Call

`Call` is an optional element that can be used to start a subroutine. If you use it, you must enclose any arguments in parentheses. For example, the `call` to `SumONumbers` in Listing 6.17 could be rewritten:

```
call SumONumbers(firstnum, secondnum)
```

There is no particular advantage to using `call`.

Exit Sub

`Exit Sub` provides a way to leave a subroutine somewhere other than `End Sub`. When `Exit Sub` is called, the program resumes running on the line after the call to the subroutine, as in Listing 6.18 (`sub02.htm`).

Listing 6.18. In sub02.htm, the program resumes after ExitSub is called.

```
Sub LoadMe()
 ' Your Code Here
 firstnum = 10
 secondnum = 30
  SumONumbers firstnum, secondnum
end sub

Sub SumONumbers(a, b)
  answer = a + b
  window.document.open
  window.document.writeln("<PRE>")
  window.document.write("The Answer is -> ")
  window.document.writeln(answer)
  window.document.writeln("</PRE>")
  window.document.close
  if (a + b) > 0 then
    exit sub
  end if
  window.document.open
  window.document.writeln("<PRE>")
  window.document.write("Error, negative sum")
  window.document.writeln("</PRE>")
  window.document.close
end sub
```

Left as it is, this page performs the exit sub in the middle of SumONumbers and displays the number 40. If you change one of the variables in the LoadMe subroutine to be a negative number, then the second message, "Error, negative sum", is displayed. I do not recommend using exit sub. I have found that in the long run, it is harder to maintain procedures with multiple exit points than procedures with a single exit.

There are a couple of things you can't do with subroutines. First, you cannot declare a subroutine inside another procedure. Second, you can not pass a reference to an argument. The variables passed to a subroutine are copies of the originals; changing these copies has no effect on the original. Third, a subroutine cannot be used as part of an expression, as in Var1 = Var2 + MySub, because a subroutine doesn't return a value. To return a value, you use the other type of procedure called a function.

User-Built Functions

A *function* has the same general structure as a subroutine but functions have different keywords as well as the capability to return a value. Type the code in Listing 6.19 (sub03.htm):

Listing 6.19. `sub03.htm` is a simple radians-to-degree function.

```
Sub LoadMe()
  ' Your Code Here
  window.document.open
  window.document.writeln("<PRE>")
  window.document.write("The Answer is -> ")
  window.document.writeln(RADtoDeg(3.14))
  window.document.writeln("</PRE>")
  window.document.close
end sub
Function RADtoDEG(Radian)
  RADtoDEG = Radian * 57.32
end Function
```

This is a simple radians-to-degrees function. Notice the keyword `Function` is at the beginning and end. Also see how the value of the function is assigned using the function name. If no value is assigned, the function value is assigned as uninitialized, which is 0 if the function is used in a numeric expression and "" if the function is used as a string.

Functions can not be declared inside other procedures. And, like subroutines, the arguments passed to the function are only copies; changing the copies has no effect on the original variables.

Functions are strung together with operators. Let's see what you can use to operate.

Operators

Operators determine what you do to variables and functions. There are five types of operators: assignment, math, string, comparison, and object. Let's start with the most used, assignments.

Assignment Operators

You use assignment operators all the time to assign one value to another; assignment variables are the heart of programming. VBScript has two ways to assign one value to another: the equal symbol (=) and Set.

The = Operator

You have already used the equal sign (=) hundreds of times in this book. I use it so much, I start to take it for granted. It does the simplest and most powerful thing you can do in a program: assigns one variable to another. The general form is `myvariable = someothervariable`, or `myvariable = somevalue`. It can be used to assign everything in VBScript except objects.

Set

The Set keyword is used to define objects. Type the following and call it set01.htm (see Listing 6.20).

Listing 6.20. set01.htm **uses the** Set **keyword to define functions.**

```
Sub LoadMe()
 ' Your Code Here
 Set MyWindow = window
 MyWindow.document.open
 MyWindow.document.writeln("<PRE>")
 MyWindow.document.writeln("Did this with my own object")
 MyWindow.document.writeln("</PRE>")
 MyWindow.document.close

end sub
```

In this example, you use the Set function to set the variable MyWindow to the object window. When setting a variable to an object, Set creates a reference to the object. You are free to create as many references to an object as you want using Set. Set does not create a new object, only a reference to it.

Set can also be used to assign a variable to a value other than a set. For example, you could write Set MyVariable = 9, and it would be the same as MyVariable = 9. Set is optional for variable assignment but required when objects are assigned.

Math Operators

The math operators are another group I tend to take for granted. The important thing to note as you go through these operators is how they work on various combinations of integer and real numbers.

Addition (+)

The + operator covers both reals and integers in that it can be used to add any two numbers together. Consider Listing 6.21:

Listing 6.21. The addition operator.

```
Sub LoadMe()
  ' Your Code Here
  example1 = 2 + 2
```

continues

Listing 6.21. continued

```
example2 = 5.67 + 1
example3 = 9.9 + 4.568

window.document.open
window.document.writeln("<PRE>")
window.document.write("example 1 = ")
window.document.writeln(example1)
window.document.write("example 2 = ")
window.document.writeln(example2)
window.document.write("example 3 = ")
window.document.writeln(example3)
window.document.writeln("</PRE>")
window.document.close

end sub
```

This produces the following result:

```
example 1 = 4
example 2 = 6.67
example 3 = 14.468
```

Here you add two integers and get an integer. You also add an integer and a real and get a real.

Subtraction (-)

Subtraction also applies to both integers and reals. Look at Listing 6.22 (math02.htm):

Listing 6.22. math02.htm illustrates the subtraction operator.

```
Sub LoadMe()
 ' Your Code Here
 example1 = 2 - 20
 example2 = 5.67 - 1
 example3 = 9.9 - 4.568

 window.document.open
 window.document.writeln("<PRE>")
 window.document.write("example 1 = ")
 window.document.writeln(example1)
 window.document.write("example 2 = ")
 window.document.writeln(example2)
 window.document.write("example 3 = ")
 window.document.writeln(example3)
 window.document.writeln("</PRE>")
 window.document.close

end sub
```

This page produces the result:

```
example 1 = -18
example 2 = 4.67
example 3 = 5.332
```

Again, an integer minus an integer is an integer. Any other combination is a real.

Exponentiation (^)

This symbol raises a number by a power, as illustrated in Listing 6.23 (math03.htm).

Listing 6.23. math03.htm **illustrates the exponentiation operator.**

```
Sub LoadMe()
  ' Your Code Here
  example1 = 2 ^ 8
  example2 = 5.67 ^ 2
  example3 = 9.9 ^ 4.568

  window.document.open
  window.document.writeln("<PRE>")
  window.document.write("example 1 = ")
  window.document.writeln(example1)
  window.document.write("example 2 = ")
  window.document.writeln(example2)
  window.document.write("example 3 = ")
  window.document.writeln(example3)
  window.document.writeln("</PRE>")
  window.document.close

end sub
```

This produces the following result:

```
example 1 = 256
example 2 = 32.1489
example 3 = 35323.3243300256
```

Modulus Arithmetic (Mod)

The Mod function divides the first number by the second number and returns the remainder, as shown in Listing 6.24 (math04.htm).

Listing 6.24. math04.htm **illustrates the** Mod **function.**

```
Sub LoadMe()
  ' Your Code Here
  example1 = 2 Mod 8
```

continues

Listing 6.24. continued

```
    example2 = 2 Mod 5.67
    example3 = 4.5 Mod 4600.9

    window.document.open
    window.document.writeln("<PRE>")
    window.document.write("example 1 = ")
    window.document.writeln(example1)
    window.document.write("example 2 = ")
    window.document.writeln(example2)
    window.document.write("example 3 = ")
    window.document.writeln(example3)
    window.document.writeln("</PRE>")
    window.document.close

end sub
```

Real numbers are rounded to integers during the Mod. The results of the above are as follows:

```
example 1 = 2
example 2 = 2
example 3 = 4
```

Multiplication (*)

This operator multiplies two numbers, as shown in Listing 6.25 (math05.htm).

Listing 6.25. math05.htm illustrates the multiplication operator.

```
Sub LoadMe()
 ' Your Code Here
  example1 = 2 * 8
  example2 = 2 * 5.67
  example3 = 4.5 * 4600.9

  window.document.open
  window.document.writeln("<PRE>")
  window.document.write("example 1 = ")
  window.document.writeln(example1)
  window.document.write("example 2 = ")
  window.document.writeln(example2)
  window.document.write("example 3 = ")
  window.document.writeln(example3)
  window.document.writeln("</PRE>")
  window.document.close

end sub
```

This returns the following result:

```
example 1 = 16
```

```
example 2 = 11.34
example 3 = 20704.05
```

Note that an integer times an integer returns an integer. All other combinations return a real.

Division (/)

Division works the same way as multiplication. See Listing 6.26 (math06.htm).

Listing 6.26. math06.htm **illustrates the division operator.**

```
Sub LoadMe()
  ' Your Code Here
  example1 = 25 / 8
  example2 = 2 / 5.67
  example3 = 4.5 / 4600.9

  window.document.open
  window.document.writeln("<PRE>")
  window.document.write("example 1 = ")
  window.document.writeln(example1)
  window.document.write("example 2 = ")
  window.document.writeln(example2)
  window.document.write("example 3 = ")
  window.document.writeln(example3)
  window.document.writeln("</PRE>")
  window.document.close

end sub
```

This page results in

```
example 1 = 3.125
example 2 = 0.352733686067019
example 3 = 9.78069508139712E-04
```

which shows that in division, all cases return a real.

Integer Division (\)

This is the companion function to Mod. Where Mod returns the remainder, the division operator returns the integer result of the division (see Listing 6.27, math07.htm).

Listing 6.27. math07.htm **illustrates integer division.**

```
Sub LoadMe()
  ' Your Code Here
  example1 = 25 \ 8
  example2 = 2000 \ 5.67
```

continues

Listing 6.27. continued

```
example3 = 400.5 \ 46.9

window.document.open
window.document.writeln("<PRE>")
window.document.write("example 1 = ")
window.document.writeln(example1)
window.document.write("example 2 = ")
window.document.writeln(example2)
window.document.write("example 3 = ")
window.document.writeln(example3)
window.document.writeln("</PRE>")
window.document.close

end sub
```

This page results in the following lines:

```
example 1 = 3
example 2 = 333
example 3 = 8
```

Negation (-)

The final math operator is negation (-). This is a straightforward concept. If you set a = 2, then write a line such as a = -a, the final value of a is -2. This operator simply returns the negative.

String

There is only one string operator: concatenation (&). This allows you to lace strings together. If a variable is not a string, using & converts it to one (see Listing 6.28, string01.htm).

Listing 6.28. string01.htm illustrates the string operator.

```
Sub LoadMe()
 ' Your Code Here
 part1 = "This is "
 part2 = "just a "
 part3 = "test"

 window.document.open
 window.document.write("Together the parts are->" & part1 & part2 & part3)
 window.document.close

end sub
```

This produces the following line:

```
Together the parts are->This is just a test
```

Comparison

Comparison operators are used inside VBScript's Control structures to test the relationship between variables. We will cover these operators using essentially the same Web page. It covers the cases of comparing number to number, number to string, and string to string.

Equality (=)

Some languages have a special symbol for testing equality to keep assignment and equality separate; VBScript does not. Instead, VBScript keeps them separate strictly by context. Look at Listing 6.29 (comp01.htm):

Listing 6.29. comp01.htm **illustrates the equality test.**

```
Sub LoadMe()
' Your Code Here
num1 = 10
num2 = 10
string1 = "10"
string2 = "Hello"
if num1 = num2 then
  Alert("num1 equals num2")
else
  Alert("num1 is not equal to num2")
end if
if num1 = string1 then
  Alert("num1 equals string1")
else
  Alert("num1 is not equal to string1")
end if
if string1 = string2 then
  Alert("string2 equals string1")
else
  Alert("string1 is not equal to string2")
end if
end sub
```

The way the preceding code is written, it will pop up alert boxes to tell you:

- [ ] Num1 equals num2
- [ ] Num1 is not equal to string1
- [ ] string2 is not equal to string1

Experiment with the numbers and the text on this and on all the following comparison examples to see what to expect from the specific comparison operator.

Inequality (<>)

The inequality test is the bookend for the equality test you just looked at. It uses the symbol <>. Check out Listing 6.30 (comp02.htm).

Listing 6.30. `comp02.htm` **illustrates the inequality test.**

```
Sub LoadMe()
' Your Code Here
num1 = 21
num2 = 10
string1 = "Hello"
string2 = "Hello"
if num1 <> num2 then
  Alert("num1 is not equal to num2")
else
  Alert("num1 equals num2")
end if
if num1 <> string1 then
  Alert("num1 is not equal to string1")
else
  Alert("num1 equals string1")
end if
if string1 <> string2 then
  Alert("string1 is not equal to string1")
else
  Alert("string2 equals string1")
end if
end sub
```

Given the numbers at the start of the subroutine, this example tells you:

- [ ] num1 is not equal to num2
- [ ] num1 is not equal to string1
- [ ] string2 equals to string1

Other Comparison Operators

These comparison operators are used frequently to compare numbers and text, usually for the purpose of sorting a list of numbers or names. Less than (<) and greater than (>) return true when the number on the left of the expression is less than but not equal to the number on the right or greater than but not equal to the number on the right. Adding an equal (=) to either one includes the number on the right. See Listing 6.31 for greater understanding (comp03.htm).

Listing 6.31. comp03.htm illustrates the less-than and greater-than comparison operators.

```
Sub LoadMe()
  ' Your Code Here
  item1 = 21
  item2 = 10

  if itme1 < item2 then
    Alert("item1 one is less than item2")
  end if
  if itme1 > item2 then
    Alert("item1 one is greater than item2")
  end if
  if item1 <= item2 then
    Alert("item1 one is less than or equal to item2")
  end if
  if item1 >= item2 then
    Alert("item1 one is greater than or equal to item2")
  end if
end sub
```

Notice you didn't call the variable num1 or string1. These comparison operators work on both strings and numbers.

Is

The Is operator compares two objects. Let's look at Listing 6.32 (comp04.htm).

Listing 6.32. comp04.htm illstrates the Is operator.

```
Sub LoadMe()
  ' Your Code Here
  set Window1 = window
  set Window2 = window.document
  set Window3 = window

  window.document.open
  window.document.writeln("<PRE>")
  if Window1 Is Window2 then
    window.document.writeln("Window1 is Window2")
  end if
  if Window1 Is Window3 then
    window.document.writeln("Window1 is Window3")
  end if

  window.document.writeln("</PRE>")
  window.document.close
end sub
```

This returns

```
Window1 is Window3
```

The result not only shows you how Is works, it also reinforces the idea of using Set to create multiple references to the same object.

and, or, **and** xor

The keywords and, or, and xor allow you to compare the results of one expression with another using boolean logic. The syntax for and, or, and xor is the same:

```
Expression1 and Expression2
```

Where *Expression* is a function that returns a boolean or a statement using one of the comparison operators similar to:

```
A >= B
```

The logic used in these three operators is described in Tables 6.1, 6.2, and 6.3.

Table 6.1. Using and.

If First Expression Is	And Second Expression Is	The Result Is
True	True	True
True	False	False
True	Null	Null
False	True	False
False	False	False
False	Null	False
Null	True	Null
Null	False	False
Null	Null	Null

Table 6.2. Using or.

If First Expression Is	And Second Expression Is	The Result Is
True	True	True
True	False	True
True	Null	True

If First Expression Is	And Second Expression Is	The Result Is
False	True	True
False	False	False
False	Null	Null
Null	True	True
Null	False	Null
Null	Null	Null

Table 6.3. Using xor.

If First Expression Is	And Second Expression Is	The Result Is
True	True	False
True	False	True
False	True	True
False	False	False

Listing 6.33 (comp05.htm) is an example using these operators.

Listing 6.33. comp05.htm illustrates the and, or, and xor keywords.

```
Sub LoadMe()
 ' Your Code Here
 A = 10
 B = 10
 C = 30

 window.document.open
 window.document.writeln("<PRE>")

 if (A = B) or (B = C) then
   window.document.writeln("Passed or")
 end if
 if (A = B) and (B = C) then
   window.document.writeln("Passed and")
 end if
 if (A = B) xor (B = C) then
   window.document.writeln("Passed xor")
 end if
 window.document.writeln("</PRE>")
 window.document.close
end sub
```

Notice how the expressions are grouped within parentheses. These operators can be used in the same expression. Two similar, but less commonly used, operators are eqv (equivalance), and imp (implication). The syntax of these two operators is the same as the group you just looked at, but the logic of these two operators is not intuitive (as illustrated in Tables 6.4 and 6.5).

Table 6.4. Using `eqv`.

If First Expression Is	And Second Expression Is	The Result Is
True	True	True
True	False	False
False	True	False
False	False	True

Table 6.5. Using `imp`.

If First Expression Is	And Second Expression Is	The Result Is
True	True	True
True	False	False
True	Null	Null
False	True	True
False	False	True
False	Null	True
Null	True	True
Null	False	Null
Null	Null	Null

Operator Precedence

You have seen that it is possible to combine several comparison operators from the arithmetic, comparison, and logical groups on one line. You have also seen that the operators can be grouped within parentheses to clarify the order of operation. What happens when expressions are not grouped within parentheses?

First, the arithmetic operators are evaluated. Within the arithmetic group, the precedence is:

- ☐ exponentiation (^)
- ☐ negation (-)

- multiplication and division (*,/)
- integer division (\)
- modulus arithmetic (Mod)
- addition and subtraction (+,-)

Next, the comparison operators are evaluated. All comparison operators have equal precedence, so they are evaluated from left to right.

Then, the logical operators are evaluated in the following order.

- not
- and
- or
- xor
- eqv
- imp

See Listing 6.34 (comp06.htm) for an example of arithmetic precedence.

Listing 6.34. comp06.htm illustrates arithmetic precedence.

```
Sub LoadMe()
 ' Your Code Here
 A = 10
 B = 20
 C = 30

 window.document.open
 window.document.writeln("<PRE>")
 Answer = A + B / C * 12
 window.document.write("A + B / C * 12 = ")
 window.document.writeln(Answer)
  window.document.writeln("</PRE>")
 window.document.close
end sub
```

Which results in:

```
A + B / C * 12 = 18
```

Use () to group your statements so they are performed in the order you want and not in the order the machine wants.

Built-In Functions

VBScript contains both user-built functions, which we have already covered, and built-in functions. These built-in functions cover several areas, including conversions, dates/times, math, arrays, strings, and variants.

Conversions

As you have seen in previous examples, working with variants can be confusing. Is it a string? Is it a number? What does the interpreter think it is? Well, conversion functions allow you to specify exactly what kind of variable the variant represents.

abs

This function converts its argument into the absolute value of the argument. Listing 6.35 (funct01.htm) contains an example.

Listing 6.35. funct01.htm **uses** abs **to convert its argument to the absolute value of the argument.**

```
Sub LoadMe()
 ' Your Code Here
 A = - 10
 window.document.open
 window.document.writeln("<PRE>")
 window.document.write("abs(A) = ")
 window.document.writeln(abs(A))
 window.document.writeln("</PRE>")
 window.document.close
end sub
```

asc, ascb **and** ascw

All these functions return the first character of the argument string. asc returns this character as a string. ascb returns it as a byte. And, on 32-bit systems (Windows 95, Windows NT), ascw returns the first character as a Unicode character (a double-byte character set that allows more complex languages to be represented).

These functions are demonstrated in Listing 6.36 (funct02.htm).

Listing 6.36. funct02.htm **illustrates the** asc, ascb, **and** ascw **functions.**

```
Sub LoadMe()
 ' Your Code Here
 Sting1 = "This is a test"
 result1 = Asc(Sting1)
```

```
result2 = Ascb(Sting1)
result3 = Ascw(Sting1)
window.document.open
window.document.writeln("<PRE>")
window.document.write("asc(string1) = ")
window.document.writeln(result1)
window.document.write("ascb(string1) = ")
window.document.writeln(result2)
window.document.write("ascw(string1) = ")
window.document.writeln(result3)
window.document.writeln("</PRE>")
window.document.close
end sub
```

The result is 84 in all three cases. In a place as international as the Web, you will need the support for new character sets that ascb and ascw give you.

chr, chrb and chrw

This is the companion group of functions for asc. chr converts a number into its ASCII character. chrb converts one byte of the character to its ASCII character. chrw provides the same function for Unicode characters. Listing 6.37 (funct03.htm) is an example.

Listing 6.37. funct03.htm **illustrates the** chr, chrb, **and** chrw **functions.**

```
Sub LoadMe()
' Your Code Here
Num1 = 73
result1 = Chr(Num1)
result2 = Chrb(Num1)
result3 = Chrw(Num1)
window.document.open
window.document.writeln("<PRE>")
window.document.write("chr(string1) = ")
window.document.writeln(result1)
window.document.write("chrb(string1) = ")
window.document.writeln(result2)
window.document.write("chrw(string1) = ")
window.document.writeln(result3)
window.document.writeln("</PRE>")
window.document.close
end sub
```

This example results in all functions returning an I. Again, remember the chrb and chrw functions, because the days of working locally are numbered. Think global.

cbool

cbool converts its argument (numeric or expression) into either TRUE or FALSE. If the argument evaluates to true or is not zero, cbool returns TRUE. If the argument evaluates to false or is zero, cbool returns FALSE. If the argument cannot be evaluated or is not a number, cbool causes a runtime error. Listing 6.38 (funct04.htm) shows how cbool works:

Listing 6.38. funct04.htm illustrates the cbool function.

```
Sub LoadMe()
 ' Your Code Here
 Num1 = 73
 Num2 = 45

 result1 = Cbool(Num1 = Num1)
 result2 = Cbool(Num1)
 result3 = Cbool(0)
 window.document.open
 window.document.writeln("<PRE>")
 window.document.write("Cbool(Num1 = Num1) is ")
 window.document.writeln(evaluate(result1))
 window.document.write("Cbool(Num1) is ")
 window.document.writeln(evaluate(result2))
 window.document.write("Cbool(0) is ")
 window.document.writeln(evaluate(result3))
 window.document.writeln("</PRE>")
 window.document.close
end sub

function evaluate(bValue)
  if(bValue) then
    evaluate = "TRUE"
  else
    evaluate = "FALSE"
  end if
end function
```

Note how the function evaluates, and how it is used in printing the results of cbool. This page displays:

```
Cbool(Num1 = Num1) is TRUE
Cbool(Num1) is TRUE
Cbool(0) is FALSE
```

Which is what you would expect.

cdate, cdbl, cint, clng, csng, cstr

These functions convert their arguments into a specific type. cdate turns its argument into a date, cdbl into a double precision number, cint into an integer, clng into a long integer, csng into a single precision number, and cstr into a string (see Listing 6.39).

Listing 6.39. Conversion functions at work.

```
Sub LoadMe()
' Your Code Here
Num1 = 73
Num2 = 45

string1 = "57.32"
string2 = "15 May 1955"
number1 = 15.78
result1 = Cdate(string2)
result2 = Cdbl(string1)
result3 = Cint(string1)
result4 = Clng(string1)
result5 = csng(string1)
result6 = CStr(number1)

window.document.open
window.document.writeln("<PRE>")
window.document.write("Cdate(string2) is ")
window.document.writeln(result1)
window.document.write("Cdbl(string1) is ")
window.document.writeln(result2)
window.document.write("Cint(string1) is ")
window.document.writeln(result3)
window.document.write("Clng(string1) is ")
window.document.writeln(result4)
window.document.write("csng(string1) is ")
window.document.writeln(result5)
window.document.write("CStr(number1) is ")
window.document.writeln(result6)
window.document.writeln("</PRE>")
window.document.close
end sub
```

This page prints out:

```
Cdate(string2) is 5/15/55
Cdbl(string1) is 57.32
Cint(string1) is 57
Clng(string1) is 57
csng(string1) is 57.32
CStr(number1) is 15.78
```

The function `datavalue` can be directly substituted for `cdate`.

DateSerial

`DateSerial` takes three numbers—year, month, and day—and converts them into a date (see Listing 6.40).

Listing 6.40. funct06.htm illustrates DateSerial.

```
Sub LoadMe()
 ' Your Code Here

 result1 = DateSerial(1994, 6, 1)

 window.document.open
 window.document.writeln("<PRE>")
 window.document.write("DateSerial(1994, 6, 1) is ")
 window.document.writeln(result1)
 window.document.writeln("</PRE>")
 window.document.close
end sub
```

This listing returns:

```
DateSerial(1994, 6, 1) is 6/1/94
```

hex and oct

These two functions convert a numeric argument into a string representation of the argument in a different number system. hex shows what the number would look like in hexadecimal form and oct shows the octal representations, as shown in Listing 6.41 (funct07.htm).

Listing 6.41. funct07.htm illustrates the hex and oct functions.

```
Sub LoadMe()
 ' Your Code Here
 number1 = 256
 result1 = hex(number1)
 result2 = oct(number1)
 window.document.open
 window.document.writeln("<PRE>")
 window.document.write("hex(number1) is ")
 window.document.writeln(result1)
 window.document.write("oct(number1) is ")
 window.document.writeln(result2)
 window.document.writeln("</PRE>")
 window.document.close
end sub
```

This shows the decimal number 256 as:

```
hex(number1) is 100
oct(number1) is 400
```

fix and int

fix and int can be used to isolate the integer parts of a number. The difference between the two is if the argument is negative, int returns the integer less than or equal to the argument, whereas fix returns the integer greater than or equal to the argument (as shown in Listing 6.42).

Listing 6.42. `funct08.htm` **illustrates** `fix` **and** `int`.

```
Sub LoadMe()
 ' Your Code Here
 number1 = -25.6
 result1 = int(number1)
 result2 = fix(number1)
 window.document.open
 window.document.writeln("<PRE>")
 window.document.write("int(number1) is ")
 window.document.writeln(result1)
 window.document.write("fix(number1) is ")
 window.document.writeln(result2)
 window.document.writeln("</PRE>")
 window.document.close
end sub
```

Notice the difference in rounding:

```
int(number1) is -26
fix(number1) is -25
```

sgn

The sgn function returns an integer that depends on the sign of its argument. If the argument is positive, sgn returns 1. If the argument is negative, sgn returns -1. And if the argument is 0, sgn returns 0.

Dates/Times

VBScript has many functions that allow you to manipulate time. (Actually, they allow you to manipulate time and date values. Manipulating time itself is beyond the scope of this book.)

date, time, now

These functions return all or part of the time and date information available from your system's hardware. date returns date information, time returns time information, and now returns time and date information. Listing 6.43 shows how these functions work.

Listing 6.43. funct09.htm **illustrates the** date, time, **and** now **functions.**

```
Sub LoadMe()
 ' Your Code Here

 result1 = date
 result2 = time
 result3 = now
 window.document.open
 window.document.writeln("<PRE>")
 window.document.write("Date is ")
 window.document.writeln(result1)
 window.document.write("Time is ")
 window.document.writeln(result2)
 window.document.write("Now is ")
 window.document.writeln(result3)
 window.document.writeln("</PRE>")
 window.document.close
end sub
```

funct09.htm returns the following:

```
Date is 9/2/96
Time is 1:14:31 PM
Now is 9/2/96 1:14:31 PM
```

day, month, weekday, year, hour, minute, second

These functions each return a part of the time and date information available from the machine. The first four, day, month, weekday, and year, derive their information from a date string. The last three, hour, minute, and second, operate on time strings. They all take one argument except weekday, which has a second argument that tells it what day of the week the week starts (1 for Sunday, 2 for Monday, and so on). If you don't give weekday a number for the second argument, it defaults to Sunday being the first day of the week. Listing 6.44 (funct10.htm) shows how these functions work.

Listing 6.44. funct10.htm **illustrates the** day, month, weekday, year, hour, minute **and** second **functions.**

```
Sub LoadMe()
 ' Your Code Here
 result1 = Day(date)
 result2 = Month(date)
 result3 = WeekDay(date)  ' Will default to Sunday
 result4 = Year(date)
 result5 = Hour(time)
 result6 = Minute(time)
 result7 = Second(time)
```

```
window.document.open
window.document.writeln("<PRE>")
window.document.write("Day(date) ")
window.document.writeln(result1)
window.document.write("Month(date) is ")
window.document.writeln(result2)
window.document.write("WeekDay(date) is ")
window.document.writeln(result3)
window.document.write("Year(date) is ")
window.document.writeln(result4)
window.document.write("Hour(time) is ")
window.document.writeln(result5)
window.document.write("Minute(time) is ")
window.document.writeln(result6)
window.document.write("Second(time) is ")
window.document.writeln(result7)
window.document.writeln("</PRE>")
window.document.close
end sub
```

The return values are:

```
Day(date) 2
Month(date) is 9
WeekDay(date) is 2
Year(date) is 1996
Hour(time) is 13
Minute(time) is 12
Second(time) is 52
```

TimeSerial

TimeSerial is a straightforward function that returns a time string given three numerical inputs, as shown in Listing 6.45 (funct11.htm).

Listing 6.45. funct11.htm illustrates TimeSerial.

```
Sub LoadMe()
 ' Your Code Here
 result1 = TimeSerial(9,59,20)

 window.document.open
 window.document.writeln("<PRE>")
 window.document.write("TimeSerial(9,59,20) is ")
 window.document.writeln(result1)
 window.document.writeln("</PRE>")
 window.document.close
end sub
```

Listing 6.45 returns:

```
TimeSerial(9,59,20) is 9:59:20 AM
```

Math

VBScript has a few math-specific functions. It isn't FORTRAN, but it should be enough for your pages.

atn, cos, sin, tan

These four trigonometric functions take a numeric argument and return trigonometric information. atn takes a ratio and returns an angle in radians. tan, sin, and cos, do just the opposite and return a ratio from an input of degrees in radians. 2PI radians (6.2830) is equal to 360 degrees. Listing 6.46 (funct12.htm) contains examples of these functions.

Listing 6.46. funct12.htm **illustrates the** atn, cos, sin, **and** tan **functions.**

```
Dim PI
PI = 3.1415
Sub LoadMe()
 ' Your Code Here
 result1 = Atn(0.707)
 result2 = Tan(PI/4)
 result3 = Sin(PI/6)
 result4 = Cos(PI/2)

 window.document.open
 window.document.writeln("<PRE>")
 window.document.write("Atn(0.707) is ")
 window.document.writeln(result1)
 window.document.write("Tan(PI/4) is ")
 window.document.writeln(result2)
 window.document.write("Sin(PI/6) is ")
 window.document.writeln(result3)
 window.document.write("Cos(PI/2) is ")
 window.document.writeln(result4)
 window.document.writeln("</PRE>")
 window.document.close
end sub
```

Note the use of the global variable PI. The result of all this is the following:

```
Atn(0.707) is 0.615408517629256
Tan(PI/4) is 0.999953674278156
Sin(PI/6) is 0.499986626546633
Cos(PI/2) is 4.63267948799578E-05
```

exp, log, sqr

These three functions return e raised to a power, the natural log of a number, and the square root of a number, respectively. Listing 6.47 (funct13.htm) contains examples of these functions.

Listing 6.47. funct13.htm **illustrates the** exp, log, **and** sqr **functions.**

```
Sub LoadMe()
 ' Your Code Here
 result1 = exp(2)
 result2 = log(150)
 result3 = sqr(5000.2)

 window.document.open
 window.document.writeln("<PRE>")
 window.document.write("exp(2) is ")
 window.document.writeln(result1)
 window.document.write("log(150) is ")
 window.document.writeln(result2)
 window.document.write("sqr(5000.2) is ")
 window.document.writeln(result3)
 window.document.close
end sub
```

Listing 6.47 illustrates the following:

```
exp(2) is 7.38905609893065
log(150) is 5.01063529409626
sqr(5000.2) is 70.7120923180753
```

randomize, rnd

The randomize statement seeds VBScript's random number generator, and rnd returns a random number with a value not greater than one, but greater than or equal to 0. If randomize is not used, or if randomize is not passed an argument, it uses a number from the system timer. Let's make some random numbers in Listing 6.48 (funct14.htm):

Listing 6.48. funct14.htm **uses the** randomize **and** rnd **functions.**

```
Sub LoadMe()
 ' Your Code Here
 randomize(second(time))

 result1 = int(rnd * 100)

 window.document.open
 window.document.writeln("<PRE>")
 window.document.write("int(rnd * 100) is ")
 window.document.writeln(result1)
 window.document.close
end sub
```

Your result will vary from the following. After all, it is a random function.

```
int(rnd * 100) is 57
```

Array Functions

VBScript provides four functions for working with arrays: IsArray, Erase, Ubound, and Lbound. These functions allow you to determine whether a variable is an array, to erase all the data in the array, and to find the lower and upper bounds of an array. IsArray and Lbound provide little useful information, and are rarely used. IsArray tells you whether or not a variable is an array (you had to declare to make it an array, so you already knew), and Lbound gives you the lower bound of any dimension of the array (the lower bound is always zero in VBScript because all arrays are zero based.

Ubound is relatively useful for finding out how big dynamically dimensioned arrays are (Redim). If the user changes the size of the array at runtime, you might need to know how many elements to check.

Erase does just what it says: It reinitializes all the data in an array. If the array is static (declared using MyArray(10) or some other size), only the data is reset. If the array is declared dynamically (using MyArray() and Redim to resize the array), the data is erased and the memory for the array is reallocated (which, when you think about it, is redundant). If Erase is used on a dynamic array, the array must be redimmed before it is used again. Listing 6.49 (funct15.htm) contains examples of these functions.

Listing 6.49. funct15.htm uses array functions.

```
Sub LoadMe()
' Your Code Here
Dim Myarray1(10)
Dim MyArray2()

window.document.open
window.document.writeln("<PRE>")

if IsArray(MyArray2) then
   window.document.writeln("Suprise! The array we declared is an array! ")
end if
MYArray1(1) = "MyStuff"

window.document.write("MYArray1(1) is ")
window.document.writeln(MYArray1(1))

erase MYArray1

window.document.write("MYArray1(1) is ")
window.document.writeln(MYArray1(1))

Redim MyArray2(4)

window.document.write("Ubound(Myarray2) is ")
```

```
window.document.writeln(uBound(Myarray2))
window.document.write("Lbound(Myarray2) is ")
window.document.writeln(LBound(Myarray2))
window.document.close
end sub
```

The results are

```
Suprise! The array we declared is an array!
MYArray1(1) is MyStuff
MYArray1(1) is
Ubound(Myarray2) is 4
Lbound(Myarray2) is 0
```

String Functions

You can tell what a language is designed for by looking at the number and type of its functions. There are two string functions for every math function in VBScript. This shows you where the emphasis of VBScript is.

Instr, InStrB

InStr takes two strings as arguments. It searches the first one for an occurrence of the second, and returns the position in the string. If the search string is not found in the target string, InStr returns 0. InStrB provides the same function for byte data. Listing 6.50 (funct16.htm) contains an example.

Listing 6.50. funct16.htm **uses** Instr **and** InStrB.

```
Sub LoadMe()
 ' Your Code Here
 Target = "This is a Target String"
 Search1 = "Tar"
 Search2 = "nada"
 result1 = Instr(Target, Search1)
 result2 = Instr(Target, Search2)

 window.document.open
 window.document.writeln("<PRE>")
 window.document.write("Instr(Target, Search1) is ")
 window.document.writeln(Result1)
 window.document.write("Instr(Target, Search2) is ")
 window.document.writeln(Result2)
 window.document.writeln("</PRE>")
 window.document.close
end sub
```

This search finds:

```
Instr(Target, Search1) is 11
Instr(Target, Search2) is 0
```

You can change where the search starts by placing a number before the search string like so:

```
Instr(5, Target, Search1, 1)
```

This would start the search on 5. The 1 at the end of the function changes the search from an exact-match search to a case-insensitive search. If these numbers are left out (as they are in the example), the defaults are to start at the first character and to use a case-sensitive search.

len, lenb

The len function and its binary counterpart, lenb, return the number of characters in a string (as shown in Listing 6.51).

Listing 6.51. funct17.htm uses the len and lenb functions.

```
Sub LoadMe()
 ' Your Code Here
 String1 = "This is a Target String"
 result1 = len(string1)

 window.document.open
 window.document.writeln("<PRE>")
 window.document.write("len(string1) is ")
 window.document.writeln(Result1)
 window.document.writeln("</PRE>")
 window.document.close
end sub
```

Listing 6.51 shows the following:

```
len(string1) is 23
```

Lcase, Ucase

Lcase and Ucase take a string as an argument and return a lower-case and an upper-case version respectively, as shown in Listing 6.52 (funct18.htm).

Listing 6.52. funct18.htm uses Lcase and Ucase.

```
Sub LoadMe()
 ' Your Code Here
 String1 = "This is Test"
```

```
    result1 = Lcase(string1)
    result2 = Ucase(string1)

    window.document.open
    window.document.writeln("<PRE>")
    window.document.write("Lcase(string1) is ")
    window.document.writeln(Result1)
    window.document.write("Ucase(string1) is ")
    window.document.writeln(Result2)
    window.document.writeln("</PRE>")
    window.document.close
 end sub
```

In Listing 6.52, Lcase and Ucase did just what they were supposed to do:

```
Lcase(string1) is this is test
Ucase(string1) is THIS IS TEST
```

Left, LeftB, Mid, MidB, Right, RightB

Left, Mid, and Right and their binary counterparts allow you to pull pieces from a string. Look at Listing 6.53 (funct19.htm):

Listing 6.53. funct19.htm uses Left, Mid, Right, and their binary counterparts.

```
Sub LoadMe()
 ' Your Code Here
 String1 = "This is Whole String"
 result1 = Left(string1, 4)
 result2 = Mid(string1, 9, 5)
 result3 = Right(string1, 6)

 window.document.open
 window.document.writeln("<PRE>")
 window.document.write("Left(string1, 4) is ")
 window.document.writeln(Result1)
 window.document.write("Mid(string1, 9, 5) is ")
 window.document.writeln(Result2)
 window.document.write("Right(string1, 6) is ")
 window.document.writeln(Result3)
 window.document.writeln("</PRE>")
 window.document.close
 end sub
```

The string was sliced up like this:

```
Left(string1, 4) is This
Mid(string1, 9, 5) is Whole
Right(string1, 6) is String
```

Space, String

Space and String are variations on the same theme. Space takes a numeric argument and returns a string composed of the same number of spaces as the argument. String takes a number and a character and returns a string containing the given number of given characters. Listing 6.54 (funct20.htm) demonstrates.

Listing 6.54. funct20.htm uses space and string.

```
Sub LoadMe()
 ' Your Code Here
 result1 = Space(10)
 result2 = String(10,45)

 window.document.open
 window.document.writeln("<PRE>")
 window.document.write("Space(10) is ")
 window.document.writeln(Result1)
 window.document.write("String(10,45) is ")
 window.document.writeln(Result2)
 window.document.writeln("</PRE>")
 window.document.close
end sub
```

It's hard to see the blank spaces in the Space function, but they are there.

```
Space(10) is
String(10,45) is ----------
```

StrComp

Where Instr finds parts of one string in another, StrComp compares two strings and returns a 0 if they are the same, a -1 if the first is closer to the front of the alphabet than the second, and a 1 if the first is closer to the end of the alphabet than the second. Listing 6.55 provides an example.

Listing 6.55. funct21.htm illustrates StrComp.

```
Sub LoadMe()
 ' Your Code Here
 string1 = "RoseBud"
 string2 = "Bud"
 string3 = "Zoom"
 result1 = StrComp(String1, String1)
 result2 = StrComp(String2, String1)
 result3 = StrComp(String3, String1)

 window.document.open
 window.document.writeln("<PRE>")
```

```
    window.document.write("StrComp(String1, String1) is ")
    window.document.writeln(Result1)
    window.document.write("StrComp(String2, String1) is ")
    window.document.writeln(Result2)
    window.document.write("StrComp(String3, String1) is ")
    window.document.writeln(Result3)
    window.document.writeln("</PRE>")
    window.document.close
end sub
```

The results of the comparisons are as follows:

```
StrComp(String1, String1) is 0
StrComp(String2, String1) is -1
StrComp(String3, String1) is 1
```

Ltrim, Rtrim, Trim

Sometimes strings have leading and trailing spaces that you need to get rid of. Ltrim takes a string argument and returns the string without leading edge spaces. Rtrim does the same to the trailing spaces. Trim removes unwanted spaces on both ends. These functions are shown in Listing 6.56 (funct22.htm).

Listing 6.56. funct22.htm uses Ltrim, Rtrim, and Trim.

```
Sub LoadMe()
  ' Your Code Here
  string1 = "   RoseBud   "
  result1 = "¦" & Ltrim(String1) & "¦"
  result2 = "¦" & Rtrim(String1) & "¦"
  result3 = "¦" & Trim(String1) & "¦"

  window.document.open
  window.document.writeln("<PRE>")
  window.document.write("Ltrim(String1) is ")
  window.document.writeln(Result1)
  window.document.write("Rtrim(String1) is ")
  window.document.writeln(Result2)
  window.document.write("Trim(String1) is ")
  window.document.writeln(Result3)
  window.document.writeln("</PRE>")
  window.document.close
end sub
```

I added the ¦ character on each end to highlight the effect:

```
Ltrim(String1) is ¦RoseBud   ¦
Rtrim(String1) is ¦   RoseBud¦
Trim(String1) is ¦RoseBud¦
```

Variants

Sometimes it is convenient to find out at runtime what kind of variant you have. To this end, VBScript provides five functions. The first four, IsArray, IsDate, IsNumeric, and IsObject, are boolean functions that return TRUE or FALSE depending on what the variant in question is. The last function, VarType, returns a number that depends on the variant type, as shown in Table 6.6.

Table 6.6. Return value of VarType.

Value of Variable	Type Description
0Empty	(uninitialized)
1Null	(no valid data)
2	integer
3	long integer
4	single-precision floating-point number
5	double-precision floating-point number
6	currency
7	date
8	string
9	automation object
10	error
11	boolean
12	variant (arrays of variants)
13	non-automation object
17	byte
8192	array

If the variant is an array, the number returned will be 8191 + the number of the type of array. For example, a date array would be 8191 + 7, for a grand total of 8198.

These functions are shown in Listing 6.57 (funct23.htm).

Listing 6.57. funct23.htm **uses variant functions.**

```
Sub LoadMe()
' Your Code Here
Dim Var1(20)
```

```
Var1(1) = "text"
Var2 = date
Var3 = 45.67
Set Var4 = window

result1 = IsArray(Var1)
result2 = IsNumeric(Var2)
result3 = IsNumeric(Var3)
result4 = IsObject(Var4)
result5 = VarType(Var1)

window.document.open
window.document.writeln("<PRE>")
window.document.write("IsArray(Var1) is ")
window.document.writeln(Result1)
window.document.write("IsNumeric(Var2) is ")
window.document.writeln(Result2)
window.document.write("IsNumeric(Var3) is ")
window.document.writeln(Result3)
window.document.write("IsObject(Var4) is ")
window.document.writeln(Result4)
window.document.write("VarType(Var1) is ")
window.document.writeln(Result5)

window.document.writeln("</PRE>")
window.document.close
end sub
```

Remember: true is -1, false is 0. Notice how vartype saw an array of variants:

```
IsArray(Var1) is -1
IsNumeric(Var2) is 0
IsNumeric(Var3) is -1
IsObject(Var4) is -1
VarType(Var1) is 8204
```

Program Flow

You have been using the If Then Else program control structure throughout the entire week. Let's look at all five control structures available to you in VBScript.

Do...Loop

If you want something done at least once before you decide to do it again, use Do...Loop with an Until at the end. If you want to make your decision before you do any looping again, your choice is Do...Loop with a While at the beginning. Listing 6.58 (flow01.htm) contains examples of both.

Listing 6.58. `flow01.htm` uses `Do...Loop` and `Do...While`.

```
Sub LoadMe()
 ' Your Code Here
 Dim count
 Count = 0

 Do While count <>0
  Count = Count + 1
 Loop

 result1 = Count
 Do
  Count = Count + 1
  LeaveNow = True
 Loop Until LeaveNow = True

 result2 = Count
 window.document.open
 window.document.writeln("<PRE>")
 window.document.write("count after first loop is ")
 window.document.writeln(Result1)
 window.document.write("count after second loop is ")
 window.document.writeln(Result2)
 window.document.writeln("</PRE>")
 window.document.close
end sub
```

Notice that the first loop was never entered, and the second was not evaluated until the end.

```
count after first loop is 0
count after second loop is 1
```

Use `Exit...Do` to leave the loop at any time. This transfers control to the first line after the `Do...Loop`. I strongly advise you to write your loops with just one exit point and avoid using `Exit...Do`.

For...Next

This function allows you to execute selected program statements a given number of times. The `For` part of the loop sets up a counter, and the `To` part of the loop sets a limit. The optional `Step` part allows you to control how you step through the counter. Listing 6.59 (`flow02.htm`) contains an example.

Listing 6.59. `flow02.htm` uses the `For...Next` function.

```
Sub LoadMe()
 ' Your Code Here

 string1 = "123456"
```

```
window.document.open
window.document.writeln("<PRE>")

For Counter = 1 To 6
 window.document.write(mid(string1,counter,1) & "*")
Next

window.document.writeln(" ")

For Counter = 6 To 1 Step -1
 window.document.write(mid(string1,counter,1) & "*")
Next

window.document.writeln(" ")

For Counter = 1 To 6 Step 2
 window.document.write(mid(string1,counter,1) & "*")
Next

window.document.writeln("</PRE>")
window.document.close
end sub
```

This produces the following:

```
1*2*3*4*5*6*
6*5*4*3*2*1*
1*3*5*
```

Notice how the string function `mid` was used to read the characters. There is also an Exit...For instruction that can be used to leave the loop prematurely. Again, I don't recommend having more than one exit from a loop.

if...then...else

You have already used this function close to a hundred times this week, but there are a few parts you haven't used. You should be familiar with the basic if...then...else. There is also an else if that can be used in place of the else statement to launch another if statement. Since you already have lots of examples of the basic use of if...then...else, Listing 6.60 (flow03.htm) contains an example of else if.

Listing 6.60. flow03.htm uses else if.

```
Sub LoadMe()
 ' Your Code Here
 choice = 3

 window.document.open
```

continues

Listing 6.60. continued

```
 window.document.writeln("<PRE>")

 if (choice = 1) then
  window.document.write("Choice is 1")
 else if (choice = 2) then
   window.document.write("Choice is 2")
  else
   window.document.write("Choice is 3")
  end if
 end if

 window.document.writeln("</PRE>")
 window.document.close
end sub
```

This page decides the following:

```
Choice is 3
```

Notice that you had to put another end if to end the second if statement started by the else if. I have seen this kind of construction used to decode a user choice. I recommend that you use Select Case (described next) instead of else if.

Select Case

Select Case allows you to execute code depending on the value of a selected case. It is most often used to handle choices. Look at Listing 6.61 (flow04.htm).

Listing 6.61. flow04.htm uses Select Case.

```
Sub LoadMe()
 ' Your Code Here
 choice = int(prompt("Input a number","4"))

 window.document.open
 window.document.writeln("<PRE>")

 Select Case Choice
  Case  1, 2, 3, 4, 5
   window.document.writeln("Number is between 1 and 5")
  Case 6, 7
   window.document.writeln("Number is  6 and 7")
  Case 8, 9
   window.document.writeln("Number is between 8 and 9")
  Case Else
   window.document.writeln("Number over 9")
 End Select
```

```
window.document.writeln("</PRE>")
window.document.close
end sub
```

The default input, (4), causes the output:

```
Number is between 1 and 5
```

While...Wend

While...Wend is a holdover from earlier versions of Visual Basic. It executes statements sandwiched between While and Wend as long as the condition after While is true. Look at Listing 6.62 (flow05.htm):

Listing 6.62. flow05.htm uses While...Wend.

```
Sub LoadMe()
 ' Your Code Here
 string1 = "Now is The Time"
 Teststring = "T"
 Dim CurrentString
 Count = 1

 window.document.open
 window.document.writeln("<PRE>")

 While StrComp(CurrentString, TestString) And Count <= len(string1)
  CurrentString = mid(String1, count, 1)
  window.document.write(CurrentString & "*")
  count = count + 1
 Wend

 window.document.writeln("</PRE>")
 window.document.close
end sub
```

The loop stops when it finds a T like so:

```
N*o*w* *i*s* *T*
```

Error Handling

The On Error statement and the Err object work hand in hand to provide error control inside your VBScript procedures. Start error handling with On Error Resume Next. In VBScript, this is the only type of On Error statement you can make. It tells the interpreter to ignore any errors that pop up and resume at the line after the error. If you have a place in your code where something risky happens, place a On Error Resume Next statement in front of it. If it causes an error, the program control will pass to the next statement (if it can; some errors are fatal) where you will have Select Case ready based on the Err object. The Err object contains three properties that allow you to deal with the error: number, description, and source. Normally, you build the Select Case around Err.number and use Err.source and Err.description to break the bad news to the user. The good thing about this is that non-fatal errors don't stop the rest of your code from executing. Listing 6.63 (err01.htm) demonstrates On Error and Err.

Listing 6.63. err01.htm **illustrates error handling.**

```
Sub LoadMe()
 ' Your Code Here
 On Error Resume Next
 window.dodah = 23 'Generate an error
 Select Case Err.Number
     Case 0
      'Nothing Happened, Go on with the program
     Case 438
       Alert("Something is wrong in" & err.source)
     Case Else
       Alert(err.Description & err.number)
 End Select
 Alert("Error Didn't stop execution!")

end sub
```

When this page is run, the interpreter throws an error 438 (no such property or method); you catch it and go on. When the last alert box goes up, you are sure the code is still running. Err also has two methods, clear (to clear the err object), and raise (to throw an exception). You can use err.raise(438) to simulate the error in the previous example.

User Interface

VBScript has two user interface elements that are redundant with Alert and Prompt. MsgBox is a little more flexible than Alert. It allows you to assign a title and predefined group of buttons; there are even provisions for assigning a help file. There are several reasons you will probably use Alert or Confirm before you use MsgBox. First, MsgBox requires more setup. Since there are no constants in VBScript, you have to know the numeric codes for the different buttons. Second, nine times out of ten you will want to produce a MsgBox that looks just like Alert. The same holds true for InputBox. Look at Listing 6.64 (output01.htm).

Listing 6.64. output01.htm uses MsgBox.

```
Sub LoadMe()
 ' Your Code Here
 result1 = MsgBox("This is the Message",0, "MyMessageBox")
 result2 = InputBox("This is the Prompt",  "MyTitle", "Default Text")
end sub
```

This will demo the `MsgBox` and `InputBox`.

Resources

The best place to go for VBScript information is the source. Start at http://www.microsoft.com/vbscript/us/vbslang/vbstoc.htm. This page changes from time to time. When in doubt, check http://www.microsoft.com.

Summary

It was a long day, but worth it. We looked at VBScript from variables to error handling, and all the stops in between. This is the final stone in your foundation if you are only going to use VBScript to build your Web pages. Tomorrow you will use everything that you have learned so far (HTML, the ActiveX Control Pad, and VBScript) to build an ActiveX-enabled Web site. Even if you don't plan on using JavaScript, I suggest you look at the JavaScript chapter and its project. With the emphasis on objects in programming, it won't hurt to know what JavaScript can teach you.

Q&A

Q Why don't all these functions work as described in the online reference you gave in resources?

A VBScript is evolving, which is one of the reasons I provided examples for every function. The best way to deal with this evolving standard is to test the functions you use with every new release and keep your eyes open for new things that are built in or old things that finally work.

Q Why are there differences between VBScript and Visual Basic? Why not just implement Visual Basic?

A The answer is security. To promote security, VBScript has no functions that interact with files on the user's machine.

Q How do you think VBScript will evolve from here?

A I predict that VBScript will mature over the next year rather than evolve. There are too many security issues in the area of OLE automation to cause changes in that area. Because of its simplicity, VBScript is well-suited to coordinating with objects on existing Web pages. I don't see VBScript getting more complicated.

Workshop

Rewrite `sub01.htm` to use conversion functions to convert the user input to numbers (remember, this is the page where 10 + 20 = 1020 because the code assumes you are working with strings).

Quiz

1. Would you be more likely to use VBScript on a math-intensive application or a string-intensive application? Why?
2. Which are illegal variables in VBScript: `MY.NAME`, `MyName`, `4Things`?
3. How can I test my error catching without generating real errors?

NOTE Refer to the appendix, "Answers," for the answers to these questions.

Week 1

Day 7

Writing JavaScripts

Today you will learn JavaScript. You have already encountered JavaScript in a couple of the examples you've done this week. You implemented JavaScript by hand-coding directly on the HTML page (covered on Day 2, "HTML & Scripting") and by using the three editing tools you looked at on Day 4, "The Tools of the Trade": Word, HoTMetaL, and the ActiveX Control Pad. JavaScript was also used in the last example on Day 5, "Programming for Internet Explorer," when you looked at programming inside the Internet Explorer. Today, after looking briefly at the background of JavaScript, you will learn all you need to know about the language, from variables to objects. By the end of the day you will have examined dozens of examples, and will be ready to use JavaScript in a project.

A Brief Background of JavaScript

JavaScript started life as LiveScript, a scripting language built specifically for Netscape Navigator. Netscape, in conjunction with Sun, changed the name to JavaScript. Microsoft's Internet Explorer also supports JavaScript. JavaScript is object oriented. The Window object you learned about on Day 5 is a native part of JavaScript. Because it is at home with objects, JavaScript can be used to manipulate ActiveX controls as well as the objects native to HTML. It is important to note that JavaScript is not Java. They are similar, but JavaScript is dedicated to Web-page scripting, whereas Java is becoming a full-blown application builder like C and C++. JavaScript's commitment to HTML and support for ActiveX controls makes learning JavaScript well worth your while.

Overview of Scripting Architecture

To learn JavaScript, you need to know about the following topics:

- Supported software platforms
- The JavaScript programming model
- Variable types
- Operators
- Variable scope
- Functions
- Program flow
- User interface

You'll be quizzed at the end of the chapter, so pay attention!

Supported Software Platforms

As of this writing, the two major Web browsers support JavaScript. Anything you learn about JavaScript is applicable to programming on both the Netscape Navigator and the Internet Explorer. You can find Netscape Navigator at http://www.netscape.com/. Find the Internet Explorer at http://www.microsoft.com/ie/ie.htm. Both are in their third version. Internet Explorer is freeware, and Netscape Navigator is available for a nominal cost on a subscription basis.

Netscape controls the JavaScript standard, and it looks like it will remain proprietary. This is not necessarily bad. Proprietary standards evolve faster and are less compromised than languages controlled by the more democratic open-standard approach.

Because JavaScript and ActiveX are currently supported on the Internet Explorer, the bottom line is that if you need to use JavaScript and ActiveX right now, use the Internet Explorer as your target software platform.

The JavaScript Programming Model

JavaScript is an object-oriented language. To those of you new to programming, an *object-oriented language* uses objects to group related properties and methods. You have already been introduced to one of the main JavaScript objects, Window (discussed in detail on Day 5). The Window object is a good example of how objects are constructed and used. The concepts of subroutines and functions that you learned on Day 6, "Writing VBScripts," also apply to JavaScript.

JavaScript and object-oriented languages in general are strong in the areas of organization and code maintenance. The downside of object-oriented languages is that they have a steeper learning curve than procedural languages. Design and maintenance are what recommend JavaScript to Web programmers. After you have used an object-oriented approach for a while, you will find it well-suited to the world of Windows and ActiveX.

Language Structure

Now you can get to know JavaScript. I'll start with a discussion of the general elements of the language, and when I'm through, you will have covered every keyword in JavaScript. Most of the examples in this chapter are run from within the framework of `template.htm`, shown in Listing 7.1.

Listing 7.1. HTML code for `template.htm`.

```
<HTML>
<HEAD>
<TITLE>Example Template</TITLE>
<SCRIPT LANGUAGE="JavaScript" FOR="window" EVENT="onLoad()">
<!--
 // Your Code Here
-->
</SCRIPT>

<SCRIPT LANGUAGE="JavaScript" FOR="window" EVENT="onUnload()">
<!--
//Your Code Here

-->
</SCRIPT>
</HEAD>
<BODY>

</BODY>
</HTML>
```

You have covered all the elements of this Web page during the previous days of the week. As you can see, there are two <SCRIPT> sections to handle two Window object events. One area is assigned to the onLoad event, which causes the code placed in this section to be run whenever the page is loaded. The second <SCRIPT> section is assigned to the onUnload event, and is fired every time you leave the page.

Are you ready? Time to learn a new language!

General

JavaScript is case sensitive. This means, for example, that the variable A is different from the variable a. Try the following in the template:

```
<SCRIPT LANGUAGE="JavaScript" FOR="window" EVENT="onLoad()">
<!--
// Your Code Here
var ROSE
var Rose
var ROse

Rose = 1
ROSE = 4
ROse = Rose + ROSE

document.open()
document.writeln("<PRE>")
document.writeln(Rose)
document.writeln(ROSE)
document.writeln(ROse)
document.writeln("</PRE>")
document.close()
-->
</SCRIPT>
```

As you would expect, given that JavaScript is case sensitive, the output from the preceding code is

```
1
4
5
```

The next question is, "How do I differentiate one line from another?" In JavaScript, all you have to do is start a new line. Look at this code:

```
</SCRIPT>
<SCRIPT LANGUAGE="JavaScript">
<!--
function CommandButton1_Click()
{
parent.frames(1).navigate TextBox2.Text
label1.caption = parent.frames(1).location.href
}
-->
</SCRIPT>
```

Notice that the lines have no visible terminator. Some languages, such as C, use a semicolon (;) as the terminator for a line. Lines of code in JavaScript use the line feed at the end of the line as a terminator.

If you feel the need to pack several lines of code on one line, use the ; to separate them, as shown in Listing 7.2.

Listing 7.2. `separate.htm` **shows how to pack several lines of code into one line.**

```
<HTML>
<HEAD>
<TITLE>Example Template</TITLE>
<SCRIPT LANGUAGE="JavaScript" FOR="window" EVENT="onLoad()">
<!--
 // Your Code Here
 var A = 0
 A = A + 1 ; A = A + 1; A = A + 1
 document.Open(); document.write(A);document.close()
-->
</SCRIPT>

<SCRIPT LANGUAGE="JavaScript" FOR="window" EVENT="onUnload()">
<!--
//Your Code Here
-->
</SCRIPT>

</HEAD>
<BODY>

</BODY>
</HTML>
```

Notice how the semicolon is used in `template.htm`. Running this program will produce the number 3. It will also annoy any programming purists with whom you work. I recommend that you keep to one statement per line (unless, of course, your goal is to annoy those who read your code).

This is the only example I will show you using the entire template. In the rest of the chapter you'll focus on the code inside.

Indentation is not required to make the language work. For example, Listing 7.3 runs identically to Listing 7.4.

Listing 7.3. Indented code.

```
<SCRIPT LANGUAGE="JavaScript" FOR="window" EVENT="onLoad()">
<!--
// Your Code Here
var A = 0
A = A + 1
A = A + 1
A = A + 1
   document.Open()
   document.write(A)
   document.close()
-->
</SCRIPT>
```

Listing 7.4. Unindented code.

```
<SCRIPT LANGUAGE="JavaScript" FOR="window" EVENT="onLoad()">
<!--
// Your Code Here
var A = 0
A = A + 1
A = A + 1
A = A + 1
document.Open()
document.write(A)
document.close()
-->
</SCRIPT>
```

Listing 7.4 runs in the same way as Listing 7.3, but Listing 7.4 won't win you many points for style. I recommend that you use indentation to organize your code so that if you have to go back and maintain it (or someone else does), it is easier to understand. You will see examples of indentation used for clarity throughout this chapter.

Comments

Comments can make your life, or the life of someone who looks at your work later, much easier. Comments are not required in JavaScript, but if you want them in your code, you have two choices: // and /* */. With //, any characters from the start of the remark to the end of the line are ignored when the script is run. With /* */, everything between /* and */ is ignored. An example of both kinds of comments follows:

```
<SCRIPT LANGUAGE="JavaScript" FOR="window" EVENT="onLoad()">
<!--
// This is ignored to the end of the line
```

```
  /* All of these lines
     will be
     ignored
  */
  var A = 0
  A = A + 1
  A = A + 1
  A = A + 1
  document.Open()
  document.write(A)
  document.close()
-->
</SCRIPT>
```

Variables

Variables are those things you learned in high school algebra—you remember, the class you knew would never apply to your "real" life. Well, you were wrong. Without variables, computer languages could do little more than power player pianos or music boxes. Variables are what allowed you to send people to the moon, build addictive games like DOOM, and make interactive Web pages. JavaScript has a simple approach to variables.

Types of Variables

JavaScript supports four variable types: numeric, string, boolean, and null. Numeric variables represent integers or floating-point numbers. Strings are arrays of characters, such as `Hello World` and `Good Bye`. For example, the following code sets `string1` to hold the string variable `hello world` and sets `mynum1` to hold the number 4:

```
var string1 = "hello world"
var mynum1 = 4
```

JavaScript is *loosely typed*, which means that you can turn around and assign these variables like this

```
string1 = 4
mynum1 = "hello world"
```

without the interpreter complaining. The advantage of a loosely typed language is that you don't have to remember lots of conversion functions. The disadvantage is that you are at the mercy of the language interpreter; it will determine what conversions need to be conducted and how. You will need to keep an eye on these automatic conversions. You might not always want what the interpreter gives you. Later today I will cover conversion functions in JavaScript that provide the capability to precisely change one type to another.

The boolean variable can be either `true` or `false`. JavaScript does not assign numbers to `true` and `false` like some other languages do.

The null variable represents a variable that has not been defined. It is not the same as a zero-length string. For example, the following code returns the value `MyUninited is null`:

```
<SCRIPT LANGUAGE="JavaScript" FOR="window" EVENT="onLoad()">
<!--
  var MyUninited
  var MyInit

  document.Open()
  MyInit = ''
  if (MyInit == null)
  {
    document.write('MyInit is null')
  }
  if (MyUninited == null)
  {
    document.write('MyUninited is null')
  }
  document.close()
-->
</SCRIPT>
```

Now you should know the difference between a null value and a zero-length string.

Variable Naming

Names of JavaScript variables must have the following two characteristics:

- They must begin with an alphabetic character or an underscore (_).
- They must be unique in the scope in which they are declared. You can't have two `MyVars` in a function.

This means a variable like `22street` would return an error like the one shown in Figure 7.1.

Figure 7.1.
Results of an improper variable.

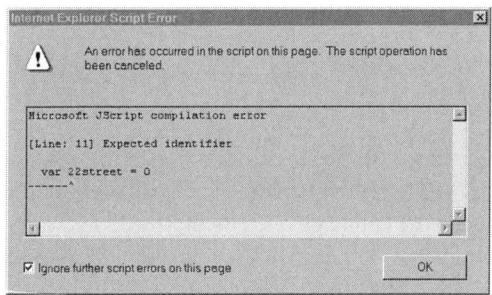

The error shown in the figure was generated by the following code:

```
<SCRIPT LANGUAGE="JavaScript" FOR="window" EVENT="onLoad()">
<!--
  var 22street = 0
  document.Open()
  document.write(22street)
  document.close()
-->
</SCRIPT>
```

var

Declaring variables is easy and optional in JavaScript. Declaring a variable is done using the key word var. Consider the following code:

```
<SCRIPT LANGUAGE="JavaScript" FOR="window" EVENT="onLoad()">
<!--
  var value1 = 1
  value2 = 'value two'

  document.Open()
  document.writeln('<PRE>')
  document.writeln(value1)
  document.writeln(value2)
  document.writeln('</PRE>')
  document.close()
-->
</SCRIPT>
```

Notice how `value1` is declared using `var`, and `value2` is not declared. The form will produce these lines:

```
1
value two
```

You can also declare a variable without assigning it a value, but you cannot have an undeclared variable without an assigned value. The interpreter doesn't initialize undeclared variables. Look at the following modification to the previous code:

```
<SCRIPT LANGUAGE="JavaScript" FOR="window" EVENT="onLoad()">
<!--
  var value1
  value2

  document.Open()
  document.writeln('<PRE>')
  document.writeln(value1)
  document.writeln(value2)
  document.writeln('</PRE>')
  document.close()
-->
</SCRIPT>
```

This causes the following error:

```
Microsoft JScript runtime error

[Line: 7] 'value2' is undefined
```

Optional declaration (bypassing the use of var) is fine, but it will not sit well with programming purists. Also, you might be working in a corporation whose programming standards require that all variables be declared.

Uninitialized Variables

If you use var to declare a variable and then print that variable, what will be in it? I have spent days in other languages tracking down bugs caused by uninitialized variables assigned some random number. JavaScript does not support this kind of frustration. Variables in JavaScript are given a value of null when they are declared without being assigned in the var statement. You saw an example of this when you looked at the null value in the "Types of Variables" section of this chapter.

Constant Variables

In general, JavaScript does not support constant variables. A *constant variable* is one of those programming oxymorons that means a variable that cannot be changed after it is declared. A constant variable is used to hold things that should not be open to the interpretation of the programmer (like the value of pi, for instance). This prevents the programmer from improving pi or accidentally changing pi.

Any variable you declare in JavaScript can be modified. If you want to implement constants in your Web pages, you must give them a unique identifier (I recommend all uppercase letters—it is the C programmer in me) and invent a stiff penalty for programmers who change them during the course of a program (I recommend reassignment as the tech writer for a group of assembly language programmers—they hate that).

Some objects within the JavaScript environment have read-only properties that can be used as constant variables. For example, the Math object, discussed later, has a property named PI, which is shown in the following code:

```
<SCRIPT LANGUAGE="JavaScript" FOR="window" EVENT="onLoad()">
<!--

  document.Open()
  document.writeln('<PRE>')
  document.writeln(Math.PI)
  document.writeln('</PRE>')
  document.close()
-->
</SCRIPT>
```

This code produces the constant 3.14159265358979.

Any attempt to change the value of Math.PI is ignored, as in the following modification to the code:

```
<SCRIPT LANGUAGE="JavaScript" FOR="window" EVENT="onLoad()">
<!--
  Math.PI = 6
  document.Open()
  document.writeln('<PRE>')
  document.writeln(Math.PI)
  document.writeln('</PRE>')
  document.close()
-->
</SCRIPT>
```

This code still produces the constant 3.14159265358979.

The bottom line here is that although there are built-in constants, the programmer cannot create a new constant.

Variable Scope and Global Variables

The scope of a variable has to do with where it is visible. The code in Listing 7.5 shows you how scope works.

Listing 7.5. HTML code for scope01.htm.

```
<SCRIPT LANGUAGE="JavaScript">
<!--
//Global Variable
var MyVariable = "Global edition of My Variable"
-->
</SCRIPT>

<SCRIPT LANGUAGE="JavaScript" FOR="window" EVENT="onLoad()">
<!--
  window.document.open()
  window.document.writeln("<PRE>")
  window.document.write("In onLoad MyVariable is ")
  window.document.writeln(MyVariable)

  ThingOne()
  ThingTwo()

  window.document.writeln("</PRE>")
  window.document.close()
-->
</SCRIPT>

<SCRIPT LANGUAGE="JavaScript">
```

continues

Listing 7.5. continued

```
<!--
function ThingOne()
{
  var MyVariable
  MyVariable = "ThingOne edition of MyVariable"
  window.document.write("In ThingOne MyVariable is ")
  window.document.writeln(MyVariable)
}
function ThingTwo()
{
  window.document.write("In ThingTwo MyVariable is ")
  window.document.writeln(MyVariable)
}

-->
</SCRIPT>
```

The code in Listing 7.5 produces the following output:

```
In onLoad MyVariable is Global edition of My Variable
In ThingOne MyVariable is ThingOne edition of MyVariable
In ThingTwo MyVariable is Global edition of My Variable
```

Notice that the `MyVariable` declared outside of the functions is visible to all functions within the <SCRIPT> tags, making it global. Then, when a variable is declared inside `ThingOne` with the same name, that local variable is used inside procedure `ThingOne`. Just to prove that the global `MyVariable` isn't overwritten, `ThingTwo` writes out its value so you can see that the global `MyVariable` hasn't changed. Also of note here is how the Window object is global.

Now change the code so that `ThingOne` and `ThingTwo` are in a different <SCRIPT> tag (see Listing 7.6).

Listing 7.6. HTML code for `scope02.htm`.

```
<HTML>
<HEAD>
<TITLE>Example Template</TITLE>

<SCRIPT LANGUAGE="JavaScript">
<!--
//Global Variable
var MyVariable = "Global edition of My Variable"
-->
</SCRIPT>

<SCRIPT LANGUAGE="JavaScript" FOR="window" EVENT="onLoad()">
<!--
  window.document.open()
  window.document.writeln("<PRE>")
```

```
  window.document.write("In onLoad MyVariable is ")
  window.document.writeln(MyVariable)

  ThingOne()
  ThingTwo()

  window.document.writeln("</PRE>")
  window.document.close()
-->
</SCRIPT>

<SCRIPT LANGUAGE="JavaScript">
<!--
function ThingOne()
{
  var MyVariable
  MyVariable = "ThingOne edition of MyVariable"
  window.document.write("In ThingOne MyVariable is ")
  window.document.writeln(MyVariable)
}
-->
</SCRIPT>

<SCRIPT LANGUAGE="JavaScript">
<!--
function ThingTwo()
{
  window.document.write("In ThingTwo MyVariable is ")
  window.document.writeln(MyVariable)
}

-->
</SCRIPT>
```

Run the page. The results are identical. Now you've seen that scope applies across <SCRIPT> sections.

Procedures

In general, a *procedure* contains programming instructions, and can be assigned to events or called from other functions. You have seen procedures in every example today. JavaScript has only one kind of procedure: the function. Let's see how it works.

Functions

A *function* has this general structure:

```
function MyFunction(arg2, arg2)
{
//Lines of code
}
```

The keyword function lets the interpreter know that what follows is a function. After the keyword function is the function name, followed by any arguments the function has enclosed in parentheses (()). The function is given copies of the arguments, which means that the function cannot change the original value of an argument.

A function can also return a value using the keyword return. Type the code found in Listing 7.7 (sub01.htm on the CD-ROM).

Listing 7.7. HTML code for sub01.htm.

```
<SCRIPT LANGUAGE="JavaScript">
<!--
function RADtoDEG (Radian)
{
  return Radian * 57.32
}
-->
</SCRIPT>

<SCRIPT LANGUAGE="JavaScript" FOR="window" EVENT="onLoad()">
<!--

  var MyRadian = Math.PI/4
  var MyDegree = RADtoDEG(MyRadian)

  document.writeln("<PRE>")
  document.writeln(MyRadian +" Rad is " + MyDegree + "degs")
  document.writeln("</PRE>")

-->
</SCRIPT>
```

This is a simple radians-to-degrees function. It returns the following value:

`0.785398163397448 Rad is 45.0190227259417degs`

JavaScript has three built-in functions: eval, parseInt, and parseFloat. The rest of the functionality in JavaScript is contained in objects, which you will learn about later today in the section called "Objects." For now, let's look at the functions.

eval

eval has this syntax:

`eval(string)`

eval takes the string argument and acts like a mini interpreter. For example, the following code returns the value 11730.

```
<BODY>
<SCRIPT LANGUAGE="JavaScript" >
<!--
  var question = '345*34'
  var answer = eval(question)
  alert(eval(question))
  document.writeln("<PRE>")
  document.writeln(answer)
  document.writeln("</PRE>")


-->
</SCRIPT>
</BODY>
```

Note how the code is in the `<BODY>` section of the form. If this code is run in the `onLoad` event, it returns the string (345*34) instead of its value.

parseInt and parseFloat

The functions `parseInt` and `parseFloat` both take a single argument: a string. The function `parseInt` takes the string and attempts to return an integer. The function `parseFloat` takes the string and attempts to return a float value. Both functions are demonstrated in Listing 7.8, `parse.htm`.

Listing 7.8. HTML code for parse.htm.

```
<SCRIPT LANGUAGE="JavaScript" FOR="window" EVENT="onLoad()">
<!--
  var MyString = "34.345"
  var MyFloat  = parseFloat(MyString)
  var MyInt = parseInt(MyString)
  document.Open()
  document.writeln('<PRE>')
  document.writeln('MyFloat = ' + MyFloat)
  document.writeln('MyInt   = '+ MyInt )
  document.writeln('</PRE>')
  document.close()

-->
</SCRIPT>
```

Listing 7.8 returns the following:

```
MyFloat = 34.345
MyInt   = 34
```

Before you go any further, look at the operators you use to string your variables and functions together.

Operators

Operators determine what is done to variables and functions. There are five types of operators: assignment, arithmetic, logical, comparison, and string. Let's start with the most used—assignment operators.

Assignment Operators

You use assignment operators all the time to assign one value to another; indeed, assignment operators are the heart of programming. JavaScript not only has the traditional =, but also includes five others: +=, -=, *=, /=, and %=. They are explained in Table 7.1.

Table 7.1. Assignment operators.

Operator	Definition
=	Assigns value of right expression to left expression
+=	Same as A = A + B
-=	Same as A = A - B
*=	Same as A = A * B
/=	Same as A = A / B
%=	Same as A = A % B (divides A and B and assigns remainder to A)

Listing 7.9 uses all of the assignment operators shown in Table 7.1.

Listing 7.9. HTML code for `assign.htm`.

```
<SCRIPT LANGUAGE="JavaScript" FOR="window" EVENT="onLoad()">
<!--
  var MyNum1 = 32
  var MyNum2  = 6

  document.Open()
  document.writeln('<PRE>')
  MyNum1 = 32
  MyNum2  = 6
  document.writeln('MyNum1 = MyNum2 is ' + (MyNum1 = MyNum2))
  MyNum1 = 32
  MyNum2  = 6
  document.writeln('MyNum1 += MyNum2 is ' + (MyNum1 += MyNum2))
  MyNum1 = 32
  MyNum2  = 6
  document.writeln('MyNum1 -= MyNum2 is ' + (MyNum1 -= MyNum2))
```

```
MyNum1 = 32
MyNum2  = 6
document.writeln('MyNum1 = MyNum2 is ' + (MyNum1 *= MyNum2))
MyNum1 = 32
MyNum2  = 6
document.writeln('MyNum1 = MyNum2 is ' + (MyNum1 /= MyNum2))
MyNum1 = 32
MyNum2  = 6
document.writeln('MyNum1 = MyNum2 is ' + (MyNum1 %= MyNum2))
document.writeln('</PRE>')
document.close()

-->
</SCRIPT>
```

Note how the numbers are reloaded between prints. This is necessary because `MyNum1` is reassigned in every `writeln`. Listing 7.9 produces the following output:

```
MyNum1 = MyNum2 is 6
MyNum1 += MyNum2 is 38
MyNum1 = MyNum2 is 26
MyNum1 = MyNum2 is 192
MyNum1 = MyNum2 is 5.33333333333333
MyNum1 = MyNum2 is 2
```

Arithmetic Operators

The arithmetic operators are another group you tend to take for granted. The important thing to note as you go through these operators is how they work on various combinations of integers and real numbers. Table 7.2 shows the arithmetic operators.

Table 7.2. Arithmetic operators.

Operator	Definition
+	Addition
-	Subtraction
*	Multiplication
/	Division
%	Modulus (assigns the remainder of a division)
++	Increments number by one
--	Decrements number by one

Listing 7.10 contains examples of the primary arithmetic operators:

Listing 7.10. HTML code for `asgmath.htm`.

```
<SCRIPT LANGUAGE="JavaScript" FOR="window" EVENT="onLoad()">
<!--
  var MyNum1 = 32
  var MyNum2  = 6

  document.Open()
  document.writeln('<PRE>')
  document.writeln("For Two integers, 32 and 6")
  document.writeln(MyNum1 +' + '+ MyNum2 +'is' + (MyNum1 + MyNum2))
  document.writeln(MyNum1 +' - '+ MyNum2 +'is' + (MyNum1 - MyNum2))
  document.writeln(MyNum1 +' * '+ MyNum2 +'is' + (MyNum1 * MyNum2))
  document.writeln(MyNum1 +' / '+ MyNum2 +'is' + (MyNum1 / MyNum2))
  document.writeln(MyNum1 +' % '+ MyNum2 +'is' + (MyNum1 % MyNum2))
  MyNum1 = 32.23
  MyNum2  = 6.98
  document.writeln("For Two Floats, 32.23 and 6.98")
  document.writeln(MyNum1 +' + '+ MyNum2 +'is' + (MyNum1 + MyNum2))
  document.writeln(MyNum1 +' - '+ MyNum2 +'is' + (MyNum1 - MyNum2))
  document.writeln(MyNum1 +' * '+ MyNum2 +'is' + (MyNum1 * MyNum2))
  document.writeln(MyNum1 +' / '+ MyNum2 +'is' + (MyNum1 / MyNum2))
  documcnt.writeln(MyNum1 +' % '+ MyNum2 +'is' + (MyNum1 % MyNum2))
  MyNum1 = 32.23
  MyNum2  = 6
  document.writeln("For Float and Int, 32.23 and 6")
  document.writeln(MyNum1 +' + '+ MyNum2 +'is' + (MyNum1 + MyNum2))
  document.writeln(MyNum1 +' - '+ MyNum2 +'is' + (MyNum1 - MyNum2))
  document.writeln(MyNum1 +' * '+ MyNum2 +'is' + (MyNum1 * MyNum2))
  document.writeln(MyNum1 +' / '+ MyNum2 +'is' + (MyNum1 / MyNum2))
  document.writeln(MyNum1 +' % '+ MyNum2 +'is' + (MyNum1 % MyNum2))
  document.writeln('</PRE>')
  document.close()

-->
</SCRIPT>
```

The following illustrates how these arithmetic operators work with various combinations of `float` and `int`.

```
For Two integers, 32 and 6
32 + 6is38
32 - 6is26
32 * 6is192
32 / 6is5.33333333333333
32 % 6is2
For Two Floats, 32.23 and 6.98
32.23 + 6.98is39.21
32.23 - 6.98is25.25
32.23 * 6.98is224.9654
32.23 / 6.98is4.61747851002865
32.23 % 6.98is4.31
```

```
For Float and Int, 32.23 and 6
32.23 + 6is38.23
32.23 - 6is26.23
32.23 * 6is193.38
32.23 / 6is5.37166666666667
32.23 % 6is2.23
```

Increment (++) and decrement(--) operators are old hat to C programmers. Listing 7.11 shows how these two features work.

Listing 7.11. HTML code for asginc.htm.

```
<SCRIPT LANGUAGE="JavaScript" FOR="window" EVENT="onLoad()">
<!--
  var result1 = 32
  result1++
  var result2 = 32
  result2--
  var a = 5
  b = ++a
  c = a++
  document.Open()
  document.writeln('<PRE>')
  document.writeln( result1)
  document.writeln( result2)
  document.writeln( a)
  document.writeln( b)
  document.writeln( c)
  document.writeln('</PRE>')
  document.close()

-->
</SCRIPT>
```

Displaying the page described in Listing 7.11 produces the following result:

```
33
31
7
6
6
```

The first two numbers, 33 (32++) and 31 (32--) are easy to understand. The last three are more difficult. Variable a is originally 5, so after two increments it becomes 7, which explains the first number. The second equation (b = ++a) causes a to change from 5 to 6 and for 6 to be assigned to b, which explains the second number. The equation c = a++ results in a, which starts as 6, to be assigned to c before it is incremented, leaving c at 6 and a at 7. Be careful when using increments and decrements with an assignment statement.

Logical Operators

Logical operators are used to combine the results of two boolean expressions. They are described in Table 7.3.

Table 7.3. Logical operators.

Operator	Definition
&&	Logical and—Returns true when both expressions are true, otherwise it returns false.
||	Logical or—Returns true if either one or both of the expressions are true. Returns false if they are both false.
!	Negation—Used on only one expression. Returns true if expression is false and false if the expression is true.

Listing 7.12 shows these logical operators at work.

Listing 7.12. HTML code for logops.htm.

```
<SCRIPT LANGUAGE="JavaScript" FOR="window" EVENT="onLoad()">
<!--

  document.Open()
  document.writeln('<PRE>')
  document.writeln( false && false)
  document.writeln( false && true)
  document.writeln( true && true)
  document.writeln( true || false)
  document.writeln( false || false)
  document.writeln( !false)
  document.writeln('</PRE>')
  document.close()

-->
</SCRIPT>
```

Listing 7.12 returns the following value where 0 is false and -1 is true:

```
0
0
-1
-1
0
-1
```

Comparison Operators

Comparison operators are used inside JavaScript's control structures to test the relationship between variables. They are described in Table 7.4.

Table 7.4. Comparison operators.

Operator	Definition
==	Comparison for equality (different from assignment statement =)
!=	Not equal to
>	Greater than
<	Less than
>=	Greater than or equal to
<=	Less than or equal to

The only unusual thing here (if you are not a C programmer) is the == operator (test for equality). In JavaScript, == always makes a comparison, and = always makes an assignment. Don't confuse the two. The statement `if (a = 5)` will ruin your whole day if you are trying to compare a and 5 rather than assign a to 5. Look for examples in the section found later in this chapter called "Program Flow."

String Operators

There is only one string operator: concatenation (+). It's funny that a language that uses = and == to give the programmer greater flexibility would also use the + to add numbers and concatenate strings. Listing 7.13 shows string operators at work.

Listing 7.13. HTML code for `strop.htm`.

```
<SCRIPT LANGUAGE="JavaScript" FOR="window" EVENT="onLoad()">
<!--
  var string1 = "Thing one "
  var string2 = "and "
  var string3 = "Thing two and "
  var mynum = 3
  document.Open()
  document.writeln('<PRE>')
  document.writeln(string1 + string2 + string3 + mynum)
  document.writeln('</PRE>')
  document.close()

-->
</SCRIPT>
```

Notice that when the number is combined with the strings, the number is automatically converted to a string, as shown in the result of running `strop.htm`:

```
Thing one and Thing two and 3
```

Operator Precedence

You have seen that it is possible to combine several comparison operators from the arithmetic, comparison, and logical groups on one line. You have also seen that the operators can be grouped within parentheses to clarify the order of operation. When expressions are not grouped within parentheses, what happens? The following order is used:

- assignment: `= += -= *= /= %= <<= >>= >>>= &= ^= |=`
- conditional: `?:`
- logical-or: `||`
- logical-and: `&&`
- bitwise-or: `|`
- bitwise-xor: `^`
- bitwise-and: `&`
- equality: `== !=`
- relational: `< <= > >=`
- bitwise shift: `<< >> >>>`
- addition/subtraction: `+ -`
- multiply/divide: `* / %`
- negation/increment: `! ~ - ++ --`

Listing 7.14 illustrates arithmetic precedence.

Listing 7.14. HTML code for `prec.htm`.

```
<SCRIPT LANGUAGE="JavaScript" FOR="window" EVENT="onLoad()">
<!--
A = 10
B = 20
C = 30
Answer1 = A + B / C * 12
Answer2 = (A + B)/(C * 12)

//window.document.open
window.document.writeln("<PRE>")
window.document.write("A + B / C * 12 = ")
window.document.writeln(Answer1)
```

```
window.document.write("(A + B) / (C * 12) = ")
window.document.writeln(Answer2)
window.document.writeln("</PRE>")
//window.document.close


-->
</SCRIPT>
```

Listing 7.14 results in the following:

```
A + B / C * 12 = 18
(A + B) / (C * 12) = 8.33333333333333E-02
```

Quite a difference. Maybe this is what is happening to my paycheck. Make a note to talk to payroll. My advice here is use parentheses to group your statements so they are performed in the order you want and not in the order the machine wants.

Objects

At the beginning of the day you saw that JavaScript is an object-oriented language. This means that you can create objects that have their own properties and methods, just like the Windows object. This allows you to group methods and properties logically. For example, the document object has properties, such as forms (an array of forms on the document) and methods like `writeln` that relate to documents. In JavaScript, it is easy for you to create your own objects.

Creating an Object

Creating an object uses the same syntax as creating a function. The following code creates a template for an object:

```
<SCRIPT LANGUAGE="JavaScript">
<!--
function MyObject(type, height, width)
{
  this.type = type
  this.height = height
  this.width = width
}
-->
</SCRIPT>
```

To create a function with this template, use the new keyword, as shown in the following code:

```
<SCRIPT LANGUAGE="JavaScript">
<!--
function MyObject(type, height, width)
{
```

```
    this.type = type
    this.height = height
    this.width = width
}
-->
</SCRIPT>

<SCRIPT LANGUAGE="JavaScript" FOR="window" EVENT="onLoad()">
<!--
  Shape1 = new MyObject("Circle", 10, 25)

  window.document.open()
  window.document.writeln("<PRE>")
  window.document.writeln(Shape1.type)
  window.document.writeln(Shape1.height)
  window.document.writeln(Shape1.width)
  window.document.writeln("</PRE>")
  window.document.close()
-->
</SCRIPT>
```

The line `MyObject("Circle",10,25)` creates the new object that runs the template you created, assigns the variables in the argument list, and names the new object `Shape1`. The output from the code verifies that the following variables were set:

```
Circle
10
25
```

Properties

These variables you set are the properties of your object. They can be accessed by the same notation you used with the Document object. For example, the type in your `Shape1` object can be referenced by `Shape1.type`, as you did in the following line:

```
window.document.writeln(Shape1.type)
```

Properties can include other objects. Look at the Listing 7.15, `object02.htm`, and notice the modifications to `MyObject`, which you created in the section titled "Creating an Object."

Listing 7.15. HTML code for `object02.htm`.

```
<SCRIPT LANGUAGE="JavaScript">
<!--
function MyObject(type, height, width, x, y)
{
  this.type = type
  this.height = height
  this.width = width
  this.pos = new Position(x,y)
}
```

```
function Position(x,y)
{
  this.x = x
  this.y = y
}
-->
</SCRIPT>

<SCRIPT LANGUAGE="JavaScript" FOR="window" EVENT="onLoad()">
<!--
  Shape1 = new MyObject("Circle", 10, 25, 24, 167)

  window.document.open()
  window.document.writeln("<PRE>")
  window.document.writeln(Shape1.type)
  window.document.writeln(Shape1.height)
  window.document.writeln(Shape1.width)
  window.document.writeln(Shape1.pos.x)
  window.document.writeln(Shape1.pos.y)
  window.document.writeln("</PRE>")
  window.document.close()
-->
</SCRIPT>
```

Notice how you added a new property, pos, of the type position to store the x and y values of MyObject. This new property is accessed through the notation Shape.pos.x. The result of this page shows that the properties did make it into Shape1:

```
Circle
10
25
24
167
```

Methods

What if you want to make your object a little more self-sufficient by adding some methods? Listing 7.16 illustrates how to make your object print itself out.

Listing 7.16. HTML code for object03.htm.

```
<SCRIPT LANGUAGE="JavaScript">
<!--
function MyObject(type, height, width, x, y)
{
  this.type = type
  this.height = height
  this.width = width
  this.pos = new Position(x,y)
```

continues

Listing 7.16. continued

```
    this.printme = Printout
}
function Position(x,y)
{
  this.x = x
  this.y = y
}
function Printout()
{
  window.document.open()
  window.document.writeln("<PRE>")
  window.document.writeln('type = ' + this.type)
  window.document.writeln('height = ' + this.height)
  window.document.writeln('width = ' + this.width)
  window.document.writeln('x value= ' + this.pos.x)
  window.document.writeln('y value = ' + this.pos.y)
  window.document.writeln("</PRE>")
  window.document.close()
}
-->
</SCRIPT>

<SCRIPT LANGUAGE="JavaScript" FOR="window" EVENT="onLoad()">
<!--
  Shape1 = new MyObject("Circle", 10, 25, 24, 167)
  Shape1.printme()

-->
</SCRIPT>
```

Here you have moved the printing to its own method, `Printout`. Inside `Printout` you used the `this` keyword to designate the internal properties of `MyObject`. If you tried to run the method, `Printout`, as a standalone function, you would get error centering on the nonexistence of the variables. The magic happens with the following line, which is found inside `MyObject`:

```
this.printme = Printout
```

This line designates `Printout` as a method of `MyObject`, and grants `Printout` access to the properties of `MyObject`. Calling `Shape1.printme` results in the following:

```
type = Circle
height = 10
width = 25
x value= 24
y value = 167
```

Associative Arrays

Internally, the data contained in an object is contained in an associative array. This allows you to associate a value from the object with the property name, as shown in Listing 7.17.

Listing 7.17. HTML code for `object04.htm`.

```
<SCRIPT LANGUAGE="JavaScript">
<!--
function MyObject(type, height, width, x, y)
{
  this.type = type
  this.height = height
  this.width = width
  this.pos = new Position(x,y)
  this.printme = Printout
}
function Position(x,y)
{
  this.x = x
  this.y = y
}
function Printout()
{

  window.document.writeln("<PRE>")
  window.document.writeln('type = ' + this.type)
  window.document.writeln('height = ' + this.height)
  window.document.writeln('width = ' + this.width)
  window.document.writeln('x value= ' + this.pos.x)
  window.document.writeln('y value = ' + this.pos.y)
  window.document.writeln("</PRE>")

}
-->
</SCRIPT>

<SCRIPT LANGUAGE="JavaScript" FOR="window" EVENT="onLoad()">
<!--
  window.document.open()
  Shape1 = new MyObject("Circle", 10, 25, 24, 167)
  Shape1.printme()
  Shape1["type"] = "Square"
  Shape1["height"] = 42
  Shape1.printme()
  window.document.close()
-->
</SCRIPT>
```

In this example, you used Shape1.["type"] to access the Shape1.type property. The results are as shown.

```
type = Circle
height = 10
width = 25
x value= 24
y value = 167
```

```
type = Square
height = 42
width = 25
x value= 24
y value = 167
```

Arrays

Those of you with a programming background are used to working with arrays. For those of you new to programming, an *array* is a collection of elements that can be accessed by an index. For example, MyArray[1] would access the element in the array with an index of one.

JavaScript does not have built-in support for arrays. If you need to use arrays, you will have to build your own. Don't panic, it isn't hard to do.

The first array you will build will allow you to enter elements into the array when you first declare it. Listing 7.18 shows this method.

Listing 7.18. HTML code for array01.htm.

```
<SCRIPT LANGUAGE="JavaScript">
<!--
function initArray()
{
 this.length = initArray.arguments.length
 for (var i = 0; i < this.length; i++)
 this[i+1] = initArray.arguments[i]
}
-->
</SCRIPT>

<SCRIPT LANGUAGE="JavaScript" FOR="window" EVENT="onLoad()">
<!--

  var MyArray = new initArray("Thing1", "Thing2", 3, 4)

  document.writeln("<PRE>")
  document.writeln("MyArray[4] = "+ MyArray[1])
```

```
    document.writeln("MyArray[4] = "+ MyArray[2])
    document.writeln("MyArray[4] = "+ MyArray[3])
    document.writeln("MyArray[4] = "+ MyArray[4])
    document.writeln("</PRE>")

-->
</SCRIPT>
```

Note that arrays are used both to find out how many arguments there are (initArray.arguments.length) and as an array of those arguments (arguments[I]). The output from this example looks like the following:

```
MyArray[1] = Thing1
MyArray[2] = Thing2
MyArray[3] = 3
MyArray[4] = 4
```

Another way to create an array is shown in Listing 7.19.

Listing 7.19. HTML code for array02.htm.

```
<SCRIPT LANGUAGE="JavaScript">
<!--
function initArray (maxnumb, initValue) {
// maxnumb: how many elements in an array
// initValue: initialize the array with this value
  this.length = maxnumb;
// you can start with j=0 for a zero based system
  for (var j=1; j <= maxnumb; j++)
  this[j] = initValue;
  return this;
}
-->
</SCRIPT>

<SCRIPT LANGUAGE="JavaScript" FOR="window" EVENT="onLoad()">
<!--
  var MyArray = new initArray(10,"*")
  MyArray[1] = "This"
  MyArray[2] = "and"
  MyArray[3] = "That"
  document.writeln("<PRE>")
  document.writeln("MyArray[1] = "+ MyArray[1])
  document.writeln("MyArray[2] = "+ MyArray[2])
  document.writeln("MyArray[3] = "+ MyArray[3])
  document.writeln("MyArray[4] = "+ MyArray[4])
  document.writeln("MyArray.lenght = "+ MyArray.length)
  document.writeln("</PRE>")

-->
</SCRIPT>
```

In this listing, you can size the array and initialize it when you declare it. The output shows both the initial values (`MyArray[4]`) and the values you set after the array was declared:

```
MyArray[1] = This
MyArray[2] = 2
MyArray[3] = That
MyArray[4] = *
MyArray.lenght = 10
```

This lack of a built-in array behavior is inconvenient but, on the plus side, you can create arrays that fit into the problems you solve with JavaScript.

Built-In Objects

JavaScript contains both user-built objects, which you have already covered, and built-in objects. You have already used the Window object; the three remaining built-in objects are String, Math, and Date.

The String Object

The JavaScript String object has one property and nineteen methods. You create a string whenever you assign a string to a variable. The following lines result in a string object with full rights to the property and functions described in Tables 7.5 and 7.6:

```
var mystring ="Hello World"
myotherstring = "Something"
```

Table 7.5. String object (properties).

Property	Definition
length	An integer containing the number of characters in the string

Table 7.6. String object (methods).

Methods	Definition
anchor(*name*)	Causes its string to behave as though it is inside an <A> section with the attribute NAME, assigned to the value of *name*.
Big()	Causes its string to behave as though it is inside a <BIG> section.
Blink()	Causes its string to behave as though it is inside a <BLINK> section.
Bold()	Causes its string to behave as though it is inside a <BOLD> section.

Methods	Definition
charAt(*index*)	Returns the character in the string at position *index*.
fixed()	Causes its string to behave as though it is inside a <FIXED> section.
fontColor(*color*)	Causes its string to behave as though it is inside a <FONT> section with the COLOR attribute set to *color*, where *color* is an RGB triplet.
fontSize(*size*)	Causes its string to behave as though it is inside a <FONTSIZE> section, where *size* is a value between 1 and 7.
indexOf(*searchstring, startindex*)	Searches its string for an occurrence of *searchstring* starting at *startindex* or, if *startindex* is not provided, at zero. Returns the index of the first occurrence or -1 if the *searchstring* is not found.
italics()	Causes its string to behave as though it is inside an <I> section.
lastindexOf(*searchstring, startindex*)	Searches its string for an occurrence of *searchstring* starting at *startindex* or, if *startindex* is not provided, at zero. Works from the back of the string to the front. Returns the index of the last occurrence or -1 if the *searchstring* is not found.
link(*href*)	Causes its string to behave as though it is inside an <A> section with the HREF attribute set to *href*.
small()	Causes its string to behave as though it is inside a <SMALL> section.
strike()	Causes its string to behave as though it is inside a <STRIKE> section.
sub()	Causes its string to behave as though it is inside a <SUB> section.
substring(*startindex, endindex*)	Returns a string that is a substring of this string object between *startindex* and *endindex*. If *startindex* is greater than *endindex*, the string is reversed.

continues

Table 7.6. continued

Methods	Definition
sup()	Causes its string to behave as though it is inside a <SUP> section.
toLowerCase()	Returns an all-lowercase version of its string.
toUpperCase()	Returns an all-uppercase version of its string.

Listing 7.20 shows how the string-manipulation functions work.

Listing 7.20. HTML code for string01.htm.

```
<SCRIPT LANGUAGE="JavaScript" FOR="window" EVENT="onLoad()">
<!--
 var Str1 = "Hello World"

 window.document.writeln("<PRE>")
 window.document.writeln("Str1.lenght = " + Str1.length)
 window.document.writeln("Str1.toUpperCase = " + Str1.toUpperCase())
 window.document.writeln("Str1.toLowerCase = " + Str1.toLowerCase())
 window.document.writeln("Str1.substring(0,5) = " + Str1.substring(0,5))
 window.document.writeln("</PRE>")
-->
</SCRIPT>
```

The Math Object

The JavaScript Math object has six properties and seventeen methods. Math functions are referenced using the object Math, as in Math.PI. The properties and functions of the Math object are described in Tables 7.7 and 7.8.

Table 7.7. Math object (properties).

Property	Definition
E	Euler's Constant, about 2.72 (base for natural logarithms)
LN10	The natural logarithm of 10, about 2.30
PI	The value of pi, about 3.14
SQRT_2	The square root of 0.5, about 7.71
SQRT2	The square root of 2, about 1.41

Table 7.8. Math object (methods).

Property	Definition
abs(*number*)	The absolute value of *number*
acos(*number*)	The arc cosine of *number* in radians
asin(*number*)	The arc sine of *number* in radians
atan(*number*)	The arc tangent of *number* in radians
ceil(*number*)	The next integer greater than *number*
cos(*number*)	The cosine where *number* is radians
exp(*number*)	The value of E raised to the *number* power
floor(*number*)	The next integer less than *number*
log(*number*)	The natural logarithm of *number*
max(*num1*, *num2*)	The greater of *num1* and *num2*
min(*num1*, *num2*)	The lesser of *num1* and *num2*
pow(*num1*, *num2*)	*num1* raised to the *num2* power
random()	A random number between zero and one
round()	Rounds to closest integer to number
sin(*number*)	The sine where *number* is radians
sqrt(*number*)	The square root of *number*
tan(*number*)	The tangent where *number* is radians

Listing 7.21 gives you a general idea about how to use these functions.

Listing 7.21. HTML code for `math.htm`.

```
<SCRIPT LANGUAGE="JavaScript" FOR="window" EVENT="onLoad()">
<!--
 var angle = Math.PI/6

 with (Math)
 {
   window.document.writeln("<PRE>")
   window.document.writeln("sin(angle) = " + sin(angle))
   window.document.writeln("cos(angle) = " + cos(angle))
   window.document.writeln("round(angle) = " + round(angle))
   window.document.writeln("exp(angle) = " + exp(angle))
   window.document.writeln("</PRE>")
 }
-->
</SCRIPT>
```

Notice how the with keyword is used. Inside the brackets of the with (Math) statement, the Math object is assumed and doesn't have to be typed. The output is as follows:

```
sin(angle) = 0.5
cos(angle) = 0.866025403784439
round(angle) = 1
exp(angle) = 1.68809179496447
```

The Date Object

The JavaScript Date object has zero properties and twenty methods. Define a new Date variable with the syntax:

```
Mydate = new Date(dateinfo)
```

where *dateinfo* is an optional indicator of the date format, which can have one of three formats:

- month day, year hours:minutes:seconds
- year, month, day
- year, month, day, hours, minutes, seconds

The methods that go with the Date object appear in Table 7.9.

Table 7.9. The Date object.

Methods	Definition
getDate()	Returns an integer representing the day of the month from its Date object
getDay()	Returns an integer representing the day of the week from its Date object where 0 is Sunday
getHours()	Returns an integer representing the hour from its Date object from 0 to 23 (military or European time)
getMinutes()	Returns an integer representing the minute from its Date object from 0 to 59
getMonth()	Returns an integer representing the minute from its Date object from 0 to 11, where 0 is January
getSeconds()	Returns an integer representing the second from its Date object from 0 to 59
getTime()	Returns an integer representing the time from its Date object since midnight, 1 January 1970, in milliseconds

Methods	Definition
`getTimezoneOffset()`	Returns an integer representing the difference in the time zone from its Date object to GMT in minutes
`getYear()`	Returns an integer representing the year from its Date object from 0 to 99, assuming 1900 as the base year
`parse(datestring)`	Like `getstring`, except datestring is used to determine the number of milliseconds since midnight, 1 January, 1970
`setDate(timevalue)`	Sets the day of the month in its Date object where *timevalue* is between 1 and 31
`setHours(timevalue)`	Sets the hour in its Date object where *timevalue* is between 0 and 23
`setMinutes(timevalue)`	Sets the minute in its Date object where *timevalue* is between 0 and 59
`setMonth(timevalue)`	Sets the month in its Date object where *timevalue* is between 0 and 11, and where 0 is January
`setSeconds(timevalue)`	Sets the seconds in its Date object where *timevalue* is between 0 and 59
`setTime(timesince)`	Sets the value of its Date object where *timesince* is milliseconds from midnight, 1 January, 1970
`setYear(timevalue)`	Sets the year in its Date object where *timevalue* is greater than 1900
`toGMTString()`	Returns a string based on the current Date object in the form Day, DD Mon YYYY HH:MM:SS GMT
`toLocalString()`	Returns a string based on the current Date object in the format specified when the Date object was created
`UTC(year, month, date, hours, minutes, seconds)`	Like `getstring`, except `UTC` is used to determine the number of milliseconds since midnight, 1 January, 1970 GMT and the entered date

Listing 7.22 shows how these functions can be used.

Listing 7.22. HTML code for `date.htm`.

```
<SCRIPT LANGUAGE="JavaScript" FOR="window" EVENT="onLoad()">
<!--
 var mydate = new Date()
 window.document.writeln("<PRE>")
 window.document.writeln("mydate = " + mydate)
 window.document.writeln("mydate.getHours() = " + mydate.getHours())
 window.document.writeln("mydate.time() = " + mydate.getTime())
 window.document.writeln("</PRE>")
-->
</SCRIPT>
```

Program Flow

JavaScript has four control structures: `if`, `for`, `while`, and `for...in`. `if`, `for` and `while` apply to general coding, and `for...in` is used to iterate through objects. Let's look at the general control structures first.

`if`

You have already used this function close to a hundred times this week, but not many in JavaScript. The general syntax is:

```
if(condition)
{
//some statements that execute if condition is true
}
else
{
//some statements that execute if condition is false
```

Listing 7.23 illustrates the `if` function.

Listing 7.23. HTML code for `flow01.htm`.

```
<SCRIPT LANGUAGE="JavaScript" FOR="window" EVENT="onLoad()">
<!--
 choice = 3

 window.document.open()
 window.document.writeln("<PRE>")

 if (choice == 1)
 {
  window.document.write("Choice is 1")
 }
```

```
  else
  {
    if (choice == 2)
    {
      window.document.write("Choice is 2")
    }
    else
    {
      window.document.write("Choice is 3")
    }
  }

  window.document.writeln("</PRE>")
  window.document.close()

-->
</SCRIPT>
```

The result of this page is as follows:

```
Choice is 3
```

Notice how you embedded a second `if` statement inside the `else` clause of the first `if` statement. I have seen this kind of construction used to decode a user choice, and it is your only option in JavaScript because there is not a `switch` clause or a `select case` clause.

for

This function allows you to perform selected program statements a given number of times. The syntax is:

```
for ([initial-expression;] [condition;] [increment-expression])
{
 statements
}
```

The initial expression usually declares an index variable that is checked against the condition and incremented (or decremented) in the last section. Listing 7.24 provides an example.

Listing 7.24. HTML code for `flow02.htm`.

```
<SCRIPT LANGUAGE="JavaScript" FOR="window" EVENT="onLoad()">
<!--
 var string1 = "12345678"
 var limit = string1.length

// window.document.open()
 window.document.writeln("<PRE>")
```

continues

Listing 7.24. continued

```
for(var i = 0;i < limit; i++)
{
  window.document.writeln(string1.charAt(i))
}
for( i = (limit - 1); i >= 0 ;i--)
{
  window.document.writeln(string1.charAt(i))
}

window.document.writeln("</PRE>")
// window.document.close()

-->
</SCRIPT>
```

Listing 7.24 produces the following:

```
1*2*3*4*5*6*7*8*
8*7*6*5*4*3*2*1*
```

Notice how the string method `charAt90` was used to read the characters.

while

The `while` statement allows you to loop through code until a condition is met. The condition is tested before the loop is entered. The syntax is:

```
while (condition)
{
 statements
}
```

Listing 7.25 provides an example of the `while` statement.

Listing 7.25. HTML code for `flow03.htm`.

```
<SCRIPT LANGUAGE="JavaScript" FOR="window" EVENT="onLoad()">
<!--
 var target = "Now is The Time"
 var Teststring = "T"
 var CurrentString = ''
 var count = 0

 window.document.open()
 window.document.writeln("<PRE>")

 while ((target.charAt(count) != 'T') && (count <= target.length))
```

```
  {
    window.document.write(target.charAt(count) + "*")
    count++
  }

  window.document.writeln("</PRE>")
  window.document.close()

-->
</SCRIPT>
```

for...in

The for...in statement is called an *iterater*. An iterater cycles through all the things in a collection. The for...in statement in JavaScript cycles through all the members of an object. The syntax is:

```
for (variable in object)
{
// program statements
}
```

Aim the result of Listing 7.26 at the object you created in object04.htm (refer to Listing 7.17).

Listing 7.26. HTML code for `flow04.htm`.

```
<SCRIPT LANGUAGE="JavaScript">
<!--
function MyObject(type, height, width, x, y)
{
  this.type = type
  this.height = height
  this.width = width
  this.pos = new Position(x,y)
  this.printme = Printout
}
function Position(x,y)
{
  this.x = x
  this.y = y
}
function Printout()
{

  window.document.writeln("<PRE>")
  window.document.writeln('type = ' + this.type)
  window.document.writeln('height = ' + this.height)
  window.document.writeln('width = ' + this.width)
  window.document.writeln('x value= ' + this.pos.x)
  window.document.writeln('y value = ' + this.pos.y)
  window.document.writeln("</PRE>")
```

continues

Listing 7.26. continued

```
  }
  -->
  </SCRIPT>

  <SCRIPT LANGUAGE="JavaScript" FOR="window" EVENT="onLoad()">
  <!--
    window.document.open()
    Shape1 = new MyObject("Circle", 10, 25, 24, 167)
    Shape1.printme()
    Shape2 = new MyObject('Shape2',1,1,0,0)
    Shape2.printme()
    for (var i in Shape1)
    {
       Shape2[i] = Shape1[i]
    }
    Shape2.printme()
    window.document.close()
  -->
  </SCRIPT>
```

Here you used the iterater to cycle through Shape1 and assign its members to Shape2, a function not uncommon in the object-oriented world.

User Interface Elements

JavaScript has three user interface elements (other than the input controls native to HTML) that you have already seen: the alert, prompt, and confirm boxes. Given that you have ActiveX to create the main screen elements, these three functions serve to display common user input dialogs. The syntax for alert is

alert(*message*)

where *message* is optional and evaluates to a printable value.

The prompt box, with the following syntax, is a little more complex:

prompt(*message*, [*Default*])

where *message* has the same characteristics as alert's *message*, and the optional default is a default value for the text box on the prompt.

The confirm box has the same syntax as alert:

confirm(*message*)

except confirm returns a distinct value for each of its two buttons (OK and Cancel).

See Listing 7.27 for a demonstration of these controls.

Listing 7.27. HTML code for `visual.htm`.

```
<SCRIPT LANGUAGE="JavaScript" FOR="window" EVENT="onLoad()">
<!--
  alert("Get Ready")
  var answer = prompt("Enter a Number","63")
  while(confirm("Pick Another Number?"))
  {
     answer = prompt("Enter another Number","63")
  }
  alert("Last item picked was" + answer)
-->
</SCRIPT>
```

This function keeps putting up prompt dialogs as long as you choose OK in the confirm dialog. When you choose Cancel in the confirm dialog, the last alert shows the last number picked.

Resources

The best place for JavaScript information is its source. Start at `http://home.netscape.com/eng/mozilla/2.0/handbook/javascript/index.html`. This is Netscape's online reference. You can find another interesting tutorial at `http://www.crs4.it/HANDBOOK/JAVASCRIPT/Voodoo/index.htm`. *Teach Yourself JavaScript in a Week* (published by Sams.net) by Arman Danesh is a also a good reference.

Summary

It was a long day, but worthwhile. You looked at JavaScript from variables to objects, and all the stops in between. This is the final stone in your language foundation (until the next new scripting language comes along). On Day 9, "A JavaScript Application," you will use these tools to build a Web site using ActiveX and JavaScript. If you skipped the VBScript pages (Day 6, "Writing VBScripts"), I strongly urge you to go back and at least skim them. VBScript has some features you might find interesting, such as error-catching and a switch-statement features.

Q&A

Q I wrote the following code; it seems to follow all the rules, but I get an error saying that Rose is undefined. What is wrong?

```
var ROSE
Rose = 1
ROSE = ROse + 4
ROse = Rose + ROSE

document.open()
document.writeln("<PRE>")
document.writeln(Rose)
document.writeln(ROSE)
document.writeln(ROse)
document.writeln("</PRE>")
document.close()
-->.
```

A On the surface, the code looks okay. You either declared or set up a new variable by assigning a value. What happened is that you used Rose by assignment before you created it. Even if you create it with the var statement, you still get an error. If you switch it with the ROse = Rose + ROSE statement, you will have the same problem. Declare the variables, then rewrite the code like this:

```
<SCRIPT LANGUAGE="JavaScript" FOR="window" EVENT="onLoad()">
<!--
 // Your Code Here
var ROSE
Rose = 1
var ROSE = 0
var ROse = 0
ROSE = ROse + 4
Rose + ROSE
document.open()
document.writeln("<PRE>")
document.writeln(Rose)
document.writeln(ROSE)
document.writeln(ROse)
document.writeln("</PRE>")
document.close()
-->
</SCRIPT>
```

Q Why are there differences between JavaScript and VBScript? Which one should I choose?

A JavaScript, as you saw today, is object oriented, whereas VBScript it a procedural language. If you have lots of C, C++, or Java experience, I suggest you use JavaScript because the syntax and the object-oriented mindset are similar. VBScript, on the other hand, has a shorter learning curve. Non-programmers can become proficient in less time. If you have little programming experience and need something fast, use VBScript.

Q How do you think JavaScript will evolve from here?

A I predict that JavaScript will mature over the next year rather than evolve. I think that the object-oriented model of JavaScript will make it the programmer's choice for Web sites, especially large, complicated Web sites. You can do a lot more than just connect the dots with JavaScript.

Q Are arrays 0 (first element is 0) or 1 (first element is 1) based?

A Since you build your own array objects, you are free to make them 0 or 1 based.

Workshop

Add a copy method to `object04.htm` that allows the user to copy the contents of another like object (hint: see `flow04`).

Quiz

1. Would you be more likely to use JavaScript on a math-intensive application or a string-intensive application? Why?
2. Which are illegal variables in JavaScript: `MY.NAME`, `MyName`, or `4Things`?
3. What control structure can I use to get information out of my homemade object?

NOTE Refer to the appendix, "Answers," for the answers to these questions.

At A Glance

During Week 2, you will apply what you have learned about scripting to the Internet. By the end of this week, you will be comfortable with ActiveX scripting and APIs. You will have touched on the concept of ActiveX controls, and will be ready to dive deeper into ActiveX controls in Week 3.

Day 8: A VBScript Application

Day 8 provides a sample Web site built using VBScript and ActiveX components. Using the tools discussed on Day 4 and the knowledge of VBScript picked up on Day 6, you will build a Web site that uses ActiveX controls.

Day 9: A JavaScript Application

Day 9 provides a sample Web site built using JavaScript and ActiveX components. Using the tools discussed on Day 4 and the knowledge of JavaScript picked up on Day 7, you will build a Web site that uses ActiveX controls.

Day 10: Setting Up an ActiveX Web Site

Day 10 introduces scenarios in which network or Web site administrators might use your ActiveX application. Day 10 also discusses the more common TCP/IP protocols and how they are used on standard and ActiveX servers.

Day 11: Server-Side Scripting with CGI and ISAPI

On Day 11, you will be introduced to CGI- and ISAPI-server scripting. This chapter will give you the skills necessary to work with existing CGIs. You will also have the information you need to learn how to create your own CGI and ISAPI scripts.

Day 12: WinSock—Windows Network Programming

Day 12 introduces some of the features of the WinSock library. You will use the WinSock TCP/UDP control from Microsoft's Internet Control Pack to create a basic WinSock application.

Day 13: Learning to Use the Win32 Internet API Library

On Day 13, you will learn the general functionality offered by the Win32 API.

Day 14: Programming with Microsoft ActiveX Conferencing APIs

On Day 14, you will learn about the NetConference API and ActiveX control as well as how to use the NetMeeting software.

Week 2

Day 8

A VBScript Application

Today you will use knowledge gained on Day 6, "Writing VBScripts," to construct an application using VBScript and ActiveX controls. You will start with the requirements for the application, do some quick design work, then implement the design.

Gathering Requirements for Your Application

You've got a friend, let's call him JP, who wants to open a bicycle store on the Internet. Ten years and forty pounds ago, he raced bicycles and has always wanted to open his own shop (or it could be that his wife wants to get rid of all the bicycles he has accumulated over the years). He has conducted some research and figures the best, least expensive way to start selling bikes is over the Internet. He wants to show an online catalog. He wants to allow customers to order the catalog. He also wants to allow the customers to order bikes and accessories online, and to track the status of their orders. He asks you, "Can you do it?"

Can You Do It?

Let's take a look at what he wants and how you might do it.

Luckily, the customer knows what he wants. The worst times I have spent programming revolved around customers who knew what they *didn't* want (normally after it was built), but couldn't quite articulate what they *did* want. Let's look at the basic requirements of the program you will write:

- ☐ a Web site
- ☐ a display catalog
- ☐ an order catalog
- ☐ the capability to handle customers' orders for bikes and accessories
- ☐ the capability to track orders

Write these down and show them to your friend. Tell him you will have something by the end of the day. First, draw a rough layout of the Web site. Sketch something that looks like Figure 8.1.

Figure 8.1.
Layout of the Web site.

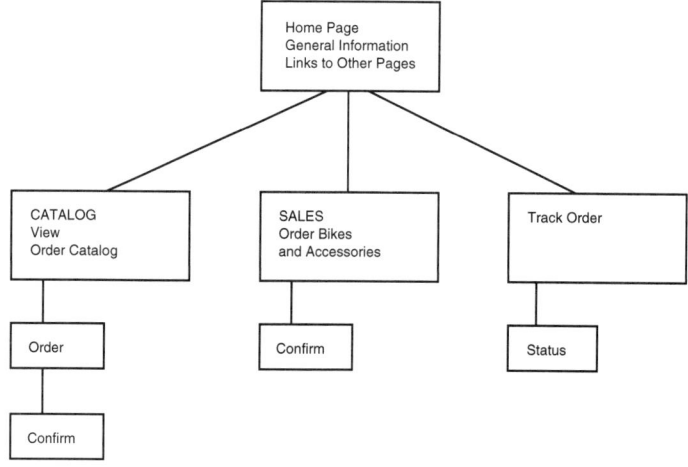

This shows a Welcome page linked to Catalog, Sales, and Order-Tracking pages. Next, follow these steps:

1. Use Word to create rough drafts of the three main pages.
2. Design the database in Access.
3. Add a driver for the bike shop database to your system's ODBC manager.

4. Use the Internet Information Server Add-In for Access to create two insert pages: one for catalog orders, and another for sales.
5. Use the Internet Information Server Add-In for Access to create a search page for order tracking.

After you finish these steps, complete the project by:

1. Customizing the pages with products from the ActiveX Control Pad.
2. Hacking your way into the scripts that Internet Information Server Add-In for Access creates, and customizing them using VBScript.

Use Word to Create Rough Drafts of the Three Main Pages

Open Word and make sure you have Internet Assistant installed (see Day 4, "The Tools of the Trade," for details). Go to File|New and select HTML.dot as your template. Add the logo (logo.bmp on the CD-ROM that came with this book), some general welcome remarks, and links to the catalog (catalog.htm), sales (sales.htm), and order-tracking (track.htm) screens. Your screen should look like Figure 8.2.

Figure 8.2.
Welcome page for JP Bikes!

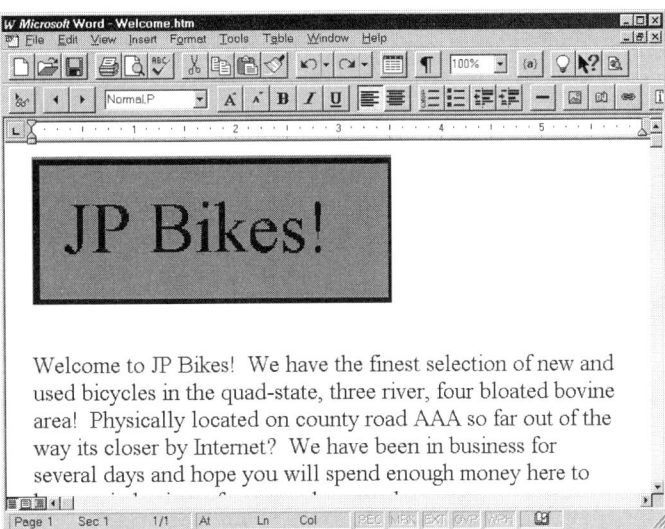

Save your work as welcome.htm. Your HTML code should look like Listing 8.1.

Listing 8.1. welcome.htm.

```
<HTML>
<HEAD>

<META NAME="GENERATOR" CONTENT="Internet Assistant for Microsoft Word 2.0z">
<TITLE>Untitled</TITLE>
</HEAD>
<BODY>
<P>
<IMG SRC="logo.bmp"><BR>
<P>
<FONT SIZE=5>Welcome to JP Bikes!  We have the finest selection
of new and used bicycles in the quad-state, three river, four
bloated bovine area!  Physically located on county road AAA so
far out of the way its closer by Internet?  We have been in business
for several days and hope you will spend enough money here to
keep us in business for a couple more days.</FONT>
<P>
<A HREF="Catalog.htm" >Visit Catalog</A>
<P>
<A HREF="Sales.htm" >Order Something</A>
<P>
<A HREF="Track.htm" >Track a Previous Order </A>
</BODY>
</HTML>
```

Next, open a new HTML page in Word. This will be the Catalog page. You will be putting ActiveX controls here later. For now, you need a logo, a return link to welcome.htm, and a link to the Catalog Order page (catord.htm, which you will generate with the Internet Information Server Add-In a bit later). Your page should look like Figure 8.3.

Figure 8.3.
Catalog page.

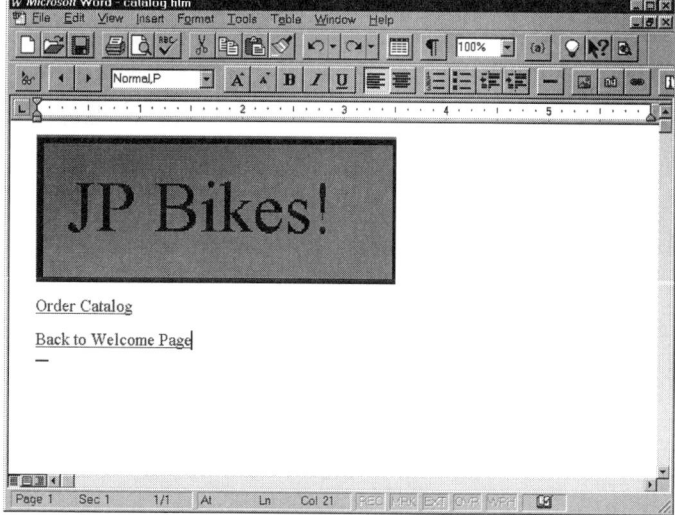

Save your work as catalog.htm. Your HTML code should look like Listing 8.2.

Listing 8.2. catalog.htm.

```
<HTML>
<HEAD>

<META NAME="GENERATOR" CONTENT="Internet Assistant for Microsoft Word 2.0z">
<TITLE>Untitled</TITLE>
</HEAD>
<BODY>
<P>
<IMG SRC="logo.bmp">
<P>
<A HREF="Catord.htm" >Order Catalog</A>
<P>
<A HREF="welcome.htm" >Back to Welcome Page</A>
</BODY>
</HTML>
```

Open a new HTML page in Word. This will be the Sales page. You will be putting ActiveX controls here to calculate the cost of the order before the user sends it. You will also add some of the code generated by Internet Information Server Add-In, and generate orders from this page. Place a logo and a return link to the Welcome page (welcome.htm) on your Sales page. Your page should look like Figure 8.4.

Figure 8.4.
Sales page.

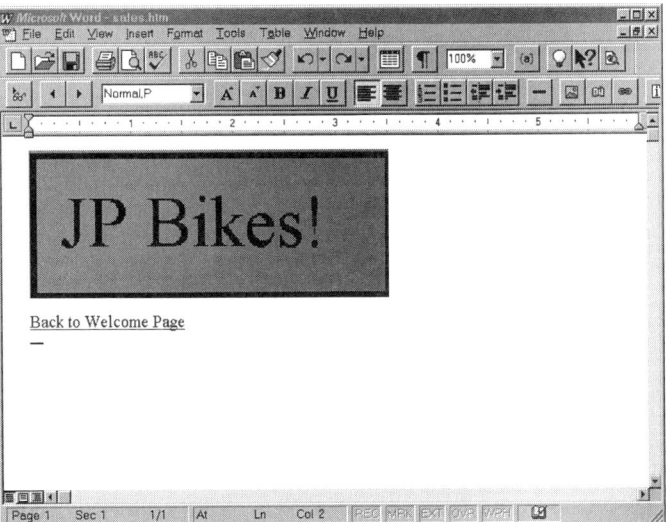

Save your work as sales.htm. Your HTML code should look like Listing 8.3.

Listing 8.3. sales.htm.

```
<HTML>
<HEAD>

<META NAME="GENERATOR" CONTENT="Internet Assistant for Microsoft Word 2.0z">
<TITLE>Untitled</TITLE>
</HEAD>
<BODY>
<P>
<IMG SRC="logo.bmp">
<P>
<A HREF="welcome.htm" >Back to Welcome Page</A>
</BODY>
</HTML>
```

Open a new HTML page in Word. This will be the Order-Tracking page. You will modify this page with frames and code generated by the Internet Information Server Add-In. Again, all you need now is a logo and a return link to the Welcome page (welcome.htm). Your page should look like Figure 8.5.

Figure 8.5.
Order-Tracking page.

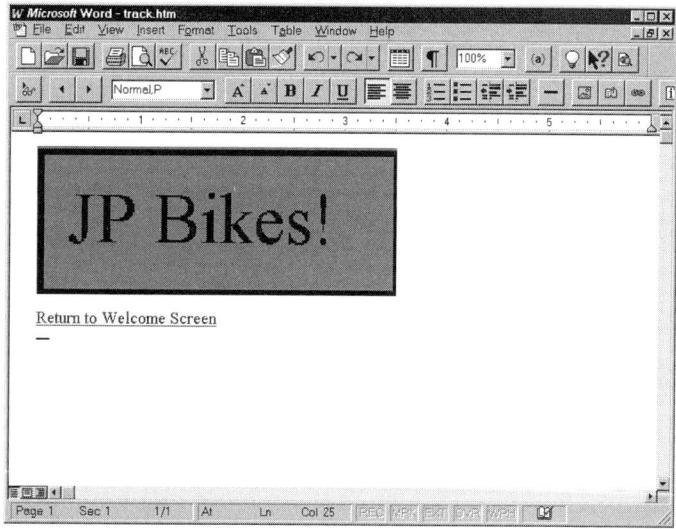

Save your work as track.htm. Your HTML code should look like Listing 8.4.

Listing 8.4. `track.htm`.

```
<HTML>
<HEAD>

<META NAME="GENERATOR" CONTENT="Internet Assistant for Microsoft Word 2.0z">
<TITLE>Untitled</TITLE>
</HEAD>
<BODY>
<P>
<IMG SRC="logo.bmp">
<P>
<A HREF="welcome.htm" >Return to Welcome Screen</A>
</BODY>
</HTML>
```

This is a good place to stop and check your work. Look at these pages and test the links in Word or in the browser. I recommend using the browser because few of your friend's customers will be using Word to look at this site. Go ahead and check.

Now, let's design a database.

Design the Database in Access

I won't go into database theory or design philosophy here. It would be fun, but it is beyond the scope of this book. You will simply create the objects you need.

NOTE

You don't need to use Access to build the database. You can use any database you have an ODBC driver for. To use another database, create the tables as described in this section. Add an ODBC entry to the system DSN, as described in the next section. Finally, type the idc and htx files generated in the upcoming section, "Using the Internet Information Server Add-In," by hand (since this tool only works in Access). The important things are the column names in the database tables and the name you give the connection in the ODBC system DSN.

Open Access and create an new database called `bikeshop.mdb`. Add two new tables, Customers and Orders, as shown in Figure 8.6.

Figure 8.6.
Bike Shop database.

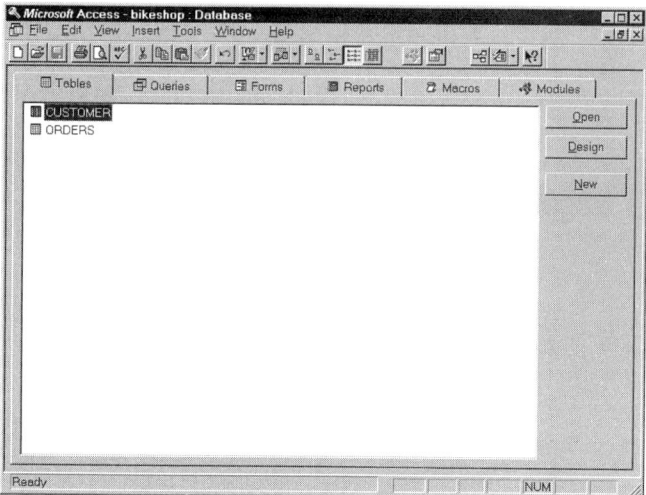

Switch to the Customers table and create the fields shown in Figure 8.7.

Figure 8.7.
Customers table.

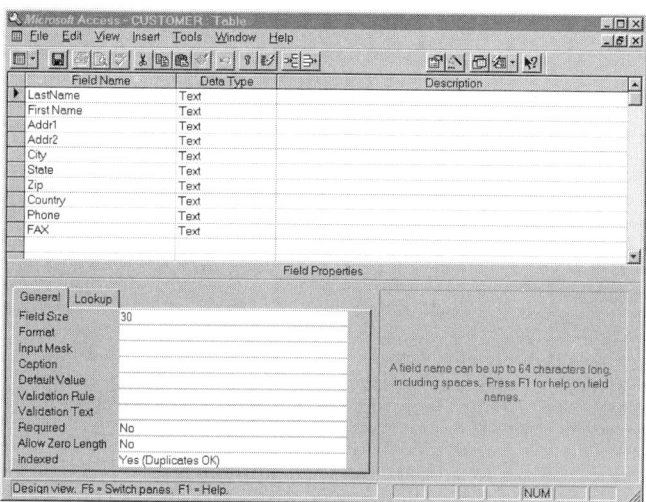

Switch to the Orders table and create the fields shown in Figure 8.8.

Figure 8.8.
Orders table.

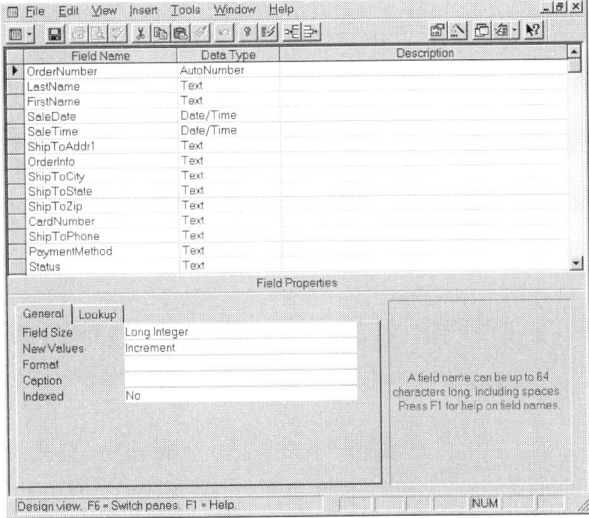

Add a Driver for the Bike Shop Database to Your System's ODBC Manager

At this point, add a reference to your database to the ODBC driver manager. Open up your ODBC administrator, click the System DSN button, and add a new entry based on an Access driver. Fill in the entry, as shown in Figure 8.9.

Figure 8.9.
ODBC administrator.

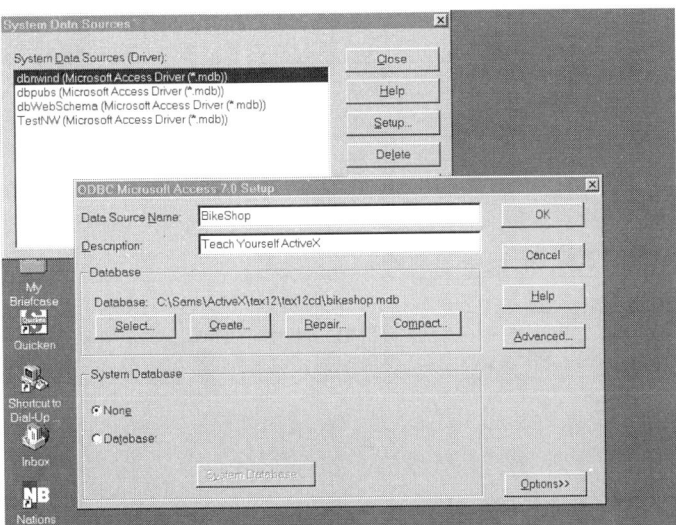

NOTE Those of you who have worked with ODBC before have probably never put an entry into the system DSN. The system DSN makes the data sources available to the system, or any other user that can log on to the system.

Now you are ready to use the Internet Information Server Add-In.

Using the Internet Information Server Add-In

Use the Internet Information Server Add-In to create a page that will insert the customer's catalog-order information into your database. Call it `catord.htm`. You must close and re-open Access for the Internet Information Server Add-In to see the new entry you made in the ODBC administrator. Open the bike shop database and launch the Internet Information Server Add-In by choosing it from Tools|Add-Ins. On the first page of the Internet Information Server Add-In Wizard, choose Insert Page Wizard. On the next screen, choose the Customers table (after all, asking customers to order catalogs is just a sneaky way of getting their names and addresses). Proceed to the field screen and add all the fields. Move to the final input page. You are going to tinker with this screen, so there is no need to add anything. Click Finish; you have created three files that resemble Listings 8.5, 8.6, and 8.7.

NOTE The Access database you just set up has not been optimized to account for multiple users. See your database documentation to determine how to tune your database to handle multiple users.

Listing 8.5. `catord.htm`.

```
<HTML>
<META NAME="GENERATOR" CONTENT="IIS Add In For Access 95">
<HEAD><Title>HTML document for the World Wide Web</Title></HEAD>
<BODY BGCOLOR="#FFFFFF">

<FORM ACTION="/scripts/catord.idc" METHOD = "POST" >
<TABLE BORDER BGCOLOR="#FFFFFF">
<TR>
<TD>LastName</TD>
```

A VBScript Application

```
<TD><INPUT NAME="LastName"</TD></TR><P>
<TR>
<TD>First Name</TD>
<TD><INPUT NAME="First Name"</TD></TR><P>
<TR>
<TD>Addr1</TD>
<TD><INPUT NAME="Addr1"</TD></TR><P>
<TR>
<TD>Addr2</TD>
<TD><INPUT NAME="Addr2"</TD></TR><P>
<TR>
<TD>City</TD>
<TD><INPUT NAME="City"</TD></TR><P>
<TR>
<TD>State</TD>
<TD><INPUT NAME="State"</TD></TR><P>
<TR>
<TD>Zip</TD>
<TD><INPUT NAME="Zip"</TD></TR><P>
<TR>
<TD>Country</TD>
<TD><INPUT NAME="Country"</TD></TR><P>
<TR>
<TD>Phone</TD>
<TD><INPUT NAME="Phone"</TD></TR><P>
<TR>
<TD>FAX</TD>
<TD><INPUT NAME="FAX"</TD></TR><P>
</TABLE>
<P><INPUT TYPE="SUBMIT" VALUE="Submit" ALIGN="MIDDLE">
<INPUT TYPE="RESET" NAME="reset" VALUE="Clear all fields"
ALIGN="MIDDLE"></P></FORM>
<HR=2>
<CENTER>This page was produced by using the <B>IIS Add-In for Access 95</B>.
<BR><I> Copyright 1996 Microsoft
Corporation</I>.</CENTER>
</BODY></HTML>
```

The htx file is the template for the page sent back by the Internet Information Server.

Listing 8.6. catord.htx.

```
<HTML>
<META NAME="GENERATOR" CONTENT="IIS Add In For Access 95">
<HEAD><Title>HTML document for the World Wide Web</Title></HEAD>
<BODY BGCOLOR="#FFFFFF">

<P><B>The following information was recieved.</B><BR>
<TABLE BORDER BGCOLOR="#FFFFFF">
<TR>
<TD ALIGN="RIGHT"><B>LastName</B></TD>
<TD><%idc.LastName%></TD></TR>
```

continues

Listing 8.6. continued

```
<TR>
<TD ALIGN="RIGHT"><B>First Name</B></TD>
<TD><%idc.First Name%></TD></TR>
<TR>
<TD ALIGN="RIGHT"><B>Addr1</B></TD>
<TD><%idc.Addr1%></TD></TR>
<TR>
<TD ALIGN="RIGHT"><B>Addr2</B></TD>
<TD><%idc.Addr2%></TD></TR>
<TR>
<TD ALIGN="RIGHT"><B>City</B></TD>
<TD><%idc.City%></TD></TR>
<TR>
<TD ALIGN="RIGHT"><B>State</B></TD>
<TD><%idc.State%></TD></TR>
<TR>
<TD ALIGN="RIGHT"><B>Zip</B></TD>
<TD><%idc.Zip%></TD></TR>
<TR>
<TD ALIGN="RIGHT"><B>Country</B></TD>
<TD><%idc.Country%></TD></TR>
<TR>
<TD ALIGN="RIGHT"><B>Phone</B></TD>
<TD><%idc.Phone%></TD></TR>
<TR>
<TD ALIGN="RIGHT"><B>FAX</B></TD>
<TD><%idc.FAX%></TD></TR>
</TABLE><P>
<A HREF="/catord.htm">Return To Data Entry Page</A>
<CENTER>This page was produced by using the <B>IIS Add-In for Access 95</B>.
<BR><I> Copyright 1996 Microsoft
Corporation</I>.</CENTER>
</BODY></HTML>
```

The idc file contains the query that will run against the database.

Listing 8.7. `catord.idc.`

```
Datasource: BikeShop
Template: catord.htx
DefaultParameters:
SQLStatement:
+INSERT INTO "CUSTOMER" ("LastName", "First Name", "Addr1",
"Addr2", "City", "State", "Zip", "Country", "Phone", "FAX")
+VALUES ('%LastName%', '%First Name%', '%Addr1%', '%Addr2%',
'%City%', '%State%', '%Zip%', '%Country%', '%Phone%', '%FAX%');
#IDC-Insert FrontHTM-catord.htm ReportHTX-catord.htx
```

Do the same for the Orders table and save the result as salord.htm (which will create the files files salord.htx and salord.idc). Generate salord.htm, salord.htx, and salord.idc as shown in Listings 8.8, 8.9, and 8.10.

Listing 8.8. salord.htm.

```
<HTML>
<META NAME="GENERATOR" CONTENT="IIS Add In For Access 95">
<HEAD><Title>HTML document for the World Wide Web</Title></HEAD>
<BODY BGCOLOR="#FFFFFF">

<FORM ACTION="/scripts/salord.idc" METHOD = "POST" >
<TABLE BORDER BGCOLOR="#FFFFFF">
<TR>
<TD>OrderNumber</TD>
<TD><INPUT NAME="OrderNumber"</TD></TR><P>
<TR>
<TD>LastName</TD>
<TD><INPUT NAME="LastName"</TD></TR><P>
<TR>
<TD>FirstName</TD>
<TD><INPUT NAME="FirstName"</TD></TR><P>
<TR>
<TD>SaleDate</TD>
<TD><INPUT NAME="SaleDate"</TD></TR><P>
<TR>
<TD>SaleTime</TD>
<TD><INPUT NAME="SaleTime"</TD></TR><P>
<TR>
<TD>ShipToAddr1</TD>
<TD><INPUT NAME="ShipToAddr1"</TD></TR><P>
<TR>
<TD>OrderInfo</TD>
<TD><INPUT NAME="OrderInfo"</TD></TR><P>
<TR>
<TD>ShipToCity</TD>
<TD><INPUT NAME="ShipToCity"</TD></TR><P>
<TR>
<TD>ShipToState</TD>
<TD><INPUT NAME="ShipToState"</TD></TR><P>
<TR>
<TD>ShipToZip</TD>
<TD><INPUT NAME="ShipToZip"</TD></TR><P>
<TR>
<TD>CardNumber</TD>
<TD><INPUT NAME="CardNumber"</TD></TR><P>
<TR>
<TD>ShipToPhone</TD>
<TD><INPUT NAME="ShipToPhone"</TD></TR><P>
<TR>
<TD>PaymentMethod</TD>
```

continues

Listing 8.8. continued

```
<TD><INPUT NAME="PaymentMethod"</TD></TR><P>
<TR>
<TD>Status</TD>
<TD><INPUT NAME="Status"</TD></TR><P>
</TABLE>
<P><INPUT TYPE="SUBMIT" VALUE="Submit" ALIGN="MIDDLE">
<INPUT TYPE="RESET" NAME="reset" VALUE="Clear all fields"
ALIGN="MIDDLE"></P></FORM>
<HR=2>
<CENTER>This page was produced by using the <B>IIS Add-In for Access 95</B>.
<BR><I> Copyright 1996 Microsoft
Corporation</I>.</CENTER>
</BODY></HTML>
```

Listing 8.9. salord.htx.

```
<HTML>
<META NAME="GENERATOR" CONTENT="IIS Add In For Access 95">
<HEAD><Title>HTML document for the World Wide Web</Title></HEAD>
<BODY BGCOLOR="#FFFFFF">

<P><B>The following information was recieved.</B><BR>
<TABLE BORDER BGCOLOR="#FFFFFF">
<TR>
<TD ALIGN="RIGHT"><B>OrderNumber</B></TD>
<%IF idc.OrderNumber EQ "NULL" %> <%else%><%idc.OrderNumber%><%endif%></TD></TR>
<TR>
<TD ALIGN="RIGHT"><B>LastName</B></TD>
<TD><%idc.LastName%></TD></TR>
<TR>
<TD ALIGN="RIGHT"><B>FirstName</B></TD>
<TD><%idc.FirstName%></TD></TR>
<TR>
<TD ALIGN="RIGHT"><B>SaleDate</B></TD>
<%IF idc.SaleDate EQ "NULL" %> <%else%><%idc.SaleDate%><%endif%></TD></TR>
<TR>
<TD ALIGN="RIGHT"><B>SaleTime</B></TD>
<%IF idc.SaleTime EQ "NULL" %> <%else%><%idc.SaleTime%><%endif%></TD></TR>
<TR>
<TD ALIGN="RIGHT"><B>ShipToAddr1</B></TD>
<TD><%idc.ShipToAddr1%></TD></TR>
<TR>
<TD ALIGN="RIGHT"><B>OrderInfo</B></TD>
<TD><%idc.OrderInfo%></TD></TR>
<TR>
<TD ALIGN="RIGHT"><B>ShipToCity</B></TD>
<TD><%idc.ShipToCity%></TD></TR>
```

```
<TR>
<TD ALIGN="RIGHT"><B>ShipToState</B></TD>
<TD><%idc.ShipToState%></TD></TR>
<TR>
<TD ALIGN="RIGHT"><B>ShipToZip</B></TD>
<TD><%idc.ShipToZip%></TD></TR>
<TR>
<TD ALIGN="RIGHT"><B>CardNumber</B></TD>
<TD><%idc.CardNumber%></TD></TR>
<TR>
<TD ALIGN="RIGHT"><B>ShipToPhone</B></TD>
<TD><%idc.ShipToPhone%></TD></TR>
<TR>
<TD ALIGN="RIGHT"><B>PaymentMethod</B></TD>
<TD><%idc.PaymentMethod%></TD></TR>
<TR>
<TD ALIGN="RIGHT"><B>Status</B></TD>
<TD><%idc.Status%></TD></TR>
</TABLE><P>
<A HREF="/salord.htm">Return To Data Entry Page</A>
<CENTER>This page was produced by using the <B>IIS Add-In for Access 95</B>.<BR>
<I> Copyright 1996 Microsoft
Corporation</I>.</CENTER>
</BODY></HTML>
```

Listing 8.10. `salord.idc`.

```
Datasource: BikeShop
Template: salord.htx
DefaultParameters: OrderNumber=NULL, SaleDate=NULL, SaleTime=NULL
SQLStatement:
+INSERT INTO "ORDERS" ("OrderNumber", "LastName", "FirstName",
"SaleDate", "SaleTime", "ShipToAddr1", "OrderInfo",
"ShipToCity", "ShipToState", "ShipToZip", "CardNumber",
 "ShipToPhone", "PaymentMethod", "Status")
+VALUES (%OrderNumber%, '%LastName%', '%FirstName%',
%SaleDate%, %SaleTime%, '%ShipToAddr1%', '%OrderInfo%',
'%ShipToCity%', '%ShipToState%', '%ShipToZip%', '%CardNumber%',
'%ShipToPhone%', '%PaymentMethod%', '%Status%');
#IDC-Insert FrontHTM-salord.htm ReportHTX-salord.htx
```

Use the Internet Information Server Add-In Wizard to generate one more group of forms: the query for the Track Order page. Call up the Wizard and choose the Query and Display option on the Wizard's first page. Then pick the Orders table. Choose the OrderNumber field as the search field. Pick the LastName, FirstName, SalesDate, and Status fields for display on the Display Web Page. All this is shown in Figure 8.10.

Figure 8.10.
Setting up the Search and Return pages.

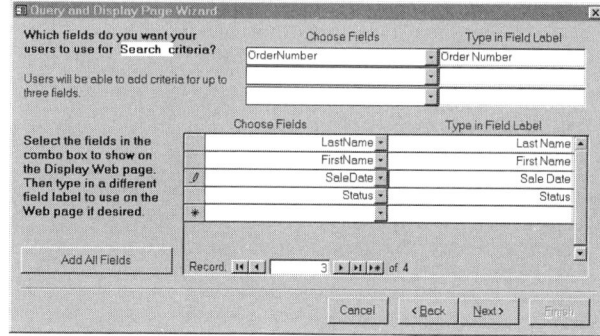

Save the file as tracord.htm, which will also save tracord.htm and tracord.idc. Your files should look like Listings 8.11, 8.12, and 8.13.

Listing 8.11. tracord.htm.

```
<HTML>
<META NAME="GENERATOR" CONTENT="IIS Add In For Access 95">
<HEAD><Title>HTML document for the World Wide Web</Title></HEAD>
<BODY BGCOLOR="#FFFFFF">

<FORM ACTION="/scripts/tracord.idc" METHOD = "POST" >
<TABLE BORDER BGCOLOR="#FFFFFF">
<TR>
<TD ALIGN="RIGHT">Order Number</TD>
<TD><INPUT NAME="OrderNumber"</TD></TR><P>
</TABLE>
<P><INPUT TYPE="SUBMIT" VALUE="Search" ALIGN="MIDDLE">
<INPUT TYPE="RESET" NAME="reset" VALUE="Clear all fields"
ALIGN="MIDDLE"></P></FORM>
<HR=2>
<CENTER>This page was produced by using the <B>IIS Add-In for Access 95</B>.
<BR><I> Copyright 1996 Microsoft
Corporation</I>.</CENTER>
</BODY></HTML>
```

Listing 8.12. tracord.htx.

```
<HTML>
<META NAME="GENERATOR" CONTENT="IIS Add In For Access 95">
<HEAD><Title>HTML document for the World Wide Web</Title></HEAD>
<BODY BGCOLOR="#FFFFFF">


<%begindetail%>
<%if CurrentRecord EQ 0 %>
```

```
<TABLE BORDER BGCOLOR="#FFFFFF">
<TR>
<TH><B>Last Name</B></TH>
<TH><B>First Name</B></TH>
<TH><B>Sale Date</B></TH>
<TH><B>Status</B></TH>
</TR>
<%endif%>
<TR>
<TD Align=Right><%LastName%></TD>
<TD Align=Left><%FirstName%></TD>
<TD Align=Right><%SaleDate%></TD>
<TD Align=Left><%Status%></TD>
</TR>
<%enddetail%>
<%if CurrentRecord EQ 0 %>
<HR=2><P>
<CENTER><B>No records were selected!<B></CENTER><P>
<%endif%>
</TABLE>
<HR=2>
<CENTER>This page was produced by using the <B>IIS Add-In for Access 95</B>.
<BR><I> Copyright 1996 Microsoft
Corporation</I>.</CENTER>
</BODY></HTML>
```

Listing 8.13. `tracord.idc`.

```
Datasource: BikeShop
Template: tracord.htx
DefaultParameters: OrderNumber="OrderNumber"
SQLStatement:
+Select "LastName", "FirstName", "SaleDate", "Status"
+From "ORDERS"
+Where "OrderNumber" = %OrderNumber%
#IDC-Search FrontHTM-tracord.htm ReportHTX-tracord.htx
```

Now you have what you need from the Internet Information Server Add-In Wizard, so let's move on.

What Do You Have So Far?

All the files you have generated are in the rough subdirectory of this chapter's entry on the CD-ROM.

The Catalog Page

The purpose of the Catalog page is two-fold. First, it displays your catalog online. Second, the Catalog page allows the user to order a catalog, which allows your friend to collect the user's address. Let's build an online catalog.

Open your ActiveX Control Pad and add an image control, seven labels, and a spin button (as shown in Figure 8.11).

Figure 8.11.
Screen setup for `catalog.alx`.

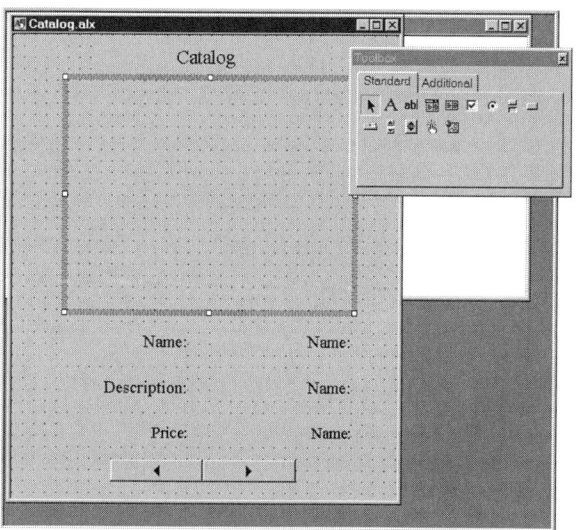

Name your variables and add the subroutines, as shown in Listing 8.14.

Listing 8.14. `catalog.alx`.

```
<SCRIPT LANGUAGE="VBScript">
<!--
'Globals
dim CatalogIndex
dim Name(6)
dim Description(6)
dim Price(6)
dim Picture(6)

Sub LoadInfo()
'CatalogIndex = 0
Description(0) = "Road Bike"
Description(1) = "Tandem Bike"
Description(2) = "Racing Bike"
Description(3) = "TriAthlon Bike"
```

```
Description(4) = "Helmet"
Description(5) = "Shorts"

Name(0) = "RB150"
Name(1) = "TB250"
Name(2) = "RC500"
Name(3) = "RR750"
Name(4) = "Hard Hat 1000"
Name(5) = "BunchUps"

Price(0) = "$450.50"
Price(1) = "$600.00"
Price(2) = "$800.95"
Price(3) = "$950.50"
Price(4) = "$39.00"
Price(5) = "$27.00"

Picture(0) = "RB150.bmp"
Picture(1) = "TB250.bmp"
Picture(2) = "RC500.bmp"
Picture(3) = "TR750.bmp"
Picture(4) = "Helmet.bmp"
Picture(5) = "Shorts.bmp"
end sub


-->
</SCRIPT>
<SCRIPT LANGUAGE="VBScript">
<!--
Sub sbtnNavigate_SpinUp()
CatalogIndex = CatalogIndex + 1
if CatalogIndex > 5 then
  CatalogIndex = 0 'Start over at 0
end if
'Load Controls with new information
lblDescription.Caption = Description(CatalogIndex)
lblName.Caption = Name(CatalogIndex)
lblPrice.Caption = Price(CatalogIndex)
imgCatalog.Picturepath = Picture(CatalogIndex)
end sub
Sub sbtnNavigate_SpinDown()
CatalogIndex = CatalogIndex - 1
if CatalogIndex < 0 then
  CatalogIndex = 5 'Start over at 5
end if
'Load Controls with new information
lblDescription.Caption = Description(CatalogIndex)
lblName.Caption = Name(CatalogIndex)
lblPrice.Caption = Price(CatalogIndex)
imgCatalog.Picturepath = Picture(CatalogIndex)
end sub
-->
</SCRIPT>
```

continues

Listing 8.14. continued

```
<SCRIPT LANGUAGE="VBScript">
<!--
Sub Layout2_OnLoad()
'initialize arrays
call LoadInfo()
'initialize controls
lblDescription.Caption = Description(CatalogIndex)
lblName.Caption = Name(CatalogIndex)
lblPrice.Caption = Price(CatalogIndex)
imgCatalog.Picturepath = Picture(CatalogIndex)


end sub
-->
</SCRIPT>
<DIV ID="Layout2" STYLE="LAYOUT:FIXED;WIDTH:274pt;HEIGHT:316pt;">
    <OBJECT ID="imgCatalog"
     CLASSID="CLSID:D4A97620-8E8F-11CF-93CD-00AA00C08FDF"
     STYLE="TOP:31pt;LEFT:39pt;WIDTH:203pt;HEIGHT:156pt;ZINDEX:0;">
        <PARAM NAME="BorderStyle" VALUE="0">
        <PARAM NAME="SizeMode" VALUE="3">
        <PARAM NAME="Size" VALUE="7161;5503">
        <PARAM NAME="PictureAlignment" VALUE="0">
        <PARAM NAME="VariousPropertyBits" VALUE="19">
    </OBJECT>
    <OBJECT ID="Label1"
     CLASSID="CLSID:978C9E23-D4B0-11CE-BF2D-00AA003F40D0"
     STYLE="TOP:203pt;LEFT:39pt;WIDTH:86pt;HEIGHT:16pt;ZINDEX:1;">
        <PARAM NAME="Caption" VALUE="Name:">
        <PARAM NAME="Size" VALUE="3034;564">
        <PARAM NAME="FontName" VALUE="Times New Roman">
        <PARAM NAME="FontHeight" VALUE="240">
        <PARAM NAME="FontCharSet" VALUE="0">
        <PARAM NAME="FontPitchAndFamily" VALUE="2">
        <PARAM NAME="ParagraphAlign" VALUE="2">
    </OBJECT>
    <OBJECT ID="Label2"
     CLASSID="CLSID:978C9E23-D4B0-11CE-BF2D-00AA003F40D0"
     STYLE="TOP:234pt;LEFT:39pt;WIDTH:86pt;HEIGHT:16pt;ZINDEX:2;">
        <PARAM NAME="Caption" VALUE="Description:">
        <PARAM NAME="Size" VALUE="3034;564">
        <PARAM NAME="FontName" VALUE="Times New Roman">
        <PARAM NAME="FontHeight" VALUE="240">
        <PARAM NAME="FontCharSet" VALUE="0">
        <PARAM NAME="FontPitchAndFamily" VALUE="2">
        <PARAM NAME="ParagraphAlign" VALUE="2">
    </OBJECT>
    <OBJECT ID="Label3"
     CLASSID="CLSID:978C9E23-D4B0-11CE-BF2D-00AA003F40D0"
     STYLE="TOP:265pt;LEFT:39pt;WIDTH:86pt;HEIGHT:16pt;ZINDEX:3;">
        <PARAM NAME="Caption" VALUE="Price:">
        <PARAM NAME="Size" VALUE="3034;564">
        <PARAM NAME="FontName" VALUE="Times New Roman">
```

A VBScript Application

```
            <PARAM NAME="FontHeight" VALUE="240">
            <PARAM NAME="FontCharSet" VALUE="0">
            <PARAM NAME="FontPitchAndFamily" VALUE="2">
            <PARAM NAME="ParagraphAlign" VALUE="2">
     </OBJECT>
     <OBJECT ID="lblName"
      CLASSID="CLSID:978C9E23-D4B0-11CE-BF2D-00AA003F40D0"
      STYLE="TOP:203pt;LEFT:148pt;WIDTH:94pt;HEIGHT:13pt;ZINDEX:4;">
            <PARAM NAME="Caption" VALUE="Name:">
            <PARAM NAME="Size" VALUE="3316;459">
            <PARAM NAME="FontName" VALUE="Times New Roman">
            <PARAM NAME="FontHeight" VALUE="240">
            <PARAM NAME="FontCharSet" VALUE="0">
            <PARAM NAME="FontPitchAndFamily" VALUE="2">
            <PARAM NAME="ParagraphAlign" VALUE="2">
     </OBJECT>
     <OBJECT ID="lblDescription"
      CLASSID="CLSID:978C9E23-D4B0-11CE-BF2D-00AA003F40D0"
      STYLE="TOP:234pt;LEFT:148pt;WIDTH:94pt;HEIGHT:13pt;ZINDEX:5;">
            <PARAM NAME="Caption" VALUE="Name:">
            <PARAM NAME="Size" VALUE="3316;459">
            <PARAM NAME="FontName" VALUE="Times New Roman">
            <PARAM NAME="FontHeight" VALUE="240">
            <PARAM NAME="FontCharSet" VALUE="0">
            <PARAM NAME="FontPitchAndFamily" VALUE="2">
            <PARAM NAME="ParagraphAlign" VALUE="2">
     </OBJECT>
     <OBJECT ID="lblPrice"
      CLASSID="CLSID:978C9E23-D4B0-11CE-BF2D-00AA003F40D0"
      STYLE="TOP:265pt;LEFT:148pt;WIDTH:94pt;HEIGHT:13pt;ZINDEX:6;">
            <PARAM NAME="Caption" VALUE="Name:">
            <PARAM NAME="Size" VALUE="3316;459">
            <PARAM NAME="FontName" VALUE="Times New Roman">
            <PARAM NAME="FontHeight" VALUE="240">
            <PARAM NAME="FontCharSet" VALUE="0">
            <PARAM NAME="FontPitchAndFamily" VALUE="2">
            <PARAM NAME="ParagraphAlign" VALUE="2">
     </OBJECT>
     <OBJECT ID="sbtnNavigate"
      CLASSID="CLSID:79176FB0-B7F2-11CE-97EF-00AA006D2776"
      STYLE="TOP:289pt;LEFT:70pt;WIDTH:133pt;HEIGHT:16pt;TABINDEX:6;ZINDEX:7;">
            <PARAM NAME="Size" VALUE="4692;564">
     </OBJECT>
     <OBJECT ID="Label4"
      CLASSID="CLSID:978C9E23-D4B0-11CE-BF2D-00AA003F40D0"
      STYLE="TOP:8pt;LEFT:55pt;WIDTH:164pt;HEIGHT:16pt;ZINDEX:8;">
            <PARAM NAME="Caption" VALUE="Catalog">
            <PARAM NAME="Size" VALUE="5786;564">
            <PARAM NAME="FontName" VALUE="Times New Roman">
            <PARAM NAME="FontHeight" VALUE="280">
            <PARAM NAME="FontCharSet" VALUE="0">
            <PARAM NAME="FontPitchAndFamily" VALUE="2">
            <PARAM NAME="ParagraphAlign" VALUE="3">
     </OBJECT>
</DIV>
```

Note the font and alignment settings of the controls inside the <OBJECT> tags. The <PARAM> tags show the differences between the default properties and the ones you put in using the property box in the ActiveX Control Pad. Use whatever fonts and alignment you want; they only change the appearance of the page. catalog.alx doesn't have anything critical hidden in this section, but some of the examples coming up take some interesting turns inside the <OBJECT> tags.

First, declare some global variables. Use catalogindex to keep track of where you are in the catalog, and declare four arrays to hold the names, descriptions, prices, and pictures from the catalog. Then create a procedure called LoadInfo (to be loaded from the OnLoad event of the Layout control) to load the arrays with the items from the catalog. The OnLoad event of the Layout control is a good place to put things you want done at the beginning of the program.

Inside the spin_up and spin_down events of the spin button, put code to cycle through the catalog. Notice how the numbers loop. When the user goes below zero on the index, it is put back to 5; when the value spun is above five, it is set back to 0. Also notice how the controls are given initial values in the OnLoad event of the Layout control.

After you save your work as catalog.alx, insert it into catalog.htm (as shown in Listing 8.15).

Listing 8.15. catalog.htm.

```
<HTML>
<HEAD>

<META NAME="GENERATOR" CONTENT="Internet Assistant for Microsoft Word 2.0z">
<TITLE>Untitled</TITLE>
</HEAD>
<BODY>
<P>
<IMG SRC="logo.bmp">
<P>

<OBJECT CLASSID="CLSID:812AE312-8B8E-11CF-93C8-00AA00C08FDF"
ID="Catalog_alx" STYLE="LEFT:0;TOP:0">
<PARAM NAME="ALXPATH" REF VALUE="file:\source\chap08\finished\Catalog.alx">
 </OBJECT>


<P>
<P>
<A HREF="Catord.htm" >Order Catalog</A>
<P>
<A HREF="welcome.htm" >Back to Welcome Page</A>
</BODY>
</HTML>
```

This is not a major change from the rough draft you made at the beginning of the day (refer to Listing 8.2). You will not change the catord files you made earlier. The catord files demonstrate the raw material generated by the Internet Information Server Add-In, and provide a good contrast to what you will do on the next page. Launch the Welcome page (welcome.htm) and pick the catalog. Your screen should look like Figure 8.12.

Figure 8.12.
Catalog page.

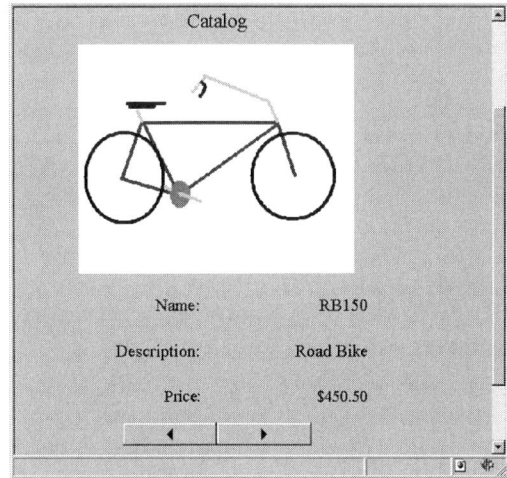

Selecting the order catalog link gives you the stock screen generated by the Internet Information Server Add-In, as shown in Figure 8.13. This is okay for a program you can download free, but you can and will improve it on the Sales and Order-Tracking pages it generates.

Figure 8.13.
Order Catalog page.

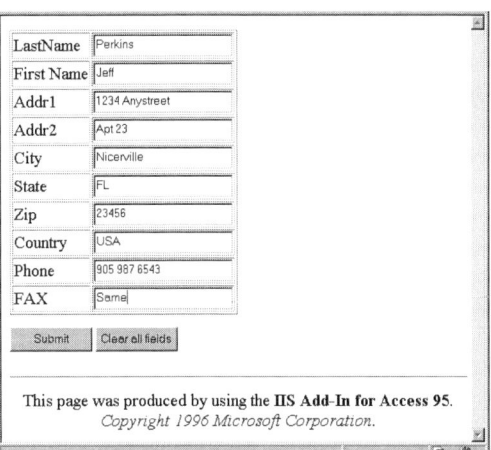

That will do it for the Catalog page. Let's move on to the Sales page.

The Sales Page

The Sales page has to do three things: It must allow the user to pick items to buy, it must allow the user to fill out an order form, and it must transmit the order form back to the bike store computer. Create a dual-list-box dialog using the ActiveX Control Pad. Use two list boxes, two buttons, and six labels, as shown in Figure 8.14.

Figure 8.14.
Layout for sales.alx.

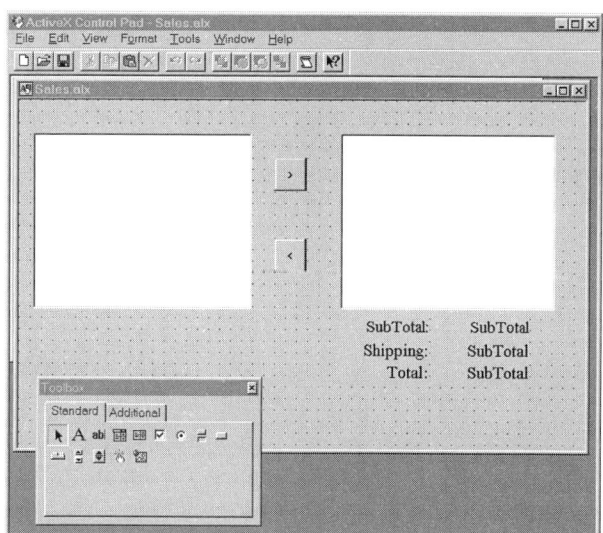

Name and configure the controls as shown in Listing 8.16.

Listing 8.16. sales.alx.

```
<SCRIPT LANGUAGE="VBScript">
<!--
'Globals
Sub Layout1_OnLoad()
  LBInventory.AddItem("RB150")
  LBInventory.List(0,1) = ("$450.50")
  LBInventory.AddItem("TB250")
  LBInventory.List(1,1) = ("$600.00")
  LBInventory.AddItem("RC500")
  LBInventory.List(2,1) = ("$800.95")
  LBInventory.AddItem("RR750")
  LBInventory.List(3,1) = ("$950.50")
  LBInventory.AddItem("Hard Hat 1000")
```

A VBScript Application

```
  LBInventory.List(4,1) = ("$039.00")
  LBInventory.AddItem("BunchUps")
  LBInventory.List(5,1) = ("$027.00")
CalcTotals()
end sub
-->
</SCRIPT>
<SCRIPT LANGUAGE="VBScript">
<!--
Sub btnInvToOrd_Click()
'Only do this if an item is selected
if LBInventory.ListIndex >= 0 then
  index = LBInventory.ListIndex
  LBOrder.AddItem(LBInventory.List(index,0))
  LBOrder.List(LBOrder.Listcount - 1,1) = LBInventory.List(index,1)
  CalcTotals()
  SetOrderInfo()
else
  Alert"Item Not Selected!"
end if

end sub
-->
</SCRIPT>
<SCRIPT LANGUAGE="VBScript">
<!--
Sub SetOrderInfo()
'This is a funcion for other Objects of the Form to call
'To get the Information from the Sales Object
  OrderInfo = "Start*"
  if LBOrder.ListCount > 0 then
    'Read in Items and Prices
    For i = 0 to LBOrder.ListCount - 1
      OrderInfo = OrderInfo & LBOrder.List(i,0) & "*"
      OrderInfo = OrderInfo & LBOrder.List(i,1) & "*"
    Next
    'Dont really need SubTotal and Shipping, we can
    'Compute those back at the factory
  end if
  OrderInfo = OrderInfo & "End*"
  window.document.ORDERFORM.OrderInfo.Value = OrderInfo
end sub
Function MakeDollar(value)
  dollars = int(value)
  cents = csng(value)- int(value)
  if cents = 0 then
    decimalpart = ".00"
  else
    decimalpart ="." & cstr(int(cents * 100))
  end if
  MakeDollar = "$" & cstr(dollars) & decimalpart

end function
Sub CalcTotals()
```

continues

Listing 8.16. continued

```
      SubTotal = 0
      Shipping = 0
      Total = 0

      if LBOrder.ListCount >= 1 then 'any items?

        for i = 0 To LBOrder.ListCount - 1
          SubTotal = SubTotal + Csng(Right(LBOrder.List(i,1), 6))
        Next

        Select Case LbOrder.ListCount
          Case 1,2
            Shipping = 5
          Case 3
            Shipping = 4
          Case Else
            Shipping = 2
        End Select
      end if
      lblShipping.Caption = MakeDollar(Shipping)
      lblSubTotal.Caption = MakeDollar(SubTotal)
      total = subtotal + Shipping
      lblTotal = MakeDollar(Total)

end sub
Sub btnDelOrd_Click()
  LBOrder.RemoveItem(LBOrder.ListIndex)
  CalcTotals()
end sub
-->
</SCRIPT>
<DIV ID="Layout1" STYLE="LAYOUT:FIXED;WIDTH:451pt;HEIGHT:239pt;">
    <OBJECT ID="btnInvToOrd"
     CLASSID="CLSID:D7053240-CE69-11CD-A777-00DD01143C57"
     STYLE="TOP:39pt;LEFT:179pt;WIDTH:23pt;HEIGHT:23pt;TABINDEX:2;ZINDEX:0;">
        <PARAM NAME="Caption" VALUE="&gt;">
        <PARAM NAME="Size" VALUE="811;811">
        <PARAM NAME="FontCharSet" VALUE="0">
        <PARAM NAME="FontPitchAndFamily" VALUE="2">
        <PARAM NAME="ParagraphAlign" VALUE="3">
    </OBJECT>
    <OBJECT ID="btnDelOrd"
     CLASSID="CLSID:D7053240-CE69-11CD-A777-00DD01143C57"
     STYLE="TOP:94pt;LEFT:179pt;WIDTH:23pt;HEIGHT:23pt;TABINDEX:3;ZINDEX:1;">
        <PARAM NAME="Caption" VALUE="&lt;">
        <PARAM NAME="Size" VALUE="811;811">
        <PARAM NAME="FontCharSet" VALUE="0">
        <PARAM NAME="FontPitchAndFamily" VALUE="2">
        <PARAM NAME="ParagraphAlign" VALUE="3">
    </OBJECT>
    <OBJECT ID="Label1"
     CLASSID="CLSID:978C9E23-D4B0-11CE-BF2D-00AA003F40D0"
     STYLE="TOP:148pt;LEFT:226pt;WIDTH:62pt;HEIGHT:16pt;ZINDEX:2;">
        <PARAM NAME="Caption" VALUE="SubTotal:">
```

A VBScript Application

```
        <PARAM NAME="Size" VALUE="2208;564">
        <PARAM NAME="FontName" VALUE="Times New Roman">
        <PARAM NAME="FontHeight" VALUE="240">
        <PARAM NAME="FontCharSet" VALUE="0">
        <PARAM NAME="FontPitchAndFamily" VALUE="2">
        <PARAM NAME="ParagraphAlign" VALUE="2">
</OBJECT>
<OBJECT ID="Label2"
 CLASSID="CLSID:978C9E23-D4B0-11CE-BF2D-00AA003F40D0"
 STYLE="TOP:164pt;LEFT:226pt;WIDTH:62pt;HEIGHT:16pt;ZINDEX:3;">
        <PARAM NAME="Caption" VALUE="Shipping:">
        <PARAM NAME="Size" VALUE="2208;564">
        <PARAM NAME="FontName" VALUE="Times New Roman">
        <PARAM NAME="FontHeight" VALUE="240">
        <PARAM NAME="FontCharSet" VALUE="0">
        <PARAM NAME="FontPitchAndFamily" VALUE="2">
        <PARAM NAME="ParagraphAlign" VALUE="2">
</OBJECT>
<OBJECT ID="Label3"
 CLASSID="CLSID:978C9E23-D4B0-11CE-BF2D-00AA003F40D0"
 STYLE="TOP:179pt;LEFT:226pt;WIDTH:62pt;HEIGHT:16pt;ZINDEX:4;">
        <PARAM NAME="Caption" VALUE="Total:">
        <PARAM NAME="Size" VALUE="2208;564">
        <PARAM NAME="FontName" VALUE="Times New Roman">
        <PARAM NAME="FontHeight" VALUE="240">
        <PARAM NAME="FontCharSet" VALUE="0">
        <PARAM NAME="FontPitchAndFamily" VALUE="2">
        <PARAM NAME="ParagraphAlign" VALUE="2">
</OBJECT>
<OBJECT ID="lblSubTotal"
 CLASSID="CLSID:978C9E23-D4B0-11CE-BF2D-00AA003F40D0"
 STYLE="TOP:148pt;LEFT:296pt;WIDTH:62pt;HEIGHT:16pt;ZINDEX:5;">
        <PARAM NAME="Caption" VALUE="SubTotal">
        <PARAM NAME="Size" VALUE="2202;564">
        <PARAM NAME="FontName" VALUE="Times New Roman">
        <PARAM NAME="FontHeight" VALUE="240">
        <PARAM NAME="FontCharSet" VALUE="0">
        <PARAM NAME="FontPitchAndFamily" VALUE="2">
        <PARAM NAME="ParagraphAlign" VALUE="2">
</OBJECT>
<OBJECT ID="lblShipping"
 CLASSID="CLSID:978C9E23-D4B0-11CE-BF2D-00AA003F40D0"
 STYLE="TOP:164pt;LEFT:296pt;WIDTH:62pt;HEIGHT:16pt;ZINDEX:6;">
        <PARAM NAME="Caption" VALUE="SubTotal">
        <PARAM NAME="Size" VALUE="2202;564">
        <PARAM NAME="FontName" VALUE="Times New Roman">
        <PARAM NAME="FontHeight" VALUE="240">
        <PARAM NAME="FontCharSet" VALUE="0">
        <PARAM NAME="FontPitchAndFamily" VALUE="2">
        <PARAM NAME="ParagraphAlign" VALUE="2">
</OBJECT>
<OBJECT ID="lblTotal"
 CLASSID="CLSID:978C9E23-D4B0-11CE-BF2D-00AA003F40D0"
 STYLE="TOP:179pt;LEFT:296pt;WIDTH:62pt;HEIGHT:16pt;ZINDEX:7;">
```

continues

Listing 8.16. continued

```
            <PARAM NAME="Caption" VALUE="SubTotal">
            <PARAM NAME="Size" VALUE="2202;564">
            <PARAM NAME="FontName" VALUE="Times New Roman">
            <PARAM NAME="FontHeight" VALUE="240">
            <PARAM NAME="FontCharSet" VALUE="0">
            <PARAM NAME="FontPitchAndFamily" VALUE="2">
            <PARAM NAME="ParagraphAlign" VALUE="2">
        </OBJECT>
        <OBJECT ID="LBOrder"
         CLASSID="CLSID:8BD21D20-EC42-11CE-9E0D-00AA006002F3"
    STYLE="TOP:23pt;LEFT:226pt;WIDTH:151pt;HEIGHT:119pt;TABINDEX:1;ZINDEX:8;">
            <PARAM NAME="ScrollBars" VALUE="3">
            <PARAM NAME="DisplayStyle" VALUE="2">
            <PARAM NAME="Size" VALUE="5341;4205">
            <PARAM NAME="ColumnCount" VALUE="2">
            <PARAM NAME="cColumnInfo" VALUE="1">
            <PARAM NAME="MatchEntry" VALUE="0">
            <PARAM NAME="FontCharSet" VALUE="0">
            <PARAM NAME="FontPitchAndFamily" VALUE="2">
            <PARAM NAME="Width" VALUE="2645">
        </OBJECT>
        <OBJECT ID="LBInventory"
         CLASSID="CLSID:8BD21D20-EC42-11CE-9E0D-00AA006002F3"
         STYLE="TOP:23pt;LEFT:10pt;WIDTH:153pt;HEIGHT:119pt;TABINDEX:0;ZINDEX:9;">
            <PARAM NAME="ScrollBars" VALUE="3">
            <PARAM NAME="DisplayStyle" VALUE="2">
            <PARAM NAME="Size" VALUE="5405;4185">
            <PARAM NAME="ColumnCount" VALUE="2">
            <PARAM NAME="cColumnInfo" VALUE="1">
            <PARAM NAME="MatchEntry" VALUE="0">
            <PARAM NAME="FontCharSet" VALUE="0">
            <PARAM NAME="FontPitchAndFamily" VALUE="2">
            <PARAM NAME="Width" VALUE="2645">
        </OBJECT>
</DIV>
```

Note that the ColumnCount property on both list boxes is set to 2. This is to provide automatic alignment in the list box for the name and price fields. It also facilitates using the list property of the list box to add and obtain information. The very first subroutine, the onload event of the Layout control, uses the list to load the Lbinventory list box with the names and prices of your inventory. The next two functions use the click events of the buttons to add to or subtract from the lbOrder list box. The subroutine CalcTotals, called inside each button's click event, calculates the subtotal, shipping, and grand total of the items in the lbOrder list box. The function MakeDollar changes this number to formatted currency strings. The most interesting function is SetOrderInfo, which writes information about the order to a text string and then uses the following line to place the Orderinfo string into the variable OrderInfo in the form named ORDERFORM:

A VBScript Application

```
window.document.ORDERFORM.OrderInfo.Value = OrderInfo
```

ORDERFORM exists on the page where sales.alx is placed, as shown in Listing 8.17.

Listing 8.17. sales.htm.

```
<HTML>
<HEAD>

<META NAME="GENERATOR" CONTENT="Internet Assistant for Microsoft Word 2.0z">
<TITLE>Untitled</TITLE>
</HEAD>
<BODY>
<P>
<IMG SRC="logo.bmp">
<HR=2><P>

<OBJECT CLASSID="CLSID:812AE312-8B8E-11CF-93C8-00AA00C08FDF"
ID="Sales_alx" STYLE="LEFT:0;TOP:0">
<PARAM NAME="ALXPATH" REF VALUE="file:\source\chap08\finished\Sales.alx"">
 </OBJECT>
<HR=2><P>

<OBJECT CLASSID="CLSID:812AE312-8B8E-11CF-93C8-00AA00C08FDF"
ID="Order_alx" STYLE="LEFT:0;TOP:0">
<PARAM NAME="ALXPATH" REF VALUE="file:\source\chap08\finished\Order.alx"">
 </OBJECT>
<HR=2><P>
    <FORM ACTION="/scripts/salord.idc" METHOD="POST" NAME="ORDERFORM">
        <INPUT TYPE=Hidden NAME="LastName">
        <INPUT TYPE=Hidden NAME="FirstName">
        <INPUT TYPE=Hidden NAME="SaleDate">
        <INPUT TYPE=Hidden NAME="SaleTime">
        <INPUT TYPE=Hidden NAME="ShipToAddr1">
      <INPUT TYPE=Hidden NAME="ShipToCity">
        <INPUT TYPE=Hidden NAME="ShipToState">
        <INPUT TYPE=Hidden NAME="ShipToZip">
        <INPUT TYPE=Hidden NAME="CardNumber">
        <INPUT TYPE=Hidden NAME="ShipToPhone">
        <INPUT TYPE=Hidden NAME="ShipVIA">
        <INPUT TYPE=Hidden NAME="OrderInfo">
        <INPUT TYPE=Hidden NAME="PaymentMethod">
        <INPUT TYPE=Hidden NAME="Status">
    </FORM>

<A HREF="welcome.htm" >Back to Welcome Page</A>
</BODY>
</HTML>
```

This new `sales.htm` evolves from the `sales.htm` you did earlier (refer to Listing 8.3) combined with `salord.htm`, which you generated with the Internet Information Service Add-In (see Listing 8.8). Access the <FORM> section from the second `alx` file on this page, `order.alx`. Use eight text boxes, ten labels, two buttons, and three radio buttons (as shown in Figure 8.15).

Figure 8.15.
Layout for `order.alx`.

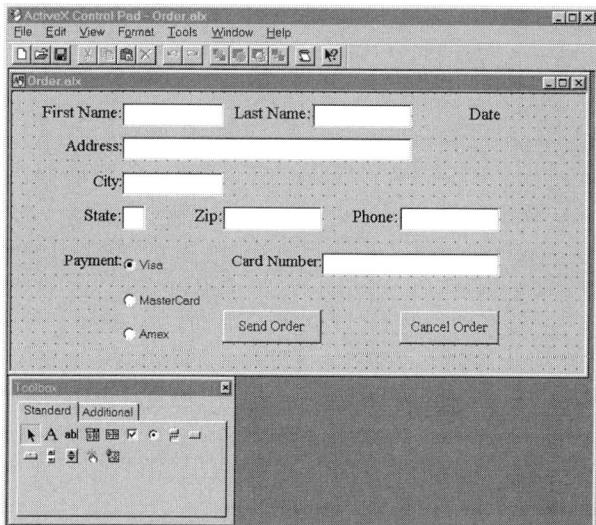

Write the code and configure the controls as a shown in Listing 8.18.

Listing 8.18. `order.alx`.

```
<SCRIPT LANGUAGE="VBScript">
<!--
Sub LoadFORM()
if window.document.forms.count > 0 then 'only if page contains forms
  For I = 0 to window.document.ORDERFORM.elements.count -1
    Select Case window.document.ORDERFORM.elements(i).name
      Case "LastName"
        window.document.ORDERFORM.LastName.Value = LastName.Text
      Case "FirstName"
        window.document.ORDERFORM.FirstName.Value = FirstName.Text
      Case "ShipToAddr1"
        window.document.ORDERFORM.ShipToAddr1.Value = ShipToAddr1.Text
      Case "ShipToCity"
        window.document.ORDERFORM.ShipToCity.Value = ShipToCity.Text
      Case "ShipToState"
        window.document.ORDERFORM.ShipToState.Value = ShipToState.Text
      Case "ShipToZip"
        window.document.ORDERFORM.ShipToZip.Value = ShipToZip.Text
```

A VBScript Application

```
        Case "ShipToPhone"
          window.document.ORDERFORM.ShipToPhone.Value = ShipToPhone.Text
        Case "PaymentMethod"
          window.document.ORDERFORM.PaymentMethod.Value = payment
        Case "SaleDate"
          window.document.ORDERFORM.SaleDate.Value = date
        Case "SaleTime"
          window.document.ORDERFORM.SaleTime.Value = time
        Case "CardNumber"
            window.document.ORDERFORM.CardNumber.Value = CardNumber.Text
        Case Else
      End Select
  Next
end if
end sub
-->
</SCRIPT>
<SCRIPT LANGUAGE="VBScript">
<!--

dim Payment

Sub btnSend_Click()
if checkfields() then
  LoadFORM()
  window.document.Forms(0).submit
end if
end sub
-->
</SCRIPT>
<SCRIPT LANGUAGE="VBScript">
<!--
Sub visa_Click()
payment = "Visa"
end sub
-->
</SCRIPT>
<SCRIPT LANGUAGE="VBScript">
<!--
Sub amex_Click()
payment = "American Express"
end sub
-->
</SCRIPT>
<SCRIPT LANGUAGE="VBScript">
<!--
Sub mc_Click()
payment = "MasterCard"
end sub
-->
</SCRIPT>
<SCRIPT LANGUAGE="VBScript">
<!--
Function CheckFields()
```

continues

Listing 8.18. continued

```
'Rotate through all the fields to
'make sure the user has filled them in

AllOK = True
ListOProblems = ""

if len(firstname.text)= 0 then
  AllOK = False
  ListOProblems = ListOProblems & "First Name, "
end if
if len(lastname.text)= 0 then
  AllOK = False
  ListOProblems = ListOProblems & "Last Name, "
end if
if len(shiptoaddr1.text)= 0 then
  AllOK = False
  ListOProblems = ListOProblems & "Address, "
end if
if len(shiptocity.text)= 0 then
  AllOK = False
  ListOProblems = ListOProblems & "City, "
end if
if len(shiptostate.text)= 0 then
  AllOK = False
  ListOProblems = ListOProblems & "State, "
end if
if len(shiptoPhone.text)= 0 then
  AllOK = False
  ListOProblems = ListOProblems & "Phone, "
end if
if len(shiptozip.text)= 0 then
  AllOK = False
  ListOProblems = ListOProblems & "Zip, "
end if
if len(cardnumber.text)= 0 then
  AllOK = False
  ListOProblems = ListOProblems & "CardNumber, "
end if
if len(window.document.ORDERFORM.OrderInfo.Value)= 0 then
  AllOK = False
  ListOProblems = ListOProblems & "No Orders, "
end if
if AllOK = True then
 CheckFields = True
else
 CheckFields = False
 Alert("The following fields need to be filled in:  " & ListOProblems)
end if
end function
Sub Layout1_OnLoad()
SaleDate.Caption = CStr(date)
payment = "VISA"
end sub
-->
```

A VBScript Application

```
</SCRIPT>
<SCRIPT LANGUAGE="VBScript">
<!--
Sub btnCancel_Click()
firstname.text = ""
lastname.text = ""
shiptoaddr1.text = ""
shiptocity.text = ""
shiptostate.text = ""
shiptoPhone.text = ""
shiptozip.text = ""
cardnumber.text = ""
end sub
-->
</SCRIPT>
<DIV ID="Layout1" STYLE="LAYOUT:FIXED;WIDTH:403pt;HEIGHT:190pt;">
    <OBJECT ID="Label1"
     CLASSID="CLSID:978C9E23-D4B0-11CE-BF2D-00AA003F40D0"
     STYLE="TOP:8pt;LEFT:16pt;WIDTH:62pt;HEIGHT:16pt;ZINDEX:0;">
        <PARAM NAME="Caption" VALUE="First Name:">
        <PARAM NAME="Size" VALUE="2187;564">
        <PARAM NAME="FontName" VALUE="Times New Roman">
        <PARAM NAME="FontHeight" VALUE="240">
        <PARAM NAME="FontCharSet" VALUE="0">
        <PARAM NAME="FontPitchAndFamily" VALUE="2">
        <PARAM NAME="ParagraphAlign" VALUE="2">
    </OBJECT>
    <OBJECT ID="Label2"
     CLASSID="CLSID:978C9E23-D4B0-11CE-BF2D-00AA003F40D0"
     STYLE="TOP:31pt;LEFT:16pt;WIDTH:62pt;HEIGHT:16pt;ZINDEX:1;">
        <PARAM NAME="Caption" VALUE="Address:">
        <PARAM NAME="Size" VALUE="2187;564">
        <PARAM NAME="FontName" VALUE="Times New Roman">
        <PARAM NAME="FontHeight" VALUE="240">
        <PARAM NAME="FontCharSet" VALUE="0">
        <PARAM NAME="FontPitchAndFamily" VALUE="2">
        <PARAM NAME="ParagraphAlign" VALUE="2">
    </OBJECT>
    <OBJECT ID="Label3"
     CLASSID="CLSID:978C9E23-D4B0-11CE-BF2D-00AA003F40D0"
     STYLE="TOP:55pt;LEFT:16pt;WIDTH:62pt;HEIGHT:16pt;ZINDEX:2;">
        <PARAM NAME="Caption" VALUE="City:">
        <PARAM NAME="Size" VALUE="2187;564">
        <PARAM NAME="FontName" VALUE="Times New Roman">
        <PARAM NAME="FontHeight" VALUE="240">
        <PARAM NAME="FontCharSet" VALUE="0">
        <PARAM NAME="FontPitchAndFamily" VALUE="2">
        <PARAM NAME="ParagraphAlign" VALUE="2">
    </OBJECT>
    <OBJECT ID="Label4"
     CLASSID="CLSID:978C9E23-D4B0-11CE-BF2D-00AA003F40D0"
     STYLE="TOP:78pt;LEFT:16pt;WIDTH:62pt;HEIGHT:16pt;ZINDEX:3;">
        <PARAM NAME="Caption" VALUE="State:">
        <PARAM NAME="Size" VALUE="2187;564">
```

continues

Listing 8.18. continued

```
        <PARAM NAME="FontName" VALUE="Times New Roman">
        <PARAM NAME="FontHeight" VALUE="240">
        <PARAM NAME="FontCharSet" VALUE="0">
        <PARAM NAME="FontPitchAndFamily" VALUE="2">
        <PARAM NAME="ParagraphAlign" VALUE="2">
</OBJECT>
<OBJECT ID="Label5"
 CLASSID="CLSID:978C9E23-D4B0-11CE-BF2D-00AA003F40D0"
 STYLE="TOP:8pt;LEFT:148pt;WIDTH:62pt;HEIGHT:16pt;ZINDEX:4;">
        <PARAM NAME="Caption" VALUE="Last Name:">
        <PARAM NAME="Size" VALUE="2187;564">
        <PARAM NAME="FontName" VALUE="Times New Roman">
        <PARAM NAME="FontHeight" VALUE="240">
        <PARAM NAME="FontCharSet" VALUE="0">
        <PARAM NAME="FontPitchAndFamily" VALUE="2">
        <PARAM NAME="ParagraphAlign" VALUE="2">
</OBJECT>
<OBJECT ID="Label6"
 CLASSID="CLSID:978C9E23-D4B0-11CE-BF2D-00AA003F40D0"
 STYLE="TOP:78pt;LEFT:117pt;WIDTH:31pt;HEIGHT:16pt;ZINDEX:5;">
        <PARAM NAME="Caption" VALUE="Zip:">
        <PARAM NAME="Size" VALUE="1094;564">
        <PARAM NAME="FontName" VALUE="Times New Roman">
        <PARAM NAME="FontHeight" VALUE="240">
        <PARAM NAME="FontCharSet" VALUE="0">
        <PARAM NAME="FontPitchAndFamily" VALUE="2">
        <PARAM NAME="ParagraphAlign" VALUE="2">
</OBJECT>
<OBJECT ID="Label7"
 CLASSID="CLSID:978C9E23-D4B0-11CE-BF2D-00AA003F40D0"
 STYLE="TOP:78pt;LEFT:234pt;WIDTH:38pt;HEIGHT:16pt;ZINDEX:6;">
        <PARAM NAME="Caption" VALUE="Phone:">
        <PARAM NAME="Size" VALUE="1341;564">
        <PARAM NAME="FontName" VALUE="Times New Roman">
        <PARAM NAME="FontHeight" VALUE="240">
        <PARAM NAME="FontCharSet" VALUE="0">
        <PARAM NAME="FontPitchAndFamily" VALUE="2">
        <PARAM NAME="ParagraphAlign" VALUE="2">
</OBJECT>
<OBJECT ID="FirstName"
 CLASSID="CLSID:8BD21D10-EC42-11CE-9E0D-00AA006002F3"
 STYLE="TOP:8pt;LEFT:78pt;WIDTH:70pt;HEIGHT:16pt;TABINDEX:7;ZINDEX:7;">
        <PARAM NAME="VariousPropertyBits" VALUE="746604571">
        <PARAM NAME="Size" VALUE="2469;564">
        <PARAM NAME="FontCharSet" VALUE="0">
        <PARAM NAME="FontPitchAndFamily" VALUE="2">
</OBJECT>
<OBJECT ID="LastName"
 CLASSID="CLSID:8BD21D10-EC42-11CE-9E0D-00AA006002F3"
 STYLE="TOP:8pt;LEFT:211pt;WIDTH:70pt;HEIGHT:16pt;TABINDEX:8;ZINDEX:8;">
        <PARAM NAME="VariousPropertyBits" VALUE="746604571">
        <PARAM NAME="Size" VALUE="2469;564">
        <PARAM NAME="FontCharSet" VALUE="0">
        <PARAM NAME="FontPitchAndFamily" VALUE="2">
```

A VBScript Application

```
    </OBJECT>
    <OBJECT ID="ShipToAddr1"
     CLASSID="CLSID:8BD21D10-EC42-11CE-9E0D-00AA006002F3"
     STYLE="TOP:31pt;LEFT:78pt;WIDTH:203pt;HEIGHT:16pt;TABINDEX:9;ZINDEX:9;">
        <PARAM NAME="VariousPropertyBits" VALUE="746604571">
        <PARAM NAME="Size" VALUE="7161;564">
        <PARAM NAME="FontCharSet" VALUE="0">
        <PARAM NAME="FontPitchAndFamily" VALUE="2">
    </OBJECT>
    <OBJECT ID="ShipToCity"
     CLASSID="CLSID:8BD21D10-EC42-11CE-9E0D-00AA006002F3"
     STYLE="TOP:55pt;LEFT:78pt;WIDTH:70pt;HEIGHT:16pt;TABINDEX:10;ZINDEX:10;">
        <PARAM NAME="VariousPropertyBits" VALUE="746604571">
        <PARAM NAME="Size" VALUE="2469;564">
        <PARAM NAME="FontCharSet" VALUE="0">
        <PARAM NAME="FontPitchAndFamily" VALUE="2">
    </OBJECT>
    <OBJECT ID="ShipToState"
     CLASSID="CLSID:8BD21D10-EC42-11CE-9E0D-00AA006002F3"
     STYLE="TOP:78pt;LEFT:78pt;WIDTH:16pt;HEIGHT:16pt;TABINDEX:11;ZINDEX:11;">
        <PARAM NAME="VariousPropertyBits" VALUE="746604571">
        <PARAM NAME="Size" VALUE="564;564">
        <PARAM NAME="FontCharSet" VALUE="0">
        <PARAM NAME="FontPitchAndFamily" VALUE="2">
    </OBJECT>
    <OBJECT ID="ShipToZip"
     CLASSID="CLSID:8BD21D10-EC42-11CE-9E0D-00AA006002F3"
STYLE="TOP:78pt;LEFT:148pt;WIDTH:70pt;HEIGHT:16pt;TABINDEX:12;ZINDEX:12;">
        <PARAM NAME="VariousPropertyBits" VALUE="746604571">
        <PARAM NAME="Size" VALUE="2469;564">
        <PARAM NAME="FontCharSet" VALUE="0">
        <PARAM NAME="FontPitchAndFamily" VALUE="2">
    </OBJECT>
    <OBJECT ID="ShipToPhone"
     CLASSID="CLSID:8BD21D10-EC42-11CE-9E0D-00AA006002F3"
STYLE="TOP:78pt;LEFT:273pt;WIDTH:70pt;HEIGHT:16pt;TABINDEX:13;ZINDEX:13;">
        <PARAM NAME="VariousPropertyBits" VALUE="746604571">
        <PARAM NAME="Size" VALUE="2469;564">
        <PARAM NAME="FontCharSet" VALUE="0">
        <PARAM NAME="FontPitchAndFamily" VALUE="2">
    </OBJECT>
    <OBJECT ID="visa"
     CLASSID="CLSID:8BD21D50-EC42-11CE-9E0D-00AA006002F3"
STYLE="TOP:109pt;LEFT:78pt;WIDTH:66pt;HEIGHT:18pt;TABINDEX:14;ZINDEX:14;">
        <PARAM NAME="BackColor" VALUE="2147483663">
        <PARAM NAME="ForeColor" VALUE="2147483666">
        <PARAM NAME="DisplayStyle" VALUE="5">
        <PARAM NAME="Size" VALUE="2328;635">
        <PARAM NAME="Value" VALUE="True">
        <PARAM NAME="Caption" VALUE="Visa">
        <PARAM NAME="GroupName" VALUE="PaymentMethod">
        <PARAM NAME="FontCharSet" VALUE="0">
        <PARAM NAME="FontPitchAndFamily" VALUE="2">
    </OBJECT>
    <OBJECT ID="amex"
```

continues

Listing 8.18. continued

```
            CLASSID="CLSID:8BD21D50-EC42-11CE-9E0D-00AA006002F3"
 STYLE="TOP:156pt;LEFT:78pt;WIDTH:68pt;HEIGHT:18pt;TABINDEX:15;ZINDEX:15;">
            <PARAM NAME="BackColor" VALUE="2147483663">
            <PARAM NAME="ForeColor" VALUE="2147483666">
            <PARAM NAME="DisplayStyle" VALUE="5">
            <PARAM NAME="Size" VALUE="2399;635">
            <PARAM NAME="Value" VALUE="False">
            <PARAM NAME="Caption" VALUE="Amex">
            <PARAM NAME="GroupName" VALUE="PaymentMethod">
            <PARAM NAME="FontCharSet" VALUE="0">
            <PARAM NAME="FontPitchAndFamily" VALUE="2">
        </OBJECT>
        <OBJECT ID="mc"
         CLASSID="CLSID:8BD21D50-EC42-11CE-9E0D-00AA006002F3"
 STYLE="TOP:133pt;LEFT:78pt;WIDTH:65pt;HEIGHT:18pt;TABINDEX:16;ZINDEX:16;">
            <PARAM NAME="BackColor" VALUE="2147483663">
            <PARAM NAME="ForeColor" VALUE="2147483666">
            <PARAM NAME="DisplayStyle" VALUE="5">
            <PARAM NAME="Size" VALUE="2293;635">
            <PARAM NAME="Value" VALUE="False">
            <PARAM NAME="Caption" VALUE="MasterCard">
            <PARAM NAME="GroupName" VALUE="PaymentMethod">
            <PARAM NAME="FontCharSet" VALUE="0">
            <PARAM NAME="FontPitchAndFamily" VALUE="2">
        </OBJECT>
        <OBJECT ID="Label8"
         CLASSID="CLSID:978C9E23-D4B0-11CE-BF2D-00AA003F40D0"
         STYLE="TOP:109pt;LEFT:16pt;WIDTH:62pt;HEIGHT:16pt;ZINDEX:17;">
            <PARAM NAME="Caption" VALUE="Payment:">
            <PARAM NAME="Size" VALUE="2187;564">
            <PARAM NAME="FontName" VALUE="Times New Roman">
            <PARAM NAME="FontHeight" VALUE="240">
            <PARAM NAME="FontCharSet" VALUE="0">
            <PARAM NAME="FontPitchAndFamily" VALUE="2">
            <PARAM NAME="ParagraphAlign" VALUE="2">
        </OBJECT>
        <OBJECT ID="Label9"
         CLASSID="CLSID:978C9E23-D4B0-11CE-BF2D-00AA003F40D0"
         STYLE="TOP:109pt;LEFT:148pt;WIDTH:70pt;HEIGHT:16pt;ZINDEX:18;">
            <PARAM NAME="Caption" VALUE="Card Number:">
            <PARAM NAME="Size" VALUE="2469;564">
            <PARAM NAME="FontName" VALUE="Times New Roman">
            <PARAM NAME="FontHeight" VALUE="240">
            <PARAM NAME="FontCharSet" VALUE="0">
            <PARAM NAME="FontPitchAndFamily" VALUE="2">
            <PARAM NAME="ParagraphAlign" VALUE="2">
        </OBJECT>
        <OBJECT ID="CardNumber"
         CLASSID="CLSID:8BD21D10-EC42-11CE-9E0D-00AA006002F3"
 STYLE="TOP:109pt;LEFT:218pt;WIDTH:125pt;HEIGHT:16pt;TABINDEX:19;ZINDEX:19;">
            <PARAM NAME="VariousPropertyBits" VALUE="746604571">
```

A VBScript Application

```
            <PARAM NAME="Size" VALUE="4410;564">
            <PARAM NAME="FontCharSet" VALUE="0">
            <PARAM NAME="FontPitchAndFamily" VALUE="2">
        </OBJECT>
        <OBJECT ID="btnSend"
          CLASSID="CLSID:D7053240-CE69-11CD-A777-00DD01143C57"
 STYLE="TOP:148pt;LEFT:148pt;WIDTH:70pt;HEIGHT:23pt;TABINDEX:20;ZINDEX:20;">
            <PARAM NAME="Caption" VALUE="Send Order">
            <PARAM NAME="Size" VALUE="2469;811">
            <PARAM NAME="FontName" VALUE="Times New Roman">
            <PARAM NAME="FontHeight" VALUE="200">
            <PARAM NAME="FontCharSet" VALUE="0">
            <PARAM NAME="FontPitchAndFamily" VALUE="2">
            <PARAM NAME="ParagraphAlign" VALUE="3">
        </OBJECT>
        <OBJECT ID="btnCancel"
          CLASSID="CLSID:D7053240-CE69-11CD-A777-00DD01143C57"
 STYLE="TOP:148pt;LEFT:273pt;WIDTH:70pt;HEIGHT:23pt;TABINDEX:21;ZINDEX:21;">
            <PARAM NAME="Caption" VALUE="Cancel Order">
            <PARAM NAME="Size" VALUE="2469;811">
            <PARAM NAME="FontName" VALUE="Times New Roman">
            <PARAM NAME="FontHeight" VALUE="200">
            <PARAM NAME="FontCharSet" VALUE="0">
            <PARAM NAME="FontPitchAndFamily" VALUE="2">
            <PARAM NAME="ParagraphAlign" VALUE="3">
        </OBJECT>
        <OBJECT ID="SaleDate"
          CLASSID="CLSID:978C9E23-D4B0-11CE-BF2D-00AA003F40D0"
            STYLE="TOP:8pt;LEFT:289pt;WIDTH:55pt;HEIGHT:16pt;ZINDEX:22;">
            <PARAM NAME="Caption" VALUE="Date">
            <PARAM NAME="Size" VALUE="1940;564">
            <PARAM NAME="FontName" VALUE="Times New Roman">
            <PARAM NAME="FontHeight" VALUE="240">
            <PARAM NAME="FontCharSet" VALUE="0">
            <PARAM NAME="FontPitchAndFamily" VALUE="2">
            <PARAM NAME="ParagraphAlign" VALUE="2">
        </OBJECT>
</DIV>
```

This code starts with a load form function that transfers the data in the controls contained in order.alx to the hidden controls in sales.htm (refer to Listing 8.17). Notice the use of the select case structure and how the variables in the <FORM> section are accessed using the elements property. The rest of the functions are straightforward. They include a function for clearing all the text, btnCancel_Click(), and another for ensuring that all the fields have been filled in, CheckFields(). The next notable code is the click event of the btnSend button. The click event for the btnSend button submits the data in the <FORM> tags to salord.idc using window.document.Forms(0).submit. This allows you to have the Submit button inside the alx object rather than on the page with the <FORM> section. salord.idc is shown in Listing 8.19.

Listing 8.19. `salord.idc`.

```
Datasource: BikeShop
Template: salord.htx
DefaultParameters: Status = "Ordered"
SQLStatement:
+INSERT INTO "ORDERS" ("LastName", "FirstName","ShipToAddr1",
"ShipToCity", "ShipToState", "ShipToZip", "ShipToPhone",
"PaymentMethod", "SaleDate", "SaleTime", "OrderInfo", "Status", "CardNumber")
+VALUES ('%LastName%','%FirstName%', '%ShipToAddr1%','%ShipToCity%',
'%ShipToState%', '%ShipToZip%', '%ShipToPhone%','%PaymentMethod%',#%SaleDate%#,
#%SaleTime%#, '%OrderInfo%','%Status%', '%CardNumber%');
#IDC-Insert FrontHTM-step2.htm ReportHTX-salord.htx
```

`salord.idc` is only slightly changed from what you saw in Listing 8.10. The real magic in this section comes in the template file, `salord.htx`, shown in Listing 8.20.

Listing 8.20. `salord.htx`.

```
<HTML>
<HEAD><Title>InterMedia</Title>
<%IF idc.LastName EQ "NULL" %>
<BODY BGCOLOR="#FFFFFF">
Nothing Happened
</BODY></HTML>
<%else%>
<SCRIPT LANGUAGE="VBScript">
<!--


Sub LoadMe()
  window.ORDERNUM.LastName.Value = "<%idc.LastName%>"
  window.ORDERNUM.SaleDate.Value = "<%idc.SaleDate%>"
  window.ORDERNUM.SaleTime.Value = "<%idc.SaleTime%>"
  window.document.Forms(0).submit
end sub
-->
</SCRIPT>

</HEAD>

<BODY BGCOLOR="#FFFFFF" Language ="VBScript"  onLoad = Loadme>

    <FORM ACTION="/scripts/ordernum.idc" METHOD="POST" NAME="ORDERNUM">
        <INPUT TYPE=Hidden NAME="LastName">
        <INPUT TYPE=Hidden NAME="SaleDate">
        <INPUT TYPE=Hidden NAME="SaleTime">
    </FORM>



</BODY></HTML>
<%endif%>
```

This is nothing like the salord.htm (refer to Listing 8.8) you generated at the beginning of the day. The new salord.htm generates a form, which in turn generates yet another form that returns an order number to the user. The Loadme subroutine, which is set to the form's onload event, loads and submits the <FORM> ORDERNUM as soon as the form is loaded, which calls ordernum.idc, shown in Listing 8.21.

Listing 8.21. ordernum.idc.

```
Datasource: BikeShop
Template: ordernum.htx
DefaultParameters:
SQLStatement:
+Select "OrderNumber"
+From "ORDERS"
+Where "LastName" Like '%LastName%'
+And "SaleTime" = #%SaleTime%#
+And "SaleDate" = #%SaleDate%#
#IDC-Insert FrontHTM-step2.htm ReportHTX-ordernum.htx
```

This code gets the order number from the database after the data is inserted by salord.idc. The order number is an auto-number data type. Access assigns a unique number to the auto-number type for every new record. The order number is presented in a straightforward way by ordernum.htx, as shown in Listing 8.22.

Listing 8.22. ordernum.htx.

```
<HTML>
<HEAD><Title>Order Number</Title></HEAD>
<BODY BGCOLOR="#FFFFFF">
<CENTER><IMG SRC="/logo.bmp"><BR></CENTER>
<%begindetail%>
<P>
<P>
<CENTER>
<P><B>Thank You For Shopping At JPBikes!</B><BR>
<P><B>Order Received from <%idc.LastName%></B><BR>
<P><B>On <%idc.SaleDate%> at <%idc.SaleTime%></B><BR>
<P><B>This is your Order Number</B><BR>
<P><B><%OrderNumber%></B><BR>
<P><B>Keep it for your records</B><BR>
</CENTER>
<%enddetail%>

<%if CurrentRecord EQ 0 %>
<HR=2><P>
```

continues

Listing 8.22. continued

```
<CENTER><B>Can't Find Order for %LastName%<B></CENTER><P>
<CENTER><B>Call us at 904 555 1010 for assistance!<B></CENTER><P>
<%endif%>

<CENTER><A HREF="/sales.htm">Return To Data Entry Page</A></CENTER>
<HR=2>
<CENTER>I Made this Page By Hand</B></CENTER>
</BODY></HTML>
```

Notice how this form uses the JPBikes! logo that you used on the other main forms. The logo is another chance to advertise your company on the order confirmation form. This form, shown in Figure 8.16, also gives the user a tracking number and shows that the order has been placed successfully in the database.

Figure 8.16.
The order-tracking number.

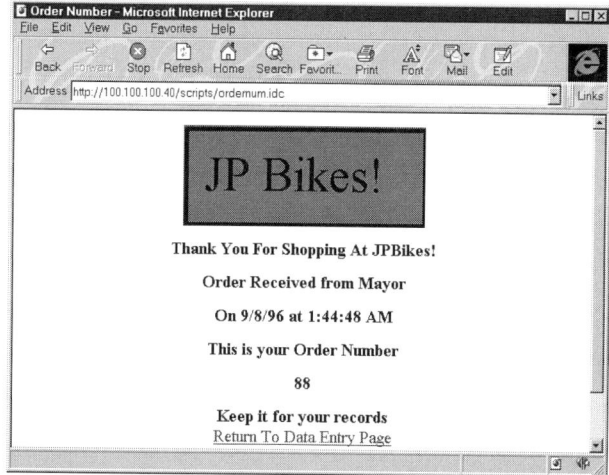

Now that you have manipulated a <FORM> section from inside an ActiveX Control Pad-built alx object and generated a file with code that enabled it to launch another job, let's finish the project.

The Order-Tracking Page

This page has a simple purpose: to let the user find out the status of an order by entering the order number you worked so hard to provide in the last section. To do this, place three buttons and a text box on an HTML insert, as shown in Figure 8.17.

A VBScript Application

Figure 8.17.
Screen layout for `track.alx`.

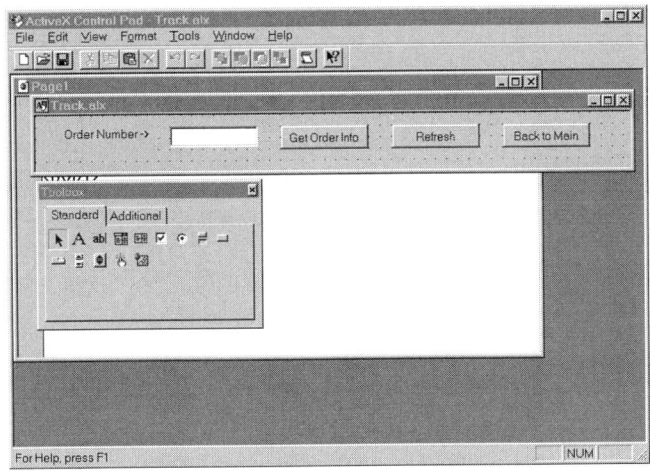

Configure and name the controls using Listing 8.23.

Listing 8.23. `track.alx`.

```
<SCRIPT LANGUAGE="VBScript">
<!--
Sub btnGetOrder_Click()
 'Build form in Second frame
  parent.secondframe.document.TRACKFORM.Ordernumber.Value = edtOrderNumber.Text
  parent.secondframe.document.TRACKFORM.submit
  btnGetOrder.Enabled = False

end sub
-->
</SCRIPT>
<SCRIPT LANGUAGE="VBScript">
<!--
Sub btnRefresh_Click()
  parent.secondframe.location.href = "/target.htm"
  btnGetOrder.Enabled = True
end sub
-->
</SCRIPT>
<SCRIPT LANGUAGE="VBScript">
<!--
Sub btnBacktoMain_Click()
  parent.location.href = "/welcome.htm"
end sub
-->
```

continues

Listing 8.23. continued

```
        </SCRIPT>
        <DIV ID="Layout1" STYLE="LAYOUT:FIXED;WIDTH:419pt;HEIGHT:38pt;">
            <OBJECT ID="btnGetOrder"
             CLASSID="CLSID:D7053240-CE69-11CD-A777-00DD01143C57"
             CODEBASE="PE"
             STYLE="TOP:8pt;LEFT:172pt;WIDTH:62pt;HEIGHT:16pt;TABINDEX:0;ZINDEX:0;">
                <PARAM NAME="Caption" VALUE="Get Order Info">
                <PARAM NAME="Size" VALUE="2187;564">
                <PARAM NAME="FontCharSet" VALUE="0">
                <PARAM NAME="FontPitchAndFamily" VALUE="2">
                <PARAM NAME="ParagraphAlign" VALUE="3">
            </OBJECT>
            <OBJECT ID="edtOrderNumber"
             CLASSID="CLSID:8BD21D10-EC42-11CE-9E0D-00AA006002F3"
             CODEBASE="PE"
             STYLE="TOP:8pt;LEFT:94pt;WIDTH:62pt;HEIGHT:14pt;TABINDEX:1;ZINDEX:1;">
                <PARAM NAME="VariousPropertyBits" VALUE="746604571">
                <PARAM NAME="Size" VALUE="2187;494">
                <PARAM NAME="FontCharSet" VALUE="0">
                <PARAM NAME="FontPitchAndFamily" VALUE="2">
            </OBJECT>
            <OBJECT ID="Label1"
             CLASSID="CLSID:978C9E23-D4B0-11CE-BF2D-00AA003F40D0"
             CODEBASE="PE" STYLE="TOP:8pt;LEFT:8pt;WIDTH:72pt;HEIGHT:18pt;ZINDEX:2;">
                <PARAM NAME="Caption" VALUE="Order Number -&gt;">
                <PARAM NAME="Size" VALUE="2540;635">
                <PARAM NAME="FontCharSet" VALUE="0">
                <PARAM NAME="FontPitchAndFamily" VALUE="2">
                <PARAM NAME="ParagraphAlign" VALUE="2">
            </OBJECT>
            <OBJECT ID="btnRefresh"
             CLASSID="CLSID:D7053240-CE69-11CD-A777-00DD01143C57"
             CODEBASE="PE"
             STYLE="TOP:8pt;LEFT:250pt;WIDTH:62pt;HEIGHT:16pt;TABINDEX:3;ZINDEX:3;">
                <PARAM NAME="Caption" VALUE="Refresh">
                <PARAM NAME="Size" VALUE="2187;564">
                <PARAM NAME="FontCharSet" VALUE="0">
                <PARAM NAME="FontPitchAndFamily" VALUE="2">
                <PARAM NAME="ParagraphAlign" VALUE="3">
            </OBJECT>
            <OBJECT ID="btnBacktoMain"
             CLASSID="CLSID:D7053240-CE69-11CD-A777-00DD01143C57"
             CODEBASE="PE"
             STYLE="TOP:8pt;LEFT:328pt;WIDTH:62pt;HEIGHT:16pt;TABINDEX:4;ZINDEX:4;">
                <PARAM NAME="Caption" VALUE="Back to Main">
                <PARAM NAME="Size" VALUE="2187;564">
                <PARAM NAME="FontCharSet" VALUE="0">
                <PARAM NAME="FontPitchAndFamily" VALUE="2">
                <PARAM NAME="ParagraphAlign" VALUE="3">
            </OBJECT>
        </DIV>
```

To explain the few lines of code in this form, let's put track.alx in context. track.alx is placed on a simple form, trakpt1.htm, shown in Listing 8.24.

Listing 8.24. trakpt1.htm.

```
<HTML>
<HEAD>
<TITLE>New Page</TITLE>
</HEAD>
<BODY>

<OBJECT CLASSID="CLSID:812AE312-8B8E-11CF-93C8-00AA00C08FDF"
ID="Track_alx" STYLE="LEFT:0;TOP:0">
<PARAM NAME="ALXPATH" REF VALUE="file:\source\chap08\finished\Track.alx">
 </OBJECT>


</BODY>
</HTML>
```

trackpt1.htm is, in turn, placed in a frame called tkodfrm.htm, shown in Listing 8.25.

Listing 8.25. tkodfrm.htm.

```
<HTML>

<FRAMESET ROWS="10%, *">
<FRAME NAME="firstframe" SRC="trackpt1.htm">
<FRAME NAME="secondframe" SRC ="target.htm" >
</FRAMESET>


</HTML>
```

From here, track.alx manipulates the other form in the frame, target.htm, shown in Listing 8.26.

Listing 8.26. target.htm.

```
<HTML>
<PRE>
<BODY>
<FORM ACTION="/scripts/tracord.idc" METHOD="POST" NAME="TRACKFORM">
<INPUT TYPE=Hidden NAME="OrderNumber">
</FORM>
</BODY>
</PRE>
</HTML>
```

target.htm sets up a <FORM> section that communicates with the tracord.idc/tracord.htx tandem that you generated earlier (refer to Listings 8.12 and 8.13). This whole setup allows track.alx to remain visible in the top frame while the response shows up in the bottom. Notice how the click event for the GetOrder button disables the button, and the click event for Refresh re-enables it. If the user can press the GetOrder button while the returned order information is displayed, there will be errors because track.alx relies on target.htm being in the bottom frame. The button is re-enabled after the bottom frame is refreshed with target.htm. The BacktoMain button is another way of navigating back to the main screen. The results of the quest for order information is shown in Figure 8.18.

Figure 8.18.
The quest for the order number.

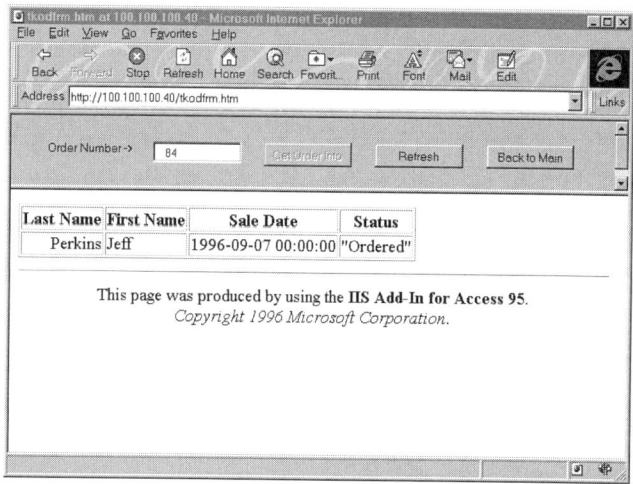

Odds and Ends

Before you implement this form on your Web site, there are a few things to consider. The first is security. The information passed in this example is plain text. You might want to implement an encryption system or keep your eyes open for an ActiveX component that encrypts for you. Second, adjust the paths on the alx objects. Note the following code:

```
<OBJECT CLASSID="CLSID:812AE312-8B8E-11CF-93C8-00AA00C08FDF"
 ID="Sales_alx" STYLE="LEFT:0;TOP:0">
<PARAM NAME="ALXPATH" REF VALUE="file:C:\Sams\ActiveX\tax08\tax08cd\Sales.alx"">
 </OBJECT>
```

The ALXPATH is set to file:C:\Sams\... (Now you know where I keep all my Sams stuff. I'll have to move it.) Unless these files are installed in exactly the same place on the client machine, they won't run. Instead, move them to the root directory of your Web site and change the reference to /Sales.alx, which will cause the client to look for the data on your Web site. On the other hand, if you are setting up an intranet or selling the components in the alx file, you might want to put this code on the client machine.

Summary

You have covered lots of ground today. Those of you who grew up with Visual Basic are probably getting pretty comfortable, while those of you who come from a C or C++ background are hoping there is an alternative in sight. Rest easy; you will spend a day building a different project in JavaScript, and the lessons learned there will expand your knowledge of and abilities with scripting and ActiveX components.

Q&A

Q Where can I find more information on how the idc and htx files work?

A http://www.microsoft.com/accessdev/accwhite/jobforpa.htm#Idc leads to a good discussion of these files. They are also covered in the Internet Information Server documentation.

Q What are the pros and cons of using alx files on Web pages?

A On the plus side, an alx file allows you to build modules that can be plugged in to many different pages. An alx file, if it is installed on the server and not the client, allows you to hide the code inside. The biggest negative is that alx files and the Layout control that reads them only work (as of this writing) on the PC platform.

Q How will alx files be used?

A I think the scripting and ActiveX components in alx files will be used to build Internet and intranet pages that look and function more like programs. I also think that as more programmers move into Internet and intranet programming, they will learn important things about layout and composition from Webmasters.

Workshop

Rewrite the Catalog order form to make it look and work like the Sales order form.

Quiz

1. On a Web site, where do the `idx`, `htx`, and `htm` files go?
2. Where can I put code that I want executed when my `alx` file starts up?
3. How do you name a `<FORM>` section of a Web page? How do you manipulate the `<FORM>` section after you have named it?

NOTE   Refer to the appendix, "Answers," for the answers to these questions.

Week 2

Day 9

A JavaScript Application

Today you will use knowledge gained yesterday to construct an application using JavaScript and ActiveX controls. You will start with the requirements for the application, do some quick design work, then implement the design.

Project Requirements

You've got a friend, let's call him JP, who runs a programming shop. He has a new project that requires daily interaction with the customer during development. The customer's headquarters are on the other coast. Both JP and the customer have an Internet connection, and JP wants to use it to facilitate the necessary technical exchange. Specifically, he wants to be able to present the current status of the project, give the user access to project documents and briefings, let the customer enter a change request, and finally, let the customer see the status of any change requests. Overall, he doesn't want this to look like a normal, billboard-type Internet site. He wants it to look and act more like one of his company's programs. He asks, "Can you do it?" You respond, "Is tomorrow too late?"

Can You Do It?

When you get back to your office, you kick yourself for your traditional, overly optimistic estimate. You start to take a look at what he wants and how you might do it.

You are lucky in that the customer knows what he wants. The worst times I have spent in the programming business revolved around customers who knew what they didn't want (normally after it was built), but couldn't quite articulate what they did want. Let's look at the basic requirements:

- A Web site
- The capability to display program status
- Access to documents and briefings
- Allowing the customer to enter a change request
- Allowing the customer to track the status of a particular change request
- A program-like look and feel

Write these down, call home, and say you will be a little late. "How late?" home asks. "Spring," you say. The first thing you want to do is create a rough layout of the Web site. On a napkin, you sketch something that looks like Figure 9.1.

Figure 9.1.
Layout of the Web site.

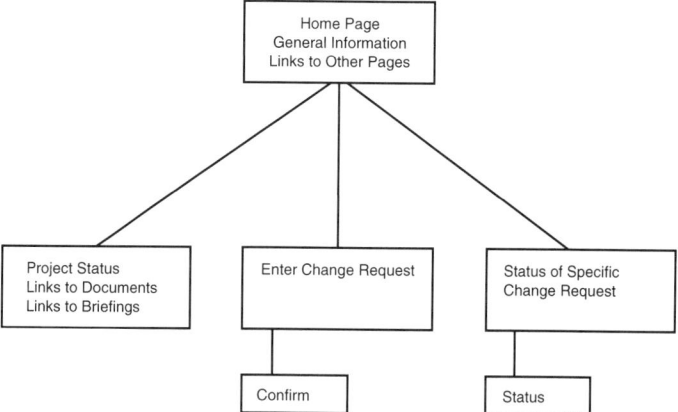

This shows a Welcome page linked to Project Status, Change Request, and Status pages. From here you will

- use Word to rough out the three main pages
- design the database in Access
- add a driver for the `BigProj` database to the system's ODBC Manager
- use the Internet Information Server Add-In for Access to create an Insert page for the Change Request page

A JavaScript Application

- [ ] use the Internet Information Server Add-In for Access to create a Search page for the Change Request Tracking page
- [ ] use the Internet Information Server Add-In for Access to create a dynamic information page

After you have done all this, you will finish the project by

- [ ] customizing the pages with products from the ActiveX Control Pad
- [ ] using a <FRAME> to give the Web site a program-like look and feel
- [ ] hacking your way into the scripts that Internet Information Server Add-In for Access creates and customizing them using JavaScript

Use Word to Rough Out the Three Main Pages

Open Word; make sure you have Internet Assistant installed (see Day 4, "The Tools of the Trade" for details). Select New from the File menu and select HTML.dot as your template. Add the logo (logo.bmp on the CD-ROM), some general welcome remarks, and links to the Project Status (projstat.htm), Change Request (chngreq.htm), and Change Request Tracking (chngtrac.htm) pages. Your screen should look like Figure 9.2.

Figure 9.2.
Welcome page for JP Programming.

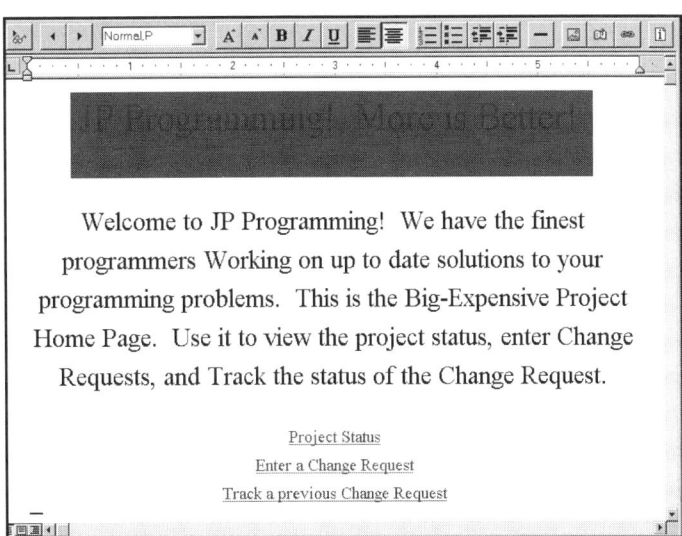

Save your work as welcome.htm. Your HTML code should look like Listing 9.1.

Listing 9.1. HTML code for `welcome.htm`.

```
<HTML>
<HEAD>
<TITLE>Untitled</TITLE>

<META NAME="GENERATOR" CONTENT="Internet Assistant for Microsoft Word 2.0z">
</HEAD>
<BODY>
<P>
<CENTER><IMG SRC="biglogo.bmp"><BR>
</CENTER>
<P>
<CENTER><FONT SIZE=5>Welcome to JP Programming!  We have the finest
</FONT></CENTER>
<P>
<CENTER><FONT SIZE=5>programmers Working on up to date solutions
to your</FONT></CENTER>
<P>
<CENTER><FONT SIZE=5>programming problems.  This is the Big-Expensive
Project</FONT></CENTER>
<P>
<CENTER><FONT SIZE=5>Home Page.  Use it to view the project status,
enter Change</FONT></CENTER>
<P>
<CENTER><FONT SIZE=5>Requests, and Track the status of the Change
Request.</FONT></CENTER>
<P>
<CENTER> </CENTER>
<P>
<CENTER><A HREF="projstat.htm" >Project Status</A></CENTER>
<P>
<CENTER><A HREF="chngreq" >Enter a Change Request</A></CENTER>
<P>
<CENTER><A HREF="chngtrac.htm" >Track a previous Change Request</A></CENTER>
</BODY>
</HTML>
```

Next, open a new HTML page in Word. This will be the Project Status page. You will be putting some ActiveX controls here later. For now, all you need is a logo, a return link to `welcome.htm`, and a link to a file called `bigproj.doc`. Your page should look like Figure 9.3.

Save your work as `projstat.htm`. Your HTML code should look like Listing 9.2.

Figure 9.3.
Project Status page.

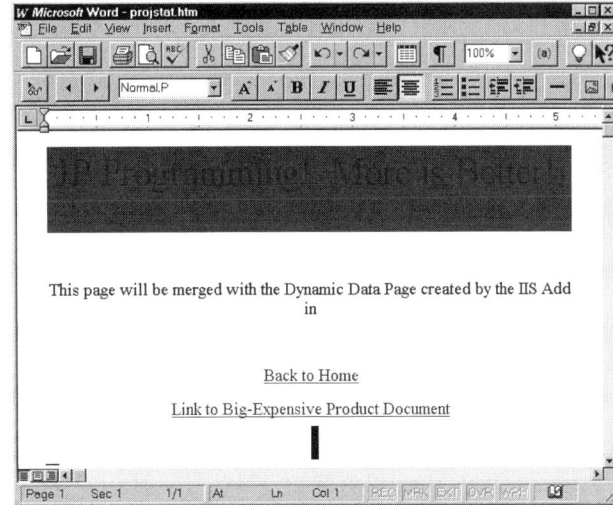

Save your work as projstat.htm. Your HTML code should look like Listing 9.2.

Listing 9.2. HTML code for projstat.htm.

```
<HTML>
<HEAD>

<META NAME="GENERATOR" CONTENT="Internet Assistant for Microsoft Word 2.0z">
<TITLE>Untitled</TITLE>
</HEAD>
<BODY>
<P>
<CENTER><IMG SRC="biglogo.bmp"><BR>
</CENTER>
<P>
<CENTER>This page will be merged with the Dynamic Data Page created
by the IIS Add in<BR>
</CENTER>
<P>
<CENTER><A HREF="welcome.htm" >Back to Home</A></CENTER>
<P>
<CENTER><A HREF="bigproj.doc" >Link to Big-Expensive Product Document</A>
<BR>
</CENTER>
</BODY>
</HTML>
```

Open a new HTML page in Word. This will be the Change Request page. You will be putting some ActiveX controls here to collect and send the Change Request. You will also add some of the code generated by Internet Information Server Add-In and generate the order from this page. Place a logo and a return link to the Welcome page (welcome.htm). Your page should look like Figure 9.4.

Figure 9.4.
Change Request page.

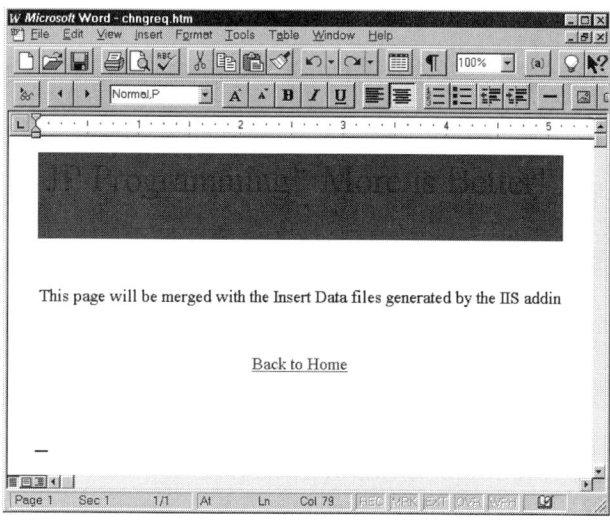

Save your work as chngreq.htm. Your HTML code should look like Listing 9.3.

Listing 9.3. HTML code for chngreq.htm.

```
<HTML>
<HEAD>

<META NAME="GENERATOR" CONTENT="Internet Assistant for Microsoft Word 2.0z">
<TITLE>Untitled</TITLE>
</HEAD>
<BODY>
<P>
<CENTER><IMG SRC="biglogo.bmp"><BR>
</CENTER>
<P>
<CENTER>This page will be merged with the Insert Data files generated
by the IIS addin<BR>
</CENTER>
<P>
<CENTER><A HREF="welcome.htm" >Back to Home</A><BR>
<BR>
</CENTER>
</BODY>
</HTML>
```

Open a new HTML page in Word. This will be the Change Tracking page (see Figure 9.5). You will modify this page with frames and code generated by the IIS Add-In. All you need is a logo and a return link to the Welcome Page (welcome.htm). Save your work as chngtrac.htm (see Listing 9.4).

Figure 9.5.
Change Request Tracking page.

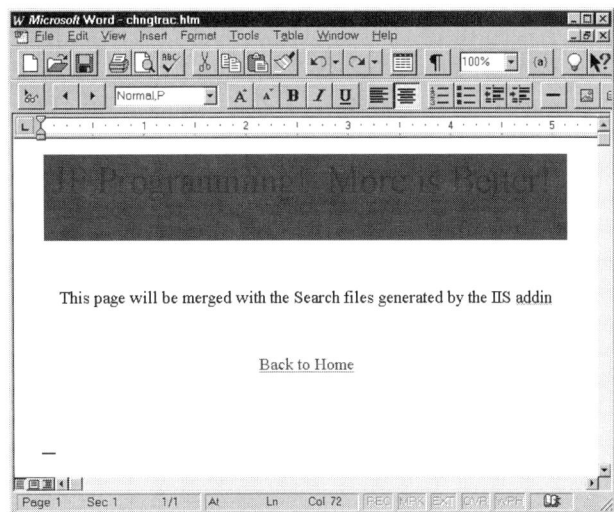

Listing 9.4. HTML code for chngtrac.htm.

```
<HTML>
<HEAD>

<META NAME="GENERATOR" CONTENT="Internet Assistant for Microsoft Word 2.0z">
<TITLE>Untitled</TITLE>
</HEAD>
<BODY>
<P>
<CENTER><IMG SRC="biglogo.bmp"><BR>
</CENTER>
<P>
<CENTER>This page will be merged with the Search files generated
by the IIS addin<BR>
</CENTER>
<P>
<CENTER><A HREF="welcome.htm" >Back to Home</A><BR>
<BR>
</CENTER>
</BODY>
</HTML>
```

Stop and check your work. Look at these pages and test the links in the browser because few of your friend's customers will be using Word to look at this site.

Design the Database in Access

I won't go into any database theory or design philosophy here—it would be fun, but it is beyond the scope of this book. In this section, you will simply create the objects you need. To do so, open Access and create a new database called `bigproj.mdb`. Add two new tables, `project` and `chngreq`, as shown in Figure 9.6.

Figure 9.6.
BigProj *database.*

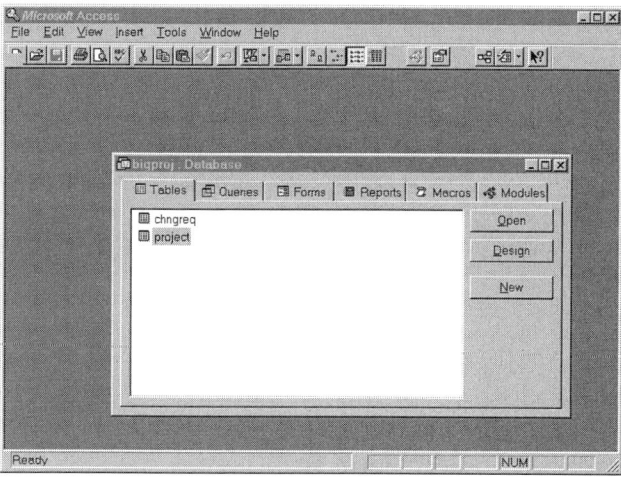

Switch to the `project` table and create the fields shown in Figure 9.7.

Figure 9.7.
`project` *table.*

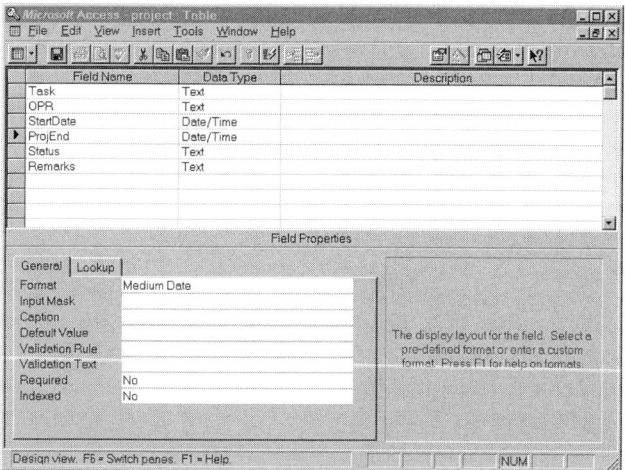

Switch to the `chngreq` table and create the fields shown in Figure 9.8.

Figure 9.8.
chngreq *table*.

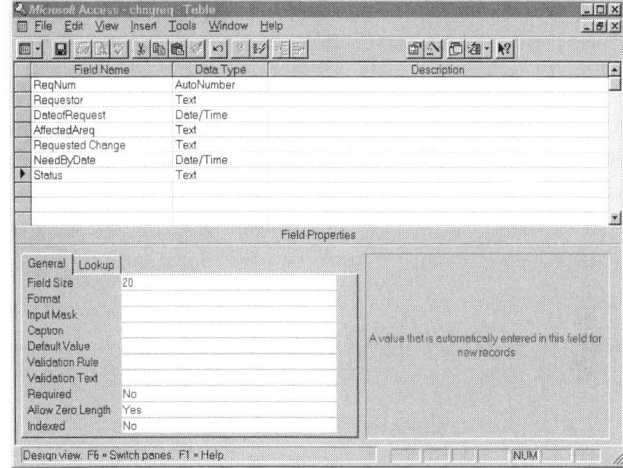

Add a Driver

Add a reference to the database to the ODBC Driver Manager. Open your ODBC Administrator, push the System DSN button, and add a new entry based on an Access driver. Fill the entry in as shown in Figure 9.9.

Figure 9.9.
ODBC Administrator.

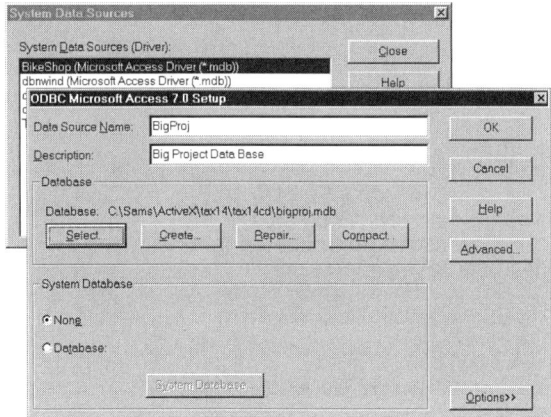

Using the Internet Information Server Add-In

Now you are ready to use the IIS Add-In to add a dynamic data page to use with the Project Status page. This new page will return a current view of the data every time the page is called. Name this new page pjdynam.htm. Close and re-open Access or the IIS Add-In will not see the new entry you just made in the ODBC Administrator. Open the BigProj database and launch the IIS Add-In by choosing it from the Tools menu under Add-ins. On the first page of the IIS Add-In wizard, choose Dynamic Display Wizard. On the next screen, choose the table project. Make sure your datasource is `BigProj`. Proceed to the field screen and add all the fields.

Move on to the final-input page. You are going to tinker with this screen, so don't add anything. Press Finish. Print the instruction sheet if you can't remember what to do with the three files you just generated. (You will have created two files like Listings 9.5 and 9.6.) `pjdynam.htx` is the template file that will show the data when requested. `pjdynam.idc` is the file you will call from the Web page to generate the up-to-date project report.

Listing 9.5. HTML code for `pjdynam.htx`.

```
<HTML>
<META NAME="GENERATOR" CONTENT="IIS Add In For Access 95">
<HEAD><Title>HTML document for the World Wide Web</Title></HEAD>
<BODY BGCOLOR="#FFFFFF">



<%begindetail%>
<%if CurrentRecord EQ 0 %>
<TABLE BORDER BGCOLOR="#FFFFFF">
<TR>
<TH><B>Task</B></TH>
<TH><B>OPR</B></TH>
<TH><B>StartDate</B></TH>
<TH><B>ProjEnd</B></TH>
<TH><B>Status</B></TH>
<TH><B>Remarks</B></TH>
</TR>
<%endif%>
<TR>
<TD Align=Left><%Task%></TD>
<TD Align=Left><%OPR%></TD>
<TD Align=Right><%StartDate%></TD>
<TD Align=Right><%ProjEnd%></TD>
<TD Align=Left><%Status%></TD>
<TD Align=Left><%Remarks%></TD>
</TR>
<%enddetail%>
<%if CurrentRecord EQ 0 %>
<HR=2><P>
<CENTER><B>No records were selected!<B></CENTER><P>
<%endif%>
</TABLE>
<HR=2>
<CENTER>This page was produced by using the <B>IIS Add-In for Access 95</B>
.<BR><I> Copyright 1996 Microsoft Corporation</I>.</CENTER>
</BODY></HTML>
```

This file will stand by itself. You will customize it later.

Listing 9.6. HTML code for `pjdynam.idc`.

```
Datasource: BigProj
Template: pjdynam.htx
SQLStatement:
+Select "Task", "OPR", "StartDate", "ProjEnd", "Status", "Remarks"
+From "project";
#IDC-DynamicDisplay FrontHTM-None ReportHTM-pjdynam.htx
```

For those of you familiar with Structured Query Language, you can see that this IDC will execute a `Select * from project`. This statement gets all the columns and rows from the database.

Now, for the Change Request page, you will need to generate an HTM, an HTX, and an IDC file to do an insert into the database. Launch the Internet Information Server Add-In again. This time, on the first page, choose Insert Page Wizard. On the next screen choose the `Custreq` table. Make sure your datasource is `BigProj`. On the next screen, choose all the fields except `reqnum`. The easiest way do this is select all the fields and then remove `reqnum`. You are going to tinker with this page, so nothing is necessary on the final screen. Save your work as `crinsrt.htm`. (The Add-In will name the other two files automatically.) You will generate `crinsrt.htm`, `crinsrt.htx`, and `crinsrt.idc` as shown in Listings 9.7, 9.8, and 9.9. Print out the file summary report.

Listing 9.7. HTML code for `crinsrt.htm`.

```
<HTML>
<META NAME="GENERATOR" CONTENT="IIS Add In For Access 95">
<HEAD><Title>HTML document for the World Wide Web</Title></HEAD>
<BODY BGCOLOR="#FFFFFF">

<FORM ACTION="/scripts/crinsrt.idc" METHOD = "POST" >
<TABLE BORDER BGCOLOR="#FFFFFF">
<TR>
<TD>Requestor</TD>
<TD><INPUT NAME="Requestor"</TD></TR><P>
<TR>
<TD>DateofRequest</TD>
<TD><INPUT NAME="DateofRequest"</TD></TR><P>
<TR>
<TD>AffectedAreq</TD>
<TD><INPUT NAME="AffectedAreq"</TD></TR><P>
<TR>
<TD>Requested Change</TD>
<TD><INPUT NAME="Requested Change"</TD></TR><P>
```

continues

Listing 9.7. continued

```
        <TR>
        <TD>NeedByDate</TD>
        <TD><INPUT NAME="NeedByDate"</TD></TR><P>
        <TR>
        <TD>Status</TD>
        <TD><INPUT NAME="Status"</TD></TR><P>
        </TABLE>
        <P><INPUT TYPE="SUBMIT" VALUE="Submit" ALIGN="MIDDLE">
        <INPUT TYPE="RESET" NAME="reset" VALUE="Clear all fields" ALIGN="MIDDLE"></P></
        FORM>
        <HR=2>
        <CENTER>This page was produced by using the <B>IIS Add-In for Access 95</B>.
        <BR><I> Copyright 1996 Microsoft Corporation</I>.</CENTER>
        </BODY></HTML>
```

Listing 9.8. HTML code for `crinsrt.htx`.

```
        <HTML>
        <META NAME="GENERATOR" CONTENT="IIS Add In For Access 95">
        <HEAD><Title>HTML document for the World Wide Web</Title></HEAD>
        <BODY BGCOLOR="#FFFFFF">

        <P><B>The following information was recieved.</B><BR>
        <TABLE BORDER BGCOLOR="#FFFFFF">
        <TR>
        <TD ALIGN="RIGHT"><B>Requestor</B></TD>
        <TD><%idc.Requestor%></TD></TR>
        <TR>
        <TD ALIGN="RIGHT"><B>DateofRequest</B></TD>
        <%IF idc.DateofRequest EQ "NULL" %> <%else%><%idc.DateofRequest%><%endif%></
        TD></TR>
        <TR>
        <TD ALIGN="RIGHT"><B>AffectedAreq</B></TD>
        <TD><%idc.AffectedAreq%></TD></TR>
        <TR>
        <TD ALIGN="RIGHT"><B>Requested Change</B></TD>
        <TD><%idc.Requested Change%></TD></TR>
        <TR>
        <TD ALIGN="RIGHT"><B>NeedByDate</B></TD>
        <%IF idc.NeedByDate EQ "NULL" %> <%else%><%idc.NeedByDate%><%endif%></TD></TR>
        <TR>
        <TD ALIGN="RIGHT"><B>Status</B></TD>
        <TD><%idc.Status%></TD></TR>
        </TABLE><P>
        <A HREF="/crinsrt.htm">Return To Data Entry Page</A>
        <CENTER>This page was produced by using the <B>IIS Add-In for Access 95</B>
        .<BR><I> Copyright 1996 Microsoft Corporation</I>.</CENTER>
        </BODY></HTML>
```

Listing 9.9. HTML code for `crinsrt.idc`.

```
Datasource: BigProj
Template: crinsrt.htx
DefaultParameters: DateofRequest=NULL, NeedByDate=NULL
SQLStatement:
+INSERT INTO "chngreq" ("Requestor", "DateofRequest", "AffectedAreq",
➥"Requested Change", "NeedByDate", "Status")
+VALUES ('%Requestor%', %DateofRequest%, '%AffectedAreq%',
➥'%Requested Change%', %NeedByDate%, '%Status%');
#IDC-Insert FrontHTM-crinsrt.htm ReportHTX-crinsrt.htx
```

You need to generate one more group of forms with the Internet Information Server Add-in Wizard—the query for the Track Status Change Order page. This time, call up the wizard and choose the Query and Display option. Pick the `Chngreq` table. Choose the `ReqNum` field to search. Pick the `Requestor`, `DateofRequest`, and `Status` field for display. These will be the fields included in the return record. All this is shown in Figure 9.10.

Figure 9.10.
Setting up the Search and Return page.

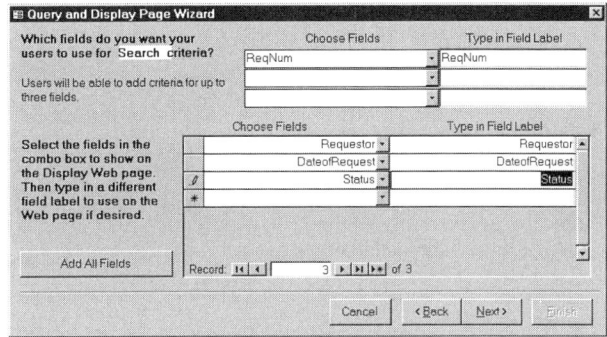

Save the file as `crtrac.htm`. This will also save `crtrac.htm` and `crtrac.idc`. Your files should look like Listings 9.10, 9.11, and 9.12.

Listing 9.10. HTML code for `crtrac.htm`.

```
<HTML>
<META NAME="GENERATOR" CONTENT="IIS Add In For Access 95">
<HEAD><Title>HTML document for the World Wide Web</Title></HEAD>
<BODY BGCOLOR="#FFFFFF">

<FORM ACTION="/scripts/crtrack.idc" METHOD = "POST" >
<TABLE BORDER BGCOLOR="#FFFFFF">
<TR>
<TD ALIGN="RIGHT">ReqNum</TD>
<TD><INPUT NAME="ReqNum"</TD></TR><P>
</TABLE>
<P><INPUT TYPE="SUBMIT" VALUE="Search" ALIGN="MIDDLE">
```

continues

Listing 9.10. continued

```
<INPUT TYPE="RESET" NAME="reset" VALUE="Clear all fields" ALIGN="MIDDLE"></P></
FORM>
<HR=2>
<CENTER>This page was produced by using the <B>IIS Add-In for Access 95</B>.
<BR><I> Copyright 1996 Microsoft Corporation</I>.</CENTER>
</BODY></HTML>
```

Listing 9.11. HTML code for `crtrac.htx`.

```
<HTML>
<META NAME="GENERATOR" CONTENT="IIS Add In For Access 95">
<HEAD><Title>HTML document for the World Wide Web</Title></HEAD>
<BODY BGCOLOR="#FFFFFF">


<%begindetail%>
<%if CurrentRecord EQ 0 %>
<TABLE BORDER BGCOLOR="#FFFFFF">
<TR>
<TH><B>Requestor</B></TH>
<TH><B>DateofRequest</B></TH>
<TH><B>Status</B></TH>
</TR>
<%endif%>
<TR>
<TD Align=Left><%Requestor%></TD>
<TD Align=Right><%DateofRequest%></TD>
<TD Align=Left><%Status%></TD>
</TR>
<%enddetail%>
<%if CurrentRecord EQ 0 %>
<HR=2><P>
<CENTER><B>No records were selected!<B></CENTER><P>
<%endif%>
</TABLE>
<HR=2>
<CENTER>This page was produced by using the <B>IIS Add-In for Access 95</B>.
<BR><I> Copyright 1996 Microsoft Corporation</I>.</CENTER>
</BODY></HTML>
```

Listing 9.12. HTML code for `crtrac.idc`.

```
Datasource: BigProj
Template: crtrack.htx
DefaultParameters: ReqNum="ReqNum"
SQLStatement:
+Select "Requestor", "DateofRequest", "Status"
+From "chngreq"
```

```
+Where "ReqNum" = %ReqNum%
#IDC-Search FrontHTM-crtrack.htm ReportHTX-crtrack.htx
```

You have what you need from the Internet Information Server Add-in Wizard. Let's move on.

What Do You Have So Far?

All the files you have generated so far are in the rough subdirectory of this chapter's entry on the CD-ROM. Feel free to link them up and put them on your Web site. This is the end of the rough-draft stage. From here you will complete each Web page using JavaScript and ActiveX controls. You will

- design an overall frame for the project
- design a Navigation bar for the Web site
- design the Change Request form
- change the IDC and HTX files for the Change Request form to return the tracking number of the request form
- add a track Change Request function to the Navigation bar

When you are done with these changes, you will have the Web site JP wanted.

The Main Frame

One of the most interesting current developments in Web-page technology is the frame. You have seen examples of frames throughout this book. Frames can make your Web site look and act more like a program. Instead of being sequential, a site with a frame can have parts that stay put while others are dynamic. For this project, to satisfy the requirement for a program-like look and feel, you will use a frame to divide the screen into four parts, as shown in Figure 9.11.

The source for this frame is pretty straightforward, as shown in Listing 9.13.

Listing 9.13. HTML code for `bigframe.htm`.

```
<HTML>
<HEAD>
<TITLE>JP Programming! Project Site</TITLE>
</HEAD>

<FRAMESET FRAMEBORDER="3" FRAMESPACING="3" ROWS="49,*">
  <FRAME MARGINWIDTH="0" MARGINHEIGHT="0"  SRC="Basic.htm"
NAME="Frame1" NORESIZE SCROLLING="no">
   <FRAMESET FRAMEBORDER="3" FRAMESPACING="3" COLS="160,*">
     <FRAMESET FRAMEBORDER="3" FRAMESPACING="3" ROWS="80,*">
       <FRAME MARGINWIDTH="0" MARGINHEIGHT="2" SRC="Basic.htm"
```

continues

Listing 9.13. continued

```
NAME="Frame2" SCROLLING="no">
    <FRAME MARGINWIDTH="4" MARGINHEIGHT="0" SRC="Basic.htm"
NAME= "Frame3" SCROLLING="yes">
    </FRAMESET>
    <FRAME MARGINWIDTH="9" MARGINHEIGHT="0" SRC="Basic.htm"
NAME="Frame4" SCROLLING="yes">
  </FRAMESET>
<NOFRAMES>
</NOFRAMES>
</FRAMESET>

</BODY>
</HTML>
```

Figure 9.11.
The main frame.

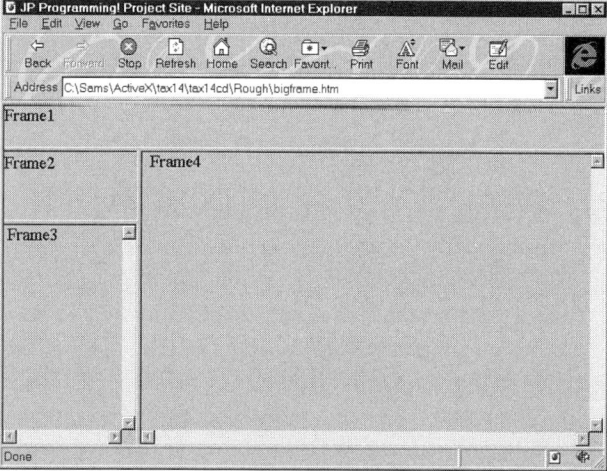

The frames are named by the NAME attribute in the <FRAME> tag. It is not obvious from the code where the frames are located. To clarify which frame is where, the page basic.htm, which is loaded into each frame, uses a JavaScript routine that runs when the window loads to print out the window name. Listing 9.14 shows how this works.

Listing 9.14. HTML code for basic.htm.

```
<HTML>
<HEAD>
    <SCRIPT LANGUAGE="JavaScript" FOR="window" EVENT="onLoad()">
<!--
window.document.open()
window.document.write(window.name)
window.document.close()
```

```
-->
    </SCRIPT>
<TITLE>New Page</TITLE>
</HEAD>
<BODY>
</BODY>
</HTML>
```

Let's solve part of this puzzle by adding the link to the document, bigproj.doc, that you put in projstat.htm. Load projstat.htm into Word or edit it by hand. Remove the logo, left-justify the links, and add new links to memo.doc (done with Memo Wizard) and briefing.ppt (done with Briefing Wizard). Then target these links to Frame4. See Listing 9.15 for details.

Listing 9.15. Revised projstat.htm.

```
<HTML>
<HEAD>
<TITLE>Untitled</TITLE>

<META NAME="GENERATOR" CONTENT="Internet Assistant for Microsoft Word

2.0z">
</HEAD>
<BODY>
<P>
<A HREF="memo.doc" TARGET = "Frame4">Memo</A>
<P>
<A HREF="bigproj.doc" TARGET = "Frame4" >Link to Big-Expensive Product

Document</A>
<P>
<A HREF="briefing.ppt" TARGET = "Frame4">Briefings</A><BR>
</BODY>
</HTML>
```

Replace basic.htm with projstat.htm in bigframe.htm. While you are at it, put the small company logo in Frame2. To do that, modify the projstat in the rough directory to logo.htm, as shown in Listing 9.16.

Listing 9.16. HTML code for logo.htm.

```
<HTML>
<HEAD>

<META NAME="GENERATOR" CONTENT="Internet Assistant for Microsoft Word
```

continues

Listing 9.16. continued

```
2.0z">
<TITLE>Logo</TITLE>
</HEAD>
<BODY>
<IMG SRC="lillogo.bmp"><BR>
</BODY>
</HTML>
```

Change bigframe.htm to load logo.htm. After changing bigframe.htm to load both logo.htm and projstat.htm, bigframe.htm should look like Listing 9.17.

Listing 9.17. HTML code for the revised bigframe.htm.

```
<HTML>
<HEAD>
<TITLE>JP Programming! Project Site</TITLE>
</HEAD>

<FRAMESET FRAMEBORDER="3" FRAMESPACING="3" ROWS="49,*">
  <FRAME MARGINWIDTH="0" MARGINHEIGHT="0"  SRC="Basic.htm" NAME="Frame1"

NORESIZE SCROLLING="no">
  <FRAMESET FRAMEBORDER="3" FRAMESPACING="3" COLS="160,*">
    <FRAMESET FRAMEBORDER="3" FRAMESPACING="3" ROWS="80,*">
      <FRAME MARGINWIDTH="0" MARGINHEIGHT="2" SRC="logo.htm"

NAME="Frame2" SCROLLING="no">
      <FRAME MARGINWIDTH="4" MARGINHEIGHT="0" SRC="projstat.htm" NAME=

"Frame3" SCROLLING="yes">
    </FRAMESET>
    <FRAME MARGINWIDTH="9" MARGINHEIGHT="0" SRC="Basic.htm" NAME="Frame4"

SCROLLING="yes">
  </FRAMESET>
<NOFRAMES>
</NOFRAMES>
</FRAMESET>

</BODY>
</HTML>
```

Your project so far should look like Figure 9.12.

Note that when you select one of the links, Frame4 acts as an OLE container and brings in Word or PowerPoint, depending on the document you chose. Tell your customer you worked for weeks to get this. The customer doesn't have to know you haven't coded a single line yet, only changed some HTML tags. Let's do some coding.

A JavaScript Application

Figure 9.12.
The project so far.

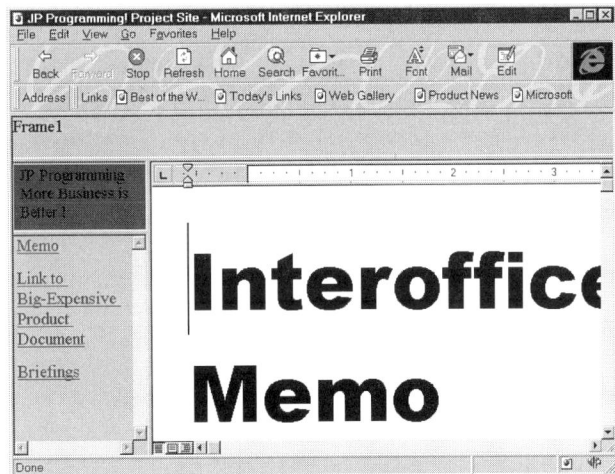

The Navigation Bar

Open the ActiveX Control Pad, make a new HTML layout, and in it place three buttons. Associate the pictures `home.gif`, `docs.gif`, and `cardfile.gif` with `btnHome`, `bntStatus`, and `btnChangeRequest`. (You can use your own pictures if you want.)

Since this is a Navigation bar, most users would expect some kind of text to come up when the mouse is over the buttons. Place code in the `onMouseMove` events of each button to put a message describing the button in the Status bar. Then put code in the `btnHome` click event to launch `welcome.htm`. Finally, put code in the `btnStatus` click event to launch the `pydynam.idc` file that generates the current status. Make both the `welcome.htm` and the `pjdynam.idc` results appear in `Frame4`. Your code should look like Listing 9.18.

Listing 9.18. HTML code for `navigate.alx`.

```
<SCRIPT LANGUAGE="JavaScript" FOR="btnChangeRequest"
EVENT="MouseMove(Button, Shift, X, Y)">
<!--
self.status = "Change Request"

-->
</SCRIPT>
<SCRIPT LANGUAGE="JavaScript" FOR="btnStatus" EVENT="Click()">
<!--

window.parent.frames[3].location.href="/scripts/pjdynam.idc?"


-->
</SCRIPT>
```

continues

Listing 9.18. continued

```
<SCRIPT LANGUAGE="JavaScript" FOR="btnHome" EVENT="Click()">
<!--

window.parent.frames[3].location.href="/tax09/welcome.htm"

-->
</SCRIPT>
<SCRIPT LANGUAGE="JavaScript" FOR="btnStatus"
EVENT="MouseMove(Button, Shift, X, Y)">
<!--
self.status = "Project Status"

-->
</SCRIPT>
<SCRIPT LANGUAGE="JavaScript" FOR="btnHome"
EVENT="MouseMove(Button, Shift, X, Y)">
<!--
self.status = "Home"

-->
</SCRIPT>
<DIV ID="Layout1" STYLE="LAYOUT:FIXED;WIDTH:394pt;HEIGHT:31pt;">
    <OBJECT ID="btnHome"
     CLASSID="CLSID:D7053240-CE69-11CD-A777-00DD01143C57"
     DATA="DATA:application/x-oleobject;BASE64,
"
     STYLE="TOP:0pt;LEFT:16pt;WIDTH:31pt;HEIGHT:31pt;TABINDEX:0;ZINDEX:0;">
    </OBJECT>
    <OBJECT ID="btnChangeRequest"
     CLASSID="CLSID:D7053240-CE69-11CD-A777-00DD01143C57"
     DATA="DATA:application/x-oleobject;BASE64,
"
     STYLE="TOP:0pt;LEFT:55pt;WIDTH:31pt;HEIGHT:31pt;TABINDEX:1;ZINDEX:1;">
    </OBJECT>
    <OBJECT ID="btnStatus"
     CLASSID="CLSID:D7053240-CE69-11CD-A777-00DD01143C57"
     DATA="DATA:application/x-oleobject;BASE64,
"
     STYLE="TOP:0pt;LEFT:94pt;WIDTH:31pt;HEIGHT:31pt;TABINDEX:2;ZINDEX:2;">
    </OBJECT>
</DIV>
```

NOTE: If you compare the navigate.alx on the disk with Listing 9.18, you will find that there are big blocks of encoded data that make up the pictures on the button. This data was omitted from the listing because it isn't something you can study and learn from, let alone something you would try to type in. Also, notice how much more data you have to send if you want graphics on your buttons. Something to consider.

A JavaScript Application

Put `navigate.alx` into `navigate.htm`, as shown in Listing 9.19.

Listing 9.19. HTML code for `navigate.htm`.

```
<HTML>
<HEAD>
<TITLE>New Page</TITLE>
</HEAD>
<BODY>

<OBJECT CLASSID="CLSID:812AE312-8B8E-11CF-93C8-00AA00C08FDF"
ID="navigate_alx" STYLE="LEFT:0;TOP:0">
<PARAM NAME="ALXPATH" REF VALUE="navigate.alx">
 </OBJECT>


</BODY>
</HTML>
```

Finally, modify `bigframe.htm` to place `navigate.htm` into `Frame1`. The line

```
<FRAME MARGINWIDTH="0" MARGINHEIGHT="0"  SRC="Navigate.htm"
➥NAME="Frame1" NORESIZE SCROLLING="no">
```

reflects the placement of `navigate.htm` into `Frame1`. Place `pjdynam.idc` and `pjdynam.htx` into the scripts directory and fire up your browser. You should see something like Figure 9.13.

Figure 9.13.
The Navigation bar in the main frame.

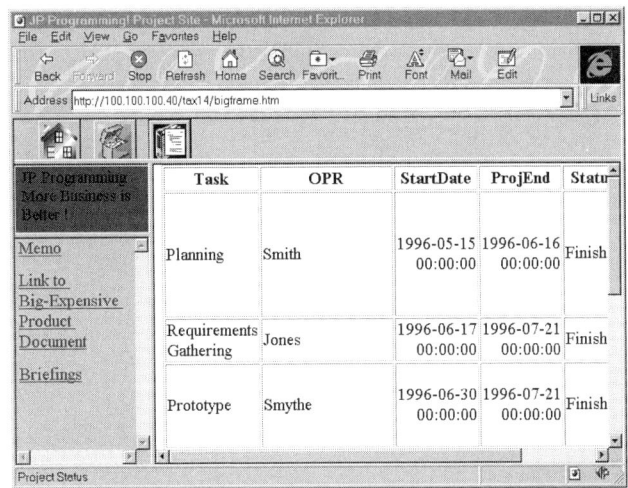

As you play with this, you will notice a couple of things. First, the welcome window we designed seems out of place in this environment. I'm not running an art class (you may have seen my bicycle pictures in an earlier chapter), and it won't further your study of design with ActiveX and JavaScript, but as you start to use frames in Web sites, you will have to rethink how you present your content. Also, the text you put in the MouseMove events does change as you float over the buttons and does communicate what the buttons are to the icon challenged. Time to build the next form.

The Change Request Form

The Change Request form needs to gather data about what the user wants to change. You will use the ActiveX Control Pad to create a Change Request form. Place four text boxes, one combo box, two buttons, and five labels (as shown in Figure 9.14).

Figure 9.14.
Change Request form.

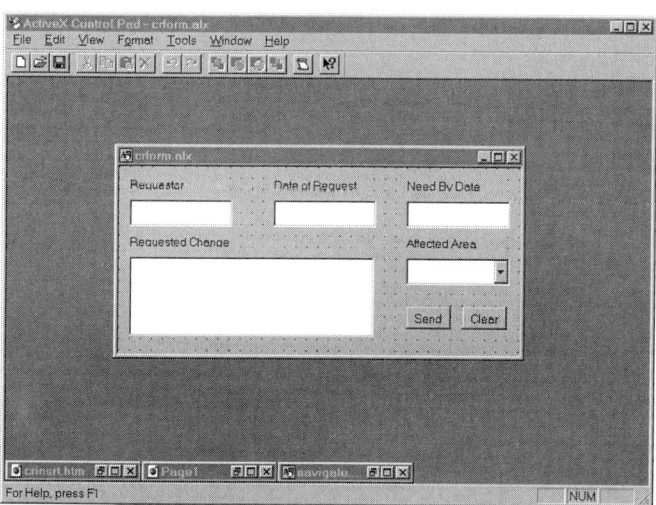

Then name the controls and add the code shown in Listing 9.20.

Listing 9.20. HTML code for crform.alx.

```
</SCRIPT>
<SCRIPT LANGUAGE="JavaScript" FOR="btnClear" EVENT="Click()">
<!--
DateofRequest.Text = ""
NeedByDate.Text = ""
RequestedChange.Text = ""
Requestor.Text = ""

-->
</SCRIPT>
<SCRIPT LANGUAGE="JavaScript" FOR="Layout1" EVENT="OnLoad()">
<!--
```

A JavaScript Application

```
AffectedArea.AddItem('GUI')
AffectedArea.AddItem('Calculations')
AffectedArea.AddItem('Timing')
AffectedArea.AddItem('Security')
-->
</SCRIPT>
<SCRIPT LANGUAGE="JavaScript" FOR="btnSend" EVENT="Click()">
<!--
if (CheckValues())
{
  //submit the data
}


-->
</SCRIPT>
<DIV ID="Layout1" STYLE="LAYOUT:FIXED;WIDTH:282pt;HEIGHT:127pt;">
    <OBJECT ID="RequestedChange"
     CLASSID="CLSID:8BD21D10-EC42-11CE-9E0D-00AA006002F3"

STYLE="TOP:62pt;LEFT:8pt;WIDTH:172pt;HEIGHT:53pt;TABINDEX:0;ZINDEX:0;">
        <PARAM NAME="VariousPropertyBits" VALUE="2894088219">
        <PARAM NAME="Size" VALUE="6053;1863">
        <PARAM NAME="FontCharSet" VALUE="0">
        <PARAM NAME="FontPitchAndFamily" VALUE="2">
    </OBJECT>
    <OBJECT ID="Label6"
     CLASSID="CLSID:978C9E23-D4B0-11CE-BF2D-00AA003F40D0"

STYLE="TOP:47pt;LEFT:8pt;WIDTH:78pt;HEIGHT:8pt;ZINDEX:1;">
        <PARAM NAME="Caption" VALUE="Requested Change">
        <PARAM NAME="Size" VALUE="2751;275">
        <PARAM NAME="FontCharSet" VALUE="0">
        <PARAM NAME="FontPitchAndFamily" VALUE="2">
    </OBJECT>
    <OBJECT ID="Label7"
     CLASSID="CLSID:978C9E23-D4B0-11CE-BF2D-00AA003F40D0"

STYLE="TOP:8pt;LEFT:8pt;WIDTH:70pt;HEIGHT:8pt;ZINDEX:2;">
        <PARAM NAME="Caption" VALUE="Requestor">
        <PARAM NAME="Size" VALUE="2476;275">
        <PARAM NAME="FontCharSet" VALUE="0">
        <PARAM NAME="FontPitchAndFamily" VALUE="2">
    </OBJECT>
    <OBJECT ID="Requestor"
     CLASSID="CLSID:8BD21D10-EC42-11CE-9E0D-00AA006002F3"

STYLE="TOP:23pt;LEFT:8pt;WIDTH:72pt;HEIGHT:18pt;TABINDEX:3;ZINDEX:3;">
        <PARAM NAME="VariousPropertyBits" VALUE="746604571">
        <PARAM NAME="Size" VALUE="2540;635">
        <PARAM NAME="FontCharSet" VALUE="0">
        <PARAM NAME="FontPitchAndFamily" VALUE="2">
    </OBJECT>
    <OBJECT ID="DateofRequest"
     CLASSID="CLSID:8BD21D10-EC42-11CE-9E0D-00AA006002F3"
```

continues

Listing 9.20. continued

```
            STYLE="TOP:23pt;LEFT:109pt;WIDTH:72pt;HEIGHT:18pt;TABINDEX:4;ZINDEX:4;">
                <PARAM NAME="VariousPropertyBits" VALUE="746604571">
                <PARAM NAME="Size" VALUE="2540;635">
                <PARAM NAME="FontCharSet" VALUE="0">
                <PARAM NAME="FontPitchAndFamily" VALUE="2">
            </OBJECT>
            <OBJECT ID="Label8"
             CLASSID="CLSID:978C9E23-D4B0-11CE-BF2D-00AA003F40D0"

            STYLE="TOP:8pt;LEFT:109pt;WIDTH:70pt;HEIGHT:8pt;ZINDEX:5;">
                <PARAM NAME="Caption" VALUE="Date of Request">
                <PARAM NAME="Size" VALUE="2476;275">
                <PARAM NAME="FontCharSet" VALUE="0">
                <PARAM NAME="FontPitchAndFamily" VALUE="2">
            </OBJECT>
            <OBJECT ID="Label9"
             CLASSID="CLSID:978C9E23-D4B0-11CE-BF2D-00AA003F40D0"

            STYLE="TOP:8pt;LEFT:203pt;WIDTH:70pt;HEIGHT:8pt;ZINDEX:6;">
                <PARAM NAME="Caption" VALUE="Need By Date">
                <PARAM NAME="Size" VALUE="2476;275">
                <PARAM NAME="FontCharSet" VALUE="0">
                <PARAM NAME="FontPitchAndFamily" VALUE="2">
            </OBJECT>
            <OBJECT ID="NeedByDate"
             CLASSID="CLSID:8BD21D10-EC42-11CE-9E0D-00AA006002F3"

            STYLE="TOP:23pt;LEFT:203pt;WIDTH:72pt;HEIGHT:18pt;TABINDEX:7;ZINDEX:7;">
                <PARAM NAME="VariousPropertyBits" VALUE="746604571">
                <PARAM NAME="Size" VALUE="2540;635">
                <PARAM NAME="FontCharSet" VALUE="0">
                <PARAM NAME="FontPitchAndFamily" VALUE="2">
            </OBJECT>
            <OBJECT ID="btnClear"
             CLASSID="CLSID:D7053240-CE69-11CD-A777-00DD01143C57"

            STYLE="TOP:94pt;LEFT:242pt;WIDTH:31pt;HEIGHT:16pt;TABINDEX:8;ZINDEX:8;">
                <PARAM NAME="Caption" VALUE="Clear">
                <PARAM NAME="Size" VALUE="1101;550">
                <PARAM NAME="FontCharSet" VALUE="0">
                <PARAM NAME="FontPitchAndFamily" VALUE="2">
                <PARAM NAME="ParagraphAlign" VALUE="3">
            </OBJECT>
            <OBJECT ID="btnSend"
             CLASSID="CLSID:D7053240-CE69-11CD-A777-00DD01143C57"

            STYLE="TOP:94pt;LEFT:203pt;WIDTH:31pt;HEIGHT:16pt;TABINDEX:9;ZINDEX:9;">
                <PARAM NAME="Caption" VALUE="Send">
                <PARAM NAME="Size" VALUE="1101;550">
                <PARAM NAME="FontCharSet" VALUE="0">
                <PARAM NAME="FontPitchAndFamily" VALUE="2">
                <PARAM NAME="ParagraphAlign" VALUE="3">
            </OBJECT>
            <OBJECT ID="AffectedArea"
             CLASSID="CLSID:8BD21D30-EC42-11CE-9E0D-00AA006002F3"
```

```
STYLE="TOP:62pt;LEFT:203pt;WIDTH:72pt;HEIGHT:18pt;TABINDEX:10;ZINDEX:10;"
>
        <PARAM NAME="DisplayStyle" VALUE="7">
        <PARAM NAME="Size" VALUE="2540;635">
        <PARAM NAME="MatchEntry" VALUE="1">
        <PARAM NAME="ShowDropButtonWhen" VALUE="2">
        <PARAM NAME="FontCharSet" VALUE="0">
        <PARAM NAME="FontPitchAndFamily" VALUE="2">
    </OBJECT>
    <OBJECT ID="Label10"
      CLASSID="CLSID:978C9E23-D4B0-11CE-BF2D-00AA003F40D0"
STYLE="TOP:47pt;LEFT:203pt;WIDTH:70pt;HEIGHT:8pt;ZINDEX:11;">
        <PARAM NAME="Caption" VALUE="Affected Area">
        <PARAM NAME="Size" VALUE="2476;275">
        <PARAM NAME="FontCharSet" VALUE="0">
        <PARAM NAME="FontPitchAndFamily" VALUE="2">
    </OBJECT>
</DIV>
```

You put code in the bntClear click event to clear the fields. You made a new function, CheckValues, that is called on the btnSend click event. CheckValues makes sure the user has put values in all the fields. You placed code in the Layout1.onload event to put items into the combo box (AffectedArea). In anticipation of the manipulation of the IDC files in the next section, add crform.alx to crinsrt.htm (the form you generated to insert the Change Request data into the database) and modify crinsrt.htm to look like Listing 9.21.

Listing 9.21. HTML code for crinsrt.htm.

```
<HTML>
<META NAME="GENERATOR" CONTENT="IIS Add In For Access 95">
<HEAD><Title>Change Request Form</Title></HEAD>
<BODY>

<OBJECT CLASSID="CLSID:812AE312-8B8E-11CF-93C8-00AA00C08FDF"
ID="crform_alx" STYLE="LEFT:0;TOP:0">
<PARAM NAME="ALXPATH" REF VALUE="crform.alx">
 </OBJECT>

<FORM ACTION="/scripts/crinsrt.idc" METHOD = "POST" NAME = "ORDERFORM" >
<INPUT TYPE = "Hidden" NAME="Requestor">
<INPUT TYPE = "Hidden" NAME="DateofRequest">
<INPUT TYPE = "Hidden" NAME="AffectedArea">
<INPUT TYPE = "Hidden"  NAME="RequestedChange">
<INPUT TYPE = "Hidden"  NAME="NeedByDate">
<INPUT TYPE = "Hidden"  NAME="Status">
</FORM>
</BODY></HTML>
```

The layout of crinst.htm will become more clear in the next section. Open navigate.alx and add this line:

```
window.parent.frames[3].location.href="/tax09/crinsrt.htm"
```

to the btnChangeRequest click method. This will enable crinsrt.htm to be placed in Frame4 by navigate.alx. Fire up bigframe.htm and test your new page. It should look like Figure 9.15.

Figure 9.15.
Change Request form in action.

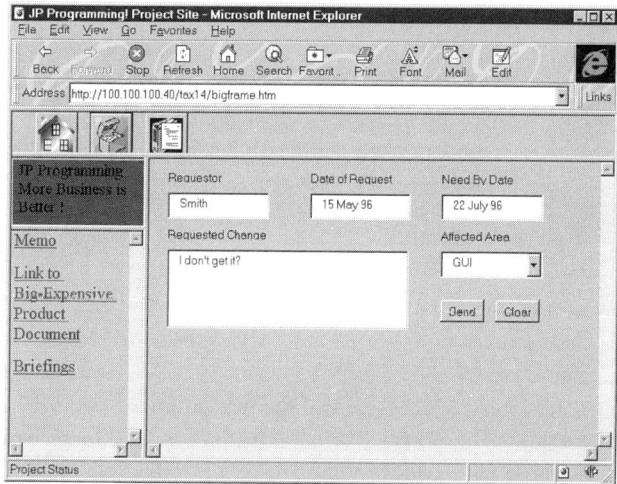

You are on the home stretch. One big and one little thing are left to clean up. Do the big thing first.

Returning the Change Request Tracking Number.

The way crinst.htx is written now, it will send a list of the data the user sends via crinst.idc. What you want to do here is have it return a unique tracking number from the field ReqNum. In the Access database bigproj.mdb, this field is of type Autonumber. This means that the database will assign it a unique value after the data is inserted. What you will do here is have crinst.htx create another request, routed through new IDC and HTX files, that will return the ReqNum. Modify crinst.htx to look like Listing 9.22.

Listing 9.22. Changed crinst.htx.

```
<HTML>
<HEAD><Title>InterMedia</Title>
<%IF idc.LastName EQ "NULL" %>
```

A JavaScript Application

```
<BODY BGCOLOR="#FFFFFF">
Nothing Happened
</BODY></HTML>
<%else%>
<SCRIPT LANGUAGE="JavaScript" FOR="window" EVENT="onLoad()">
<!--
  window.document.forms[0].elements[0].Value = "<%idc.DateofRequest%>"
  window.document.forms[0].elements[1].Value = "<%idc.Requestor%>"
  window.document.forms[0].submit()

-->
</SCRIPT>
</HEAD>
<BODY>

    <FORM ACTION="/scripts/crreqnum.idc" METHOD="POST" NAME="ORDERNUM">
        <INPUT TYPE=Hidden NAME="DateofRequest">
        <INPUT TYPE=Hidden NAME="Requestor">
    </FORM>


</BODY></HTML>
<%endif%>
```

Here, you have embedded script in the template file that loads up another request and submits it when the `window.onload` event occurs. Write a new file, `crreqnum.idc`, that will use `RequestDate` and `Requestor` to return a `ReqNum`. Name it `crreqnum.idc`. It should look like Listing 9.23.

Listing 9.23. HTML code for `crreqnum.idc`.

```
Datasource: BigProj
Template: crreqnum.htx
DefaultParameters:
SQLStatement:
+Select "Reqnum"
+From "chngreq"
+Where "Requestor" Like '%Requestor%'
+And "DateofRequest" = '%DateofRequest%'
#IDC-Insert FrontHTM-crinstr.htm ReportHTX-crreqnum.htx
```

Notice this is a SQL statement that returns a `chngreq` (which has been created by the database because it is an Autonumber) and passes the results to the template `crreqnum.htx`. What you need here is a simple template that will present the user with the change request number. Try the code in Listing 9.24.

Listing 9.24. HTML code for `crreqnum.htx`.

```
<HTML>
<HEAD><Title>Order Number</Title></HEAD>
<BODY BGCOLOR="#FFFFFF">
<%begindetail%>
<P>
<P>
<CENTER>
<P><B>Thank You For You Attention</B><BR>
<P><B>Change Request Received from <%idc.Requestor%></B><BR>
<P><B>On <%idc.DateofRequest%> </B><BR>
<P><B>This is your Order Number</B><BR>
<P><B><%Reqnum%></B><BR>
<P><B>Keep it for your records</B><BR>
</CENTER>
<%enddetail%>

<%if CurrentRecord EQ 0 %>
<HR=2><P>
<CENTER><B>Can't Find Order for %Requestor%<B></CENTER><P>
<CENTER><B>Call us at 904 555 1010 for assistance!<B></CENTER><P>
<%endif%>

<HR=2>
<CENTER>I Made this Page By Hand</B></CENTER>
</BODY></HTML>
```

Upon closer examination, this is a simple HTML that just presents the change request number. The project now looks like Figure 9.16.

Figure 9.16.

The returned change tracking number.

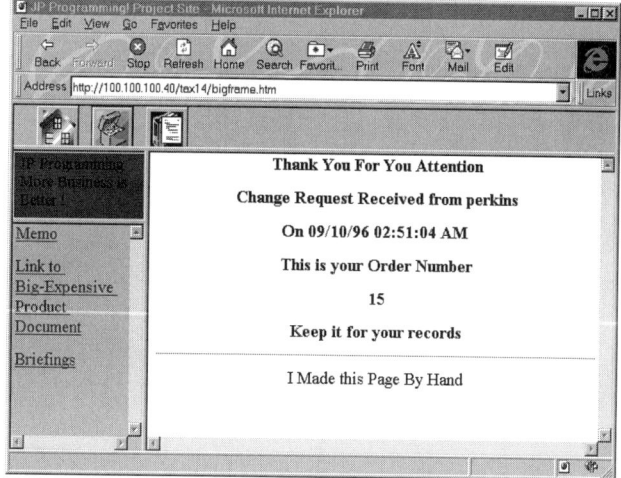

A JavaScript Application

Now that you have given the users a change request number, which they will probably lose (that is a different project), you need to give them a way to use it.

Adding a Track Change Request to the Navigation Bar.

Add another button to the Navigation bar. Name it `btnfind`. Use picture `findpeps.gif`. Your Navigation bar should now look like Figure 9.17.

Figure 9.17.
Final navigation bar.

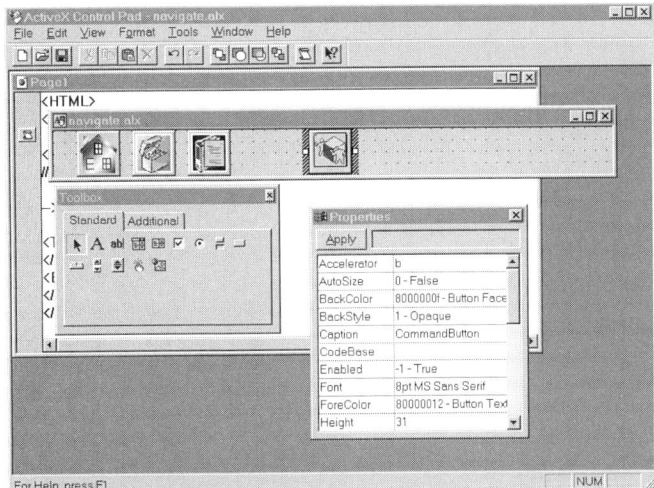

Add code to the `MouseMove` and `onclick` events of `btnfind`. In `MouseMove`, add a line to print a message to the Status bar. In the click event, add code to launch the form `crtrac.htm` that you generated at the start of this process. You are now done with the project. The code section of `navigate.alx` should look like Listing 9.25.

Listing 9.25. New `navigate.alx`.

```
<SCRIPT LANGUAGE="JavaScript" FOR="btnChangeRequest"
EVENT="MouseMove(Button, Shift, X, Y)">
<!--
self.status = "Change Request"

-->
</SCRIPT>
<SCRIPT LANGUAGE="JavaScript" FOR="btnStatus" EVENT="Click()">
<!--

window.parent.frames[3].location.href="/scripts/pjdynam.idc?"
```

continues

Listing 9.25. continued

```
-->
</SCRIPT>
<SCRIPT LANGUAGE="JavaScript" FOR="btnHome" EVENT="Click()">
<!--

window.parent.frames[3].location.href="/tax09/welcome.htm"

-->
</SCRIPT>
<SCRIPT LANGUAGE="JavaScript" FOR="btnStatus"
EVENT="MouseMove(Button, Shift, X, Y)">
<!--
self.status = "Project Status"

-->
</SCRIPT>
<SCRIPT LANGUAGE="JavaScript" FOR="btnHome"
EVENT="MouseMove(Button, Shift, X, Y)">
<!--
self.status = "Home"

-->
</SCRIPT>
<SCRIPT LANGUAGE="JavaScript" FOR="btnChangeRequest" EVENT="Click()">
<!--
window.parent.frames[3].location.href="/tax09/crinsrt.htm"

-->
</SCRIPT>
<SCRIPT LANGUAGE="JavaScript" FOR="btnFind" EVENT="Click()">
<!--
window.parent.frames[3].location.href="/tax09/crtrack.htm"

-->
</SCRIPT>
<SCRIPT LANGUAGE="JavaScript" FOR="btnFind"
EVENT="MouseDown(Button, Shift, X, Y)">
<!--
self.status = "Find Change Request"

-->
</SCRIPT>
```

Remember that the pictures in the <OBJECT> tags generate lots of lines of characters that you don't need to see. If you fire up your Web site and hit the Find button, your screen will look like Figure 9.18.

Figure 9.18.
Finding a change request number.

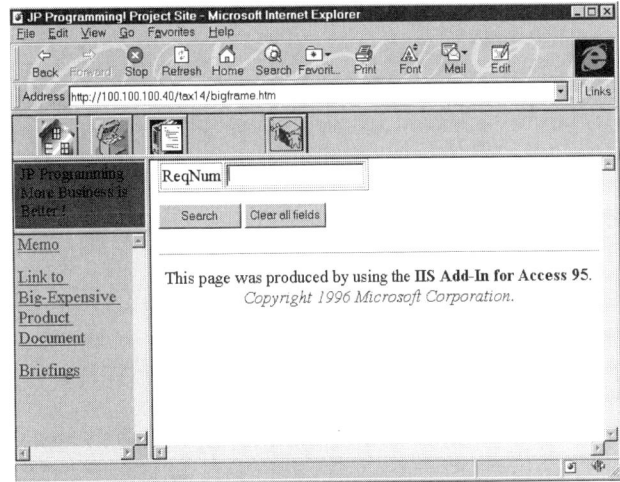

Summary

You have covered lots of ground today. You used all your acquired skills to build a project using ActiveX and JavaScript. The application you built looks more like a program than a traditional Web site, a trend I suspect will continue. At this point you have had the opportunity to use both scripting languages. You should probably have some initial feelings about which one will suit your purpose. Tomorrow your ActiveX education will continue.

Q&A

Q I noticed the application we built today didn't use ToolTips (windows that float above controls when the mouse passes overhead). Can I use ToolTips?

A Not with the ActiveX controls we used. If you need ToolTips, I suggest you visit the Web sites of some ActiveX component builders.

Q I noticed some different notation today for changing the values of the variables inside <FORM> tags. Was that just for variety?

A No. Something you always have to watch out for is how a language is implemented versus the specification for the language. Some properties that work on Internet Explorer using VBScript do not work with Internet Explorer and JavaScript and vice versa.

Workshop

Make the Bike Shop Web site you did with VBScript on Day 8, "A VBScript Application," but use frames and a Navigation bar like the example in this chapter.

Hint: Modify the Navigation bar from this application to launch the order, sales, and tracking screens used in the bike shop example.

Quiz

1. Where, in crfrom.alx, would be a good place to check the validity of the user inputs?
2. What is the syntax for triggering the submit event in a <FORM> section on the first frame in collection of frames?
3. Which of the following lines will work in JavaScript?
   ```
   window.document.forms(0).elements[0].Value = "Launch"
   window.document.forms[0].elements[0].Value = "Launch"
   window.document.forms[0].submit
   ```

NOTE Refer to the appendix, "Answers," for the answers to these questions.

Week 2

Day 10

Setting Up an ActiveX Web Site

Until now, we have approached the Internet from a user's perspective and, to some extent, from a programmer's perspective. In this section we'll take a more holistic approach and view it from a Web-site administrator's perspective.

The ActiveX features were, after all, designed with a focus on empowering the Web-site administrator. ActiveX allows the administrator to command "Give me this and that" and for the programmer to respond with, "How high and when?" Knowing the parts and pieces with which the administrators are working will help the programmers provide them with better tools.

In this chapter you will be introduced to some of the requirements for operating Web and other Internet servers. I will focus on three major pieces of a Web site and what ingredients go into them, and will discuss how they relate to ActiveX programming. These pieces include

- ☐ The hardware components
- ☐ The site administrator
- ☐ The network connection

System Requirements

When setting up a system to access the Internet, you will need a certain mix of hardware and software, installed and configured to meet your specific purposes. To determine this mix, you first need to know what the *purpose* of the Web site is going to be. A site can be set up for several reasons.

Every business, of course, can find a commercial purpose geared to its specific industry. The company could use it to peddle its wares, or just to publish information about its product.

Individuals also like to post their own home pages. Using the Web in this way gives every family (that has access to a computer) an Internet presence. Folks like to publish the goings-on and interests of their family to keep friends updated. It's like having your own family newspaper!

If you're going to have a dedicated Internet server, there are certain site-management features you may find important to have. If you're going to have an office desktop PC, you will want to make sure that it has a Web-browsing and news capabilities. If you're going to have a portable device, like a laptop or PDA (Personal Digital Assistant), you will probably need scaled-down network services such as simple e-mail and text browsing.

TIP

When you set up a Web presence, it's tempting to try to take advantage of every single piece of technology out there. This can give your users a very cool site that uses audio, video, and inline images, with buttons, arrows, and little circles describing what each one is. When you do this, try not to leave your less-activated users out in the cold.

All these powerful features become null and void to a user who has just simple text access to Web pages. (Don't laugh. Scientists are still finding "living dinosaurs" in various backwater parts of the world.)

Always include an option on your pages to allow users without ActiveX capabilities to interact with the content (see Figure 10.1).

Hardware

The hardware used for client and server machines, logically, should be different from each other. This is because their missions are different. A standard client, like a desktop PC, does not need a dedicated LAN-type connection to the Internet (but it helps). A standard server, like an HTTP Web server, will need that dedicated connection, but may not need to be able to make outgoing calls.

Figure 10.1.
Users will access your site with a variety of different types of terminals.

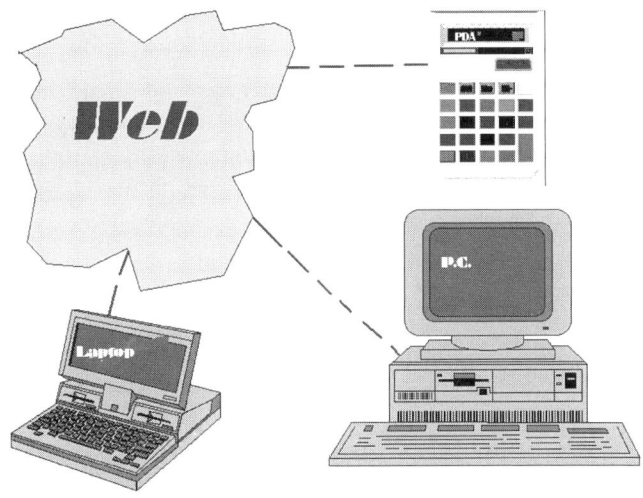

Network Access Devices

There is a tremendous variety of Web browsers and other Internet-access programs out there, but in the next few years some of these programs will be ported to smaller, hand-held, or even the new Internet TV-top devices (refer to Figure 10.1).

Some of these hand-held devices use a tiny LCD screen, while many of the proposed TV-top devices include very limited text input. Few, if any, of these devices will be able to access your other, expensive, programs like Microsoft Office or Shockwave.

The Client System

The most basic of hardware required for any system is pretty standard stuff—a console (monitor, mouse, keyboard, printer, case, and power supply) and a CPU (Motorola, Intel, and so on). Although you may be operating your own servers, you will want to do so through a remote client. You can administer the server from its console, but remember that the server may be too busy doing other server things to act effectively as a local terminal as well.

Along with the basic box just described, you will need multimedia hardware (which you probably already have) such as a joystick, sound card, and high-quality video card and monitor. You can get really carried away with the multimedia and add MIDI keyboards, radio and television cards, and CD-ROMs—all of which can be then coordinated through ActiveX programming.

Finally, the most important part of the client system is its network connection. The client can be attached to the Net in a variety of ways.

Modems can be used to access the Internet through a dial-up account. This type of account usually provides for a dynamically assigned IP address. Some providers will go as far as to assign dial-up users a static IP address (usually for an added fee). On standard telephone lines, modems can be used that are rated in speed from 2,400baud to 14,400bps. In most areas of the United States, that number can go as high as 28,800 or 36,600. For additional fees to the ISP and your phone company, you can use a higher-speed modem and ISDN line to gain access as fast as 57,600baud.

> **Dynamic and Static IPs**
>
> IP (Internet Protocol) addresses are unique numbers used to define a specific host (computer) on the Internet. Your IP is assigned to you by your ISP from its block of available numbers.
>
> If an ISP has a block of 1,024 IP addresses and has 500 users, it will have no problem giving each one of those users his own IP address.
>
> If that ISP has 2,000 users, some of them will have to share an address. It works like this: The provider assumes that fewer than 1,024 users will be logged on at any time, and dynamically assigns each user an address when he logs on. The ISP then frees up that address when the user logs off, making it available for the next client.
>
> Some users, however, will want or need a *static* IP address. This gives him the same IP every time he accesses his account. If you plan to use server-type software, this can be very useful for speeding up the system. Efficiency is increased with a dedicated IP address by not forcing the client to do a DNS (domain name service) check to locate the server.
>
> In ActiveX programming, you will want your code to intelligently allow your users to use domain names (such as bucky.com) or addresses (such as 204.181.96.53) to access different sites.

WARNING

> Often, users get very frustrated with trying to assign a domain name to a dynamic IP. It can't be done. To do so would require the updating of every single DNS in the world every time that user logged on to his ISP dial-up account.

Besides connecting through a modem, a client may be hooked up to the Internet through its LAN. This will usually happen in a corporate or other institutional setting—but hey, it could happen at home, too.

With a dedicated connection through a network card, your LAN would probably be hooked up to the Net through a dedicated ISDN or T1 line. As a rule of thumb, ISDN gives you at least twice the speed of a regular modem, and a T1 will give you about twice the speed of an ISDN connection. (See Figure 10.2.)

Figure 10.2.
If you have a dedicated connection (such as a network card), every station on your entire LAN is probably connected to the Internet.

The Server System

If your network needs are aimed more toward making information available rather than retrieving it, your system needs to reflect that mission.

The basic hardware for a server is similar to that of a desktop machine—a console (monitor, mouse, keyboard, printer, case, and power supply) and a CPU (Motorola, Intel, and so on). That's pretty much where the similarity stops.

Most servers have very little need for multimedia hardware. Unless the purpose of your server is multimedia-related (such as a RealAudio or TrueSpeech network), you can get by fine with an 8- or 16-bit sound card, or even no sound card at all.

You will probably want some kind of audio, though, so that you can hear the alarms when something goes wrong. For the most part, however, most ActiveX programming does not require any multimedia on the server at all. There are a few exceptions to the multimedia requirements on Windows NT IIS (Internet Information Server) systems. Since these systems usually run unattended, they may require no more multimedia than a CD-ROM— and that is usually to hold the installation disks.

You will also want to have plenty of storage and memory resources. On an Internet server that receives a lot of simultaneous hits, you should have very fast hard drive access—SCSI (Small Computer Systems Integration) hard drives are great for this. You should also have an abundance of memory to handle several instances of several programs working together with some degree of speed. If your server has to constantly swap between memory and storage, it is going to become bogged down, and users will timeout.

Finally, the most important part of any server is its network connection. No network, no server. For this reason, an Internet server is almost always on a dedicated connection (ISDN or T1) to the ISP. This is usually handled with a network card in the computer case. A cable comes out of this card and goes to a router that passes the signal on through a T1 or ISDN and out to the ISP.

Server Software

When you have a computer that is all hooked up to the Internet, you are ready to start setting up your Internet site, or "Net presence."

E-mail

If you are managing your own server, one of the most important services to install on your network server is e-mail. Users who want to send feedback to a Web-site administrator will often address their comments to `webmaster@whatever.net` (or some such address).

To enable these services you will need a POP3 server and an SMTP server. (See Figure 10.3.) An SMTP server will allow your users to *send* e-mail. A POP3 server is used to store *incoming* mail for your users until they are ready to retrieve it themselves. The two are usually integrated into one software package.

TIP When working with ActiveX products, it's usually a good idea to stay with Microsoft's server products—but not always.

Microsoft offers a wonderful e-mail server package: Microsoft Mail Server. It has tons of really great features and allows for plenty of different e-mail accounts over a number of different types of networks. To enable the SMTP features, however, requires (or did at the time of this writing) a *very* expensive gateway in addition to the server software itself. There lies the rub.

If you are going to be servicing only a limited number of accounts, and they will all use SMTP, Microsoft Mail is a heck of a lot more bang than you need. All its wonderful features will go completely unused and may even serve as an obstacle to productivity as you try to work around all of its features just to enable the few you need.

ActiveX does not require any specialized e-mail services—and, in fact, it is best if e-mail processes stick to the established standards. After all, SMTP is short for *Simple* Mail Transfer Protocol!

Figure 10.3.
SMTP and POP3 are used to send and receive e-mail.

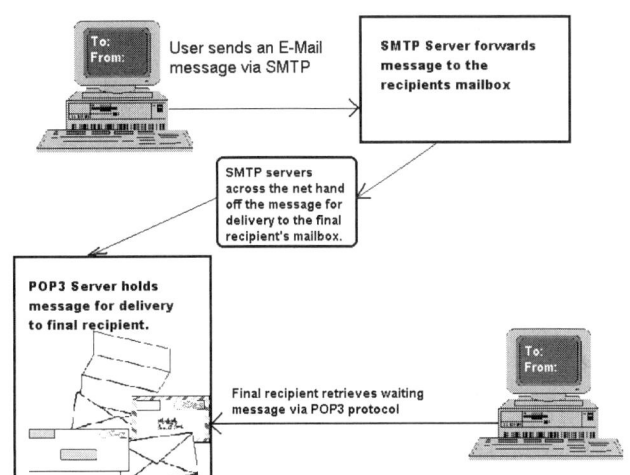

News

Internet News (Usenet) is very similar to e-mail. You compose a message, called an *article* in NNTP (Network News Transfer Protocol) lingo, and send it to a server. The recipients then retrieve the article at their leisure. This is where Usenet and e-mail branch off: You don't specify a recipient for a news article; you specify a newsgroup to which the article will be posted. The article is then retrieved by anybody who subscribes to that newsgroup. Now you're a published author!

 **NOTE** For you WinSock programmers, you should know that e-mail works over TCP/IP port 25, and NNTP works over TCP/IP port 119.

It is seldom necessary to set up a Usenet news server—unless you are operating an ISP yourself. Also, in some instances, you may want to use one to create a public forum to host a discussion of a topic relevant to you or your business.

Usenet news servers can be difficult to manage. Keeping the message counters correct and maintaining a feed with other Usenet hosts can be quite time-consuming. Also, bandwidth can be used up quickly with the more than 14,000 public newsgroups available to your users.

> **Microsoft's Internet Mail and News**
>
> This is about as good a time as any to install Microsoft's Internet Mail and News client onto your machine. You can find it on the CD-ROM that accompanies this book in the setup file named `MailNews95.exe`.
>
> Here's how to install the client:
>
> 1. Double-click the setup file `MailNews95.exe`.
> 2. After accepting the EULA (End User License Agreement), you are prompted for your name and organization. Of course, if you are not affiliated with any organization, you do not need to put anything in that space!
> 3. Next you are prompted as to whether you want to install the news client, the mail client, or both. For now, you need only select the news client, but you can install the mail client also, if you like.
> 4. Now the installation routine will copy the necessary files to your computer and prompt you to reboot. Do so.
> 5. When your system comes back to you after the reboot, you're ready to configure the system. To do so, right-click your Internet Explorer icon (on the desktop) and select the Properties option from the pop-up menu. A tabbed configuration dialog box appears; select the Programs tab.
> 6. The Programs tab has a section that allows you to specify which programs you want to use for Mail and for News. Select Internet News for your newsreader.
> 7. Run Internet Explorer. When it's fired up, you should notice a new Mail icon on your toolbar. When you click it, a pull-down menu will appear. Select the Read News option from that menu. The Internet News program will fire up, and you will be ready to configure the reader.
> 8. When your newsreader is loaded, you can exit from the Web browser if you choose. The newsreader will still be there. From the newsreader's menu, select News and then Options to go to the configuration for the client.
> 9. The news options are many, but there is only one tab with to concern yourself with here: the Server tab. Click it.
> 10. Enter your personal data—name, e-mail address, and organization (if appropriate). Then, at the bottom of the tab box, you should see three buttons, one of which is Add. Click it.

> 11. A News Server Properties dialog box will appear with three tabs. In the general tab, enter the name of Microsoft's NNTP server, msnews.microsoft.com.
> 12. Click the Connection tab and enter the properties for your specific type of Internet connection.
> 13. There is not much to put in the Advanced tab, but you should check it to make sure that it is using TCP/IP port 119 and that it is not set to use a secure connection.
>
> You are now finished installing Microsoft's NNTP client, and are ready to participate in Microsoft's newsgroups.

Transfer

Another service you will most certainly find necessary is FTP (File Transfer Protocol). This will allow you to make ZIP and other files available for downloading. To make this easy, Windows NT comes with a built-in FTP server. With it, you can provide anonymous or password-protected access to your FTP server directories. The anonymous access feature allows all users to access files and directories. The password-protected feature allows special file privileges to be assigned to individual accounts. It also has features for enabling various levels of security to fit a particular need.

Web Server

This is the service that enables users on the Net to access your Internet site with a Web browser such as Netscape. It is also one of the more complex of server systems to operate and maintain. Security features must be monitored and, as with most other servers, the logs must be monitored and user configurations kept current.

Each Web server package available has its own tips, tricks, and features. All of them enable users to retrieve hypertext documents, and most even have features for allowing CGI, Perl, or other server-side scripting.

Microsoft has introduced its IIS (Internet Information Server) as a part of Windows NT Server 4.0. This is the first complete ActiveX Web server released, and allows for such features as ISAPI and trust verification as well as other secure transaction features. As you develop ActiveX applications (both server and client), you will find the use of an IIS server invaluable in testing and debugging your processes.

Database Server

The idea of a database server is not new, but only with the development of ActiveX has it become powerful for everyday users as well as advanced programmers. Microsoft BackOffice includes SQL Server and is a very powerful tool for any large or small corporation. dbWeb is a relatively new product from Microsoft that is designed specifically for enabling database queries and responses by way of the Internet. If SQL Server is a bit more than you need, there are also more Web-centric packages such as dbWeb. These enable user interaction with ActiveX databases over a network.

Web-Site Administrator Requirements

Basic management of a Web site is relatively safe and simple. The managing and monitoring of user activity logs and other similar functions tends to be fairly routine stuff *once the server is configured properly*. That is why most ISPs will provide their users with facilities to set up and maintain their own Web pages instead of forcing them to operate their own Web servers.

The tougher issues, like security and directory structure, are handled by the network administrator, but sometimes even those functions are handed down to the individual Web-site administrators.

Technical Skills

The focus in ActiveX programming is to treat everything on the Net as a bunch of objects—each having its own properties, methods, events, interfaces, and so on. The definition of a Web-site administrator is expanded somewhat because of this.

Administrators need not be programmers themselves, but it helps to have access to one to help write client and server scripts. They also need not be hardware specialists, again, as long as there is one available. Finally, they need not be certified network specialists—as long as they have access to one.

It would seem that a Web-site administrator needs to be a jack of all these trades, but a basic familiarity with ActiveX and OLE is all an ActiveX Web-site administrator needs to have in the way of technical skills. A better analogy is that the Web-site administrator is a conductor, constantly trying to balance the different parts of his symphony (see Figure 10.4). The real talent as an ActiveX-site administrator comes in providing *content* rather than being an engineer.

Hardware

The hardware for an ActiveX Web site is very much the same as for any other Web site. The major difference between the two is the use of interactive multimedia, or *active content*.

ActiveX Web sites will tend to manage more multimedia content, and for debugging purposes may need some degree of multimedia capability.

An ActiveX Web-site administrator is faced with very few hardware issues. A few of them that one may face include

- [ ] Maintaining the connection to the Internet (by way of modem or network card)
- [ ] Maintaining hardware capable of handling any multimedia content (that is, sound card, video, and so on)
- [ ] Basic cleaning of equipment

Figure 10.4.
ActiveX Web-site administrators coordinate the efforts of a team of technicians (locally and remotely).

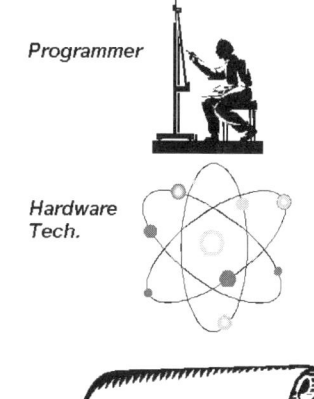

Software

An ActiveX Web-site administrator needs to be familiar with the wide variety of different types of Web browsers that will be used to access his site. This is usually limited to Microsoft Internet Explorer and Netscape, but can include a great many others.

To send files to and retrieve files from a Web site, the administrator will probably need to use an FTP client. If you enable your users to have FTP access, each user will be able to manage his own accounts, such as WWW and FTP accounts.

Most importantly, you must be familiar to some extent with all the software running on your servers. This is not as important if you are using your ISP's servers rather than your own. Two times you will definitely want to be familiar with your ISP's server software are

- [ ] When using an ActiveX server (that is, Microsoft Internet Information Server).
- [ ] When using an FTP server. Different servers use different logon/logoff processes, and, especially when performing automated tasks, the commands and responses are different among them.

Networking

Managing a Web site really does not require a very in-depth knowledge of networking. In fact, most HTML authors do not know or care much at all about networking as a technology. They just do it. There are, however, a couple of key networking features about which you, as an ActiveX programmer, need to be aware.

- Hostnames and IP Addresses—You have seen that most Internet hosts are referred to by their *domain name*, such as bucky.com or www.microsoft.com. You also know that every host on the Internet has an IP address, such as 204.181.96.53 or 207.68.137.43. DNS is where the two come together.

- DNS—By referencing the DNS, you can find out the IP address of a domain, or vice versa. (See Figure 10.5.) This is done on the Internet by registering a domain with your server's IP address through the services at InterNIC (Internet Network Information Center). The URL for InterNIC is http://www.internic.net.

Figure 10.5.
DNS resolves hostnames to IP addresses and back.

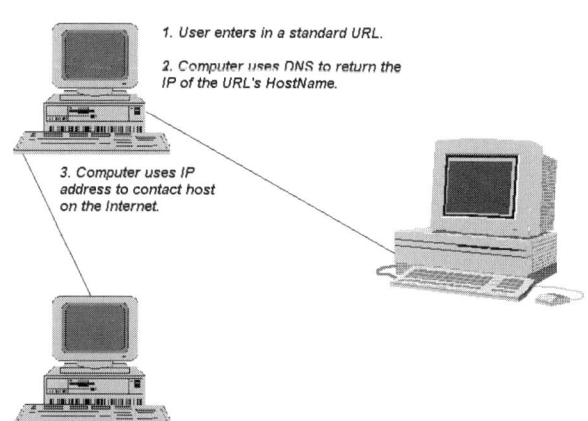

When your domain is registered through InterNIC, other users can connect to you with a relatively easy-to-remember name such as MyHost.MyDomain.Net instead of having to use a mix of your hostname and your IP address like MyHost.123.45.67.890.

NOTE: In an *intra*net, such as an office LAN, you can usually omit the domain name of a machine within your own domain, using only its hostname to refer to it. For example, if you are operating a machine named MyHost.MyDomain.Net and want to access another machine at MyDomain.Net named YourHost.MyDomain.Net, you could simply refer to the other machine as YourHost.

Network Protocols

TCP/IP (Transmission Control Protocol/Internet Protocol) is the language of the Net. It is the protocol used to communicate between hosts. Whether you use a dial-up, ISDN, Frame Relay, or T1, you will use TCP/IP.

There are a variety of other services that can also be run on the Net, but these would still use TCP/IP to communicate. Some of the services that you can run over TCP/IP include SNMP (Simple Network Management Protocol) and any or all the standard Internet services (FTP, SMTP, HTTP, and so on). Often these services are referred to, not incorrectly, as *protocols*. (See Figure 10.6.)

Figure 10.6.
FTP is working over TCP/IP. TCP/IP is working over ISDN. ISDN is working over the telephone network.

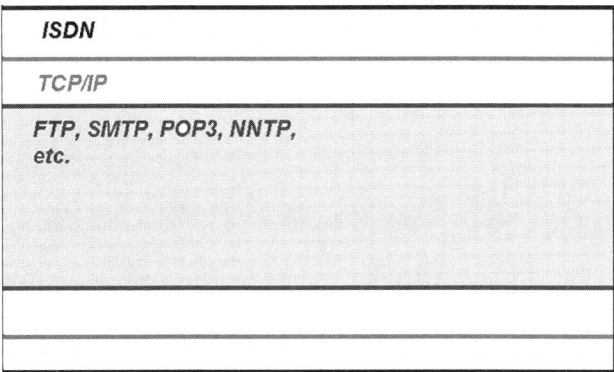

 **NOTE** You should remember that a *protocol* is a language or syntax, and a *service* is the implementation of that protocol (or set of protocols).

To *use* these services, you need not know too much about how they work. However, to *program* with them using ActiveX controls, you will want to have a fairly thorough understanding of the respective standard.

Wear Your Socks

Prior to ActiveX, there was one library within windows that gave programmers a facility for programming Internet applications for Windows: the WinSock.DLL, which is based on the Berkeley Sockets specification. Now, with ActiveX, we have a bucket-load of libraries and controls with which we can very easily program the same applications.

With the WinSock, the programmer needed to be quite expert in the hows and whys of TCP/IP. Often, when creating custom Internet applications, programmers

> found it easier (if not better) to create their own protocol rather than to stick with the established ones. Programmers are not known for being conformists, and learning how everybody else did mail or file transfers was actually more difficult than creating one's own, proprietary method.
>
> Of course, this failure to comply with established standards meant that many programs written for the Internet were actually only usable for a specific purpose and were not generally compatible with other Internet applications. By releasing such a rich and wide variety of Internet programming tools, Microsoft has given us a way to stick to established protocols without having to be a network guru. We just end up looking like one.
>
> You will learn more about these powerful controls in the final chapters of this book as you create News, Mail, FTP, and other standard network utilities.

Internet Service Providers

An Internet service provider (ISP) is an organization that provides a user with a connection to the Internet, usually for a fee. Most cities have at least one ISP operating locally, and almost every metropolitan area has more than a dozen small and large providers.

Most ISPs can be broken down into two categories:

- ☐ Those who cater to individual dial-up customers—These ISPs tend to offer a full package of Internet user services, including an e-mail account and a Web site. One downside to using this type of service is the use of dynamic IP addressing, which gives you a different IP address every time you log on to the service. Also, some of the providers charge as much as $2.50 for every hour you are online.
- ☐ Those who cater to commercial and leased-line customers—These ISPs tend to offer fewer user services and a more technical level of LAN-to-Internet connection. One downside to using this type of service is that you do not usually have the use of your ISP's Web and mail servers, with the possible exception of a few administrative e-mail accounts.

Usually a provider will offer both commercial and individual network services, concentrating on one and offering the other on the side.

> **Yeah, but where does an ISP get *its* connection?**
>
> Some of the more established services, such as CompuTek.Net and MCI.Net, offer such a high grade of service that other ISPs get their connections from them.

A good example of this ISP-to-ISP service is FishNet, a dial-up ISP in little Greenville, Texas. FishNet provides individual and commercial users in its area with dial-up Internet connections.

FishNet, in turn, gets its Internet connection from CompuTek in Dallas over ISDN lines. CompuTek, then, gets its connection from SprintLink Network over several T1 lines.

Sprintlink and CompuNet have the rare advantage of being located in the Richardson, Texas "Telecom Corridor." Richardson, Texas and Raleigh, North Carolina are the hubs of North America's two main Telecom R&D networks and, as such, are referred to as *corridors*.

Sprintlink runs backbones that connect nodes all over the world—linking many networks, LANs, and ISPs together in one big Internet. There are also several other backbones, such as MCI, AT&T, and UUNet, as well as several FreeNets—each providing a connection, of one sort or another, to the Internet.

So where did the connection *originate*? Well, the final mass of connections *is* the beginning and the end. The Internet does not "exist" anywhere, and there is no original source. When you connect to somebody who connects to somebody who connects to somebody…you're Internetting! So when you connect to an ISP, you are opening a path to everyone else who can open a path to your ISP.

Sometimes *portions* of the Net will go down for a time, but stocks do not necessarily plummet, and businesses do not necessarily fail. In early August 1996, AOL (America Online) went down for a while. Users could not access the Net, but the Internet itself did not collapse. Portions of the phone network go down from time to time also, but they always restore the lines.

So, as long as you can call your ISP, and your ISP is connected to somebody—even if it's just connecting its subscribers to each other—the Net is not "down" for you.

Building a Bomb-Proof Network: A Modern Fable

Once upon a time, there was a great country. The people of the country had spent the last 50 years at war, and there seemed no end in sight. In fact the bombs they made for their enemy were so big, the leaders decided to live underground for fear of fallout. They decided also that they would talk to other leaders on the phone and wouldn't be lonely.

> They knew that the bombs, when they came, would land everywhere. The buildings would be gone, and their phones would stop working. So they went to their scientists and asked them to build a bomb-proof phone system.
>
> "That would be a very interesting task," the scientists said, "but we've been building bombs. We don't know anything about telephones." So half of the scientists that were building bombs started building telephones.
>
> Stumped, the scientists approached the professors at the universities and asked them how they talk to each other. The professors had been using phones and told them so.
>
> "So let's get this right," the scientists said to the professors. "You talk over the telephone to each other. And if your phone stops working, and it would if a bomb hit, you would wait and use your phone later, when it works again?"
>
> "That's right," replied the professors.
>
> The scientists then went to the leaders and said, "We found it. We have your bomb-proof network!"
>
> "We are going to use the commercial telecommunications infrastructure. It is reliable, because there are teams across the country working day and night to support it. When one section of it goes down, only that section is disabled. All the non-bombed areas are still working."
>
> Excited, the leaders discussed among themselves their plans for the new network. But when they tried to predict how and when they would need it, they found that they would not.
>
> So many scientists had focused for so long on building the bomb-proof network, that there were no more scientists working on bombs.

Selecting an ISP

There are many ways to obtain a connection to the Internet. There are an even greater number of companies that will help you obtain that connection. Selecting the right connection for your specific site's needs is key in maintaining a polished Web presence. To do that you will have to have some sort of relationship with a local or distant ISP.

Because of the anonymous features of the Internet, it is often difficult to tell what kind of operation an ISP is running until you actually use its service or visit its shop. For this reason, you will want to physically visit its facilities and meet its people before you invest much more than the cost of a dial-up account. On the outside, this may seem frivolous. However, one year of dedicated service can cost upwards of $3000. A few dollars, or even a few hundred dollars, is well-spent to ensure that you don't pay for several thousand dollars' worth of someone else's mistakes.

Levels of Service

The level of service you require is not necessarily a case of "more is better." Very few people find the Internet useless, but not everybody needs a 10megabyte-per-second Ethernet connection. Consider what your *current* needs are. When a dial-up connection costs $25 and dedicated access costs $250, you must assess what you truly require before going big.

> **TIP** If you are just getting started, consider a high-speed dial-up connection for a few months. This will give you time to see just what the heck the Internet is before you go trying to program over it.

Dial-Up

If you are managing a Web site on your ISP's server, you can do so with as little as a dial-up account. Your ISP will usually provide you with an FTP site where you can post your Web pages, images, and ActiveX controls and scripts.

You *can* operate a Web server over a dial-up connection, but only while you are online. When you log off, your server can no longer process requests from the Net.

Dedicated

If you operate your own servers, there are three major differences from having dial-up service. First, you will not need your ISP's Web server. Second, you will have a local drive on which to put your Web stuff—you can set it up for FTP or whatever type of access you desire. Third, and most important, your Web site will be up as long as your dedicated connection is working.

Summary

In this chapter you have been exposed to some of the issues confronting ActiveX Web-site and network administrators in selecting and working with an Internet service provider. These issues include networking, hardware and software, and user-specific considerations.

You know that both a client and a server system must have a console with a CPU and a network connection, be it dedicated or dial-up. You also know that a dial-up connection is not very effective for running server software because the server will be disconnected whenever the dial-up session is concluded.

You have also learned about the different kinds of services that you may run on your server, such as FTP, News, and e-mail. Each service is designed to fit a particular need, and you need only install the ones you want your users to be able to access, and which provide the best format for the delivery of your content.

You also know about some of the technical skills required of Web-site administrators. Although they need not be specialists in hardware, software, or networking, they still need a general mix of all of those skills to maintain their systems. The real focus for the Web-site administrator is on the *content*.

Finally, you learned a little about how to select an ISP by visiting its site and selecting a level of service.

Q&A

Q Why would an ActiveX programmer care what an ActiveX site administrator does, as long as he creates programs that "Meet the spec"?

A The programmer not only responds to requests from the administrator; he must also anticipate the administrator's needs. For instance, if your administrator asks you to create a control that keeps track of how many hits his users' pages receive, it will benefit you to be familiar with the capabilities of his different servers to process and log that type of data. If you don't know where this data is logged, you won't know how to retrieve it.

Q I can't get my 28,800 modem to connect higher than 9600, and I know the modem is in good shape. Why is it so slow?

A Many TelCos (telephone companies) only guarantee 2,400baud connections (Southwestern Bell in Addison, Texas is one example). To avoid embarrassment, they will usually work with users to "condition the lines." This involves putting a circuit in at your phone box and another in at your connection to the phone company. This "black box" will usually bring you up to speed.

Q I want to set up an Internet server, but I only have a dial-up connection and 16-bit Windows. Can I do it?

A Yes. You *can* run a server over a dial-up connection, but your users will experience *very* slow responses. Also, some providers charge for access by the hour. You may want to switch to a less costly unlimited-access dial-up account if you operate your server on the Net more than a few hours per week.

Workshop

Develop a brief plan of a Web site for a real or fictional company. Show the directory structure and which standard and ActiveX servers you would use. Identify what personnel are needed to develop and maintain the site.

Quiz

1. What is the first thing you must do to set up a Web presence?
2. What two hardware components are common to servers as well as standalone or client computers?
3. What hardware features are generally associated with ActiveX servers and clients?
4. How often does a dynamic IP address change?
5. What is the benefit to having a static IP address?
6. What three ways can be used by Me.Our.Net with an IP of 204.001.001.001 to refer to You.Our.Net with an IP of 204.001.001.002?
7. What protocols are used to send and retrieve mail, respectively?
8. What makes an NNTP server difficult to manage?
9. What does a database server do?
10. For what two types of customers do ISPs provide Internet access services?

NOTE See the appendix, "Answers," for the answers to these questions.

Week 2

Day 11

Server-Side Scripting with CGI and ISAPI

The Internet Server Application Programmers Interface (ISAPI) is a tool with which ActiveX programmers can write server-side scripts. These server scripts are the "next generation" of the CGI (Common Gateway Interface).

These kinds of scripts are run through your HTTP daemon (server). The scripts act as an interface between the users (and their software) and the server (and its software).

Without server scripting, Web surfing is relegated to simply serving up and viewing static documents. The users can't interact with these documents, and features such as HTML forms and clickable image maps become impossible.

In this chapter you will become acquainted with writing both CGI and ISAPI applications.

CGI

Before we get into the meat and potatoes of this, let's take a look at the words CGI represents: Common Gateway Interface.

Common means that this scripting specification is used with a variety of different HTTP server software packages. This allows programmers to be relatively certain that a CGI script that is written for a package like O'Reilly's WebSite will still work on Microsoft's Internet Information Server as well as Netscape HTTP server or any of the shareware and freeware servers out there—as long as they support CGI.

NOTE You will frequently hear of an Internet server (be it SMTP, FTP, or HTTP) referred to as a *daemon* (pronounced *dee*-muhn). They get this name from the early days of the commercial Internet, when server packages were mostly limited to use on UNIX. Any UNIX-hound can tell you that these suckers were devilishly difficult to set up and maintain. Since then, they have become much simpler to operate—although most features have become much more powerful.

Gateway interface means that this scripting specification is used to allow network access to local programs (see Figure 11.1). In and of itself this is not very spectacular, but in the interest of security, you do not want to allow network access to just any old program or data file. Some of these files are just too sensitive.

Figure 11.1.
CGI and ISAPI Scripts act as an interface between a local user and an external program located on the remote HTTP server.

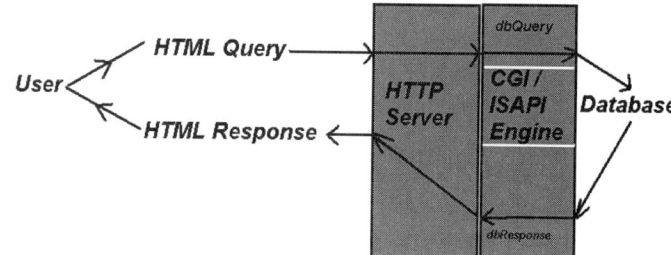

Gateways also provide the interface for allowing users to interact with Web content through clickable images and forms. Then, when the user selects whatever options he wants in the forms and images, the gateway can take that input and return *dynamic content*. This means that the document that is returned to the client may not actually exist until the user requests it. The gateway does this by taking the input provided by the user and creating a document that meets the user's request on-the-fly.

One example of these gateway interfaces is *ODBC* (Open DataBase Connectivity). ODBC is the database feature of Windows that allows the system to access any of a number of different kinds of databases without having to launch a full-blown database application. Web services do not generally know how to access a database, so they need a gateway between the user and the ODBC driver.

Tip

Microsoft has been very good about ensuring that powerful database features have been implemented in every evolution of the ActiveX technologies. This especially includes its ODBC system, which is designed to make databases accessible from a large number of interfaces (thus the word *Open* in Open Database Connectivity).

Included in the Microsoft Internet Information Server installation is a `.DLL` appropriately named `HTTPODBC..DLL`. It works with any of a number of IDCs (Internet Database Connectors) for different kinds of databases. This `.IDC` file is then used to specify a data source, define allowable queries, and specify the file that will act as an HTML template within which the results of the query will be returned to the client. The template will usually have an `.HTX` (hypertext extension) filename extension.

The user's request is translated by the gateway into a process that the ODBC system can understand. Then, when ODBC returns its results, the gateway creates an HTML document based on those results. That's dynamic content.

Tip

As you create your CGI and ISAPI applications, bear in mind that most Web surfers require instant gratification. When a user requests a document (that is, runs a script), he won't wait very long for your program to return the results.

Make sure to test your applications for speed as well as for accuracy and bugginess. A slow server is a server that users will avoid.

CGI Creation

CGIs can be created with any of a number of different languages. They come in two flavors—scripted and compiled. Either way they will work in the same manner, which I will describe throughout this chapter.

If you want to compile your CGI script into an .EXE or .DLL file, you will need to use a programming language like C, C++, or Visual Basic. These languages create a binary file that many newer programmers prefer.

The preference of a programming language over a scripting language is due, for the most part, to the power and ease with which compiled applications are developed. Most have some sort of windowed design interface that aids in the creation of the CGI. Visual Basic, for instance, uses a context-sensitive help system and will even reformat and capitalize your code *as you type.* (See Figure 11.2.)

Figure 11.2.
Visual Basic includes a context-sensitive help system and will alert you to many errors even while you are making them.

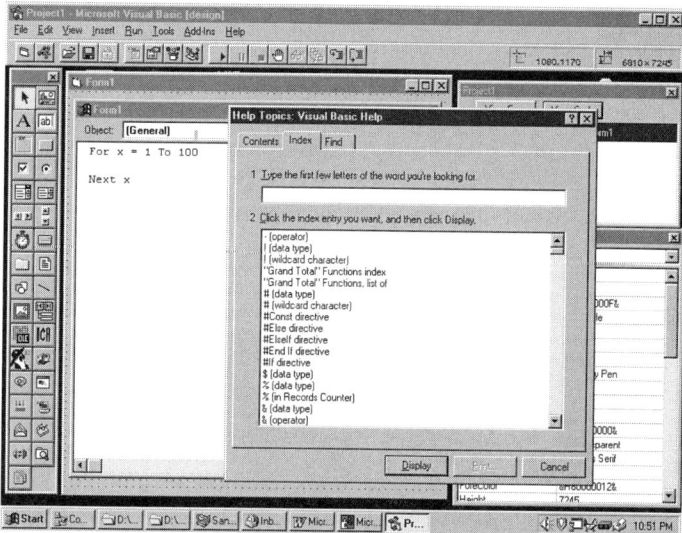

Alternatively, most seasoned Internet programmers prefer to use one of the scripting languages of the Internet such as Perl, UNIX shell, or even AppleScript. There are several good reasons for using a script instead of a compiled application. For one, scripts are just text files.

Real-time editing and debugging of these scripts is quick and simple because you don't have to recompile every time. Also, because they are text files, they can usually be edited and tested from a remote location, whereas compiled binaries have to be deleted from the CGI-BIN directory, recompiled, and then re-sent to the server before they can be tested.

CGI Script Installation

For security reasons, CGIs are normally kept in a restricted-access directory. This directory is usually named something like \cgi-bin\ or a derivative thereof. Most ISPs will not allow users to upload their CGIs directly to this directory, although they can always retrieve information from that directory.

The potential threat from which ISPs want to protect themselves comes in the form of malicious or undesirable functions being called by the script. For example, if you were to create a script, and it had a bug that placed it into some sort of endless loop, the system resources used by that script could not be recovered until a human being came along and reset the server.

If the flawed CGI script is called several times before the Webmaster gets around to fixing it, the system can hang and crash. This would crash the Web site for every single one of the ISP's users. Such a disaster would put the ISP in hot water with hundreds of users, and would cost them and their users several more thousands of dollars each. It would also, most likely, cost them their Web privileges. This is a good argument for debugging programs.

For this reason, many ISPs require you to send your CGI to an individual within its organization. That individual has the responsibility of crash-testing the script to find hidden hazards before they can cause any serious grief. Only then is the script posted to the CGI directory. This process can take days or weeks. This is a good argument for having a strong, trusting relationship with your Internet provider.

CGI Operation

The concept behind CGI programming is pretty simple. The CGI takes command-line parameters and environment variables and something called StdIn (standard input) and returns a document through the StdOut (standard output).

Command-Line Parameters and Environment Variables

In a standard DOS or Windows environment, programs can be launched with a command-line parameter. This means, for example, that if you were to type the following at a prompt:

```
MyProgram.exe Parameter1 Parameter2
```

the program MyProgram.exe would be launched, and it would use the parameters Parameter1 and Parameter2 as part of the start process.

When a user requests a CGI from an HTTP server, he usually does so while passing a set of parameters. However, these may not always be passed to the CGI as *command-line* parameters. Usually, the URL parameters are passed to the CGI through environment variables instead. For example, say you entered the URL Http://www.MyDomain.Net/MyDir/MyCGI.exe?Bucky. In this example, Bucky would be passed to the CGI application MyCGI.exe as a command-line parameter. This would cause the server to execute the command MyCGI.exe Bucky. An example of a CGI request that would pass the parameters through an environment variable instead of a command line would look like the URL Http://www.MyDomain.Net/MyDir/MyCGI.exe?MyName=Bucky.

In this example, Bucky would not be passed to the CGI application as a parameter. Instead the HTTP daemon would set an *environment variable* called MyName to the value Bucky. This would cause the server to execute the command MyCGI.exe all by itself. It is up to the CGI script itself to retrieve data from the variable.

The = is the key here. If there is no equal sign, the query string (everything after the ?) is passed to the CGI application as a command-line parameter.

If an = exists anywhere in the query string, everything to the left of the equal sign is treated as an environment variable to be set. Everything to the right of the equal sign is treated as a value to be assigned to that environment variable.

HTTP Query Syntax

> [URL]\[CGI]?[parameter]
>
> or
>
> [URL]\[CGI]? [Environment Variable]=[Value] &[Environment Variable]=[Value]

A CGI program is usually launched by a client request in the form of an HTTP query. The query can be formatted to send a command-line variable to the CGI or to set one or more environment variables to be used by the CGI in its operation. The parameter will be sent to the CGI on the command line unless there is an = in the query string. If there is an equal sign, the parameters will be used to send environment variables.

Example:

The following line would launch MyCGI.exe Parm1 from the command line:

```
http://www.MyDomain.net/MyCGI.exe?Parm1
```

The following line would launch MyCGI.exe from the command line and set the environment variable for Couple to the value of 2 and for Few to the value of 3:

```
http://www.MyDomain.net/MyCGI.exe?Couple=2&Few=3
```

This is a good time to mention the & (ampersand) character as well. Some of the more popular search engines such as Yahoo! (Figure 11.3) and WebCrawler use CGIs that require several different environment variables to be set. Each variable and its associated value is set off from the one before it with an ampersand, as in the URL Http://www.MyDomain.net/MyDir/MyCGI.exe?DOSCommand=Format&Drive=C&Parm=u.

In this example, the server would set three environment variables. The variable DOSCommand would be set to the value Format, the variable Drive would be set to C, and the variable Parm would be set to u. It would not pass any command-line parameters to MyCGI.exe because there is an = in the query string.

Another way the & character is used is in string concatenation. *String concatenation* is when you append an entire string to the end of another string. For example, suppose you had to form fields (HTML or VB—it doesn't matter). One of them contains an AreaCode value and the other contains a PhoneNumber value. You may not care to separate the two for this particular form since you are treating both as one string; therefore, you *concatenate* the two with an & character like so:

```
Dim strAreaCode as String
Dim strPhoneNumber as String
Dim strBothNumbers as String
strBothNumbers = strAreaCode & strPhoneNumber
```

This would set the value of strBothNumbers to the area code with the phone number appended to it.

Many tutorials teach that the + sign can be used instead of the & sign to achieve the same concatenation results. This is sometimes true. If you use the + sign with two string values, both of which begin with letters instead of numbers, the two may concatenate well. If, however, one of those variables has not already been defined as a string or begins with an integer, unexpected results may occur.

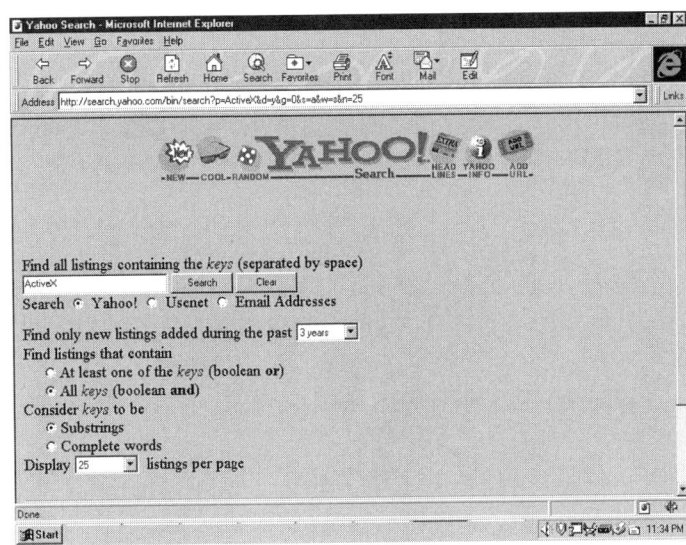

Figure 11.3.
The Yahoo! search server uses a CGI format that sends the data used in the search through environment variables.

Standard Input

Standard input (StdIn) is the information that is sent from the client to the script server with an HTTP Put or Post method. It refers to two variables—Content_Length and Content_Type.

Content_Type is the MIME type for the object that is being sent to the server script as data. This could be a picture, video, sound, or just about anything that can exist on a computer (except, maybe, a dust cover). If the data being sent is a Web form, the MIME type is application/x-www-form-urlencoded.

Content_Length is the size of the data stream being sent to the script server. This is represented in bytes—not bits or kilobytes.

Standard Output

After the script server receives the StdIn, it performs any functions contained within the script and returns the standard output (StdOut). This can be a document that goes back to the client that made the CGI request, or it can be instructions to the HTTP daemon as to what information the daemon should send back to the client. Either way, the StdOut consists of just a few headers and a data stream of some kind.

In the StdOut you can perform any one of four functions:

- Return a reference to a remote document
- Return a reference to a local document
- Return a document
- Return a document with headers

If the end result of the CGI is to simply send a file that already exists on some remote server to the client, all you have to do is send a Location: header followed by the full URL of the remote document, like this:

```
Location: http://www.OtherDomain.net/OtherDir/Other.html
```

If the result of the CGI is to send a file that already exists on the same server as the CGI, you send that same Location: header, only this time you need only follow it with the relative path, like this:

```
Location: /MyDir/MyFile.html
```

If the CGI result is to send a file it created by itself on-the-fly, send the Content-Type: header followed by a blank line and the document data:

```
Content-type: text/iuls
```

This line would let the server take care of passing the HTTP header information to the client, but in some cases it may be necessary, expedient, or just downright fun to send the header information yourself while preventing the HTTP daemon from sending that same type of header information. Also, by not requiring the HTTP daemon to process your HTTP headers, the execution speed of the CGI is increased somewhat.

Should you choose to send the header information yourself, you can report various information back to the client. This includes the level of HTML that you support and the name and version number of the application you are using. This information can be important when your users are scanning through their log files, trying to identify which programs performed what actions on their machines.

The way you tell the server that your CGI is going to talk to the client directly is to meet these two requirements:

- ☐ Prefix the filename of your CGI with nph- (for example, nph-MyScript.exe).
- ☐ Have the script send the appropriate HTTP headers that the server would have.

A StdOut that the CGI returns in this manner would look something like this:

```
HTTP/1.0 200 OK
Server: MyProprietaryServer/1.9b1
Content-type: text/html

<HTML>
<HEAD> <TITLE> My Document </TITLE> </HEAD>
<BODY>
<p>This is my document</p>
</BODY>
</HTML>
```

Using CGIs with HTML Forms

Now that you know how data is sent to the script server from the client, as well as how response data is sent back to the client from the script server, you can learn how an HTML form is used to command a client to start sending that data.

How these forms are placed within an HTML document is a topic that will be covered in the last seven chapters of this book. An example of one, however, can be seen in Figure 11.3.

For now, it should be enough to know that there are two different methods that an HTML Form can use to interact with CGI—Get and Post.

In the Get method, all the information that follows the ? on the URL line is placed in the environment variable Query_String. It is then up to the CGI program to parse that string appropriately to retrieve the data that the user entered into the HTML form.

In the Post method, the user-specified HTML form information is sent to StdOut. This is sent as a block of HTTP data rather than an extended URL as in the Get method.

From the data stream of a Post method itself, there is really no way for your CGI to automatically know when it has received all data that was sent from the client. As a result, your CGI must determine the length of the string in bytes from the Content_Length environment variable. Then it will use that byte count to figure out when it has received everything that was to be transmitted.

ISAPI Programming

Repeating what I mentioned earlier, ISAPI is not just a replacement for CGI—it's a strong enhancement to it. CGI is used on almost every kind of HTTP daemon, but it is not OLE capable like ISAPI. As a result, CGI scripts require more overhead in terms of memory and system resources.

Executables Versus Dynamic Link Libraries

A gateway interface can be compiled in one of two ways. It can be compiled into an executable (.EXE) or into a dynamic link library (.DLL). Although each has its own benefits as well as drawbacks, .DLLs are the preferred form. Both are referred to as PEs (portable executables).

Executables

If you are at all familiar with compiling programs (as you should be if you are reading this book), you already know how to compile an executable (.EXE) file.

When you create this type of file, you are creating something that can be run from the operating system's command line.

Dynamic Link Libraries

A dynamic link library (.DLL file) is a bit more complex to create. When you create this type of file, you are creating something that cannot be run from the operating system's command line, but rather is called by some other process external to the .DLL itself.

When an external process makes a call to a .DLL, it does not actually "run" the library, but rather makes reference to a procedure within that library. These calls are often referred to as *API calls*. When you create an ISAPI .DLL, you are creating an ActiveX OLE control. This calling of a process within a .DLL is called *linking*. Two types of linking can be used with ActiveX .DLLs—runtime and load-time.

In the case of load-time linking, the library sits idle until an explicit call is made to it. When this happens, the program that called it will perform whatever functions it needs and then, when the library is no longer needed, it is unloaded and remains idle until called again. These types of libraries are also referred to as *out-of-process* or *new-process* servers.

Runtime linking is very similar to load-time linking; however, when the library is a runtime library, it is called with the LoadLibrary function. It then uses the GetProcAddress method to identify the address that is used in launching the library's functions.

Server-Side Scripting with CGI and ISAPI

Tip The Microsoft documentation often refers to libraries that use runtime linking as *ISAPI .DLLs*, but this can be confusing. Remembering that ISAPI stands for "Internet Server API," understand that a runtime library can be used in a number of ways that are completely unrelated to Microsoft's Internet Server, or even the Internet itself. An ISAPI .DLL is not limited to use on an ActiveX Web server.

In an HTTP server, runtime ISAPI libraries are loaded when the HTTP server is loaded, then share resources with it by running in the server's process. This eliminates a significant amount of overhead normally associated with CGI scripts. CGIs run in a process separate from the server—demanding equal access to the system resources. Finally, when the library is no longer needed, it can be unloaded.

Note A simple printout of the code for an OLE .DLL could continue for a hundred or more pages, and the documentation on all of its features could extend much farther. Therefore, in the following sections I will focus on the parts of an OLE .DLL that is specific to ISAPI.

As you see, ISAPI .DLLs are loaded and unloaded as necessary by the HTTP daemon. When a call is made to an ISAPI library it is loaded into memory. Then, when the server decides that it no longer needs that process, it unloads it, freeing up memory and resources for other processes. Alternatively, the .DLL can be "preloaded" by the server so that when the first user attempts to access it, there won't be a pause when it's loaded.

In-Process Versus New Process

A significant difference between the way CGI and ISAPI .DLLs are run is the addresses in which they are loaded. CGIs are loaded completely separate from the server process. This is called running in a new process. ISAPIs are loaded into the same process as the HTTP server. This economizes memory use by avoiding all of the overhead associated with running several different processes in several different areas of memory.

From a system administrator's standpoint, the whole daemon will run smoother and will be less prone to bottlenecks when multiple simultaneous connections are initiated by remote clients.

There is another, very powerful advantage to running ISAPI processes. When a .DLL is first called, be it CGI or ISAPI, it is loaded into memory and run. In ISAPI, if the .DLL is still loaded and several other clients also request it, it will not need to load another copy of itself for each request. CGI needs to run a separate instance for each request, but ISAPI does not.

HTTP and ISAPI Interaction

From a user standpoint, the making of a request to and the receiving of data from an ISAPI server is done exactly the same as with CGI. This is as it ought to be, because the client's browsers are using the HTML and HTTP standards for queries and responses.

The browsers don't know or care if the server script is CGI, ISAPI, Perl, or a custom proprietary script. They send and receive their data according to the World Wide Web Consortium's standards—not some unofficial "standard" proposed by Microsoft, Netscape, or anyone else.

> **The Browser Wars**
>
> As Netscape continues to try to win Microsoft's market share and Microsoft tries to create globally acceptable Internet products, the competition has become so fierce that Netscape has even gone so far as to complain to the U.S. Department of Justice about Microsoft's progress.
>
> In their eagerness to beat the competition, however, each has implemented features in its own browser that have not been accepted by the Internet standards committees. Microsoft (with its BGSound tag) and Netscape (with its strange use of the Object tag) have made the presentation of Internet content inconsistent between browsers. (Although Microsoft's visual display remains compliant, Netscape does not currently display embedded objects properly. Netscape won't play Microsoft's BGSounds, but this usually will not interfere with content presentation.)
>
> This extreme competition has, in many cases, forced content providers to keep what amounts to two or three copies of their Web site available online so that Netscape users can view content geared toward that browser, Internet Explorer users can view content geared toward that browser, and users with text-only browsers can view content geared toward their browsers.
>
> These inconsistencies are a prime example of how Internet consumers can suffer when individual companies forsake established standards and try to lead the pack instead of working with it.

Although the data and procedures used by ISAPI are similar to those of CGI, from a programmer's standpoint the information is passed back and forth in a very different way.

The reason for this is the OLE nature of ISAPIs.

These advanced OLE features also make the process much more complex, and fall well outside the scope of anything with which a new user may be familiar. However, because ISAPI is such a powerful feature of the ActiveX family of technologies, I am including it here.

TIP If you want to go on to develop these and other types of OLE applications, it is recommended that you make use of the MSDN (Microsoft Developer's Network) line of CD-ROMs. There are several levels to MSDN, but you will find most of what you need for OLE programming at Level 2. When you obtain an MSDN subscription, Microsoft provides you with (depending on your subscription level) copies of all of their APIs, copies of all of their operating systems, and copies of all of their BackOffice network servers.

The Extension Control Block

The Extension Control Block (ECB) is ISAPI's equivalent of StdIn and StdOut. It is a data structure that performs the passing of data from a client to the script and back. The actual data that is in this includes everything you would have sent and received through StdIn/StdOut plus some.

In the ECB structure are variables such as Query_String, Path_Info, and Path_Translated. In addition, this structure includes several functions that are used to pass information back and forth. These functions include GetServerVariable, WriteClient, and ReadClient.

NOTE For you OLE programmers out there, you will need to keep in mind as you write your ISAPI servers that the files must be multithreadable. Complete information on this can be found in the MSDN Level 2 CD-ROMs or just about any manual on Win32 OLE programming. If you are not already an OLE Programmer, you may wish to explore this area of programming.

Entry Points

Every ISAPI .DLL requires certain *entry points*. Entry points are features of an object server through which the .DLL will interact with the rest of the system. They include GetExtensionVersion, HTTPExtensionProc, TerminateExtension, and a set of return values.

GetExtensionVersion

This is the first process called when the HTTP daemon attempts to run an ISAPI server. If the .DLL does not support it, the whole process will fail.

HTTPExtensionProc

This process is called in response to every client request. It can be compared to Visual Basic's Sub_Main feature because it runs as soon as the .DLL is loaded. It uses the ReadClient callback functions to read the client data.

When the ISAPI server gets this data, it can then go about figuring out what it is supposed to do with it.

Return Values

After the ISAPI server has done whatever it was written to do, it needs to return a value indicating its status to the daemon. This status will indicate whether the request is still pending, if there was an error, or that the process has been completed successfully.

One type of return value that you will want to make sure to use is the data to be sent back to the client using the WriteClient or ServerSupportFunction.

TerminateExtension

This process is the exact opposite of the HTTPExtensionProc process. It is run when the .DLL is to be shut down and is very useful for freeing up system resources.

Just because your program has run its course and is ready to be unloaded doesn't necessarily mean that every process it initiated is complete. When the .DLL makes a call to other OLE servers on the machine, those servers may get hung up or otherwise fail to exit properly. The TerminateExtension process provides a place where programmers can put any code to clean up the mess left behind when these errors occur.

Failure to take advantage of this process can put your system in a resource crunch. As each of the different programs and processes are executed, they take up a certain amount of memory and/or processor time. If these keep getting loaded and are never unloaded, they will tie up more and more of your system. Eventually, your 128MB Web server could be left with only 2MB or 3MB of memory available—the rest being reserved for those incomplete processes and threads that were not cleaned up.

ISAPI Functions

Within the HTTPExtensionProc process are several functions that can be called to read and set information about the current connection.

GetServerVariable

`GetServerVariable` is the function ISAPIs use to retrieve information for which a CGI would have used an environment variable. This includes information about the current connection as well as any server-specific information.

WriteClient

This function, like its namesake and counterpart in CGI, is used to send output to the client host. When the function is complete, it will return a boolean (`True`/`False`) value indicating whether the operation was successful. If it was not, and it returns a `False` value, you can use the `GetLastError` function to find out the nature of the problem.

ReadClient

The `ReadClient` function is another function that has a namesake counterpart. It is very similar to the `WriteClient` CGI process. It is used to read the information that the client sends through the HTTP connection. When this function is used, it will return a boolean response indicating whether it was successful.

If the `ReadClient` function returns a `False` response, it means that there was some sort of problem. The server can then use the `GetLastError` function to determine the nature of the problem. The opposite would seem to be indicated by a `True` response, but this is not necessarily going to be the case every time.

When the `ReadClient` function returns a `True` response, it can either mean that the function was successful, or it could mean that the Windows socket closed before the operation was complete. If the latter is the case and the socket timed out or was otherwise shut down prematurely, the `ReadClient` will return a `True` response, but at the same time, the data it retrieves will be 0 bytes in length.

The reason for this seemingly illogical way of handling a premature closure of the socket is due to the fact that in the event of a failure without a closed socket, you may want to retry the `ReadClient` function until it works properly. However, if you keep retrying to `ReadClient` when the socket is closed and you keep returning a `False` value, the server will get stuck in an infinite loop.

When the function reports the process as successful but with a 0-length output, then a retry won't be triggered. The server will then try to read the data that was returned (or the data that was not returned, in this case) and, seeing that it is 0 bytes long, this result can be used as a trigger to check for a closed socket.

Considerations for Building an ISAPI .DLL

After you have completed the basic functionality of your ISAPI OLE server, there are a few points you should take into consideration. These points are best left for the rewriting and debugging process. How they are implemented depends on the purpose of the server. They are not supposed to be the framework within which to write the program.

HTTPExtensionProc

Avoiding confusion of the `HTTPExtensionProc` with the CGI `StdIn`, you will want to make sure that each of the server variables is taken from the ECB data structure and that you are not referencing environment variables—as you would do with CGI.

In this process you will receive a pointer to the ECB data, which is the only parameter passed. Then you can use the `GetServerVariable` feature to access whichever variables you need in your ISAPI. The ISAPI can also use the `ReadClient` feature to retrieve data from the remote host that requested the process.

Access Violations

You can't debug an OLE server enough, but you sure better try. In the case of ISAPI servers, this is particularly critical because an ill-performing ISAPI that runs in the same process as the daemon can bring the system down if it tries to perform an OLE function on something that is not ready for it. One area where this type of debugging is of special importance is in an environment where several ISAPI OLE servers are used.

As with CGIs, there can be (and usually is) more than one ISAPI server that you will want to make available to your users. When multiple ISAPIs are running, they stand a risk of bumping into each other and trying to modify the same bit of data at the same time.

When testing your ISAPI server, make sure that you test it—not only alone, but also in combination with other ISAPI servers that will be on the same machine. To resolve access violations, and to prevent them in the first place, you should obtain a copy of the Win32 API. This document details many different features of Windows that keep the OLE programmer and his project out of trouble. A few of them are described here.

DLLMain

This type of entry function is called by an ActiveX Web daemon during the `LoadLibrary` and `FreeLibrary` processes. In it you should have any information necessary to both get the ISAPI server up and running, and to bring it back down and unload it.

Logging

The ECB structure uses a field named `lpszLogData` to provide information for logging of activity by the ISAPI OLE server. When your ISAPI needs to record log data, it is usually best to log at least some information to the server's log. Doing this provides the system administrators for the Web daemons the information they need to determine the cause of any mysterious ISAPI-related problems.

If you log your information where the system administrators can see it, they will be better equipped to lay blame in the proper place without too much fishing around. It is very easy for a system administrator to kick your ISAPI server back to you and blame it for all kinds of problems if you are not logging to his logs and a problem occurs. Logging to this file also provides a way for the system administrator to track the use of different OLE servers and determine which ones are used and which are not.

Converting CGI to ISAPI

CGIs and ISAPIs share a common purpose—server-side scripting. Although they perform very similar purposes, converting your older CGI applications to new ISAPI ones involves a technological shift from command-line-oriented programming to object-oriented programming.

You won't have to change the logic of your gateway interface—although you will have to change much of the programming syntax used to create it.

Converting the other way however, from ISAPI to CGI, is not quite so simple—it is sometimes even impossible. Taking an ISAPI and converting it to CGI is impossible in many cases because ISAPI takes advantage of many OLE features with which CGI is utterly incapable of dealing.

Let's take a look at some of the considerations you will need to take in converting your CGI into an ISAPI OLE server.

The following conversion points are by no means to be used as a complete process for creating an OLE server. To create an OLE server requires many advanced OLE skills that are not unique to ActiveX.

StdIn/StdOut to ECB

CGI receives its input from the StdIn features. You should go through your ISAPI project to ensure that it retrieves this data from the lpbData field of the ECB through use of the ReadClient callback function instead of StdIn.

When execution of the CGI is complete and it is ready to return its results, it sends signals through StdOut. This is done by sending Status: ### xxxx (where # is an integer and x is a character) through the WriteClient method.

You should find these places within your project and make sure that you use one of the ISAPI methods to send data to the client. This is done by using the WriteClient method, defined in the ECB. This method is very similar to the CGI equivalent by the same name. Alternatively, you can use the HSW_REQ_SEND_RESPONSE_HEADER feature of the ServerSupportFunction.

If your CGI uses Location: or URL: to return a prior existing file, these processes need to be replaced with their ISAPI equivalents within the ServerSupportFunction. This includes HSE_REQ_SEND_URL for files that are local to the server and HSE_REQ_SEND_URL_REDIRECT_RESP for files that are on a remote server or other unknown location.

Summary

Today you have become acquainted with server-side scripting. The lessons here deal with CGI and ISAPI scripts, but other scripts (such as Perl and LISP) can be used also.

Both CGI and ISAPI pass information between a Web server and a Web client (usually a browser). The information for CGI is formatted exactly the same as for ISAPI because the information that flows back and forth across the Net must conform to the HTTP standard. The difference between CGI and ISAPI is in how the information is handled on the server.

Most CGI parameters can be sent through environment variables; if not, information can be passed on the command line.

In the case of ISAPI, information is passed through OLE interfaces defined in the ISAPI library file.

ISAPI is a feature of ActiveX that works on an Internet server. It has certain benefits over CGI. When several clients request the same CGI process at the same time, a separate instance of the CGI must be run for each client request. An ISAPI need only have one instance of itself loaded to service multiple simultaneous requests. Also, a CGI runs in a process separate from the server, while ISAPIs run within the server process.

All in all, this allows a server to run more server scripts faster using ISAPI over CGI.

Q&A

Q When creating an OLE ISAPI into a .EXE file and attempting to register it with the RegSvr32 utility, I get application errors. Why is this?

A This is an error that has been reported frequently throughout alpha, beta, and even the final release phases of the ActiveX SDK. Compiling your OLE server as a .DLL instead of an .EXE always seems to cure it, but nobody can say for sure yet why this is so.

Q This chapter talked about ISAPI as an extension to CGI; is this the same as an ISAPI filter?

A No, but there are many similarities. They both are compiled into .DLL files and the syntax for their functions is very similar (for example, filters use GetFilterVersion and HTTPFilterProc, whereas ISAPI extensions use GetExtensionVersion and HTTPExtensionProc).

The purpose of an ISAPI filter is to monitor all incoming requests to the HTTP server. If a condition you specified in the filter occurs (such as a request from a specific IP), the filter process is run. This can be extremely useful for monitoring activity or rejecting certain hosts from the server.

Q Are there any tools for making the creation of ISAPI extensions any easier?

A Yes, thank goodness. Visual C++ 4.1 introduced an AppWizard (Application Wizard) that can be used to create ISAPI extensions—as well as a number of other ActiveX aids. Without this tool, manually coding all of the features of an ActiveX OLE server can be tremendously time-consuming.

Q I'm not a C++ programmer, but I have written many OLE applications in Visual Basic. Will I need to rewrite them for C++ to make use of their OLE features over the Web?

A No. Microsoft provides a .DLL called OLEISAPI..DLL that allows you to run processes that are exposed to OLE without rewriting them for ISAPI. This is done through the action attribute of the <FORM> tag. The action is specified like so:

```
Action = OLEISAPI..DLL/[ServerName].[ClassName].[MethodName]
```

If you have a server that is registered as TheServer, a class called DoIt, and a method called FastReturn, you would write out the action attribute parameter like so:

```
Action = OLEISAPI..DLL/TheServer.DoIt.FastReturn
```

Q I wrote an OLE .DLL in Visual Basic that I am running on my Internet Information Server. I decided to change a few things in it and recompile. This resulted in an Access Denied error. What happened?

A When OLE ISAPI calls your .DLL and then finishes with it, it leaves the library in memory. To recompile your VB .DLL, you will need to shut down the Web service before you try to recompile your library. Note that in Windows NT, network server applications can be run as a "service." This means that they do not require any program to be run. They are practically part of the operating system and are as transparent to the user as File and Printer Sharing is to the Windows 95 user.

Workshop

Using a site such as Yahoo! (http://www.yahoo.com) or Deja News (http://www.dejanews.com), create a customized HTML form that will search its database. Visit its site and observe the HTML source for its forms. This is called reverse engineering.

Quiz

1. What do CGI and ISAPI stand for?
2. What is the purpose shared by an ISAPI extension and a CGI?
3. What file extension identifies a file as an interface to ODBC?
4. What file extension identifies a file as a template within which to return the results of an IDC query?
5. Can Visual Basic be used to create ISAPI .DLLs?
6. What commands are used by ISAPI .DLLs to retrieve information from and send information to a client connection?
7. Why are CGIs and ISAPIs kept in a directory apart from the rest of the Web pages?
8. What character, when present, causes the HTTP daemon to pass the query string as environment variables rather than command-line parameters?
9. What two types of files can be used as ISAPI extensions?
10. What is the advantage of running an in-process server rather than a new-process or out-of-process server?

NOTE Refer to the appendix, "Answers," for the answers to these questions.

Week 2

Day 12

WinSock—Windows Network Programming

In this chapter you will learn what WinSock is. You will also learn how the WinSock control is used to create applications for TCP and UDP. When you are finished, you will be able to create:

- ☐ A TCP server and a TCP client application
- ☐ A UDP server and a UDP client application

What Is WinSock?

WinSock (short for Windows Sockets) is the standard for programming network applications in Windows. All ActiveX programs use the routines in the WinSock DLLs to access the TCP/IP stack. WinSock is meant to be a universal interface to the TCP/IP stream.

From a computer's perspective, sockets in programming work just like electric sockets. When a piece of software wants to get some juice from the network, it plugs into a stream and gets whatever it needs. You can never have any more connections than you have sockets, but the sockets are easy to install. Each additional connection requires more and more power (or bandwidth).

Background

Before I go into the nuts and bolts of how to use ActiveX WinSock features, here's a little background on WinSock.

History

The University of California at Berkeley is known for all kinds of creative innovations (some more productive than others). The "sockets" concept of networking is one of the best.

Berkeley Software Distribution's UNIX was the first to incorporate socket style-routines. BSD UNIX was developed to be the universal interface to TCP/IP. Although it is still in wide use, it has fallen into a small niche as other network systems such as NetWare and Windows NT have taken a dominant position. The TCP/IP aspect of UNIX remains, though.

The task of taking this TCP/IP implementation to a Microsoft Windows machine was undertaken by a group of hobbyists and professionals. The planning sessions were held during a series of conferences in the early part of this decade. The WinSock standard was proposed in September of 1991. Research on it continued on until January 1993, when the version 1.1 specification was released. WinSock 2 is currently in its test phases and is planned for release in late 1996 or early 1997. It will be significantly, if not completely, backwards compatible with version 1.1.

Current Implementation

The WinSock standard has been accepted by Microsoft as the official standard for programming TCP/IP applications in Windows. It is not, however, owned by Microsoft, as ActiveX is. While Microsoft did have a very strong voice in how WinSock was developed as a standard, WinSock has always been maintained by an independent organization. According to Microsoft's press releases, ActiveX will also be handed over to an independent standards body for continued maintenance and development.

NOTE Although the WinSock standard can, theoretically, provide an interface for programming over any network, it has mostly been used for programming Internet applications through TCP/IP.

WinSock Vocabulary and Context

A WinSock *supplier* is the individual or organization that creates an application based on the Windows Sockets API.

An *application* is WinSock compliant if it adheres to all provisions in the WinSock 1.1 specification (about 200 pages). It must have at least one WinSock interface (or there is no reason to go through the trouble of adhering to the WinSock specification!). Any application that is WinSock compliant is called a WinSock application (of course).

WinSock Technical Description

WinSock routines are only one level in the hierarchy of objects between you (the person) and the TCP/IP stream (see Figure 12.1).

Figure 12.1.
There are many levels of communication that enable a user to retrieve remote data through a WinSock connection.

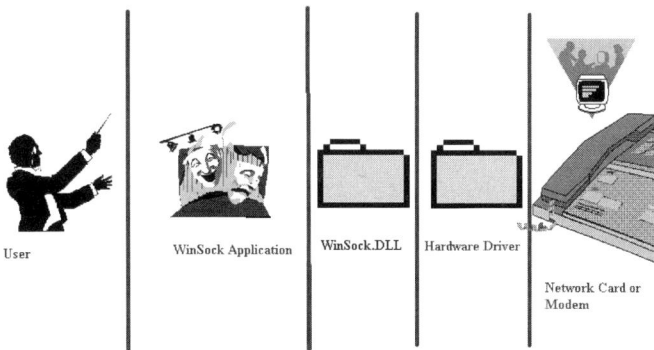

Hierarchy

First there is you, the user, and you are using a WinSock application (say it's your Web browser). You want to use this thing to get some information from the Internet, so your Web browser will need to access the TCP/IP stream, which is the lowest level of the hierarchy.

The TCP/IP stream has to come up from "out there" on the Net to your computer through a hardware interface. This is your modem or your network card—whichever you use to access the Internet.

After the stream gets in through the hardware, there is a piece of software that is usually part of the operating system. That is the *driver* for your network hardware.

This hardware driver monitors the network device as well as the application's software to determine what is talking to whom. "On top" of this hardware driver are the network *stacks* for whatever protocols you use on your computer. On a Windows95 machine, these are usually NetBEUI, NetBIOS, and IPX/SPX. TCP/IP is also included for any Internet hosts.

Whatever other network stacks are used on a computer, every machine that accesses the Internet will have to have a TCP/IP stack as well. Your Web browser communicates with this stack. Obtaining this communication between your Web browser and the TCP/IP stack is the purpose of WinSock routines.

Functions

WinSock.DLL (also known as The WinSock Library) is a file on your hard drive that contains the socket functions. This library is the *hard* code for making the computer send the zeros and ones to the correct parts and pieces of your computer. By making calls to this file and monitoring its states, you can perform all the socket functions for communicating with TCP/IP. You will look at some of C>nSoa'.DLL's more basic functions to acquaint yourself with its features.

When you run your Web browser, you are telling it to view different pages on the Web. This is conducted by typing a URL (Uniform Resource Locator). Within this URL is the name of the specific host on the Net from which you wish to retrieve the page. The name portion of the URL can be in the domain-name format (www.mcp.com) or in IP format (206.246.150.10).

If the domain name format is used, it will need to be resolved into the IP format, which is how hosts on the Net are uniquely identified to each other. Only humans need the domain-name format to make this identification easier to remember. To get the IP address, use the GetHostByName() function.

The WinSock GetHostByName() Function

GetHostByName(*Hostname*)

The GetHostByName() function is used to retrieve the IP address of a specified host. This must be done before the connection can be made to the other system because computers use IP addresses instead of domain names to identify themselves to each other.

Example:

GetHostByName(mcp.com)

This function would return:

206.246.150.10

On a similar note, if you need to convert an IP Address to a host name, use the GetHostName() function.

The WinSock GetHostName() Function

GetHostName(*IP Address*)

The GetHostName() function is used to retrieve the domain name that is assigned to the specified host's IP address. This is used to make the identification of a specific host easy for the user.

Example:

GetHostName(206.246.150.10)

This function would return:

mcp.com

WinSck.OCX

Implementation of the WinSock API into a user application can be quite complex because a tremendous number of interfaces are available. Requesting a connection, making the connection, communicating, and so on are each processes that involve many steps. States change as these steps are taken, and the application must monitor these states, acting accordingly.

In spite of this complexity, Windows Internet applications can be developed with relative ease when using a plug-in control such as the WinSck.OCX. This control takes over most of the difficult and repetitive tasks. This leaves the programmer free to code only the most application-specific features.

Purpose of the WinSock Control

The WinSock control can be used to program client or server machines. It can also be used in a special third mode called *broadcast*, which is a hybrid of the previous two modes.

Installation

The ICP (Internet Control Pack), included on the enclosed CD-ROM, contains controls for most of the more popular Internet protocols. The most powerful of these, and perhaps the most difficult to use, is the WinSock TCP/UDP control.

 **NOTE** To install the Internet Control Pack, double click the MSICPB.exe icon on the CD. When the automatic installation is complete, reboot your system as prompted.

All other controls in this package are *client controls*; they are used to connect to other machines that are waiting and monitoring the Net for connection requests. The WinSock UDP and TCP controls, however, can act as either client or server controls. If your application conforms to the proper specifications, it can even act as a server control for HTTP, FTP, SMTP, and all the others.

In the following sections you will examine the WinSock control's features for creating both a client and a server application in Visual Basic.

The first sample projects you will create are a message server and a client application. A message server takes messages for you while you are away from your computer, and a client application is used by others to send those messages to you.

Creating a WinSock TCP Server

To create the WinSock server, start with a brand new Visual Basic form. In the References option of the project, select Microsoft WinSock Controls. Then add the controls to the Visual Basic toolbar.

 **NOTE** Adding the Microsoft WinSock controls to the toolbar places two icons on the toolbar. One is the TCP control, and the other is the UDP control.

 **TIP** If the WinSock control is not on the list and you have installed the Internet Control Pack, follow these instructions:

1. Locate the WinSck.ocx file on your hard drive.
2. Run RegSvr32.exe and the location of the file from the command prompt (for example: RegSvr32 C:\Windows\System\WinSck.ocx).
3. Pull up the References option in Visual Basic, and the control should be listed.

Next, add the labels, text boxes, buttons, and so on (see Figure 12.2). These will include:

- [ ] Two command buttons; one named cmdClose and the other cmdListen
- [ ] Two labels; one named lblConnections with a caption of 0
- [ ] One list box named lstMessages
- [ ] One TCP control named tcpListener
- [ ] One TCP control array named tcpReceiver with a 0 index property

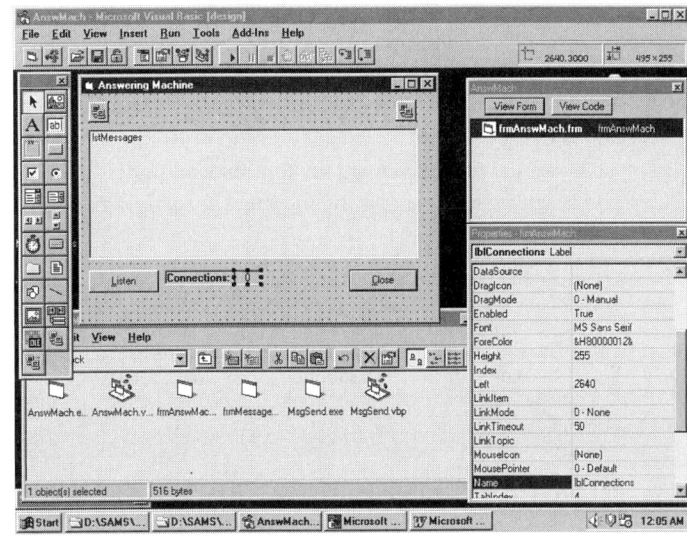

Figure 12.2.
The WinSock answering machine application uses several labels, text boxes and buttons as well as two copies of the WinSock control.

Now add code to the appropriate controls so that this application will take your messages for you.

First of all, tell the control to monitor one TCP/IP port to any incoming messages. For your answering machine, choose the random 1023 port. To tell the WinSock control to monitor that port, set the LocalPort property, then invoke the Listen method like so:

```
Private Sub cmdListen_Click
    'Server starts monitoring port 1023when the Listen button is clicked
    tcpListener.LocalPort = 1023
    tcpListener.Listen
End Sub
```

The WinSock TCP Control's Listen Method

WinSock Control.LocalPort = *Unused Port*

WinSock Control.Listen

The WinSock control's Listen method is used to command the control to monitor the local TCP/IP port as specified in the LocalPort property.

Example:

```
tcpWinSock.LocalPort = 1025
tcpWinSock.Listen
```

When a user sends a message (using the client application that you will write later in this chapter) the ConnectionRequest event is fired. When this happens, load a copy of the tcpReceiver control, leaving the tcpListener control free to handle any other incoming calls. To track how many incoming messages are arriving at one time, update the lblConnections counter.

```
Private Sub tcpListener_ConnectionRequest (ByVal requestID as Long)
    'When a connection is requested, a Receiver control is loaded
    `and the Connections counter incremented.
    lblConnections.Caption=lblConnections.Caption + 1
    Load tcpReceiver(lblConnections.Caption)
    tcpReceiver(lblConnections.Caption).Accept requestID
End Sub
```

The WinSock TCP Control's Accept Method

WinSock Control(Index).Accept *Connection ID*

The WinSock control's Accept method is used to tell a control to accept an incoming request for a connection. A link to the connection request is passed to the control that is to accept the request.

Example:

```
tcpWinSock(3).Accept 25
```

This will tell the fourth WinSock control to accept a connection request, identified as an integer.

After this code has executed, the connection between the client and the server is set.

The next step is to wait for the client application to send its message. When the server receives the message, the DataArrival event is fired. When this happens, invoke the WinSock control's GetData method to retrieve the message. The message is then added to the lstMessages list box for you to view. The message-taking code looks something like this:

WinSock—Windows Network Programming

```
Private Sub tcpReceiver_DataArrival(Index as Integer, ByVal bytesTotal as Long)
Dim msgDataIn
'When data arrives it is sent directly to the Message List
    tcpReceiver(lblConnections.Caption).GetData msgDataIn, vbString
    lstMessages.AddItem msgDataIn
End Sub
```

The WinSock TCP Control's GetData Method

SYNTAX

WinSock Control(Index).GetData *Variable*, *VariableType*

The WinSock control's GetData method is used to retrieve any data sent to the control from the remote client. The data is then sent to the user-specified variable.

Example:

tcpWinSock(1).GetData strMyVariable, vbString

This will tell the second WinSock control to set the string-type value of vbMyVariable to whatever was received through the WinSock connection.

As soon as the client sends its message, it closes the socket. When this happens, decrease the Connections counter and unload the WinSock control that was using it like so:

```
Private Sub tcpReceiver_Close(Index as Integer)
    'When the socket closes
    `the control is unloaded and the Connections counter is decreased.
    tcpReceiver(Index).Close
    Unload tcpReceiver(Index)
    lblConnections.Caption = lblConnections.Caption - 1
End Sub
```

The WinSock TCP Control's Close Method

SYNTAX

WinSock Control(Index).Close

The WinSock control's Close method shuts down the connection between client and server. The control can then be unloaded, freeing network resources.

Example:

tcpWinSock(25).Close
UnLoad tcpWinSock(26)

 This closes the 27th WinSock connection, then unloads the control.

TIP The WinSock control's Close method might seem to be a redundant feature because the control is unloaded whenever the form is unloaded.

Actually, the Close method is important because it cleans and closes any loose connections to the network. This frees your network resources as soon as they are no longer needed.

After you compile this into an .EXE, your computer will be able to run the program and, after you press the Listen button, it will take incoming messages from the client program (which I will discuss now).

Creating a WinSock Client

To create the WinSock client, start with a brand new Visual Basic form. In the References option of the project, select Microsoft WinSock Controls. Then add the controls to the Visual Basic toolbar.

The next step is to add the labels, text boxes, buttons, and such (see Figure 12.3). These will include:

- ☐ Two labels
- ☐ Two text boxes; one named txtRemoteHost and the other named txtMessage
- ☐ One command button named cmdSend
- ☐ One TCP control named tcpSender

Figure 12.3.
Since it does not have to monitor a port, the WinSock message-sending application only uses one copy of the WinSock control.

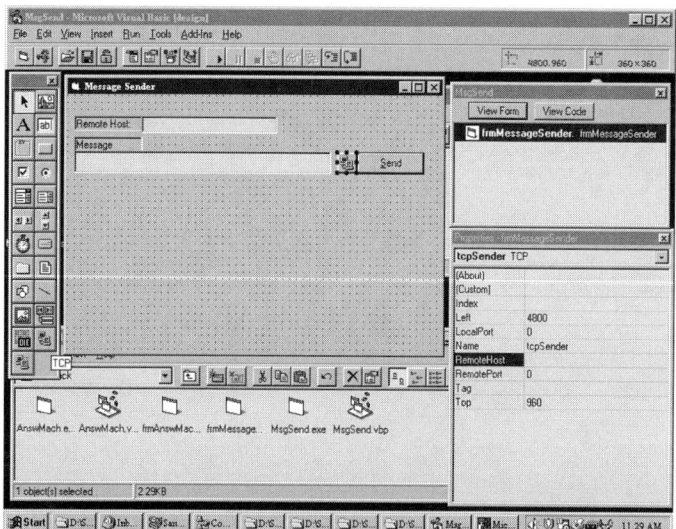

Now add code to the appropriate controls so that you can send messages to the server program.

When the user has identified the IP address of the answering machine and entered his message in the text box, he presses the Send button to transmit the message to the server.

Since the program does not do anything until the user presses the button, you must add code to the Send button's `Click` event that tells it to connect to the answering machine like so:

```
Private Sub cmdSend_Click
    'The user specified Answering Machine is called on port 1023
    tcpSender.Connect tcpRemoteHost, 1023
End Sub
```

The WinSock TCP Control's Connect Method

```
WinSock Control(Index) Server IP, Server Port
```

or

```
WinSock Control(Index) RemoteHost = Server IP
WinSock Control(Index) RemotePort = Server Port
WinSock Control(Index) Connect
```

The WinSock control's `Connect` method is used by a control that is acting in client mode to request a connection to an Internet server. The IP address and the port on which it is listening can either be passed on the `Connect` command line, or their respective properties can be set before the `Connect` method is invoked.

Example:

```
tcpMyClient. "204.181.96.53", 25
```

or

```
tcpMyClient RemoteHost = "204.181.96.53"
tcpMyClient RemotePort = 25
tcpMyClient Connect
```

This instructs the WinSock control to request a client connection to the server at `204.181.96.53` on port 25.

As soon as the connection is made, send your data, and log off. This is done in the `tcpSender` control's `Connect` event like so:

```
Private Sub tcpSender_Connect()
    'When a connection is made
    'the Message is transmitted and the socket is then closed.
    tcpSender.SendData txtMessage.Text
    tcpSender.Close
End Sub
```

The WinSock TCP Control's SendData Method

WinSock Control(Index).SendData *Data String*

The WinSock control's SendData method is used by the control in either client or server mode to transmit data to the remote connection.

Example:

tcpMyClient.SendData "I think therefore I am."

This instructs the WinSock control to send the data string "I think therefore I am." to a WinSock application running on the remote host.

After you compile this into an .EXE, you will be able to send a message from the Message box to any Internet host that is running the server program.

> **NOTE**: A working sample of this WinSock client program can be found in the \VB4\WinSock directory on the CD-ROM included with this book.

WinSock UDP

When you load the WinSock control onto your Visual Basic toolbar, notice that it adds two icons—TCP and UDP. Each is capable of transferring data over the Internet.

The TCP control requires a user to request a connection to a server and have that connection accepted. The UDP control, however, does not require the request or acceptance of a connection; it simply broadcasts from a port to a host (or an array of hosts) on the network. If the hosts are listening, they receive the broadcast.

UDP Server

To create the WinSock UDP server, start with a brand new Visual Basic form. In the References option of the project, select the Microsoft WinSock Controls reference. Then add the controls to the Visual Basic toolbar using Ctrl_T from Visual Basic's main window.

After you select the right tools and references, add the labels, text boxes, buttons and so on (see Figure 12.4). For the server, these include:

- [ ] Two command buttons (named cmdClose and cmdListen)
- [ ] One list box named lstMessages
- [ ] One text box named txtLocalPort
- [ ] One WinSock UDP control named UDP

Figure 12.4.
The WinSock UDP server answering machine form with the controls loaded and displayed.

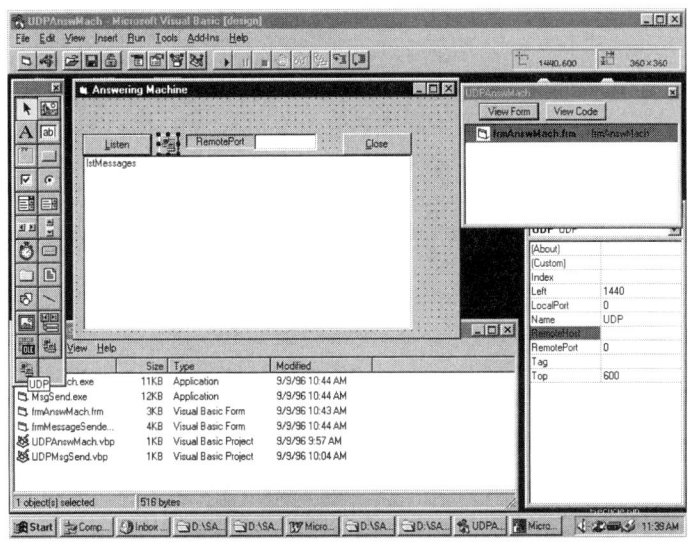

When the form is laid out, add the code that allows the answering machine application to wait for incoming messages. In a UDP connection, this involves nothing more than setting the LocalPort property of the control. To make the Listen button await a connection, add the following code:

```
Private Sub cmdListen_Click()
   UDP.LocalPort=872
End Sub
```

When you have set the LocalPort of the UDP control, it fires a DataArrival event for each string received. In your answering machine application, add the incoming messages to the lstMessages list box.

```
Private Sub UDP_DataArrival(ByVal bytesTotal as Long)
   Dim strDataIn
   UDP.GetData strDataIn, 8
   lstMessages.AddItem strDataIn
End Sub
```

This application monitors the local port specified in the txtLocalPort.Text property. When data comes in through that port, it fires the DataArrival event, which adds the data string to the lstMessages list box.

UDP Client

To create the WinSock UDP client, start with a brand new Visual Basic form. In the References option of the project, select the Microsoft WinSock Controls reference. Then add the controls to the Visual Basic toolbar using Ctrl_T from Visual Basic's main window.

After you select the right tools and references, add the labels, text boxes, buttons, and so on (see Figure 12.5). For the message-sending application, these include:

- ☐ Four command buttons named cmdSend, cmdQuit, cmdAdd and cmdRemove
- ☐ One list box named lstHosts
- ☐ One text box named txtMessage
- ☐ One WinSock UDP control array named UDP

Figure 12.5.
WinSock UDP control loaded into the UDP message-sending project.

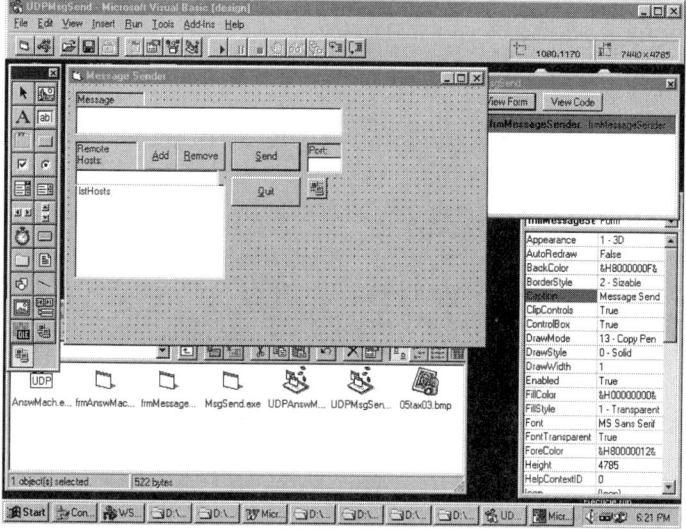

When the form is laid out, add the code that allows this message-sending application to broadcast its message to a number of waiting answering machines.

In a UDP connection, this involves nothing more than setting the RemotePort and RemoteHost properties of the control and invoking the SendData method. Thus, to make the Send button broadcast a message, add the following code:

```
Private Sub cmdSend_Click()
   For x = 1 to lstHosts.ListCount
      Load UDP(x)
      UDP(x).RemotePort = txtRemotePort.Text
      UDP(x).RemoteHost = lstHosts.ItemData(x-1)
      UDP(x).SendData txtMessage.Text
   Next x
End Sub
```

The WinSock UDP Control's SendData Method

```
WinSockLib.UDP(Index).RemoteHost = Remote IP
WinSockLib.UDP(Index).RemotePort = Remote Port
WinSockLib.UDP(Index).SendData Data String
```

The WinSock UDP control's SendData method is used by the server data to the remote connection(s) and on the specified port.

Example:

```
udpMyClient.RemoteHost = "204.181.96.53"
udpMyClient.RemotePort = 25
udpMyClient.SendData "I think therefore I am."
```

This instructs the WinSock UDP control to send the data string "I think therefore I am." The message is broadcasted to the remote machine only if the remote machine is currently monitoring the port.

This application sends one message to each RemoteHost in an array of UDP connections. Each of those hosts must be monitoring the same port as the message sender at the time of the broadcast to receive the message.

Summary

In this chapter you learned about WinSock programming and how it applies to the Internet. You know about its beginnings as a proposed standard in 1991, and its future release in the WinSock 2 specification.

WinSock is used as a Windows programmer's interface to the TCP/IP suite of network protocols, including SMTP, FTP, NNTP, HTTP, and others. Using the WinSock interface frees the programmer from having to coordinate a variety of network management functions that are automated in the WinSock library.

The `WinSck.OCX` file is one of the ActiveX custom controls installed with Microsoft's Internet Control Pack. It provides a simplified interface to the WinSock library to programmers in languages such as Visual Basic, Microsoft Access, and Visual FoxPro.

The WinSock control exposes features for two different kinds of Internet connections—TCP (Transmission Control Protocol) and UDP (User Datagram Protocol). TCP is host-to-host communication, and UDP is a broadcasted, "connectionless" form of communication.

Both TCP and UDP controls require a host on one system that is sitting idle, awaiting a connection, and a client on another host that initiates the transaction.

Q&A

Q Can the WinSock control be used as a complete WinSock interface?

A No. The WinSock control only exposes an *interface* to the WinSock DLL file. If your want to access the WinSock routines directly, make API calls to the WinSock library through an interface such as a Visual Basic or Microsoft Access Module.

Q How many connections (UDP and TCP) can you make at the same time?

A This is limited by your system's resources. Each programming environment only allows a certain number of controls to be loaded at the same time. The number of connections is also limited by such factors as your system memory and the bandwidth of your network connection.

Q What changes will I have to make to work with the upcoming WinSock 2 specification?

A Ideally, none. The implementation of the WinSock 2 API is planned to be backwards compatible. If you use the ICP WinSock control as your WinSock interface, your code will remain the same. But when it comes out, you will want to use the updated control to take advantage of any enhanced features of WinSock 2.

Q How can I tell when a program is finished using the WinSock control?

A The WinSock control, unlike others in the ICP, does not have a `State` or `ProtocolState` property. If you use this control, your application must determine when the transactions are complete. When they are, your application can unload the control, freeing system resources for other processes.

Workshop

The WinSock UDP control can be a very powerful tool for broadcasting information in real-time to a number of different users. For this exercise, you will create a broadcast server and a redistributable client that your users will run to receive those real-time broadcasts. Try to meet the following specifications:

- ☐ The program will use a TCP control in Listen mode, which will receive requests from each of the users when they wish to begin receiving your broadcasts.
- ☐ When the connection is requested, the control will identify the user's IP address, check it, and add it to a list object.
- ☐ The broadcast will be in audio format. To do this, add a wave audio control to your project. The operator will use your interface to the wave audio control to record a message, which will be stored to a file on disk.
- ☐ When the user initially connects to the server, the server will transmit the last audio file recorded back to the user. Then, whenever the audio file is updated, it will be broadcasted to each client identified in the list object.

Quiz

1. What is the original operating system that was designed as an interface to the TCP/IP network?
2. What is the name given to an application that uses a WinSock interface?
3. What two formats can be used to identify a host on the Internet?
4. What is the WinSock function that determines the IP address of a domain?
5. What two client/server interfaces are presented by the WinSock custom control in Visual Basic and Microsoft Access?
6. Which property on the WinSock TCP control is used by a server to identify the port it will monitor?
7. Which property of the WinSock UDP control is used by a server to identify the port it will monitor?
8. When a control is notified of an incoming connection request, what parameter(s) will it receive to take control of that connection?
9. When invoking the GetData method, what two parameters must be specified?
10. What method is used to terminate a WinSock session?

NOTE Refer to the appendix, "Answers," for the answers to these questions.

Week 2

Day 13

Learning to Use the Win32 Internet API Library

The Win32 Internet API is designed to handle the client side of the Internet connection. A familiar application that uses client-side technology is your browser. Unlike the ISAPI Server API, the Internet API (also know as WinInet) can be used in any normal application. The executable file does not have to be placed in a special directory with special permissions. In this chapter, you will learn the general functionality offered by this WinInet API and learn how to use the Microsoft programming classes to use this WinInet API.

Overview

Using the Internet requires a connection from a client (your browser, for example) to a server. The API supports a connection that can be a request to a server that understands HTTP, FTP, or Gopher. While there are other kinds of Internet connections, these three are the most widely used. Each kind of connection has a different but similar use.

What Is the File Transfer Protocol (FTP)?

FTP is a File Transfer Protocol. It allows servers to make files available to clients, and it lets the client give the server files. It transfers files from one computer to another, regardless of the operating system on either machine. This is important because operating systems that don't know how to talk to each other can use the FTP service to place or get files to each other. For example, a student in Texas using a Macintosh computer can retrieve or put files on a UNIX machine in California. FTP files are generally laid out in a tree structure, just like a directory system. This allows the client to place or retrieve files from the appropriate location.

In the Windows NT and Windows 95 operating systems, FTP commands are supported at the command prompt. The Microsoft Internet Explorer (Microsoft's browser) support for FTP is built in the address box. It can be accessed by typing FTP://ftp.server-name.

Figure 13.1 is an example of an FTP site. Notice the name and explanation of the site. They appear to use HTML, but in fact it is Internet Explorer doing the formatting. Look at how the files list the date and time of last modification as well as the file size. The directories are also listed. When using FTP, you have to know what file you are looking for and where to find it. There is no searching capability.

Figure 13.1.
This is how Microsoft Internet Explorer displays an FTP site.

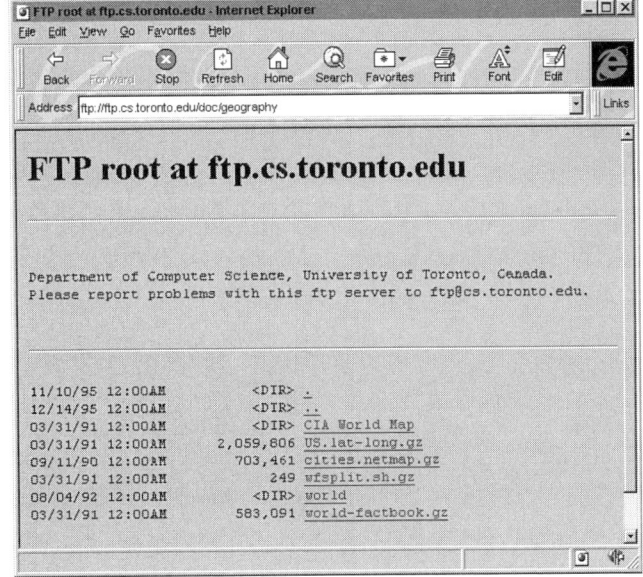

The Gopher Protocol

Compared to FTP, Gopher offers a little more to the client but also requires more from the server. FTP does not have any capability to jump from one server to another, but Gopher and HTTP have the capability to jump to other servers using links. Gopher also offers the capability to annotate files and directories, and create custom menus. However, it does not allow the client to place files on the server.

Gopher servers have a tag file. This tag file keeps the name of the file the directory system uses: a "friendly" name that would be useful to the client (for example, the administrator's name, modification date, and type of file, such as a text file or binary executable file). An example of a friendly name would be The 1996 Acme Stock Report, where the file name is actually 1996stpt.txt. The client doesn't see the tag file, but information in the tag file can be sent back to the client along with the file itself. The tag file has to be constructed by an administrator of the Gopher site. The Microsoft Internet Information Server uses the command line application GDSSET.EXE to make tag files for the Gopher server it supports. A tag file would have to be built for each file retrievable by Gopher.

Gopher allows searches through the wide area information search (WAIS). WAIS is a full-text information retrieval system. In order for the file to be searchable, the server administrator has to create a WAIS index.

The Microsoft Internet Explorer's support for Gopher is built in the address box. It can be accessed by typing Gopher://gopher.*server-name*.

Figure 13.2 is an example of a Gopher site. Notice the name and explanation of the site. This page appears to use HTML, but in fact it is Internet Explorer doing the formatting. This site offers directories and searches to clients. The Gopher server differentiates between files, directories, and searches. This particular Gopher site doesn't have any files at the root directory, but it does have several directories and searches. Figure 13.3 shows how a Gopher site searches an index, as presented through Micorsoft Internet Explorer, and Figure 13.4 shows a Gopher site's search results (based on the search from Figure 13.3).

The Gopher search capabilities are not as advanced as some of the searches that are *now* available through HTTP/HTML, but the Gopher search was a good resource in its time.

Figure 13.2.

This is how Microsoft Internet Explorer displays a Gopher site.

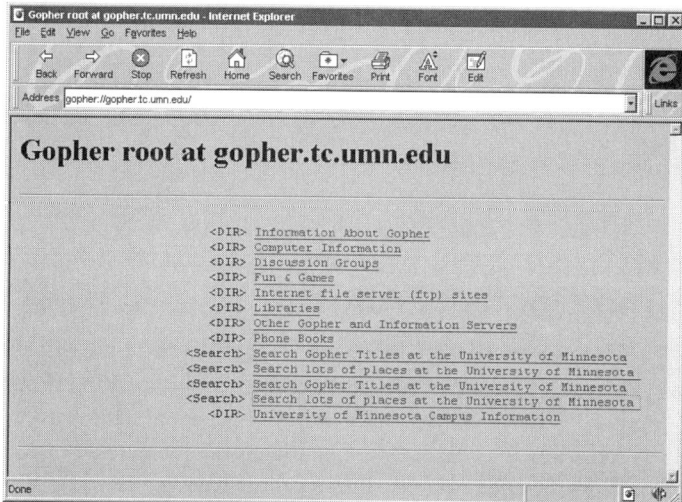

Figure 13.3.

This is how a Gopher site searches an index, as presented through Microsoft Internet Explorer.

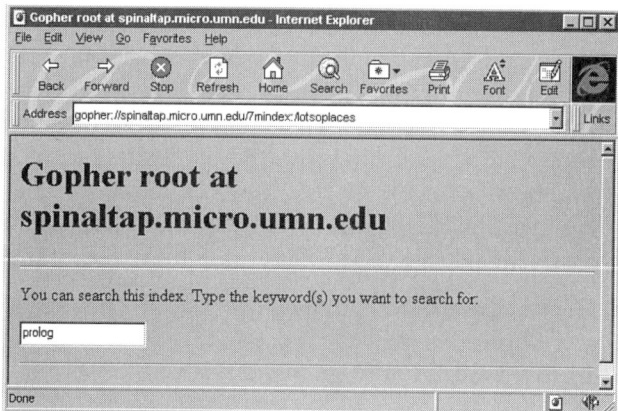

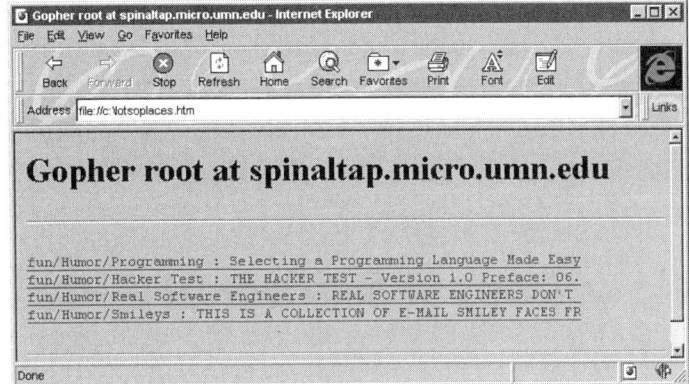

Figure 13.4.
This is a Gopher site's search results, based on the search from Figure 13.3. The search results let the client know where to go in the Gopher file system to find the file.

HTTP and HTML

Both FTP and Gopher offer useful services, but they lack a few qualities. Both are basically file systems with only files and searches to offer. To see the information, the client must download the file to his computer and open it with the correct application. HTTP and HTML offer the client the information without having to open the file. Actually, the concept of choosing files is replaced with the concept of moving to other pages.

HTTP servers offer much more to a client. While FTP and Gopher are file server systems, HTTP can be a complete server system. It can offer unlimited capabilities such as database access, true search engines, and calculations. The list is only limited by your imagination. The HTTP server does its work and then sends the client's browser a file to display the result of whatever work it was requested to do.

The HTTP server's work is far more versatile than FTP and Gopher because it can *act* on the request. An example (one of many) is the request for information, such as the Yellow Pages on the Web. The request goes from your browser to the server. The server can filter the request for valid data or passwords. If the request is invalid, the server returns an HTML page notifying you. If the request is valid, the server can look through a file server, look through an e-mail server, look through a database, or do just about anything else.

FTP and Gopher in the Future

The services offered by FTP and Gopher are quickly being replaced by Web pages served up by HTTP and written in HTML. If you search for Gopher or FTP pages, you are probably using a search engine behind an HTML form. Why would someone keep these servers around? Converting an existing (and probably extensive) server to HTML is not hard, but there are several costs involved. These costs involve hardware, software, labor, training, and administration of the new system. Many of these systems reside in governments or schools, and the resources to update the systems are not available.

HTML doesn't solve every problem either. The capability of a client to place a file on a server (as FTP can do) is not allowed. The Microsoft Internet Information Server comes with all three services.

How Does the WinInet API Fit In?

The WinInet API is designed to allow applications access to Internet (or intranet) information, without requiring detailed knowledge of how the connection works (such as TCP/IP or sockets). The API makes reading a file from the Internet as easy as reading a file from your hard drive. If you are familiar with other Win32 APIs, the buffer and error handling of this API should look familiar. If you want to have all the detailed information of the WinInet specification, check out http://www.microsoft.com/intdev/sdk/docs/wininet/.

The difficulty with Internet technology is that it changes very quickly. Who wants to learn a set of functions that will soon be obsolete? The WinInet API is written to flexibly change the underlying technology and yet have a consistent set of functions for programmers to use.

Microsoft has written a set of classes that incorporate the WinInet API functionality into the Microsoft Foundation Class (MFC) classes. The benefit of these classes is that they fit nicely into the MFC hierarchy of classes, thereby giving the programmer more functionality than what the WinInet API functions afford. If you are familiar with MFC, learning these new classes will be a snap. In order to use these classes, you have to use the Microsoft Visual C++ version 4.2. Prior versions of Visual C++ will not have these classes.

The API Functions

Before looking at the MFC classes, let's look at the functions in the WinInet API. The main functions a client should be concerned with are connecting to the server, having the server do something, and closing the connection to the server.

Check whether the hardware and software in your operating system are correctly configured before you begin programming with this API. Connecting to a Web site with your browser would be a good test of whether your machine's hardware and software are working correctly. This API takes advantage of the software you already have installed on your system, so instead of having to install the protocols and software to use this API, the API assumes that you already have connectivity with these three protocols.

Learning to Use the Win32 Internet API Library

While there are only three technologies supported by the API, there are several functions that you need to accomplish regardless of which protocol you use. The general functions are:

- InternetOpen—The first function you need to call. It initializes the WinInet API. Without this function call, the results could be unpredictable.
- InternetOpenUrl—Makes a connection to the server and prepares for the information to be retrieved.
- InternetCrackUrl—Parses a URL string into components such as server name, path in server, user name, password, and any parameters.
- InternetCreateUrl—Creates a URL string from components such as server name, path in server, user name, password, and any parameters.
- InternetCanonicalizeUrl—Converts a URL string into a "safe" form. This safe form can include replacing invalid characters, converting characters to other characters, and encoding.
- InternetCombineUrl—Combines the base and path of a URL into a single string that will be made "safe" by canonicalizing the URL.
- InternetConnect—Begins a session for any protocol to make a connection. The session information can include server name, user name, and password, and connection protocol (HTTP, FTP, Gopher). You do not need to open a session for each request. A single session can handle all your requests. You need to balance the session per request for your particular use.
- InternetQueryOption—Returns information about your Internet session such as user name, password, time-out features, asynchronous features, callback features, and other security features.
- InternetSetOption—Sets information about your Internet session such as user name, password, time-out features, asynchronous features, callback features, and other security features.
- InternetErrorDlg—Displays message box for error occurring from the HttpSendRequest error conditions. The dialog displays the error message and gives the button options of OK, Cancel, or Retry.
- InternetCloseHandle—Used to terminate an Internet handle and free any associated resources. If the handle is a parent of other handles, this function can be used to close all the child handles of the parent. This function closes the handle opened by InternetOpen.
- InternetReadFile—Reads a buffer of data. InternetOpenUrl, FtpOpenFile, GopherOpenFile, and HttpOpenRequest will create the buffer. Make sure your buffer size is large enough for requested information. If the requested information is not available (for example, this function is waiting on the server), the function will not return until the information is available.

- `InternetSetFilePointer`—Moves the position of the file pointer by a number of bytes. You can move the position relative to the file pointer's current position, the beginning of the file, or the end of the file.
- `InternetWriteFile`—Writes a number of bytes to a file and returns the number of bytes written. It is useful to know how many bytes were actually written to a file if (for some reason) the function could not write all the bytes.
- `InternetFindNextFile`—Finds the next file where the first file was found with either `FtpFindFirstFile` or `GopherFindFirstFile`.
- `InternetSetStatusCallback`—Sets the function address to call when there is status information. This function address is of a function you write. This function would do something with the status information, such as let the user know what the status is.
- `InternetConfirmZoneCrossing`—Lets the user know if he is moving from a secured Web page to an unsecured Web page.
- `InternetTimeFromSystemTime`—Formats the date and time from a specified HTTP format (as noted in the HTTP specification) to a string.
- `InternetTimeToSystemTime`—Formats a string into a specified HTTP format (as noted in the HTTP specification).
- `InternetAttemptConnect`—Lets the client attempt to connect to the server before a file request is attempted. The method of connecting takes less time than connecting and then requesting a file.

NOTE URL stands for *universal resource locator*. In terms of the Internet, that would be the server name, such as www.microsoft.com.

NOTE `SYSTEMTIME` is a data structure that contains the following information: year, month, day of week (where Sunday is 0), day of month, hour, minute, second, and millisecond.

To get to specific files or other information, use the functions that coincide with your particular need. There are functions specific to each of the three connections supported: HTTP, FTP, and Gopher.

The HTTP functions are

- HttpOpenRequest—Creates a handle to an HTTP server by setting the type of action (such as GET), the object of that action (file, ISAPI filter, template, and so on), the object making the request (generally the Web page), and the type of data you can accept (such as text).
- HttpAddRequestHeaders—Adds or removes information to the handle created by HttpOpenRequest. This information is in the form of headers. In general, a Web browser will send information about itself such as manufacturer and version of product. Web servers can act on this information as well as log this information.
- HttpSendRequest—Sends the request created in HttpOpenRequest and HttpAddRequestHeaders to the server. This function also always asks you to specify additional headers.
- HttpQueryInfo—Returns information about the sent header (you created), returned header (server created) or the returned request (server created). The last two pieces are probably more interesting. The header information is important because it can tell you things like when the file was last modified, when the file expires, what format type is the returned request, etc.

The FTP functions include the following:

- FtpFindFirstFile—Can find either the first file or the first directory on the FTP server starting at a specified path. You can only call this function once per FTP session; any other calls will be a waste of your time. To find more files or directories, use the InternetFindNextFile function. The FTP protocol can not guarantee correct file information such as create date and time, so it returns the most accurate information based on available information.
- FtpGetFile—Retrieves a file from the FTP server and puts it on your local system. You can control where the file goes, what the new file name is, what the new file attributes are, and other conditions of the file transfer.
- FtpPutFile—Sends a file to the FTP server and puts it in a specific directory that you choose. You must have appropriate permissions for this function to succeed.
- FtpDeleteFile—Deletes a file from the FTP server. You must have appropriate permissions for this function to succeed.
- FtpRenameFile—Renames a file on the FTP server. You must have appropriate permissions for this function to succeed.
- FtpOpenFile—Opens a file on the FTP server for reading or writing. Use this function if you need to control how the data is sent to the server or read from the server. This function gives you a more granular control over the process.

- `FtpCreateDirectory`—Creates a directory on the FTP server. You must have appropriate permissions to use this function.
- `FtpRemoveDirectory`—Deletes a directory on the FTP server. You must have appropriate permissions to use this function.
- `FtpSetCurrentDirectory`—Changes the current directory. You should find out where you are by using `FtpGetCurrentDirectory`.
- `FtpGetCurrentDirectory`—Gives you the name of the FTP server directory you are in.

The Gopher functions include the following:

- `GopherFindFirstFile`—Can find the first file based on a Gopher locater, an indexed search, or the top-level information in the Gopher server. After the first call to `GopherFindFirstFile`, any other calls to find files should use the `InternetFindNextFile` function.
- `GopherOpenFile`—Starts reading a Gopher file.
- `GopherCreateLocator`—Creates a locator string. Information necessary to create a locator string includes server name, friendly name of file, and file name.
- `GopherGetAttribute`—Returns information about the file on the Gopher server.

Notice that once you get the files enumerated, based on your connection type, the rest of the enumeration is used with `InternetFindNextFile`.

Examples of function calls used to download from an HTTP server include

- `InternetOpen`
- `InternetConnect`
- `HTTPOpenRequest`
- `HTTPSendRequest`
- `InternetReadFile`
- `InternetCloseHandle`

The MFC Classes and WinInet

If a programmer wanted to write an application using this API, a lot of programming would be required to handle non-WinInet aspects of the application, such as the graphical user interface (GUI), any database connectivity, and just about anything else the application needs to do. You could write a WinInet program without MFC (or some other programming class library), but for rapid application development (RAD), this is probably unrealistic. Knowledge of C++ class usage is mandatory for using these classes.

The MFC classes that work with this functionality are

- `CInternetSession`—Creates and initializes the Internet session you need, regardless of the protocol you are using.
- `CInternetConnection`—The base class for all three protocol connection types. This class manages the common functionality and low-level details of the connection.
- `CFtpConnection`—Used to connect to an FTP server. This class handles most of the directory and file tasks.
- `CGopherConnection`—Used to connect to a Gopher server. This class handles the locator and attribute information.
- `CHttpConnection`—Used to connect to an HTTP server. This class handles the initial request to the server.
- `CInternetFile`—Inherits from CStdioFile and is the base class for `CGopherFile` and `CHttpFile`. This base class handles the file manipulation for the Gopher and HTTP protocols.
- `CGopherFile`—Handles Gopher files but has little functionality. Its only methods are contructor and `Close()`.
- `CHttpFile`—Handles HTTP files. It sends the request to the HTTP server, reads the headers and the HTML data stream that the server sends back.
- `CFileFind`—The base class for `CGopherFindFile` and `CFtpFindFile`. It handles file searches and file information.
- `CFtpFileFind`—Finds FTP files on an FTP server.
- `CGopherFileFind`—Finds Gopher files on a Gopher server and returns information in the tag file.
- `CGopherLocator`—Creates the Locator object to access Gopher files.
- `CInternetException`—Handles Internet programming exceptions.

Global functions for the WinInet in MFC include the following:

- `AfxParseURL`—Tells you what kind of protocol server, file, port and what type of protocol the URL will go to: HTTP, FTP, or Gopher.
- `AfxGetInternetHandleType`—Returns the type of HTTP, FTP, or Gopher request handle you have, such as finding a file versus connecting to a server.
- `AfxThrowInternetException`—Throws a memory exception, such as when a call to memory allocation fails.

Programming with MFC

To follow the code snippets and exercises in the rest of the chapter, make sure that the Internet connectivity to HTTP and FTP is working. You can use your browser to verify this. You also need to have Microsoft Visual C++ version 4.2 or later installed. The help files and sample application of Microsoft Visual C++ go into great detail about what these new classes do. Please see these resources for additional information.

The First Sample Program

This first sample program will connect to a HTTP server and read the HTML file (`default.htm`). As it reads the file, the application will print the information to a screen. This is not a sophisticated program, but you will actually connect to a server and read a file. There are three types of operations you will be doing. You will open a connection to the server, make a request of the server, and read a file. As you go through this example, look for the differences between these three pieces.

You will need to find a Web server that has a Web page in the root directory to exchange for the names I use in this example. In the sample code, I chose a server I could get to at the time this chapter was written. The danger in this is that the server might not be working now. Before you begin, find a Web server (any will do) that has the `default.htm` document. Some of the more advanced servers don't have this file. As long as you know the name of a server and the name of a file in the root directory of that server, you can exchange those names for the ones I use in the code.

Let's create an application. Open Microsoft Visual C++ and make a new project workspace. Name the workspace HTTPexam. Make sure the project is a *console application.* The reason it should be a console application is because I don't want you to be confused by seeing any classes that are not closely related to these WinInet classes. Because a console application doesn't use MFC by default, you need to change the project so that it does use MFC. In your project, change your project settings (Build Menu / Settings) to use MFC in a shared DLL (General tab / MFC drop-down list). If you don't let the project know you need to use the MFC DLL, when you build, you will get link errors regarding `beginthread` and `endthread` functions.

NOTE A *console application* is a DOS-type application where there are no windows.

Create a header file `httpex.h` that looks like Listing 13.1.

Listing 13.1. httpex.h (create a header file).

```
#include <afx.h>     // header file for MFC
#include <afxinet.h> // header file for WinInet
#include <iostream.h> // header file for input/output stream
#include <stdlib.h>  // header file for standard library functions

class CHttpExample : public CInternetSession
{
public:
    CHttpExample(LPCTSTR pszAppName, int nMethod);
};
```

Create a code file httpex.cpp that looks like Listing 13.2.

Listing 13.2. httpex.cpp (write bare application).

```
#include "httpex.h" // header file for Project

// CHttpExample class implementation

void main()
{

// variables

// running code implementation

}
```

Make sure httpex.cpp has been added to the project files, and update project dependencies. The CHttpExample class's only base class is CInternetSession. The derived class you made (CHttpExample) only has one method. You don't need anything more in your header file to make a connection and to retrieve information from a server.

Now let's add the implementation code that is associated with the function defined in the header file. Add Listing 13.3 to httpex.cpp after the line

```
//CHttpExample class implementation
```

Listing 13.3. httpex.cpp (add class implementation code).

```
CHttpExample::CHttpExample(LPCTSTR pszAppName, int nMethod)
    : CInternetSession(pszAppName, 1, nMethod)
{
}
```

There is no code in the constructor for your CHttpExample class because the base class does everything you need. All you have to do is pass this information to it when you declare a variable of CHttpExample type.

At this point, the project should build with no errors or warnings. If it does have errors or warnings, now is a good time to fix your project settings and debug your code. However, the main function is still empty, so the program will do nothing. Let's add some useful code to make the program do something.

You need to declare a few variables that you want to work with. The first and most obvious is to instantiate your class by having a variable of CHttpExample type. The second variable you need is for your connection type and will be of type CHttpConnection. The third variable you need will help you read the file and will need to be of type CHttpFile. You also need to add a few character strings to handle the server name, filename, header information you send, header information you request, and the text of the file in which you are interested. The last variables will hold the status of functions you are executing. Add Listing 13.4 below the line with // variables on it.

Listing 13.4. httpex.cpp (declare variables).

```
CHttpExample        session(_T("Http Example"), INTERNET_OPEN_TYPE_PRECONFIG);
CHttpConnection*    pServer=NULL;
CHttpFile*          pFile=NULL;
CString             serverName(_T("dinaf2"));
CString             fileName(_T("/default.htm"));
CString             headerInfo(_T("Accept: text/\r\nUserAgent:HTTPExample\
                    r\n"));
CString             newLocation;
CString             returnedFileText;
DWORD               dwReturnCode;
BOOL                fSuccess;
```

TIP You may be asking what the _T("*string*") syntax does. By using the _T macro, I can compile my code as Unicode, MultiByteCharacterSet, or ANSI (single-byte character set) without having to change the way I have my hard-coded strings. The CString class handles how the string is kept based on which type of string I am interested in. To compile your code in a particular setting, have one of the following defined in your project settings: _UNICODE, _MBCS, or _SBCS. If you plan to have your code used outside the English language, this is important.

The way you declared the session variable will pass the information from the `CHttpExample` class to the `CInternetSession` class. A `CString` can be initialized when it is declared or later. Both methods are used here. The variables `pServer` and `pFile` will be initialized in the code. Also notice that the server does not have to be prefixed with `http://`. If you prefix the name, a connection will not be established.

The second parameter to the constructor for your session variable is the type of Internet access you want. This has nothing to do with the server you are trying to get to. This parameter tells the software how to configure your machine's side of the connection. You have three choices here. I chose the one that will work with my machine. If you are not running on a Windows NT or Windows 95 operating system, you will have to choose the flag that is best for you. The three flags are

- `INTERNET_OPEN_TYPE_PRECONFIG`—Access information is preconfigured in your operating system's registry. This is a safe choice for WinNT and Win95.
- `INTERNET_OPEN_TYPE_DIRECT`—Direct access to the Internet.
- `INTERNET_OPEN_TYPE_PROXY`—Access through a proxy or gateway. For corporate situations, this might be what you need.

If you do not know what type of access you have, contact your system administrator or Internet service provider (ISP).

Now let's write some code to get you connected. Add Listing 13.5 to your main function just below the `// running code implementation` line.

Listing 13.5. `httpex.cpp` (add connection and request code).

```
pServer = session.GetHttpConnection(serverName);
pFile = pServer->OpenRequest(CHttpConnection::HTTP_VERB_GET,
    fileName,NULL,1,NULL,NULL,INTERNET_FLAG_EXISTING_CONNECT);

// connection to server
pFile->Close();
if(pFile)
    delete pFile;

pServer->Close();
if(pServer)
    delete pServer;

session.Close();
```

Let's look at each line of code. The first line initializes your connection to the name of the HTTP server and returns a pointer to a `CHttpConnection` object. But what if the server had some sort of security? The code didn't pass a user name or password, so a secured connection would fail. The function parameters for `GetHttpConnection` are *serverName*, *portNumber*, *userName*, and *password*. But because I'm using the default system registry, I don't need to set the port number. The function definition defaults this to INTERNET_INVALID_PORT_NUMBER. The user name and password also default to NULL, so if I don't need them, I don't need to pass them as parameters. If a connection to the server could not be established, the pServer pointer would be null. It is a good idea to check that the pointer is not null before continuing; however, I don't do that here. With any real-world program, you would want to check the pointer before proceeding. This will save you from possible exceptions in your code.

The second line of code requests the file default.htm from the server. The first parameter CHttpExample::HTTP_VERB_GET tells the server what kind of request you are making. If you pass this parameter as NULL, the HTTP_VERB_GET is used. The other choices correspond with normal requests that can be made to a Web server:

- HTTP_VERB_POST = 0
- HTTP_VERB_GET = 1
- HTTP_VERB_HEAD = 2
- HTTP_VERB_PUT = 3
- HTTP_VERB_LINK = 4
- HTTP_VERB_DELETE = 5
- HTTP_VERB_UNLINK = 6

The object or filename you are interested in is the second parameter. The rest of the parameters take default values, but to let you know what they are, I included them in the function call. The other parameters handle issues such as what type of file you can accept (text-only is an example), what the URL address of the object is (if the object is not in the Web's root directory), and how you want the file returned (don't cache, make it secure with encryption, and so on).

The last few lines of code close the connection to the server and gracefully close your CInternetSession object. You should be able to build and run the code. The application at this point connects to the server, requests the file, and closes down. To look at the file, you need to add more code. Insert Listing 13.6 just below the line //connection to server.

Listing 13.6. httpex.cpp (add file handling code).

```
if(fSuccess = pFile->AddRequestHeaders(headerInfo))
{
    if(fSuccess = pFile->SendRequest())
    {
        if(fSuccess = pFile->QueryInfoStatusCode(dwReturnCode))
        {
            if(dwReturnCode==200)
```

```
            {
                if(fSuccess = pFile->QueryInfo(HTTP_QUERY_RAW_HEADERS_
                ➥CRLF,newLocation))
                {
                    if(newLocation != _T(""))
                        cout << _T("Header Info: ") << newLocation
                            ➥<< endl << endl;
                }
                pFile->SetReadBufferSize(2000);
                while(pFile->ReadString(returnedFileText))
                    cout << returnedFileText;
            }
        }
    }
}
```

You have now written the entire application to read an HTML file and write it to the screen. Let's look at the code from Listing 13.6 in detail.

The first line adds information to the header you send to the server. You would use this if you wanted control over the exact request sent to the server. Our CString variable headerInfo tells the server you accept text information, and tells the server the name of the application making the request. If the function fails, it returns a 0 to fSuccess. You need to check every function that returns a success code before continuing.

The second line sends the request. The function is empty because you have already set the filename and location. However, if you were executing a CGI script or ISAPI filter on the server, this is the function you would pass the information to. This information could include the name of the script and parameters to that script.

The next line returns information on how well our request was satisfied. This is important because if there was a problem, you would need to find out why. The return code dwReturnCode will be a number representing that success or failure. In the code, I only check for 200 (the request was fulfilled without any errors) because that means my request was satisfied. The return codes are broken down in Table 13.1.

Table 13.1. Return codes.

Return Code	Meaning
200	Request completed.
201	Object created, reason = new URI.
202	Asynchronous completion.
203	Partial completion.

continues

Table 13.1. continued

Return Code	Meaning
204	No information to return.
300	Server couldn't decide what to return.
301	Object permanently moved.
302	Object temporarily moved.
303	Redirection with new access method.
304	If-modified-since was not modified.
400	Invalid syntax.
401	Access denied.
402	Payment required.
403	Request forbidden.
404	Object not found.
405	Method is not allowed.
406	No response acceptable to client found.
407	Proxy authentication required.
408	Server timed out waiting for request.
409	User should resubmit with more information.
410	The resource is no longer available.
411	Couldn't authorize client.
500	Internal server error.
501	Required not supported.
502	Error response received from gateway.
503	Temporarily overloaded.
504	Request timed out waiting for gateway to respond.

The next line of code in Listing 13.6 uses the `QueryInfo` method from the `CHttpFile` class. This method retrieves information from the header that was returned from the server. The server can supply you with different kinds of information that may be useful to a client application. The complete list is

- [ ] HTTP_QUERY_MIME_VERSION
- [ ] HTTP_QUERY_CONTENT_TYPE
- [ ] HTTP_QUERY_CONTENT_TRANSFER_ENCODING

- HTTP_QUERY_CONTENT_ID
- HTTP_QUERY_CONTENT_DESCRIPTION
- HTTP_QUERY_CONTENT_LENGTH
- HTTP_QUERY_ALLOWED_METHODS
- HTTP_QUERY_PUBLIC_METHODS
- HTTP_QUERY_DATE
- HTTP_QUERY_EXPIRES
- HTTP_QUERY_LAST_MODIFIED
- HTTP_QUERY_MESSAGE_ID
- HTTP_QUERY_URI
- HTTP_QUERY_DERIVED_FROM
- HTTP_QUERY_LANGUAGE
- HTTP_QUERY_COST
- HTTP_QUERY_WWW_LINK
- HTTP_QUERY_PRAGMA
- HTTP_QUERY_VERSION
- HTTP_QUERY_STATUS_CODE
- HTTP_QUERY_STATUS_TEXT
- HTTP_QUERY_RAW_HEADERS
- HTTP_QUERY_RAW_HEADERS_CRLF

The last two methods of code to discuss are the SetReadBufferSize and ReadString. The SetReadBufferSize lets MFC know how large a buffer of information you want each time you look at the file. ReadString reads the number of bytes you specified in SetReadBufferSize.

TIP   The default for the buffer, if you choose not to call SetReadBufferSize, is 4,096 bytes. Do not depend on CStrings to manage the size of your buffer. I suggest that you always set your buffer size.

The buffer size is in bytes. If your character type is larger than one byte, remember to increase the size of the buffer to accommodate the character size. Consider an example of a Unicode character. Assuming the Unicode character is two bytes, and that our string is 2,000 characters, the math would be 2 * 2000 = total buffer size needed.

In this example the program connected to a server, read a file and header information returned from the server, and printed to the screen. Figure 13.5 is a screen shot of this application. Notice the header information and the body of the HTML. The HTML isn't formatted because the ReadString method doesn't know or care about formatting.

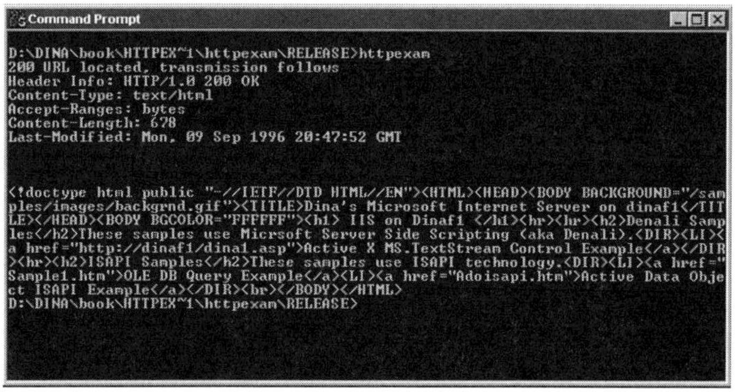

Figure 13.5.
The HTTP example application output.

It seems like there is a lot of work put into this example, but the code has so few lines. The MFC class inheritance provides the power behind the code. Let's take a closer look.

CInternetSession

The program only used three functions from the CInternetSession class in the HTTP example: the constructor, GetHttpConnection, and Close. This class is flexible enough to handle all three connection types, set any options, and handle any call backs. CInternetSession inherits from the MFC's CObject class. The CObject class has nothing to do with the Internet, but it does have the methods necessary for memory allocation, debugging, and serialization including new, delete, and the equals operator (=). These are basic functions, but they are helpful here because you don't have to write them yourself.

CInternetConnection and the Connection Classes

CInternetConnection is the base class for CHttpConnection, CFtpConnection, and CGopherConnection. It provides methods to get the server name, server context number, and session object. The CHttpConnection class doesn't do much more. It only has two methods: a constructor and OpenRequest. The same is true for the CGopherConnection class. These classes don't need many functions because most of the work is done on the server.

Why would a programmer write an application for HTTP or Gopher when they probably already have a Web browser or Gopher reader? There are a variety of reasons, only limited by your needs. One interesting capability of these classes is getting a file to display the information unlike a browser would. However, if that is what you want to do, go for it. Imagine you are a Web site administrator and you need to check all the links on your pages to see whether those pages, images, audio files, and so on are working. You could write a program to analyze the links on each page by finding the reference to the file and attempting to retrieve that file. If you can't get the file, neither can your browser. Another example is that many Web sites want the current information on their Web pages to be attractive. It would be easy to write a program that lists all files that have not been modified in the last 30 days. These applications can be anywhere, not necessarily on the Web server.

The `CFtpConnection` Class

Although the classes for HTTP and Gopher do not have many methods, the `CFtpConnection` class does because the client has more control and choices about what it does on the server when it uses FTP. It can create or delete files and directories. This is a powerful class because it allows greater flexibility that can be controlled.

Imagine you know you will need every file and subdirectory in the \computer-club directory. With a browser such as Microsoft Internet Explorer, you would just have to click on each subdirectory and pull down each file. Wouldn't it be nice if you could start one program and then go on to more interesting things? When the program is finished, the files would appear on your hard drive just as they appeared on the server. This would save you the time and the trouble of having to do it yourself. Your program could even check to see whether you had enough space on your hard drive before bringing down each file.

The FTP Sample Application

This sample application will connect to an FTP server, read all the files and directories in the root, and get a file named Welcome.txt. The output of the application should look something like Figure 13.6.

Figure 13.6.
The FTP sample application output. The URL of the location is included.

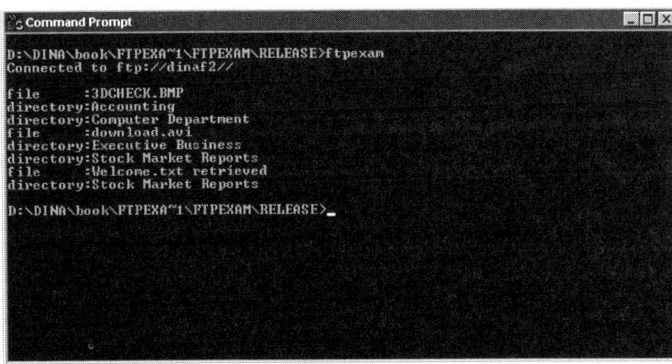

As with the previous example, you will need to find an FTP server and a file you want to retrieve from that server. If you have permissions to write to that server, try to put a file on the server instead of getting a file.

To start, first create an application in the same manner as the previous example. Open Microsoft Visual C++ and make a new project workspace. Name the workspace FTPexam. Make sure the project is a console application; I don't want you to be confused by seeing classes that are not closely related to these WinInet classes. Because a console application doesn't use MFC by default, you need to change the project so that it does use MFC. In your project, change your project settings (Build Menu / Settings) to use MFC in a shared DLL (General tab / MFC drop-down list). If you don't let the project know you need to use the MFC DLL, when you build, you will get link errors regarding beginthread and endthread functions.

Because you have already written one application, enter all the code for the second application. The general flow of the application should make sense to you.

Create a header file ftpex.h that looks like Listing 13.7.

Listing 13.7. ftpex.h (create header file).

```
#include <afx.h>     // header file for MFC
#include <afxinet.h> // header file for WinInet
#include <iostream.h> // header file for input/output stream
#include <stdlib.h>  // header file for standard library functions

class CFtpExample : public CInternetSession
{
public:
    CFtpExample(LPCTSTR pszAppName, int nMethod);
};
```

Create a code file ftpex.cpp that looks like Listing 13.8.

Listing 13.8. ftpex.cpp (write the entire application).

```
#include "ftpex.h"   // header file for Project

// CFtpExample class implementation
CFtpExample::CFtpExample(LPCTSTR pszAppName, int nMethod)
    : CInternetSession(pszAppName, 1, nMethod)
{
}

void main()
{
```

```
// variables
CFtpExample       session(_T("Ftp Example"), INTERNET_OPEN_TYPE_PRECONFIG);
CFtpConnection*   pServer=NULL;
CString            serverName(_T("dinaf2"));
CString            fileName;
CString            subdirectoryName;
CString            currentDirectory;
BOOL               fSuccess;

// running code implementation
pServer = session.GetFtpConnection(serverName);

    if(fSuccess = pServer->GetCurrentDirectoryAsURL(currentDirectory))
    {
        cout << _T("Connected to ") << currentDirectory << endl << endl;
        CFtpFileFind ftpFind(pServer);
        if(fSuccess = ftpFind.FindFile(_T("/*")))
        {
            while(fSuccess)
            {
                fSuccess = ftpFind.FindNextFile();
                if(ftpFind.IsDirectory())
                {
                    fileName = ftpFind.GetFileName();
                    cout << _T("directory: ") << fileName << endl;
                }
                else
                {
                    fileName = ftpFind.GetFileName();
                    if(fileName==_T("Welcome.txt"))
                    {
                        if(fSuccess = pServer->GetFile(fileName,fileName,TRUE,
                            FILE_ATTRIBUTE_NORMAL,FTP_TRANSFER_TYPE_ASCII))
                                cout << _T(" retrieved") << endl;
                        else
                            cout << endl;
                    }
                    else
                        cout << endl;
                }
            }
            ftpFind.Close();
        }
        else
        {
            ftpFind.Close();
        }
    }

pServer->Close();
if(pServer)
    delete pServer;

session.Close();
}
```

The connection code is very similar to the HTTP example's connection code. The major differences between this example and the previous one are the use of `CFtpFindFile` and the methods used from `CFtpConnection`.

The `CFtpConnection` class has quite a few functions for manipulating where the client is and what the client is doing on the server. The methods of `CFTPConnection` are

- `CFtpConnection`—The class constructor. All general initialization of class members happens here.
- `SetCurrentDirectory`—Sets the current directory for this connection.
- `GetCurrentDirectory`—Gets the current directory for this connection.
- `GetCurrentDirectoryAsURL`—Gets the current directory in relation to the root of server, and includes the server's name.
- `RemoveDirectory`—Removes the directory from the server.
- `CreateDirectory`—Creates the directory on the server.
- `Rename`—Renames a file on the server.
- `Remove`—Removes a file on the server.
- `PutFile`—Puts the file on the server.
- `GetFile`—Gets the file from the server.
- `OpenFile`—Opens the file.
- `Close`—Closes the connection to the server.

Also notice that instead of using `CInternetFile` (as in the CHTTP example), you used the `CFtpFindFile` class. Its members are

- `CFtpFileFind`—The class constructor. Any intialization of class members happens here.
- `FindFile`—Finds a file on the FTP server.
- `FindNextFile`—Finds the next file.
- `GetFileURL`—Gets the URL of a file, including the path.

What about some of the functions we used to manipulate the file that are not in the preceding class method list for `CFtpFindFile`, such as `IsDir`? Because `CFtpFindFile` inherits from `CFileFind`, the codes get all the functionality of this base class. The class is used by the Gopher and FTP connection types. It gives the code some neat functionality; it also does the normal file stuff, such as determining whether the file is a directory, whether it is marked with the read-only attribute, when the file was last accessed, and the size of the file. These are just a few of our choices; the rest of the methods of `CFileFind` I'll leave for you to discover.

Notice that the `GetFile` function's first two parameters in Listing 13.8 were both `fileName`. The first variable defines the name of the file I want to retrieve and the second variable defines the file on the local hard drive I want. The fourth and fifth parameters are flags. The fourth parameter is what attributes we want the file to have on our hard drive. Your choices are

- `FILE_ATTRIBUTE_ARCHIVE`
- `FILE_ATTRIBUTE_COMPRESSED`
- `FILE_ATTRIBUTE_DIRECTORY`
- `FILE_ATTRIBUTE_NORMAL`
- `FILE_ATTRIBUTE_HIDDEN`
- `FILE_ATTRIBUTE_READONLY`
- `FILE_ATTRIBUTE_SYSTEM`
- `FILE_ATTRIBUTE_TEMPORARY`

The fifth parameter specifies the condition of the transfer of the file. Your choices are text or binary:

- `FTP_TRANSFER_TYPE_ASCII`
- `FTP_TRANSFER_TYPE_BINARY`

TIP Use the `FTP_TRANSFER_TYPE_BINARY` when you want the file to be of the same type as it is when stored on the server. This is also the default choice if you don't specify a type.

TIP If you just want to read a file from an FTP server, use the `CInternetFile::Read` along with the `CFtpConnection::OpenFile` functions.

Listing 13.9 displays `httpex.cpp` in its entirety.

Listing 13.9. The HTTP example (entire `http ex.cpp` file).

```
#include "httpex.h" // header file for Project

// CHttpExample class implementation
```

continues

Listing 13.9. continued

```
CHttpExample::CHttpExample(LPCTSTR pszAppName, int nMethod)
    : CInternetSession(pszAppName, 1, nMethod)
{
}

void main()
{
// variables
CHttpExample      session(_T("Http Example"), INTERNET_OPEN_TYPE_PRECONFIG);
CHttpConnection*  pServer=NULL;
CHttpFile*        pFile=NULL;
CString           serverName(_T("dinaf2"));
CString           fileName(_T("/default.htm"));
CString           headerInfo(_T("Accept: text/*\r\nUser-Agent:
                   ➥ HTTP Example\r\n"));
CString           newLocation;
CString           returnedFileText;
DWORD             dwReturnCode;
BOOL              fSuccess;


// running code implementation
pServer = session.GetHttpConnection(serverName);
pFile = pServer->OpenRequest(CHttpConnection::HTTP_VERB_GET,
    fileName,NULL,1,NULL,NULL,INTERNET_FLAG_EXISTING_CONNECT);

if(fSuccess = pFile->AddRequestHeaders(headerInfo))
{
    if(fSuccess = pFile->SendRequest())
    {
        if(fSuccess = pFile->QueryInfoStatusCode(dwReturnCode))
        {
            if(dwReturnCode==200)
            {
                if(fSuccess = pFile->QueryInfo(HTTP_QUERY_RAW_HEADERS_
                ➥CRLF,newLocation))
                {
                    if(newLocation != _T(""))
                        cout << _T("Header Info: ") << newLocation << endl
                        ➥<< endl;
                }

                pFile->SetReadBufferSize(2000);
                while(pFile->ReadString(returnedFileText))
                    cout << returnedFileText;
            }
        }
    }
}

// connection to server
pFile->Close();
```

```
if(pFile)
    delete pFile;

pServer->Close();
if(pServer)
    delete pServer;

session.Close();

}
```

Summary

In this chapter you learned about the Win32 Internet API and the MFC classes corresponding to this API. These functions allow the client to make a connection to a server. With these MFC classes, a programmer can make a connection to a server and manipulate files. The neat feature of these classes is that a programmer doesn't have to understand TCP/IP programming or any other low level functionality because the classes abstract and manipulate this work for you.

The HTTP classes help you get files from a Web server. The FTP classes let you do all the file and directory manipulation that an FTP server will allow. The Gopher classes cover a little of the other two classes.

Q&A

Q Where do you download the Win32 API?

A Download from `http://www.microsoft.com/intdev/sdk/docs/wininet/`.

Q What version of Microsoft Visual C++ do you need to use these cool classes?

A Use version 4.2, which is only available through subscription.

Q What is the base class for connecting to a server?

A `CInternetSession`.

Q What is the base class for the three connection types?

A `CInternetConnection`.

Q What class do you need to read an HTML file?

A `CHttpFile`.

Q What classes do you need to read an FTP or a Gopher file?

A `CFtpFileFind` and `CGopherFileFind`, respectively.

Workshop

In your own browser, try to connect to an FTP site. You may have to change the options of your browser. Also try to connect to the FTP site through any commands supported by your operating system. Once you are connected, try downloading a file. If you have a Web server, configure it for FTP, connect to it, and put a file in its directory. Next, try to connect to a Gopher site. You may have to change the options of your browser. Also try to connect to the Gopher site through any commands supported by your operating system. Once you are connected, try downloading a file. If you have a Web server, configure it for Gopher, connect to it, and get a file from its directory. Try to use a search engine. Attempt to create a WAIS search on your Web server (if you have one).

Quiz

1. Why will a normal console application not link with MFC, even if you have the proper #include?
2. What methods do I need to connect to a server?
3. Why do I have to check the return value from CFtpConnection::GetCurrentDirectory()?
4. What is the class I should use to handle an exception?
5. What is the _T macro used for?

NOTE Refer to the appendix, "Answers," for the answers to these questions.

Week 2

Day 14

Programming with Microsoft ActiveX Conferencing APIs

The Internet has made way for new kinds of communications. The goal is to make communication as simple as possible, but flexible and full of features. The Microsoft ActiveX Conferencing API is a great new tool because it allows people to participate in conference calls and meetings over their computers.

The Goal

The goal of Microsoft ActiveX Conferencing APIs is to allow real-time voice and data communications, application sharing, file-transferring, whiteboard usage (the computer equivalent of using a chalk board in a meeting), and text-based chats. This functionality is nothing new. Each piece or several pieces of Microsoft's ActiveX Conferencing APIs are currently bundled in software by vendors (Microsoft being one of them). You might be wondering why software vendors don't create a single application instead of using one component of

Microsoft's ActiveX Conferencing APIs to accomplish one goal. Unfortunately, applications require a great deal of vendor money and resources, and are often outdated six months after their release. Many problems related to what I call *shrink-wrap software* are solved with component software. To make this component software "Internet aware," it must be an Active X product.

The Standard

The Microsoft ActiveX Conferencing API and control are based on communications standards governed by an international committee. Many companies are trying to conform to this standard when creating their applications, which means that any other product that conforms to the same standard should be compatible with their product. The Microsoft ActiveX Conferencing API and control are based on standards passed by the International Telecommunications Union (formerly CCITT).

The Technology

The *party host* and the *party members* are the two main elements of conferencing technology. The party host manages the party members joining or leaving the conference, and manages how information is transferred to each party member. The party host can be a locator service that lists all people that you can connect with (see Figure 14.2 for an example), or a party host can be you calling your business associate in another town (you would be the party host). An example of this technology is a chat service. Most chat servers operate either as an open room, where anyone can join the discussion, or a private room, where one member specifically invites a newcomer. Everything is centrally managed by the chat server, but made available to anyone who joins.

Microsoft NetMeeting

The NetConference APIs and ActiveX control assume that central host management is handled by another party, namely Microsoft NetMeeting (see Figure 14.1 for the user interface of NetMeeting). NetMeeting is the central host and keeps track of who is available to be called or conferenced (see Figure 14.2 for NetMeeting's directory list). NetMeeting has a locator service that sits on a server (probably not your machine). When you install NetMeeting, tell it who and where you are (see Figure 14.3). If you leave your NetMeeting software running in the background, your software lets you know when someone calls you (see Figure 14.4). NetMeeting keeps a list of all NetMeeting users, and acts as an address book that contains NetMeeting contacts. Also, you need NetMeeting because NetConferencing has no way to make a direct connection to necessary protocols. NetConferencing passes requests to NetMeeting, and NetMeeting, in turn, passes the information to the protocols

(see Figure 14.5). NetMeeting also allows you to configure audio and compression (see Figure 14.6). It appears that the next release of NetConferencing will not require the use of NetMeeting.

Figure 14.1.
NetMeeting main user interface.

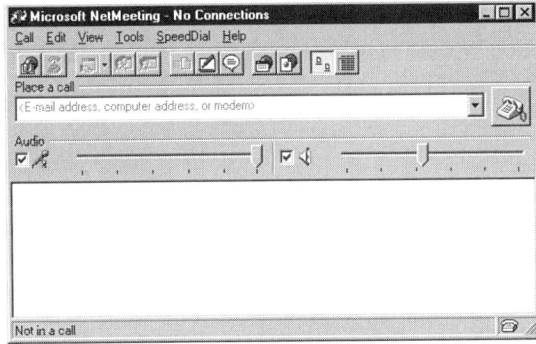

Figure 14.2.
This is the directory service listing in NetMeeting. This lists the party members of a conference.

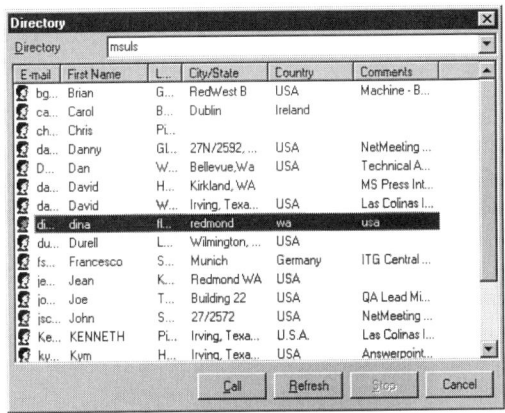

Figure 14.3.
Personal information and e-mail information is available to other members in NetMeeting.

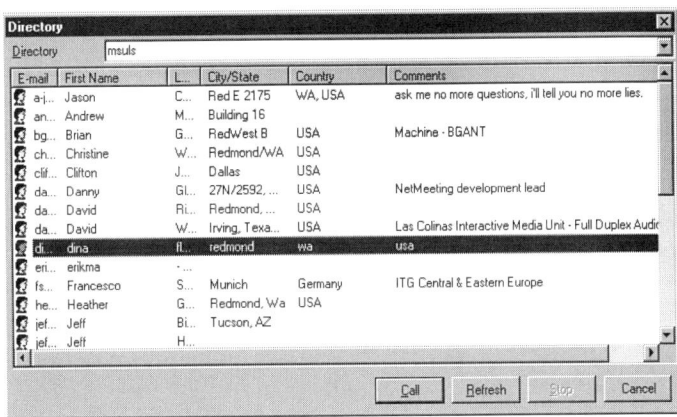

Figure 14.4.
The General property of NetMeeting includes your preferences for the handling of incoming calls and files.

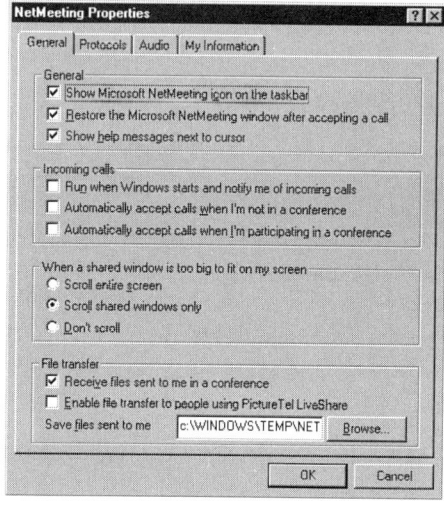

Figure 14.5.
The Protocols property of NetMeeting allows the user to choose what protocols are available and what protocols he wants NetMeeting to use.

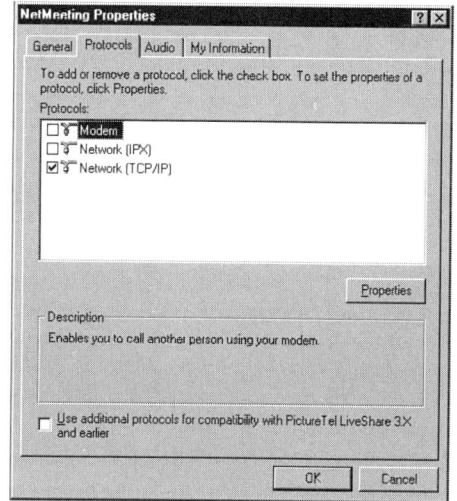

So if you don't need NetConferencing to manage the host activities, what do you need it for? Simply put, NetConferencing allows you to function as a member of a conference. A member can

- ☐ create a new conference and invite someone to join
- ☐ call someone (make a connection)
- ☐ request information about a connection

- set information about a connection
- send a file
- send a data-stream
- cancel a file or data-stream transfer
- activate a remote computer's application
- listen for other calls

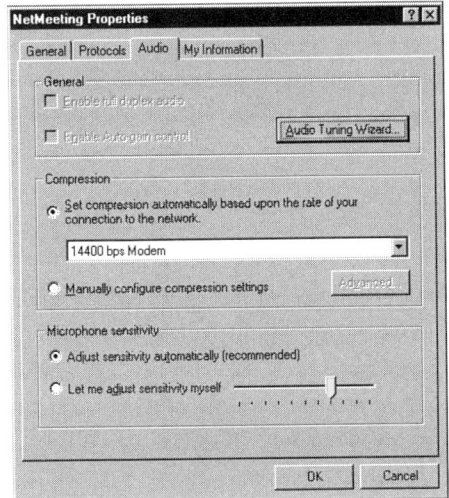

Figure 14.6.
The Audio and Compression properties of NetMeeting.

Let's Get Started

There's a lot to cover about NetConferencing and NetMeeting, including system requirements, the functions in the API, coding issues and other important points.

System Requirements

NetConferencing and NetMeeting should work on Windows 95 and Windows NT. At the time of this writing, both products were in beta and only supported on Windows 95. You can get Microsoft NetMeeting and Microsoft NetConference at http://www.microsoft.com/intdev/, which is the Internet Developer page on the Microsoft site. Install the NetMeeting software before installing the NetConference SDK.

The Functions in the API

The functions of the API are few at this time, but you can expect more functionality as this product grows. The entire list of APIs follows:

- `ConferenceConnect` establishes a conference connection between two systems. This is important because without it, you can't do anything.
- `ConferenceDisconnect` stops an existing conference. If you don't end the conference, you will lose system resources.
- `ConferenceGetInfo` obtains information about a conference or the users in a conference. The host of the conference might do this to find out information about members and to keep statistics. The members of the conference might do this to find information about specific members.
- `ConferenceSetInfo` changes conference settings. Use this function to set either the default directory, where you want to receive files, or the application GUID (special unique identifier) for the application that would be shared between two users.
- `ConferenceSetNotify` establishes a notification callback routine for an application. This function lets you assign a function of yours that you want called (the caller is this API) for status information or other notifications.
- `ConferenceRemoveNotify` turns off function callbacks for the function set in `ConferenceSetNotify`.
- `ConferenceLaunchRemote` tries to start the application associated with the application GUID. This application does not sit on your machine; rather, it sits on another member of the conference's machine. Use this function to guide that conference member by using his software but letting him see *how* you are using it.
- `ConferenceListen` starts the application on your system so that it listens for calls. The only other way the application can be activated is with an active call.
- `ConferenceShareWindow` lets other members of the conference view your window (any object that has a window handle) by passing the window handle to that conference member.

NOTE In Microsoft Windows operating systems, every window has a *handle*. This handle is used to give the programmer access to the window, yet the programmer doesn't have to know the details of what a handle is. Every object is a window: the desktop, the application interface, even a button. So being able to access the object via its handle is very fundamental to Microsoft operating systems.

- `ConferenceSendData` sends a block of data to the specified members of the conference. This is different from sending a file. Data could be associated with a chat-based conversation.
- `ConferenceSendFile` sends a file to the members of the conference. This is different from `ConferenceSendData`. A file generally has information associated with it that is also sent. Data in a file might include the date of last modification, or read-versus-write capability.
- `ConferenceCancelTransfer` stops a file from being transferred. If the process is fast, you might not be able to cancel the transfer because it might be already finished. This depends on the speed of your machine, the speed of the network, and the speed of the conference members' machines (speed also includes reads and writes to the hard drive).

Before You Get Started

You might have noticed that some of the functions have management qualities, such as being able to terminate a conference. How is that possible without a central host?

There are three scenarios:

- a first caller terminates the call
- someone who joined in the middle of the conference terminates the call
- the last person to join the conference terminates the call

Assume the last person to join the conference terminates the call. Because he was the last person to join the conference, no other callers or nodes depend on him for connection. That means there are no side effects from terminating the call.

The middle person, on the other hand, has callers dependent on him. If he terminates, callers who joined after him are terminated by default.

If the first caller terminates, the entire conference is shut down. This seems like a steep condition for a conference call, but it does follow the standard. The standard does allow for the "splitting" of conferences into two, but that is beyond the scope of this chapter.

So now you see why a permanent host is necessary: so the conference never dies. People can join and leave without terminating the conference or being dependent on each other to join.

Broadcasts and personal connections to other members of the conference are also ways to participate in conferences. I might want to send my status to my boss only, or I might want to send the network traffic report to everyone in the conference are also ways to participate in conferences. When sending data or a file, you must specify whether you want the entire conference to receive it, or whether you want an individual member of the conference to receive it.

Let's Get to Coding

To use the Conferencing API, include the windows.h and msconf.h header files. You must include the windows.h header file so you can share your applications window; you'll need to be able to pass the window handle. Make sure that msconf.lib is in the path (for library files) for your compiler. msconf.h and msconf.lib are included in the NetConference SDK (software development kit). The windows.h file should be in your c:\msdev\include directory if you are using Microsoft Visual C++ 4.2. If you don't include the header file or library, NetConferencing will dynamically link to any NetMeeting functionality it needs. Your header files should look something like Listing 14.1. Listing 14.2 is the implementation code for a simple application that connects to a computer, and then disconnects.

Listing 14.1. Use netconf.h to create header file.

```
#include <windows.h> // header file for windows
#include <msconf.h> // header file for MS NetConferencing
```

Listing 14.2. Use netconf.cpp to create codefile to connect.

```
#include "include netconf.h"

void main()
{
    HCONF hconf;
    CONFADDR confAddr;
    CONFINFO confInfo;

if(CONFERR_SUCCESS == ConferenceConnect(&hconf, &confAddr, &confInfo, NULL))
{
    if(CONFERR_SUCCESS == ConferenceDisconnect(hconf))
        cout << _T("Connection disconnected successfully") << endl;
    else
        cout << _T("Connection could not be disconnected") << endl;
}
else
    cout << _T("Connection could not be established") << endl;
}
```

The function ConferenceConnect has the parameters shown in Table 14.1.

NOTE  DWORD is a standard in Microsoft Visual C++. Please see the product help files for this and any other data type you don't understand.

NOTE
If you want to see what a user-defined type like DWORD resolves to, make sure your project supports Microsoft Visual C++'s browser information file component. The browser builds a set of data that includes definitions. Make sure your code can compile and build this data. When you are at that stage, right-click the highlighted word DWORD. A pop-up menu will appear, with one of the choices being the definition. Click this to see the definition.

Table 14.1. DWORD WINAPI ConferenceConnect.

Parameter	Description
HCONF * phConf	This is the conference handle; without a reference to the handle, you can't access any members or information about the conference.
CONFADDR * lpConfAddr	This is the machine to connect to; it is generally the machine of another member of the conference or the conference host.
CONFINFO * lpConfInfo	This sets the initial information (such as audio and video, and whether you are starting or stopping the conference) for the conference.
CONFNOTIFY * lpConfNotify	This sets information about your call-back function, such as the function address and the application GUID.

In Listing 14.2, I left the fourth parameter (CONFNOTIFY * lpConfNotify) as NULL instead of passing a CONFNOTIFY pointer because callback information isn't necessary at this time.

So what do you put in these new data types? The HCONF is a handle to a conference. There can be more than one conference, each identified by its handle, which makes it easy to get to each conference. What is actually inside this variable is not very interesting; it is only important that the other conferencing functions recognize this handle.

The conference address (CONFADDR * lpConfAddr) for the machine is a structure that has a DWORD for the total size of the structure and a union. The union contains one of two members: the IP address or a character string of the computer name. Which member of the union is used depends on where the union member is assigned (see Table 14.2).

Table 14.2. Assignments and resulting union members.

Assignment	Resulting Union Member
CONF_ADDR_IP	the DWORD member holds the IP address
CONF_ADDR_MACHINENAME	the string member holds the name of the machine on the local network
CONF_ADDR_PSTN	the string member holds telephone number
CONF_ADDR_UNKNOWN	neither member is used

For a local network, the CONF_ADDR_MACHINENAME computer name (dinaf, for instance) is probably sufficient.

NOTE In this chapter, I use the computer name dinaf as a placeholder. You want to change dinaf to a machine name for another member of the conference.

NOTE The NetConferencing API takes Unicode strings. Good macros to brush up on are L"x", _T("x"), where x is a string such as "Joe". Examples are L"Joe" or _T("Joe").

The status code CONFERR_SUCCESS means the function successfully completed its task. Check for this return code on each NetConferencing function. The rest of the return codes appear in Table 14.3. In this table, the word *object* refers to a file, application or other item. It does not refer to an ActiveX object.

Table 14.3. NetConferencing function return codes.

Return Code	Definition
CONFERR_ACCESS_DENIED	Access to the object was denied. This usually means you (or whoever) don't have permission to perform the operation. This is a system-level event.
CONFERR_ALREADY_SHARED	The application is already being shared. The application can't be shared more than once.
CONFERR_BUFFER_TOO_SMALL	The amount of storage (memory) was too small to handle the request.

Return Code	Definition
CONFERR_ENUM_COMPLETE	The enumeration (itemization) of the requested objects (conferences, members, and so on) is complete.
CONFERR_FILE_NOT_FOUND	The requested file was not found. It either doesn't exist or exists someplace else.
CONFERR_FILE_RECEIVE_ABORT	The transfer of the file was canceled by the receiver.
CONFERR_FILE_SEND_ABORT	The transfer of the file was canceled by the sender.
CONFERR_FILE_TRANSFER	There was a problem transferring the file.
CONFERR_INVALID_ADDRESS	The specified address (machine) was invalid.
CONFERR_INVALID_BUFFER	For some reason, the buffer cannot be read or written to.
CONFERR_INVALID_HCONF	The conference handle is invalid. Be careful. This is a unique identifier that the software creates. Don't mess with it.
CONFERR_INVALID_HWND	The window handle is invalid. Be careful. This is a unique identifier that the operating system creates. Don't mess with it.
CONFERR_INVALID_OPERATION	The request was invalid. There can be several reasons, including trying to cancel a conference before you have created one.
CONFERR_INVALID_PARAMETER	One of the parameters is incorrect. This could be a variety of things, so check every parameter. If it is computed, check computation.
CONFERR_NO_APP_SHARING	You can't share this application because it is not valid. Be careful what application GUID you set or pass.
CONFERR_NOT_SHARED	The application window is not currently being shared.
CONFERR_NOT_SHAREABLE	You can't share the application window because it is not allowed.
CONFERR_OUT_OUT_MEMORY	There is not enough memory to complete the operation. This is a good indication of a system with memory leaks or without enough resources.

continues

Table 14.3. continued

Return Code	Definition
CONFERR_PATH_NOT_FOUND	The path of the object (file, application, and so on) was not found. This could be a reference to a directory or hard drive that is not valid.
CONFERR_RECEIVE_DIR	There is a problem with the directory where the file is to be placed. It could be that the directory doesn't exist or is misspelled.
CONFERR_SUCCESS	The request succeeded completely with no significant errors or problems.

Now that you can connect, let's get information about the conference. Listing 14.3 adds to the code that allows you to connect to a conference.

Listing 14.3. Use `netconf.cpp` to create codefile to connect to and get information about a conference.

```
#include "include netconf.h"

void main()
{
    HCONF hconf;
    CONFADDR confAddr;
    CONFINFO confInfo;

if(CONFERR_SUCCESS == ConferenceConnect(&hconf, &confAddr, &confInfo, NULL))
{
        if(CONFERR_SUCCESS == ConferenceDisconnect(hconf))
        {
            cout << _T("Connection disconnected successfully") << endl;

            DWORD dwCode;
            VOID vRequestedInfo;

            if(CONFERR_SUCCESS == ConferenceGetInfo(hconf,dwCode,&vRequestedInfo))
            {
                cout << _T("Connection Information retrieved") << endl;
            }
            else
                cout << _T("Connection Information NOT retrieved") << endl;
        }
        else
            cout << _T("Connection could not be disconnected") << endl;
}
else
    cout << _T("Connection could not be established") << endl;
}
```

The `ConferenceGetInfo` function has three parameters, which are listed in Table 14.4. The function definition (without parameters) looks like the DWORD WINAPI ConferenceGetInfo.

Table 14.4. Parameter information for `ConferenceGetInfo`.

Parameter	Description
HCONF * phConf	This is the unique conference handle.
DWORD dwCode	This is the type of information you are requesting, such as information on a conference or information on a particular member of the conference.
VOID * pvoid	This is the actual information you requested.

The last two parameters work in unison. dwCode indicates a type of information. Each type of information is kept in its own structure. You will need to cast pvoid to the correct structure to retrieve the information you requested. The first row in Table 14.5 can be understood to mean that if you want to get information about the user, you need to cast pvoid to a CONFUSERINFO structure, then read the specific members of that structure. For more details on these structures, refer to the NetConference SDK product specification. The dwCode and pvoid parameters can appear as one of the following structures:

Table 14.5. `dwCode` and `pvoid`.

dwCode	pvoid
CONF_GET_USER	CONFUSERINFO structure
CONF_ENUM_USER	CONFUSERINFO structure
CONF_GET_CONF	CONFINFO structure
CONF_ENUM_CONF	CONFINFO structure
CONF_ENUM_PEER	CONFDEST structure
CONF_GET_RECDIR	CONFRECDIR structure
CONF_GET_FILEINFO	CONFFILEINFO structure

You might have to fill in part of the structure before casting to a void *, and many of the functions take an all-or-nothing approach. Say you want information on either one user or on all users; placing a zero in the appropriate field of the structure indicates that you are requesting information on all users. See the end of this chapter of a listing of each structure.

NOTE The specification has types like LPCONFDEST and LPCTSTR. LP refers to a local pointer, and the data type LPCONFDEST is usually #defined like this:

```
#define LPCONFDEST CONFDEST *
```

The NetConferencing ActiveX Control

The NetConferencing ActiveX control is another way to access a conference. The ActiveX control dynamic link library is IMSCONF.DLL. The NetConferencing ActiveX control can be used like any other, meaning it can be used in an HTML document or a script (such as VBScript or JavaScript). The control sits on top of the MSCONF.DLL (SCRAPI, using the XXXAPI naming convention, such as MAPI or TAPI). SCRAPI is the codename for the API technology.

NOTE Some of the methods return a BSTR. A *BSTR* is a specific system string type in OLE. A BSTR is a CHAR *, but the type holds its count of characters after the string. Don't try to manipulate BSTRs yourself. OLE provides several functions: SysAllocString, SysAllocStringLen, SysFreeString, SysReAllocString, SysReAllocStringLen, and SysStringLen. There is a certain amount of bytes cached by OLE, so when you do the final SysFreeString on a variable, you won't see the memory freed. Don't worry. OLE has some built-in memory cache and BSTRs are included.

The objects in the Active X control are the conference manager, user, conference, member, and channel. A *conference manager* is the host that I referred to in the beginning of this chapter. The *user* is any potential member of a conference; this could be someone who has the NetMeeting software running in the background listening for a call. A *conference* is exactly what it sounds like. A *member* is an active participant in the conference. The *channel* is a media-specific pipe for communicating, such as an audio channel or a video channel. If you have put stereo equipment together, the channel should be a familiar concept. For the first beta release of NetMeeting, four channels are supported: data transfer, file transfer, application sharing, and application control. The audio and video channels will be supplied in future releases. The channel control doesn't always support the user-to-user concept in each method, and the default behavior is a broadcast message to everyone in the conference. Check each method call in the SDK for broadcast versus peer-to-peer connection information.

Let's write a Web page that uses this NetConference ActiveX control. You need a
`Window_OnLoad` subprocedure to get things started, and a `Window_OnUnload` subprocedure to
get things cleaned up. You also need a text box to show user names in the conference, two
buttons (one to join the conference and one to leave the conference), and procedures for these
buttons. Listing 14.4. shows the HTML code for the text box, buttons, and procedures.
Figure 14.5. illustrates how the Web page looks in the Microsoft Internet Explorer 3.0
browser.

Listing 14.4. Use `conf.htm` to configure VBScript to use the NetConference ActiveX control.

```
<HTML>

    <HEAD>
        <TITLE> NetConference ActiveX Sample </TITLE>
    </HEAD>

    <BODY>
        <CENTER>
            <H1> NetConference ActiveX Sample </H1>
        </CENTER>
        <HR>
        <B> Members of conference: </B>
        <BR>
        <PRE><TEXTAREA NAME = MyTextBox COLS = 80 ROWS = 10></TEXTAREA></PRE>
        <PRE>
            <INPUT NAME=Join TYPE=BUTTON VALUE="Join">
            <INPUT NAME=Leave TYPE=BUTTON VALUE="Leave">
        </PRE>

<!-- Here the is NetConference ActiveX control -->
<OBJECT
    ID = ConfMgr
    CLASSID="clsid:53D22820-D7E8-11CF-ADOA-0080C7137C82">
</OBJECT>

<SCRIPT LANGUAGE="VBScript">
Option Explicit

Dim Conference <!-- Global Conference Object -->

Sub Window_OnLoad

    <!-- Window_OnLoad code goes here -->

End Sub
```

continues

Listing 14.4. continued

```
Sub Window_OnUnload
    <!-- Window_OnUnload code goes here -->
End Sub
Sub Join_onClick()
    <!-- Window_OnLoad code goes here -->
End Sub
Sub Leave_onClick()
    <!-- Window_OnLoad code goes here -->
End Sub
</SCRIPT> </HTML>
```

Now that you have the basic code, add code to create and delete the conference, and to join or leave the conference. Notice in Listing 14.4 that you created a conference manager object (`ConfMgr`) and conference object (`Conference`). Because they are not declared in a subprocedure, they are global to the script and can be accessed by any subprocedure in the script.

To initialize the ActiveX control, add Listing 14.5 to the `Window_OnLoad` subprocedure. In Listing 14.5, you create a conference collection object (`Conferences`) because there can be many conferences running simultaneously. After you declare your variables, initialize your conference manager object. Pass the GUID of the calling application, then go through the conference collection and grab the first one you find. If there are members already in the conference, add them to the text box. The `ConfMgr.Advise` and `Conference.Advise` variables let the ActiveX control listen for notifications.

Listing 14.5. Add the `Window_OnLoad` code to `conf.htm`.

```
Sub Window_OnLoad
    Dim Conferences 'Conference collection
    Set Conference = Nothing
    On Error Resume Next
    If Not ConfMgr.Initialize
    ➥("{00021191-0000-0000-C000-000000000046}") Then
        MsgBox "Can't Initialize Conference Manager !!!"
        Exit Sub
    End If

    ConfMgr.Advise
    Set Conferences = ConfMgr.Conferences
```

```
    If Not(Conferences Is Nothing) Then
        'Get first conference in conference collection
        Set Conference = Conferences(0)
        If Not (Conference Is Nothing) Then
            Conference.Advise
            'GetCurrent Members in the first conference
            Dim Members
            Dim ThisMember
            Dim arrayIndex
            If Members Is Nothing Then
                MyTextBox.Value = "Error" & Hex(Err.Number)
            Else
                MyTextBox.Value = "" 'Initialize text box
                For arrayIndex = 0 To Members.Count -1
                    MyTextBox.Value = MyTextBox.Value &
                    ➥Members(arrayIndex).Name & Chr(13) & Chr(10)
                Next
            End If
        End If
    End If
End Sub
```

Listing 14.6 adds the cleanup code you need. Because you have opened a conference and a conference manager, it makes sense that you would have to close them down. There is no need to clean up the text box, but it is a nice thing to do for users of the Web page.

Listing 14.6. Add the `Window_OnUnload` code to `conf.htm`.

```
Sub Window_OnUnload
    MyTextBox.Value = "" <!— Make the text box have no names, ie blank →
    If Not (Conference Is Nothing) Then
        Conference.Unadvise
        Set Conference = Nothing
    End If
    ConfMgr.Unadvise
    ConfMgr.Uninitialize
End Sub
```

Listing 14.7 adds the code you need to join the conference. Notice that if a conference was not previously created, you create one here. Then you create a user and invite the user to join the conference. The user in this case is a computer name. You would want to enter the correct name in place of *MyMachineNameOrIPAddress*. After a user joins a conference, he changes from a user to a member. At this point, you want to reassemble all the members of the conference and put their names in the text box. The code to do this is presented in Listing 14.7.

Listing 14.7. Add the `Join` code to `conf.htm`.

```
Sub Join_onClick
    Dim User
    On Error Resume Next
    If Conference Is Nothing Then
    <!-- Create the conference if it doesn't exist (1 means a data conference)→
        Set Conference = ConfMgr.CreateConference("MyConference",1)
        If Conference Is Nothing Then
            MsgBox "Couldn't create conference"
            Exit Sub
        End If
        Conference.Advise
    End If
    <!-- Create the user if it doesn't exist (2 means machine name)→
    Set User = ConfMgr.CreateUser("MyMachineNameOrIPAddress",2)
    If User Is Nothing Then
        MsgBox "Couldn't create user "
    Else
        If Not Conference.Invite(User) Then
            MsgBox "Couldn't invite user"
        End If
    End If
```

To do the necessary cleanup, you need some code to handle when you close the browser or leave this page to load another. So the `Leave` code is fairly straightforward, as Listing 14.8 illustrates.

Listing 14.8. Add the `Leave` code to `conf.htm`.

```
Sub Leave_onClick
    On Error Resume Next
    If Conference Is Nothing Then
        MsgBox "Conference isn't active"
    Else
        If Not Conference.Leave Then
            MsgBox "Couldn't leave conference"
        End If
End Sub
```

To use a conference in this ActiveX control, you must create a conference object, but you only need one per application instance. You can create the other objects by having a method return that object as instantiated (user, conference, communication channel and file transfer) or by having an enumeration create that object (member, client application, shareable application). For a list of objects, please see the end of this chapter.

When you attempt to open this page in your Internet Explorer 3.0, you will notice a message box (see Figure 14.7) asking whether you want to activate the control. This is a nice way for the user to be aware that something is going on with his computer, and to have a degree of control over it.

Figure 14.7.
NetConference asks you how you would like to use it.

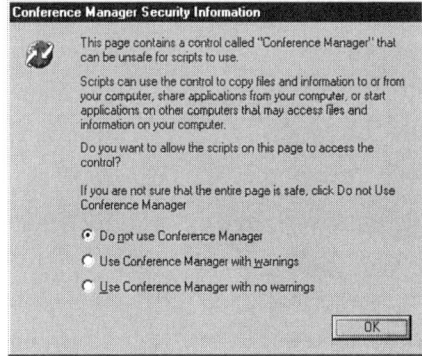

NetConference will be very useful in scripts. Imagine that you go to a conference HTML page. You find a list of people involved in the conference, a text box for you to enter a message to send, and a text box for you to read messages as they are entered by other members of the conference. Joining a conference is as simple as clicking a button on an HTML page! For complete information on this control, refer to the specification you will get when you download and install the SDK.

NetConference API Structures

All dwSize variables are the size of the structure in bytes. When you look at the API parameters in more detail, remember that you might have to pass the size or count of an object.

NOTE

When dealing with string characters, a variable can refer to the count of characters or the count of bytes. This is important when dealing with any character that is larger than one byte. Most API function parameters expect counts of bytes, regardless of data type, but it is important to check anyway. The parameter cb refers to count of bytes.

Table 14.6 contains the structure members for the CONFUSERINFO structure.

Table 14.6. Specification: the structure of CONFUSERINFO members.

Member	Description
DWORD dwSize	size of this entire structure
DWORD dwUserID	unique value for user in conference
DWORD dwFlags	combination of:
CONF_UF_DATA	user is in a data conference
CONF_UF_AUDIO	user is in an audio conference
CONF_UF_VIDEO	user is displaying a video image
CONF_UF_LOCAL	indicates a local user
DWORD dwReserved	reserved for future use, must be 0
DWORD szUserName	null-terminated string of user's name

Table 14.7 contains the members of the CONFINFO structure.

Table 14.7. Specification: the structure of CONFINFO members.

Member	Definition
DWORD dwSize	size of this entire structure
HCONF hconf	conference handle
DWORD dwMediaType	combination of:
CONF_MT_DATA	data conference
CONF_MT_AUDIO	audio conference
CONF_MT_STOPPING	stopping the conference
DWORD dwState	current conference state, combination of:
CONF_CS_INVALID	state of conference is invalid
CONF_CS_INITIALIZING	state of conference is initialized
CONF_CS_ACTIVE	state of conference is active
CONF_CS_STOPPING	state of conference is stopped
DWORD cUsers	number of people in conference
DWORD dwGCCID	GCC identifier
DWORD szConferenceName	null-terminated name of conference
CONF_MAX_CONFERENCENAME	

Programming with Microsoft ActiveX Conferencing APIs

`CONF_MAX_CONFERENCENAME` refers to a constant number defined for the maximum characters in a conference name.

Table 14.8 contains the members of the `CONFDEST` structure.

Table 14.8. Specification: the structure of `CONFDEST` members.

Member	Description
DWORD dwSize	size of this entire structure
DWORD dwFlags	destination flags for transfer when receiving `CONFN_DATA_SENT` or `CONFNDATA_RECEIVED` notifications; combination of:
CONF_DF_BROADCAST	data sent to everyone
CONF_DF_PRIVATE	data sent to one person
CONF_DF_DATA_SEGMENT_BEGIN	start of data
CONF_DF_DATA_SEGMENT_END	end of data
DWORD dwUserId	specific person or 0 (0 represents broadcast)
DWORD dwReserved	application GUID or 0 (0 represents it does not apply)

Table 14.9 contains the members of the `CONFRECFIR` structure.

Table 14.9. Specification: the structure of `CONFRECDIR` members.

Member	Description
DWORD dwSize	size of this entire structure
TCHAR szRecDir[MAX_PATH]	full path of default directory for received files

`MAX_PATH` refers to the constant number defined for the maximum number of characters for this string.

Table 14.10 contains the members of the `CONFFILEINFO` structure.

Table 14.10. Specification: the structure of `CONFFILEINFO` members.

Member	Description
DWORD dwSize	size of this entire structure
DWORD dwFileID	unique file ID

continues

Table 14.10. continued

Member	Description
`DWORD dwReserved1`	reserved for later use
`DWORD dwFileSize`	size of the file in bytes
`DWORD dwReserved2`	reserved for later use
`DWORD dwBytesTransferred`	count of bytes transferred
`DWORD dwFileAttributes`	file attributes such as read, archive, hidden, or system
`FILETIME ftCreationTime`	time the file was created
`FILETIME ftLastAccessTime`	last time the file was opened
`FILETIME ftLastWriteTime`	last time the file was modified
`TCHAR szFileNameSrc[MAX_PATH]`	name of the original file
`TCHAR szFileNameDest`	name of the file as it is put in the receiving directory

`MAX_PATH` refers to the maximum number of characters that can be in the string `szFileNameSrc`.

NetConference ActiveX Objects, Properties, Methods, and Events

NetConference ActiveX objects are conference manager, user, conference, member, and communication channel. Remember that *properties* are information about the object such as what the text is in a text box. A *method* acts on the object, such as capitalizing all characters in a text box. An *event* is a piece of code that does something when a specific event happens. For example, when you click the text box to change it, all characters in the text box are automatically highlighted. Table 14.11 is a list of properties, methods, and events for the `IConferenceManagerX` object.

Table 14.11. `IConferenceManagerX` properties, methods, and events.

Properties	Methods	Events
`ConferenceCapabilities`	`Initialize`	`InvitedToConference`
`RemoteConference`	`Uninitialize`	`ConferenceCreated`
`Conferences`	`CreateConference`	`StateChanged`
`Users`	`CreateUser`	`RequestToJoin`

Properties	Methods	Events
NullObject	Advise	MemberChanged
	Unadvise	InvitedToConference
		ConferenceCreated
		StateChanged
		RequestToJoin
		MemberChanged
		ChannelChanged
		DataSent
		DataReceived
		FileSent
		FileReceived
		AppSharingStatusChanged
		AppControlStatusChanged

Table 14.12 is a list of properties for the IConfUserX object. This object has no events or methods.

Table 14.12. IConfUserX properties (no events or methods).

Properties
Name
Type
ConferenceCapabilities
IsMCU
Conferences
Applications

Table 14.13 is a list of IConferenceX properties and methods. This object has no events.

Table 14.13. IConferenceX properties and methods (no events).

Properties	Methods
Name	Invite
Capabilities	AcceptInvite

continues

Table 14.13. continued

Properties	Methods
State	RejectInvite
Members	Join
Applications	AcceptJoin
ChannelInterfaces	RejectJoin
Channels	CreateChannel
	Leave
	IsSameAs
	Advise
	Unadvise

Table 14.14 is a list of `IConfMemberX` object's properties and methods. This object has no events.

Table 14.14. `IConfMemberX` properties and methods (no events).

Properties	Methods
Name	IsSameAs
Type	
ConferenceCapabilities	
IsMCU	
Conferences	
Applications	
Conference	
IsSelf	

Table 14.15 is a list of `IConfChannelX`'s properties and methods. This object has no events.

Table 14.15. `IConfChannelX` properties and methods (no events).

Properties	Methods
Conference	IncludeMember
Interface	ExcludeMember
Members	IsSameAs
Objects	

Table 14.16 is a list of `IconfDataExchangeX` methods. This object has no properties or events.

Table 14.16. `IConfDataExchangeX` **methods (no properties or events).**

Methods
SendData
Advise
Unadvise

Table 14.17 is a list of `IConfFileExchangeX` properties and methods. This object has no events.

Table 14.17. `IConfFileExchangeX` **properties and methods (no events).**

Properties	Methods
ReceiveFileDir	SendFile
	Cancel
	Advise
	Unadvise

Table 14.18 is a list of `IConfAppSharingX` properties and methods. This object has no events.

Table 14.18. `IConfAppSharingX` **properties and methods (no events).**

Properties	Methods
SharableApps	Advise
	Unadvise

Table 14.19 is a list of `IConfAppControlX` methods. This object has no properties or events.

Table 14.19. `IConfAppControlX` **methods (no properties or events).**

Methods
StartRemoteInstance
Advise
Unadvise

Table 14.20 is a list of `IConfApplicationX` properties. This object has no events or methods.

Table 14.20. `IConfApplicationX` properties (no events or methods).

Properties
GUID
Name

Table 14.21 is a list of `IConfShareAppX` properties and methods. This object has no events.

Table 14.21. `IConfShareAppX` properties and methods (no events).

Properties	Methods
Name	Share
ShareState	Unshare

Table 14.22 is a list of `IConferenceX` properties. This object has no events or methods.

Table 14.22. `IConferenceX` properties (no events or methods).

Properties
BytesTransferred
String
Array

Table 14.23 is a list of `IConfFileTransferX` properties and methods. This object has no events.

Table 14.23. `IConfFileTransferX` properties and methods (no events).

Properties	Methods
Name	IsSameAs
BytesTransferred	
TotalSize	
State	

Summary

The NetConferencing APIs and the NetConferencing ActiveX control extract the know-how from the programmer while leaving a great deal of functionality for the user. This functionality is not for the timid. The product is in its earliest stages, and a great deal remains to be fleshed out.

This software allows an application (Web page or windows GUI interface) to let people join a conference, transfer data or files, and disconnect from the conference. Conference management functionality is also included, but you must depend on NetMeeting to make this software work.

Q&A

Q Where do you get the NetConferencing and NetMeeting software?

A NetConferencing and NetMeeting can be found at http://www.microsoft.com/intdev/. This is the Internet Developer Studio on the Microsoft site.

Q What do NetConferencing and NetMeeting give you?

A NetConferencing and NetMeeting give you the ability to have multiway conferencing through your Internet browser or other applications.

Q What are the system requirements?

A For beta release: Win95

For product release: WinNT and Win95

Q What is the main object in the NetConference ActiveX control?

A Conference manager is the main object in the NetConference ActiveX control.

Workshop

Develop a cool application or Web page that uses NetConference to transfer data and files between your computer and someone else's computer.

Quiz

1. What is the difference between a conference manager and a conference?
2. What is the difference between a user and a member?
3. What software is a requirement of NetConference?

NOTE: Refer to the appendix, "Answers," for the answers to these questions.

At A Glance

Week 3 focuses on the ActiveX controls that you can use to create dynamic Web pages.

Day 15: What Is an ActiveX Control?

Day 15 explores background information that will prove useful when you are learning to use ActiveX controls. Day 15 covers how ActiveX controls came to be, how these controls are used, where you can find ActiveX controls on the Internet, and the system requirements for using ActiveX controls.

Day 16: Installing ActiveX Controls

Day 16 teaches you about the <OBJECT> container tag, as well as how to use an ActiveX control within a Web page and how to add an ActiveX control to a Visual Basic project. You will create a basic Web site for a fictitious company and build your first, and possibly most exciting, ActiveX Visual Basic application: a Web browser.

Day 17: ActiveX Control Downloading

During Day 17, you will learn about the actual process of installing Internet components and a few ways to prevent the installation of unwanted code or content.

Day 18: Customizing ActiveX Control Properties

During Day 18, you will learn more about what ActiveX controls are, what they can do, and how to make them do it. This chapter covers the controls that come with the Internet Explorer, and teaches you how to manipulate options (or parameters) available with the different ActiveX objects.

Day 19: User Interaction with ActiveX Controls

During Day 19, you will learn how to enable people who access your ActiveX utility to interact with the controls covered on previous days. When you are finished with this chapter, you will be able to create an interactive ActiveX HTML document and an interactive ActiveX Visual Basic application.

Day 20: Using the Internet Control Pack

During Day 20, you will learn how the Internet Control Pack came into being, what protocols this pack includes, and what programs support this feature. You will use the Internet Control Pack with Visual Basic to create several Internet projects, including a POP3 mail checker, an SMTP mail-sending utility, an HTML Web browser, an HTTP keyword-search utility, an FTP directory-information utility, and an NNTP newsgroup-information utility.

Day 21: Creating an ActiveX Control

In this chapter, you will be exposed to some of the advanced features of COM and DCOM OLE programming. This chapter also reviews some of the features of control creation and how they apply to ActiveX. You will learn how and why to edit the system registry, some of the features and requirements of a COM/DCOM control, and OLE interface design for objects and classes.

Week 3

Day 15

What Is an ActiveX Control?

ActiveX controls have evolved from object linking and embedding technologies. They allow user access and interaction with shared documents over the Internet or an enterprise's intranet. ActiveX, in general, consists of a number of processes that allow many varied technologies to operate over a distributed environment such as the Internet (see Figure 15.1).

With object linking and embedding, a spreadsheet from an application such as Excel and a database from an application such as Access can be made a part of the content of a document in Word. Without object linking and embedding, those objects would be kept separate, and you would need to run all three applications to access the data.

Figure 15.1.
ActiveX is a method for implementing various technologies over the Internet.

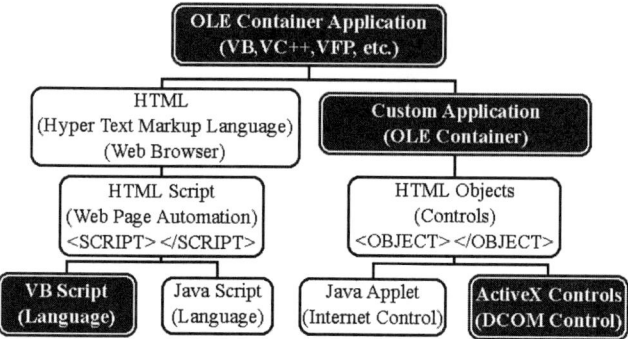

Before you can learn how to program with ActiveX controls, there is some background information with which you should be familiar. In today's lesson, you will learn

- How ActiveX controls came to be
- How ActiveX controls are used
- Where to find ActiveX controls
- The system requirements for using ActiveX controls

Evolution of ActiveX Controls

ActiveX controls come from half a century of software development, beginning with research at companies such as Xerox/PARC and Bell Labs. ActiveX controls are a marriage of an innovative method of allowing applications to interact with each other (OLE) and Microsoft's response to the demand for a simple way to implement that interaction.

OLE

OLE (Object Linking and Embedding) is what sets the advanced programmer apart from the merely experienced. To understand just what it means (no, it's not what the crowd says at a bullfight!), let's dissect the phrase:

Object—Every "thing" on a computer system is called an *object*. This includes the console, applications, libraries (like many of the .DLL files in your \Windows\System directory), and so on.

Linking—Sometimes a *link* is created between two separate objects on a system, which allows them to share each other's information and resources. For instance, if

you have a mailing list and a form letter, you can create a link between the two so that the form letter can go out to everyone on the list. If the list is modified in some way, the changes will be reflected in the mailings.

In Figure 15.2 you see a document from a doctor in a remote location ordering new Yeti Restraints from his medical supplies company. Because he wants to include a graph in his document, and because he is using the WordPad utility that has no graphing support, he can create a link to a previously created Excel chart. This is done through the menu option Insert | Object and then by selecting the Create from File option.

Figure 15.2.
The WordPad dialog box for creating a link to external data or embedding a new object within a document.

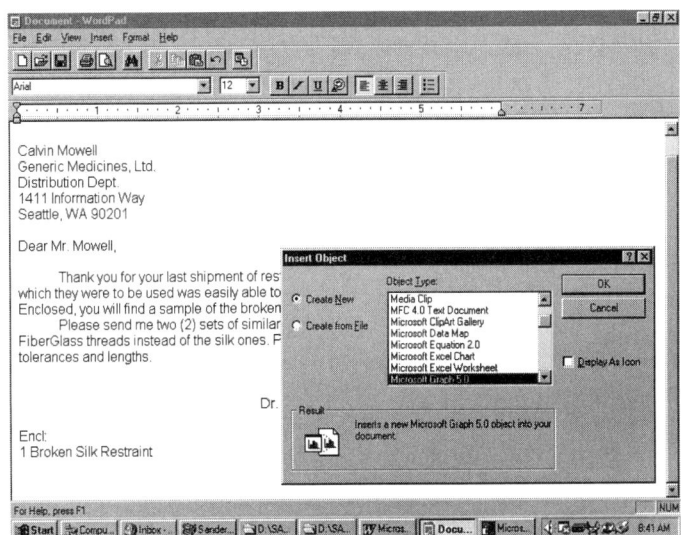

Embedding—When you create a document in one application, sometimes you will find that the application does not allow you to work with or edit a particular kind of document.

Referring again to Figure 15.2, if Dr. Kirbymeister had not previously created an external graph, the doctor would choose the menu option Insert | Object—but this time, he would select the Create New option instead of Create from File. Then he could create and edit the chart from within WordPad as though he were using the Excel program itself.

The History of OLE

OOP (Object Oriented Programming) was developed around the middle of the century. At that time, most of its use was limited to the military, research labs, universities, and large corporations.

OLE, as a generally accepted technology, was not introduced to the public until Apple Corporation developed and marketed the later versions of the Macintosh. The Mac used the first widely accepted GUI (Graphical User Interface), and its natural programming environment was object oriented.

It was a few more years before it found global acceptance, when Microsoft incorporated OLE and OOP into millions of NT Servers and Windows 95 Workstations. Now OLE is the state-of-the-art in programming—almost 50 years after it was introduced.

Uses of OLE

OLE is the technology that allows applications on a computer to interact with each other. An example of OLE is when you view an Excel spreadsheet or a Word document in a PowerPoint presentation or an Office Binder. (See Figure 15.3.)

The Office binder is a utility that comes with Microsoft Office for Windows 95. It allows a user to place several documents in one shell. This shell then provides a method for linking the various object so that they can all reference a common set of data. This is one of the first implementations of DCOM-type technologies into a Windows95 product, since the different documents can reside on remote servers.

Figure 15.3.
OLE between Office95 applications.

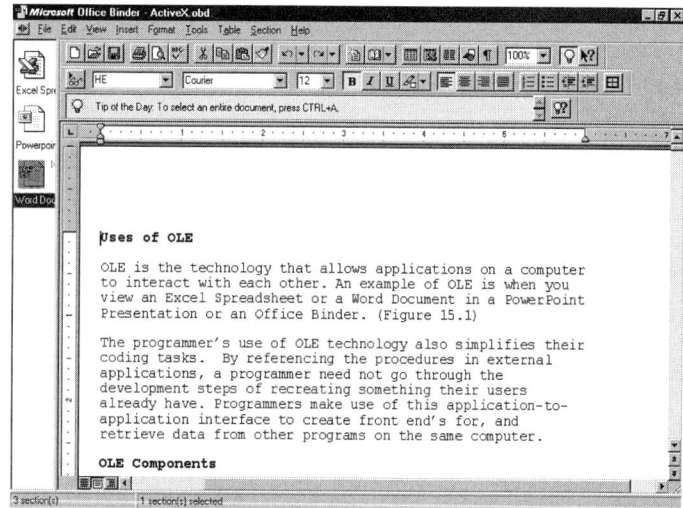

Using OLE technology also simplifies programmers' coding tasks. By referencing the procedures in external applications, a programmer need not go through the development steps of re-creating something his users already have. Programmers make use of this application-to-application interface to create front ends for, and retrieve data from, other programs on the same computer.

You can see another instance of OLE by following these steps:

1. Start a new Word document.
2. From the pull-down menu, select Insert and then Object. You should see a list of many different objects you can insert into the otherwise all-text document.
3. From the list, select Bitmap Image. You should see that your menus and button bars have switched from the standard Microsoft Word features to tools from Microsoft Paint (or whatever OLE bitmap editor your system uses).
4. By clicking outside of the image area, you can return to the standard Word setup.

OLE Components

The application whose features one wants to access would need to support a certain set of functions. The presence or absence of these features is what makes an application OLE-enabled or not. The host application is an OLE *server*, and the system accessing it is the OLE *client*. Although the OLE server is usually a full-blown application, it could be as simple as a DLL or two. As long as the server supports the interconnectivity features of OLE, other OLE-enabled applications can use it.

The widest uses of OLE are based on COM (Component Object Model). COM defines a basic structure and set of rules for developing object-oriented programs. When a Windows OOP programmer develops his application, it is the structure of the COM model upon which his program acts.

NOTE I only gave a brief discussion of COM here. After you are more familiar with ActiveX and OLE programming, you may wish to reference the entire specification for the Component Object Model, as well as information about its ongoing development, at Microsoft's OLE Developers' Site at `http://www.microsoft.com/oledev`.

When creating an ActiveX control, you must implement the `IUnknown` interface, which must be self registering. The controls are then instantiated and uninstantiated through the `AddRef()` and `Release()` methods in whatever programming language you use.

OLE also proved to be of great benefit to software manufacturers who wanted to increase the value of their products by allowing other applications to access the features of their software. A manufacturer would publish an API (Application Programmers Interface) for its product, and developers would reference that document to see how to make their programs interact with that product. Using this complex API, the programmers would develop their own front ends for others' software, tailoring them to the specific needs of their customers.

> **Sharing or Stealing?**
>
> The shared nature of OOP makes it very easy for a programmer to breach the barrier between using and taking credit for another programmer's work.
>
> When an OLE programmer creates an interface to another programmer's software, the features add value to that application. If, however, the new application is nothing more than a front end to another application, credit should be given to the original programmer.

The only real drawback to this is that the API can be very difficult to understand for a programmer who is not familiar with the program. Although OLE coding is complex, it is still not as complex as it would be without the standardization of OLE features.

VBX—16-bit Custom Control

VBX was the first "custom control." It incorporated the features of an API into a single item that could be added to a program. This item would enable the programmer to access the features of a given item without needing to know the more complex features of OLE. Each control enabled users to interact with a specific OLE component or set of components.

Visual programming systems (like Visual Basic and Access), which are OLE container applications, could now access complex features of an external object with just a few lines of code. Although the processes the VBX uses are not true OLE in the strictest sense, this "mock OLE" is still quite powerful.

The development of custom controls brought an additional benefit to programmers, many of whom were working with programming languages that were not true OOP. Although the VBX was not a true OLE component, it broke ground in enabling programmers to access functionality within external software components.

OCX—16/32-bit Object Controls

OCX controls were developed in response to the need for simpler, yet more powerful, access to control and OLE functionality. Lower-level VBXs just did not do it. Although most of these controls are still not, by definition, true OLE controls, many of them incorporate the more complex (and frequently needed) OLE functions. The enhanced "mock OLE" of the first OCX's filled most of this demand.

Custom controls like VBXs and OCXs provided an excellent way of incorporating complex features into a simple package. As with any technology that proves valuable, programmers began demanding more from these tools—demanding that developers incorporate actual OLE features into them. Indeed, OCXs met this demand so well that there is still some confusion and debate among programmers about whether OCXs are true OLE controls.

ActiveX Controls

ActiveX controls were introduced to combine two distinct areas in the evolution of computer technologies: custom controls and a rethinking of the basic ideas behind OLE and OOP.

These new controls are the first DCOM (Distributed Component Object Model)-based OLE controls. As I've mentioned, prior OLE interfaces were based on COM; therefore, ActiveX is the first true OLE control.

In DCOM, the programmer no longer programs for an individual computer, but rather for the environment, or network, within which computers operate. In the older COM model, a programmer need only follow a set of rules on how the computer and the user would interact. With DCOM, the programmer is provided with a set of rules by which computers, in general, interact with each other over the Internet or an intranet.

How ActiveX Controls Are Used

Two similar methods are used to interact with ActiveX controls—programmatically and through script. When using VBScript, the line between the two is blurred because it so closely follows the structure of the Visual Basic programming language.

Programmatic

One of the neatest things about ActiveX controls is the way they blur the line between Internet controls and regular programming controls such as command buttons and drop-down list boxes. ActiveX controls can be used within hypertext documents as well as within full-blown programs. The major difference between the two uses is that scripting uses a degree of restricted functionality for many controls when used in a network document. When these same controls are used in an OLE container application (such as Visual Basic or Visual C++), they can be programmed with all the power of the programming language used.

Using ActiveX with Visual Basic/VBA

Although the programming of ActiveX controls is possible today through Visual Basic 4.0, the integration of ActiveX into a programming language is mature only in versions of Visual Basic after version 4. Visual Basic and VBA (Visual Basic for Applications) will be the first programming languages to incorporate ActiveX into their environments.

Programmers who make use of Visual Basic to program with ActiveX will find it simple to port their applications to the Web by replacing their VB code with VBScript. Most of the syntax and other conventions will remain the same, and most of the code will need very minor revisions to work the same as it did in the compiled version. In fact, VBScript is actually just a subset of VBA.

This code will send 100 alerts to the user in Visual Basic:

```
Sub cmdWarnUser
     For x = 1 to 100
         msgbox "Alert!"
     Next X
End Sub
```

This code will do the same thing in VBScript:

```
Sub cmdWarnUser
   For x = 1 to 100
      alert "Alert!"
   Next x
End Sub
```

Using ActiveX in Other Languages

Visual Basic and VBA are the programming environments in which most of the ActiveX controls are designed to be used. They can be used, however, in any programming environment that supports DCOM-based OLE. These programming environments are called OLE *container* applications. A few of these are Visual Basic, Access, Visual FoxPro, Turbo C++, and Visual C++.

ActiveX Scripting

ActiveX scripting adds a level of control to Internet documents and allows the programmer to automate and activate Web pages. It does this through the use of server-side and client-

side scripts (covered earlier in this book). The HTML page itself can have bits of script (client-side) such as VBScript and JScript, which provide a level of automation for use on the client machine. The server then can have its own scripts, such as ISAPI and CGI, which provide a level of automation for use on the server machine.

Server Scripts

Without client scripting, the only way to program a Web document is through a server script such as ActiveX ISAPI, HTTP CGI, or UNIX Perl. These scripts are very powerful, but they require a Web page manager to have access to a server's executable files.

> **Loading CGI Scripts on an ISP's Server**
>
> Unless you operate your own HTTP server locally, it can be very time-consuming to upload, test, and configure your own server scripts.
>
> First you must select the language in which you are going to write your script. Most (if not all) ISPs (Internet service providers) use UNIX as their server operating system—and most users do not. Perl scripts usually work best on those systems. Some systems also support CGI scripting, but those scripts must be written in C++. Some HTTP servers support CGIs that are written in VB as well. Microsoft Internet Information Servers support the new ActiveX Server Scripting, called ISAPI. The language you choose depends on the HTTP server software. Should your ISP change its system, you may need to rewrite and re-compile your server scripts.
>
> After you have written your script(s), you must put it into your HTTP server's script directory (usually something like \CGI-BIN\). You will need special permission from your ISP to access this directory because its other users will be using the same directory. Consideration should be paid to those other users by not bothering the other scripts in the directory.
>
> Most scripts will need to be uploaded to the server (and made public to the world) just to enable testing on them. Testing a server script on a local machine would result in some unexpected results.
>
> All this makes scripting within HTML documents (that is, client-side scripting) easier on the Web page author and safer for the ISP and its users.

For many ISPs, this level of user access to their servers is unacceptable and they disallow it (or charge a premium for it). Server scripting gives the scriptwriter access to a large portion of the ISP's server configuration. The malicious or uninformed writer could cause problems—not only on the ISP's servers, but to its customers' machines as well.

HTML Script

The IETF (Internet Engineering Task Force) has established a standardized method for coding script within an HTML document. This standard defines how all scripts are supposed to work within a Web document.

> **NOTE** The IETF site contains the full text of all the current Internet Standards (RFCs) in their final forms as well as proposed specifications. The site is located at IETF http://www.ietf.org.

JavaScript

JavaScript is the first widely used language based on the HTML scripting standard. It was developed by Sun Microsystems to support Java applets. The similar naming of the scripts and the objects often causes confusion when talking about either in conversation—but they are two completely different beasts.

> **NOTE** Sun Microsystems provides information on the Java specification (which it developed) on its Web site at JavaSoft http://www.javasoft.com.

ActiveX honors the JavaScript standard and allows interaction between JavaScript, VBScript, Java controls, and ActiveX controls.

VBScript

VBScript, which you learned about earlier, is Microsoft's answer to JavaScript. It also allows a programmer to place his code and objects in an HTML document. Because VBScript is part of the ActiveX line of technologies, it supports programmatic control of both Java applets and ActiveX controls. Anyone with a Microsoft Internet Explorer Web browser can run VBScript.

> **NOTE** Microsoft's VBScript site contains information on the VBScript language. You can find it at http://www.microsoft.com/vbscript.

Security

Parents, guardians, employers, and others provide those in their charge with Internet access to increase their productivity and overall value. However, with this added power comes a need to be protected from inappropriate, dangerous, or downright malicious activity. ActiveX provides a framework over which a very effective security system can be laid.

Threats

Because scripting is such a powerful tool, it is of great value in distributing information according to a multitude of client-system requests. This punches a wide hole in the security of most enterprises.

Security can be breached by allowing foreign programs access to internal information systems. Dangerous or malicious activity by scripts can be brought on through programmatic events such as file I/O. The threat is not less for an individual system than it is for a larger network.

Protection

To protect yourself from malicious programs, there are a couple of security policies you will want to implement on your system. These should protect you against

- ☐ Users who wish to gain unauthorized access to your system.
- ☐ Malicious code, in the form of viri.
- ☐ Bad behavior on the part of downloaded ActiveX Components.

Standard

Because most security boils down to three basic levels (UserID, password and/or physical location), the wise administrator will keep the most sensitive information *unavailable to the Net*. Each user and system administrator should determine the level of protection (and the resultant impact upon interoperability) within which their particular system should operate.

AntiVirus

Any system that has a disk drive, network connection, or other way of accessing files (and being accessed for files) is exposed to threats from viral infection. An AntiVirus program should be running on any system with such interconnectivity. Microsoft AntiVirus, Norton AV, McAfee AntiVirus, and many other utilities provide a basic level of security that should catch most threats from viral infection.

>
> **NOTE**
>
> McAfee has dominated the anti-virus market throughout the last decade. Learn where to get the latest copies of their anti-virus software at http://www.mcafee.com.

ActiveX

In response to the threat that scripting exposes, a wide variety of methods have been developed with and without the ActiveX technologies to protect systems against threats such as malignant code and corrupt controls. Some of these methods include Internet ratings, code signing, trust verification, and user locator services.

Where to Find ActiveX Controls

ActiveX controls are available from many sources. Controls that software manufacturers, corporate marketers, and even hobbyists post on their Web pages can automagically find their way to systems all over the world. The nature of ActiveX controls makes it almost too simple for users to load and install them on their machines.

World Wide Web

The easiest way to obtain new software of any kind, especially ActiveX controls, is by way of the World Wide Web (also known as *WWW* or *The Web*). As ActiveX is being implemented all over the world, the Web is turning out to be the most effective distribution channel as well as a way to communicate. (Why order something through the mail, with all of its overhead, cost, and inefficiencies, when it can be downloaded as needed with immediacy?)

Automatic Installation from Web Pages

When a user points his browser to a standard Web page (or HTML document), the page of text is displayed in the browser window. This is the quickest, cheapest, easiest way to acquire a new ActiveX control. When a user views a page containing ActiveX controls while using an ActiveX-enabled browser, activities to load and use those controls are launched. Users are prompted whether they want to load and install the controls (and, of course, expose themselves to the threat those controls may pose).

NOTE  If the control does not require a user license, you can immediately start programming with it. In fact, you *can* program with it immediately anyway. You just cannot distribute your application *until you have a license to do so.*

During the installation, the control is loaded onto the user's system. If the Web-page creator referenced an .INF file, that file will tell the user's system what files to get, where to get them, and how to add them to the system registry as necessary. At this point, a number of different security activities are performed to assure the integrity of the control.

Software Distributors

At the time of this writing, Microsoft has ActiveX in the beta test phase of its development. Still, many software developers have already released their ActiveX applications. It's probably safe to say that ActiveX (or DCOM) is a standard that will be developed upon heavily—even if Microsoft never releases it in a final form!

ActiveX Web Browsers

There are a wide variety of Web browsers on the market—each capable of viewing hypertext documents.

In the earliest days of the Web, text-only browsers such as Lynx were the standard. These browsers allow users to read the content of a Web page over a slow (less than 9600 baud) connection. Any graphic content (which can swell the size of a document significantly) is not retrieved unless the user specifically asks for it.

In the early 1990's, the National Center for Supercomputing at the University of Illinois at Urbana-Champaign developed a graphical Web browser called Mosaic that proved very popular on the net. Soon afterward, Netscape jumped on the WWW bandwagon, developing and releasing its Navigator Web browser. By this time, use of the Web by previous nonusers was increasing by leaps and bounds, and a wide variety of (sometimes incompatible) Internet utilities was being released to the general market.

To maintain dominance in the computing industry, Microsoft followed suit in a big way with the development of ActiveX browsers that not only allow text and graphics, but a plethora of other types of content, such as music, video, and a special Internet flavor of SQL (Structured Query Language).

Internet Explorer

Beginning with version 3.0 of MSIE, Microsoft has chosen its free Web browser as the developmental and presentation platform for the introduction of ActiveX technologies. Needing no plug-ins or additional software, it is the most effective tool for applying the features of activated HTML pages.

The term "ActiveX" comes from Bill Gates' directive to his staff to "Activate the Internet." Internet programmers will often refer to a standard Web feature, such as text browsing and file transfer, as "activated" if it has the OLE or other advanced features of ActiveX.

NOTE: Regularly upadated information on MSIE and its related technologies can be found on the Internet Explorer home page at www.microsoft.com/ie.

The Netscape home page is found at http://www.netscape.com. Information on Netscape Navigator and its plug-ins and accessories can be found here, and is updated regularly.

Netscape Navigator

There is a wide variety of Web browsers used to access the World Wide Web, and Netscape Navigator is currently the Web browser of choice for most users. In spite of this wide use, however, it does not internally support ActiveX.

Installing Netscape and MSIE on the Same Machine

As a developer, you will need to be able to see how others will view your pages. As long as competition is alive and well, users will access your pages with a variety of different browsers. Netscape and MSIE are the two most popular (for now).

On a Windows95 machine, you can enable the use of both browsers by following these instructions:

1. Obtain the most recent copy of MSIE from its Web site. (The CD-ROM that came with this book has a copy of the version that was current at the time of printing.)
2. Obtain the most recent copy of Netscape Navigator from its Web site.
3. Run the installation process for MSIE. When it is done, reboot your machine.
4. Run MSIE by double-clicking the Internet icon on your desktop. Customize the settings from the View | Options menu. Exit the program and continue to the next step.
5. Run the installation process for Netscape Navigator. When it is done, reboot your machine.
6. Run Netscape by double-clicking the Netscape Navigator icon on your desktop. Customize the settings from the Options menu.
7. At this point, Netscape will ask you if you want to use it as your default browser. If you will be doing your development work in ActiveX, you should select No and check the box that says Do not ask this question again. Exit the program and continue to the next step.
8. Run MSIE one more time by double-clicking the desktop icon.
9. At this point, Windows will ask you if you want to use MSIE as your default browser. If you will be doing your development work in ActiveX, you should select Yes and check the box that says Do not ask this question again. Leave MSIE running and continue to the next step.
10. Select the View | Options menu item. Then select the File Types tab, select the Internet Document (HTML) item, and press the Edit button. This should bring up a window with a section titled Actions.
11. Press the New button.
12. For Action, enter `View with Netscape`.
13. For Application, enter `netscape.exe`.

Now, when you right-click an Internet document, you will have the option of viewing it with Netscape or opening it with MSIE.

NCompass Labs

NCompass Labs makes a plug-in for Netscape that adds some ActiveX functionality to it. Because Netscape does not yet have ActiveX functionality, a plug-in such as this is necessary to browse ActiveX documents with that browser.

> **NOTE**  Find the NCompass Labs home page at http://www.ncompasslabs.com. You can find the company's ActiveX plug-in as well as its other products here.

ActiveX Controls

Microsoft has released a number of ActiveX controls into the public domain. Any developer may use most of these tools, royalty free, to develop and distribute his applications. Some of these include the HTML Layout Control, the Active Marquee Control, and (possibly the most important of all) the ICP (Internet Control Pack).

The ICP is a set of ActiveX controls, incorporating the standard Internet protocols. These controls are listed in Table 15.1.

Table 15.1. ActiveX controls found in the ICP.

Name of control	Stands for
FTP control	File Transfer Protocol
NNTP control	Network News Transfer Protocol
POP3 control	Post Office Protocol
SMTP control	Simple Mail Transfer Protocol
HTTP control	Hypertext Transfer Protocol
HTML control	Hypertext Markup Language
WinSock control	Windows Sockets API

Microsoft licensed the controls in the ICP from NetManage, who has also has placed them in the public domain. You will learn more about the ICP later.

ActiveX System Requirements

The DCOM model behind ActiveX is designed to be usable across a variety of systems. Cross-platform compatibility has always been the holy grail of systems development. The variety of systems and the exponentially higher number of possible configurations and software packages installed on those systems makes this task all but impossible.

Operating Systems

ActiveX controls are usable on any system that supports DCOM. The first to incorporate this technology is Windows 95, with Windows NT version 4.0 following close behind. Microsoft is working with software vendors to enable ActiveX on UNIX and Macintosh in the near future.

Required Files

In the following lessons, you will be introduced to some specific ActiveX controls; any files required to run them will be noted. A few are basic to the use of ActiveX.

For a Windows 95 installation, the files that may need to be made available to the user are discussed in the sidebar titled "ActiveX File Dependencies." If you use any other controls, you may want to keep a similar chart as a reference for what other files those controls may require.

There is no one file or one group of files that you can use to make your system a complete ActiveX or DCOM system. Each feature has its own requirements. Windows NT 4.0 is based on DCOM, and others will certainly follow, but other operating systems must use an add-in (such as the Internet Explorer version 3.x for Windows 95) to use ActiveX features.

ActiveX File Dependencies

Microsoft Foundation Class-based custom controls (OCXs) require `MFC40.dll`, `MSVCRT.dll`, and `OLEPro32.dll`.

Trust verification services require `WinTrust.dll` and `digsig.dll`.

ICP Controls

All of the controls in the Internet Control Pack require the `NMSCKN.dll` in addition to their `.OCX` control, and all but the `WinSck.ocx` requires `NMORENU.dll` and `NMOCOD.dll`.

The `FTPct.ocx` requires the additional `NMFTPSN.dll`. The `HTML.ocx` requires the additional `NMW3VWN.dll`.

Many ActiveX packages may also require the installation of DirectX to operate. DirectX was originally developed as Microsoft's Game SDK (Software Developer's Kit). DirectX gives the programmer a powerful tool for accessing the more complex features of 3D video and sound.

> **Other ActiveX Controls**
>
> Included with the ActiveX SDK are two redistributable, packaged, self-installing files that will install the controls most important for ActiveX on Windows 32-bit machines.
>
> `WintDist.exe` (WinINet) installs the most basic Windows Internet files—`WinInet.dll` and `InLoader.dll`.
>
> `AXDist.exe` (ActiveX) will install the WinINet files and the additional ActiveX controls—`WinINet.dll`, `InLoader.dll`, `URLMon.dll`, `HLink.dll`, `HLinkPrx.dll`, `OLEAut32.dll`, and `STDOLE2.tlb`.

Summary

In this chapter, you have been introduced to ActiveX controls, the concept of COM (Component Object Modeling), and the emerging DCOM (Distributed Component Object Model).

ActiveX controls are the first wide implementation of DCOM, and provide the programmer with a simplified interface to the highly complex features of OLE in an internetworked environment. These controls are the product of the evolution of custom controls and OLE and the market demand for a system that combines the two.

ActiveX controls can be embedded within an HTML document or in an application developed in an OLE container IDE (integrated development environment) such as Visual Basic. The programmer can then develop a user interface to those controls using VBScript or another scripting language. The programmer can also use those same ActiveX controls, programmatically, to develop standalone client or server applications.

ActiveX controls can be acquired quite easily, and almost by accident. An individual who is browsing the Web and accesses a page with embedded ActiveX controls may receive a prompt asking if he wants to install the custom control. Also, when a user installs an application that uses ActiveX controls, those controls are installed on and made available to his system.

Although the ActiveX controls themselves will not necessarily work on every machine, a user's Windows 95 system can be easily upgraded and modified to support them. This is done by installing a few freely redistributable files on the user's system.

Q&A

Q How complicated are OLE and the COM model?

A Very! One could go as far as to say they are the most complex to understand, yet the most basic to use, concepts in object-oriented programming. This is because they are the basis of OOP. Most of your ActiveX programming will be in a scripting language like VBScript or JavaScript, or in an interpreted programming environment like Visual Basic or Access. The most important features of OLE are exposed to these programming systems through the properties, methods, and events of ActiveX controls. To access the lower-level features of OLE, a program must support the interaction with MFC (Microsoft Foundation Classes). If you do not use MFC, you will have to make sure your code implements the many classes required of an OLE server. For this you would need a much lower level of language, such as Visual C++.

Q Is a Java applet the same as an ActiveX control?

A No. Java applets could best be defined as Internet-aware custom controls. Because these applets are not OLE enabled, they are not true ActiveX controls. From a scripting or interpreted language standpoint, however, working with Java applets is very similar to working with ActiveX controls. ActiveX will support the Java Virtual Machine.

Q Is it possible to receive a control that will perform maliciously on my machine?

A Yes—if you are not careful. Different Web browsers have varying degrees of security that the user can enable or disable as he sees fit. There are a number of methods an ActiveX control developer can use to assure the users of his product that they are receiving a genuine product. It remains up to the user, for the most part, to let those features work and not disable them.

Workshop

Retrieve copies of, or create shortcuts to, the following ActiveX-related specifications (the URLs mentioned only show the specification's sponsor's home page):

HTML 3.2—http://www.w3.org
Win32 Internet API—http://www.microsoft.com
MSIE Object Model for Scripting—http://www.microsoft.com
Internet Ratings API—http://www.microsoft.com
COM Specification—http://www.microsoft.com
WinSock API—http://www.microsoft.com

Quiz

1. Explain the significance of each of the following:
   a. OLE
   b. VBX
   c. OCX
2. When was object-oriented programming developed?
3. What are the two methods for interacting with ActiveX controls?
4. What is the name of the new technology behind ActiveX controls?
5. If you develop an HTML document with embedded ActiveX controls, what scripting language, besides VBScript, can you use to program the user interface to those controls?
6. If you develop an ActiveX application for a Web document, what would be the easiest programming language to use to make it a standalone application?
7. What is the most common file that must be installed on a user's machine to enable Windows Internet functionality?
8. What do COM and DCOM mean?
9. Name one operating system that has built-in support for DCOM.
10. Within what two types of items can an ActiveX object be incorporated?
11. What company developed the Java technologies?
12. An ActiveX control must support what two features?
13. What basic concept is behind the shift from COM to DCOM?
14. What operating systems are able to implement DCOM?
15. What operating systems are able to run ActiveX?
16. What features are used in the most basic level of security?
17. What filetype tells an ActiveX browser how to register a control?
18. What must a user obtain, after he installs the control, in order to redistribute his applications?
19. What is the difference between JavaScript and a Java applet?
20. Of what programming language is VBScript a subset?

NOTE   Refer to the appendix, "Answers," for the answers to these questions.

Week 3

Day 16

Installing ActiveX Controls

In this lesson you will learn:

- About the `<OBJECT>` container tag.
- How to use an ActiveX control within a Web page.
- How to add an ActiveX control to a Visual Basic project.

You will also go through the steps involved in:

- Creating a basic Web site for a fictitious company.
- Building your first, and possibly most exciting, ActiveX Visual Basic application—a Web browser.

HTML—Hypertext Markup Language

Web pages are simple text documents with special commands that you can put within brackets (such as <COMMAND>). These commands tell a Web browser information about the page, such as its title and type, and formatting information, such as what characters are bold or italic. A few commands, or *tags*, are common to every HTML document. The basic structure of an HTML document should contain the following information:

```
<HTML>
<HEAD>
<TITLE>Title of your document</TITLE>
</HEAD>
<BODY>
Document information…
</BODY>
</HTML>
```

As you can see, the document begins with <HTML> and ends with </HTML>. These *container* commands tell the browser where the document begins and where it ends. Also, within the head container tag are the title tags, defining `Title of your document` as the title of this document. The body container comes after the head container, and defines `Document information…` as the body of the document. On a standard, graphical Web browser, the document would be displayed as in Figure 16.1.

Figure 16.1.
Web view of a basic HTML document.

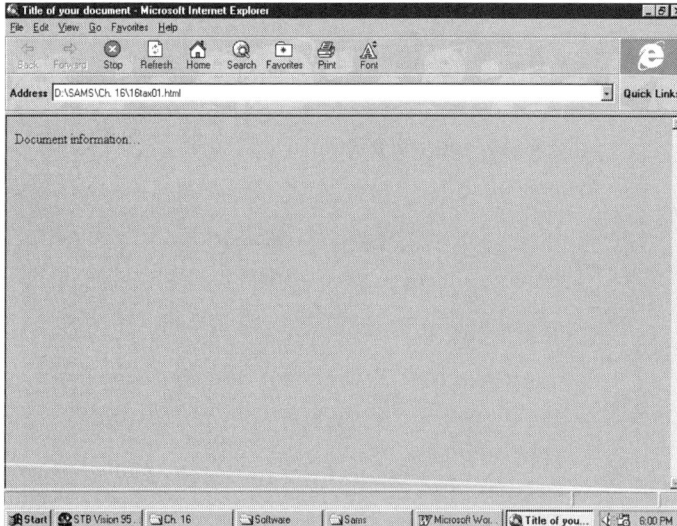

WARNING

If you forget to use the closing tag for a container tag (such as `<OBJECT>` `</OBJECT>`, where `</OBJECT>` is the closing tag), you will probably encounter some unexpected and undesirable results.

Frames Support

A standard for displaying several different pages (or frames) within one window was introduced by Netscape and adopted by the WWW Consortium. This feature has also been adopted in the Microsoft Internet Explorer beginning with version 3.x.

Using a few additional container tags (`<FRAME>`, `<FRAMESET>`, `<NOFRAMES>`) in place of the `<BODY>` container, an HTML author can customize the height, width and placement of these disparate pages.

Now you will create the Web page for your fictitious company. The scenario for creating this page follows:

- You are the newly hired Webmaster for Wonderland Industries—a manufacturer of a variety of products. Your job is to set up a Web presence for the company.
- The directory from which visitors will browse the site is on your personal machine in the `C:\W3` directory.
- The default page for your particular Web server's software is `index.html`.

Here are the steps you must complete to create your Web page:

1. Create a directory on your hard drive called `C:\W3`.
2. Install the ActiveX Control Pad by double-clicking `SetupPad.EXE` on the enclosed CD-ROM. Windows Notepad is an excellent HTML editor, but Microsoft has developed the ActiveX Control Pad to make the insertion of ActiveX controls and scripting easier.
3. Open a window to the `C:\W3` directory, then right click the empty directory and select New from the pop-up menu.
4. You will see a menu with the selection of items you can create anew. Select the one titled Internet Document (HTML) and name the new document `index.html`. You might be prompted as to whether or not you are sure you want this name. The answer is yes. If you do not see Internet Document (HTML) as a choice from the pop-up menu, install the HTML Wizard from the enclosed CD-ROM.

5. Right-click the file you just created and select the option titled Edit with ActiveX Control Pad. The ActiveX Control Pad will be launched to edit your new document.
6. Edit the document so that it appears exactly as in Figure 16.2.

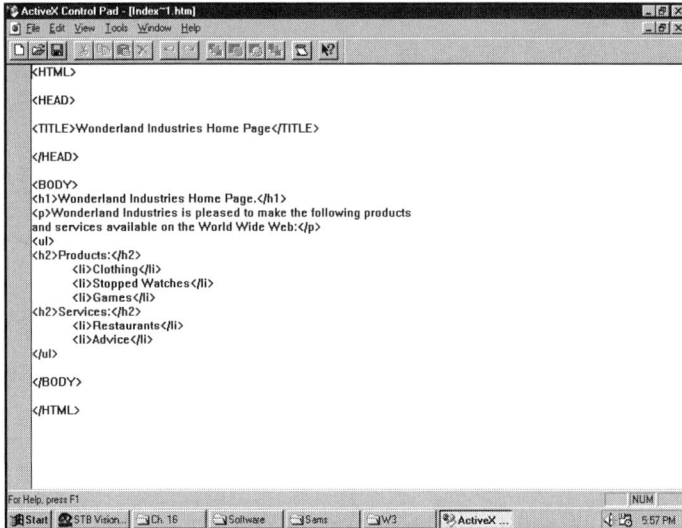

Figure 16.2.
Home page viewed with ActiveX Control Pad.

Now you have created the initial home page for your company. Double-click the desktop icon for C:\W3\index.html to launch your Web browser, and you will be able to see the document as it will appear on the Web (see Figure 16.3).

This is a fairly simple page, and is similar to the first page with which many businesses begin their Web presence. HTML provides many more typesetting and other formatting options to customize the display of text. However, even with an e-mail hyperlink, the page lacks activity.

The <OBJECT> Tag

The <IMG> tag was the first to enable basic multimedia within an HTML document. Using a command such as <IMG SRC=image.gif> allows you to place a static image within a document.

The <OBJECT> tag, once known as the <INSERT> tag, is a container tag. This means that whenever it is used within a hypertext document, there will be an <OBJECT> tag at the beginning of the object and a </OBJECT> tag at the end of the object. The space between the tags is where you code the properties and parameters of the object.

Figure 16.3.
Home page viewed with a Web browser. Bare as it might seem, many businesses start with a page much like this one.

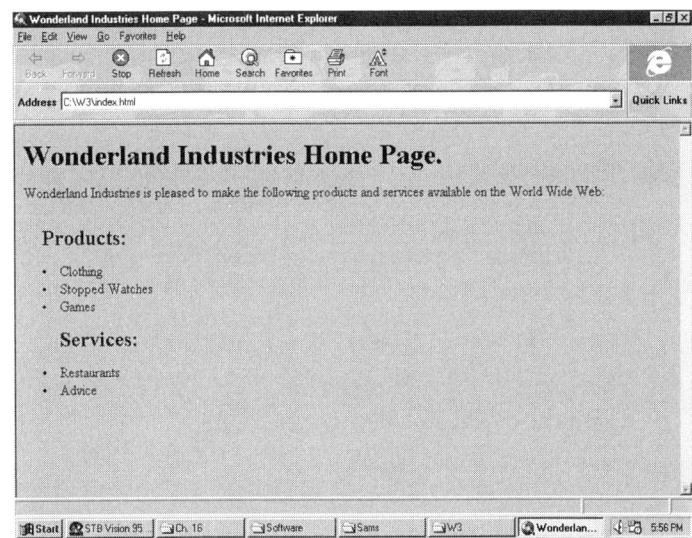

The World Wide Web Consortium (the organization that defines the standards for Internet operations), located at http://www.w3.org, established the <OBJECT> tag to enable rich forms of media content within Web pages. Using the object tag, you can specify the MIME (Multimedia Internet Mail Extension) type for the object.

The object tag is part of the HTML 3.2 specification for hypertext documents. It is used to make OLE and multimedia content available in HTML pages over the Internet or over an intranet. Within this container tag, any parameters for the current instance of the control are defined. Listing 16.1 is a sample object-tag syntax.

Listing 16.1. A sample object-tag syntax.

```
<Object
    ID="MyControl"
    Width=640
    Height=480
    ClassID="CLSID:hhhhhhhh-hhhh-hhhh-hhhhhhhhhhhh"
    CODEBASE="ftp://ftp.domain.net/mycontrol.ocx#version=xx,xx,xx,xx x"
    Type="application/x-oleobject"
>
<Param Name="Enabled" Value="True">
</Object>
```

Using the <OBJECT> tag, you can add active content to your home page. In your Wonderland example, you will add a PowerPoint Presentation to enhance the look and feel of the page.

To do this, copy the PowerPoint animation that your Public Relations Director, White Rabbit, gave you for your Web directory. (You'll find a copy on the enclosed CD-ROM at \W3\wndrland.ppz. Copy that file to C:\W3 on your local hard drive.)

Now that you have a copy of the presentation, you need to write an HTML document within which browsers can view the animation. To do this, create a basic HTML document with a basic <OBJECT> tag defining the presentation's properties.

First, define the ClassID parameter for a PowerPoint Animation. Then, define the size of the presentation. The format for the ClassID is

```
ClassID = "clsid:[Class ID]"
```

The <OBJECT> tag for the White Rabbit's PowerPoint animation within the HTML document should look like this:

```
<OBJECT
    CLASSID="clsid:EFBD14F0-6BFB-11CF-9177-00805F8813FF"
    WIDTH=640
    HEIGHT=480>
<PARAM NAME="File" VALUE="wndrland.ppz">
</OBJECT>
```

> **How to Determine an Object's ClassID**
>
> There are a variety of methods you can use to determine an object's ClassID.
>
> 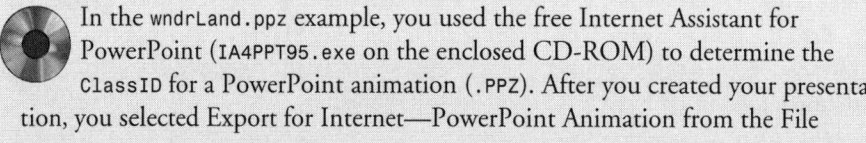 In the wndrLand.ppz example, you used the free Internet Assistant for PowerPoint (IA4PPT95.exe on the enclosed CD-ROM) to determine the ClassID for a PowerPoint animation (.PPZ). After you created your presentation, you selected Export for Internet—PowerPoint Animation from the File menu.
>
> Another way to determine the ClassID of a control or object is to use the Visual Basic IDE to create a project and add the item reference or control to it. Then, viewing the project file with a text editor such as Notepad, you can see what CLSID was used in the .VBP file.
>
> If you are familiar with the registry settings, you can use Windows RegEdit to look for the CLSID of the control you wish to use.
>
> The best way to get the CLSID of an ActiveX control is to use the ActiveX Control Pad to insert your control into a Web page. The Control Pad will insert the CLSID and any necessary parameters into your document.

Now you will create a Web page for Mr. Rabbit's presentation and create a link to it in the Wonderland home page. To do this, create a basic HTML document and insert the `<OBJECT>` tag for the presentation into the page. Call the HTML document `wndrland.html`. Use the following code to create the new page. (See Listing 16.2.)

Listing 16.2. `wndrland.html`.

```
<HTML>
<HEAD><TITLE>About Wonderland</TITLE></HEAD>
<BODY>
<CENTER>
<OBJECT
    CLASSID="clsid:EFBD14F0-6BFB-11CF-9177-00805F8813FF"
    WIDTH=640
    HEIGHT=480>
<PARAM NAME="File" VALUE="wndrland.ppz">
</OBJECT>
</CENTER>
<HR>
Click <A HREF="wndrland.ppz">here</A> to view the presentation with Powerpoint
</BODY>
</HTML>
```

Internet Explorer ActiveX Controls

When you have made it this far, you will be able to insert very powerful active content into an HTML document. The preceding example, using a PowerPoint animation, is fairly simple and, as you can see, requires no scripting. However, it requires the user to have the very large PowerPoint Viewer (or PowerPoint itself) installed on the local machine.

Let's work with some slightly smaller, but more commonly used, ActiveX controls. These controls are installed from the `AXDist.exe` file in the ActiveX SDK on the enclosed CD-ROM. The latest versions can be downloaded from Microsoft's ActiveX Server (the URL is `http://www.microsoft.com/intdev/sdk`). These controls provide dialog, display and command features that are not normally part of an HTML document.

The CyberTime Page

Three useful ActiveX controls are the Label, Timer, and Pop-up Window controls.

To learn how these controls are used, you'll create an HTML file that displays the current time, and retrieves the current time from the U.S. Department of Commerce Atomic Time Server (cool, eh?). Using Windows Notepad or the ActiveX Control Pad, you will create a text file that begins like this:

```
<HTML>
<Head> <title>CyberTime</Title> </Head>
<Body>
```

Next, insert a Label control called `"lblClock"` into the document. Notice that you use the TYPE attribute to identify the MIME type of the control as an OLE object. The CODEBASE attribute tells the user's browser where it can obtain a copy of the control. All this is done using the <OBJECT> container tag as shown in Listing 16.3:

Listing 16.3. Inserting `lblClock`.

```
<OBJECT
    ID="lblClock"
    WIDTH=400
    HEIGHT=25
    CLASSID="CLSID:99B42120-6EC7-11CF-A6C7-00AA00A47DD2"
    CODEBASE="http://activex.microsoft.com/controls/iexplorer/ielabel.ocx"
>
```

After you finish, this the control is automatically created on the local machine. However, you still need to define the parameters of the particular object as shown in Listing 16.4:

Listing 16.4. Defining the parameters of `lblClock`.

```
<PARAM NAME="Caption" VALUE="Dept. of Commerce Time Server">
<PARAM NAME="FontName" VALUE="Arial">
<PARAM NAME="FontBold" VALUE="1">
<PARAM NAME="FontSize" VALUE="12">
<PARAM NAME="backcolor" VALUE="1">
<PARAM NAME="forecolor" VALUE="1">
<PARAM NAME="Alignment" VALUE="Left">
```

Don't forget to use the closing `</Object>` tag to avoid unpredictable results. That's all there is to inserting an ActiveX control.

Warning

Although you can create and edit controls and scripts by clicking the left margin, you may still need to edit the properties, values, and parameters manually in the Control Pad window. To do this, click the Script or Object icon in the left margin, set any values allowed through the Control Pad's interface, then exit the Control Editor and return to the Control Pad window. Now you can modify, add, or delete

> whichever properties you need. Also, be careful about going back to the left-margin icon to edit your control or script. The wizard may zap any changes you made that it doesn't recognize.

Now you'll add a Timer control to the page. Both the Label and the Timer controls should be very familiar to Visual Basic programmers. The Timer control is added in much the same way as the Label control (as shown in Listing 16.5):

Listing 16.5. Adding the Timer control.

```
<Object
    ID="Timer"
    ClassID="clsid:59CCB4A0-727D-11CF-AC36-00AA00A47DD2"
    CodeBase="http://activex.microsoft.com/controls/iexplorer/ietimer.ocx"
    Type=application/x-oleobject"
    Align=Middle
>
    <Param Name="Interval" Value="100">
    <Param Name="Enbaled" Value="True">
</Object>
```

Finally, you'll add a new control, the Pop-up Window. This clever utility displays an HTML file in a temporary window. The window will display all the formatting correctly, and disappears when the user clicks the screen. The <OBJECT> tag for this control looks like Listing 16.6:

Listing 16.6. Adding the Pop-up Window control.

```
<Object
    ID="PopUpWindow"
    ClassID="clsid:A23D7C20-CABA-11CF-A5D4-00AA00A47DD2"
    CodeBase="http://activex.microsoft.com/controls/iexplorer/iepopwnd.ocx"
    Type="application/x-oleobject"
> </Object>
```

After you have all the objects in place, add a bit of code that displays the information from the U.S. Department of Commerce's atomic clock when the user clicks the time (as shown in Listing 16.7):

Listing 16.7. This displays information from the U.S. Department of Commerce's atomic clock.

```
<SCRIPT LANGUAGE="VBScript">
<!--
Sub lblClock_Click
    PopUpWindow.Popup "http://132.163.135.130:14/"
End Sub
Sub Timer_Timer()
    lblClock.caption=time
End Sub
-->
</SCRIPT>
```

When you've entered all this code, you will have a Web page that displays the local time and, when the user clicks the time, information from an atomic clock is displayed in a pop-up window (see Figure 16.4). A working example of this page can be found in the \W3\ directory of your CD-ROM in the file titled CyberTime.html.

Figure 16.4.
A browser view of a CyberTime page using ActiveX controls.

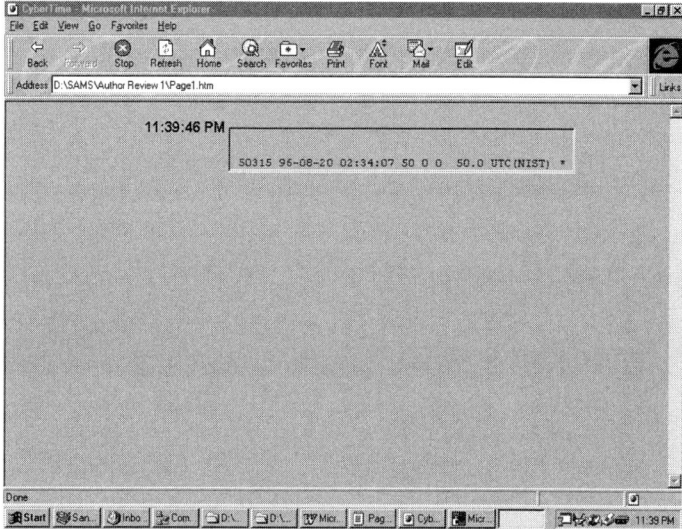

Programmatic Installation of ActiveX Controls

Now that you know how an HTML author uses ActiveX controls, you can get acquainted with how a programmer uses them. Remember, though, that the use of ActiveX controls is not limited to Web browsers and programming languages. They can be used by any program that uses OLE (such as Word or Excel).

Visual Basic

Installation of an ActiveX control into a Visual Basic project is exactly the same as with any other custom control. In this section, you will create a Web browser using the HTML control from the Internet Control Pack (ICP) on the enclosed CD-ROM. If you have not already installed the ICP, simply double-click the MSICPB.exe file on the CD-ROM, and when the installation is complete, reboot your computer to allow changes to take effect.

After you install the ICP, create a new Visual Basic project called WebView.vbp. This will be Wonderland's corporate Web browser.

With the project loaded into Visual Basic, press Ctl+T to see what objects and controls are referenced (see Figure 16.5). Clear the check box next to each control except for the Microsoft HTML Client Control control—that one should be checked. This will remove any unnecessary controls from, and add the HTML control to, the Visual Basic toolbox.

Figure 16.5.
Visual Basic project with the Microsoft HTML Client Control loaded.

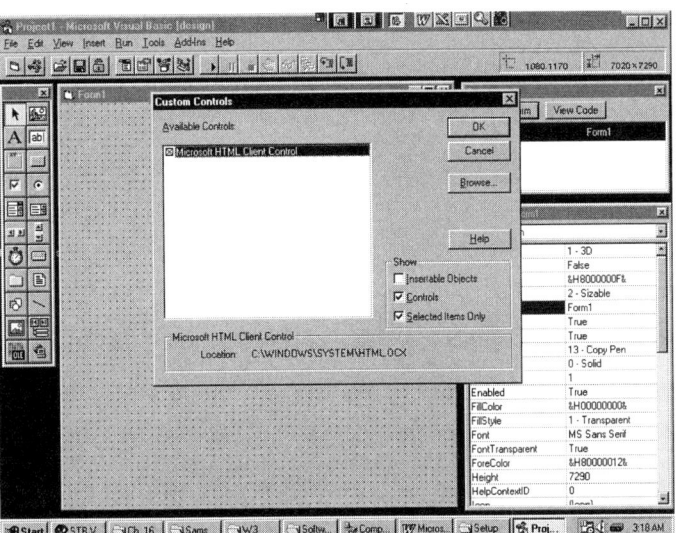

Next, insert the control into a form. You should also change the form's caption, identifying it as the Wonderland Web Browser. Add two menu items, File Exit and View Source, an empty text box, and a command button labeled &Go. The form should appear as in Figure 16.6.

Figure 16.6.
Form layout for the Wonderland Web Browser.

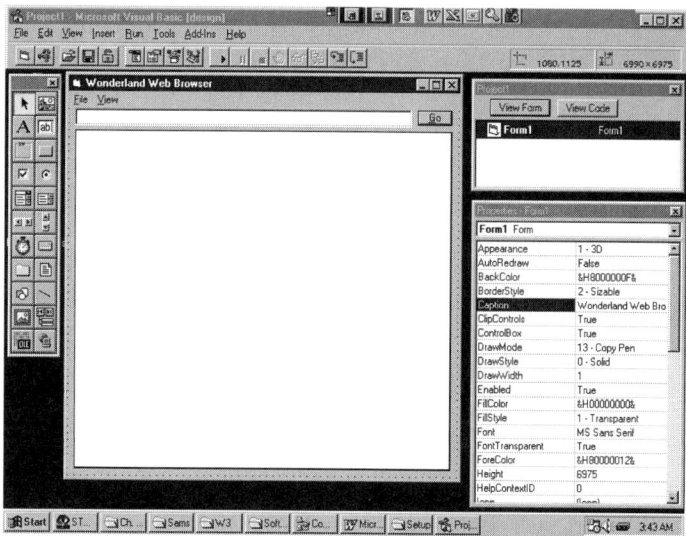

Add a bit of code to support the browser activities. The code for the important subroutines of the Web browser follows, but you can add other features to meet your needs (see Listing 16.8).

Listing 16.8. This is the code for subroutines of the Web browser.

```
Private Sub Command1_Click()
    HTML1.RequestDoc Text1.Text
End Sub
Private Sub mnuFileExit_Click()
    End
End Sub
Private Sub mnuViewSource()
    Select Case mnuViewSource.Checked
        Case True
            mnuViewSource.Checked=False
            HTML1.ViewSource = False
        Case False
            mnuViewSource.Checked = True
            HTML1.ViewSource = True
    End Select
End Sub
```

As you can see, most of the work is done by the HTML control. The only thing you really needed to code was one menu option to exit the program, and another to toggle between Code View and Web View modes.

Registering Controls with `RegSvr32.exe`

Before most other applications can use the features of a control (.DLL or .OCX), the control must be added to the system registry. You can manually view and edit the system registry using the `RegEdit.exe` file that comes with Windows.

The system registry contains a great deal of information about your system, including its configuration and the software installed on it. Editing the registry can be quite complicated—especially if you are not very familiar with it.

To make the registration of OLE controls easier, Microsoft provides the `RegSvr32.exe` utility. There might be several copies of this file on your machine, so make sure that the most recent one is in your `C:\Windows` directory.

The rules for using the utility are pretty much self-explanatory. To register the OLE server, use:

```
RegSvr32 [DLL or OCX Filename]
```

This will register the OLE Server.

You can also use the optional command-line parameter to unregister an OLE Server as necessary:

```
RegSvr32 /u [DLL or OCX Filename]
```

Finally, you can use a parameter to force the program into "silent" mode. This is useful for processes where you may not want the user to be bothered with the results of the registration process. Use this option sparingly, though. You wouldn't have tried to register a control unless you expected it to succeed. If it doesn't work, there may be other actions you will want to take.

When you have added all the controls and coded the program, you are ready to browse simple Web documents. Because this program uses the simple Microsoft HTML control, it does not yet support all of ActiveX. This is not a bug, though. The HTML control is a very powerful ActiveX control, and you can program many advanced features into the project using it.

For example, you added a menu item to allow the viewing of source code for HTML pages. By clicking the View|Source menu item, you can toggle between Code View and Web View. For those of you who have learned HTML by observing the ways that other people do it, this can be a very valuable learning tool!

Other Languages

Installation of an ActiveX control into IDEs other than Visual Basic projects is different for each language. If you can use a custom control in your favorite programming language, you should have no problem using ActiveX controls because they install like any other custom control.

Using ActiveX Controls within ActiveX Documents

As I mentioned earlier, the quickest, cheapest, easiest way to acquire ActiveX controls is to browse an ActiveX document with an ActiveX browser, such as MSIE. To better understand this, you will create a Web document for your fictitious company that contains a redistributable ActiveX control.

In the example with the PowerPoint presentation, you used an inserted control and a linked object. Remember that an object (such as a PowerPoint presentation) must be controlled by something (such as the PowerPoint program or the free PowerPoint viewer). In that example, you referenced the control via the ClassID (already installed on the user's machine), then pointed toward the specific animation via the File parameter.

In the following scenario, the powers that be at Wonderland Industries have asked you to create another Web page.

Business Case

The queen of hearts has asked you to develop a page for her gaming division. She would like a home page that allows users to select a site to view from a list of sites.

On this Web page, she wants a list box showing several other entertainment sites. Your task is to create a Web page that allows users with ActiveX browsers to select a site from the list and be transported to the new site. This can be done with HTML alone, but for learning purposes, you'll do it in ActiveX. To accomplish this, complete the following steps:

1. To begin, create a blank HTML page (hearts.html). Include the basic HTML tags (<HTML>, <HEAD>, <TITLE> and <BODY>). The <HTML> container tag defines the beginning and ending of a hypertext document. Each HTML document should have <HEAD>, <TITLE>, and <BODY> containers. Or, in place of a <BODY> container, your document can have a <FRAMESET> container. Listing 16.9 is a sample HTML document. The title of the document you are creating for the queen of hearts is Hearts Gaming and is illustrated in Listing 16.10.

Listing 16.9. A sample HTML syntax.

```
<HTML>
<Head>
<Title>My Document</Title>
</Head>
<Body>
My Content
</Body>
</HTML>
```

Listing 16.10. hearts.html.

```
<HTML>
<Head>
<Title>My Document (Frames Version)</Title>
<Base Target=_top>
</Head>
<FrameSet Rows="85%, 15%">
<FrameSet Cols="15%,85%">
<Frame
    SRC="TopLeft.html"
    Name="fmTopLeft">
<Frame
    SRC="TopRight.html"
    Name="fmTopRight">
</FrameSet>
<Frame
    SRC="Bottom.html"
    Name="fmBottom">
</FrameSet>
<NoFrames>To view this page, you must have &quotFrames&quot enabled.</NoFrames>
</HTML>
```

2. Now, using the ActiveX Control Pad, add a list box control to the file. To do this, select the menu option Edit | Insert ActiveX Control. This displays a window that lists all ActiveX controls and OLE objects currently installed on your system. Select the Microsoft Forms List Box control from the list of object types.

    When you select the control you want to insert into your document, the Object Type dialog box is replaced by two new windows, Properties and Edit ActiveX Control. For the List Box control, only customize a few of the properties—height, width, and ID.

3. Set the height and width properties to 128 and 256 respectively. This gives the list box the correct proportions to show all of the sites you'll be listing. Change the ID property to URLList.

4. When you've set these properties, close both the Properties and the Edit ActiveX Control windows to return to the ActiveX Control Pad's editing window. You should see that an <OBJECT> tag container has been added with a variety of parameters defined (see Figure 16.7). You can manually edit the properties for the object parameters without returning to the dialog boxes. If you want to use the dialog boxes to help you edit the parameters after you've already returned to the document, click the icon displayed in the left margin of the editor next to the opening <OBJECT> tag.

Figure 16.7.
The <OBJECT> *tag for the list box control as created within the ActiveX Control Pad.*

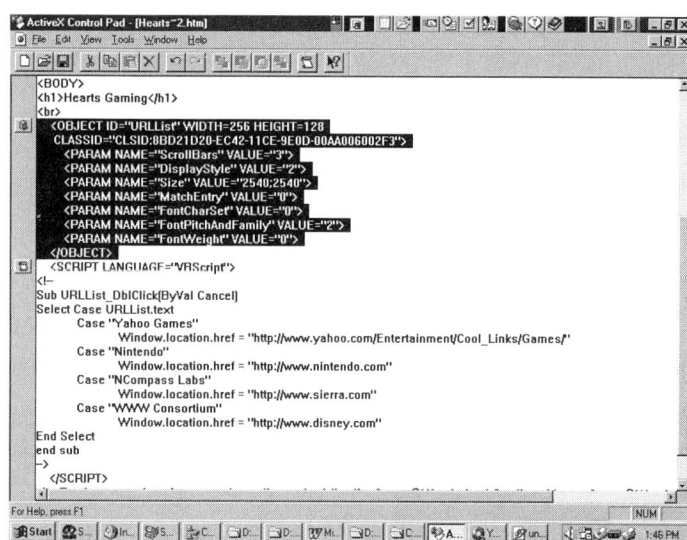

Next, add code to fill the list box. You'll use this control to list the sites that the queen wants her visitors to be able to view.

Even though you've added these objects to the form, there is no code behind them. You must add a script that will populate the list box with the queen's URLs. For this, you'll add a bit of VBScript (which you learned about earlier). See Listing 16.11 for relevant code.

Listing 16.11. This script populates the list box with the queen's URLs.

```
<SCRIPT LANGUAGE="VBScript">
<!--
Sub Window_onLoad()
   URLList.Enabled = True
   URLList.Additem "Yahoo Games"
   URLList.Additem "Nintendo"
```

```
    URLList.Additem "Sierra On-Line"
    URLList.Additem "Disney"
end sub
-->
</SCRIPT>
```

Finally, add a bit of code to tell the browser to jump to the associated URL when the user double-clicks an item within the text box (as shown in Listing 16.12):

Listing 16.12. This code tells the browser to jump to the associated URL.

```
<SCRIPT LANGUAGE="VBScript">
<!--
Sub URLList_DblClick(ByVal Cancel)
    Select Case URLList.text
       Case "Yahoo Games"
          Dim strLocation as String
          strLocation="http://www.yahoo.com/Entertainment/Cool_Links/Games/"
          Window.location.href = strLocation
       Case "Nintendo"
          Window.location.href = "http://www.nintendo.com"
       Case "NCompass Labs"
          Window.location.href = "http://www.sierra.com"
       Case "WWW Consortium"
          Window.location.href = "http://www.disney.com"
    End Select
end sub
-->
</SCRIPT>
```

When you finish with the HEARTS.HTML page, your completed project should resemble the \W3\HEARTS.HTML file on the on the enclosed CD-ROM. You will have created an ActiveX-enabled Web page with an embedded control. For this page, the user must have the list box control already installed on his machine. The next chapter discusses ActiveX control downloading to distribute controls over the network.

Summary

In this chapter, you have learned about the <OBJECT> container tag and how it is used to insert active content into an HTML page. This feature allows an HTML author to reference objects that are installed on a user's machine. It also provides an object against which a VB or Java script can act.

You have also learned the basics of using an ActiveX control within a programming environment such as Visual Basic. Using an ActiveX control exactly like any other custom control you can create your own proprietary, standalone Internet applications and distribute them to your users.

Q&A

Q What is the significance of a `ClassID`?

A A `ClassID` is the unique code assigned to an OLE control. This lengthy number is used by OLE-enabled applications to identify its installation on a local machine.

Q Can I use ActiveX controls in any old programming language?

A No. ActiveX controls are usable in an OLE container application such as MSIE, Visual C++, or Visual Basic, not within programming environments that do not support of OLE functionality, such as Turbo Basic version 1.

Q How can I tell whether a custom control is an ActiveX control?

A It's very difficult for the new programmer to tell whether a custom control is based on the DCOM model. Basically, you must rely on the developer to identify it as such. If you are familiar with building OLE controls, you can determine whether a suspect control is ActiveX-compatible by checking for the existence of the `Iunknown` interface, and seeing whether it has self-registering routines within it.

Q Must a control on a Web page be an ActiveX control?

A No, but other controls can be unreliable over a network connection—especially a slow one. ActiveX (or DCOM OLE) considers the unavailability of remote data or data sources, whereas other controls might not. In the hearts example in this chapter, you used a list box control that is not a true ActiveX control. Because the data you used to work with the control was contained within the HTML page, you did not need to worry about whether or not data at a remote site would be available and could therefore use the control safely.

Workshop

Create a Web page and insert a list box, a text box, and a video (`.AVI`) file.

Quiz

1. What are the four container tags required in every HTML document?
2. Which of the required container tags can be replaced by the <FRAME> tags?
3. What container tag, formerly known as the <INSERT> tag, is required for the use of ActiveX controls?
4. What are two items in an HTML page that have a graphical icon in the margin of the ActiveX Control Pad?
5. What two parameters within the <OBJECT> tag define the size of the object?
6. What was the first tag to allow multimedia content within an HTML document?
7. What organization publishes the standards for HTML tags?
8. What hotkey combination within Visual Basic allows a programmer to define what controls are loaded into a Visual Basic project?
9. What utility is used to register and unregister controls on a PC?
10. Must an ActiveX HTML author define the location where an ActiveX control can be downloaded?

NOTE Refer to the appendix, "Answers," for the answers to these questions.

Week 3

Day 17

ActiveX Control Downloading

Earlier lessons discussed briefly some of the processes involved in downloading controls via the Internet and the security threats posed by the shared nature of the Internet. In this chapter, you will learn about the actual process of installing Internet components and a few ways to prevent the installation of unwanted code or content. This process involves three stages:

- ☐ First, the control is downloaded to the local machine.
- ☐ Second, the control undergoes a verification process to ensure its integrity.
- ☐ Finally, the control is installed onto the machine and added to the system registry.

The following sections of this chapter define these steps and describe in greater detail the various application program interfaces (APIs) that apply to them.

OLE Objects

ActiveX objects within an HTML document go through several stages before they are installed on a user's local machine.

Acquisition

The first step, downloading or acquiring of the component, can happen in a couple of different ways. A few of these ways (as they relate to the Web) were discussed earlier (when installing an application such as Internet Explorer, for instance). Remember in this network-centric lesson that ActiveX controls can be installed via floppy disks, data tape, and so on. The usual method of installing these components, however, is from within an HTML document via an ActiveX Web browser—using the <OBJECT> tag.

Verification

The second step, verification, can use any or none of the following steps (installation and component downloading) to ensure that the control will not act maliciously on your system. Because the verification process is not mandatory, each individual user, programmer, and administrator must decide which, if any, of the processes will be used.

Installation

The third step, installation, depends on which selected verification process the control has successfully passed through. Even if a control has no programmed security features, users will be prompted on whether or not they wish to install that object. This is because objects with no security features cannot identify themselves as safe.

Not every installed object is necessarily an OLE object. When the object is an OLE control, there are several considerations for ensuring its integrity.

Component Downloading

There are two primary HTML tags that can be used to download an item from the Internet: <OBJECT> and HREF.

Minimal security via ActiveX is available within the HREF tag because HREF is treated as a hyperlink rather than an OLE object. An example of this would be a CGI server script; the hypertext reference would look like the following:

```
<A HREF="http://www.domain.net/CGIScript.exe">CGI Script</A>
```

The browser, treating CGIScript.exe as a hyperlinked document, would download and launch the .EXE without conducting any real security activity.

To enable the majority of ActiveX security features, you must identify an item as an object. (CGI scripts are not normally OLE objects). Identify the item as an OLE object using the <OBJECT> tag.

NOTE The ActiveX Gallery, located at http://www.www.microsoft.com/activex/gallery, is Microsoft's display gallery for its ActiveX controls. You can observe the code download and verification processes in action as you download the controls from this site.

The CodeBase Attribute

After identifying an object via the <OBJECT> tag (and setting its parameters if necessary), use the CodeBase attribute of the <OBJECT> tag to inform the user's system of the location of the control. The format of the Code attribute closely resembles the format for any URL:

```
CODEBASE="http://www.domain.net/control.ocx"
```

Version Control

As time goes by, computer programs are either phased out or, preferably, upgraded. This can cause some problems with conflicting versions of the same control. When a software manufacturer decides to upgrade its control, applications or scripts written around that code might not work with versions other than the one for which it was written. To manage the installation of different versions of the same control, the Code attribute enables content providers (HTML authors) to specify which version their pages need.

This version identification information is tacked onto the end of the Code URL in bold in the following example:

```
CODEBASE="http://www.domain.net/control.ocx#Version=1,2,3"
```

Using this attribute, you can identify all versions for which your application is usable. If your application was written for Version 1 and is still usable with Versions 2 and 3, the preceding example is how you should format the attribute. If the user has Version 1 installed on his machine, his browser will attempt to obtain the most recent version specified (here, Version 3) when it hits this tag.

> **Backwards Compatibility**
>
> For the most part, software vendors try to keep their products backwards compatible. This allows users of the product to perform minimum modifications to their programs when a control is upgraded. One example of this is the evolution of Visual Basic.
>
> Basic began gaining wide acceptance before object-oriented programming was very popular. These early versions of Basic used line numbers and REM statements. During this time, the first major burst of growth in the training, education and employment of programmers was occurring. As a result, the majority of programmers used line numbers and REM statements to identify the location of subroutines and comments to be ignored by the compiler.
>
> As Visual Basic came into being, REM statements were replaced by the apostrophe ('), and the use of line numbers to maintain the sequence in which code was to be executed became obsolete.
>
> To maintain backwards compatibility, the choice between long and short commands was made an option. A programmer could use the simple apostrophe to identify a remark, or he could use the REM statement. To the compiler, they are the same. Line numbers also became optional.
>
> By allowing programmers to use these conventions, Microsoft ensured that a programmer who spent days, months, or years developing an application could still use all or most of his code in the new programming environment. This is backwards compatibility.

PE, .CAB and .INF Files

There are several types of objects that can be used as ActiveX objects within the <OBJECT> tag of an HTML document. Each object has its own specific features and drawbacks.

- .CAB—Compressed cabinet file
- Portable Executables (PEs)—(.OCX: custom control; .EXE: standalone executable; .DLL: dynamic link library)
- .INF—Setup information file

ActiveX Control Downloading

About the time Windows95 was released, users began seeing .CAB files on a variety of Microsoft products' installation disks. The ActiveX SDK includes a tool, diantz.exe, which is used to create these active archives. *Active* means that the archives have more power and utility than the previously popular shareware compression standards (such as ZIP, LZH, ARJ, ARC, XX_ and so on).

.CAB—Compressed Cabinet Files

NOTE

For you hard-core hackers out there, the compression type used for .CAB files is based on the Lempel-Ziv compression algorithm. This is a "lossless" algorithm that was developed in 1977. Where some other compression algorithms look for whitespace, Lempel-Ziv looks for repeated binary sequences. Then it uses an offset value to refer to the first instance of the sequence.

NOTE

Microsoft maintains a newsgroup forum where individuals discuss issues related to .CABinet development. Answers to unique problems, as well as pointers to Frequently Asked Questions (FAQs) can be found in this newsgroup, located at news://msnews.microsoft.com/ microsoft.public.internetexplorer.java.cabdevkit

With the CABView utility (available in the Windows95 PowerToys on the enclosed CD-ROM), users can double click a CABinet file to make their system view and treat the archive as a subdirectory of its current directory. Drag and drop, execution of PEs, and file editing are all supported within a CABinet.

If a .CAB file has an .INF file in it, it can inform the user's systems of all necessary information to install the control onto the local machine.

WARNING

The .CAB file should only contain one .INF file if it is to be used as a self-installing ActiveX object. If the cabinet contains two .INF files, undesirable and unpredictable results may occur.

Now you're going to learn how to use Microsoft's two command-line utilities for working with cabinet file compression—Diantz.exe and Extract.exe. These can be found in the \InetSDK\bin directory.

Diantz.exe

Diantz.exe is the utility for *creating* .CAB files. It's very easy to use from a prompt. Simply follow .exe with the name of the file you want to add to a cabinet, and the name of the cabinet to which you want the compressed file added.

The Diantz Utility

SYNTAX

Diantz source *destination*
Diantz /F directive_file

The Diantz utility is used to create and update compressed file .CABinets. There are two methods that can be used with this utility. The first is to add files one by one like so:

Diantz.exe MyFile.dat MyCab.cab

This would add MyFile.dat to MyCab.cab, creating MyCab.cab if it doesn't already exist. If you don't specify a .CABinet file, it'll just compress the file alone, and name the compressed file the same as the original, except that the last character will be an underscore (_).

The other way is to use a directive file on the command line like so:

Diantz.exe /F MyDirec.ddf

This will build the .CABinet according to the instructions in the Diamond directives file (MyDirec.ddf).

Several other command-line parameters can be used with either of these methods, including the following:

- [ ] /V#—Where # is the level of verbosity (1-3)
- [ ] /D VAR=MyValue—this sets the environment variable VAR to the value in MyValue
- [ ] /L DIR—where DIR is the destination directory for the archive

TIP The name of the file in the `InetSDK` is `Diantz.exe`, but if you type the `.EXE` name alone at a prompt, you will see that it returns the help information for a command called `Diamond.exe`. You might want to rename `Diantz.exe` to `Diamond.exe` because that's the file's "real" name.

Extract.exe

This is the utility used for *extracting* files from a `.CAB` file. It is also very simple to use from a prompt. Just follow `.exe` with the name of the `.CABinet` from which you want a file extracted, and the name of file.

The Extract Utility

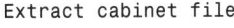
Extract cabinet file

The `Extract` utility is used to extract files from compressed file `.CABinets`. To use it, follow the executable name with the name of the compressed cabinet and the name of the file you wish to extract, like so:

`Extract.exe MyCab.cab MyFile.dat`

 This will extract the file `MyFile.dat` from the cabinet `MyCab.cab`.

Using Cabinets

Let's try an example of the `Diantz.exe` and `Extract.exe` cabinet manipulation utilities.

First, create a directory within which to work. Let's use a directory called `\CabZip\` on the C drive.

 You can find an example of the files with which you will be working on the CD-ROM in a similarly named directory.

Next, make sure that the Diamond compression utility (`Diantz.exe`) is available within this directory. Since this utility is in the `\INetSDK\Bin\` directory, just make sure it's in the path. To verify that `Diantz.exe` is in the path and available from within any directory, type `path` at the DOS command prompt. If you do not see the `\INetSDK\Bin\` in the list of directories returned by the path statement, add a line to your `autoexec.bat` file as follows:

`path=%path%;C:\Dev\InetSDK\Bin`

The previous line appends the \InetSDK\Bin\ directory to your default program search path. Make sure this statement is on a line after all other path statements in your autoexec.bat. This ensures that other directories are searched first. This way, as your programs become updated (and they will!), the \INetSDK\Bin\ directory will be the last place your system looks for a program that it can't find elsewhere.

 The next step is to copy the files from the CD-ROM into this new directory. The files are listed in the following table:

Table 8.3. CD-ROM files.

(DOS) Filename	Long Filename
ACTIVEX.CCC	ActiveX.ccc
ALICE1.JPG	Alice1.jpg
CHESHIRE.AVI	Cheshire.avi
RESUME.DOC	resume.doc
ANDTHA~1.WAV	and that's done with.wav
OFFICE95.XLS	Office95.xls
OLE-OC~1.MCC	OLE-OCX ActiveX Programming.mcc
VBINTE~1.URL	VB Internet Controls News.url
COPYME.TXT	copyme.txt

Next, create a cabinet for each file. Place each file in its own cabinet to observe the compression ratios for the different kinds of files.

NOTE
This demonstration shows that text-based and bitmapped files compress very well. On the other hand, binary files, such as audio applications, don't compress as well. Also, once you have created a cabinet (or used any other form of compression on a file), you will not be able to compress it again to reduce it further.

 To make this compression process go a little faster, you can create the following batch file (a sample has already been created on the CD-ROM called CabZip.bat):

```
diantz /v3 "ActiveX.ccc"  activex.cab
diantz /v3 "Alice1.jpg"   alice1.cab
diantz /v3 "Cheshire.avi" Cheshire.cab
diantz /v3 "resume.doc"   resume.cab
```

```
diantz /v3 "Office95.xls" Office95.cab
diantz /v3 "OLE-OCX ActiveX Programming.mcc" "OLE-OCX ActiveX Programming.cab"
diantz /v3 "VB Internet Controls News.url"    "VB Internet Controls News.cab"
diantz /v3 "and that's done with.wav"         "and that's done with.cab"
```

NOTE Notice the quotation marks (") around some of the files. When working from a DOS command prompt, it is often necessary to place these marks around files with long filenames, long file extensions, case sensitivity, and embedded spaces.

Next, extract each one of the cabinet files. If you extract them into the current directory (where copies already exist), you will be prompted as to whether you wish to overwrite the current copy or not. To automate this process, create a batch file with the following command (a copy of this batch file, named CabUnZip.bat is in the \CabZip\ directory on the CD-ROM):

```
for %%x in (ACTIVEX.CAB ALICE1.CAB CHESHIRE.CAB RESUME.CAB OFFICE95.CAB
➥ OLE-OC~1.CAB VBINTE~1.CAB ANDTHA~1.CAB) do extract.exe %%x
```

Type the whole thing on one line. Perform this function from the command prompt as well as from within a batch file. From a prompt, replace the batch variable identifier (%%) with a command line variable identifier (%).

PEs

The .OCX, .EXE and .DLL files are referred to, collectively, as PE (portable executable) files. These files are the simplest to use as ActiveX controls because they require no other files (that is, they are standalone utilities), and they can be run automatically.

A PE cannot be cross-platform compatible. It can only run on the machine type for which it was compiled. For this reason, content providers who use PEs as embedded objects need to consider the type of machine with which their users will be accessing the document.

Over a distributed environment such as the Internet, these BLOBs (binary large objects) can take a long time to download. If the code is tight, or the file is compressed using a compression algorithm, this significantly reduces the amount of time it takes to download them. But if the file is compressed, it can not be self-executing. It first must be uncompressed, or returned to its original form. The exception to this is .CAB files—they can be self-executing when used as ActiveX objects.

.INF—Setup Information Files

.INF files are used to tell the local machine how to set up the control and where to get its components. By specifying the files that various machines might need (such as Mac, UNIX, Win95), the .INF file can be used to install a different package for each type of system.

These .INF files are very similar to the old .INI (INItialization) files, as illustrated by the following code:

```
; Setup File for Sample.INF

[Add Code]
sample.ocx=sample.ocx
sample.dll=sample.dll

[sample.ocx]
file=http://www.domain.net/sample.ocx
clsid={xxxxxxx-xxx-xxxx-xxxxxxxxxxxx}
fileversion=1,0,0,0
destdir=11
file_win32_x86= http://www.domain.net/win32.cab
file_win32_mips= http://www.domain.net/winNT.cab
file_mac_ppc= http://www.domain.net/mac.cab

[sample.dll]
file=sample.dll
destdir=10
file_win32_x86= http://www.domain.net/win32.cab
file_win32_mips= http://www.domain.net/winNT.cab
file_mac_ppc= http://www.domain.net/mac.cab
```

Referring to the preceding sample .INF file, note that when launched by an ActiveX browser, the commands within an .INF file would install two files: sample.ocx and sample.dll. The .OCX would be retrieved from www.domain.net, while the .DLL would come from the same directory as the .INF (because no external site or directory was specified). The destdir setting has two options: 10 for the Windows directory, and 11 for the Windows\System directory. If no destination directory is specified, the control is kept in a cache until purged by automatic (that is, space-saving) or manual means.

You can also see in the sample that the file version is 1.0.0.0 (note that commas are used instead of dots in the .INF file version settings). If the machine has version 0.9 installed, it will still download the newer version. If, however, the local machine has a newer version, 1.0.1.0 for instance, it will not bother to install the older version. That would be a bug.

Cross-Platform Compatibility

An attribute of the <OBJECT> tag, called the CODETYPE attribute, can be used to further inform the system about the object's requirements. CODETYPE identifies the object's MIME type. An example of the CODETYPE attribute, defining an audio-video interface animation, would look like this:

```
CODETYPE="video/avi"
```

ActiveX uses another MIME type to identify the machine for which the code was written.

This feature of the Code tag is perhaps one of the most exciting. The Holy Grail of programming has been the use of one program on a variety of systems. Although this is still not possible (and probably never will be), features of the Code tag do allow the user's machine to retrieve a copy of the control designed for the user's individual system—whether it is a Mac, UNIX box, PC, or whatever. The format for this is a MIME type that conforms to the following specification:

```
application/x-FileType_OS_CPU
```

where the options for each field include:

```
FileType - pe, cabinet or setupscript
OS - win32 or mac
CPU - x86, ppc, mips or alpha
```

Referring to the preceding sample, note that this MIME- type format is extended to allow an .INF file to specify which files would be required on different machines. In this example, the controls for a Win95 MIPS machine would be in Win95.cab, the controls for a WinNT Alpha machine would be in WinNT.cab, and the controls for a Macintosh would be in MAC.cab. In each case, the entire cabinet would be downloaded, but only the necessary files would be installed. Also, it keeps a Mac from having to download the code for a PC and vice-versa.

Internet Security

The threats to system security manifest themselves in three items: OLE objects, non-OLE objects, and document content. The first two are of primary significance to the system developer. The last, document content, allows parents, employers, and other individuals to determine the type of content their users view without actually censoring every item his users can access (an impossible task).

Prior to ActiveX, the installation and configuration of software was completely controlled by the user or his system administrator. Now, through simply looking at a Web page, a control or other object can find its way to the user's machine with very little user interaction. This exposes the user to the threat of malicious or simply undesirable code being installed on his local machine.

WARNING

Internet Explorer, Netscape, and most other browsers allow the users, not the system administrator, to select the level of security they wish to observe. Internet Explorer ships with the highest level of security enabled by default.

Some users disable their security features to avoid those pesky confirmation dialog boxes. You might want to think twice before disabling any of them.

Although a determined hacker can still create a Web page that gives the user this kind of grief, the use of ActiveX security measures helps ensure that the developer of the code is identifiable. In the event that the developer's software creates an undesirable effect, the user will have information to contact the developer and inform him of his code's apparent bugs.

Another feature of ActiveX security is that it allows users to determine whether they want to install a piece of code in the first place. If the control does not have security features enabled, the user is told that the code might not be safe, and prompts him as to whether or not he wants it installed on his machine. If the security features are enabled, it gives the user's machine certain information about the code and its developer, and that information is verified over the Net through certifying authorities such as Dun & Bradstreet or GTE.

See trust verification in action when you visit Microsoft's ActiveX control site at http://www.microsoft.com/activex/controls. When you download a page with an ActiveX control that is not already installed on your system, Internet Explorer begins downloading the control to your cache (see Figure 17.1). First, a small icon is displayed where the ActiveX control is located (A). Second, the browser's status line tells you that it is installing components (B). A progress indicator reports the percentage of the control that has been downloaded (C). If you are connected via a modem, the indicator lights on your modem show activity (D).

Figure 17.1.
When downloading an ActiveX control, several things happen in Internet Explorer.

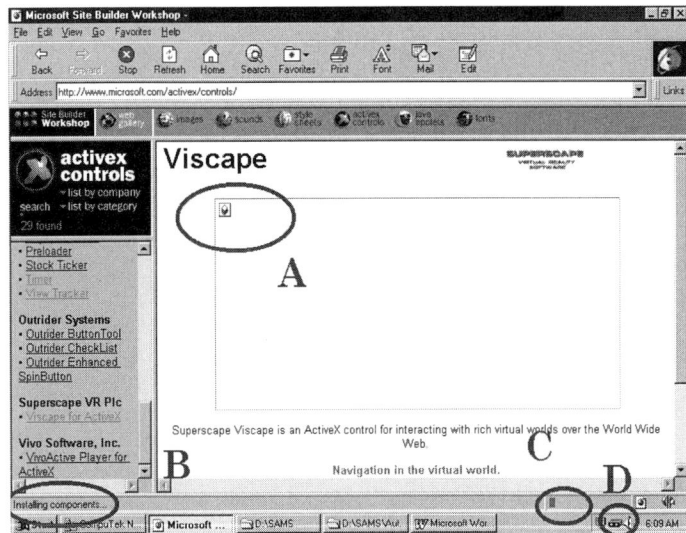

When the control has been retrieved, a pop-up window appears (see Figure 17.2) with a prompt that asks whether you want to install the control (A). The pop-up box also contains the program name and version number (B), the name of the CA (certification authority) that issued the certificate (C), and the expiration date of the downloaded version of the control (D).

Figure 17.2.
After an ActiveX control is downloaded, a pop-up window appears.

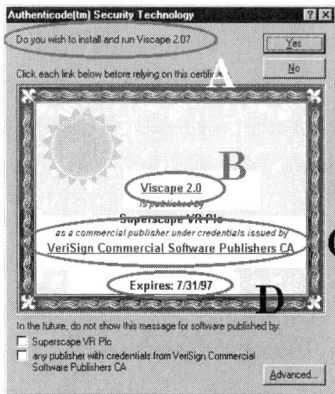

 **Note** Companies such as Verisign have Web sites set up to allow individuals and companies to use their trust verification services to issue and validate digital IDs. Verisign is located at http://www.verisign.com.

Finally, ActiveX security has a feature called Internet Ratings, which provides a degree of parental, administrative, or employer control to define which sites are not to be accessed by their users. Web page developers can place code within their HTML pages or their ActiveX controls to inform systems attempting access of any risqué content on that page. Administrators can then determine what level of freedom their users have in accessing pages with various levels of violent or sexual content.

On the enclosed CD-ROM, a directory called \Ratings\ contains several HTML files. If you load the ratings.html file into Internet Explorer, you can view different pages with the ratings system enabled on them. For more information about having your site rated, you should contact a ratings service.

Certificates

When you buy a software product off the shelf at your local store, you have certain assurances that the product will perform as stated on the box. This assurance (or "Implied Warranty of Merchantability") comes in the form of a product logo. Microsoft uses a very high-tech hologram to mark its products. If a knock-off artist wants to copy a Microsoft product and sell it on shelves, he would need more than a simple printing press—he'd need a hologram copying program as well (or a box of Microsoft hologram stickers).

This logo-on-a-box method is not as reliable with software that is distributed via the Net. Instead, several other methods of verifying security come into play in ActiveX programming. Information for verifying authenticity and integrity is contained within the object itself. It might come in the form of X.509 security certificates or other embedded information.

Base Security Layer

Microsoft's Base Security Layer SDK provides the means whereby a control can be certified as safe. This happens through the System Certificate Store. I will only briefly discuss the System Certificate Store here. The full specification can be found in the ActiveX SDK in the `\INetSDK\Help\Security\BSLH` directory.

When you download and install code that has a Certificate of Authenticity, this software vendor's certificate is stored in the local machine's System Certificate Store. Certificates from a variety of vendors can be found here.

Some of the API calls for accessing this store are as follows:

- `WinGetSystemCertificateStore`—Returns a handle to the local System Certificate Store.
- `WinInsertCertificate` or `CertStoreAddCert`—Adds a new certificate to the System Certificate Store.
- `FindCertificateByIssuerName`—Queries the System Certificate Store for a certificate issued by a certain agency.

Using these API calls, a programmer can query the Base Security Layer for the existence of a security certificate and retrieve the information within that certificate to validate a control as authentic. This certificate is used by the trust verification service.

Trust Verification Service

Trust verification service is the set of API calls that determines whether a requested object can be trusted. It provides features whereby a trust administrator can define what is and is not allowed to be installed on a machine.

It also provides a means whereby the administrator of a system can define the types of processes, controls and other objects that will be allowed. Although the security certificate will provide information about an object, it is still up to the trust administrator to make the final call.

To take advantage of trust-verification services, the trust administrator must work with a trust provider. This provider maintains a server or group of servers that provides authentication of certificates. This provider determines the methods used in validating a certificate, thus freeing users and their system administrators from the complexities of producing and verifying trust certificates.

When an application on a user's machine attempts to use an object that requires trust verification, the service contacts the software provider, its agent and/or any other trust providers to validate or update the certificate.

Safety API

Now that you know a little about the behind-the-scenes processes used to identify safe objects, let's go into how local users and administrators can implement these features in their own systems. As I stated earlier, security of all kinds boils down to a few basic features: UserID, password and, occasionally, physical location. Still, these can be very powerful when any or all of them are kept secret.

The Safety API has its first implementation in the Microsoft Internet Explorer. Users can designate the degree of security they wish to observe by selecting the Security tab of the View|Options menu in MSIE and pressing the Programs button (see Figure 17.3). The three options are

- Expert—Every control that is marked as safe requires the user to decide whether it will be loaded. Controls that are not marked as safe cannot be loaded.
- Normal—Only controls marked as safe will be loaded; the user will be prompted to load unmarked controls.
- None—No warnings…no security.

Figure 17.3.
Internet Explorer configuration menu to select the level of security.

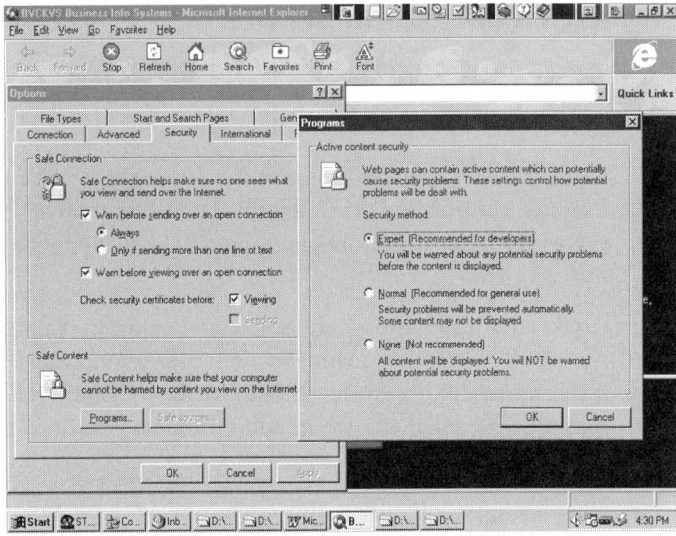

The complexities of ActiveX security boil down to two basic questions:

- ☐ Creation—Is this control still safe when scripted?
- ☐ Initialization—Is the control, standing alone, safe?

The Safety API provides the means to evaluate these hazards during creation and initialization.

Creation—Is This Control Still Safe When Scripted?

When creating an OLE control, programmers define a set of interfaces with which they want that control to operate.

An example of this type of safe control is the Marquee control. Its only function is to display animated text in a box. There is no way for this cutesy little display to harm your machine, so it is safe with any code.

An example of a potentially unsafe control is the SMTP control from the Internet Control Pack. This control could be scripted to send an e-mail resignation letter to your boss, or worse—your spouse!

To identify the control as safe for scripting, add it to the CATID_SafeForScripting component category in the system registry. Additionally, you can add code to the control's internal registration and unregistration routines to ensure its management in the proper component category.

Initialization—Is the Control, Standing Alone, Safe?

Controls go through several phases, each phase having its own risks and strengths.

When controls are first created (or initialized) on a system, certain properties define them. In turn, these properties are defined by the data from an IPersist* interface. The data in this interface can come from just about anywhere, including some remote server.

The danger here is twofold: the control can initialize in an undesirable way, or worse, it can send your private data to an untrusted system.

To identify the control as safe for initializing, add it to the CATID_SafeForInitializing component category in the system registry.

IObjectSafety

A more versatile, although higher level, method that works with registry settings is the IObjectSafety interface. In addition to marking a control as safe or unsafe, it can be manipulated programmatically to command a control to change its safety level.

To make a control safe for initializing, set the SetInterfaceSafetyOptions of this interface to INTERFACE_SAFE_FOR_UNTRUSTED_CALLER.

To make a control safe for scripting, set the SetInterfaceSafetyOptions of this interface to INTERFACE_SAFE_FOR_UNTRUSTED_DATA.

Of course, a particularly brilliant and malicious programmer can build, rebuild, or reverse-engineer any control to report itself as safe for scripting, and cause all kinds of damage. That makes trust verification of the source of the control all the more important.

The Code-Signing Tool Kit

The ActiveX SDK includes a set of tools to assist the programmer in signing code as safe. This reduces the preceding complex steps to a few simple steps. This kit helps the programmer certify PEs, cabinets, controls and class files.

This tool kit uses public key encryption and digital signatures to determine both the true source of a control and the integrity of that control (because it was released by the source). The following details each step required for signing a control as safe:

1. Obtaining a *.CER (X.509 certificate)—Before you can digitally sign your code, you must obtain a software publishing certificate through a CA (certification authority) such as Microsoft or GTE, or through an LRA (local registration agency) such as your employer or university. The CA determines whether you are who you say you are and issues an X.509 certificate with the public key that you provided embedded

within it. The certificate also has additional information embedded within it identifying your organization. Distribute this certificate with all signed software.

A control author can choose from two levels of certification. Other levels might present themselves in time, but the current choices are individual certification or commercial certification.

To obtain individual certification, an applicant needs only to submit positive identification (as defined by the CA) and promise that the software he publishes won't be malicious.

To obtain commercial certification, software vendors must complete the steps required for individual certification, but must also obtain a D-U-N-S® number from Dun & Bradstreet and must generate and store a private key on a dedicated piece of hardware.

For training purposes, the ActiveX SDK includes a utility called MakeCert.exe, which generates a test (that is, not real) x.509 certificate under your name and generates a public and a private key (also known as a *keypair*). The Makecert utility will then generate a *.CER (certificate) file.

> **Do**
>
> Do—Use the Makecert utility to generate pretend certificates.
>
> **Don't**
>
> Don't—Continue to use the Makecert utility after you obtain a real certificate from an LRA or CA.

2. Obtaining an .SPC (Software Publishing Certificate)—When you obtain an X.509 certificate, you will use the Cert2SPC.EXE utility to generate a Signed-Data object in the PKCS#7 format (Private Key Cryptography Standard #7). This object contains information from however many certificates you want to use (you can use more than one certificate to sign code if you like).

3. Signing a File—The SignCode Wizard walks you through the steps of adding your digital signature to your code. When you complete this step, you can begin to distribute your signed code safely over the Net.

When a user whose ActiveX security features are enabled loads a page that has one of your signed objects (OCX, DLL, EXE, CAB or class), a dialog box will prompt him as to whether he wishes to load your object. When this dialog appears, it will contain information you specified when you created the .SPC file. This could include your name, address, phone, Web site, logo and a variety of other information. When you have gone completely through the wizard, you will be able to sign your controls and code using public key encryption (see Figure 17.4).

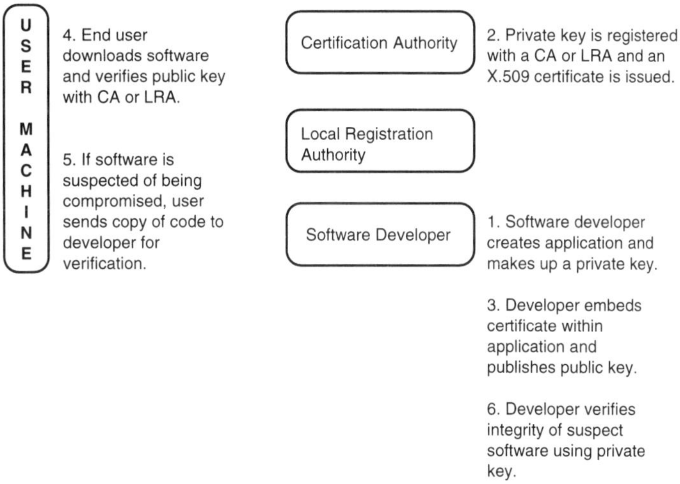

Figure 17.4.
The processes behind public key encryption go through many levels to ensure integrity.

USER MACHINE

4. End user downloads software and verifies public key with CA or LRA.

5. If software is suspected of being compromised, user sends copy of code to developer for verification.

Certification Authority — 2. Private key is registered with a CA or LRA and an X.509 certificate is issued.

Local Registration Authority

Software Developer — 1. Software developer creates application and makes up a private key.

3. Developer embeds certificate within application and publishes public key.

6. Developer verifies integrity of suspect software using private key.

Public Key Encryption

To be confident that your code is safe, you should know a little about the theory and process behind public key encryption. It is actually little more than a password-protected password. You must know the first password (the public key) to get the second password (the private key). The process is shown graphically in Figure 17.4.

As simple as that sounds, its use over the last five years has prompted several government agencies to consider restricting it.

In simple terms, public key encryption takes an item through several steps:

1. A user makes up a password—this can be as small as a word or as large as a passage from a book. The user then creates an object that he wishes to encrypt, such as a letter to his bank.

2. The user invokes a routine that creates a cross-section (or *hash*) of the object. This routine (such as an RSA scheme) might read every fourth character, or every even-numbered character on every other odd-numbered line or some such algorithm. (In reality, encryption schemes are much more complex!) The hash then becomes that object's "digital signature."

3. Because the object and the password are combined to create the signature, each object generates a unique signature and, if the object is altered, its signature changes. A talented vandal can use the public key to generate a new signature, and the end user has no way of knowing that the package was altered from its original state. This is where the magic comes in.

> 4. Either the public key or the private key can be used to determine the integrity of a file. Anyone can find out the public key (because it's embedded within the .SPC file). The private key, however, is known only to the vendor (and perhaps the CA or its agent). When you receive a copy of suspicious software, check it against its private key to determine whether it was altered.

4. Determining File Integrity—When you have distributed your signed code, there is no guarantee that someone will not corrupt your code and distribute it with the public key signature. If one of your users reports a bug and you think the fault lies with a hacker (instead of your program), obtain a copy of that user's suspect code. Then test it to determine its integrity.

The ChkTrust utility can tell you whether your code has been tampered with. It does this by extracting the PKCS#7 object from the file and extracting the X.509 certificate from that. It then creates a new hash, and checks it against the one in the PKCS#7 object.

If the hash (digital signature) created with both the public and the private keys is deemed valid, the suspect program is proven to be the same as the one that the author originally distributed. If one or both of the signatures is found to be invalid, then the code is proven to have been altered.

For a walk through the steps of signing a control, along with links to a certification authority, check out Microsoft's Authenticode site at http://www.microsoft.com/intdev/security/authcode/sixsteps.htm.

Internet Ratings

Many different government actions (such as the Computer Decency Act and the Clipper chip in the United States, and Germany's temporary ban on Compuserve) have tried, without success, to regulate violent or sexually oriented content on the Internet. Each effort has failed due to the distributed nature of the Net and public outrage at anything that smacks of governmental censorship.

The World Wide Web Consortium has been working to allow parental, employer and administrative control over this type of material. Self-regulation is expected to prove much more successful than governmental action because it empowers people closer to home to determine what material is or is not acceptable.

PICS—Platform for Internet Content Selection

The PICS standard is the result of several conferences addressing the conflicting needs of censorship and free speech. By implementing a standard system of rating content (much like in the film industry), content developers can post labels on their network content, describing the level of risqué material it contains.

NOTE http://www.w3.org/pub/WWW/PICS/ is the home page for the development of the PICS standard. The World Wide Web Consortium has taken on the effort of establishing a method for implementing rating systems for Internet content that is more dynamic than the system used in theaters.

Rating Systems

PICS is not attempting to establish how ratings are assigned, but rather how rating systems are implemented.

NOTE http://www.rsac.org is the home of the Recreational Standards Advisory Council. The RSAC provides a PICS-compliant rating system and a Web interface for registering the content of Web sites and individual Web pages.

Rating Labels

Web site administrators can register the content of their Web pages with an entity such as the RSAC. When you receive your ratings, they should be placed within the <HEAD> container tag of an HTML document. An example of this tag follows:

```
<META http-equiv="PICS-Label" content='
(PICS-1.1 "http://www.rsac.org/ratingsv01.html"
l gen true comment "RSACi North America Server"
by "user@domain.net"
for "http://www.domain.net/user"
on "1996.08.16T08:15-0500"
exp "1997.01.01T08:15-0500"
r (n 0 s 0 v 0 l 0))'>
```

This example rates the URL http://WWW.Domain.Net/User as a 0 (completely safe) for nudity, sex, violence and language. It was registered in the name of User@Domain.Net, and is good from August 16, 1996 until January 1, 1997 between the hours of 8:15 AM and 5:00 PM. It's everything a parent could ask for.

Internet Ratings API

Microsoft's Internet Ratings API exposes certain features of the PICS standard to the programmer. This API is also part of Nashville (Microsoft's code name for their Internet add-on pack).

With this API you can, of course, enable or disable the ratings features. You can also check the authorized level of access enjoyed by the current user. This access is defined by the PICS standard. If the user does not have a level of access appropriate for the page, a Request Denied dialog is displayed.

Using this API, you can determine the rating of a site or compare the ratings on two different sites. In this way, you can assure a user (no guarantees, though) that a site that reports a set of ratings has been verified by a trusted third party.

Summary

In this chapter you have learned about the processes involved in downloading, verifying and installing ActiveX controls.

You have learned about two of the <OBJECT> tag's parameters—Code and CODETYPE, and how they can be used to identify the location, version and machine type for a control. Files of several kinds can be used as ActiveX controls, including portable executables, custom controls and cabinet archives. You can add an .INF file to a cabinet or place it all by itself on a Web page to tell a user's machine the where, how and what of installing ActiveX controls and their required files.

ActiveX uses an enhanced MIME type to identify the type of computer, be it Mac, UNIX or Windows. This format allows a content provider to enable a user to reap the benefits of an ActiveX Web site, no matter what type of computer he prefers.

You are also familiar with many of the features of ActiveX security. This set of APIs enables users of your control to rest assured that the code they download from the Net is the same code that you posted.

ActiveX security relies on the use of X.509 and PKCS#7 security certificates. These certificates are verified with a trusted authority, such as a commercial or individual issuer. These security measures can reassure, but not guarantee, a user that his copy of your code is intact. The only way to guarantee its integrity is to process it against your top-secret private key. You can, but do not have to, use the Base Security Layer SDK to enable these security features.

ActiveX has another type of security, based on the PICS standard, to allow parents, employers, and other authorities to censor access to content they feel is not appropriate for their users. Using the Internet Ratings API, you can add this level of security to your own standalone applications. Use the HTML implementation of PICS to rate the content of your own Web pages.

Q&A

Q What other compression formats will work with ActiveX besides Microsoft's cabinets?

A Any compression method can be used to reduce the size of a file. Cabinets are the only ones that can be used as true ActiveX controls. This is because cabinets are the only ones that are self-installing.

Q Does the ActiveX MIME type for identifying a user's CPU and OS allow other platforms besides Mac and Windows?

A Yes. There are tentative plans to extend this to include UNIX and other systems, but not soon.

Q Is there an ActiveX security measure to protect against viral infection?

A No. ActiveX does not include antivirus security. The public key encryption can help a user identify when a program has been altered, but that's as far as it goes. To enable antivirus protection, you would need a utility such as Norton Antivirus or Mcafee Virusscan.

Q Does ActiveX allow a network administrator to define what can be installed on the machines under his charge?

A No. In a highly secure organization, such as a bank or defense installation, firewalls and proxy servers can be set up to avoid many threats. If users within the organization have access to the World Wide Web, the administrator must train users about the threats and trust them to heed those warnings or disallow Web access altogether. The whole point of ActiveX security is to allow the client, rather than the server, to define what is or is not trusted.

Q Is it possible for a malicious programmer to create a fake X.509 certificate and distribute hazardous software that is signed with that certificate?

A Yes, but it won't work. When an object is marked as safe with an X.509 certificate, the client machine will verify the certificate with the CA or LRA. Even if the x.509 certificate is perfect, if there is no confirmation by a third party trust-verification service, the object will not be treated as trusted software. (The exception to this is when a user turns off his security features.)

Workshop

Create an .INF file that performs the following functions:

Installs FooBar.OCX (Version 3.1.0.1) from the current Web directory into the user's \Windows\System directory.

Installs FooBar.DLL (Version 1.0.0.0) from the current Web directory into the user's \Windows directory.

Quiz

1. What are the three phases in ActiveX component downloading?
2. What container tag is used to identify an ActiveX control?
3. What attribute of the tag from Question 2 is used to identify the location and version of an ActiveX control?
4. What attribute of the tag from Question 2 is used to identify the MIME type of the control in Question 3?
5. What three types of files are referred to as portable executables?
6. What file contains the information required to install an ActiveX control and its related files?
7. What code is used within the Setup Information file to tell the system to load a control into the \Windows\System directory?
8. What three parts of a Web page present opportunities for security threats?
9. Which SDK provides the tools for certifying a control as safe?
10. What service provides the means for verifying that a control signed with the SDK from Question 9 is safe for the user?
11. What two issues are addressed by the Safety API for determining the level of safety within an ActiveX control?
12. What OLE property programmatically defines the level of safety enjoyed by a control?

13. What two facts about a vendor can be determined from the signed control to validate its integrity?
14. What level of security is obtained from the CA or the LRA, respectively?
15. What two types of "passwords" are used in public key encryption?
16. What is the Internet standard for enabling security measures dealing with the content of a site?
17. What API is used to work with content security?

Week 3

Day 18

Customizing ActiveX Control Properties

By now you should have a strong familiarity with the processes involved in inserting objects into an HTML document and ensuring that those objects are verifiably intact (or trusted).

In this chapter, you will learn more about what ActiveX controls are, what they can do, and how to make them do it. This chapter covers

- ☐ The controls that come with the Internet Explorer
- ☐ How to manipulate options (or parameters) available with the different ActiveX objects

Built-In Controls

Chapter 15, "What Is an ActiveX Control?" discusses the COM and DCOM models for object-oriented programming. The DCOM model provides the programmer with a hierarchical, standard set of objects that would be found in an intranet-connected machine. Programmers can manipulate the properties of these objects to enable customized networking features within their applications.

This hierarchy follows the structure shown in Figure 18.1. I refer to this structure interchangeably as the Object Model for Scripting and the Internet Explorer Object. For a full explanation of each of the objects in the hierarchy, you should refer to the documents in the ActiveX SDK under `\INetSDK\Help\ScriptOM\`.

Figure 18.1.
The Object Model for Scripting.

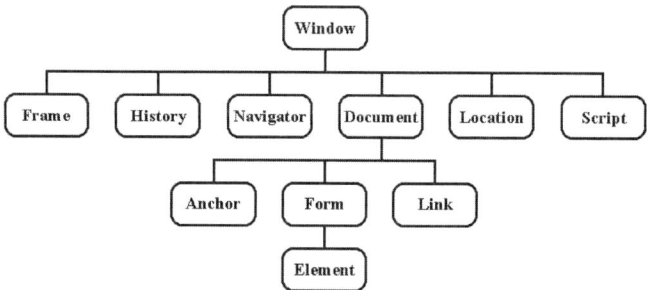

To easily identify the objects within the Object Model for Scripting, naming conventions are quite valuable. By naming your objects in a consistent manner, you can easily tell what type of object something is.

Using the conventions in the following table, you can have many separate instances of a given object in use at the same time. You will still be able to refer to each of them directly, and in a way that makes sense to someone who is not already familiar with your code.

> **NOTE**
>
> Naming conventions are not written in stone. These are provided as a guide. If you (or your supervisor) have a preferred way of naming your objects, go ahead and use that. The important thing is that each name be unique and that they follow *some* sort of convention.

Table 18.1. Object Model for Scripting naming conventions.

Object	Prefix	Sample
Anchor	a	aAnchor
Document	doc	docDocument
Form	frm	frmForm
Frames	fr	frFrame
History	hst	hstHistory
Link	lk	lkLink
Location	loc	locLocation
Navigator	nav	navNavigator
Script	scr	scrScript
Window	w	wWindow

NOTE

Throughout this chapter, you will see several examples of how to reference the various objects built into the Explorer model. You can use the ActiveX Control Pad, included on the enclosed CD-ROM, to explore these features—the way they were meant to be used.

The Control Pad has the different objects, properties, events, and methods built into its artificial intelligence engine. This enables it to prompt you, through the use of wizards, in the steps for referencing and manipulating the objects built into the Explorer. It also gives you a way to use other controls that are plugged into your system registry.

Window Object

The topmost object within the Object Model For Scripting is the Window object. The Window object is the container within which programs or scripts will run. This is the primary object against which you will be programming. The "window" to which it refers is the main window of your Web browser.

If you wanted to refer to an object such as the current location or URL within the current window, you would address it as follows:

```
window.location.href
```

Extending this out,

```
window.location.href="http://www.domain.net"
```

or

```
location="http://www.domain.net"
```

would set the `location.href` of the current window to www.domain.net.

Notice that the default parent of this Location object is the Window object, and the default property of the Location object is `href`.

> **NOTE**
>
> Multiple windows may be visible at any one time. To refer to the current window, you do not have to specify to which window object you are referring, so
>
> ```
> window.location.href="http://www.domain.net"
> ```
>
> is the same, for our purposes, as
>
> ```
> location.href="http://www.domain.net"
> ```

By assigning the window a name, you can make your code easier to read by adding something like this:

```
window.name = "wDomain"
```

Then you can refer to it elsewhere in the program like this:

```
wDomain.location.href="http://www.domain.net"
```

Just like people, objects within the Internet Explorer Object can be referred to in many ways. Each has its own name, as well as other ways to refer to it that are relative to the context in which they are used.

A window's *parent* is the window within which it was created. If you have a window named `wChild` contained within a frame that is contained within a top-level window named `wParent`, it would have the full name:

```
wParent.frFrame.wChild
```

If you were to have a bit of script within `wChild` that addresses its parent, you could refer to it as `wParent` or `wChild.Parent`. If you wanted to refer to the top-most window, you could use the property `Top` and refer to it as `wChild.Top`. There are other context-relative properties defined in the Object Model for Scripting, such as `Self`, that work in a similar way.

The Window Object

SYNTAX

window.[*]

The Window object refers to browser window. If no Window object is specified, the current window is assumed. This object contains all the objects in the Object Model for Scripting.

Example:

strURL=Window.location

and

strURL=location

 will set the value of strURL to the location of the current window.

Frames Object

The Frames object is a property of the Window object. Some Web pages make use of a type of window display known as *frames* that enables the display of several different Web pages within one window. (See Figure 18.2.) Since several frames can be used within one window, the Frames object is used as an array.

Figure 18.2.
Frames allow the display of multiple Web pages within one window.

When a browser loads a page with frames, a hyperlink can instruct the client browser to change one or more of the pages while leaving the other pages intact.

Do	Don't
DO remember to use `Frames(0)` to refer to the first frame. DON'T use `Window.Frames(1)` to refer to the first frame.	

Do	Don't
DO remember to use the plural form, `Frames`. DON'T use the singular form, `Frame`, since there should never be only one frame within a window if frames are used on a page.	

When you reference `Window.Frames(x)` within a script or program, it returns an entire Window object. If you want to reference the URL of the document in the second frame of a window, you would phrase it like this:

`wWindow.frFrames(1).Location.href`

In this way you are, for all practical purposes, treating the `wWindow.frFrames(1)` object as a Window object.

The Frames Collection Object

`window.frames()`

The Frames Collection object references any of the frames in a given window. Each frame in a given window is numbered consecutively, beginning with the first one, numbered 0 rather than 1.

Example:

`Window.Frames(0)`

would refer to the first frame and

`Window.Frames(1)`

would refer to the second frame.

Location Object

Another important property of the Window object is the Location object. Providing more than just the simple URL, this object enables you to use several powerful features that would

not otherwise be available through straight HTML. This includes the capability to reference the port on which the connection is accepted, and the full filename of the specific file that was returned (if it had one).

The Location Object

`window.location`

The Location object references each of the parts of a URL, including:

Parameter	Description
HRef	The complete URL
Protocol	HTTP, FTP, and so on
Host	The local hostname of the computer
HostName	The full host and domain name
Port	The TCP/IP port of a connection
PathName	The full filepath on a host
Search	Any search parameters specified in the URL after a ?
Hash	Any index parameters specified in the URL after a #

Example:

`strURL=Window.Location.HREF`

would return the full URL of the current window.

WARNING

The `Hash` and `Search` properties always return the question mark (?) or pound sign (#) along with the parameter. If you set the variable `strMyString` to the value within a `Hash` property, it will return something like `#Place` instead of just `Place`.

History Object

A really great property of the Window object is the History object. A simple line like

`window.history = intX`

will set the variable `intX` to the number of pages that were accessed by the browser window (or window frame).

This object has two particularly powerful methods, `Back` and `Forward`. These enable you to tell the browser to go back to a previous page, or forward (if you have already gone back one or more pages).

Unlike the `Frames()` property array, the number in the History object starts counting with 1. If no pages have been accessed yet, the value of the `history` property is set to d.

Another method of the History object, `Go`, enables you to select a specific site in the history and jump to that page. The format for this would go something like

```
Window.Go 5    'Assuming there are at least 5 sites in the history
```

The History Object

`Window.History`

The History object references each or all the sites visited during the current session of the browser (even longer with some browsers). The length of the list can be determined through the aptly named `Length` property.

Example:

`intHistList = Window.History.Length`

would return the total number of sites loaded during the current session of the browser.

The browser can be commanded to go backwards and forwards in this list, using the `Back` and `Forward` methods.

`Window.History.Back`

would load the previously loaded page.

`Window.History.Forward`

would load the page you were on before you used the `Back` method.

If you already know which history item you want to hit, specify it with the `Go` method like so:

`Window.History.Go 3`

Document Object

The most important (and complex) property of the Window object is the Document object. This is where the actual content of a Web page resides. The next sections go into some of the details of `Object` properties.

The Color Object

A group of properties (LinkColor, aLinkColor, vLinkColor) enables you to customize the color in which hyperlinks will appear. You can use BGColor and FGColor to customize the color of the background and foreground, respectively, of the document as a whole.

For example, you can set the background color of a page to all black using the following format:

```
wWindow.docDocument.BGColor="Black"
```

Or, if you are referring to a document within the current window, use:

```
docDocument.BGColor="Black"
```

Several different color names are supported by the Explorer Object Model including black, white, and gray; the primary colors red, yellow and blue; and several tertiary colors such as green and orange.

The Anchor Object

The Anchor object returns an array of all the hyperlink anchors within the document. *Anchors* are the pages and locations, referenced within the document, to which a user may jump.

An anchor, as typed within an HTML document, would look like this:

```
<a href="http://www.domain.net">Jump to Domain Network</a>
```

To reference the third anchor within an HTML document, your code would look like this:

```
document.anchors(2)
```

This property would return a Window object containing the properties of the referenced page.

The Link Object

The Link object is another property array of the Document object. It is very similar to the Anchors object, but it returns all the hyperlinks within a document.

The Form Object

The Form object is also an array. Anyone familiar with Visual Basic or other Windows programming languages might find the Form object confusing because a form in Windows is not the same as a form in HTML. In HTML, which is the context used here, a *form* is an item such as a check box or a list box or other user-input item.

The Forms Collection Object

`Window.Document.Forms`

The Forms collection object references an array of all the HTML forms in the current document. The length of the list can be determined through the Length property.

Example:

`intFormList = Window.Document.Form.Length`

would return the total number of HTML forms in the current document.

`Window.Document.Forms(0)`

would return the first HTML form in the current document.

The Location Object

The Location object is a property of the Window object, which we will go into in some detail. It is very powerful for determining and/or setting the various options for accessing a given site.

You should know that a URL consists of several parts, even though it is presented as one long string, such as `http://www.domain.net/directory/filename.ext:80`.

In the Location object, these can be set or retrieved using the properties shown in Table 18.2.

Table 18.2. Properties for setting and retrieving URLs in the Location object.

Property	Sample
href	http://www.domain.net/filename.ext:80
protocol	http:
host	www.domain.net:80
hostname	www.domain.net
port	80
pathname	directory

There are two other properties, `Hash` and `Search`, that apply to special features of an HTML document or CGI script that I do not go into here. (Again, for full explanation of those objects, refer to the document "Object Model For Scripting" in the ActiveX SDK.)

The `LastModified` Property

The `LastModified` property of the Document object is just what it appears to be—the date when this file was last saved. There are currently a variety of methods used by Netscape and others, who use `<META>` tags that are not part of the HTML standard, to enable the author to set this date. Unless the W3 Consortium decides to adopt another standard, this property is obtained from the file date of the specific file on the server.

The `Title` Property

The `Title` property of the Document object is obtained from within the HTML document itself. It is set by the author of the HTML file by enclosing it within the `<TITLE> </TITLE>` container tag. Should the author neglect to assign a title to a document, the `Title` property will return an empty string, `""`.

The `Referrer` Property

The `Referrer` property of the Document object is a very interesting item. It provides the ActiveX programmer with a method of determining how the user found your page. A command line such as

```
strSource = document.referrer
```

would return the URL of the page that had a hyperlink that took the user to your page. If you track this information and are listed with a service such as Yahoo! or WebCrawler, you can tell how often a user was referred by one of them, or if they were referred by a link in some other company's or user's page. If the user got to your page by typing in the URL directly, this property will return a `NULL` value.

> **Meta-Information**
>
> Not to be confused with the `<META>` tag, meta-information is certain to be one of the most valuable types of information with which companies developing an Internet presence could work. This is the beginning of what is hoped to be the Information Age.

Internet-acquired information comes in three major forms. First, some companies want a presence on the Internet so that they can put their products into a new vehicle for distribution, such as online ordering. Second, some companies want a presence on the Internet so that they can get information about the people that are interested in their products. The third major form of information is information about information, or *meta-information*.

NOTE Companies such as Paradysz Matela & Co. specialize in extracting information about information, and reselling that data as meta-information. Paradysz Matela & Company's URL is `http://www.pmmclists.com`.

You have heard the old question, "Who watches the watchers?" This is meta-information. Companies such as Dallas-based Intactix or New York City-based Paradysz Matela & Co. market this type of information-about-information quite successfully. Meta-information can tell you where, when, why, or how information is acquired—whether the information is about babies, ballet, bandages, or bullets.

You can take a (sometimes very large) database and give the user meta-information about that database. Some of this information could answer questions such as "In what states do my users live and work?" or "How much does my average user spend on online services?" or "Do products in green packages sell better on the top shelf, or the bottom?"

Talking to the Document

The next thing you need to know is how to tell the document what it will tell the user. This is where GIGO (Garbage In/Garbage Out) comes into play. The coolest interface in the world cannot hide bad content. In the following sections you will review a couple of methods for sending content, whatever the quality, to the user through the document.

The `Document.Write` Method

By using the `Document.Write` method, you can have your application create the content of an HTML page on-the-fly. This written text will not be saved to the copy of the HTML page, but rather, it will be simply added to the local copy of the page, as viewed by the client browser.

Using the `Document.Write` Method

Document.Write [*string*]

The command Write is used to write a character string to a document. The string will be entered into the current position in the document.

It uses one string value parameter to specify the text that should be written. This parameter can be a named variable, like `strMyVariable`, or it can be the actual text string enclosed in quotes, like `"My Paragraph"`.

Example:

```
Document.Write "My Paragraph"
```

This example would write the text "My Paragraph" to the document.

Example:

```
strMyString = "Hello world!"
Document.Write strMyString
```

This example would write the text "Hello world!" to the document, since that is the value of the variable `strMyString`.

Open/Close

Before you can write to a document, you need to open the document for editing and then close it again. Thus, to perform the Write action shown in the preceding section, you would have to have to format it something like this:

```
Document.Open
Document.Write "Hello World!"
Document.Close
```

Control Attributes and Parameters

Now that you have learned a little about ActiveX's built-in objects, we will refer again to the `<OBJECT>` tag. In earlier chapters you learned how to insert objects, and even a little about customizing their size with the Height and Width keywords. The next section gets a little deeper into the parameters that are used to customize other control features.

Attributes—ID, ClassID, Data

Every object that is inserted into an HTML page should have an ID attribute. This is the unique name that will be used within the HTML page, and any script within the page, to identify it. This name should follow the conventions set forth in the previous section.

If the object is an OLE object (such as an ActiveX control), it should also name the ClassID attribute for the object. As you remember, the ClassID is the unique name used within the local machine to identify the object within the registry. While the HTML author determines the ID, the ClassID is set by the control.

No two controls should ever have the same ClassID. If you have two different timers, for example, and each has different behavior, you can refer to each of them by its unique ClassID rather than by easily confused names like Timer and IETimer.

Finally, the <OBJECT> tag should identify the data that the object will use. This Data attribute can be identified by using one of two methods.

The first method points to the URL where the data is stored:

Data = [URL]

The second method is to put the actual data within the Data attribute of the <OBJECT> tag:

Data = "data:[MIME Type];[Data]

Now, let's bring these properties of the <OBJECT> tag together to see how they work.

```
<OBJECT
  ID=objMyTextBox
  ClassID="clsid:12345678-1234-1234-1234-123456789012"
  Data="data:text/txt:Hello world"
>
```

This <OBJECT> tag would insert an object called objMyTextBox into the document. The ClassID is a pretend one, but it follows the format for a real one. The data that would be used to initialize the control is contained in the Data parameter, and is identified as the MIME type text/txt. The actual data is simply the phrase, Hello world.

Parameters

Most ActiveX controls have several other options that can be defined and that are not specified within the <OBJECT> tag itself—although they are defined within the <OBJECT> container tags. These control-specific parameters are defined within the <PARAM> tag and enable you to define the name of a parameter, such as Enabled, and the value of the named parameter, such as True or False.

The HTML <OBJECT> Container Tag

```
<OBJECT
    ID = [Object Name]
    WIDTH = [Pixels 0 - 800]
    HEIGHT = [Pixels 0 - 600]
    CLASSID = "CLSID:hhhhhhhh-hhhh-hhhh-hhhh-hhhhhhhhhhhh"
    CODEBASE = [URL FilePathName]
    Type = [MIME Type]
    Data = [String of Data]
>
<PARAM
    NAME=[Variable Name]
    VALUE=[String Value]
>
</OBJECT>
```

The <OBJECT> container tags define the properties of the control when it is created on the local machine. Before closing the control with the </OBJECT> tag, any additional control-specific information is added through the <PARAM> tag.

Example:

```
<Object
    ID="Timer"
    ClassID="clsid:59CCB4A0-727D-11CF-AC36-00AA00A47DD2"
    CodeBase="http://activex.microsoft.com/controls/iexplorer/ietimer.ocx"
    Type=application/x-oleobject"
>
<Param Name="Interval" Value="100">
<Param Name="Enbaled" Value="True">
</Object>
```

This would use the Internet Explorer Timer control to create an object called `"Timer"`. If the ActiveX control is not available on the current machine, an attempt will be made to retrieve the it from Microsoft's Web server. When it is loaded, it will `tick` (`Enabled=True`) every 100 beats (`Interval=100`).

Parameter	Description
ID	The name by which this particular control is to be referred
Width	The width of the control on the page
Height	The height of the control on the page
ClassID	The unique ID by which this OLE object is referred
CodeBase	The URL from which this control may be installed
Data	Data that is used by the control (a page or image can be contained in the data attribute's parameter)
Type	The MIME type of the control object (for ActiveX OCXs, this will usually be `"application/x-oleobject"`)
Param	Control-specific parameters
Name	Parameter's variable name
Value	Value to be referenced by parameter's variable name

WARNING

> Sometimes you may be tempted to calculate the passing of time through the Timer control. This is not always such a good idea.
>
> The ticking away of the Timer control, although pretty darn regular, is still subject to the availability of system resources. If your system is already bogged down with other events, the Timer control may "hiccup" and fire after 123.7 beats instead of the 100 for which you set it.
>
> If you need to do calculations based on real time, it is best to use the system clock. It's there; it's built into the hardware; and best of all, it remains accurate even after the computer loses power.

Summary

In this chapter you have learned something about the Object Model for Scripting, also called the Internet Explorer Object. This is the basic structure against which ActiveX controls operate. It has several properties, most of which are entire objects unto themselves.

The main (or top-most) object is the Window object. Each Window object contains several objects, including the Frame, History, Navigator, Location, Script, and Document. Not all of these objects are applicable to every single instance of the Window object.

The most significant subsidiary object (or property) of the Window object is the Document object (also called the DocObject). The Document object contains the actual content of a Web page. It is also composed of several objects, including the Link, Anchor, and Form objects.

You also should have a slightly better understanding of the <OBJECT> tag, most importantly, the Data attribute. Using this attribute, you can specify the persistent data with which an ActiveX control is loaded. Using this attribute, you can reference one control and have it instantiated many times, with a different purpose on each instance.

For more information on instantiation of ActiveX OLE controls as well as other ActiveX OLE features, see Day 21, "Creating an ActiveX Control," and the Microsoft Developer's Network Level 2 Documentation.

Q&A

Q How did Microsoft come up with the Object Model for Scripting as it is used in the Internet Explorer Object?

A The Object Model for Scripting is based on the World Wide Web Consortium's working draft titled "Inserting Objects into HTML" (http://www.w3.org/pub/WWW/TR/WD-object). This specification was developed in cooperation with Microsoft, Netscape, Sun Microsystems, and others with a great interest in the growth of the World Wide Web. It provides the basis under which ANY object can be inserted into a Web page, including Java applets, ActiveX controls, and similar OLE components.

Q I have heard of the <INSERT> tag from HTML 2.0. When did it become the <OBJECT> tag and why?

A HTML 3 introduced the <OBJECT> tag in response to market demand for a more object-oriented approach to Web page design. Programmers who are familiar with object-oriented programming will appreciate the added power provided by this interface in activating their Web pages and Internet applications.

Q I invest a lot of time and money in learning Internet technologies, only to have them change at every turn. If I create Web pages and applications based on this changed tag, will I have to relearn everything—again?

A Change is a difficult thing on which to keep a handle. The only thing definite about Internet technologies is that they WILL change. However, the folks who are making these changes do so only to enhance what was previously there. Apologies aside, they make extensive use of backwards compatibility. If you go through the trouble of integrating these new, powerful features into your own project, you can rest assured that each modification of the standard will incorporate some degree of backwards compatibility. In most cases, this means you will need to perform little or no redesign of your applications—unless you want to incorporate whatever NEW features are added.

Workshop

Create a Web page using the <OBJECT> tag and its Data parameter. Make this object a text box, and using the Data parameter, fill the text box with some sort of text, such as Hello World!.

Quiz

1. What is defined by the Object Model for Scripting?
2. What naming conventions (that is, prefixes) are used for the following objects:
   a. Document
   b. Window
   c. Script
   d. Frames
   e. Form
3. What is the top-most object within the Object Model for Scripting?
4. Which object array allows the display of several Web pages within one Window?
5. What attribute of the <OBJECT> tag provides a way to assign a unique name for each object?
6. What number is used to reference the first frame of a frames array?
7. What property of the Window object is used to reference previously displayed documents?

Questions 5-7 refer to the Location object, using the URL `http://www.domain.net/directory/subdirectory/filename.ext:80` as an example:

8. What property would return with `80`?
9. What property would return with `www.domain.net:80`?
10. What property would return with `www.domain.net`?

> **NOTE**
> Refer to the appendix, "Answers," for the answers to these questions.

Week 3

Day 19

User Interaction with ActiveX Controls

By now you have a pretty good idea how to insert controls into Web pages and Visual Basic applications. You also know how to modify the properties of these controls—both programmatically and within the `<OBJECT>` tag. In this chapter, you will take the next step and learn how to enable people who access your ActiveX utility to interact with these controls.

When you are finished with this chapter, you will be able to create:

- ☐ an interactive ActiveX HTML document.
- ☐ an interactive ActiveX Visual Basic application.

Interactive HTML

When you create a Web page, there is nothing but content—some words and maybe some graphics. When you insert a control, be it ActiveX or something else, you do little more than enhance the content.

To truly *activate* your page, you must allow the user to interact with it. HTML provides a few different ways to allow user input: the <FORM> and <INPUT> tags.

The <FORM> Container Tag

When you want to code a user-input interface, you use the Form object. It is defined within the <FORM> tag, and has several attributes that define what the interface does (actions) and how it does it (methods).

NOTE Different programming environments have different ways of allowing user input. Unfortunately, each one uses the word *form* to define a different part of the user input interface.

Where the word form is used in this chapter, make sure to understand the context in which it is used. For example, a Visual Basic form has a Caption attribute, but an HTML form does not.

The Action attribute points to the URL of the Web item that will perform the selected function. This Web item can be just about anything that can be passed as a URL or preferably, as a named object. If you do not specify a URL to handle the action, it is assumed that the current document will be handling the request.

The Method attribute defines whether the user request is for receiving information or for submitting it. The value for the Method attribute can be either Post or Get.

NOTE Text should be contained within the <FORM> container tags to describe the purpose of the form (unless the purpose is going to be obvious to the user).

If you have an HTML document loaded, and want to load another page using the <FORM> tag to retrieve that document, it looks something like this:

```
<FORM Method = GET Action = "http://www.domain.net/other.html">
Load other HTML Document
</FORM>
```

This HTML code by itself does not allow users to tell the browser they want to launch that event. To do that, add an <INPUT> tag within the <FORM> container tag.

Using the <FORM> Container Tag

▼ SYNTAX

```
<FORM
    Method = [Get/Post]
    Action = [URL]
>
<INPUT
   Name = [String Value]
   Type = [Form Type]
   Value = [String Value]
>
</FORM>
```

The <FORM> container tag is used to define an area that allows for user input. The <INPUT> tags within the <FORM> container tag specify what type of input the user may enter.

<FORM> tags define the action taken upon submission of user input as either "GET" (append data to the Action URL with a # prefix) or "POST" (append data to the Action URL with a ? prefix).

GET Example:

```
<FORM Method = "GET" Action = "http://www.domain.net/MyIndex.html">
<INPUT Type = "Text" Value = "MyHeading">
<INPUT Type = "Submit" Value = "Submit">
</FORM>
```

This submits a request for the URL http://www.domain.net/MyIndex.html#MyHeading.

The pound (#) sign is automatically added because the Get method is used.

POST Example:

```
<FORM Method = "POST" Action = "http://www.domain.net/MyIndex.html">
<INPUT Name = "Info" Type = "Text" Value = "MyData">
<INPUT Type = "Submit" Value = "Submit">
</FORM>
```

This submits a request for the URL http://www.domain.net/MyIndex.html?Info=MyData.

▲ The question mark (?) is automatically added because the Post method is used.

The `<INPUT>` Tag

The `<INPUT>` tag allows you to specify the *type* of user input to be allowed in the form. It does this through the `Type` and `Value` attributes of the `<INPUT>` tag. Several of these types can be seen in Figure 19.1.

Figure 19.1.
Several different input types on a Web page.

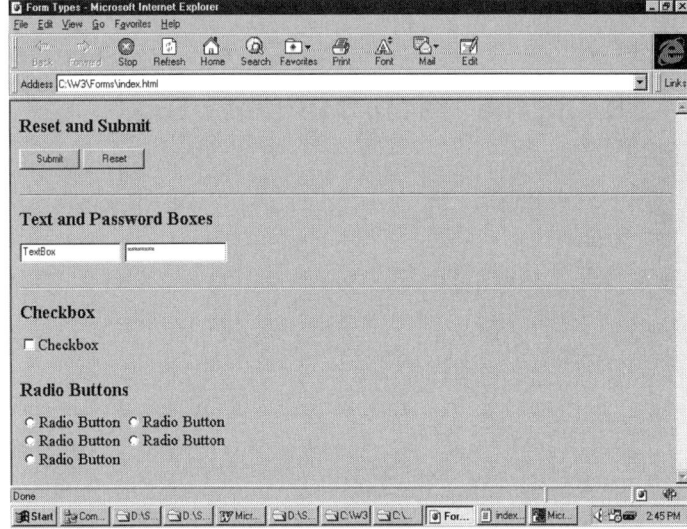

The `Type` attribute specifies what kind of input the user will provide. To select how the data input form is to be presented, use `submit`, `checkbox`, `radio`, or `text` as the value of the `Type` attribute. `textarea`, `password`, `reset` and `image` are also input types that you can use.

Input Type: `submit`

In the earlier example, you created a form that commanded that another Web page be loaded, but did not give the user a way to launch that action. To rectify this, add a Submit button to tell the browser to perform the action like so:

```
<FORM Method = GET Action = "http://www.domain.net/other.html">
<INPUT TYPE=submit VALUE="Load other HTML Document">
</FORM>
```

User Interaction with ActiveX Controls

In this example, a Submit button is displayed on the page and the text Load other HTML Document is displayed on the face of the button. When the user clicks the button, other.html is loaded. An example of this page can be seen in Figure 19.2.

Figure 19.2.
An HTML form's Submit button.

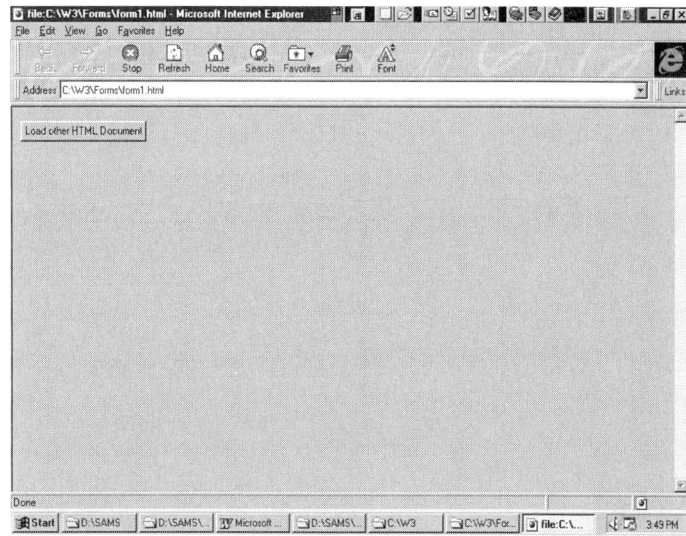

A sister to the Submit button is the Reset button. It is used in exactly the same way as the Submit button, except that when this button is pressed, all of the values on the current form are reset to their defaults.

Input Type: checkbox

Another input type is checkbox, which allows user input of a simple true/false status. This feature allows you to get simple yes/no answers out of your users. In the following example, the user can answer the question Are You Sure? by clicking the box:

```
<FORM>
<INPUT TYPE=checkbox NAME=ckCertainty VALUE=False>Are You Sure?
</FORM>
```

A sample of how this check box form would look in a Web browser can be seen in Figure 19.3.

The preceding sample defaults to a value of False—the user is not sure. An ActiveX object can be programmed to set the value of this item with the command ckCheckbox = True or ckCheckbox = False. It can also read the value by referencing the value of ckCheckbox as if it were any other true/false variable.

Figure 19.3.
An HTML form's check box.

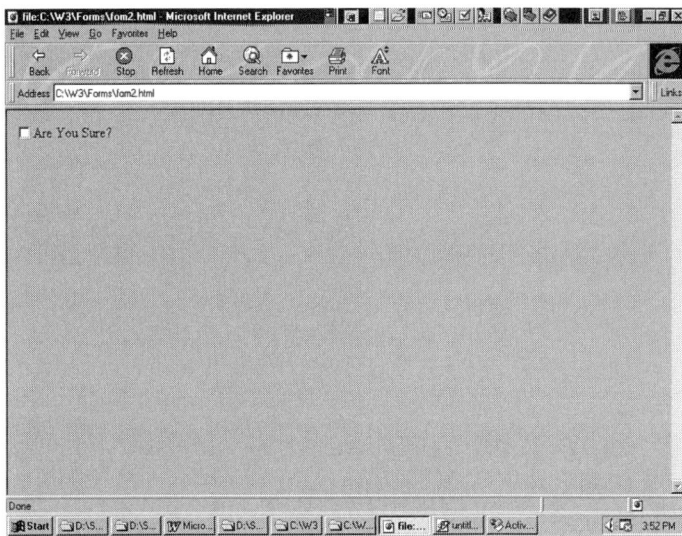

Input Type: radio

Another input type is the radio button. Several radio buttons can be placed within one <FORM> container tag to allow the user to select from a series of options; however, the controls do not have to be grouped together. To specify that a radio button is part of a group, assign the same value in the Name attribute to every button in the group. Then the user will only be able to select one of them.

In this example, the user can select a value that will represent the state he is in by selecting the appropriate radio button (see Figure 19.4).

```
<FORM>
<INPUT TYPE=radio NAME="State" Value="TX">Texas<br>
<INPUT TYPE=radio NAME="State" Value="NJ">New Jersey<br>
<INPUT TYPE=radio NAME="State" Value="IL">Illinois<br>
<INPUT TYPE=radio NAME="State" Value="GA">Georgia<br>
<INPUT TYPE=radio NAME="State" Value="HI">Hawaii
</FORM>
```

Figure 19.4.
Radio buttons on an HTML form.

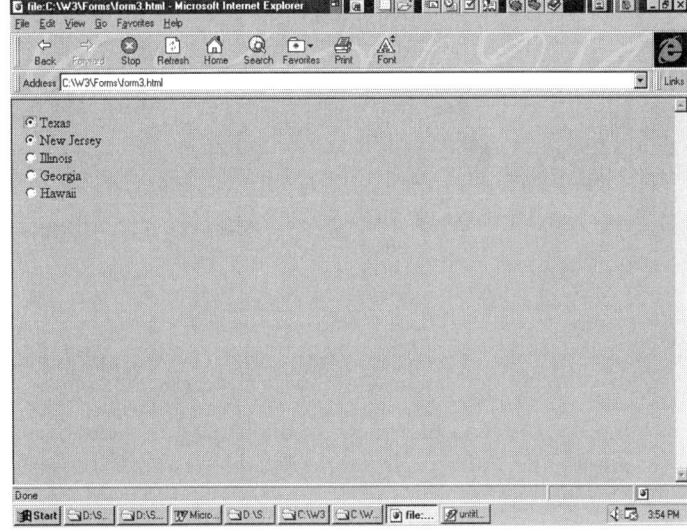

Input Type: text

Another input type is called text. The text box allows users to input a string of characters instead of selecting from predefined options. This input type uses two additional attributes: SIZE and MAXLENGTH. SIZE defines how many characters the text box can display. MAXLENGTH defines the maximum number of characters allowed in the text box.

The SIZE attribute can be set to one number, such as 24, while the user can still enter more than 24 characters into the form. This is because the SIZE attribute only defines how many character can be *shown*. The MAXLENGTH attribute defines how long the character string can be, and in this case, if it is set to more than 24 characters, the user will be able to enter a data string that is longer than the text box can display.

If you do not specify the MAXLENGTH value, there will be no limit to the length of the string. Actually there is, but depending on the environment, you won't want to use a string longer than 255 characters, and the maximum is close to 65,000 characters. If you want to send an information stream that long, you should consider breaking it up into parts, or submitting it as a binary file.

In the following example, the text box is set to request the user's name. The text box will show 24 characters, and will allow a maximum of 32 characters:

```
<FORM>
User Name:
<INPUT TYPE="textT NAME="txtUserName" SIZE=24 MAXLENGTH=32>
</FORM>
```

> **Using the Yahoo! Search Form**
>
> Yahoo!, Inc. allows users to place HTML on its pages to perform a search on its database of Web sites. This code uses the default text type and the Submit button:
>
> ```
> <FORM METHOD=GET ACTION = "http://search.yahoo.com/bin/search">
> ```
>
> Yahoo Search:
>
> ```
> <INPUT SIZE=30 NAME=p>
> <INPUT TYPE="submit" VALUE="Submit">
> </FORM>
> ```

An alternative to the text type of input is the `textarea` type. This works exactly the same as `text`, except that it allows multiline entries by the users.

If the text that the user is expected to enter is of a sensitive nature, use the password type of input form. This one also works exactly like a text box, except every character is replaced by an asterisk (*).

By no means does this cover all types of user input used within forms, but it gives a good summary of some of the ways users are able to input data. As the HTML specification grows and the market comes up with new ways to request user input, one day there just might be an input type called `RetinaScan`!

NOTE Any Form object input type can have a name. In fact, if it does not have a name, other objects cannot interact with it.

The previous chapter talked about giving each Form object a name and conforming to a naming standard, such as `frmForm`. Input types should also follow a naming convention. Here are a few suggestions, but there are many, many more controls as well:

Table 19.1. Naming conventions: Form object input types.

Object	Prefix	Sample
Button	cmd	cmdCommand
Ani button	ani	aniButton
Image	img	imgImage
Vertical line	lin	linVertical
3D panel	pnl	pnlPanel
Check box	chk	chkBox

Object	Prefix	Sample
Slider	sld	sldProgressBar
Combo box	cbo	cboListBox
List box	lst	lstListBox
Horizontal Scroll	hsb	hsbHorizontalScrollBar
Vertical Scroll	vsb	vsbVerticalScrollBar
Spinner	spn	spnSpinControl
Text box	txt	txtTextBox
Label	lbl	lblLabel

WARNING

If the user puts information into an HTML form, later pages might be able to reference the History object and retrieve this information—even though the user never meant for the new page to have access to it. The wise HTML author does his users a great service by ensuring that this information is cleared, obscured or otherwise made unavailable to later pages. This can be done by scripting some code in the onUnLoad event in the HTML document. When the page is unloaded, the code can set the values of the form to other values from what the user supplied. Be sure to do this *after* any processes that reference the form values are complete.

Input types allow a variety of ways for the user to enter information. Even if the user enters his data, the value of these data-input features can still be rendered null without something to retrieve the information. Then the item that retrieved the information must either store it for future use (such as in a cookie), or act on it before or while the user passes on to the next page (such as through a bit of VBScript).

Because input types such as the textarea and password do not in and of themselves DO anything, some sort of client or server script or an ActiveX control must reference the information provided. If the METHOD attribute of the <FORM> tag is POST instead of GET, information in named objects contained within the named form are passed to another HTML item, such as a CGI script or Web page.

In a `Post` (or `Query`) method, named values are sent after a `?`, and each value is separated from the others by an `&`. A URL would look something like this:

```
http://www.cnct.com/~davidk/cgi/search.exe?Name=David&Daughter=Shaina
```

This URL would access the fictional server script `search.exe` on the server `www.cnct.com` in the directory `/~davidk/cgi/`. It would then submit the value of the `Name` and `Daughter` variables (`David` and `Shaina`, respectively) and wait for a confirmation or other document to be returned to the browser.

Image Maps

A very *graphical* method of providing user input is the clickable image map. Users can click a portion of an image, and the HTTP server or client will use the coordinates within the image on which the user clicked. To enable this feature you need, along with your Web page, an image and a defined map of that image.

The `<IMG>` Tag

As you begin writing with HTML, one of the first things you become familiar with is the `<IMG>` tag. This tag allows you to insert a graphic (usually `.GIF` or `.JPG`) into your document. The following example would insert an image called `sample.gif` into your document:

```
<img src="http://www.domain.net/sample.gif">
```

Specify the dimensions of the graphic with the `height` and `width` attributes like so:

```
<img src="http://www.domain.net/sample.gif" height=64 width=64>
```

Let's assume that 128×128 is the actual size of the graphic, so you don't need to bother with these sizing attributes. Just remember that you are not restricted to the original size of the graphic.

`ISMAP` and `UseMap` Map Names

To identify an image as a server-side clickable map, add the `ISMAP` attribute to the `<IMG>` tag:

```
<img src="http://www.domain.net/sample.gif" ISMAP>
```

To identify an image as a client-side clickable map, add the `USEMAP="mapname"` attribute to the `<IMG>` tag:

```
<img src="http://www.domain.net/sample.gif" USEMAP="sample.map">
```

After you designate your image as a clickable image map, define the attributes of the map. These attributes define which portions of the map perform which actions. This map information can be contained within the Web page itself, or the data could be in an external `.MAP` file.

WARNING

If you don't define the location of the map information within the document using the USEMAP attribute, make sure that the HTTP server software supports the passing of the click coordinates correctly, and use the ISMAP attribute.

Map Information Within HTML

To place map information within an HTML document, use the `<MAP> <MAP>` container tag. Ideally, this should appear in the `<HEAD>` of the document.

One or more `<AREA>` tags should appear within the `<MAP>` container tags. `<AREA>` tags define the shape of each area within the image, and what action will be taken when the user clicks within those areas. The `<AREA>` tag uses three attributes to do this: SHAPE, COORDS and HREF.

SHAPE

There are three shapes you can use in an image map—rectangle (RECT), polygon (POLY) and circle (CIRC). If no SHAPE attribute is specified, the default is rectangle.

COORDS

Coordinates are determined based on the standard x,y format. In our example, the graphic is 128×128 pixels in size. So, the coordinates for the upper-left corner of the image are 0,0, and the coordinates for the lower-right corner of the image are 128,128.

The COORD attribute to define the *entire* rectangle of an image would appear as `0,0,128,128`. To define only the left side of the image, use `0,0,64,128`. To define only the right side of the image, use `64,0,128,128`.

NOTE

The x1,x2,x3,x4 (left, top, bottom, right) format is good for a rectangle.

A circle would use x,x,x (CenterX, CenterY, radius).

A polygon would use x1,x2,x3,x4...x1 (each point of the polygon, ending with the original point).

Do	Don't
Do remember that the order of these numbers is left, top, bottom, right.	Don't get the numbers out of order, or you will experience unexpected results.

HREF

Finally, the <AREA> tag uses the HREF attribute. This defines the action that will be taken when a user clicks the specified area. In its simplest form, the HREF attribute points to an HTML document, such as gohere.html. Alternatively, it could point to a named anchor in the current document (such as <A NAME = gohere>). To specify one of these anchors, preface the name with the pound sign (#) (such as <a href="#MyLocation">My Location</a>).

The UseMap Image Attribute

```
<IMG
    SRC = [Image File]
    UseMap = [Map File]
>
```

The UseMap attribute of the <IMG> tag is used to assign hyperlinks to regions defined within an image map. The image map can be contained in the current document or in an external .MAP file.

Example:

```
<IMG SRC=MyImage.JPG Height=64 width=64 UseMap="MyMap.MAP">
```

This tag inserts a 64×64 image into the current position in the page. When the user clicks an area within the image, an action will be taken based on the <AREA> tags in the map file "MyMap.MAP".

Now let's take a look at the maps themselves. Figure 19.5 has a 128×128 graphic containing four distinctive areas. The event that is performed depends on which quadrant is clicked by the user's mouse.

```
<MAP NAME="FourSquare">
<AREA SHAPE="RECT" COORDS="0,0,32,32" href="TopLeft.html >
<AREA SHAPE="RECT" COORDS="0,32,32,64" href="BottomLeft.html >
<AREA SHAPE="RECT" COORDS="32,0,64,32" href="TopRight.html >
<AREA SHAPE="RECT" COORDS="32,32,64,64" href="BottomRight.html >
</MAP>
<IMG SRC="foursquare.gif" USEMAP="#FourSquare">
```

The <MAP> Container Tag

```
<MAP NAME=[Map Name]>
<AREA SHAPE=[Shape] COORDS= [Left], [Top], [Bottom], [Right] HREF=[HyperLink]>
</MAP>
```

The <MAP> container tag defines a hyperlink for different areas within an image. These areas, or *hotspots*, are defined with one or more <AREA> tags.

Example:

```
<MAP NAME="MyMap">
<AREA SHAPE="Rect" COORDS= "0,0,64,64" HREF="NewPage.html">
</MAP>
```

This map specifies a rectangle, 64×64 pixels, in the top-left corner of the image. When the user clicks this rectangle, "NewPage.html" is loaded.

Figure 19.5.
A clickable image map. Each quadrant is identical in size, and the entire graphic is 128×128 pixels.

Map Information Within an External .MAP File

To place map information within an external .MAP file, you must create a text file. The extension for the map file can be anything you want, but the file itself must be a text file. The map file consists of the same <AREA> tags found in the attributes of a <MAP> container described previously.

WARNING

> If you use an external map file, you will not be able to test your page locally. You must post the test pages on a live server so that the server can process your mouse clicks. The only way to test your image maps locally is to use the <MAP> </MAP> tags within the document so the browser can process the mouse clicks.

> **TIP** A good reason to use client-side processing rather than server-side processing is that it's just plain good writing to keep the demand on server resources to a minimum. Distributed data processing is almost always more efficient than centralized data processing.

User Input Via HTML Scripting

Let's briefly discuss some ways that you can obtain user input via a scripting engine, such as JavaScript (JScript) or VBScript. Bear in mind that whether you use VBScript, JavaScript, Perl, LISP, or a generic public domain script, each requires a scripting engine (usually a .DLL or two). These engines are based on the guidelines published by the WWW Consortium (http://www.w3.org).

User Input with VBScript

VBScript offers several different methods for providing user input. The more complex ones involve using embedded objects, but I want to focus on how to provide objects with user input, or how to get data from the objects themselves. This means you will be dealing with very basic forms of user input.

Intrinsic Events

Each object has its own built-in events. These events are routines that are run whenever the user performs a given action, or when a particular state that is being monitored changes.

Some of these events, such as onLoad and onUnload, are pretty obvious. I want to cover those related to the Form's collection object.

- OnClick—Fires within a mapped image that the user clicks.
- OnFocus—Fires within the select, input or textarea object when the user clicks or tabs to it.
- OnBlur—Fires within the select, input or textarea element when the user focuses on an object outside the Form object.
- OnSubmit—Fires within the Form object when the user selects the submit action.
- OnSelect—Fires within the input or textarea element when the user highlights (or selects) text.

User Interaction with ActiveX Controls

WARNING

A script can perform almost any of these functions, even if the user does not actually request it through the pushing of a button or whatever. The script can do this by sending a command, such as Button_Click, instead of waiting for the user to actually click a button. This adds a level of power to the script writer, but has no way of proving that the user wants the data sent. You must verify that another way—by using code that has been validated through a trust verification service, for example.

Intrinsic Events

SYNTAX
```
Sub [Object]_[Event]
End Sub
```

Several events are built into most, if not all, ActiveX controls. These events can be scripted through an engine, such as VBScript, to respond to a particular event in a particular way.

Example:

If, for example, you want to play a *tick* sound every time the user selects an object, and a *tock* sound whenever he deselects it, create a subroutine for each event that looks something like the following bit of code:

```
Sub MyControl_OnFocus
    PlaySound(Tick)
End Sub
Sub MyControl_OnBlur
    PlaySound(Tock)
End Sub
```

User Input Via Visual Basic

Although HTML forms provide programmers with a rich set of tools with which a user input interface can be created, they don't hold a candle to the ones available from within a programming language like Visual Basic (see Figure 19.6). This is because HTML was developed to be usable on any and every computer. Visual Basic is used to program only within the Windows environment.

The beauty of Visual Basic, when it comes to ActiveX programming, is that you are no longer limited to performing Internet functions through a Web browser or a command-line utility (blech!). All of the parts and pieces of Windows are exposed to Visual Basic, and the programmer can reference these objects in conjunction with the appropriate WinSock interfaces. These parts and pieces include the Common Dialog controls and the routines in the Visual Basic Runtime library, as well as any other very complex and powerful libraries that may be installed on the user's machine, like Remote Access.

> **Remote Access Service**
>
> A Windows NT domain can be managed completely over TCP/IP connections. Powerful as this is, it also provides a path for malicious guests to spray virtual graffiti all over your servers.
>
> To minimize this risk, there is a set of APIs called *Remote Access*. The Remote Access Service provides an interface where an NT server and all of its workstations can make the other system services available, while limiting control of security operations to those with appropriate access permissions.
>
> When creating Visual Basic applications that will be run over a WAN, LAN or other NT domain, it is a good idea to use the features of RAS (Remote Access Service) whenever possible. Your program will then be usable by folks who are limited to RAS access to their systems, while still being usable to those with Internet connections.

Figure 19.6.
The Visual Basic IDE provides the programmer with a variety of rich features for facilitating user input.

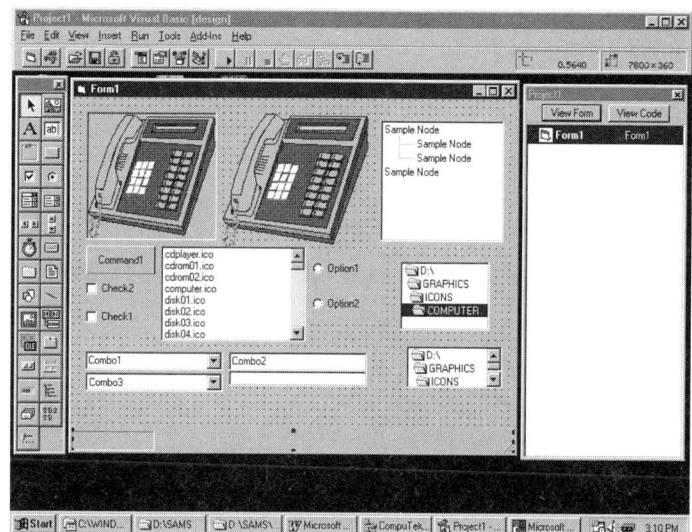

Figure 19.6 is a Visual Basic form. From it, you can see that Visual Basic has a number of different methods for providing user input. Drop-down and scrolling lists, images, and buttons are all familiar from standard HTML forms. There are also a few others: Tree view and directory view are part of the user's Windows environment, not part of the HTML specification (yet).

This bit of code in a Visual Basic project will display a message box when the user presses a command button named cmdPressMe.

```
Private Sub cmdPressMe_Click()
    MsgBox ("I'm Pressed")
End Sub
```

Activate your own Visual Basic I/O interfaces through the simple addition of an ActiveX control, such as one that comes in the Internet Control Pack. These controls allow you to create standalone applications that work over your machine's WinSock to support FTP, NNTP, HTTP, SMTP/POP3, and so on within your own application.

Summary

This chapter familiarized you with the available user-input mechanisms that allow the use of user-supplied data with ActiveX controls.

In HTML, INPUT items are contained within the <FORM> </FORM> container tags. Each INPUT item has a Name and a Type, as well as a Value. The first two are defined within the HTML document. The third, Value, is defined either programmatically (through a script) or by the users when they click a button or enter text.

Some input types that you can use include

- reset—Clears all data from the current form.
- submit—Sends all data from the current form to the URL defined in ACTION.
- checkbox—Toggles a value as true or false.
- radio—Allows an interface to select one of many.
- text—Allows entry of a string of characters by the user.
- textarea—Same as a text box, but allows multiline entry.
- password—Allows entry of masked text.

Q&A

Q There are a lot of different browsers made by a lot of different companies. What browser supports ActiveX objects?

A To create a clickable image map, your Web page must be hosted by an HTTP server that supports this feature. In all other cases, the objects reviewed in this chapter require only that the browser supports ActiveX. Microsoft Internet Explorer supports ActiveX controls as well as HTML, Java and VBScript.

Q What makes a browser or utility "ActiveX enabled"?

A A browser or application is ActiveX enabled when it supports the object and scripting conventions of ActiveX.

Q Where can I find support for the specifications of ActiveX objects and controls?

A The best site for up-to-date information on ActiveX specifications is `http://www.microsoft.com/intdev`. This is the Microsoft ActiveX Developers Web Site.

Q How is ActiveX different from Java or HTML?

A HTML provides the framework under which OOP is implemented in Web pages. Java was one implementation of that framework. ActiveX provides the framework under which a client machine is defined, as well as its component objects. This allows a Web page to call on features within the user's machine (such as PowerPoint, Word, Excel, Access, Project, Schedule+, and so on) as well as within objects on the Net (through FTP, HTTP, and so on).

Workshop

Create a Web page to be used for sending mailing-list information. Include the following features within a form:

Text boxes for first name and last name.

Radio button to select state.

Text boxes for address, city, zip code and phone number.

Spinner button for age.

Add a Submit button to the document, and code it to send the information from the form to an imaginary CGI called `MailList.exe`.

Quiz

1. Which container tag is used to define a Form object?
2. What tag and attributes define an input item, such as a command button or a text box?
3. What object returns the data entered by the user?
4. What would you name a list box called AllofUs?
5. Which object is used to allow a basic true/false input?
6. What property defines the maximum input for a text box?
7. Which methods of an HTML form allow the posting and requesting of data?
8. Which attribute of the <INPUT> tag defines the I/O control to be used?
9. Which attribute of the <IMG> tag defines an image as being associated with a clickable map?
10. When defining the coordinates of a mouse click, with what do the positions in the x1,x2,x3,x4 format correspond?

NOTE Refer to the appendix, "Answers," for the answers to these questions.

Week 3

Day 20

Using the Internet Control Pack

Microsoft licensed a set of controls from NetManage that allows programmers to add standard Internet features to their applications. Supported protocols of this control pack include FTP, NNTP, SMTP, POP3, HTTP, and, of course, straight WinSock.

Any IDE that is an OLE container application and supports custom controls can use this control pack. Some of these programs include Visual Basic, Access, Visual FoxPro, Visual C++, and many more. For demonstration purposes (and because of its similarity to VBScript, with which you are familiar), you will use Visual Basic.

You will use Visual Basic to create several Internet projects, including

- A POP3 mail checker
- An SMTP mail-sending utility
- An HTML Web browser

☐ An HTTP keyword-search utility
☐ An FTP directory-information utility
☐ An NNTP newsgroup-information utility

HTML.OCX—Hypertext Markup Language Control

The HTML control is a powerful Web-page-viewing tool that can request, retrieve, parse and display a Web document. Figure 20.1 shows the HTML control loaded in Visual Basic.

NOTE If you are creating a project for distribution, make sure the dependent files, including NMOCOD.DLL, NMORENU.DLL, NMSCKN.DLL, NMW3VWN.DLL, and HTML.OCX, are distributed as well.

Figure 20.1.
The HTML control, shown in the lower-right corner of the tool box.

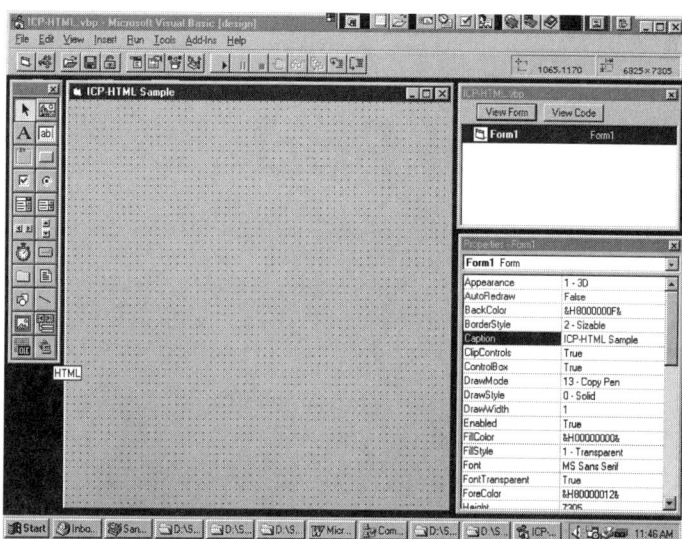

To learn to use the functions of the HTML control within Visual Basic, you will create a basic Web-browser program using the following steps:

1. Create a new form with an HTML control, then add a simple text box and command button (see Figure 20.2). The user enters his URL in the text box and, after pressing the command button, the URL is launched in the HTML control.

2. Code the action to be taken (in this case, when the user presses the command button). You need only add code on the command button's Click event:

```
Private Sub cmdGo_Click()
    HTML.RequestDoc txtURL.Text
End Sub
```

The HTML Control's RequestDoc Method

SYNTAX

HTML.RequestDoc URL

The HTML.RequestDoc method is used to retrieve and display the HTML document returned by an HTTP request from the supplied URL. For example, HTML.RequestDoc http://www.microsoft.com/activex will retrieve and display Microsoft's ActiveX home page.

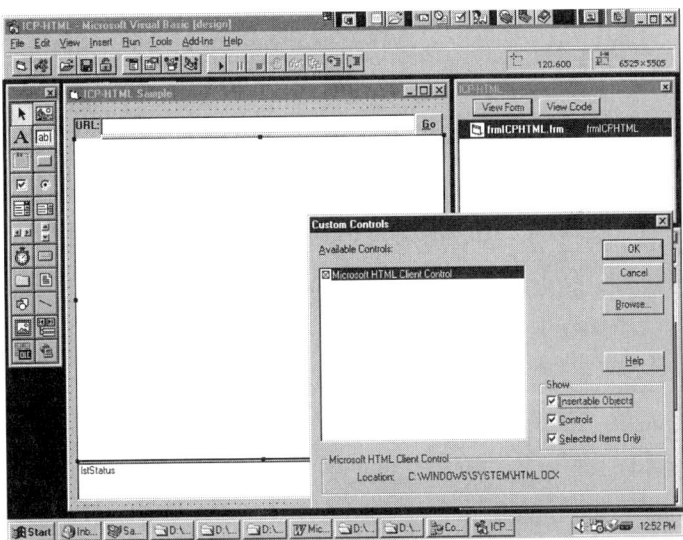

Figure 20.2.
A simple Web browser application using Visual Basic and the ICP HTML control.

3. Enable different status indicators. In Figure 20.2, you added a list box named lstStatus. You will now add status indicators to this list box to log certain activities; add the code as follows:

```
Private Sub HTML_BeginRetrieval()
    lstStatus.AddItem "Retrieving: " & txtURL.Text
End Sub

Private Sub HTML_DoRequestDoc(ByVal URL As String, ByVal Element
➥As HTMLElement, ByVal
 DocInput As DocInput, EnableDefault As Boolean)
    lstStatus.AddItem "Connecting to: " & txtURL.Text
    txtURL = URL
End Sub
```

```
Private Sub HTML_EndRetrieval()
    lstStatus.AddItem "Document Complete"
End Sub
```

 To see a working example of this sample application, refer to the \vb4\icp- directory on the enclosed CD-ROM.

For the basic meat and potatoes of a Web browser, that's all there is to it. However, several additional properties, methods and events are available within the HTML control; I suggest you acquaint yourself with them to add powerful functionality to the display of your Web content.

HTTPct.OCX—Hypertext Transfer Protocol Client Control

The HTTP control (see Figure 20.3) can perform low-level HTTP commands with the GET and PUT methods. It does not, however, perform any kind of interpretation on the markup.

The HTTP control is one of those tools that is useful for digging up *meta-information* (information about information). Even if you've never used a professional Web browser, you've seen the basics of what they can do in the previous sample (refer to Figure 20.2).

Figure 20.3.
The cursor is pointing to the HTTP control in the lower-right corner of the tool box.

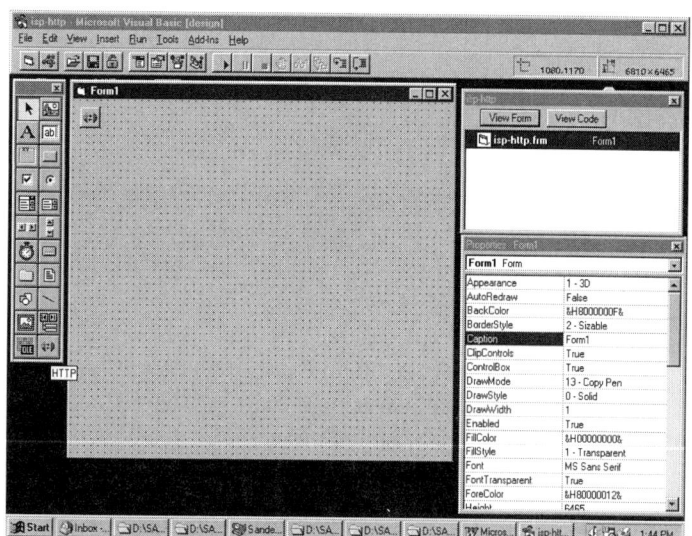

NOTE Remember: HTTP is a protocol; HTML is a document format.

Millions of individuals and organizations that want to distribute information have put graphical information presentations on the Web. Although these presentations are very end-user-friendly, there is no predefined, global, everybody-does-it *format* for these displays. There is, however, a predefined, global, everybody-uses-it *stream* for transferring these displays; it's called *HTTP*.

By tapping into the HTTP stream, you can capture information within the document or data being transferred. Then you can perform programmatic functions on that information, such as a keyword search.

To demonstrate how the HTTP control works, let's create a simple application. This application takes a user-defined URL and searches for instances of a user-defined keyword within the URL's pages. Follow these steps to create the application:

1. Create a new project in Visual Basic. Add a form with text boxes, list boxes, and labels, as shown in Figure 20.4.

NOTE If you are creating a project for distribution, make sure the dependent files, including NMOCOD.DLL, NMORENU.DLL, NMSCKN.DLL, and HTTPct.OCX, are distributed as well.

Figure 20.4.
The shell for a Web-search application using Visual Basic and the ICP HTTP control.

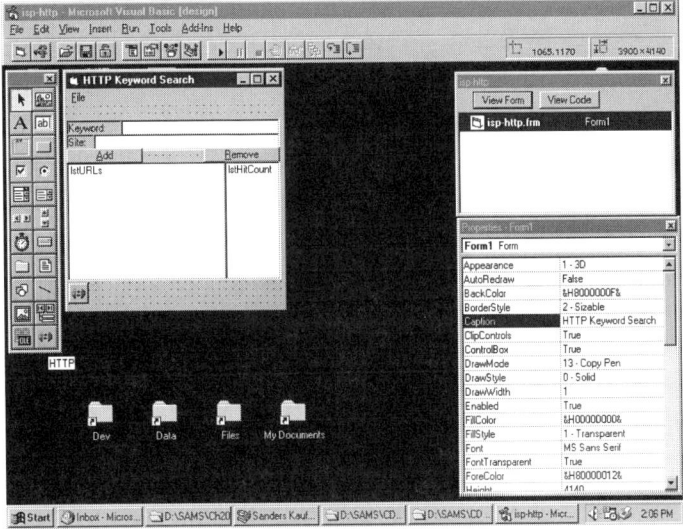

2. Add your standard features (such as Ctrl+X and File|Exit commands for closing the application). Then add functionality to the program. The function of the application you are creating is to send a request for a Web document and to search the resulting character stream for occurrences of the keyword.

3. Code the command button. When the form is initially run, it waits for the user to enter a URL into the text bar and to press the Add button. This will add this site and its results to the list of search results. The code to do this is contained within the Add button's `Click` event:

```
Private Sub cmdAddSite_Click()
    lblStatus = "Searching: " & txtURL.Text
    HTTP.URL = txtURL.Text
    HTTP.GetDoc txtURL.Text
    lstURLs.AddItem txtURL.Text
    lstHitCount.AddItem "Searching"
End Sub
```

Now, when the user clicks the Add button (line 1), the status bar indicates that a search is in progress (line 2). In lines 3 and 4, the HTTP control is told to request the Web page at the URL in the text box. When this request is made, one of two things happens: Either it works or it doesn't.

4. If it doesn't work, put a line in the search results and the status bar defining the error as reported by the `HTTP_Error` event:

```
Private Sub HTTP_Error(Number As Integer, Description As String,
➥ Scode As Long, Source As
String, HelpFile As String, HelpContext As Long, CancelDisplay As Boolean)
    lblStatus.Caption = Description
    lstURLs.AddItem txtURL
    lstHitCount.AddItem "Error"
End Sub
```

5. If it does work, the `DocOutput` event will fire. Within this event, code the process that reads the incoming data into a buffer, and add the process that scans the buffer for the keyword.

In the following example, look for the state to change to `Data` mode. Then scan whatever comes in for the value of the `Text` property of the text box (such as a user-defined keyword). If there's a match, log it to the results display. When the state changes to `Transfer Complete` mode, log that to the display as well.

```
Private Sub HTTP_DocOutput(ByVal DocOutput As DocOutput)
    Select Case DocOutput.State
        Case 0   'No Activity
        Case 1   'Beginning Transfer
        Case 2   'DocHeader Transfer Beginning
        Case 3   'Data transferred
            DocOutput.GetData Content, 8
            If InStr(1, Content, txtKeyword.Text, 1) Then
                lstURLs.AddItem HTTP.URL
                lstHitCount.AddItem "Match"
            End If
```

```
            Case 4  'Error
            Case 5  'Transfer Complete
                    lstURLs.AddItem HTTP.URL
                    lstHitCount.AddItem "Finished"
        End Select
End Sub
```

 To see a working example of this sample application, refer to the \vb4\icp- directory on the enclosed CD-ROM.

Using this code as is, you can create a basic application that will search Web sites for key phrases. Companies such as Yahoo!, WebCrawler, and even Microsoft use these kinds of search methods to find content, without having to deal with the variations in individual styles of presentation.

SMTPct.OCX—Simple Mail Transfer Protocol Client Control

The SMTP control (see Figure 20.5) can perform both basic and high-level e-mail *sending* functions. Using this control, you can make various e-mail reporting functions automatic, acquiring information for the message programmatically through Visual Basic.

Figure 20.5.
The cursor is pointing to the SMTP control in the lower-right corner of the tool box. Also, an SMTP control is shown loaded onto the form.

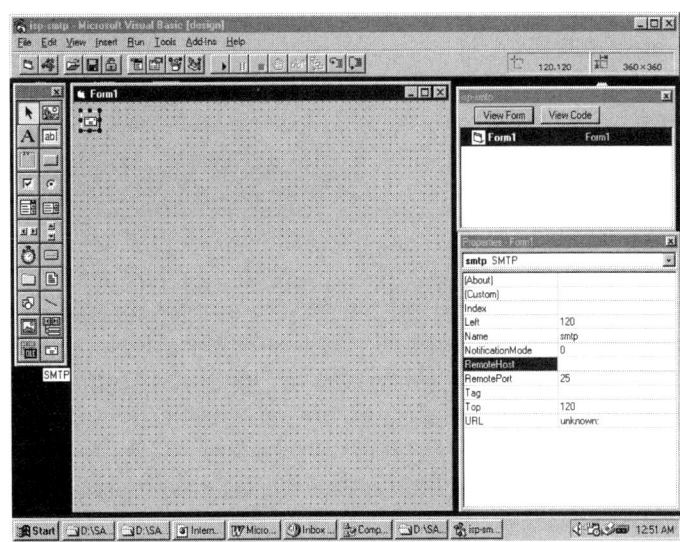

To demonstrate the use of this control, let's make a simple mail-sending program. It will use basic fields (To, From, and Subject) and will have a multiline text box for the message body.

The user will have to supply the name of the mail server. To create this application, perform the following steps:

1. Create a Visual Basic form with text boxes, labels, and so on (see Figure 20.6). These text boxes will define the areas within which the user will enter the header and body information for the message.

Note: If you are creating a project for distribution, make sure that the dependent files, including NMOCOD.DLL, NMORENU.DLL, NMSCKN.DLL, and SMTPct.OCX, are distributed as well.

Figure 20.6.
The shell for a mail-sending utility using Visual Basic and the ICP SMTP control.

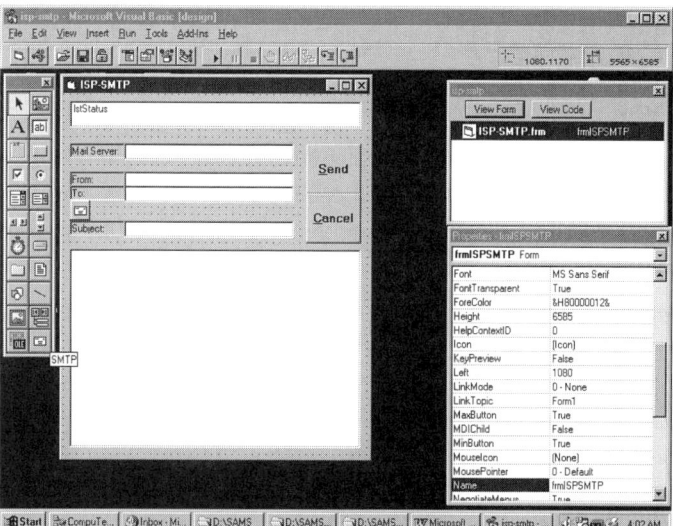

2. Add some code behind the Send button. When the user finishes composing his message, he presses the Send button; the code that you have added launches a series of activities that transmits the message from the user to the destination e-mail address.

The code behind the Send button looks something like this:

```
Private Sub cmdSend_Click()
'Fill in the Document Headers
   With SMTP.DocInput.Headers
       .Add "From", txtFrom.Text
       .Add "To", txtFrom.Text
       .Add "Subject", txtFrom.Text
   End With
```

```
'Send the Message
    SMTP.RemoteHost = txtMailHost.Text
    SMTP.SendDoc , , txtMessage.Text
End Sub
```

In the first part of this code, the document headers are defined. These are the meat and potatoes of an Internet mail message. They are also the foundation for other network applications (such as HTTP and MIME).

In the second part of the code, the SMTP control connects to the mail server and sends the text of the message.

To see a working example of this sample application, refer to the \vb4\icp-directory on the enclosed CD-ROM.

For the full text of the SMTP protocol, including some of the magical optional headers, refer to RFC-822 (http://ds0.internic.net/rfc/rfc822.txt).

Mail headers *must* include From and To headers, *should* include a Subject header, and the last section *can be* the body of the message. There are some additional, optional headers: CC to send a carbon copy to another recipient, BCC to send a blind carbon copy, Return-Receipt-To to receive confirmation of a message receipt, or Reply To to allow the receiver reply to an address other than the originator's.

Some interesting headers with which you can work include:

- X-Mailer—Defines which mailer program is sending the message.
- Keywords—Defines a few words, relative to the message topic, from which a search can be performed quickly.
- Comments—Allows an area in which miscellaneous notes can be embedded in the message.
- Content-Type—Allows for MIME-encoded multimedia mail.

POP3ct.OCX—Post Office Protocol Client Control

In the previous section, you used SMTP to send an e-mail message to another person on the Net. What you might not realize is that your message probably didn't go directly to the addressee's computer; rather, it probably went to that person's post office, where it waited until the user retrieved it using his preferred mail program (see Figure 20.7).

Figure 20.7.
Several different mail programs are available, including Microsoft Internet Mail and News and Microsoft Exchange.

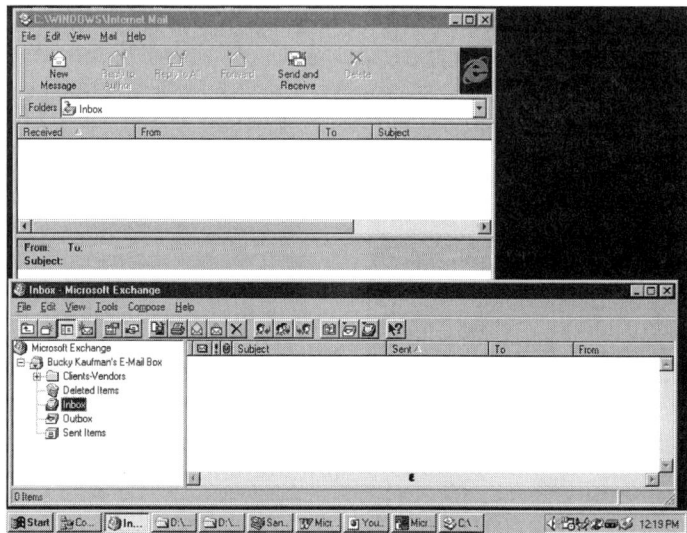

If you use an e-mail program such as Eudora, Internet Mail and News, or Microsoft Exchange (see Figure 20.7), you probably download your mail from a mail server (your post office), and then read it when you're darn good and ready.

Using an e-mail program is the easy way to read mail, as opposed to checking your mail via Telnet and a UNIX shell. When you access your mail server with those kinds of Rlogin (remote login) utilities, you are reading your mail directly from the server. To retrieve the messages and read them at your leisure offline, you need to use an e-mail client that supports the POP3 Post Office Protocol.

The POP3 control is used to retrieve mail or information about mail from an Internet server. To demonstrate the use of this control, let's create a simple application to check mail and see how many messages are waiting.

1. Create a Visual Basic form with text boxes, labels, and so on (see Figure 20.8).

> **NOTE**
>
> If you are creating a project for distribution, make sure the dependent files, including NMOCOD.DLL, NMORENU.DLL, NMSCKN.DLL, and POP3ct.OCX, are distributed as well.

Figure 20.8.
The shell for a mail-checking utility using Visual Basic and the ICP POP3 control.

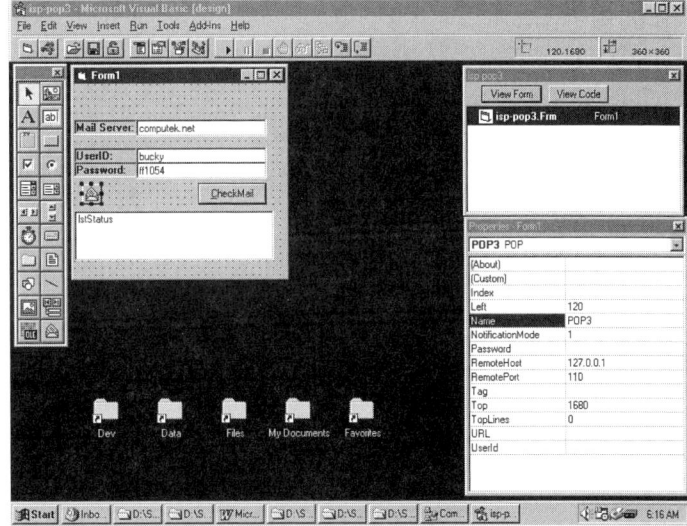

2. Code the procedures that occur when the user clicks the command button labeled Check Mail.

   In this sample, the user supplies certain basic information (UserID, Password, and Mail Host). He then presses the Check Mail button whenever he wants to check his e-mail. As with the earlier samples in this chapter, you are making this application to perform one function—check the mail. Therefore, the code that starts the process is in the Check Mail button.

   ```
   Private Sub cmdCheckMail_Click()
       POP3.Connect txtRemotehost.Text
   End Sub
   ```

   This begins the logon process. When the systems connect, the ProtocolStateChanged event fires and returns a value of 1 (Authorizing). At this point, you are connected to the POP server, but you need to fire off your authentication before you can do anything there.

NOTE If you want to see what goes on in the background of an SMTP transfer, use Telnet to connect to your mail host on port 25. Then you can log in manually (with your logon name and password). To see what commands your mail host supports, enter help or ? when prompted. (Remember: *be very, very careful.*) You can also perform this on port 21 to an FTP server and, to some extent, with your Usenet news server on port 119 without even logging in.

3. Monitor the state of the protocol to determine the proper time to send your UserID and Password for the server to authenticate. This is conducted using a bit of code in the `ProtocolStateChanged` event like so:

```
Private Sub POP3_ProtocolStateChanged(ByVal ProtocolState As Integer)
If ProtocolState = 1 Then
    POP3.Authenticate txtUserID.Text, txtPassword.Text
End If
End Sub
```

4. Code the way the computer handles the response when the server tells it how many messages are waiting.

When you are logged on and authenticated, the server sends you information—such as the number of messages waiting. Retrieve this information from the `RefreshMessageCount` event. This event fires immediately after logon:

```
Private Sub POP3_RefreshMessageCount(ByVal Number As Long)
    lstStatus.AddItem "Message Count: " & Number
End Sub
```

To see a working example of this sample application, refer to the \vb4\icp- directory on the enclosed CD-ROM.

Now that you are familiar with the POP3 and SMTP controls, you should be able to create your own e-mail programs instead of requiring bulky and expensive third-party programs.

NNTPct.OCX—Network News Transfer Protocol Client Control

In the previous section, you used SMTP to send an e-mail message to another person on the Net and POP3 to retrieve your own messages. You had to use two different controls because the sending and receiving of private e-mail occurs through two different protocols. News messages, however, only require one protocol (and thus, one control) because they are not sent to one individual; they are broadcasted to anyone who happens to be listening.

NOTE Microsoft operates a public news server at news://msnews.microsoft.com. This server provides a forum for users of Microsoft products (in other words, everybody) to discuss and receive tech support on Microsoft products and technologies. Microsoft even has a cadre of MVPs (Most Valued Professionals) who unofficially monitor these groups and provide assistance.

If you have Internet access, you probably already have the use of an NNTP, or Usenet news server. Each server makes all incoming messages to a particular newsgroup available to the subscribers of that newsgroup. Each server also broadcasts articles (messages) posted by subscribers and makes them available to all the servers that request it. For this reason, a news provider must either maintain *only* its own newsgroups (like Microsoft does), or accept all news traffic (like most ISP news servers do). These newsgroups can be read by any of the NNTP news readers, of which Microsoft's Internet Mail and News client is only one (see Figure 20.9).

Figure 20.9.
Microsoft's Internet Mail and News Client.

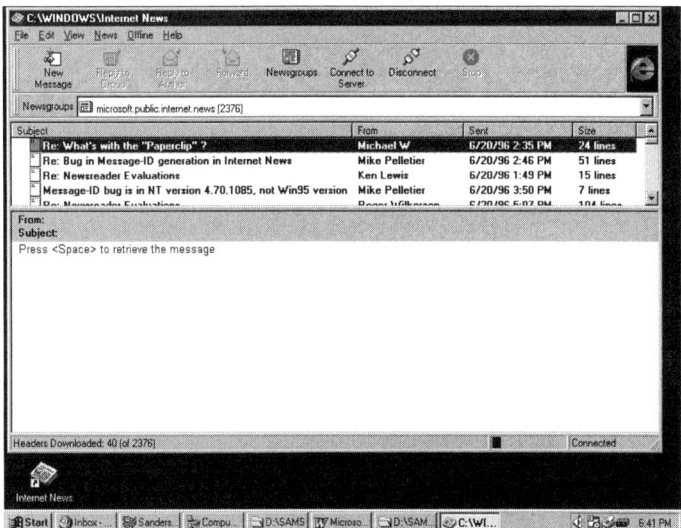

The NNTP control is used to post articles to and retrieve articles from a news server. To demonstrate a few of the basic functions of this control, let's make a simple application to log on to Microsoft's news server and report information about the articles available.

1. Create a Visual Basic form with text boxes, labels, and so on (see Figure 20.10).

NOTE If you are creating a project for distribution, make sure the dependent files, including NMOCOD.DLL, NMORENU.DLL, NMSCKN.DLL, and NNTPct.OCX are distributed as well.

Figure 20.10.
The shell for a Usenet meta-information utility using Visual Basic and the ICP NNTP control.

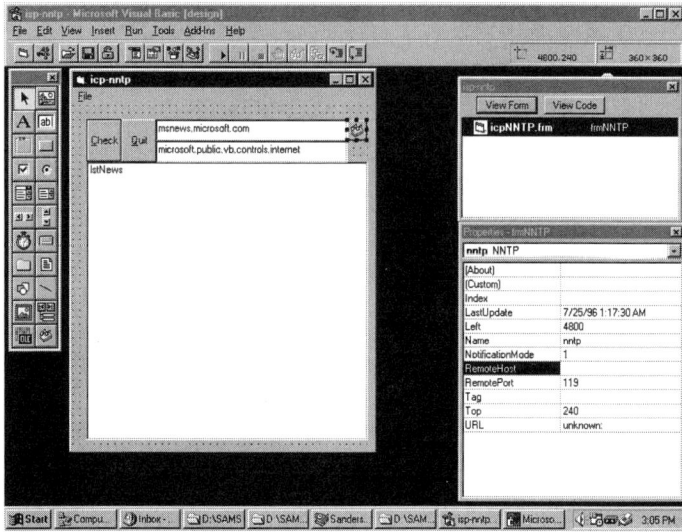

In the NNTP example, the users enter the news server and name of the newsgroup from which they wish to retrieve message information. When data is entered in both, they press the Check button to poll the server.

2. Code how the program will behave when the user clicks the Check button. In this case, the program allows the user to connect to the news server.

   To poll the server, connect to it, and provide any UserID and Password information required by your Usenet provider. For the most part, connecting is done simply by coding the connect button as follows:

   ```
   Private Sub cmdCheck_Click()
       NNTP.Connect txtNewsHost.Text
   End Sub
   ```

3. Monitor the `ProtocolStateChanged` event of the NNTP control. After the connection request is made and the remote server responds, the state of the protocol changes. This fires the `ProtocolStateChanged` event. When this event fires with a protocol state of 1 (Connected), you must have a bit of code that immediately tells the server which group you want to access:

   ```
   Private Sub NNTP_ProtocolStateChanged(ByVal ProtocolState As Integer)
       If ProtocolState = 1 Then NNTP.SelectGroup txtNewsGroup.Text
   End Sub
   ```

4. After your program successfully executes the `SelectGroup` method, the control will respond by firing the `SelectGroup` event.

NOTE Remember: A *method* is the way you tell a control to do something; an *event* is the way the control tells you it did something.

5. After you tell the server which group you want to access, the server responds with information about that group, including the number of the first article, the number of the last article, and the total number of articles it is holding for that group. Retrieve that information in the SelectGroup event. To do this, code the NNTP_SelectGroup event as follows:

```
Private Sub NNTP_SelectGroup(ByVal groupName As String, ByVal firstMessage
➥As Long, ByVal lastMessage As Long, ByVal msgCount As Long)
    lstNews.AddItem "GroupName: " & groupName
    lstNews.AddItem "First Msg: " & firstMessage
    lstNews.AddItem "Last Msg:  " & lastMessage
    lstNews.AddItem "Total:     " & msgCount
    NNTP.Quit
End Sub
```

6. You're ready to test the project. If you are not already connected to the Internet, get there—then run the project. In the News Server box, enter msnews.microsoft.com. In the Newsgroup box, enter MSNBC.BreakingNews.

In this example, you performed the simplest of news functions. Explore the power of this utility in the retrieving and posting of articles, and in the decoding, formatting and displaying of news postings.

To see a working example of this sample application, refer to the \vb4\icp- directory on the enclosed CD-ROM.

Usenet News

Tens of thousands of Usenet newsgroups are available on most commercial services. Of those, several thousand are active. Many have traffic as high as several hundred messages per day.

Many professionals in a broad spectrum of disciplines use Usenet to keep in touch and to discuss the latest concerns in their field. Search tools (such as DejaNews) provide users with a powerful means of researching any topic. It's all discussed on Usenet.

`FTPct.OCX`—File Transfer Protocol Client Control

In the previous section, you used NNTP to retrieve information about a newsgroup (and you learned that this type of data is called *meta-information*). In this section, you will learn how to extract meta-information from an FTP server.

FTP servers are used to make files accessible over the Internet for individuals or the public. In fact, many users with dial-up accounts set up their own private FTP sites on their local machines to make files available for a short period of time (only while they're online, for example).

When you post information to any kind of Internet server (be it HTTP, FTP, Gopher, or whatever), you will usually post it via FTP. Several very popular FTP utilities are available for this operation. One of the best is the WinSock FTP-32 client (see Figure 20.11). In fact, most Web browsers, including Microsoft Internet Explorer and Netscape Navigator, already contain FTP client capabilities.

Figure 20.11.
The WinSock FTP-32 client application.

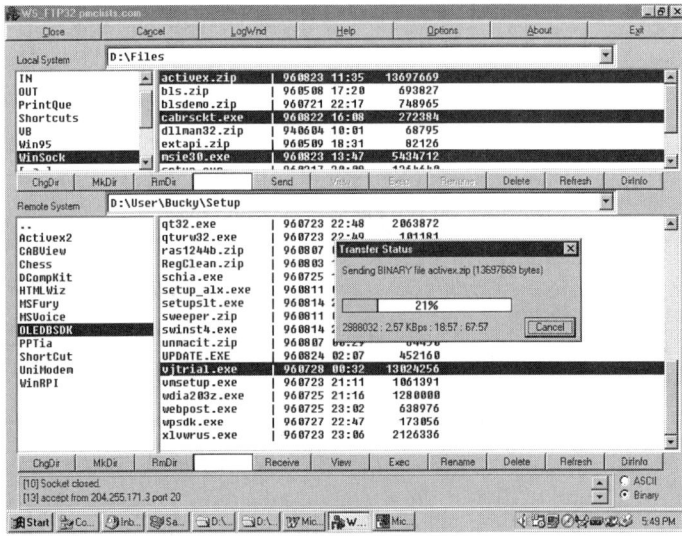

The Internet Control Pack's FTP control is a *client* control, not a *host* control. That means it is used to *retrieve* files, not make them available. However, with this control, you can add FTP retrieval features into your own applications—making the Internet portion of any application you write virtually invisible to the user. The following illustrates this:

1. From an MS-DOS command prompt, type FTP.exe FTP.Microsoft.Com. The output will be as follows:

   ```
   Connected to ftp.microsoft.com
   220 ftp Microsoft FTP Service (Version 2.0)
   User(ftp.microsoft.com:(none)): _
   ```

2. Respond to the User prompt as Anonymous. The output will be as follows:

   ```
   Password: _
   ```

3. Respond to the Password prompt with your e-mail address (*user@domain*.net). The output will be as follows:

   ```
   230-This is FTP.MICROSOFT.COM please read the file index.txt for additional
   ➥details.
   230 Anonymous user logged in.
   ftp>
   ```

4. Quit the FTP session by typing Quit. The output will be as follows:

   ```
   C:\Windows> _
   ```

Logging on to and off of an FTP server using the command line involves a great many steps. Placing those or any other processes in a graphical environment can greatly reduce the intimidation factor involved in getting your application accepted by potential users.

The FTP client control is terrific when you're building an Internet application that demands minimal user interaction. Command-line (see Figure 20.12) and graphical FTP (refer to Figure 20.11), as done today, is intimidating to users who are not familiar with basic Internet features such as directory trees and client/server connections.

Figure 20.12.
The Windows 95 command-line FTP Client.

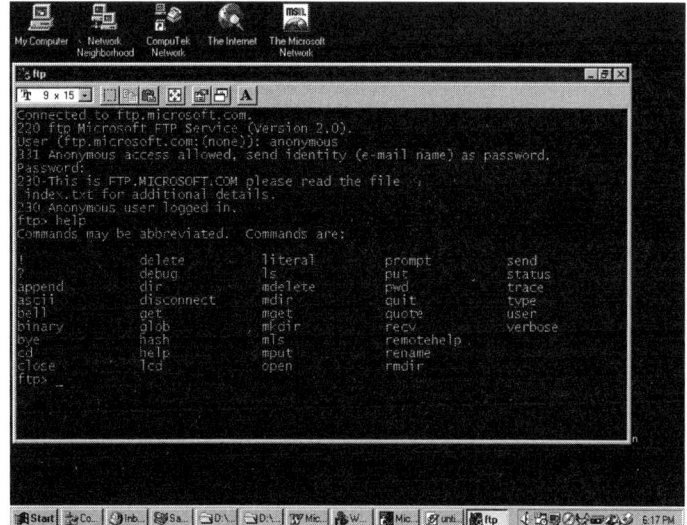

The FTP control is used to upload and download files from an FTP server. To demonstrate the basic functions of this control, let's create a simple application to log on to Microsoft's FTP server and report information about the available files. Follow these steps:

1. Create a Visual Basic form with text boxes, labels, and so on (see Figure 20.13).

NOTE If you are creating a project for distribution, make sure the dependent files, including NMFTPSN.DLL, NMOCOD.DLL, NMORENU.DLL, NMSCKN.DLL, and FTPct.OCX, are distributed as well.

Figure 20.13.
The shell for an FTP directory-information utility using Visual Basic and the ICP FTP control.

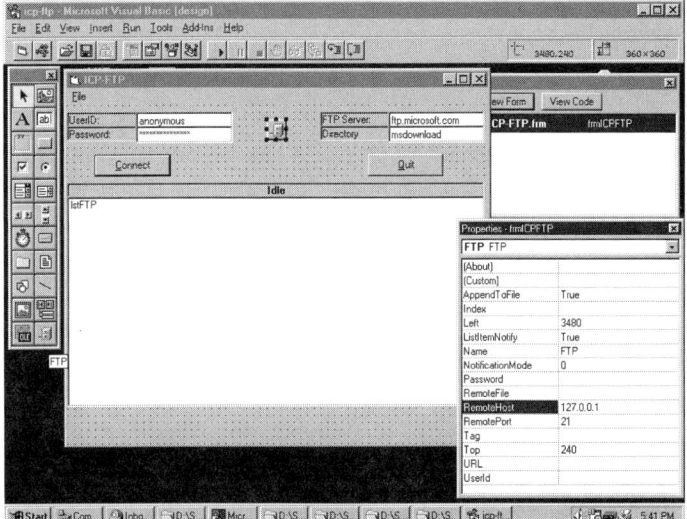

2. After the objects have been placed on the form, add the code that starts the process. This happens after the users have entered their data in the text boxes and pressed the Connect button. Behind that button is one command:

```
Sub cmdConnect_Click
    FTP.Connect txtFTPServer.Text
End Sub
```

In this example, users specify a server, their login information, and a directory on that server. When they click the Connect button, information about that directory is displayed in the window. The login process for the FTP control works the same as if it were being conducted from the command line.

WARNING Different types of FTP servers respond differently. You might have to refer to the documentation of the FTP protocol (RFC 959).

NOTE FTP Protocol (RFC 959)

http://ds0.internic.net/std/std9.txt

Although every FTP server has its own custom prompts and menus, each must conform to this FTP standard.

3. Monitor the protocol for a change in its state. When the control enters the Authorizing state, respond with the UserID and Password for this connection.

   To perform this logon step, add a bit of code to the FTP_ProtocolStateChanged event like so:

   ```
   Private Sub FTP_ProtocolStateChanged(ByVal ProtocolState As Integer)
   Select Case FTP.ProtocolState
       Case 0   'Idle
       Case 1   'Authorizing
           lblStatus.Caption = "Authorizing: " & txtPassword.Text
           FTP.Authenticate txtUserID.Text, txtPassword.Text
       Case 2   'Authorized
   End Select
   End Sub
   ```

4. Add a bit of code to determine when your connection is authenticated. In this case, go immediately to the user-defined directory on the FTP server. As soon as the FTP_Authenticate event fires, respond by telling it which directory you want to visit with the FTP.ChangeDir method like so:

   ```
   Private Sub FTP_Authenticate()
       FTP.ChangeDir txtFTPDir.Text
   End Sub
   ```

5. Monitor the FTP_ChangeDir event. This event fires as soon as the server enters the requested directory. When this happens, request a listing of the current directory using the FTP.List method like so:

   ```
   Private Sub FTP_ChangeDir()
       FTP.List "*"
   End Sub
   ```

WARNING: Not all FTP servers work the same. On some, the List method doesn't work, but the PrintDir method does. Use the DocObject properties and methods whenever possible to accommodate these variations. The DocObject will allow you to take any and all data that is returned, but the PrintDir method may not return any data at all. It is best to code procedures that will analyze the DocObject properties and identify what type of data is being returned from the server.

6. After you invoke the FTP.List method, monitor the FTP_ListItem event. This event fires as each item in the list comes down the pipe. These items are passed through the control as an FTPDirItem object. The FTPDirItem is an object that is specific to the FTP client control. In this example, you are retrieving the value of the Detail property from the FTPDirItem. Add this Detail property with a bit of code in the ListItem event like so:

```
Private Sub FTP_ListItem(ByVal Item As FTPDirItem)
    If ItemDetail <> "" Then lstFTP.AddItem Item.Detail
End Sub
```

To see a working example of this sample application, refer to the \vb4\icp- directory on the enclosed CD-ROM.

WARNING: If you are working with the ICP FTP control, you may encounter errors when you attempt to manipulate the FTPDirItem through your code. If you do, try registering the FTP control and its dependent files with the RegSvr32.exe utility. This will register the OLE controls in your operating system as well as your development environment. Also, ensure that the FTP control and any dependent libraries are referenced in your development's OLE references. In Visual Basic, this can be done from the menu using the Tools|References menu option.

Again, the real power of a control, such as the FTP client, is the retrieval of meta-information instead of just raw data. With this control, you can produce other reports, such as an Archie report or even the files themselves. This is an automatic or manually updated database that contains listings of the billions of megabytes of redundant files found on remote FTP servers. When you query this utility for a file, it will be able to give you several options to help you find it.

State Logic

The ICP begs to use state logic. The ICP uses of three different kinds of states:

- [ ] The state of the control
- [ ] The state of the protocol
- [ ] The state of the DocObjects

The Control State

The state of the control is returned in the control's State property (such as FTP.State). These control states are:

- [ ] Connection requested
- [ ] Resolving Host
- [ ] Host Resolved
- [ ] Established Connection
- [ ] Disconnecting
- [ ] Idle

The Protocol State

The state of the protocol is returned in the control's ProtocolState property (such as FTP.ProtocolState). Different protocols share similar states; the following states are specific to the named protocols:

FTP

- [ ] 0—Idle
- [ ] 1—Authorizing
- [ ] 2—Authorized

HTTP

- [ ] 0—Idle
- [ ] 1—Connection Established

POP

- ☐ 0—Idle
- ☐ 1—Authorizing
- ☐ 2—Authorized
- ☐ 3—Quitting

The DocObject State

The state of the items being transferred are returned in the object's State property (such as `DocInput.State`).

- ☐ 0—Idle
- ☐ 1—Initiating Transfer
- ☐ 2—DocHeader Transfer
- ☐ 3—DataBlock Transfer
- ☐ 4—Error During Transfer
- ☐ 5—Transfer Complete

Summary

In this chapter you have been introduced to the controls distributed with the Microsoft Internet Control Pack. These ActiveX controls are useful for performing standard Internet functions—such as news, mail and file transfers—through a custom interface. Among other things, these controls allow the programmer to add Internet functions to the background of his own applications—which means the user need not be Internet-savvy to benefit from the Net.

With the FTP control you can perform file transfer functions.

With the NNTP control, you can search for and retrieve articles from Usenet news services.

With the SMTP and POP3 controls, you can send e-mail to and receive e-mail from anyone that has an Internet address.

With the HTTP control you can perform Web functions, such as posting information to a CGI script or retrieving Web documents.

With the HTML control you can retrieve, parse, and display Web documents.

Q&A

Q What `.DLL`s need to be installed on a user's machine to work with the Internet Control Pack?

A Each control in the ICP needs its `.OCX` file (of course).

The `WinSck.OCX` needs only itself and the `NMSCKN.DLL`.

Each of the rest needs `NMSCKN.DLL`, `NMORENU.DLL`, and `NMOCOD.DLL` (in addition to its `.OCX`).

The FTP control needs the additional `NMFTPSN.DLL`.

The HTML control needs the additional `NMW3VWN.DLL`.

Q What is the DocObject?

A The DocObject, as it relates to the Internet Control Pack, is a block of data that is transferred over the Internet. Depending on what information the server is sending, you can reference its properties to identify properties such as headers, file sizes, filenames, and so on.

Q What are DocInput/DocOutput?

A The DocInput and DocOutput objects (and their properties, methods, and events) are streams of incoming and outgoing Internet data. They are common to all controls in the ICP, and are the context within which the Object Model for Scripting is implemented within applications (as opposed to within HTML).

Q With all these client controls, the next logical step is to build servers and hosts for these protocols. How is this done with the ICP?

A The WinSock control is the one to use when building a server (applications that wait for connections rather than initiating them). This control taps directly into the Windows interface from the TCP/IP stream. To build a server for one of the established protocols (such as SMTP or POP3), you must build a WinSock-based application that can properly respond to the SMTP and POP3 standard commands. You can do this with a protocol-specific control that references the WinSock library, or a WinSock control that references the WinSock library.

Fax-2-Fax

You are, by now, familiar with the standard TCP/IP protocols—SMTP/POP3, NNTP, FTP, HTTP, and so on. A wonderful benefit of the WinSock control is the ability it gives a programmer to produce his own "proprietary" protocols.

> In 1995, Lawrence Kern, a Telecom Corridor CPA, and a couple of Telecom lawyers from the pre-regulation days got together to address the opportunities in telephony on the emerging Internet. They began with the idea that a fax transmission is not all that different from an e-mail or other message transmission; thus it could be sent over the Internet more quickly, more cheaply, and more reliably than over long-distance telephone lines.
>
> The system they eventually developed went through many trial phases before a final demonstration of the process was completed. They wanted to determine which protocol to use to transmit a fax image and its associated data over the Net. Several were tried, including FTP, SMTP/POP3, and a brief try with uuencoding as is used in NNTP.
>
> No pre-established protocol fit the need. Although the development of this project was before the development of ActiveX, there were still several utilities out there that could be used to program against the WinSock interface. Using a shareware .VBX control, Mr. Kern and his team were able to create their own proprietary protocol. Their product was a little bit SMTP, a little bit FTP, and a little bit rock-and-roll.
>
> In the few years since the Fax-2-Fax network was researched and developed, many other fax services have become popular. Among these are The Internet Phone Company (www.tpc.int) and Faxaway (www.faxaway.com). Although these services provide a fast and economical e-mail-to-fax gateway, the Fax-2-Fax network remains the best interface for completing a fax transmission to a remote fax over the Internet.
>
> By forsaking *public* standards, they were able to create the right tool for the job. They showed tremendous innovation and initiative to create something new. This is the same spirit that brought us things like the Internet, the Public Service Telephone Network, railroads and sliced bread. This is what you can do with the WinSock control.

Workshop

Create an SMTP utility that will automatically mail copies of your Autoexec.Bat, Config.SYS, and Win.INI files to yourself with Delete Me in the subject line. Observe the potential risks. Add a POP3 control that will delete the message you just sent to yourself.

Quiz

1. What two procedures must be invoked to log on to an FTP server?
2. What three values must be loaded into the SMTP.DocInput.Headers object to send a message?
3. What method is invoked to change directories during an FTP session?
4. What method must be invoked to return the first, last and total article numbers from an NNTP server?
5. What method is used to log on to an NNTP server?
6. Must a password be used with all news servers?
7. What event returns the message count from a POP3 server?
8. What state must a DocObject be in to retrieve the headers information?
9. The State property of what object identifies whether or not a hostname has been resolved?

Note

Refer to the appendix, "Answers," for the answers to these questions.

Week 3

Day 21

Creating an ActiveX Control

In this chapter you will be exposed to some of the advanced features of COM and DCOM OLE programming. First, you should know just what those two words mean.

Until now, you have been learning how to use OLE features within programs, and to use controls written by other people. For example, you *used* the marquee control, but you did not *create* the marquee control. Programs such as Visual Basic (the next version) and Visual C++ enable you to create class objects (objects that are derived from classes) and OCX controls that others can use in their own applications.

A survey of the technologies that go into creating an OLE control would fill a volume much larger than this one. However, for those of you who will go on to creating these controls, this chapter reviews some of the features of control creation and how they apply to ActiveX. You will learn

- How and why to edit the system registry
- Some of the features and requirements of a COM/DCOM control
- OLE interface design for objects and classes

Editing the System Registry

The system registry is the location for all the system settings on an NT or Win95 machine. Actually, any system that supports OLE will need to have some sort of equivalent to the system registry. When Microsoft introduced it in Windows 3.0, it allowed third-party programmers to write applications for Windows, which allowed Microsoft to sell more Windows, and so on.

Windows 3.0

Windows 3.0 has two sections of the Win.INI to enable OLE-like features—[Embedding] and [Extensions]. These sections tell the OLE system what features are enabled and what file extensions are associated with those features, respectively.

The format for the [Extensions] section follows a standard *keyname = value* format. An example section would look like this:

```
[Extensions]
crd=cardfile.exe ^.crd
doc=C:\MSOFFICE\WINWORD\WINWORD.EXE ^.doc
MDB=C:\MSOFFICE\ACCESS\MSACCESS.EXE ^.MDB
mpp=C:\MSOFFICE\WINPROJ\winproj.exe ^.mpp
msg=C:\PROGRA~1\MICROS~1\exchng32.exe /f ^.msg
ppt=C:\MSOFFICE\POWERPNT\POWERPNT.EXE ^.ppt
qry=C:\WINDOWS\MSAPPS\MSQUERY\msquery.exe ^.qry
vbp=C:\VB\vb.exe ^.vbp
wri=write.exe ^.wri
```

The Win.INI [Extensions] Section

Extension = Application FilePath ^.Extension

The [Extensions] section of the Win.INI file defines the application that is automatically associated with a given file extension. The INI file itself takes precedence over any similar settings in the system registry.

Example:

```
foo = C:\FooDir\FooApp.exe ^.foo
```

In this example, an entry is made that will cause the computer to use the FooApp.exe program to handle FOO files.

The format in the [Embedding] section of the Win.INI tells the system the name of the control, the name of the object, the path to the control, and the type of object. An [Embedding] section would look like this:

```
[embedding]
Mplayer = Media Clip, Media Clip, mplayer.exe, picture
ComicChat.Room.1 = Comic Chat Room, Comic Chat Room, C:\MSN\CCHAT\CHAT.EXE,
➥picture
```

The Win.INI [Embedding] Section

[ServerObject] = [Description 1], [Description 2] [OLE Server] [Format]

The [Embedding] section of the Win.INI file defines the OLE servers that can manipulate a given object. This file is only used for backwards-compatibility with older Windows 3.0-style programs.

Example:

```
My Object  = My Object, My Object, C:\MyAppDir\MyApp.exe, picture
```

In this example, an entry is made that tells the operating system about a new type of server object called My Object [ServerObject].

Next it gives the creatable object two descriptions. The first is a general name for the object; the second is a more generally readable description for it that will appear in menus and dialogs that refer to the object.

It also tells the system where there is an OLE server that is capable of creating one of these server objects [OLE Server].

 Finally, it says what kind of file the data file will be. This is almost always picture.

Windows 3.1

Windows 3.1 added speed and OLE features to the access of the system registry components. Instead of keeping the information in diverse sections of multiple files, it keeps the most important parts of the registry in a few fast-access binary files. Also, in response to the glut of programs being written for the Windows brand of OLE, Microsoft pre-added entries for several third-party OLE applications to the distribution copies of Windows 3.1. This made the installation of OLE-capable programs go more easily.

Windows 95

In Windows 95, access to the registry files is speeded up considerably. This is to allow for the network feature of having dynamic keys. These keys make it possible for counters and various other real-time and metered data to be kept close to the processing environment.

Registry Components

The system registry is made up of information from three files. These files contain user-specific, computer-specific, and system-specific information. It would be difficult to show just what these files look like. They are not very human-readable, but they still contain the binary representation of a whole data structure. You have to use a tool like the RegEdit utility to read and manipulate the registry database.

System.DAT

The System.DAT file contains the system-specific information for the system, such as what type of monitor is installed and how many keys are on your keyboard.

Reg.DAT

The Reg.DAT file is the computer-specific registration database of information for the system. It is through this database that changes to the registry are made, and is where support for OLE happens in Windows 95. Drag and Drop, OLE, and Compound Documents all refer to this database to perform their operations.

User.DAT

The User.DAT file contains the user-specific information about the user profile. This magic feature of Windows 95 enables each user to have a desktop customized to his own taste.

The information for each user's particular setup is contained in the policy-settings portion of this file. User profiles make it possible for Mom to access newsgroups that are pointed to her favorites, and Dad's are still pointed to his when he logs on to the system. They can also manage the ratings for Junior. One computer, multiple configurations.

The last registries file to be loaded during boot-up is the Policy.POL (System Policies) file. It can be edited with the System Policy Editor (distributed with the Windows 95 Resource Kit). The settings in the system policy override all other policies. It is usually loaded from the network so that all the systems can be managed in the same way.

Editing the Registry Database

There are several good utilities that come with the Windows 3.1, 95, and NT systems that can assist you in editing the registry settings.

RegEdit

Windows 3.1 and 95 come with RegEdit.exe (see Figure 21.1), usually in the \Windows\ directory. In Windows 3.1 you had the command-line option of /v to toggle between normal and advanced modes. In Windows 95 there is just one mode: Power User.

WARNING

For you diagnosticians out there, when you trace a problem with a client machine to a "mysterious" registry problem, try to find out whether someone went running around loose in the RegEdit program. It's a good place for someone who does not know what he is doing to really hurt himself.

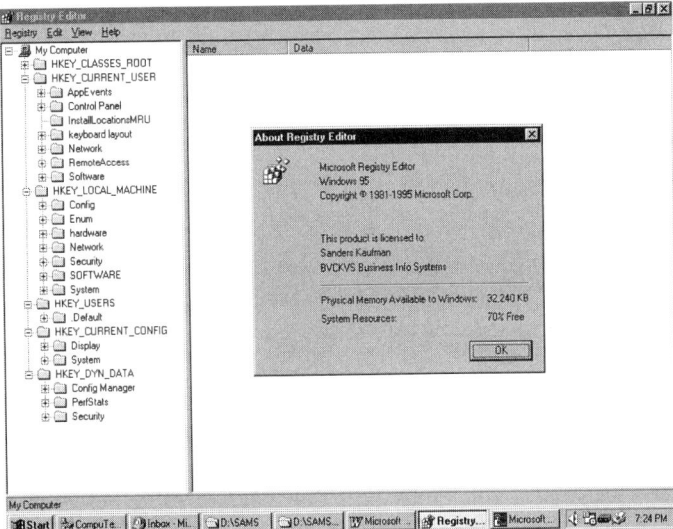

Figure 21.1.
The Windows 95 Registry Editor.

The RegEdit utility is handy for editing the way OLE is carried out on a system. The functions that can be customized through RegEdit include Open, Close, Delete, Print, Edit, and other functions you might find on the File menu of an application.

When you have an OLE application on your system, you will want to make sure that it's registered in the registration database. Ideally, the software author included processes to automatically register and unregister the OLE server.

If the author did not include this process, or if the program somehow becomes unregistered on your system, there should be a REG file somewhere. These files are associated with the

RegEdit utility to register the software component. This can also be done from the RegEdit Merge-Registration Info menu.

Listing 21.1 is a sample REG file for the Windows Media Player (also see Figure 21.2):

Listing 21.1. A sample REG file.

```
REGEDIT
HKEY_CLASSES_ROOT\mplayer = Media Clip
HKEY_CLASSES_ROOT\mplayer\protocol\StdExecute\server = mplayer.exe
HKEY_CLASSES_ROOT\mplayer\protocol\StdFileEditing\Handler = mciole.dll
HKEY_CLASSES_ROOT\mplayer\protocol\StdFileEditing\server = mplayer.exe
HKEY_CLASSES_ROOT\mplayer\protocol\StdFileEditing\PackageObjects =
HKEY_CLASSES_ROOT\mplayer\protocol\StdFileEditing\verb\1 = &Edit
HKEY_CLASSES_ROOT\mplayer\protocol\StdFileEditing\verb\0 = &Play
HKEY_CLASSES_ROOT\mplayer\shell\open\command = mplayer.exe /play /close %1

;OLE2 Compatibility entries.
HKEY_CLASSES_ROOT\MPlayer\CLSID = {0003000E-0000-0000-C000-000000000046}
HKEY_CLASSES_ROOT\CLSID\{0003000E-0000-0000-C000-000000000046}
HKEY_CLASSES_ROOT\CLSID\{0003000E-0000-0000-C000-000000000046} = Media Clip
HKEY_CLASSES_ROOT\CLSID\{0003000E-0000-0000-C000-000000000046}
➥\InprocHandler = mciole.dll
HKEY_CLASSES_ROOT\CLSID\{0003000E-0000-0000-C000-000000000046}\ProgID =
MPlayer
HKEY_CLASSES_ROOT\CLSID\{0003000E-0000-0000-C000-000000000046}
➥\Ole1Class = MPlayer

HKEY_CLASSES_ROOT\.avi = mplayer
HKEY_CLASSES_ROOT\.mmm = mplayer
HKEY_CLASSES_ROOT\.mid = mplayer
HKEY_CLASSES_ROOT\.rmi = mplayer
```

Figure 21.2.
The registry entries for MPLAYER *from the MPlayer registry file.*

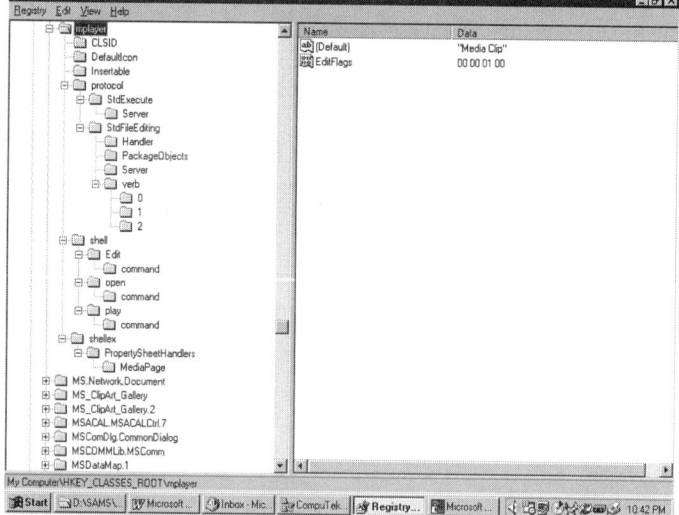

Creating an ActiveX Control

For the truly advanced or daring administrator, the RegEdit utility includes a menu option, Add|File Type, which enables you to manually add the OLE registration information that should have been in the REG file—or to modify it to your own preferences. It is very similar to Windows 95's View|Options|File Types.

RegSvr32

You may have seen the RegSvr32.exe utility being distributed in the setup disks for different programs. This is the command line utility to register the OLE server features of an OCX or DLL file.

By typing RegSvr32 and the filename of an OLE server, you can register that item in the system registry. This registration process will make its features available to all the other OLE-capable programs on your system.

The RegSvr32 Utility

▼ SYNTAX

RegSvr32.exe [/u] [/s] [/c] [OLE Server]

The 32-bit server registration utility is used to register and unregister OLE servers (such as OCX and DLL files) in the system registry.

Example:

RegSvr32.exe /c MyServer.DLL

This will register the OLE server MyServer.DLL and output the results to the console (monitor).

RegSvr32.exe /u /s MyServer.OCX

▲ This will unregister the OLE server MyServer.OCX and do it in silent mode (no output to the console).

RegClean

The RegClean utility (see Figure 21.3) is available from Microsoft's Software Library (ftp://ftp.microsoft.com/SoftLib/MSLFiles). It includes a Registry Cleanup utility that, among other things, will remove entries in your system registry for components or OCX files that are no longer available to your system.

Figure 21.3.
Microsoft's Registry Cleaning Wizard.

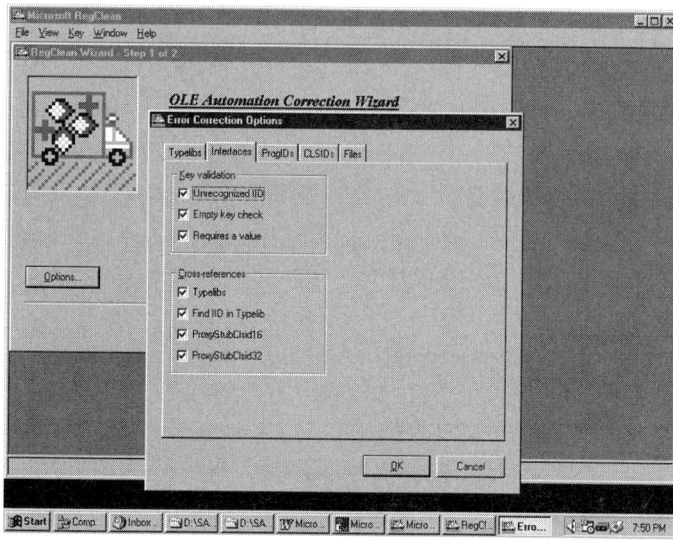

ActiveX and the System Registry

There are many OLE controls out there that work just fine as they are, ActiveX environment or not. To attain the title of ActiveX control, your OCX or DLL file must support certain features—which the following sections introduce.

> **NOTE**
>
> The following sections introduce you to the APIs and SDKs involved in creating an ActiveX control. There are a variety of these tools that you may wish to use (such as security and versioning). Some can be quite complex and are included here for the truly daring programmer.
>
> Microsoft makes its Internet APIs and SDKs publicly available on its Web site. Also, most of the documentation files on these tools were installed on your computer by the ActiveX SDK in the \IntDev\ directory.

Self-Registering and Versioning

An ActiveX control's API must support the standard calls for registering and unregistering a control.

The DLL Register Server Standard API feature (STDAPI DLLRegisterServer()) loads all the .CLASS information (from the DLL or OCX file) into the system registry.

The DLL UnRegister Server Standard API feature (STDAPI DLLUnRegister Server()) removes all the previously loaded .CLASS information from the System Registry.

Ver.DLL

Ver.DLL contains the Windows versioning features. It supports three important functions:

- GetFileVersionInfoSize—Returns the size (in bytes) of the versioning information. This is useful to the programmer for reserving an appropriate buffer into which he should retrieve this data. For instance, if you were working in Visual Basic and retrieved this data into a string value (for whatever reason), you could reserve a three-character string variable instead of a memory-hogging variant.
- GetFileVersionInfo—Whether or not you make use of the *size* of the versioning information, you can retrieve the data itself with this function.
- VerQueryValue—After you have retrieved the versioning information, use this function to retrieve VersionInfo, which contains, among other things, FileVersion, ProductVersion, and two additional blocks of data. These two blocks work together to identify the self-registering properties of the control.
- VerFileInfo—Contains a pointer to the location of the OLESelfRegister key within StringFileInfo.

Remote Procedure Calls (RPCs)

RPCs provide the programmer with a series of functions to access the Win32 registry. At this level, network functions such as SNMP procedures can be used. The client machine would need to have the Microsoft RPC service installed. Use of this feature is not *required* for ActiveX controls, but it sure is powerful.

Programmers add utility for users whose machines are running the RPC service. If the user with whom you wish to interact is running the Windows RPC service (included with the Windows 95 CD-ROM in \Admin\NetTools), this allows programmatic access to the OLE procedure calls within Windows API. This is how features such as SNMP can be accessed.

Base Security Layer SDK

Another feature programmers can make use of is the Base Security Layer of Windows. You were introduced to various parts of this feature in earlier chapters. What should be made clear here is that much of the information that is read from and written to ActiveX objects is stored in the system registry. This goes for all ActiveX security features such as code signing, ratings, trust verification, and user locator services.

ActiveX Control Features

For a control to be truly ActiveX/OLE-enabled, it must support the central features of OLE—aggregation, marshaling, and reference counting—and support IUnknown interfaces. Briefly, these can be defined as follows:

- Aggregation—This feature enables one control to incorporate into itself the features of another control. Without aggregation, the control code must be recompiled for each instance of the object (in other words, one object—one control). With aggregation, you only need one control to manage any number of instances of an object. This is an overly simplified definition, since there are all kinds of things that must go on in order to perform this function.

> **NOTE**
>
> The Java Virtual Machine (VM) uses a Garbage Collector rather than reference counting to determine whether it is being used and if so, how many times.
>
> Microsoft's implementation of the Java Virtual Machine combines OLE reference counting with the Java Garbage Collector. This relieves the programmer of the burden of coding when a reference to a control should be added, deleted, loaded, or unloaded. Also, Java allows for exception handling, whereas COM does not. These are perfect examples of how Java makes OLE programming a lot easier!

- Marshaling—The process in which select features from one object are used within another object.
- Reference counting—This feature helps manage memory use. When a COM object is loaded, it can be used to manipulate any number of instances of that object. By keeping count of how many different ways it is being used, the object can be unloaded when all other instances are cleared from use. (For you C++ programmers, that means you must use the AddRef and Release member functions when instantiating your controls.)
- IUnknown—All COM interfaces are based on this interface. It is through these interfaces that OLE applications talk with each other. The three primary interfaces implemented through IUnknown are QueryInterface, AddRef, and Release.

To actually compile your control for use, you need to use an OLE-aware programming environment such as Visual C++, Visual Basic, or Visual Java++.

Visual J++ (Jakarta)

Visual J++ (which Microsoft code-named "Jakarta") is the first full-blown IDE (integrated development environment) to make Internet programming fully available to OLE developers. (See Figure 21.4 for a view of the Jakarta IDE.) This programming language is based on the Java language developed by Sun Microsystems and integrates the features of OLE.

In this marriage, COM objects are exposed to Java as Java objects, and a public Java class is exposed to OLE as COM objects. Although you can program COM objects in a variety of languages, you still must use a Java compiler to create Java objects. This, however, may not be true for Java compilers other than Jakarta since it is based on the Microsoft Java VM.

One security feature for running Java applets in ActiveX browsers is that they are *hobbled*. Hobbling restricts the control from calling code or classes that cannot be verified by the Java byte code verifier. Also, any interface that cannot be defined in a type library (TLB file) will be hobbled.

You can find more information about Visual J++ at Microsoft's Web site, http://www.microsoft.com/visualj.

Figure 21.4.
Microsoft's Visual J++ IDE.

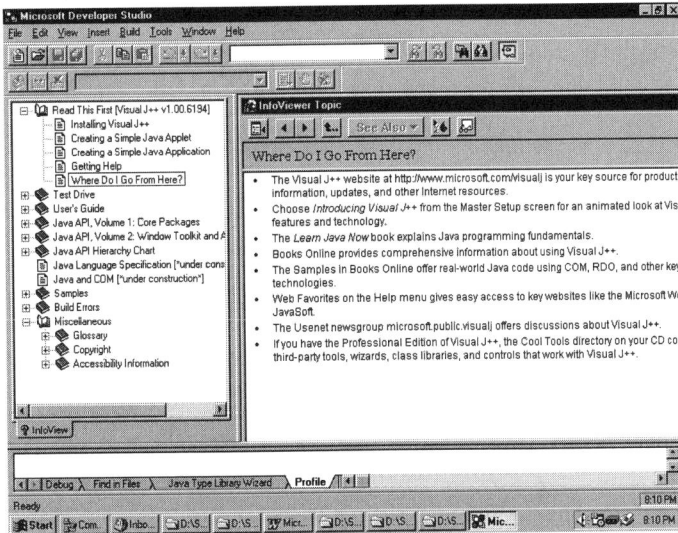

Visual Basic

Visual Basic (see Figure 21.5) supports various levels of OLE connectivity with COM objects, depending on the version of VB you are using. Even Visual Basic 4 enables you to program against a previously registered object.

A powerful feature of Visual Basic is its capability to make API calls to OLE servers. This feature enables 16-bit VB applications to make calls to 32-bit OLE out-of-process servers, and 32-bit VB applications to make calls to 16-bit OLE out-of-process servers. When using in-process servers, you still must consider bitness.

Figure 21.5.
Microsoft's Visual Basic IDE.

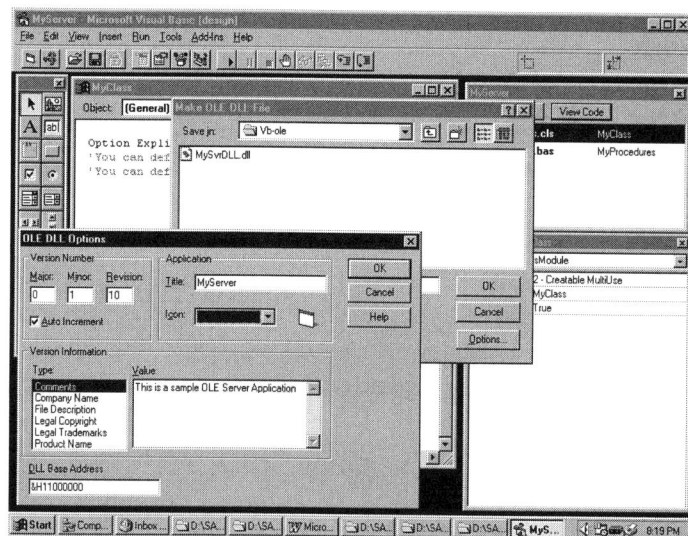

Learn more about Visual Basic at Microsoft's Web site, http://www.microsoft.com/vbasic.

WARNING

> When making API calls over a distributed network (such as with the Microsoft RPC Service API), performance is slowed considerably as remote connections are established and disconnected.

VB is wonderful for using OLE servers. On the enclosed CD-ROM, you should find a sample VB application, MyServer, for creating an OLE server in VB4. It does not *do* anything, but if you view the source code with Notepad, you will see comments about what *should* be done in a particular part.

Visual C++

Visual C++ has always (until now, anyway) been the language of choice for OLE programmers. Versions 4 and later enable you to program with foundation classes (predefined OLE classes) or templates (programming language-specific code snippets). Each has its own features for accessing COM.

Microsoft Foundation Classes (MFCs)

C programmers do most of their OLE programming with the classes supported in Microsoft's Foundation Classes Library. Be sure to include the dependent files with your distribution disks. These include

- [ ] MFC40.DLL—May be different, depending on your MFC version
- [ ] MSVCRT.DLL—Visual C++ RunTime libraries
- [ ] OLEPro32.DLL—Required for OLE

ActiveX Template Library (ATL)

The ATL is distributed by Microsoft to enable programmers to use API calls instead of relying on foundation classes. The most current version can be found at http://www.microsoft.com/visualc/v42/atl/default.htm.

This is a set of Visual C++ templates that enables quick and easy programmatic access to the ActiveX OLE features. This library is not at all a comprehensive library of functions, but it will enable you to create redistributable functioning COM class objects.

Dual Interfaces

The ATL enables you to add support for dual interfaces to your C++ program. This makes possible access to features by way of both the IDispatch interface and vtable entries. This enables interaction through third-party features such as scripting.

Tear-Off Interfaces

This library also allows for support of Tear-Off Interfaces. This means that an object can be enumerated (defined) within the system with an IEnum... interface, BUT you do not have to worry about the resource demand on your OLE connection. The OLE connection is not actually instantiated (loaded) until it is used. It can be used many times after that and will stay loaded. When all the objects that were using it report that they are no longer using it (that is, the reference count hits 0), it is unloaded (uninstantiated).

IUnknown—The Center of ActiveX OLE

When you create an OLE interface for an object, there is one standard, IUnknown, with which most of your calls will work. (For a graphical representation of how IUnknown is used as an interface, refer to Figure 21.6.) Determining the number of references (current implementations of this interface) and querying the interface (asking about a specific implementation) are determined by the processes that occur through this interface.

The basic model of the IUnknown interface would support the QueryInterface, AddRef, and Release methods:

```
Interface IUnknown {
    Virtual HResult QueryInterface(REFID, VOID FAR *) = 0;
    Virtual ULong AddRef()=0;
    Virtual ULong Release()=0;
};
```

An example of C++ code that would implement a DragDrop function by way of the IUnknown interface would look like this:

```
Interface IDropTarget:IUnknown {
    Virtual HResult DragDrop()=0;
    Virtual HResult DragEnter()=0;
    Virtual HResult DragLeave()=0;
    Virtual HResult DragOver()=0;
};
```

NOTE: Make sure your program makes AddRef and Release calls as necessary. This will inform the system when it is using an object and when it isn't. Then the system can load and unload it as necessary. If you keep opening interfaces and not closing them, you could easily run out of memory and hang your system.

Every interface, IUnknown or not, implements three methods:

- AddRef—When an object is instantiated, it calls the AddRef method to let COM increase the use count.
- QueryInterface—Returns data based on a query from the Interface Identification (IID) specified in a parameter.
- Release—Tells COM that the object is no longer needed and to decrease the use count for that interface. If the count is 0, the interface will be uninstantiated altogether.

Figure 21.6.
Graphical representation of how programmers and their programs interact with COM.

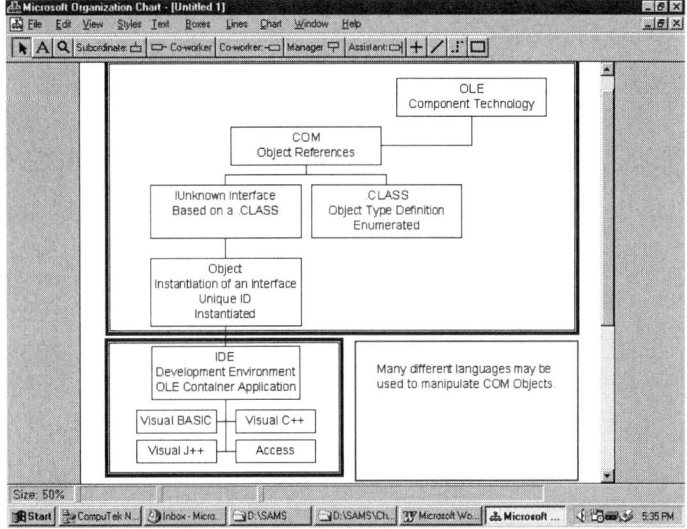

OLE Definitions

OLE is a component technology (a theory).

COM is a convention for referring to computer objects.

A *class* is the definition of how one object behaves. The object it defines does not exist until it is instantiated. Each has a 128-bit Uniform Unique Identifier property (UUID).

An *interface* is any class based on the IUnknown class. This class will be the contract under which any objects created with it will operate.

The *IUnknown class* provides the details of a user-defined object, but it cannot be loaded itself. It only provides the definitions by which other objects are loaded.

An *ActiveX IDE* (Integrated Design Environment) is a program that enables interaction with COM objects.

A *language* is the syntax and vocabulary used in an IDE to reference objects and procedures.

An *object* is the instantiation of an interface. It is usually contained in an EXE or a DLL file, but it can be contained on a remote machine (using RPC).

Summary

Taken as a whole, these features are a bit much to swallow in one gulp. However, whether you are a control programmer who uses controls or a control programmer who creates them, it is important to have an exposure to the design considerations in ActiveX controls.

Your ActiveX controls will be working closely with your system registry, and you may have to use a utility such as RegEdit or RegClean to fix something. Also, if other programmers' controls are running rampant in your registry, you may find it necessary to remove or edit them manually.

If you design ActiveX controls, you have a wide choice of programming languages with which to work. Microsoft makes Visual Basic, Visual C++, and Visual J++ with control-creation features.

Also, you will need to include certain interfaces based on the IUnknown interface. They will need to be self-registering, using the API calls for DLLRegisterServer and DLLUnRegisterServer. The controls will also need to support versioning through API calls to Ver.DLL. Several other interfaces can be added to the control to enable enhanced features such as RPCs (Remote Procedure Calls) and code signing.

Q&A

Q What's the difference between a class, a control, and an object?

A A *class* is a description of how an OLE object works (a contract).

A *control* is the code, usually compiled into a DLL or an OCX file, that contains the machine-level instructions (in other words, Mac-, PC-, or UNIX-specific) on how an object interacts with the system (a transaction manager).

An *object* is created when a program tells a control to create one, following the rules defined in a class.

Q Can I change the system registry by editing the [Embedding] and [Extensions] sections of my Win.INI file?

A No. Only older programs that cannot use OLE reference those sections. They expose a default Open process.

Q Can I assign two or more programs to one file extension in the [Extensions] section?

A No. You can use the FileTypes tab from Explorer to do this, but not the Win.INI file. An example would be that you cannot assign both Notepad and Write to open a text file.

Q Can I assign two or more file extensions to one program in the [Extensions] section?

A Yes. One program may be capable of opening up a variety of files. An example would be that you can use Word to open DOC files as well as RTF, TXT, and even HTML files.

Q How can I back up my system registry *alone*?

A Archive the three registry files—Reg.DAT, User.DAT, and System.DAT—to a safe place. You might also want to include your Autoexec.BAT and your Config.SYS, as well as your Win.INI and System.INI while you are at it, since they affect how your system registry will react.

Q How does automatic registration work for the user?

A When a program such as the Setup utility installs its controls, it should make an API call to the DLL and OCX files to tell them to register themselves. This can also be done manually in one of two ways:

Using the RegSvr32.exe utility, included with Windows, run RegSvr32 [Filename]. The control, if it supports self-registration, should be added to your system registry.

If the control author did not include self-registration interfaces in the control, it will need to have a REG file with it. This file should have the information necessary to add the OLE server to the system registry. The filename for this can be used as a command-line parameter for the RegEdit.exe utility (for example, RegEdit [Filename]).

If the control is not self-registering and does not have a REG file, other programs will only be able to access it while it is running.

Q What, exactly, will RegClean.exe do to my system?

A Fix it. You can select options to allow or disallow such features as the following:

- ☐ Validation of unrecognized or obsolete entries
- ☐ Validation of optional keys
- ☐ Check for empty keys
- ☐ Validation of type libraries
- ☐ Validation of cross-references
- ☐ Check OLE servers
- ☐ Check ProgIDs, ClassIDs, and Handlers
- ☐ Check OLE conversions
- ☐ Check remote automation

Workshop

Create an OLE server that supports self-registering and versioning, using any or all the following IDEs:

Visual C++ with MFC
Visual C++ with ATL
Visual Basic
Visual J++

Quiz

1. What section of the Win.INI file identifies OLE objects?
2. Which file used by the system registry identifies the hardware that is installed on a local machine?
3. Which utility is used to remove invalid and obsolete entries from the system registry?
4. What two interfaces must a control support to be considered self-registering?
5. What DLL file supports the API calls used in versioning?
6. Which programs will create both Java and COM objects?
7. What dependent files must be installed on a user's machine to use an ActiveX control that is based on MFCs (Microsoft Foundation Classes)?
8. What COM interfaces are derived from IUnknown?
9. What three methods must be supported by any interface based on IUnknown?
10. An *object* is an _____ of an interface.

NOTE

Refer to the appendix, "Answers," for the answers to these questions.

Answers

Chapter 1

1. An Internet service provider that charges a fee based on a metered rate
2. HyperTerminal and dial-up networking
3. To integrate pre-existing technologies, and to enhance Windows features used over the Internet
4. From computer-oriented to document-oriented program design
5. Its class
6. Properties, methods and events
7. Because it is based on a standard, and is viewable by users on a variety of machines
8. MIME (RFC 1521 & 1522)

Chapter 2

1. You use the BACKGROUND attribute of the <BODY> tag.
2. The BORDER attribute
3. Use the regedit.exe program under the CLSID directory.

Chapter 3

1. It relieves a server of the burden of having to process multiple simultaneous requests to run an application.
2. JScript and VBScript
3. To prevent malicious or undesirable effects from network scripts
4. A computer connected to the Internet, and a program that coordinates the interaction between a script and a script engine
5. A script, host, and engine
6. All the objects in the VBScript script engine and the Microsoft Internet Explorer Object Model for Scripting
7. The Language attribute
8. Enclose the script within comment tags.
9. Within the head element
10. You must acknowledge Microsoft in the About box.

Chapter 4

1. No, it has no facility to interpret these tags and will ignore them.
2. The procedure for both is the same. Select or highlight the elements you want to align and press the appropriate alignment button on the tool bar. The three settings are left, right, and center.
3. Not automatically. You can use the text editor part of the ActiveX Control Pad and enter them manually, but there is no automated support.

Chapter 5

1. If you run window.mane in the browser, you get an error telling you that the object Window doesn't support a member called mane. If you use just mane, VBScript makes a new variable, and your value is blank.
2. windows.document.write and windows.document.writeln
3. <SETFRAME> is the tag and TARGET is the attribute.

Chapter 6

1. The string-intensive application, because string functions outnumber math functions two-to-one in VBScript
2. MY.NAME is illegal because it has a period in it; 4Things is illegal because it starts with a number.
3. Use the Raise method of the Err object. This will allow you to raise an error with a specific number and not risk crashing your machine.

Chapter 7

1. JavaScript is well suited for both. The string and math functions are evenly balanced.
2. MY.NAME is illegal because it has a period in it. The interpreter will think it is a property or method of an object. 4Things is illegal because it starts with a number.
3. The for...in loop is specifically designed to loop through the values of your object.

Chapter 8

1. The idx and htx files go into the `scripts` subdirectory. The htm files go into the root directory.
2. You can put startup and initialization code in the `onload` event of the Layout control.
3. You name a form section using the following syntax:

   `<FORM ACTION="/scripts/salord.idc" METHOD="POST" NAME="ORDERFORM">`

   Where NAME = "MYNAMEHERE" names the section. You manipulate it through the Document object of the window. The Document object maintains a list of all the <FORM> sections on the Web page. To submit the form, you would type `document.MYNAMEHERE.submit`. (Remember, the case is not important.)

Chapter 9

1. The `CheckValues()` function would be the perfect place to check the validity of the user inputs. This function already looks at all the controls.
2. `window.parent.frames[0].document.forms[0].submit()`
3. Only the middle one will work. The first one uses `()` instead of `[]`. The last doesn't use `submit()`, and will not work.

Chapter 10

1. The specific purposes of the server must be defined.
2. The console and CPU are common to both a server and a client.
3. Multimedia components (CD-ROM, sound card, graphics) are generally associated with, but not necessarily required for, ActiveX systems.
4. A dynamic IP address is assigned every time the user logs on, but remains the same throughout a given session.
5. An easy-to-remember domain name can be assigned to the address.
6. You

   You.Our.Net

   You.204.001.001.002
7. Send: SMTP

   Retrieve: POP3

8. It requires a great deal of attention.
9. A database server processes queries over a network to a database and returns their results. Additionally, a number of higher-end database-management processes are available, depending on the server software.
10. Individual dial-up customers

    Commercial and leased-line customers

Chapter 11

1. CGI—Common Gateway Interface

   ISAPI—Internet Server Application Programmer's Interface
2. Both are used as an interface between a remote user and an external program on the server.
3. `.IDC` (Internet database connector)
4. `.HTX` (hypertext extension)
5. No, but by using the `OLEISAPI.DLL`, you can reference OLE DLLs compiled with Visual Basic.
6. `ReadClient` and `WriteClient`
7. Web pages, alone, are very safe. CGIs and ISAPIs, however, can be written to work all kinds of damage on a server, and the result of that damage can cascade down to every user serviced by the IPP (Internet Presence Provider).
8. The equal sign (=)
9. `.EXE` and `.DLL`
10. Reduced system resource overhead. The ISAPI DLL will run in the same space as the HTTP server itself.

Chapter 12

1. (BSD) Berkeley Software Development UNIX
2. A WinSock application
3. Domain format and IP address format
4. `GetHostByName()`
5. TCP and UDP
6. `LocalPort`
7. `RemotePort`

8. `RequestID` or `Connection ID`
9. The name of the variable into which the data is to be read, and the data type of the incoming stream
10. The `Quit` method

Chapter 13

1. A normal console application will not link with MFC because Microsoft Visual C++ doesn't set the MFC library as required in the project settings.
2. `GetFtpConnection`, `GetHttpConnection`, `GetGopherConnection`
3. If you don't check and you continue with the code execution, you may have an exception and your code will terminate improperly.
4. `CInternetException`
5. The `_T` macro lets you compile code in the three character types (Unicode, MBCS, and SBCS) without having to handle each case specifically.

Chapter 14

1. There can be many conferences managed by only one conference manager.
2. A user is a potential member of a conference but has not joined the conference yet, while a member has joined the conference.
3. NetMeeting

Chapter 15

1. a. OLE is the basis for object-oriented programming.
   b. VBXs were the first custom controls. They are used to allow programming environments such as Visual Basic to interact with complex features of their machines (that is, networks, modems, and so on).
   c. OCXs are very similar to VBXs with the additional capability to more powerfully interact with a machine and, often, to provide a way of interacting with more powerful OLE features than those used by VBXs.
2. The middle of the century
3. Programmatic and scripting
4. DCOM
5. JavaScript or JScript

6. Visual Basic
7. ShDocVW.DLL
8. Component object model and distributed COM, respectively
9. Windows NT 4.0
10. HTML pages and OLE Container applications
11. Sun Microsystems
12. IUnknown and self-registering
13. The addition of machine-to-machine programming methods
14. All operating systems that are run on networked machines
15. Windows 95 and Windows NT 4.0+
16. (UserID, Password, Location(Optional))
17. .INF files
18. A designer's license
19. JavaScript is an HTML script, and a Java applet is an HTML object
20. Visual Basic for Applications

Chapter 16

1. <HTML>/<HTML>, <HEAD></HEAD>, <TITLE></TITLE>, <BODY></BODY>
2. <BODY></BODY>
3. <OBJECT></OBJECT>
4. scripts, objects
5. height, width
6. <IMG>
7. World Wide Web Consortium (W3 Organization)
8. Ctrl+T
9. RegSvr32.exe
10. No. A programmer might wish to reference a control that the user already has installed on the machine without making it available on the Net. If the user does not have the control, it will not be enabled on the Web page when the user views it. Control developers who develop proprietary controls might wish to ensure that those without a license to use the control can't use it. To do this, the control developer simply declines to include a reference to the control's distribution site; the content can have this small level of security.

Chapter 17

1. Acquisition, Verification, Installation
2. `<OBJECT>`
3. `Code`
4. `CODETYPE`
5. `.OCX, .DLL, .EXE`
6. `.INF`
7. `DestDir=11`
8. OLE objects, Non-OLE objects, document content
9. Base Security Layer SDK
10. Trust verification service
11. Creation—Safe when scripted.
    Initialization—Safe when standing alone.
12. `IObjectSafety`
13. The original source of the control
    Integrity of the control since its release
14. Commercial certification and individual certification
15. Private key and public key
16. PICS—Platform for Internet Content Security
17. Internet Ratings API

Chapter 18

1. A standard hierarchy of objects against which an ActiveX Program operates
2. a. `doc—docDocument`
    b. `w—wWindow`
    c. `scr—scrScript`
    d. `fr—frFrames(0)`
    e. `frm—frmForm(0)`
3. The Window object
4. `Frames()`
5. `Frames()`

6. `0 (Frames(0))`
7. History
8. Port
9. host
10. hostname

Chapter 19

1. `<FORM></FORM>`
2. `<INPUT TYPE = … NAME = …>`
3. `Value`
4. `lstAllOfUs`
5. `CheckBox`
6. `MaxLength` property
7. `GET` to retrieve data; `SEND` to post data
8. The `TYPE` attribute
9. The `ISMAP` attribute
10. X1—Left; X2—Top; X3—Bottom; X4—Right

Chapter 20

1. `FTP.Connect` *RemoteHost*
   `FTP.Authenticate` *UserID*, *Password*
2. `From, To, Subject`
3. `FTP.ChangeDir`
4. `NNTP.SelectGroup`
5. `NNTP.Connect` *RemoteHost*
6. No. Some news servers require a UserID and password, but most only allow access from within their own network and, therefore, do not require a UserID or password.
7. `POP3_RefreshMessageCount`
8. `2 - DocHeaders`
9. `Control`

Chapter 21

1. `[Embedding]`
2. `System.DAT`
3. `RegClean.EXE`
4. `DLLRegisterServer` and `DLLUnRegisterServer`
5. `Ver.DLL`
6. Visual Basic
   Visual C++
7. `MFC40.DLL`
   `MSVCRT.DLL`
   `OLEPro32.DLL`
8. All of them.
9. QueryInterface
   AddRef
   Release
10. Instantiation

Index

Symbols

?, 332

A

\<A\> tag, 24
Accept method, 338
Access, 266
Access wrap-up, 78
Active control, 413
ActiveX
 accessing
  files, 8
   messages, 8
   browsers, 419-420
 built-in controls, 474
 client-side scripting, 42-45
 code-signing toolkit, 463
 Conferencing APIs, 377-378
 conference manager, 391
 controls
  attributes and parameters, 485
  overview, 407
 Control Pad, 79, 84
 creating Web pages, 429
 document objects, 10
 editing system registry, 538
 forms, 81
 FTP (File Transfer Protocol), 299
 ICP controls, 423
 installing from Web pages, 418
 interactive HTML, 492, 503
 IP (Internet Protocol) addresses, 294
 NetConference ActiveX objects, 398
 NetConferencing ActiveX control, 390, 398
 release, 7
 script engines, 50-53
  as OLE/COM object, 52
  creation, 51
  states, 53
  host and engine interfaces, 51-52
  required interfaces, 52
  running the script, 52
  script invocation, 52
  script item loading, 52
  script loading, 51
 scripting, 41, 414, 418
  server scripts, 415
 search engines (system registry), 52
 self-registering, 544

setting up Web sites
  hardware, 292
  server software, 296
  system requirements, 292-299
Software Developers' Kit, 8
software distributors, 419
system requirements, 422-424
tour of the Control Pad, 79, 83
using with Visual Basic/VBA, 414
version identification information, 449
Visual J++ (Jakarta), 547
Web sites, 300-302
World Wide Web, 418
writing VBScript, 107

ActiveX controls
  creating, 412
  creating conference objects, 395
  downloading, 447
  evolution of, 408
  features, 546
  ICP, 422
  installation, 49, 427-429
  locating, 418, 422
  navigation bar, 277
  OLE (Object Linking and Embedding), 408
  parameters, 486
  programmatic installation, 437
  properties, 480
  transporting to new sites, 440
  using within ActiveX document, 440
  VBX custom control, 412

ActiveX Layout control, 49
ActiveX OLE
  IUnknown, 550
ActiveX programming, 3
ActiveX script engine, 54
ActiveX Template Library (ATL), 549
aggregation, 546
Alert dialog boxes, 100
Anchors property Document object, 481
API functions (WinInet), 354-358
APIs
  creating ActiveX control, 544
  Remote Access Service (RAS), 506
  Remote Procedure Calls (RPCs), 545
  Win32 Internet API Library, 350-354
  WinInet API, 354-358
applications
  console applications, 360
  creating with JavaScript, 259, 261
<AREA> tag, 502
arithmetic operators (JavaScript), 183-185, 189
arrays
  array01.htm (Listing 7.18), 194
  array02.htm (Listing 7.19), 195-196
  associative, 193-194
  VBScript, 123
assignments in JavaScript operators, 182-183
associative arrays, 193-194
attributes
  BACKGROUND, 21
  BORDER, 30
  ClassID, 486
  CODEBASE, 434, 449
  CODETYPE, 456
  COORD, 501
  Data, 486
  HREF, 502
  ID, 486
  INPUT attributes dialog, 70
  Language, 46, 110
  SHAPE, 501
  SRC, 46
  Type, 29, 47, 494
  UseMap, 502

B

<BODY> tag, 20
BACKGROUND attribute, 21
backward compatibility, 450
Base Security Layer SDK, 545
boolean variables (JavaScript), 173
BORDER attribute, 30
browsers
  ActiveX, 419-420
  creating Web-browser programs, 512
  Internet Explorer, 88, 101
  Lists.html, 69
  Netscape Navigator, 88, 101
  subroutines, 438
  within browsers, 99
buffers, 355
building
  HTML inserts, 91
  ISAPI DLL, 325
buttons, 337
bytes, writing to files, 356

C

.CAB (Compressed Cabinet Files), 451
CABView utility, 451
case sensitivity of JavaScript, 170
CD-ROM files, 454
CFtpConnection class, 369
CGI
  converting to ISAPI, 327-328
  creating, 313
  loading process, 321
  programming, 315
  scripting, 312, 415
  script installation, 314
  scripting with HTML forms, 319
  security, 314
Change Request form, 280
Change Request Tracking page, 265

extension control block (ECB) 567

CInternetConnection class, 368-369
CInternetSession class, 368
classes
   MFC, 358-375
   objects, 9
ClassID attribute, 432, 486
Client-side scripting, 42-45
Close method, 339
Code-Signing Tool Kit, 463
CODEBASE attribute, 434, 449
codes, comments, 172
CODETYPE attribute, 456
color, customizing, 481
command-line parameters, 315
commands, container, 428
comment tags, 22
comments
   JavaScript code, 172
   VBScript, 111
comparison operators, 135, 187
components of system registry, 540
CompuNet, 305
CONFDEST members, 397
ConferenceGetInfo function parameters, 389
Conferencing APIs (ActiveX), 377-378
CONFFILEINFO members, 397
CONFINFO members, 396
Confirm dialog boxes, 100
CONFRECDIR members, 397
CONFUSERINFO members, 396
Connect method, 341
connections (servers), 355, 359
   closing, 364
   FTP servers, 359
   Gopher servers, 359
connection classes, 368-369
console applications, 360
constant variables, 119, 176
container commands, 428
control attributes and parameters, 485
Control Pad (ActiveX), 79

control states, 531
conversion functions, 142
converting
   CGI to ISAPI, 327-328
   URL strings to safe form, 355
COORD attribute, 501
create
creating
   .CAB files, 452
   ActiveX control, 412
   applications
     for Microsoft FTP server, 528
     with JavaScript, 259-261
   CGIs, 313
   databases with Access, 266
   frame pages to hold minibrs.htm, 99
   links to Web pages, 433
   mail-sending program, 517
   OLE control, 462
   Web-browser programs, 512
   Web pages, 429
   WinSock server, 340-341
   WinSock TCP server, 336
customizing
   ActiveX control properties, 480
   color, 481
   with HTML, 429

D

Data attribute, 486
database servers (overview), 300
databases
   adding to ODBC Driver Manager, 266
   designing with Access, 266
date (formatting), 356
Date object (JavaScript), 200-202
declarations (VBScript), 123
declaring variables, 362
deleting
   directories (FTP servers), 358
   files (FTP servers), 357
dial-up accounts, 294

Diantz.exe, 452
Dim statements, 115
directories (FTP servers), 358
DLL Register Server, 545
DLLMain entry function, 326
DNS (domain name system), 302
DocObject states, 532
Document object
   Anchors property, 481
   LastModified property, 483
   Links object, 481
   Title property, 483
document objects (ActiveX), 10
Document.Write method, 485
documents
   adding links, 275
   communicating between, 485
   enhanced objects, 8
   hypertext, 11-12
domain names, assigning to dynamic IP, 294
downloading from the Internet, 448
drivers (monitoring the network), 334
dwCode, 389
dynamic link libraries (DLLs) vs. executables, 320

E

e-mail, 296-297
editing
   registry databases, 540
   system registry, 538
embedding, 409
Empty keyword, 119
encryption, 465
engines, scripting, 43-45
environment variables, 315
error handling (VBScript), 163
events
   IConferenceManagerX, 398
   window object events, 101
executables vs. dynamic link libraries (DLLs), 320
extension control block (ECB), 323

F

file pointers, 356
File Transfer Protocol, *see* FTP
File Transfer Protocol (FTP)
    Client control, 526
files
    .INF files, 455
    bytes, writing to, 356
    CD-ROM, 454
    FTP servers, 357
        renaming, 357
        retrieving from, 357
    Gopher, 358
    reading, WinInet API, 354
    tag files, 351
FishNet ISP, 305
<FORM> container tag, 493
<FORM> tag, 31
formatting
    date, 356
    strings in HTTP format, 356
    time, 356
forms
    ActiveX, 81
    Change Request form, 280
Forms collection object, 482
Forms object, 482
<Frame> tag, 274
Frames Collection object, 478
Frames object, 477
Frankenstein model programming overview, 9
FTP (File Transfer Protocol), 299, 350, 353
    servers, 530
        connecting to MFC class, 359
        directories, 358
        files, 357
        logging on using the command line, 527
        renaming files, 357
        retrieving files, 357
        sample application, 369-375
        sending files to, 357
FTP sites (Microsoft's Software Library), 543
ftpex.cpp file, 370-371

ftpex.h header file, 370
function keyword, 180
functions
    array functions, 152
    conversion functions, 142
    for-in, 205
    GetHostByName( ) function, 334
    GetHostName( ) function, 335
    GetServerVariable, 325
    HTTP (WinInet API), 357
    if, 202-203
    ISAPI, 324
    JavaScript procedures, 179-181
    math functions, 129
    ReadClient, 325
    string functions, 153
    while, 204
    WinInet API, 354
    WinSock, 334
    WriteClient, 325

G

gateway interface scripting, 312
GetData method, 339
GetExtensionVersion, 324
GetHostByName() function, 334
GetHostName() function, 335
GetServerVariable, 325
GIGO (garbage in/garbage out), 484
Gopher, 351-353
    files, reading, 358
    functions, 358
    locator strings, 358
    servers, connecting to, 359

H

handles
    HTTP servers, 357
    Internet, terminating, 355

hardware
    drivers, 334
    setting up Web sites, 292
heading tags, 22
History object, 479
hosts, scripting, 43-45
HoTMetaL, 64-67
HTML (HyperText Markup Language), 353
    building inserts, 91
    ClassID, 432
    CODEBASE attribute, 434
    container commands, 428
    customizing with, 429
    documents, 428
    elements of, 17, 39
    filename extensions, 16
    installation of ActiveX control into Visual Basic, 437
    interactive HTML, 492, 503
    Internet Explorer ActiveX controls, 433
    JavaScript, 416
    lists, 27
    <OBJECT> tag, 430-432
    <SCRIPT> tag, 46
    scripting, 45, 50
    servers, 353
    tags, 17-18, 39, 440
    toolbars, 68
    transporting to new sites, 440
    VBScript, 416
    version identification information, 449
HTML control, 512
HTTP, 353
    example (httpex.cpp file), 373
    format, 356
    servers, 353
        connecting to MFC class, 359
        handles, creating, 357
HTTP control
    demonstration, 515
    perform low-level HTTP commands, 514
httpex.ccp
    code file, 361
    connection and request code, 363

IObjectSafety interface   569

declaring variables, 362
file handling code, 364
HTTP example, 373
implementation file, 361
httpex.h header file, 361
HTTPExtensionProc, 324-326
hypertext, 11-12
HyperText Markup Language (HTML), 15

I

IConfAppControlX methods, 401
IConfApplicationX properties, 402
IConfAppSharingX properties, 401
IConfChannelX properties, 400
IConfDataExchangeX methods, 401
IConferenceManagerX events, 398
IConferenceManagerX methods, 398
IConferenceManagerX properties, 398
IConferenceX properties, 399, 402
IConfFileExchangeX properties, 401
IConfFileTransferX properties, 402
IConfMemberX properties, 400
IConfShareAppX properties, 402
IConfUserX properties, 399
ICP (Internet Control Pack)
    ActiveX controls, 422
    control states, 531
    controls, 423
    DocObject states, 532
    FTP control, 528
    protocol states, 531
    state logic, 531
    installing, 335-336

ICP HTML control, 513
ICP HTTP control, 515
ICP POP3 control, 521
ICP SMTP control, 518
ID attribute, 486
IETF (Internet Engineering Task Force), 416
IIS Add-In
    Access wrap-up, 78
    adding format, 74
    Microsoft Access, 71
image control, 103
image maps, 500
<IMG> tag, 500
implementation files, 361
increment operators (JavaScript), 185
indented code (JavaScript), 171-172
.INF files, 455
initializing
    ActiveX control, 392
    Internet sessions, 359
    WinInet API, 355
INPUT attributes dialog, 70
<INPUT> tag, 31, 494
input types, 494-497
inserting
    buttons, 337
    databases to ODBC Driver Manager, 266
    data pages with Internet Information Server Add-In, 267
    ISMAP attribute to the <IMG> tag, 500
    labels, 337
    links to documents, 275
    text boxes, 337
    Timer control to Web pages, 435
    Track Change Request to the Navigation bar, 287
installing
    ActiveX Control Pad, 49, 429
    ActiveX controls into Visual Basic, 437
    ActiveX from Web pages, 418

ActiveX Software Developers' Kit, 8
CGI script, 314
ICP (Internet Control Pack), 335-336
Internet Mail and News client, 298-299
MSN (The Microsoft Network), 4-5
Netscape and MSIE, 420-421
NNTP client, 299
OLE objects, 448, 453
verification process, 448
integrating network technologies, 7
interactive HTML, 492, 503
Internet
    ActiveX programming for, 3
    downloading from, 448
    organizations for standards and practice, 7
    Query and Display Page Wizard, 73
    security, 457, 466
Internet Assistant
    HTML view, 60
    overview, 58
    tour, 59, 64
Internet Explorer
    ActiveX controls, 433
    JavaScript support, 168
    object model, 88
    Web sites, 88, 420
Internet handles, terminating, 355
Internet Information Server Add-In, 267
Internet Mail and News client, installing, 298-299
Internet News (Usenet), 297
Internet Ratings, security, 459
Internet service providers, *see* **ISPs**
Internet sessions, initializing, 359
InternetOpen WinInet API function, 355
intranets, 302
IObjectSafety interface, 463

IP (Internet Protocol)
  addresses, 294
IPersist* interfaces, 52
Is operator, 137
ISAPI
  DLL entry points, 323
  executables vs. dynamic link
    libraries, 320
  extension control block
    (ECB), 323
  functions, 324
  loading process, 321
  programming, 320
  return values, 324
  servers, 322
    access violations, 326
  scripting overview, 311
ISAPI DLL, building, 325
ISPs (Internet server providers), 4
  CompuNet, 305
  connections, 304
  FishNet, 305
  levels of service, 307
  selecting an ISP, 306
  servers, 415
  Sprintlink, 305
iterater (for-in statement), 205
IUnknown (ActiveX OLE), 550

J

Jakarta (Visual J++), 547
Java Virtual Machine (VM),
  546
JavaScript, 416
  as an object-oriented
    language, 169
  built-in objects, 196-198
    Date, 200-202
    Math, 198-200
  case sensitivity, 170
  comments (in code), 172
  creating applications,
    259-261
  for function, 203
  for-in function, 205
  history, 168
  if function, 202

  indented code (Listing 7.3),
    171-172
  Internet Explorer support,
    168
  Navigator support, 168
  objects, 189
    arrays, 194-196
    associative arrays, 193-194
    built-in, 196-202
    creating, 189
    methods, 191-192
    properties, 190-191
  online resources, 207
  operators
    assignments, 182-183
    comparison, 187
    increment, 185
    logical, 186
    math functions, 183
    precedence, 188-189
    string, 187
  procedures, 179
    eval function, 180-181
    functions in, 179
    parseFloat function, 181
    parseInt function, 181
  separate.htm (Listing 7.2),
    171
  template.htm (Listing 7.1),
    169-170
  unindented code (Listing
    7.3), 171-172
  user interface, 206
  user interface, 207
  variables
    boolean, 173
    constant, 176
    declaring (var keyword),
      175
    naming, 174
    null, 173
    numeric, 173
    scope, 177-179
    string, 173
    types, 173
    uninitialized, 176
  while function, 204
JP programming, 262
JScript, 47-50

K–L

keywords
  function, 180
  new, 189

labels, 337
Language attribute, 46, 110
LastModified property, 483
Layout control, 103
libraries, 350-354
linking separate objects on a
  system, 408
links
  adding to documents, 275
  creating to Web pages, 433
Links object (Document
  object), 481
List box control, 442
Listen method, 338
lists
  HTML, 27
  TYPE attribute, 29
Location object, 478, 482
locator strings, creating, 358
logical operators (JavaScript),
  186

M

<MAP> container tag, 502
math functions, 129, 183
Math object (JavaScript),
  198-200
methods
  Accept method, 338
  Close method, 339
  Connect method, 341
  Document.Write method,
    485
  GetData method, 339
  HTML.RequestDoc method,
    513
  IConfAppControlX, 401
  IConfDataExchangeX
    methods, 401
  IConferenceManagerX, 398
  Listen method, 338

SendData method, 342
UDP control's SendData
  method, 345
Window object, 100
MFC (Microsoft Foundation Class), 354, 549
  classes, 358-375
    CFtpConnection, 369
    CInternetSession, 368
    connection classes, 368-369
    return codes, 365
  programming with, 360-368
Microsoft
  ActiveX control Web sites, 458
  Access, 71
  Base Security Layer SDK, 460
  HTML Client control, 437
  integration of network technologies, 7
  Internet Explorer, 461
  Internet Ratings API, 468
  operating system overview, 4
  public news server, 522
  Software Library FTP sites, 543
MIME (multimedia Internet mail extensions), 11
modems, dial-up accounts, 294
moving file pointers, 356
MPlayer registry file entries, 542
MSDN, 323
MSN (The Microsoft Network), 4-5

N

NAME attribute, 274
naming conventions
  Form object input types, 498
  Object Model, 475
Navigation bar
  ActiveX Control Pad, 277
  adding to Track Change Request, 287
  in main frame, 280

Navigator, 168
NCompass Labs, 422
NetConference, 395
  ActiveX
    control Web pages, 390, 398
    objects, 398
    return codes, 386-388
NetConferencing APIs
  functions, 382-383
  main user interface, 378-380
  msconf.h header file (Listing 14.1), 384-385
  windows.h header file (Listing 14.1), 384-385
  system requirements, 382
  windows.h header file, 384
NetMeeting APIs
  functions, 382-383
  msconf.h header files (Listing 14.1), 384-385
  system requirements, 382
  windows.h header files (Listing 14.1), 384-385
Netscape Navigator, 168
  hypertext documents, 11
  Web sites, 88, 420
  see also Navigator
Network News Transfer Protocol Client control, 522
networking, 302-305
network procotols, 303
New Document dialog, 59
new keyword, 189
NNTP client, installing, 299
NNTP control, 523
nothing (VBScript), 120
null constant, 120
null variables (in JavaScript), 173
numeric variables (in JavaScript), 173

O

object model, 475
object-oriented programming, 169

<OBJECT> tag, 37, 430-432
  list box control, 442
objects
  built-in
    Date, 200-202
    Math, 198-200
    String, 196-198
  classes, 9
  JavaScript, 189
    arrays, 194-196
    associative arrays, 193-194
    creating, 189
    methods, 191-192
    properties, 190-191
OCX controls, 413
ODBC (Open Database Connectivity), 313
ODBC Administrator, 72, 268
ODBC Driver Manager, 266
<OL> tag, 27
OLE (Object Linking and Embedding)
  applications, developing, 323
  components, 411
  control, creating, 462
  definitions, 551
  history, 410
  installing, 448, 453
  IUnknown, 550
  RegEdit utility, 541
  ActiveX controls, 408
online resources (JavaScript), 207
opening files on FTP servers, 357
operators
  comparison, 135
  string, 134
  VBScript, 128, 186
    assignments, 182-183
    comparison, 187
    increment, 185
    logical, 186
    math functions, 183
    precedence, 188-189
    string, 187
Option Explicit (VBScript), 116

P

paragraph tags, 23
parsing strings (URLs), 355
party hosts (Conferencing APIs), 378
PICS (Platform for Internet Content Selection), 467
POP3 Post Office Protocol, 520
positioning file pointers, 356
Post Office Protocol Client control, 519
precedence (of JavaScript operators), 188-189
procedures
    JavaScript, 179-181
    VBScript, 125
processes
    GetExtensionVersion, 324
    HTTPExtensionProc, 324
    TerminateExtension, 324
programming
    ActiveX controls, 413
    ActiveX for Internet, 3
    CGI, 315
    creating to hold minibrs.htm, 99
    Frankenstein model, 9
    ISAPI, 320
    OLE controls, 10
    Script Wizard, 97
    string concantenation, 317
    transporting to new sites, 440
    WinSock, 303, 332
    with MFC, 360-368
Project Status page, 263
Prompt dialog box, 101
properties
    building with VBScript, 91
    IConfApplicationX, 402
    IConfAppSharingX properties, 401
    IConfChannelX properties, 400
    IConferenceManagerX, 398
    IConferenceX, 402
    IConferenceX properties, 399
    IConfFileExchangeX properties, 401
    IConfFileTransferX, 402
    IConfMemberX properties, 400
    IConfShareAppX, 402
    IConfUserX, 399
    status change, 96
    window properties, 88-90
protocols
    FTP, 350
    Gopher, 351-352
    TCP/IP, 303
    states, 531
public key encryption, 465
pvoid, 389

Q-R

Query and Display Page Wizard, 73

radio (input types), 496
rating systems (security), 467
ReadClient function, 325
reading
    buffers (WinInet API functions), 355
    files
        Gopher, 358
        WinInet API, 354
Referrer property (Document object), 483
Reg.DAT file, 540
RegClean utility, 543
RegEdit, 541
RegEdit utility, 541
registering controls with RegSvr32.exe, 439
RegSvr32 (system registry), 543
RegSvr32.exe, 439
Remote Access Service, 506
Remote Procedure Calls (RPCs), 545
return codes (MFC class), 365
Returned Change tracking number, 287

S

Safety API, 461
scope (JavaScript variables), 177-179
<SCRIPT> tag, 36, 46
script engines, 50, 53
script files, hacking, 76
Script Wizard, 84, 97
scripting
    ActiveX, 41, 414, 418
    ActiveX Control Pad, 84
    CGI, 312
    CGIs with HTML forms, 319
    changing options, 91
    client-side scripting, 42-45
    hosts and engines, 43-45
    HTML, 45, 50
    HTML scripting, 504
    JScript, 47-50
    object models, 474
    ODBC (Open Database Connectivity), 313
    standard input, 317
    standard output, 318
    Telix, 48
    VBScript, 47-50
scripts (NetConference), 395
SDKs (Base Security Layer SDK), 544-545
Search and Return page, 271
security, 417-418
    certificates, 460
    CGIs, 314
    Internet, 457, 466
    Internet Explorer configuration, 462
    Internet ratings, 459
    PICS (Platform for Internet Content Selection), 467
    public key encryption, 465
    rating systems, 467
    Safety API, 461
    trust verification service, 461
    World Wide Web Consortium, 466
SendData method, 342, 345

separate.htm (JavaScript), Listing 7.2, 171
servers
  connections
    closing, 364
    WinInet API functions, 355
  creating WinSock TCP server, 336
  FTP servers, 530
  Gopher, connecting to, 359
  HTML, 353
  HTTP, 353
    connecting to, 359
    creating handles, 357
  ISAPI, 322
  system overview, 295
sessions
  information (WinInet API functions), 355
  Internet, initializing, 359
  starting, WinInet API functions, 355
setting up
  Search and Return page, 271
  Web sites, 292-299
SHAPE attribute, 501
sites
  administrator requirements, 300-304
  Internet Explorer, 88, 420
  Microsoft's ActiveX control, 458
  Netscape, 420
  Netscape Navigator, 88
  network protocols, 303
  setting up, 292-299
    administrator requirements, 300-304
    hardware, 292
    server software, 296
    technical skills, 300
  transporting to new sites, 440
  VBScript, 165
  Visual Basic, 548
SMTP control, 517
SoftQuad home page, 65
software distributors, 419
Sprintlink ISP, 305
SRC attribute, 46
standard output, 317-318
starting sessions (WinInet API functions), 355
state logic, 531
static IP address, 294
status change (properties), 96
String object (JavaScript), 196-198
strings
  concatenation, 317
  formatting (HTTP format), 356
  functions, 153
  locator (Gopher), 358
  operators, 134, 187
  URLs, 355
  variables (in JavaScript), 173
submit (Input Types), 494
subroutines
  VBScript, 125
  Web browsers, 438
system registry
  components, 540
  editing, 538
  editing registry databases, 540
  Reg.DAT file, 540
  RegSvr32, 543
  System.DAT file, 540
  User.DAT file, 540
  Ver.DLL, 545
  Windows 3.0, 539
  Windows 3.1, 539
  Windows 95, 539
System.DAT file, 540

T

<TABLE> tag, 29
<TAG> tag, 17
tag files, 351
tags
  <A> tag, 24
  <BODY> tag, 20
  <FORM> tag, 31
  <HTML> tag, 18
  <IMG> tag, 500
  <INPUT> tag, 31
  <MAP> Container Tag, 502
  <OBJECT> tag, 37
  <OL> tag, 27
  <SCRIPT> tag, 36, 46
  <TABLE> tag, 29
  <TAG>, 17
  <UL> tag, 27
  comment tags, 22
  <FRAME> tag, 274
  heading tags, 22
  HTML tags, 440
  <INPUT> tag, 494
  <OBJECT> tag, 430-432
  paragraph tags, 23
TCP/IP (Transmission Control Protocol/Internet Protocol), 303
Telix (scripting), 48
template.htm (JavaScript), Listing 7.1, 169-170
TerminateExtension, 324
terminating Internet handles, 355
text (input types), 497
text boxes, adding, 337
time (formatting), 356
Timer control, adding to Web pages, 435
Title property (Document object), 483
toolbar
  HoTMetaL, 67
  HTML, 68
Track Change Request, 287
True and False constants, 121
trust verification service, 461
TYPE attribute, 29, 47, 494

U

UDP
  client, 344
  control, 342
  server answering machine form, 343
<UL> tag, 27
unindented code (JavaScript), 171-172

uninitialized variables, 118
uninitialized variables
   (JavaScript), 176
universal resource locator, *see*
   URL
URL (universal resource
   locator), 356
   strings, 355
   version identification
      information, 449
UseMap attribute (<IMG> tag),
   502
UseNet newsgroups, 525
User Input
   HTML scripting, 504
   VBScript, 504
   Visual Basic, 505
user interfaces for JavaScript,
   206-207
User.DAT file, 540

V

variables
   constant, 119, 176
   declaring, 362
   declaring (var keyword), 175
   environment variables, 315
   improper variable name, 114
   naming, 114, 174
   scope of, 122
   scope, 177-179
   types, 173
   uninitialized, 118, 176
   VBScript, 112
variants (VBScript), 158
VB (Visual Basic), 50
VBScript, 47-50, 416
   array functions, 152
   arrays and declarations, 123
   background information, 107
   building with, 91
   built-in functions, 142
   comments, 111
   control structures, 159
   conversion functions, 142
   error handling, 163
   Is operator, 137
   language structure, 109

math functions, 129
math-specific functions, 150
nothing, 120
null constant, 120
operator precedence, 140-141
operators, 128
   comparison, 135
   string, 134
Option Explicit, 116
overview of scripting
   architecture, 108
procedural languages, 108
procedures, 125
randomize statement, 151
<SCRIPT> tag, 110
Select Case, 162
string functions, 153
subroutines, 125-126
supported software platforms,
   108
time and date values, 147
True and False constants, 121
user input, 504
user interface elements, 164
user-built functions, 127
using keywords, 138-139
using new variable names, 97
variables, 112
variants, 158
Visual Basic programming
   model, 108-109
Web sites, 165
VBX custom control, 412
Ver.DLL, 545
verifying installation process,
   448
version identification information, 449
Visual Basic, 548
   error alert, 314
   ICP POP3 control, 521
   installation of ActiveX
      controls, 437
   mail-sending utility, 518
   Microsoft HTML Client
      control, 437
   SMTP control, 517
   user input, 505
   Web sites, 548
   Web-search application, 515

Visual Basic IDE, 506
Visual C++, 549
Visual J++ (Jakarta), 547

W-Z

WAIS (wide area information
   search), 351
Web browsers
   ActiveX, 419-420
   creating Web-browser
      programs, 512
   Internet Explorer, 88, 101
   Lists.html, 69
   Netscape Navigator, 88, 101
   subroutines, 438
   within browsers, 99
Web pages
   adding Timer control, 435
   creating, 429
   creating links to, 433
   NetConference ActiveX
      control, 391
   structure, 18
Web servers
   creating WinSock TCP
      server, 336
   ISAPI, 322
   overview, 299
   system overview, 295
Web sites
   administrator requirements,
      300-304
   Internet Explorer, 88, 420
   Microsoft's ActiveX control,
      458
   Netscape, 420
   Netscape Navigator, 88
   network protocols, 303
   setting up, 292-299
      administrator require-
         ments, 300-304
      server software, 296
      technical skills, 300
   transporting to new sites, 440
   VBScript, 165
   Visual Basic, 548
Welcome page, JP programming, 262

wide area information search (WAIS), 351
Win.INI files, 539
  extensions, 538
Win32 Internet API Library, 350-354
Window object, 475
  Frames object, 477
  History object, 479
  Location object, 478, 482
Window object, methods, 100
Window object events, 101
Window objects properties, 88-90
Windows
  Base Security Layer SDK, 545
  installing MSN, 6
  operating system overview, 4
  WinSock overview, 332
Windows 3.0, 538
Windows 3.1 system registry, 539
Windows 95
  command line FTP client, 527
  system registry, 539
Windows Media Player sample REG file, 542
WinInet
  MFC classes, 358-375
WinInet API, 354-358
WinInet API functions, 357-358
WinSck.OCX plug-in, 335
WinSock
  Accept method, 338
  answering machine application, 337
  Close method, 339
  Connect method, 341
  creating servers, 340-341
  creating TCP server, 336
  FTP-32 client application, 526
  functions, 334
  GetData method, 339
  hierarchy, 333
  Listen method, 338

  overview, 332
  programming, 303, 332
  SendData method, 342
  UDP client, 344
  UDP control, 342
  UDP control's SendData method, 345
  UDP server answering machine form, 343
Word
  Internet Assistant installation, 261
  Project Status page, 263
World Wide Web Consortium, 466
WriteClient, 325
writing bytes to files, 356

A VIACOM SERVICE

The Information SuperLibrary™

Bookstore   Search   What's New   Reference   Software   Newsletter   Company Overviews

Yellow Pages   Internet Starter Kit   HTML Workshop   Win a Free T-Shirt!   Macmillan Computer Publishing   Site Map   Talk to Us

CHECK OUT THE BOOKS IN THIS LIBRARY.

You'll find thousands of shareware files and over 1600 computer books designed for both technowizards and technophobes. You can browse through 700 sample chapters, get the latest news on the Net, and find just about anything using our massive search directories.

All Macmillan Computer Publishing books are available at your local bookstore.

We're open 24-hours a day, 365 days a year.

You don't need a card.

We don't charge fines.

And you can be as **LOUD** as you want.

The Information SuperLibrary
http://www.mcp.com/mcp/   ftp.mcp.com

Teach Yourself JavaScript 1.1 in a Week, Second Edition

—Arman Danesh

Teach Yourself JavaScript in a Week, Second Edition, is a new edition of the best-selling JavaScript tutorial. It has been revised and updated for the latest version of JavaScript from Netscape, and includes detailed coverage of new features, such as how to work with Java applets with LiveConnect, writing JavaScript for Microsoft's Internet Explorer, in-depth instructions on how to use Netscape Navigator Gold, and more! The CD-ROM includes a full version of Netscape Navigator Gold, additional tools, and ready-to-use sample scripts. This book covers JavaScript 1.1.

Price: $39.99 USA/$56.95 CDN   User Level: Beginning–Intermediate
ISBN: 1-57521-195-5   600 pages

Teach Yourself VBScript in 21 Days

—Keith Brophy & Tim Koets

Learn how to use VBScript to create living, interactive Web pages. This unique scripting language from Microsoft is taught with clarity and precision, providing you with the best and latest information on this popular language. This book teaches advanced OLE object techniques, and explores VBScript's animation, interaction, and mathematical capabilities. The CD-ROM contains all the source code from the book and examples of third-party software.

Price: $39.99 USA/$56.95 CDN   User Level: New–Casual
ISBN: 1-57521-120-3   720 pages

Presenting ActiveX

—Warren Ernst and John J. Kottler

This book provides a hands-on glimpse of Microsoft's new ActiveX technologies, and describes the roles that existing Microsoft technologies play in this new architecture. *Presenting ActiveX* illustrates how ActiveX lets Web publishers and developers add "active" elements to their Web pages and Web applications, and shows how to use existing technologies to create ActiveX-powered Web pages today. The CD-ROM contains source code from the book and powerful ActiveX utilities.

Price: $29.99 USA/$42.95 CDN   User Level: Casual–Accomplished
ISBN: 1-57521-156-4   336 pages

Laura Lemay's Web Workshop: JavaScript

—Laura Lemay

Explore various aspects of Web publishing, CGI scripting, interactivity, graphics design, and Netscape Gold. *Laura Lemay's Web Workshop: JavaScript* provides a clear, hands-on guide to creating sophisticated Web pages. The CD-ROM includes the complete book in HTML format, publishing tools, templates, graphics, backgrounds, and more!

Price: $39.99 USA/$56.95 CDN   User Level: Casual–Accomplished
ISBN: 1-57521-141-6   400 pages

JavaScript Unleashed

—*Richard Wagner, et al.*

Programming JavaScript is much simpler than programming for Java, since JavaScript code can be embedded directly into an HTML document. *JavaScript Unleashed* unveils the mysteries of this new code, allowing programmers to exploit its full potential in their Web applications. Learn to use JavaScript to create dynamic Web pages. This book covers Netscape LiveWire server system, Netscape Navigator Gold, and more! The CD-ROM includes source code from the book, sample applications, and third-party utilities.

Price: $49.99 USA/$70.95 CDN   User Level: Casual–Accomplished–Expert
ISBN: 1-57521-118-1   900 pages

Web Programming with Visual Basic

—*Craig Eddy & Brad Haasch*

This book is a reference that quickly and efficiently shows the experienced developer how to develop Web applications using the 32-bit power of Visual Basic 4. It includes an introduction and overview of Web programming, and quickly delves into the specifics, teaching readers how to incorporate animation, sound, and more into their Web applications. This book includes coverage of Netscape Navigator, how to create CGI applications with Visual Basic, spiders, agents, crawlers, and other Internet aids. The CD-ROM contains all the examples from the book, plus additional Visual Basic programs.

Price: $39.99 USA/$56.95 CDN   User Level: Accomplished–Expert
ISBN: 1-57521-106-8   400 pages

Web Programming with Java

—*Harris & Jones*

This book gets readers on the road to developing robust, real-world Java applications. Various cutting-edge applications are presented, allowing the reader to quickly learn all aspects of programming Java for the Internet. Readers will be able to create live, interactive Web pages. The CD-ROM contains source code and powerful utilities.

Price: $39.99 USA/$56.95 CDN   User Level: Accomplished–Expert
ISBN: 1-57521-113-0   500 pages

JavaScript Developer's Guide

—*Wes Tatters*

JavaScript Developer's Guide is the professional reference for enhancing commercial-grade Web sites with JavaScript. Packed with real-world JavaScript examples, the book shows the developer how to use JavaScript to glue together Java applets, multimedia programs, plug-ins, and more on a Web site. Readers discover ways to add interactivity and Java applets to Web pages. The CD-ROM includes source code and powerful utilities.

Price: $49.99 USA/$70.95 CDN   Accomplished–Expert
ISBN: 1-57521-084-3   600 pages

Add to Your Sams.net Library Today
with the Best Books for Internet Technologies

ISBN	Quantity	Description of Item	Unit Cost	Total Cost
1-57521-195-5		Teach Yourself JavaScript 1.1 in a Week, Second Edition (Book/CD-ROM)	$39.99	
1-57521-120-3		Teach Yourself VBScript in 21 Days (Book/CD-ROM)	$39.99	
1-57521-156-4		Presenting ActiveX (Book/CD-ROM)	$29.99	
1-57521-141-6		Laura Lemay's Web Workshop: JavaScript (Book/CD-ROM)	$39.99	
1-57521-118-1		JavaScript Unleashed (Book/CD-ROM)	$49.99	
1-57521-106-8		Web Programming with Visual Basic (Book/CD-ROM)	$39.99	
1-57521-113-0		Web Programming with Java (Book/CD-ROM)	$39.99	
1-57521-084-3		JavaScript Developer's Guide (Book/CD-ROM)	$49.99	
		Shipping and Handling: See information below.		
		TOTAL		

Shipping and Handling: $4.00 for the first book, and $1.75 for each additional book. If you need to have it NOW, we can ship product to you in 24 hours for an additional charge of approximately $18.00, and you will receive your item overnight or in two days. Overseas shipping and handling adds $2.00. Prices subject to change. Call between 9:00 a.m. and 5:00 p.m. EST for availability and pricing information on latest editions.

201 W. 103rd Street, Indianapolis, Indiana 46290

1-800-428-5331 — Orders   1-800-835-3202 — FAX   1-800-858-7674 — Customer Service

Book ISBN 1-57521-163-7

What's on the Disc

The companion CD-ROM contains the authors' source code and samples from the book, as well as many third-party software products.

Windows 95 Installation Instructions

1. Insert the CD-ROM disc into your CD-ROM drive.
2. From the Windows 95 desktop, double-click the My Computer icon.
3. Double-click the icon representing your CD-ROM drive.
4. Double-click the icon titled CDSETUP.EXE to run the installation program.
5. Installation creates a program group named Teach Yourself ActiveX Programming in 21 Days. This group will contain icons to browse the CD-ROM.

NOTE If Windows 95 is installed on your computer and you have the AutoPlay feature enabled, the CDSETUP.EXE program starts automatically when you insert the disc into your CD-ROM drive.

Windows NT Installation Instructions

1. Insert the CD-ROM disc into your CD-ROM drive.
2. From File Manager or Program Manager, choose Run from the File menu.
3. Type <drive>\CDSETUP.EXE and press Enter, where <drive> corresponds to the drive letter of your CD-ROM. For example, if your CD-ROM is drive D:, type D:\CDSETUP.EXE and press Enter.
4. Installation creates a program group named /Teach Yourself ActiveX Programming in 21 Days. This group will contain icons to browse the CD-ROM.